**W9-CAO-925**

# DATE DUE

OCT 30 2013

# Open for Business

**American and Comparative Environmental Policy**
Sheldon Kamieniecki and Michael E. Kraft, series editors

For a complete list of books in the series, please see the back of the book.

# Open for Business

Conservatives' Opposition to Environmental Regulation

Judith A. Layzer

The MIT Press
Cambridge, Massachusetts
London, England

© 2012 Massachusetts Institute of Technology

MIT Press books may be purchased at special quantity discounts for business or sales promotional use. For information, please email special_sales@mitpress.mit.edu or write to Special Sales Department, The MIT Press, 55 Hayward Street, Cambridge, MA 02142.

This book was set in Sabon by Toppan Best-set Premedia Limited. Printed on recycled paper and bound in the United States of America.

Library of Congress Cataloging-in-Publication Data

Layzer, Judith A.
Open for business : conservatives' opposition to environmental regulation / Judith A. Layzer.
    p.   cm.—(American and comparative environmental policy)
Includes bibliographical references and index.
ISBN 978-0-262-01827-2 (hardcover : alk. paper)
1. Environmental policy—United States. 2. Conservatism—United States.
3. Environmental legislation—United States. 4. United States—Environmental conditions. 5. United States—Politics and governemnt. I. Title.
GE180.L394   2013
363.7'05610973—dc23
2012012948

10  9  8  7  6  5  4  3  2  1

# Contents

# Series Foreword: Conservative Ideas and Their Consequences

Corporate leaders and conservative analysts have long been critics of U.S. environmental policy. They maintain that environmentalists exaggerate problems and predict dire consequences in order to alarm Americans unnecessarily, raise money for their cause, and shape public policy to their liking. In addition, they contend that many laws, regulations, and government programs are excessively burdensome and costly, will result in only modest—if any—improvements in environmental quality, and, therefore, are unnecessary. In their view, corporations have a great deal at stake financially (as do their shareholders), and they have every right to express their positions and lobby government to protect their interests.

Environmentalists counter these arguments in several ways. They point out that the true costs of environmental damage (e.g., to public health and property) often are excluded from cost-benefit and other economic assessments as well as from the actual costs of manufacturing processes and goods. When they are included in such calculations, efforts to protect the environment and public health, as well as to promote natural resource conservation, are more than worth the effort and expense. Moreover, at the global level, environmentalists say that the United States is not playing a major role in forging an effective international agreement to control climate change because of the political power of certain domestic industries, primarily the energy companies. They accuse conservative leaders and business of derailing efforts to enact legislation to protect the environment in Congress through the kinds of lobbying tactics they use and by the vast sums of money they contribute to U.S. House and Senate campaigns. Following the passage of environmental protection laws, they remind us, business interests frequently seek to influence rulemaking in government agencies and, if unsuccessful, challenge the laws in court.

In addition, environmentalists charge that business groups spend large sums of money to frame issues in a manner that serves their narrow interests while often misleading the public. Firms do this, according to environmentalists, by manipulating media coverage, filling the airwaves and print media with advertisements that tout their green credentials, and writing editorials that slant the truth. In addition, a number of large companies, including Koch Industries, ExxonMobil, Philip Morris, General Motors, General Electric, and Archer Daniels Midland, have developed and heavily funded several conservative think tanks such as the Cato Institute, Citizens for a Sound Economy, and the Federalist Society. The money is primarily used to fund policy and scientific research, produce publications and mailings, and hire "neutral" experts to write articles and editorials that support business interests. Several think tanks have sponsored scientific studies that minimize the severity of environmental threats posed by air and water pollution, acid rain, and climate change. Findings from these studies are being used to undermine the precautionary principle, undercut adaptive management, and argue that only "complete" scientific knowledge can serve as a basis for environmental regulation. Policy and economic analyses conducted by industry-funded think tanks almost always contend that current and proposed environmental and natural resource rules and regulations are extremely costly and provide little or no benefit.

Conservatives and business leaders reject these accusations and point to the progress the country has made since the early 1970s in improving air and water quality, conserving energy, keeping the price of energy relatively low, and encouraging the safe transportation and disposal of chemical wastes. Companies have spent billions of dollars to retool their plants and manufacturing processes in order to control emissions, save energy, and safely dispose of toxic wastes. The reduction of sulfur dioxide ($SO_2$) emissions by power plants in the mid-Atlantic states has significantly reduced acid rain, thereby protecting forests, lakes, and streams in the United States and Canada. The timber industry has hired numerous ecologists and conservation biologists and is now managing forests more wisely by protecting critical habitats. Large agricultural firms are effectively managing soil erosion and are containing feedlot waste and chemical runoff from cropland. Unlike in the past, firms are cooperating more closely with government regulators and maintain that a "greening of industry" is currently taking place.

Using this ongoing battle over environmental protection and resource conservation between opposing political groups as a backdrop, Judith

Layzer asks: how, and to what extent, have conservatives influenced U.S. environmental politics and policy? Have they, despite the acquisition of substantial political power, truly failed to make a significant difference in the environmental regulatory framework? Have their efforts had a discernible effect on Americans' exposure to environmental risks?

As Layzer points out at the beginning of her book, American conservatives have consistently voiced skepticism about the ability of government to solve the country's social and economic ills. Instead, they have favored minimizing the regulatory burden on the private sector and devolving responsibility to state and local governments and private entities. While they disagree on certain issues, for the most part conservative leaders have succeeded in building an enduring political coalition among libertarians, pro-business Hamiltonians, and a populist faction that in the 1980s called itself "the New Right" and in the 2000s is known as the Tea Party. According to Layzer, this has been accomplished through the vilification of government and portrayal of business leaders as "entrepreneurs," the virtuous engines of economic growth and prosperity.

She explains that, for the conservative coalition, the two core and unifying values are freedom of individuals from government interference and economic efficiency, viewed as the product of markets unencumbered by government regulation. From this perspective, government intervention in the economy must be opposed because it reduces personal freedom and creativity; impairs the ability of business to maximize profits and create jobs, thereby hampering overall economic growth; and is almost invariably ineffective while causing negative, unintended consequences. Proponents of government action must demonstrate that the benefits exceed the costs, and that the intervention mitigates a serious risk. Conservatives believe that when government does enact environmental rules and regulations, it should do so in a way that is minimally coercive and least costly and burdensome to business, for example, by relying on incentives and market-like systems, or, preferably, encouraging compliance through voluntary programs.

Likewise, government should minimize impediments to the use of public land and natural resources and refrain from restricting the use of private property. On the rare occasions when government is compelled to enact restrictions on private property, policymakers should compensate landowners for any reduction in the market value of their property. Layzer argues that since the 1970s, conservative activists have worked hard to promote these antiregulatory ideas in hopes of rolling back—or at least substantially changing—the environmental regulatory framework fostered by landmark legislation such as the Clean Air Act and Endangered Species Act, and preventing or delaying action on newly identified problems like climate change.

Drawing on a detailed historical analysis of both conservative ideas and their political and policy consequences, Layzer argues that conservatives' inability to enact wholesale reform masks their true impact on both policy and politics. To make that case, she examines the role that conservatives' antiregulatory ideas have played in shaping the United States' response to environmental issues since 1970. The main focus of the analysis concerns innovations in and contests over the use of administrative discretion. Conservative policymakers have devised new ways to relax existing rules and delay or prevent the adoption of new ones. In response, members of Congress who support environmental protection have sought to limit administrators' ability to undermine regulatory stringency. When in power, political appointees who favor improving environmental quality have used their discretion to advance environmental protection in the face of hostility from a conservative Congress.

A second focus involves policy learning, defined as revising policy goals or techniques in response to experience. Some environmentalists have been genuinely convinced by arguments about the need for less prescriptive mechanisms, such as inducements, collaboration, and programs that facilitate voluntary stewardship; others have reluctantly accepted new analytic tools and policy mechanisms in deference to apparently intractable opposition.

A third focus is political learning—in other words, adjustments in tactics in response to experience. Conservatives have learned to employ environmentally friendly language and avoid confrontation, while environmentalists have adopted the rhetoric of "balance," "common sense," and "efficiency" out of similar notions of political expediency. In Layzer's view, over time, the use of administrative discretion by conservative officials, combined with policy and political learning among both advocates and officials, has yielded an environmental policy regime that is increasingly inadequate relative to the global risks we face.

The book illustrates well the goals of the MIT Press series in American and Comparative Environmental Policy. We encourage work that examines a broad range of environmental policy issues. We are particularly interested in volumes that incorporate interdisciplinary research and focus on the linkages between public policy and environmental problems and issues both within the United States and in cross-national settings. We welcome contributions that analyze the policy dimensions of relationships between humans and the environment from either a theoretical or empirical perspective. At a time when environmental policies are increasingly seen as controversial and new approaches are being implemented widely, we especially encourage studies that assess policy successes and failures, evaluate new institutional arrangements and policy tools, and clarify new directions for environmental politics and policy. The books in this series are written for a wide audience that includes academics, policymakers, environmental scientists and professionals, business and labor leaders, environmental activists, and students concerned with environmental issues. We hope they contribute to public understanding of environmental problems, issues, and policies of concern today and also suggest promising actions for the future.

Sheldon Kamieniecki, University of California, Santa Cruz
Michael Kraft, University of Wisconsin-Green Bay
American and Comparative Environmental Policy Series Editors

# Preface

Upon assuming the governorship of New Jersey in January 1994, Christine Todd Whitman announced that the state would be "open for business." Like many Republicans, Whitman shared the conservative belief that environmental regulations ought to be curtailed to enable business to thrive. Subsequently, as administrator of the Environmental Protection Agency under President George W. Bush, Whitman discovered that her views were moderate compared to those of antiregulatory conservatives like Vice President Dick Cheney. In mid-2003, Whitman resigned her position, and two years later she published a book entitled *It's My Party, Too,* in which she criticized the efforts of the Bush White House to weaken environmental regulations. Whitman's experience is emblematic of a decades-long struggle within the Republican Party over how to address the environment in the face of a conservative coalition determined to free business of regulatory constraints.

I was motivated to write this book by puzzlement over what, exactly, that coalition had accomplished since the 1980s, when they began to dominate both the Republican Party and American politics. It seemed likely to me that, although they had failed to dismantle the existing regulatory framework, conservatives had influenced environmental politics and policymaking in discernible ways. For example, by the 2000s, most of my students were reluctant to describe themselves as "environmentalists," even though they clearly shared the values of many environmental activists. In addition, most of the tools employed in the environmental policies of the 1960s and 1970s had fallen out of favor, even within the environmental community. Were these the consequences of learning from experience, an effective antienvironmental campaign, or some combination of the two? This book is an effort to sort out that quandary.

The theoretical framework of the book rests on the understanding that the conservative movement is rooted in ideas—in particular, ideas about the importance of individual freedom and unfettered markets. According to Alfred Regnery, one of the patrons of the conservative movement, the intellectual founders of contemporary conservatism "wanted to use their ideas to change the world."[1] Yet one early reviewer of the manuscript for this book asked whether the conservative movement is really motivated by ideas at all, or is instead just a coalition of self-interested groups. As evidence of the latter, he pointed to the "hypocrisy" of ranchers who claim to oppose government intervention yet accept subsidies for their own activities. As I try to make clear, while conservatism is far from a coherent ideology, it is unfair to suggest that it is simply a cloak for unprincipled self-interest.

Moreover, although conservatives tend to agree on a small set of ideas, history does not suggest the existence of a "vast right-wing conspiracy" that has inexorably executed a well-formulated plan to take over American politics. Political development is far more contingent than such a vision would allow. That said, there is strong evidence that over the past forty years a well-funded and relentlessly ambitious core of political operatives has sought to craft, articulate, and disseminate ideas that will resonate among political elites and ordinary Americans. Those operatives have also devised effective tactics for dismantling, dislodging, or at least getting around the policies and programs they abhor.

It is also worth noting that although conservatives have gained ascendance in the Republican Party, the terms "conservative" and "Republican" are not synonymous. Many moderate Republicans, mostly concentrated in the Northeast, have been staunch defenders of environmental protection throughout the period of conservative ascendancy. Even some avowed conservatives do not subscribe to the particular views of the antiregulatory activists that dominate the movement. Divisions among industry, religious conservatives, and antiregulatory activists over endangered species conservation and climate change have occasionally riven the Republican Party.

This book fills a gap in the literature on the conservative movement. The dozens of books about conservatives that have been published since the 1980s say little to nothing about environmental issues. In part, this is because for many conservatives environmental issues are not a top concern; in fact, that is why those who do care about these issues have had virtually free rein. With its detailed exploration of the low-profile tactics employed by conservative activists, as well as the policy and political impacts of those tactics, this book also adds to the small but growing literature in political science about incremental institutional change. And finally, this book deepens the environmental policy literature. As environmental historian Samuel Hays observes, most scholars are "inclined to engage in close examination of the environmental movement itself and to ignore the equally vast subject of the environmental opposition."[2] Hays contends:

> The environmental opposition is far more complex than the environmental impulse. Its components are far more diffuse; it uses more varied strategies to express opposition; it develops and evolves over time to establish a coherent, persistent force for countering environmental initiatives. . . . Contemporary observers identify the environmental impulse as a coherent force in modern society, but they rarely speak of the environmental opposition in similar fashion as a movement having like features of distinctive social, economic, and political roots. The subject remains an untapped exploration for environmental historians.[3]

Hays goes on to say that analysis of the environmental opposition is an intricate undertaking that requires varied analysis and careful gathering of evidence to figure out how it arises piecemeal from various sectors of the economy and society and then comes together as a larger political movement. He asks: What distinguishes those who see environmentalists as beyond the pale and those who "see themselves as engaged in pragmatic contests for the allocation of public and private resources?"[4] These are the challenges and questions I set for myself in writing this book.

# Acknowledgments

In the pages that follow, I recount a history but do not provide a comprehensive historical treatise; instead, I have tried to understand a forty-plus-year period through the lens of an analytic framework that captures the interplay among contemporary ideas and institutions. In reconstructing the events of the conservative era, I am indebted to the journalists, historians, and policy scholars who have traced the development of the conservative movement, as well as those who have documented decision making in particular presidential administrations. Over the past five years, my research assistants at MIT—particularly Molly Mowery, Sarah Madden, Rachel Henschel, Kate Van Tassel, Joshua Sklarsky, and Kate Dineen—tracked down information that contributed to this volume. Alexis Schulman was a thorough fact checker and dogged investigator of details.

Some of my colleagues deserve thanks as well. Steve Teles, who several years ago asked me to write a chapter based on this research, reminded me to put myself in the shoes of conservative activists. This book is likely more (although still not completely) even-handed as a result. Gus Speth read an early draft of the manuscript and gave helpful feedback. Erik Bleich and Kathleen Thelen read drafts of the "theory" chapter, and Andrea Campbell talked through some of the concepts in the analytic framework. Kateri Carmola provided extremely thoughtful editorial comments on chapters 1 and 2. Richard Lazarus—on short notice and in the midst of the holiday rush—gave powerful advice about portraying jurisprudence. Richard Andrews of the University of North Carolina, as well as two anonymous reviewers, provided extraordinarily thorough and incisive comments on the original draft of the manuscript. Mike Kraft, Sheldon Kamieniecki, and Clay Morgan gathered reviews and did their best to help me produce a high-quality book.

I am fortunate to have brilliant friends and family who have not only supported me but actually read and edited chapters. Liz Phillips and Bill Rodriguez read portions of an early draft. Bill also provided excellent suggestions on a near-final version of the concluding chapter. Emmy Rubin, Melissa Shufro, and others talked through nettlesome sections, and Melissa took a day out of her busy life to help me copyedit. Daphne Kalotay generously proofread a chapter on short notice as well. Most important of all: my brother, Nick, read the entire first draft; his enthusiasm gave me the confidence to submit the book for review. And my parents, Jean and David, read every word of the next-to-final draft, providing thoughtful (and encouraging) reactions and wonderful editorial suggestions.

Finally, there are the all-important people who helped produce the book itself. Lee Zamir sacrificed a chilly afternoon to capture the wonderful image that graces the front of the book. Yasuyo Iguchi, at the MIT Press, performed wizardry to transform that image into a bold, clear cover. I agonized over the title, exchanging countless emails, texts, and phone calls with a team of consultants: Steve Almond, Eve Bridburg, Daphne Kalotay, Rishi Reddi, Bill Rodriguez, Julie Rold, Judy Sharkey, Larry Vale, and, of course, Jean, David, Carolyn, and Nick Layzer. Clay Morgan at the MIT Press suffered through all of this with enormous patience. Marcy Ross did yeoman's work to format and copyedit not only the prose but also the extensive endnotes and references. And I'm particularly grateful to Sandra Minkkinen, who gracefully tolerated my penchant for endless editing and selflessly engineered a tight production schedule to give me even *more* time to make last-minute changes.

# 1

# Introduction

On November 5, 2008, voters elected Barack Obama the forty-fourth president of the United States. Environmental concerns played a minimal role in the twenty-two-month-long presidential campaign, despite their growing prominence in popular culture during that period. In some respects this was not surprising. Historically, the environment has not been a deciding factor in national elections. Moreover, in the months leading up to the 2008 election, the near collapse of the global financial system dominated the news and the presidential debates. The campaigns' lack of focus on the environment also reflected the relatively small differences between the two candidates' positions on the preeminent environmental issue, global climate change. Both Obama and his rival, Republican John McCain, acknowledged that global climate change is real and caused by human activity. Both candidates also supported a cap-and-trade system for carbon dioxide, the most prominent of the greenhouse gases that cause climate change.[1] In fact, during his years in the Senate, McCain had repeatedly cosponsored legislation to limit carbon dioxide emissions using a cap-and-trade mechanism. But McCain's leadership on climate change made him anomalous within the Republican Party. More important, it was inconsistent with the views of a vocal contingent within the party that decried global warming as a hoax and had long deplored environmental regulation as a ploy by liberal activists to impose government control over every aspect of American life.[2] Such antiregulatory conservatism dominated the Republican Party from 1980 to 2008; it receded only briefly before reappearing with a vengeance in 2009, not long after President Obama took office.

In the United States, conservatives share a skepticism about the ability of the federal government to solve social and economic problems; they favor minimizing the regulatory burden on the private sector and devolving responsibility to state and local governments and private enterprises. They define themselves in reaction to New Deal liberalism, which is hopeful about the ability of government programs to ameliorate the inequality and environmental degradation caused by unregulated markets.[3] Although united on broad principles, contemporary conservatives differ on particulars. One of the most important disagreements concerns the desirability of government support for business. Because they believe that human progress is the result of individual creativity, libertarians esteem individual liberty and are deeply suspicious of concentrated political power, whether public or private. By contrast, "Hamiltonian" conservatives support a strong central government that uses its power to promote business and economic growth.[4] Such discrepancies have, at times, threatened the unity of the conservative movement. For the most part, though, conservative leaders have succeeded in maintaining a political coalition among libertarians, probusiness Hamiltonians, and a populist faction that in the 1980s called itself the New Right and in 2009 became known as the Tea Party. Enabling this synergy has been the vilification of government and portrayal of businesspeople, particularly "entrepreneurs," as the virtuous engines of economic growth.

For the conservative coalition, the two transcendent and unifying values are freedom of individuals from government interference and economic efficiency, assumed to result from markets unfettered by government regulation. Government intervention in the economy must be resisted because it reduces individual freedom and creativity; impairs the ability of business to maximize profits and create jobs, dampening overall economic growth; is almost invariably ineffective; and causes perverse, unintended consequences. The burden of proof is on proponents of government action to demonstrate that the benefits exceed the costs, and that the intervention mitigates a quantifiably serious risk whose existence is empirically verified with conclusive empirical data. When government does enact environmental regulations, it should do so in a way that is minimally coercive and least costly and burdensome to business—relying on incentives and market-like systems, or, even better, encouraging compliance through voluntary programs. Similarly, government should minimize impediments to the use of public land and natural resources and refrain from restricting the use of private property. On the rare occasions when government is compelled to enact restrictions on private property, policymakers should compensate landowners for any reduction in the market value of their holdings.[5]

Since the 1970s, conservative activists have worked hard to promote these antiregulatory ideas, in hopes of rolling back—or at least substantially modifying—landmark legislation such as the Clean Air Act and the Endangered Species Act, and preventing action on newly identified problems like climate change. They have had sound political reasons to expect their views would have an impact. When Republicans gained control of both the White House and the Senate in 1981, it was thanks largely to the power of the conservative coalition that had come together in the mid-1970s. Over the next two decades, conservatives developed an impressive ideological network; according to one admirer, by 2000, they "controlled the Republican Party, could count on a majority of federal judges of various shades of conservatism, had a substantial presence in every media sector, and had developed a vast array of public policy, activist, and grassroots organizations, among other assets."[6] Throughout the 1980s and 1990s, conservatives used this political apparatus to launch attacks on environmental laws and regulations in the White House, Congress, and the courts. In response, environmentalists and their allies raised alarms about the unraveling of the nation's system of environmental protection.

And yet, in 2000, conservative journalist David Mastio ruefully observed that "conservatives have struggled to deal with the environment as a political issue. And with the exception of occasional tactical victories, we have failed miserably."[7] In some respects Mastio's despair was well founded: between 1980 and 2000, conservatives were unable to repeal or fundamentally revamp any of the nation's major environmental statutes. Furthermore, public opinion on the issue barely budged during this period: more than 75 percent of Americans consistently told pollsters they sympathized with the goals of the environmental movement, and nearly every year a majority claimed to support environmental protection, even at the risk of curbing economic growth.[8]

Even after Republicans gained control of both Congress and the White House in 2003, and public support for environmental protection softened, conservatives struggled to advance their legislative agenda.[9] In fact, historian Julian Zelizer has remarked that, despite their striking political success, conservatives have not succeeded in changing policy.[10] With respect to environmental policy in particular, political scientists Christopher Klyza and David Sousa contend that even during an era of conservative dominance the "green state" has continued to evolve, albeit slowly and haltingly, in a direction favored by environmentalists.[11]

Given the apparent paradox of mounting political clout and minimal policy impact, this book asks: how, and to what extent, have conservatives influenced U.S. environmental politics and policy? Have they, despite the acquisition of substantial political power, truly failed to make a significant difference in the environmental regulatory framework? Have their efforts had a discernible effect on Americans' exposure to environmental risk? Drawing on a detailed historical analysis of both conservative ideas and their political and policy consequences, I argue that, despite their inability to enact wholesale reform, conservatives have had a substantial impact on both policy and politics. Conservatives have exerted influence in several ways. Since the 1970s, conservative activists have disseminated a compelling antiregulatory storyline to counter the environmentalist narrative, mobilized grassroots opposition to environmental regulations, and undertaken sophisticated legal challenges to the basis for and implementation of environmental laws. Over time, these activities have imparted legitimacy to a new antiregulatory rhetoric, one that emphasizes distrust of the federal bureaucracy, admiration for unfettered private property rights and markets, skepticism about science, and disdain for environmental advocates. By employing arguments rooted in this formula, conservatives have been instrumental in blocking efforts to pass major new environmental legislation or increase the stringency of existing laws, despite the emergence of scientific evidence suggesting serious new problems and growing risk from previously identified concerns.

Direct attacks on existing laws have proven less fruitful, however, instead provoking countermobilization by environmentalists, public criticism, and legislative resistance. So, over time, conservatives have adopted a more subtle strategy aimed at ensuring that laws are implemented and enforced in ways that reduce the stringency of federal environmental protection. Couching their challenges in the language of reason and moderation, they have used procedural requirements—such as cost-benefit analysis, risk assessment, risk "balancing," and regulatory review—to discourage new regulations. They have also modified the wording and interpretation of rules in ways that have limited their stringency.

Moreover, in the 1990s, a federal judiciary populated by a growing number of conservative judges began to retreat from its predecessor's stance of holding regulators' feet to the fire. With increasing frequency, federal judges limited environmentalists' standing to sue, required agencies to consider economic and risk trade-offs when promulgating rules, and insisted that government compensate property owners if regulation reduced the value of their property. Although these changes in judicial interpretation were not as dramatic as conservatives would have liked, they prompted retrenchment by environmental activists and discouraged administrators from taking aggressive action.

In short, conservatives have obstructed new legal mandates and capitalized on the relatively low visibility of bureaucratic and judicial decision making to weaken existing policies or prevent adjustments to address new or growing risks—an approach similar in nature and impact to the one they have employed in the realm of social welfare policy.[12] They have been most successful in relaxing biodiversity conservation policies because conflicting mandates to both conserve biodiversity and facilitate development are institutionalized in the nation's resource management agencies. In addition, the media tend to treat biodiversity conservation conflicts as regional and to emphasize their economic implications, making it difficult to mobilize national coalitions capable of defending or advancing restrictive policies. Conservatives have had less impact on pollution control policies, in part because the responsible agency officials have a singular mission and clear statutory mandates to protect public health and the environment. In addition, environmentalists can more easily raise public concern about human health threats from pollution, making it less difficult to galvanize a national coalition backing protective policies.

Conservative activism has also had more subtle political effects. Above all, it has wrought changes in the perceptions of and discourse about the federal government's role in environmental protection. Once seen as the hero, capable of saving Americans from industrial polluters, the government is now widely regarded as an agent of ineffective, inefficient policies. Conservative activism has breathed life into a view of the federal government as an overbearing monolith, impinging on the freedom of hardworking Americans. While environmentalists are considered extremists, inclined to promote their elite interests above those of the public, businesspeople are admired as entrepreneurs, job creators, and effective managers. Perhaps most seriously, as the debate over the environment has become more vitriolic and polarized, the prospects for regulatory reform that might improve the working of environmental policy have faded.

If this argument is correct, its practical implications are profound. Historically, the United States has enacted stringent policies to address local and global environmental problems, from curbing air and water pollution to phasing out chemicals that destroy the stratospheric ozone layer. Largely in response to pressure from conservatives, however, federal officials increasingly rely on voluntarism and corporate social responsibility. Yet abundant evidence suggests that such approaches typically yield only marginal environmental benefits.[13] Furthermore, instead of pioneering solutions to environmental problems and positioning itself to lead the world in pursuit of a more sustainable global economy, the United States is scrambling to catch up with countries like Germany, Denmark, and China, all of which have stimulated commercial development of environmentally benign technologies with a robust mix of policies.[14]

The argument has implications for political theory as well, particularly our understanding of the interplay between ideas and institutions in contemporary policymaking. The conservative movement is rooted in the view that "ideas matter." In fact, political scientist Stephen Skowronek contends that "[f]ew other reconstructive movements in American politics have drawn inspiration so directly from disciplined thinkers and holistic systems of thought."[15] Following the publication of Richard Weaver's 1948 treatise *Ideas Have Consequences*, conservatives honed a set of arguments that attracted a diverse group of adherents, built an elaborate web of organizations for incubating and disseminating those claims, and gained clout in both electoral politics and the judicial realm. These developments led many commentators to observe that conservatives were "winning the war of ideas." But translating that political dominance into *policy* has been another matter altogether.

This disconnect between political power and apparently limited policy impact is emblematic of a more generic puzzle. It is widely recognized that institutions can prevent the wholesale transformation of policies, even when challengers wielding new ideas gain control of the policymaking apparatus.[16] Yet political scientists have found that on occasion ideas provide the content for major policy change;[17] they have also identified several mechanisms by which political officials can make incremental adjustments that undermine institutions over time.[18] The analysis that follows reflects the interplay between existing institutions, which both structure and foil efforts at policy change; the ideas that intermittently provide the impetus for major policy change; and efforts to modify policy without directly revoking or reforming it.

## Roadmap

The remainder of the book consists of a detailed political analysis of the role that conservatives' antiregulatory ideas have played in shaping the United States' response to environmental issues since 1980.[19] The main theme of this story concerns innovations in and contests over the use of administrative discretion. Conservative policymakers have devised new ways to weaken existing rules and delay or prevent the adoption of new ones. Similarly, proenvironmental officials have used their discretion to devise novel mechanisms to advance environmental protection in the face of hostility from a conservative Congress. A second theme involves policy learning, defined as revising policy goals or techniques in response to experience. In particular, some environmentalists have been genuinely convinced by arguments about the need for less prescriptive mechanisms, such as inducements, collaboration, and programs that facilitate voluntary stewardship; others have reluctantly accepted new analytic tools and policy mechanisms in deference to apparently intractable opposition. At least some conservatives have learned from experience that relying exclusively on private stewardship does not yield high levels of environmental protection. A third theme is political learning—that is, tactical adjustments in response to experience. Conservatives have become more savvy about employing environmentally friendly language and avoiding confrontation, while environmentalists have adopted the rhetoric of "balance," "common sense," and "efficiency" out of similar notions of political expediency. Over time, the use of administrative discretion by conservative officials, combined with policy and political learning among both advocates and officials, has yielded an environmental policy regime that is increasingly inadequate relative to the global risks we face.

These themes emerge out of a historical analysis guided by the theoretical framework laid out in chapter 2. Rooted in political science, sociology, and communications studies, that framework provides a set of empirical expectations about the interaction between ideas and institutions in bringing about (or resisting) policy change. It identifies three ways advocates and policy elites wielding new ideas try to influence politics and policy: (1) by helping allies attain positions of power in order to change the context in which policy decisions are made; (2) by challenging the status quo *directly* through attempts to change a law; or (3) by employing *low-profile* challenges, such as riders attached to must-pass legislation or adjustments in how a law is implemented and enforced, or interpreted by the courts.

Familiarity with the framework deepens the analysis that follows, but impatient readers may want to jump directly to chapter 3, which describes the simultaneous institutionalization of environmental ideas and growth of conservatives' capacity to challenge the status quo. As this chapter details, in the late 1960s and early 1970s, an environmental storyline emerged in which rapacious development was threatening the life-support systems of a fragile earth. That storyline prompted an eruption of public concern, to which politicians responded by enacting a series of environmentally protective laws. But environmentalism infuriated both industrialists and the members of a nascent conservative movement, who began popularizing an alternative storyline that disparaged environmentalists, downplayed environmental threats, and highlighted the costs of regulation. They recommended forcing proponents of government intervention in the economy to face much stiffer analytic tests, in hopes of greatly reducing the number and stringency of regulations. Although policymakers made some concessions in response to this critique, by the end of the decade environmental values had been institutionalized in federal agencies, congressional committees, and federal statutes. New laws and their attendant regulations and judicial interpretations, in turn, had prompted the development of a professional environmental advocacy community. At the same time, an increasingly cohesive conservative movement was amassing weapons to challenge the nation's newly created environmental regulatory framework.

Subsequent chapters examine how, beginning in 1981, conservative activists and political elites tackled the two pillars of the U.S. environmental regulatory framework—pollution control and conservation of natural resources and biodiversity—as well as how they obstructed efforts to address emerging problems, particularly climate change. Chapter 4 analyzes the Reagan years from 1981 to early 1989. At the beginning of this period, after gaining control of the White House, conservatives made a series of highly publicized attempts to roll back environmental regulations. A proenvironmental majority in Congress managed to fend off many of the Reagan administration's most aggressive antiregulatory initiatives, while the courts blocked others. Nevertheless, the White House was able to prevent action on the most prominent newly identified problem, acid rain, while slowing the pace of new regulations and curbing enforcement of existing rules. Moreover, nearly a decade of conservative dominance in the White House weakened the vigor with which many environmental laws were administered. Just as important, by promoting an antiregulatory storyline at the elite and grassroots levels, conservatives made environmentalism controversial, eroding the prospects for reforms designed to enhance the effectiveness of existing laws.

Chapter 5 documents how the presidency of George H. W. Bush coincided with the flowering in the late 1980s and 1990s of a grassroots movement to legitimize the antiregulatory storyline. Even as environmentalism experienced a resurgence in response to Reagan, conservative popularizers disseminated strident criticism of environmentalism and its policy consequences that was buttressed by academic critiques of the nation's pollution control framework. For his part, President Bush struggled to maintain a balance between these two powerful forces. In 1990, he signed the Clean Air Act Amendments, a major piece of environmental legislation that included an acid rain provision, and it briefly appeared that the proenvironmental storyline was again ascendant. Under pressure from his conservative advisors, however, Bush eventually backed away from the environmental commitments made during his campaign, and in 1992, he ran for reelection on an antiregulatory platform. Meanwhile, a challenge to federal rules aimed at conserving biodiversity gained traction with the emergence of a national property rights campaign and the wise use movement in the West. During this period, the courts also gave a boost to the conservative cause, particularly in the realm of land-use regulation.

By the time President Clinton took office in 1993, the antiregulatory mobilization was in full swing. The Reagan era had bolstered conservatives' confidence, while Bush's efforts to placate them had failed to quell demands for regulatory relief by an increasingly strident community of activists. Chapter 6 chronicles how changes in the media enhanced conservatives' ability to recruit a committed national constituency, as Web sites critical of environmentalism proliferated, and Fox News and talk radio commentators joined the fray. Riding a wave of antiregulatory activism in the West, conservative politicians gained control of Congress and used their new position to launch an aggressive attack on federal environmental regulations. In the process, they mistakenly assumed the public did not care about environmental issues. As they did under Reagan, environmentalists succeeded in stimulating public concern while their allies in Congress parried legislative challenges to the status quo. The attacks deepened the stalemate over reform, however; they also prompted efforts by the Clinton administration to appease conservatives and thereby defuse their attacks. By the end of the Clinton era, elite polarization on environmental issues was severe, and environmentalists' paramount concern—climate change—was controversial among the public and bogged down in Congress.

Chapter 7 analyzes the years from 2001 to 2008, the presidency of George W. Bush and the high-water mark of conservative governance. Control of both the White House and Congress by conservatives during much of this period emboldened them to attempt another round of legislative revisions—albeit this time couched in environmentally friendly language. Although most of the bills were unsuccessful, fending them off kept environmentalists fully occupied. In the meantime, tactical adjustments combined with distraction facilitated low-profile efforts by conservative appointees to weaken existing environmental rules and prevent action to address both well-known and newly recognized threats, particularly climate change. The courts circumscribed conservative achievements during this period, however. Furthermore, as the Bush era drew to a close, the enactment of policy to address climate change seemed almost inevitable. Democrats had regained the majority in Congress; popular concern appeared to have reached a tipping point; the Supreme Court had rejected the Bush administration's efforts to skirt the issue; and the conservative coalition was fracturing, as some business and religious groups vocally rejected Bush-era environmental policies.

Chapter 8 begins by providing an overall assessment of conservatives' accomplishments and failures between 1980 and 2008. Although they did not succeed in unraveling the regulatory framework established in the 1970s, conservatives did manage to relax the stringency of existing rules and stave off policies to address newly identified threats. In addition, by introducing an alternative storyline, conservatives forced environmentalists to reconsider both the substance of their appeals and their tactics; as a result of their continuing inability to bring about federal action on climate change, by the mid-2000s the environmental community was in turmoil, and diagnoses and prescriptions abounded. Perhaps most important, conservatives succeeded in making environmentalism controversial; although most Americans still claim to be sympathetic to environmental goals, resistance to government action in pursuit of those goals is widespread. So, as this chapter explains, although Obama took office promising a reversal of Bush-era policies on energy and the environment, the global recession, an ambivalent public, and a revitalized conservative movement stymied efforts to enact legislation to curb U.S. emissions of greenhouse gases in the 111th Congress. As a result, the president has been confined almost entirely to administrative adjustments aimed at reducing the nation's energy consumption. He has also exploited his discretion to advance some restrictive air-pollution-control policies, but has moved more cautiously on biodiversity conservation. The chapter concludes by reflecting on the prospects for environmentalism and environmental protection in the coming decades and considering what environmentalists can learn from the conservative movement.

# 2
# Discerning the Impact of Conservative Ideas

This chapter proposes a framework for thinking about how an emerging set of conservative ideas has interacted with recently created environmental institutions in the United States since 1970. The framework maps the tactical choices facing both proponents of new ideas and defenders of the status quo; it also suggests when and how different kinds of challenges are likely to prompt policy and political change. It is particularly relevant to the contemporary historical era, in which governance is fragmented into relatively autonomous policy systems, and competition within those systems among advocates and policymakers with a range of values and preferences is the norm, rather than the exception.[1]

The framework treats policy contests as struggles to define problems and characterize solutions within a rhetorical and institutional context that both constrains and provides opportunities for particular arguments and tactics. But an exclusive focus on overt policy debates and formal decisions can obscure "the subterranean political processes that shape ground-level policy effects,"[2] as well as the ways that powerful actors shape and restrict the political agenda, ensuring that some issues are never seriously considered.[3] Therefore, the framework accounts for the possibility that simply gaining control of the policymaking apparatus can enable decision makers to modify policy in important ways, even if they are unable to prevail in their efforts to redefine problems or furnish compelling portraits of their preferred policies.

## Ideas, Institutions, and Policy Change

Political scientists trying to explain policy stability and change increasingly invoke an interaction between ideas and institutions, rather than positing the overriding importance of either one. The first of these, ideas, includes thoughts, impressions, concepts, and strategies for action. As the internal contents of an individual mind, ideas filter perceptions of the physical world; when communicated in speeches, books, articles, correspondence, and other kinds of rhetoric, they are the means by which people and organizations shape the perceptions of others. Ideas take different forms depending on whether they have been packaged for consumption by popular or technical audiences.[4] Communicating an idea to the public involves translating technical jargon about problems and policies into narratives using symbols and images. The credibility and persuasiveness of a public narrative is a function not just of the quality of the story and its resonance with the cultural values of the audience, but also of the storyteller's credentials, recognition by peers, and associational membership—that is, his or her perceived authority. By contrast, communicating an idea to a technical audience—one consisting of academics/experts, bureaucrats, and judges—involves providing detailed explanations and using specialized language. The credibility and persuasiveness of a technical idea comes not just from the extent to which its content resolves an important technical puzzle, but also from the communicator's apparent evenhandedness, command of disciplinary concepts and analytic techniques, and professional stature.

Three basic kinds of ideas are especially relevant to the analysis in this book (see table 2.1): (1) overarching ideas about the political system, such as conservatism or liberalism; (2) ideas about specific policy systems, such as the environmental policy system; and (3) even more specific ideas about the nature of particular problems, like air pollution, and the workings of particular policies, like regulation or emissions trading.[5] At the level of the overarching political system, *worldviews* are internally held ideas about the relationship between government and the economy—conceptions of possibility that are "embedded in the symbolism of a culture and deeply affect modes of thought and discourse."[6] The translation of a worldview to a scholarly treatise is known as a *political philosophy*. Its public expression takes the more accessible form of a *public philosophy*, which Samuel Beer has defined as "an outlook on public affairs [that] is accepted within a nation by a wide coalition and [that] serves to give definition to problems and direction to government policies dealing with them."[7] At the policy-system level, *principled beliefs* consist of assumptions and the "theories" that flow from them about how a particular aspect of the world works. In their technical form, such beliefs are embedded in *analytic frameworks*; when communicated to the public, they take the form of *storylines*. Within any given policy system, a variety of analytic frameworks and storylines can coexist. At the level of indi-

**Table 2.1**
Categories of political ideas

| | Form of expression/type of audience | | |
| --- | --- | --- | --- |
| Political level | Internal-cognitive/ self | Technical/expert | Communicative/ public |
| (1) Overall political system | Worldview (Ideology) (Pre-analytic vision) | Political philosophy | Public philosophy |
| (2) Policy system | Principled beliefs (Core beliefs) | Analytic framework (Systemic framework) | Storyline (Commonsense reasoning) |
| | | (Policy paradigm) | |
| (3) Policy | Explanation for a problem, Solution to a problem (Policy mechanism) (Secondary beliefs) | Policy analysis  Policy prescription (Programmatic idea) (Sectoral idea) | Problem definition  Policy image |

vidual policies, two kinds of ideas are important. First, there are beliefs about the magnitude of a particular problem and the cause-and-effect mechanisms that underlie it. These constitute *policy analysis* in the technical realm and *problem definition* in public discourse. Also at this level are explanations of the workings of policies, which are *policy prescriptions* among technical audiences and *policy images* when communicated to the general public.[8]

All three levels of ideas can affect politics in a variety of ways, but most fundamentally, they structure people's perceptions of their interests—that is, their understandings of what is important to them—and, in turn, their policy goals, or preferences. Scholars working in the rational-choice tradition portray policymakers as rational, self-interested individuals whose preferences are fixed, and for whom ideas merely furnish "the hooks on which politicians hang their objectives and by which they further their interests."[9] Such a barren view is difficult to sustain, however. John Kingdon points out that people need to attach meaning to their behavior, even if that behavior is motivated by self-interest; he goes on to observe that, in any case, self-interest cannot be a sure guide to political decisions because policymakers often face considerable uncertainty.[10] Even more trenchant is Deborah Stone's observation that ideas and interests are deeply and fundamentally connected because people cannot determine their interests objectively, without reference to others. "In real societies," she argues, "where people are psychologically and materially dependent, where they are connected through emotional bonds, traditions, and social groups, their preferences are based on loyalties and comparisons of images. How people define their preferences depends to a large extent on how choices are presented to them and by whom."[11]

Although contemporary ideas clearly shape people's conceptions of their interests, they do so within the context of existing institutions, which structure those perceptions as well. Institutions comprise the "*relatively enduring* features of political and social life"[12]—the formal rules and practices of governance,[13] as well as the "informal rules and procedures that structure conduct" in an agency or organization.[14] Institutions arise when winning coalitions in a political struggle cement their victories in the design and operation of laws and organizations, creating policy legacies that, by design, protect their interests[15]—although the outcome of a political struggle may be a compromise that does not precisely reflect the interest of any particular group. In a phenomenon known as policy feedback, policy legacies shape subsequent participants' expectations, as well as their conceptions of what actions are reasonable, possible, and desirable; help determine who is a legitimate participant in a policy struggle; and provide opportunities for group mobilization by furnishing access and veto points.[16] Additional self-reinforcing mechanisms embedded in institutions, such as path dependence, similarly dampen the effects of contemporary efforts to change policy.[17] These stabilizing forces also "unbalance" the playing field for competitors in a policy debate, channeling policy decisions onto some paths and not others.[18]

While acknowledging the potent braking and channeling effects of institutions, many political scientists have observed that, during periods of apparent crisis, uncertain policymakers are susceptible to contemporary ideas that promise to restore stability and predictability to the system. According to John Ikenberry, at such branching points, or "critical junctures," typically caused by events outside an institution or policy system, "uncertainties about power structures and dissatisfaction with prevailing definitions of interests create opportunities for the recasting of interests."[19] As Mark Blyth observes, in situations of deep uncertainty, in which people do not know their interests, never mind how to realize them, "the set of available ideas with which to interpret the environment, reduce uncertainty, and make purposeful collective action possible becomes crucially important in determining the form of new institutions."[20] For example, the Great Depression created enormous uncertainty about the workings of the macroeconomic system, opening the door for Keynesian ideas; forty years later, stagflation destabilized the New Deal order, creating an intellectual opening for monetarist ideas.[21]

These insights, although useful, understate the propensity for internally generated institutional change and therefore the extent to which contemporary ideas may influence the outputs of policy systems. As James Mahoney and Kathleen Thelen point out, there is a great deal of "play" in the implementation and enforcement of existing rules.[22] Political coalitions seek not only to dislodge existing institutions but also to influence how those institutions interpret ambiguous rules. What is more, there is considerable evidence that, over time, policy analysis, deliberation, persuasion, and experience can prompt "policy learning," defined as "a deliberate attempt to adjust the goals or techniques of policy in response to past experience and new information."[23] That adjustment may be the result of a genuine change in beliefs, or it may be a pragmatic response to political conditions.[24] Even more common than policy learning is political learning, in which advocates and policy elites adjust their political strategies or tactics in response to the perceived effectiveness of the strategy and tactics of their opponents.

## Promoting Policy Change: How Ideas and Institutions Interact

Although their efforts are circumscribed by existing institutions, contemporary actors motivated by new ideas have a variety of options for effecting policy change. They can try to change the rhetorical or institutional context of a policy subsystem, in hopes of shaping subsequent policy battles. Alternatively, they can work within the existing context—either by challenging problem definitions and policy images directly, or by modifying the content of policies in low-profile ways that are unlikely to provoke widespread public opposition.[25] Importantly, proponents' ability to overturn the status quo, whether directly or through low-profile means, depends not just on the institutional context and the nature of the ideas they espouse, but on the response by defenders of the status quo. The outcome of a challenge also depends on factors external to the policy system, such as the state of the economy, the fortuitous occurrence of focusing events, and the overall partisan balance of power.

**Advancing Policy Change by Modifying the Policymaking Context**
Changing the context in which a policy debate arises can provide powerful levers for influencing the outcome of that debate. As has been widely
recognized, the U.S. political system is extremely (and purposefully)
fragmented. Each branch provides numerous access and veto points, and
it is extraordinarily difficult for one party to control simultaneously the
executive branch, both chambers of Congress, and the courts. In any
case, the parties themselves are not ideologically cohesive but rather are
loose coalitions whose ability to discipline their members is limited. As
a result, even when the same party gains control of the executive and
legislative branches, a rarity in the contemporary United States, it cannot
necessarily enact a legislative program without the cooperation of the
minority.

Nevertheless, if proponents of a particular public philosophy control
Congress, the White House, or both, they can enhance their ability to
defend or overturn the status quo by modifying the *institutional* context
within which policy decisions are made and carried out. Presidents establish the overall contours of the budget and appoint agency heads who
share their worldview. Although administrators can shape the implementation of laws in the short run, the appointment of judges is the best
means a president has for extending his impact in the long run;[26] for
example, the appointment of relatively liberal judges in the 1940s and
1950s made possible a series of decisions that extended federal protections for whole classes of people. Presidents can also issue executive
orders creating new organizational structures (such as task forces) or
procedures (such as centralized review) within the office of the White
House.

For its part, the majority party in Congress can modify either chamber's processes and rules, and elevate legislative leaders with particular
ideologies and strategic inclinations. If controlled by a single party, Congress has broad leeway in responding to the president's budget. And
Congress can pass laws requiring new procedures or eliminating existing
ones, thereby privileging some approaches to implementation over others.
For instance, the processes mandated by the Administrative Procedures
Act of 1946 increased public access to governmental decision making,
empowering those wielding ideas that had formerly been excluded from
consideration.

The *rhetorical* context of a policy system also creates limits on and
opportunities for defending or overturning the status quo. Recognizing
this, advocates and political elites who aspire to make policy more con-

sistent with their principled beliefs strive to create and disseminate a compelling alternative to the dominant storyline—typically a long-term endeavor. To be effective, a storyline should be rooted in an analytic framework that is supported by credible policy experts and contains a broad vision of the public good that draws on the existing cultural reservoir of ideas.[27] The dominant storyline constrains the types of problem definitions and policy images regarded as plausible; it also determines who is considered a legitimate participant in policymaking and shapes the public's and policymakers' perceptions of their political interests.[28] But a persuasive alternative storyline can generate a social movement and create new public norms guiding private action.[29] One signal that a competing storyline has gained traction is that the opposition incorporates elements of it into their own narrative.

### Advancing Policy Change by Challenging a Policy Directly

Changes in the institutional or rhetorical context of a policy system, though important, do not translate automatically into changes in particular policies. To dislodge the status quo, proponents must make several tactical choices. The first decision concerns the venue in which to mount a challenge: Congress, an agency, or the courts.[30] Each forum operates according to a different set of rules and on different timelines, and each has its own norms, language, and professional ethos.[31] A related decision concerns whether or not to attack directly. Although they occasionally result in major policy change, direct attacks on an institutionalized status quo are costly to mount and face long odds in the fragmented U.S. political system. In Congress, defenders of the status quo—if they are in the majority—possess a welter of institutional means to deflect direct legislative challenges: leaders can bottle up a measure in committee, refuse to schedule a floor vote, or allow unfriendly amendments on the floor. Even if they are in the minority, senators can block new legislation with a filibuster. A president who supports the status quo can impede legislative change simply by failing to propose or endorse a policy or, if necessary, by threatening or actually using a veto. In short, the status quo retains an enormous advantage in U.S. politics.

But challengers can create momentum for change if they can convince legislators that an issue is salient—that is, of widespread concern to voters—by redefining the problem. Redefining a problem entails furnishing a compelling and credible causal story—ideally one that posits a simple, direct relationship between cause and effect, identifies sympathetic victims and loathsome villains, suggests an imminent crisis, and gains the endorsement of authoritative experts.[32] For example, Rachel Carson's *Silent Spring* redefined pesticides, initially portrayed as salvation from devastating insects, as poisons that, used indiscriminately, threaten the web of life. An effective problem definition can turn an ongoing phenomenon into a public-policy concern and shape perceptions of its severity and urgency.[33] It can also influence people's conceptions of their interests and what is at stake, and thus prompt or inhibit political mobilization and facilitate or obstruct the formation of alliances.[34] Just as a particular definition of a problem underpins the status quo, a redefinition can enable challengers to get a new issue onto the political agenda.[35] Finally, because it provides a causal explanation and fixes responsibility, a widely accepted problem definition can limit the range and type of solutions the public and policymakers are likely to regard as legitimate.[36]

Although politicians ordinarily prefer to avoid uncertain political fallout by adjusting policy incrementally, if a problem appears to be widely salient, aspiring leaders may choose to expend their political capital building a coalition that is large enough to enact policy change.[37] Moreover, rank-and-file legislators are likely to get on the bandwagon because salience reduces the electoral uncertainty of taking a position on an issue.[38] Of course, policymakers do not simply respond to advocates' formulations. As Larry Jacobs and Robert Shapiro explain, politicians try to shape public perceptions using rhetoric they believe will resonate, based on the results of polls and focus groups and the advice of lobbyists and staff. They use "crafted talk" to raise the priority and increase the weight that individuals assign to particular attitudes they already hold, in order to affect the yardstick voters use to evaluate a proposal.[39]

The media play a central role in facilitating (or impeding) efforts by advocates or policymakers to raise the salience of a particular problem definition.[40] To a large extent, the media set the public agenda; through framing, they also shape the way people think about problems, especially on issues about which they have no firsthand experience.[41] Therefore, journalists' assessments of what constitutes a newsworthy story, as well as their selection of trustworthy sources, exerts a powerful influence on their audiences' adherence to a particular problem definition. (At the same time, journalists' quest for balance can bolster the credibility of a competing problem definition.) Policymakers and advocates are well aware of the incentives and constraints facing journalists, and they create "events," such as speeches, demonstrations, press conferences, and hearings. For example, according to Representative Henry Waxman, legislative hearings present "a golden opportunity to bring public attention to an issue, which instantly [makes] it a higher priority for Congress."[42] The practical effect of a successful hearing, he says, is that the media immediately want to know what is being done to remedy the problem.

Should proponents of policy change succeed in raising the salience of a problem definition, having an appealing policy solution on hand further improves their prospects. Crafting a policy image involves far more than simply choosing from a toolkit of potential policy mechanisms. As Anne Schneider and Helen Ingram point out, "Public officials must explain and justify their policy positions to the electorate by articulating a vision of the public interest and then showing how a proposed policy is logically connected to these widely shared public values. . . . They need to have a believable causal logic connecting the various aspects of the policy design to desired outcomes."[43] The construction of a policy image follows logic similar to problem definition: initially, policy prescriptions are vetted in the expert community, where they may be "softened up" for years.[44] To survive this process, policy prescriptions must be technically sound and have the support of credible analysts. "It is not clear reasoning or carefully developed and interpreted facts that make [policy] ideas convincing"; rather, policy images "seem to become anchored in people's minds through illustrative anecdotes, simple diagrams and pictures, or connections with broad commonsense ideologies that define human nature and social responsibilities."[45]

Timothy Conlan, Margaret Wrightson, and David Beam illuminate the process of developing and propagating a policy image in their description of the politics of tax reform in the early 1980s.[46] They contend that "the release of Treasury's proposals gave the media a new and sharper angle, a story in stark black and white that pitted special interests and the status quo in tax policy against the public interest and tax reform." At the same time, the Treasury Department's "uncompromising application of economic principles gave the study credibility among the press, while Reagan's subsequent emphasis on 'fairness, simplicity, and economic growth' gave journalists the hooks needed to make front-page news." The media turned tax reform into a "tar baby"; the tax-reform battle became an epic struggle between good and evil. Like all good political stories, this one was highly personalized, singling out, for example, Robert Packwood (dubbed "Senator Hackwood") as a foe of reform. The authors conclude: "[I]t is clear that populist rhetoric, bright lights, and the casting of tax reform as something legislators could only be 'for' or 'against' converted many who would not have sympathized with the cause under other circumstances."[47]

Occasionally, legislative leaders may sponsor a policy prescription even if it lacks a well-crafted image and the problem it purports to address is not salient. Sometimes leaders are motivated by anticipation of public concern; alternatively, agencies or courts may put an issue on the legislative agenda by making a decision to which Congress feels compelled to respond. In such cases, technical analysis rather than public approbation may be central to the process of legitimizing a particular policy. For example, Martha Derthick and Paul Quirk observe that analysis played a key role in the economic deregulation debate of the 1980s because it was grounded in expert agreement and offered relatively complete guidance for officeholders' actions.[48] The authors acknowledge, however, that like tax reform, economic deregulation made for good politics because proponents could portray it in simple, symbolic, and relatively intuitive terms. They point to another crucial feature of the politics of economic deregulation as well: the regulatory commissions had already made economic deregulation the status quo. As a result, Congress felt its prerogatives had been challenged; under pressure from regulated industries to restore stability, it merely needed to codify reform measures already instituted.

Perhaps most important, Derthick and Quirk observe, proponents of economic deregulation were aided by the fact that their opponents were relatively disorganized and had no defensible idea with which to buttress the status quo. Such a situation is increasingly rare, however, especially as policy monopolies have become less common and competitive policy systems the norm.[49] More commonly, defenders of the status quo are prepared to mobilize and respond to a direct challenge. They can do this by attacking both the persuasiveness and the credibility of challengers' problem definition and policy image.[50] An effective counter-narrative downplays the extent and magnitude of the harmful effects associated with a problem, casts doubt on opponents' cause-and-effect framing, and highlights the costs and unintended consequences of the policy proposed to remediate the problem. Like challengers, defenders of the status quo craft problem definitions and policy images that feature victims, villains, and heroes, along with a straightforward causal story; ideally, they posit that a crisis will ensue if the proposed policy is enacted. To enhance their credibility, they cite experts who share their worldview.

**Advancing Policy Change through Low-Profile Policy Challenges**

Overt policy battles make for good political theater but can require massive expenditures of political and financial capital. Therefore, as Jacob Hacker points out, sometimes those motivated by ideas that are incompatible with popular institutions "may find it prudent not to attack such institutions directly. Instead, they may seek to shift those institutions' ground-level operations, prevent their adaptation to shifting external circumstances, or build new institutions on top of them."[51] The central attribute of low-profile challenges is that they tend to undermine opposition, or contain conflict: it is difficult to garner publicity for such challenges and therefore to make them salient. The more arcane they are, the more difficult it is to mobilize resistance.

Members of Congress have a variety of low-profile means to challenge the status quo. They can communicate directly with high-level agency officials or adjust an agency's budgetary level or allocation to reflect their own preferences. One of the most effective low-profile tactics legislators can employ is to attach a rider—or nongermane amendment—to popular legislation. Legislators can use riders to prohibit agency spending on particular activities, forbid citizen suits or judicial review of an agency decision, or make other, more substantive policy adjustments. Because they must pass if government is to be funded, appropriations and other budget bills are particularly effective vehicles for provisions that would not withstand public scrutiny. Klyza and Sousa explain: "Submerged in the voluminous language and figures of a multi-billion dollar appropriations bill, riders may move through the legislative process quietly, with little or no debate. Congressional opponents may not be able to muster their forces to fight riders when there are so many other issues at stake in a huge appropriations bill, and presidents may hesitate to veto must-pass appropriations bills to kill one or a few noxious riders."[52] Although House and Senate rules technically reserve substantive policymaking for authorizing legislation, in practice legislators can attach provisions to appropriations bills with relative impunity.

Proponents of the status quo can fend off low-profile legislative challenges by drawing attention to them, thereby expanding the scope of the conflict.[53] If advocates succeed in making a low-profile challenge sufficiently salient, its allies in Congress are likely to demand its removal. Alternatively, the president can veto the bill containing the offending provision. The mere threat of a veto may be enough to prompt legislators to withdraw the measure.

Low-profile challenges are not restricted to the legislative branch. The president has a variety of tools with which to change policy quietly and unilaterally: executive orders, proclamations, presidential memoranda (less formal and therefore simpler to execute than executive orders), and presidential signing statements. As political scientist Phillip Cooper points out, such presidential directives "are quick, convenient, and relatively easy mechanisms for moving significant policy initiatives."[54] For example, Abraham Lincoln used a proclamation to free the slaves in 1863; Franklin D. Roosevelt placed Japanese-Americans in detention camps by executive order in 1942; Richard Nixon used a proclamation to levy a 10 percent surcharge on imports in 1971; and President Clinton used his executive prerogative to apply a patients' bill of rights to all federal health plans.[55]

Administrators also have numerous options for low-profile challenges to the status quo. Most obviously, they can try to modify the way a law is implemented by instituting new rules or repealing or substantially revising existing ones; they can also expedite or delay a rulemaking process. In formulating a rule, they can choose to consult with (or ignore) particular interests or to infuse the rulemaking process with a new analytic perspective. The option of challenging the status quo through rulemaking may appear especially desirable if proponents have a technically compelling policy analysis that does not translate into a publicly appealing problem definition, or if they anticipate a successful defensive mobilization in response to their policy prescription. Of course, proposed rules must be published and the public allowed to comment; on the other hand, the rulemaking process is arcane and the language used technical. As *Washington Post* journalist Joanne Omang explains, "Major policies are hidden in small phrases, subordinate clauses and fine gray print in all existing environmental legislation. And even more so in its regulations." Because proposed rules or rule changes "are put forward in jargon and on a level of detail guaranteed to confuse non-experts," it is difficult to persuade the media and therefore the public of their significance.[56]

Nevertheless, rulemaking is cumbersome, so indirect approaches may be more expedient. Administrators may decide instead to shift an agency's programmatic emphasis by changing the allocation of the budget. As Richard Waterman observes, "Since Congress is often limited in its ability to force agencies to spend funds exactly as specified in the budget, presidents and their subordinates have a great deal of freedom to determine how funds will be allocated after the budget has officially been set."[57] Administrators can also increase, cut, or reorganize personnel; take on new functions or privatize functions previously performed by the bureaucracy; and hire and promote, or demote and transfer, critical personnel. Alternatively, agency heads can centralize authority over a program or devolve responsibility for implementing or enforcing it to the states, capitalizing on the fact that states have different priorities and capacities. Or they can modify the decision-making process—by adjusting the membership or size of a decision-making body or an advisory panel, or the rules by which such a group reaches closure—in hopes that the new process will yield a definition of the problem that warrants a different kind of solution.[58]

Agency heads have a host of even more covert means of challenging the status quo at their disposal. They can direct their staff to change the interpretation or enforcement of rules. They can adjust agency operating procedures through internal memos and unpublished directives. They can reopen rules by soliciting new public comment, or postpone a rule's effective date of implementation. In concert with the Department of Justice, agency heads can adopt a variety of legal positions that affect how a policy is implemented, such as adjusting the aggressiveness with which criminal and civil violations are pursued, defending or declining to defend an agency against legal challenges, or settling on terms that are favorable to the plaintiffs. Finally, agency officials can take an analytic stance that undermines or buttresses a particular policy: they have the discretion to interpret evidence in the course of a formal analysis, such as a cost-benefit analysis or risk assessment; refer an issue to an advisory committee or request a peer review; demand additional information or make do without it; or alter, suppress, or publicize information generated by agency staff.

Although administrators have substantial discretion, their ability to change unilaterally the way a rule is written or implemented is limited by opponents' ability to jeopardize their autonomy—that is, their ability to take actions consistent with their own wishes without interference from politicians, courts, and organized interests.[59] Administrators value their autonomy because they believe in their own expertise, fear losing control of their turf, and dislike uncertainty.[60] A credible threat to her autonomy can compel an administrator to seek alternative solutions, if only to regain control of decision making. As former Environmental Protection Agency (EPA) legal counsel Jon Cannon observes, in the interest of maintaining control over its own decision making, an agency engages in a complex dance with its overseers: if it anticipates attracting attention from Congress or the White House, and so is vulnerable to reversal or having its authority curtailed, the agency may decide to modify its behavior to avoid or minimize those risks.[61]

Raising the salience of a problem or highlighting a new way of addressing it is one way advocates and policymakers can threaten an administrator's autonomy because once an issue becomes highly visible, political appointees and legislative overseers are more likely to intervene in agency decision making.[62] To raise an issue's salience, outside advocates can launch public relations campaigns that publicize low-profile challenges; they can support whistleblowers who reveal details of agencies' internal operations. Opponents in Congress can raise the salience of low-profile tactics by administrators as well—by launching investigations into agency behavior, submitting a barrage of questions that consume bureaucrats' time, or holding hearings that require extensive preparation and at which legislators chastise agency officials. If actions by one member of the executive branch become salient, other political appointees or members of the White House staff may intervene by threatening agency resources or personnel, or by appealing to the president. Congress may retaliate by passing legislation that changes an agency's legal mandate or reduces its discretion by imposing more detailed requirements. It may give citizens more access to agency decision making, hold up appointments of key agency personnel, or reduce an agency's appropriations. Alternatively, since the passage in 1996 of the Congressional Review Act, Congress can reverse a rule, as long as a simple majority in both houses votes for and the president signs a "resolution of disapproval" within sixty legislative days of its submission.[63]

A second way advocates can threaten an administrator's autonomy is by filing a lawsuit that demonstrates persuasively that the agency is acting unlawfully—because its action transgresses limitations set by Congress (via statute), lacks statutory authority, or is "arbitrary and capricious" because it exceeds permissible bounds for the exercise of agency discretion At the very least, a lawsuit—or the credible threat of one—can stall implementation of an agency rule or decision and serve as a bargaining chip in a dispute; at most, a court ruling can force an agency to reconsider and even alter the premises underlying its decision. To be successful, however, litigants must present a persuasive legal argument that is supported by the plain meaning of constitutional, statutory, or regulatory language, or by settled judicial precedent interpreting that language.[64] That said, sometimes the application of the law to a particular agency action is unclear, either because the case presents novel facts or because the relevance of particular constitutional, statutory, or regulatory language, or of previous judicial rulings (precedent) is not obvious.[65] In the face of such ambiguity, litigants' ability to prevail depends not only on the defendants' skill at furnishing a compelling counter-narrative but also on the identity of the specific federal judges, particularly their ability and ideology, and—in the appeals courts, where the vast majority of controversial cases are resolved—the composition of the judicial panel.[66]

## Policy and Political Outcomes

Because direct challenges face long odds, major policy change is rare. To be successful, policy entrepreneurs who launch a direct challenge to the status quo must not only prevail in the struggle to define a problem but must link that problem to their preferred policy image when a policy window opens.[67] Basic attributes of the U.S. political system, including divided control of the political branches and inter- and intraparty differences, as well as numerous structural veto points, exacerbate the difficulties associated with direct challenges. Because of feedback effects, policies that confer substantial and long-lived benefits on large groups of beneficiaries are likely to be particularly resistant to a direct challenge.[68]

That said, singly or in combination, direct and low-profile challenges can produce incremental policy changes, which result in "gradual institutional transformations that add up to major historical discontinuities."[69] Such transformations can arise through "layering," "conversion," or "drift." Layering is the introduction of new rules alongside or atop existing ones; it can lead to significant change if it alters the logic of an institution or compromises its stable reproduction.[70] Conversion occurs in situations where "existing institutions are redirected to new purposes, driving changes in the role they perform and/or the functions they serve."[71] Like conversion, drift involves "changes in the operation or effect of policies that occur without significant changes in these policies' structures."[72] The major cause of drift is decisions by policymakers to "prevent the recalibration of . . . programs" despite a change in the social context;[73] as a result, there is a growing gap between the aims of a policy and new conditions.

Building on work by Jacob Hacker, James Mahoney and Kathleen Thelen hypothesize that two factors determine the nature of change that is likely to occur: the *strength of veto possibilities* in the political context and the *level of discretion* within the institution.[74] They posit that layering is likely when there are strong veto possibilities but a low level

**Table 2.2**
Contextual and institutional factors that facilitate institutional change

|  |  | Characteristics of targeted institutions | |
|  |  | Low levels of discretion | High levels of discretion |
|---|---|---|---|
| Characteristics of the policy context | Strong veto possibilities | Layering | Drift |
|  | Weak veto possibilities | Displacement/ revision | Conversion |

*Source*: James Mahoney and Kathleen Thelen, eds., *Explaining Institutional Change: Ambiguity, Agency, and Power* (New York: Cambridge University Press, 2010).

of discretion within the institution; drift is more likely when there are strong veto possibilities but a high level of administrative discretion; and conversion is more likely when there are weak veto possibilities and a high level of discretion (see table 2.2). Whatever the process by which change occurs, the net result is that a new idea gains a foothold in the administration of policy—in place of or alongside the older ones—without a significant public debate. For example, layering occurred in the 1980s and 1990s, as new policies fostered the rapid growth of employer-sponsored and individual retirement accounts—a development that dramatically shifted the retirement-savings landscape and over time threatened to undermine support for Social Security.[75] During the same period, the impacts of drift and conversion were evident in health care policy: private health insurance coverage fell as a result of declines in employer-based insurance, and public insurance programs failed to fill the gaps. The failure of the Clinton health care reform plan in 1994 reinforced a tendency toward drift that was only arrested with the passage of health care reform in 2009.

When combined with long-term efforts to change the rhetorical context, direct and low-profile challenges can facilitate political as well as policy changes. In particular, as Mark Smith observes, policymakers may respond to effective challenges by reprioritizing, reframing, or repositioning.[76] Reprioritizing involves taking an issue formerly low on the agenda and raising its prominence, in hopes of appealing to a new or disaffected audience. Reframing involves shuffling the hierarchy of arguments used to justify a position on an issue, again in order to broaden one's appeal. Repositioning, the most drastic step, entails revising a policy position in order "to align oneself with the rhetorical possibilities and constraints of the day."[77] Such adjustments, in turn, create new possibilities for policies that might once have seemed unthinkable or at least improbable.

## Using the Framework to Make Sense of Politics

The argument about the impact of conservative ideas on environmental politics and policy that unfolds in the next five chapters is rooted in the framework described above. It draws for support on evidence from a wide variety of primary and secondary sources, including speeches and campaign platforms; testimony in legislative hearings, legislative committee reports, floor debates, conference committee reports, and veto messages; newspaper and journal coverage; documents and commentary from conservative Web sites, journals, and books; a broad range of scholarship on the ideas, history, and values of American conservatism, including biographies of prominent conservative figures; and scores of in-depth, semi-structured interviews with conservative activists, environmentalists, and political officials.[78]

To illuminate which factors have been most influential in determining the impact of conservative ideas, I compare efforts—both direct and low-profile—to make the Clean Air Act, the Endangered Species Act (ESA), and climate change policy more restrictive or more permissive. Although focusing on specific policies narrows the scope of the book, doing so facilitates systematic comparison; it also inhibits the tendency to cherry-pick examples that support the view that conservative ideas have (or have not) been influential. In each of the policy areas I examine, conservative activists formed alliances with industries affected by environmental regulation. In two of the three, those coalitions confronted environmentally protective policies that were institutionalized in federal agencies. The Clean Air Act has been a thorn in the side of conservatives since 1970, when the federal government instituted a much more restrictive standards-and-deadlines-based approach than had existed previously. At the same time, it has remained among the most consistently popular of the nation's environmental laws. Moreover, the EPA, which administers the Clean Air Act, has a singular mission to protect the environment and public health. Federal efforts to conserve biodiversity through the Endangered Species Act have also provoked conservative ire, particularly since the late 1980s. Like the Clean Air Act, the ESA transformed a relatively permissive status quo into a highly restrictive one. Because of their primary focus on ecological rather than human health, however, ESA-related actions have been much less salient among the general public than those related to the Clean Air Act. Complicating matters further, the agencies responsible for implementing the Endangered Species Act, the Fish and Wildlife Service and the National Marine Fisheries Service, reside within departments with historic resource development mandates.

The third issue, climate change, gained prominence in the 1980s, by which time conservatives had developed a formula for rebuffing calls for environmental regulation. Importantly, in this policy area environmentalists have been the challengers, demanding more restrictive policy, while conservatives have defended a permissive status quo. Therefore, the struggle has revolved around whether or not climate change is a problem at all, with environmentalists trying to heighten its perceived importance and enhance the palatability of proposed solutions, and conservatives trying to downplay its significance and tarnish the image of policies to address it.

The central analytic task of the chapters that follow is to demonstrate a causal connection between contemporary conservative ideas and policy or political outcomes, while accounting for the mediating impacts of institutions and environmentalists' responses. To this end, first and foremost, I investigate the extent to which specific policy outcomes are consistent with the stated preferences of conservative activists. For the Clean Air Act, key outcomes include the stringency of air quality standards relative to scientists' recommendations, the pollution-reduction capacity of emission regulations and other rules relative to the options available, and the level and nature of enforcement activities. For the Endangered Species Act, I examine decisions about whether or not to list species as threatened or endangered, the amount and quality of critical habitat designated, and the extent to which biological opinions and recovery plans are environmentally risk-averse.[79] For climate change, I consider the extent and nature of the United States' participation in international deliberations and agreements, the existence and level of domestic limits on or charges for greenhouse gas emissions, and the level of federal support for alternative fuels and energy efficiency measures.

Many of my informants strongly cautioned against relying too heavily on statistics—from enforcement and budget figures to species listings— as measures of performance because such figures are easy to manipulate and because implementation is far more complex than quantitative data can convey. For example, any attempt to standardize enforcement at the EPA is confounded by the enormous variety of conditions and circumstances that individual cases involve. As a result, enforcement officials must make a large number of subjective choices in deciding how to proceed.[80] Furthermore, because influence often occurs early in the decision-making process, its impact may be masked by the use of quantitative indicators. Therefore, I assemble a variety of qualitative data to supplement quantitative measures of policy outcomes.

In addition to evaluating the correlation between conservative preferences and policy outcomes, I also assess the correspondence between the rhetoric of conservative advocates and the language employed by politicians and political appointees to explain their positions and decisions. For legislative challenges, I trace the relationships among ideas propagated by conservatives, media coverage of issues, public opinion, and justifications offered by policymakers. In evaluating administrative challenges, I consider administrators' rationales as well as judges' reasoning where relevant. I also seek evidence that decision makers did (or did not) debate the relative merits of competing ideas while considering their own position, as well as the extent to which they were constrained in doing so by institutional forces.

In the chapters that follow I weave comparisons among efforts to revise the Clean Air Act and the ESA, as well as efforts to prevent policies to address climate change, into a chronological narrative. In detecting the relative causal force of conservative ideas and existing institutions amid a wealth of data, chronology is central.[81] At a minimum, we can attribute causal force to an idea only if that idea was articulated prior to the action in question. But even this requirement is complicated in practice. Ideas often bubble up in various places before they are formally articulated and disseminated; by the time a book or journal article is published, the ideas it contains may have been circulating for some time in white papers, conference papers, and informal conversations. On the other hand, the release of a new book or article may provoke a wider discussion of an idea that has been around for years. I have adopted the relatively conservative analytic approach of considering an idea influential only if it was demonstrably in the public realm prior to its articulation by a decision maker.

Chronology also matters in assessing the magnitude of changes in policy outcomes. Simple comparisons from one administration to the next of measures like acreage conserved, dollars spent, or number of enforcement actions are almost certain to be misleading. For example, legal scholar John Leshy argues that the Reagan administration did not meaningfully accelerate coal and gas leasing, notwithstanding its claims to that effect. As Leshy explains, the federal government had already taken the better part of a decade to come up with a coal-leasing program that was both legal and politically acceptable. Federal coal leasing, he says, "was *bound* to have increased sharply after 1981 simply because all the pieces had finally been put into place" (emphasis mine).[82] Similarly, the federal offshore oil- and gas-leasing program was in upheaval during the 1970s, and in 1980, Carter's interior secretary Cecil Andrus proposed to double oil and gas leasing on the outer continental shelf over the subsequent five years. Therefore the question is: how much did the Reagan administration increase leasing *beyond what was likely to happen anyway*, given the institutional context of the time.

Complicating the effort to isolate the impact of conservative ideas on politics and policy is the fact that in the U.S. political system the ideological composition of any single institution—the White House, Congress, an agency, or an appellate court—is rarely monolithic. In fact, some of the most interesting episodes occur when there is disagreement within an administration over the proper course of action. Moreover, whatever the reigning ideology within a particular institution, political actors are constrained at any given time by events in the political context that they do not control and by general perceptions of what is politically feasible. Finally, outcomes produced by the system are both provisional and a result of a complex interplay among the branches. For example, an agency decision may stand for several years before being overturned by the courts; therefore, the lag time between the initial impact of an idea and its ultimate consequences can be substantial.

# 3

# The Environmental Decade and the Conservative Backlash, 1970–1980

*For the first two-thirds of the twentieth century, environmental protection in the United States was primarily a state and local affair, and one that—with occasional exceptions—garnered little national attention. But in the 1960s, a new storyline rooted in an environmental worldview gained traction. In response to an outpouring of public concern, in the early 1970s, Republican president Richard M. Nixon worked with a Democratic Congress to pass a series of laws that launched the "environmental decade." Those laws layered biodiversity conservation directives on top of the resource conservation and development mandates of the nation's land-management agencies. They also created a spate of new pollution control requirements, to be administered by the recently created Environmental Protection Agency.*

*Even as environmentalism was becoming institutionalized in the federal government, conservatives were popularizing an alternative storyline that they hoped would furnish a rationale for rolling back new environmental laws. In the face of criticism from industry and its conservative allies, as well as changing economic conditions and waning public attention, policymakers retreated from some of their most ambitious environmental commitments. Nevertheless, by the end of the 1970s, environmentalism was embedded in federal agencies, laws, and regulations. In addition, a policy community comprising experts, environmental activists, and sympathetic journalists had taken shape. At the same time, a well-funded conservative movement, intent on dismantling the recently installed environmental status quo, was gaining momentum.*

## Institutionalizing the Environmental Storyline

The modern environmental movement emerged during the late 1960s and early 1970s, a tumultuous period in U.S. history. In April 1968, Martin Luther King Jr. was assassinated, and a spate of riots broke out in cities across the country. A few months later, presidential hopeful Robert Kennedy was shot. Growing opposition to the war in Vietnam fed a "counterculture" skeptical of all the nation's major institutions, but particularly business. Protests erupted on college campuses. Meanwhile, national polls documented an extraordinary rise in popular concern about the environment that cut across nearly all segments of society.[1] According to historian Samuel Hays, three impulses drove the emergence of modern environmentalism: the search for a better life associated with home, community, and leisure; rising expectations about health and well-being; and the spread of an "ecological perspective that arose out of the popularization of knowledge about natural processes."[2] These impulses, in turn, followed on the heels of a series of societal changes, notably rising education levels and affluence.[3]

The original environmental storyline, as articulated by activists and scientific popularizers, described a fragile earth whose ability to provide resources to meet human demands was constrained by physical limits. Drawing on a risk-averse interpretation of the available science, the emerging storyline emphasized the potentially severe impacts of human activity—both extracting natural resources and dumping wastes—on human health and the environment. According to some versions, as a result of unchecked growth, the human economy was approaching (or had already exceeded) the earth's carrying capacity. The storyline also expressed skepticism about the ability of technology to solve problems or mitigate scarcity. In fact, it portrayed technology as the foremost cause of the planet's decline. Suspicious of private-sector innovation, environmentalists prescribed strong federal action to overcome the inertia of a political system controlled by parochial and industrial interests. The ultimate goal was a better quality of life rather than ever-increasing levels of consumption.

Not just advocates but also high-level political officials articulated versions of the environmental storyline. A 1965 message to Congress by President Lyndon Johnson captured its essence:

For centuries Americans have drawn strength and inspiration from the beauty of our country. . . . Yet the storm of modern change is threatening to blight and diminish in a few decades what has been cherished and protected for generations. A growing population is swallowing up areas of natural beauty with its demands for living space, and is placing increased demand on our overburdened areas of recreation and pleasure. The increasing tempo of urbanization and growth is already depriving many Americans of the right to live in decent surroundings. More of our people are crowding into cities and being cut off from nature. Cities themselves reach out into the countryside, destroying streams and trees and meadows as they go. A modern highway may wipe out the equivalent of a fifty acre park with every mile. And people move out from the city to get closer to nature only to find that nature has moved farther from them.

The modern technology, which has added much to our lives, can also have a darker side. Its uncontrolled waste products are menacing the world we live in, our enjoyment and our health. The air we breathe, our water, our soil and wildlife, are being blighted by the poisons and chemicals which are the by-products of technology and industry. . . . [4]

Stewart Udall, who served as interior secretary under Presidents Kennedy and Johnson, explicitly argued for limits on economic growth to avoid destroying the environment. In particular, he advocated putting the brakes on "mechanization, affluence, and on all kinds of useless and conspicuous consumption."[5]

### The Nixon Administration Passes Landmark Environmental Laws

Although not personally an environmentalist, President Nixon responded to the issue's burgeoning popularity by adopting it as his own. On January 1, 1970, he took the first step toward institutionalizing environmentalism in the federal government by signing the National Environmental Policy Act (NEPA). The purpose of NEPA was to "encourage productive and enjoyable harmony between man and his environment" as well as "to promote efforts which will prevent or eliminate damage to the environment and biosphere and stimulate the health and welfare of man." To these ends, NEPA mandated the creation of a Council on Environmental Quality (CEQ) to advise the president and generate a yearly status report on efforts to improve the nation's environmental quality. In addition, NEPA required all federal agencies to integrate environmental values into their decision making by considering the environmental impacts of their proposals and articulating reasonable alternative actions. Nixon's CEQ translated the latter provision into a requirement that a formal environmental impact statement (EIS) accompany every major federally funded project.

After signing NEPA, Nixon delivered a series of speeches in which he employed rhetoric that was strikingly consistent with the environmental storyline. For example, he devoted much of his 1970 State of the Union address to the environment, stressing the urgency of taking action. He decried the effects of unfettered economic growth and returned several times to two themes: that happiness was not to be found in personal economic wealth and that the economic indicators of government did not reflect citizens' well-being. (At the same time, he argued not for limiting but for redirecting growth, on the grounds that increasing prosperity provides the means to protect the environment.) In his February 1970 Special Message to the Congress on Environmental Quality, Nixon warned: "We in this century have too casually and too long abused our natural environment." The task ahead, he went on to say, called for "fundamentally new philosophies of land, air and water use, for stricter regulation, for expanded government action, for greater citizen involvement . . ."

On April 22, 1970, popular support for environmentalism reached a tipping point, as millions of people across the country poured into the streets to celebrate Earth Day. Nixon's August 1970 message to Congress on the transmittal of the First Annual Report of the CEQ, perhaps his most eloquent, revealed the political impact of Earth Day. In it the president asserted: "The recent upsurge of public concern over environmental questions reflects a belated recognition that man has been too cavalier in his relations with nature." Without prompt action, he continued, "we face the prospect of ecological disaster." He pointed out that the environment was not an abstract concern or a matter of aesthetics or personal taste. Rather, "[o]ur physical nature, our mental health, our culture and institutions, our opportunities for challenge and fulfillment, our very survival—all of these are directly related to and affected by the environment in which we live. They depend upon the continued healthy functioning of the natural systems of the Earth."

To the dismay of many of his conservative and business supporters, Nixon proceeded to oversee the creation of a set of institutions that embodied the environmental storyline, thereby changing the context for pollution-control decision making. In July 1970, he established the Environmental Protection Agency (EPA) through administrative reorganization, thereby bringing coherence to what had been a fragmented and ineffectual federal pollution-control policy system. Initially, the EPA's mission was simply to establish and enforce environmental protection standards and conduct research to facilitate that process; over time, its mission became more ambitious: to protect human health and the environment. Nixon went on to issue a slew of executive orders that prohibited killing endangered species, restricted the use of off-road vehicles on federal lands, increased protection for historically and culturally important sites, and imposed safeguards for controlling predators on federal land.

In collaboration with large, bipartisan majorities in Congress, Nixon also approved a series of ambitious environmental laws that reflected the principles of environmentalism: holism, interconnectedness, and human dependence on natural systems. These laws departed dramatically from their predecessors in a variety of ways. They clearly established federal supremacy in a realm that had previously been primarily the purview of the states. They also rejected the common-law paradigm of balancing competing rights and entitlements, substituting in its place a presumption against pollution.[6] And they featured a host of action-forcing provisions— including strict deadlines and stringent standards—that greatly increased environmentalists' legal leverage over developers and polluters.

Most of the new statutes also contained citizen-suit provisions, which allow any person to pursue civil enforcement against alleged violators or against any agency that does not enforce the law. These provisions gave environmentalists unprecedented access to the courts. The federal courts had opened up to environmentalists in the 1960s, as judges relaxed standing requirements to include aesthetic, not just material, consider-ations. But government agencies continued to routinely assert lack of standing as a defense, forcing environmental groups to go through the time-consuming and expensive process of demonstrating it.[7] Citizen-suit provisions eliminated such barriers. In short, the nation's new environ-mental laws were, as legal scholar Richard Lazarus describes them, "dramatic, sweeping, and uncompromising, consistent with the nation's spiritual and moral resolution on the issue."[8] More prosaically, they made environmentalists "permanent players in the regulatory game."[9]

The Clean Air Act, signed on December 31, 1970, was the first and most expansive pollution control law of the contemporary era; it sig-naled a radical shift in the definition of the air pollution problem. As political scientist Helen Ingram points out, with the passage of the act, "[t]he programmatic, functional definition of air quality, restricted to what was economically and technologically feasible, was abandoned, and clean air was legislated a fundamental, national value."[10] The Clean Air Act also embodied a new policy image: its strict timelines and uncompromising—some said unrealistic—technology-forcing standards were consistent with the view of environmental protection as a right.

The avowed purpose of the statute was to "protect and enhance the quality of the Nation's air resources so as to promote the public health and welfare and the productive capacity of its population." To that end, it required the EPA to set minimum national ambient air quality stan-dards (NAAQS) that would safeguard public health (primary standards) and welfare (secondary standards) without considering economic costs. To meet those standards, new stationary pollution sources (factories, power plants) were required to install the best available pollution control technology—the so-called New Source Performance Standards, or NSPS. The law exempted *existing* stationary sources from this requirement, however; instead, it required each state to devise an implementation plan that specified how it would attain federal air quality standards and ensure compliance by local polluters. The act also mandated that auto-makers reduce tailpipe emissions of hydrocarbons and carbon monoxide 90 percent by 1975 and nitrogen oxides 90 percent by 1976. It gave the EPA the authority to set limits as low as zero on emissions of hazardous substances and to seek jail terms and court fines against recalcitrant facilities. And it allowed citizen suits to compel enforcement if the EPA failed to act.

Three years after enacting the Clean Air Act, Congress passed the Endangered Species Act, one of the earliest and most significant environmental-era laws to address the issue of biological diversity.[11] Like the Clean Air Act, the Endangered Species Act was overwhelmingly popular in Congress: it passed the Senate without dissent in a voice vote, and the House approved it by a vote of 355–4. Also like the Clean Air Act, the Endangered Species Act constituted a sharp departure from its predecessors in its bold purpose and highly restrictive enforcement mechanisms. Section 2 of the act declared that "various species of fish, wildlife, and plants in the United States have been rendered extinct as a consequence of economic growth and development untempered by adequate concern and conservation"; that other species were in danger of extinction; and that "these species of fish, wildlife, and plants are of esthetic, ecological, educational, historical, recreational, and scientific value to the Nation and its people." To address these deficiencies, Congress established the goals of providing "a means whereby the ecosystems upon which endangered species and threatened species depend may be conserved," creating "a program for the conservation of such endangered species and threatened species," and taking "such steps as may be appropriate to achieve the purposes of the [international] treaties and conventions" under which the United States pledged to conserve endangered species.

To carry out the law, the act established procedures for listing species as threatened or endangered, designating areas of habitat critical to their survival, and preparing plans to ensure their recovery and eventual delist-ing. It firmly prohibited capturing or harming a listed species. It also required any federal agency that was contemplating funding or permit-ting a project that could affect a listed species to consult with the Interior Department's Fish and Wildlife Service or, in the case of marine species, the National Marine Fisheries Service (NMFS, pronounced "nymphs") within the Commerce Department. If NMFS or the Fish and Wildlife Service finds the project will harm the species, the agency must propose alternatives.

Importantly, although the Endangered Species Act is highly restrictive, the wildlife agencies that administer it are relatively small players within departments historically tasked with facilitating the orderly development of the nation's natural resources. In particular, the Fish and Wildlife Service—which bears most of the responsibility for implementing the act—has a chaotic history and a meek organizational character; it has been chronically underfunded and lacks a clientele aside from hunters and fishermen. As a result, according to political scientists Jeanne Nienaber Clark and Daniel McCool, it regards itself as a "secondary service organization" rather than as a leader in the environmental movement.[12]

Nixon's willingness to sign restrictive new laws notwithstanding, there is overwhelming evidence that he advocated on behalf of the environment out of political expedience, rather than conviction.[13] According to former EPA administrator Russell Train, "There is no evidence of which I am aware that Nixon had any real personal interest in environmental matters. I certainly never heard him express any. His reaction to these issues was that of a highly political animal. He read the polls and had to be aware that concern for the environment was rapidly rising among the American people. His political instincts told him that he and the Republican Party could not afford to be seen as anti-environment."[14] Several of the president's key advisors who genuinely cared about the environment—including Train, John Whitaker, Christopher DeMuth, and John Ehrlichmann—also recognized its salience.[15] They urged him to capitalize on rising public concern, reckoning that by doing so he could thwart the ambitions of Democratic presidential hopeful Edmund Muskie, who had made environmental protection his cause. In fact, Nixon got little political credit for his leadership on the issue because environmentalists were always suspicious of his motives; he did, however, succeed in provoking the ire of the business community.

Given Nixon's tenuous environmental commitment and his desire to regain the support of industry, it was hardly surprising when in 1971—as the economy sagged and public attention to the issue declined—he began injecting concerns about the costs of environmental protection into his speeches. In his 1971 environmental message to Congress, he said: "As our nation comes to grips with our environmental problems, we will find that difficult choices have to be made, that substantial costs have to be met, and that sacrifices have to be made. Environmental quality cannot be achieved cheaply or easily." Similarly, his message transmitting the CEQ's second annual report to Congress contained a section called "A Sense of Realism" that focused on the costs of environmental protection, saying "[i]t is simplistic to seek ecological perfection at the cost of bankrupting the very tax-paying enterprises which must pay for the social advances the nation seeks." At a speech delivered to the Detroit Economic Club in late September, Nixon went even further, suggesting that demands for environmental protection threatened to "destroy the system" and asking, "How many jobs is it going to cost?"[16]

Although he continued to submit ambitious environmental programs to Congress, including a national land-use bill and a sulfur dioxide tax, Nixon declined to invest political capital in their passage.[17] The CEQ began to encounter White House resistance when it proposed new executive orders. During his third environmental message to Congress in early February 1972, Nixon declined to offer any new proposals and emphasized that the federal government could not do everything. Then, on October 17, 1972, Nixon vetoed the Clean Water Act, saying the price tag was "unconscionable" and would exacerbate inflation, which was a growing concern.[18] The following day, Congress easily overrode his veto. (Nixon retaliated by impounding half of the $18 million Congress had authorized for implementing the act.)

The White House also took a variety of steps to limit the impact of the Clean Air Act during implementation, retreating from the lofty objectives Nixon had originally espoused. EPA administrator William Ruckelshaus sought to establish his agency's protective mission, as well as its independence from the White House, and despite pressure from members of Nixon's cabinet, he issued a series of restrictive rules. In late April 1971, for example, Ruckelshaus announced stringent air quality standards for the six "criteria" pollutants specified in the Clean Air Act: sulfur dioxide, particulates, carbon monoxide, hydrocarbons, nitrogen oxides, and photochemical oxidants. Two months later, the EPA issued final regulations prescribing the testing procedures for complying with automobile emissions limits. In December, the EPA set emissions limits for five major industries. And twice—in January and again in May 1972—Ruckelshaus denied highly publicized requests by the auto industry to extend the deadlines for reducing their emissions. Finally, in April 1973, Ruckelshaus agreed to a one-year extension, explaining that he feared production breakdowns that could provoke a backlash against environmental protection. Later that year he granted the automakers a one-year suspension of the standard for nitrogen oxides that was to have become effective for 1976-model-year cars—although in both cases he established relatively strict interim standards.

Ruckelshaus faced almost daily efforts by the White House to limit the power and independence of the EPA, however, and the sharpest disputes arose over the Clean Air Act.[19] Ruckelshaus and CEQ chair Russell Train, both of whom were well respected in the environmental community, were often on the losing side of clashes with more conservative members of the administration—particularly commerce secretary Maurice Stans and presidential assistant Peter Flanigan—who consistently intervened on behalf of industry and sought to undermine environmental protection.[20] John Quarles, former deputy administrator for enforcement, contends that as a result of these conflicts, the "EPA [was] forced to establish a balance in its decisions. It [had] to be sufficiently sensitive to the economic, social, and other impacts of the environmental regulations to preserve a degree of harmony with the rest of the government."[21]

Hoping to rein in the environmentalists within his administration, Nixon initiated a process of centralization that would give him some measure of control over the complex regulatory apparatus he had helped to create. He instituted an interagency "Quality of Life" review, to be conducted by the recently created Office of Management and Budget (OMB), the purpose of which was to reduce the costs of regulation.[22] The OMB review quickly became a powerful force in the environmental regulatory process by forcing the EPA to perform extensive analyses of costs and other factors, delaying regulations for months and sometimes longer. In one prominent struggle, the OMB changed the guidelines proposed by the EPA for states as they prepared their implementation plans—changes that made the guidelines more permissive by taking the costs of emissions limits into account. Congress fought back in defense of the EPA's prerogatives, however. In mid-February 1972, Democratic senator Tom Eagleton of Missouri convened hearings to investigate environmentalists' complaints that the OMB was weakening implementation of the Clean Air Act. The conflicts became so severe that Ruckelshaus threatened to resign unless the president vested final authority over EPA rules in his office, rather than the OMB.[23]

At the urging of commerce secretary Stans, Nixon altered the institutional context in another way as well: he assembled the National Industrial Pollution Control Council (NIPCC), a group of sixty-three industry leaders, to advise him on health, safety, and environmental regulations.

The NIPCC, which was housed in the Department of Commerce, proceeded to complain bitterly about the government's overzealous response to public concern about the environment—sentiment they claimed was producing environmental standards "incompatible with the economic health of our society," "unachievable with presently available technology," or "unattainable at economically tolerable costs."[24] Again, however, Congress intervened, after many legislators expressed concern about the "fox-in-the-henhouse" potential of having polluters advise regulators on pollution abatement strategies in exclusive, closed-door meetings.[25] Nixon was forced to disband the NIPCC after Congress declined to appropriate funding for fiscal year 1974.

Nixon also tried to rein in the EPA by limiting its budget. In early 1971, Nixon asked Congress to appropriate roughly twice as much for environmental protection in fiscal year 1972 as it had appropriated for 1971; in addition, he called for enlarging the EPA's staff from 6,223 to 8,863.[26] Nixon's 1973 budget request for the EPA was almost the same as his 1972 request, however, despite the addition of significant new responsibilities. Moreover, as in his previous two budgets, he requested far less money for air pollution control than Congress had authorized; at $171.5 million, Nixon's budget request for air pollution was, in fact, just over half of what the administration had estimated during congressional deliberations it would cost to implement the law. Congress appropriated more than the president asked for, but Ruckelshaus—on the advice of the OMB—declined to spend the additional money.[27]

By early 1973, E. W. Kenworthy of the *New York Times* was writing of "ecological retrenching"[28] and *Washington Post* journalist Lou Cannon was declaring that the easy victories for ecology had ended. "Both within and outside the administration," Cannon explained, "the euphoria of the early Earth Days has been replaced by the hard realities of the budget squeeze, the conflict between the environment and the energy shortage, and the growing anxiety within industry against economic constraints."[29] The oil crisis of October 1973, in which the Organization of Arab Petroleum Exporting Countries (OAPEC) declared an embargo against the United States, increased the sense of vulnerability among the public and prompted growing concern about securing energy supplies (and low prices), even if doing so meant relaxing environmental standards. Sprinkled throughout Nixon's budget for fiscal year 1974 were cuts in various environmental programs. At the same time, the Interior Department rushed to open up remote areas to oil drilling. Even in Congress, which had generally sought to defend environmental rules from infringement by the administration, the drive to supply more domestic energy threatened to weaken many of the nation's recently installed environmental safeguards. For example, capitalizing on the sense of urgency created by the oil embargo, in late 1973, proponents convinced Congress to suspend NEPA and allow construction of the trans-Alaska pipeline, and to delay a bill that would regulate strip mining.[30]

By the time Congress reconvened in January 1974, the furor around energy had abated, but the momentum behind environmental protection had been lost.[31] The Nixon administration was emboldened by the declining salience of the environmental storyline to attempt a direct challenge to the Clean Air Act. In early 1974, without consulting the EPA, the Federal Energy Office and the OMB assembled a legislative package of thirteen amendments relaxing some of the act's most stringent regulations. Among them was a two-year extension of the auto emissions standards deadline; permission to use tall smokestacks that diffuse pollution as a permanent, rather than an interim, way of meeting air quality standards; a requirement that the EPA take economic and social impacts, not just health effects, into account when setting air quality standards; and federal preemption if states set more rigorous standards than the federal government.[32] After a public confrontation between the recently appointed EPA administrator Russell Train and treasury secretary William Simon, the White House dropped the most egregious provisions. In any case, the package was dead on arrival in Congress, where most of the members responsible for passing the original law continued to defend it.[33]

### Institutionalization of the Environmental Storyline Continues under Gerald Ford

In August 1974, after his role in the Watergate affair was revealed, Nixon resigned in disgrace. Vice President Gerald Ford assumed the presidency in the midst of a recession, with inflation at 12 percent and the stock market in turmoil.[34] Despite the uncertain economic conditions, observers expected Ford to take an interest in environmental protection; after all, he had been a National Park ranger in his youth. Instead, during his brief tenure Ford made a small number of bland statements emphasizing the need for "balance" while doing little to maintain a favorable rhetorical context for environmental protection. For instance, his 1975 State of the Union address did not even mention the environment, except in the context of energy production (noting, "We must strike a reasonable compromise on environmental concerns with coal").

In a brief proclamation on Earth Day 1975, Ford emphasized individual stewardship rather than government action, saying, "Through voluntary action each of us can join in building a productive land in harmony with nature." And in a speech delivered in Cincinnati in July 1975, he said: "I pursue the goal of clean air and pure water, but I must also pursue the objective of maximum jobs and continued economic progress. Unemployment is as real and sickening a blight as any pollutant that threatens the Nation."[35] Still, the continuing salience of the environment was evident on World Environment Day (June 4, 1976), just six months before the presidential election, when Ford concluded an admittedly tepid statement by saying: "As we look forward to our third century as a nation, we must keep a global perspective. We must recognize the inescapable interdependence of human beings and the dependence of all on the fragile planet we share."

Whatever Ford's worldview, in the summer of 1976, Russell Train mused in his journal that Ford was "surrounded by doctrinaire anti-environmentalists."[36] So it is unsurprising that Ford used his executive powers to prevent any effort to make environmental policy more restrictive. As a result, the League of Conservation Voters (LCV) characterized Ford's environmental record as "hopeless," noting that he sided with industry on almost every major issue.[37] Specifically, the LCV pointed out, he worked to cripple the law protecting wild horses in the West, declined to use the Marine Mammal Protection Act to prevent the slaughter of dolphins by tuna fishermen, and slowed down the listing of endangered species. He also restored funding for a variety of large-scale, environmentally damaging water projects, such as the Tennessee-Tombigbee Waterway, while cutting back funding for parks and wildlife conservation. He twice vetoed strip-mining legislation because he was concerned about its impacts on the coal industry, the nation's energy supply, and inflation. And he sought to weaken the Toxic Substances Control Act working its way through Congress by eliminating premarket testing of potentially dangerous chemicals.

Ford also backed the auto industry's request to delay the Clean Air Act's standards for emissions from automobiles and new power plants from 1977 to 1982, suggested that the EPA allow states to extend compliance schedules for existing facilities, and opposed the EPA policy of preventing deterioration of air quality in clean-air regions.[38] With respect to federal land-use planning, Ford declined to advance new legislation, saying, "I am opposed to it, period." On energy, Ford favored a major commitment to nuclear energy, offshore oil drilling with minimal consultation with the states, and a $6 billion subsidy program to develop oil shale and synthetic fuels from coal. He also perpetuated Nixon's efforts to make the institutional context less hospitable to regulation by establishing the Council on Wage and Price Stability, which reviewed government programs for their impact on inflation. In addition, with Executive Order 11821, Ford created the Inflation Impact Statement—a mechanism that the OMB used to press agencies to submit cost-benefit analyses of major regulatory proposals.

Despite these apparent retreats from ambitious environmental protection goals by the White House, the institutionalization of environmentalism in the federal government continued through the mid-1970s, thanks in part to the ascent in 1975 of an extremely motivated and proenvironmental Democratic Congress. (Democrats held a 291 to 144 advantage in the House and a 61 to 38, plus one Independent, majority in the Senate.) Proposed changes to the Clean Air Act died in October 1976, after a Senate filibuster in the final hours of the legislative session. The main bone of contention was a provision that would clamp down on pollution in national parks and other relatively clean areas, even if there was no immediate threat to public health. With largely bipartisan support, however, Congress passed—and Ford reluctantly signed—a series of restrictive environmental laws, including the Safe Drinking Water Act (1974), which required the EPA to set national drinking-water standards; the National Forest Management Act (1976), which established a planning framework for and prohibited large-scale clear-cutting on the national forests; the Federal Land Policy and Management Act (1976), which provided a framework for managing Bureau of Land Management property; the Toxic Substances Control Act (TOSCA, 1976), which regulated the production, use, and disposal of toxic chemicals; and the Resource Conservation and Recovery Act (RCRA, 1976), which regulated the disposal of solid and hazardous waste.

Implementation of these laws proceeded apace. Former EPA administrator Russell Train contends that, although the agency was critically short of money and personnel, and despite White House indifference and sometimes outright opposition, "EPA and its programs kept on track."[39] In addition to promulgating rules, the agency established a substantial "enforcement presence."[40] During its first two years, the EPA's enforcement staff grew by nearly five times, to almost 1,500 people, many of them in the agency's regional offices. Between 1973 and 1976, the agency began enforcing the Clean Air Act—sending out requests for information, conducting inspections and stack tests, and issuing formal notices of violation and administrative orders to pollution sources.

When the EPA wavered in its resolve, the courts generally upheld a restrictive interpretation of the new laws, particularly the Clean Air Act.[41] For example, in response to environmentalists' lawsuits, the courts repeatedly ordered the EPA to promulgate emissions limitations, as explicitly required by the act. The courts also rebuffed industry challenges to air quality standards. For example, in March 1976, the U.S. Court of Appeals for the D.C. Circuit (en banc, 5–4) upheld the authority of the EPA to phase out lead in gasoline, reversing a 1974 opinion by a three-member panel of the same court (*U.S. Environmental Protection Agency v. Ethyl Corp et al.*). Lead manufacturers and oil companies had challenged the proposed regulations on the grounds that the health danger from lead could not be specifically linked to automobile emissions. But the majority opinion upheld the regulation in its entirety, pointing out that "awaiting certainty will often allow for only reactive, not preventive regulation."[42]

In one of the most significant cases of the early 1970s, environmental groups, led by the Sierra Club, argued that the Clean Air Act required a program to prevent the deterioration of air that was cleaner than the secondary (welfare) standards. The issue had been debated intensely during rulemaking in 1971, and when the EPA issued guidelines that provided no instructions to the states about establishing a Prevention of Significant Deterioration (PSD) program, environmentalists sued. The Supreme Court affirmed by an equally divided court (4–4) the rulings of the lower courts in 1973 (*Sierra Club v. Ruckelshaus*), which had held that the Clean Air Act did not allow "significant deterioration" of air quality in regions that already exceeded Clean Air Act standards, and commanded the EPA to issue PSD regulations.[43] In another important case, decided in 1974, the Fifth Circuit prohibited polluters from using "dispersion enhancement" (in other words, tall stacks) or intermittent controls rather than installing pollution control devices to achieve air quality standards, unless the appropriate technology was "unavailable or infeasible" (*Natural Resources Defense Council v. Environmental Protection Agency*). As political scientist R. Shep Melnick observed: "By establishing a new policy status quo, the court shifted what might be called the political burden of proof within Congress. No longer was the burden on those favoring national uniformity and program expansion to build a coalition broad enough to pass new legislation. Now the burden was on their opponents to pass legislation to overturn the courts."[44]

Buttressing the newly institutionalized status quo was a dense network of advocacy organizations and policy experts for whom ensuring the restrictive implementation of environmental statutes was a central preoccupation. Earth Day, along with the new laws that followed it, sparked the creation or expansion of a host of groups, including the Environmental Defense Fund (founded in 1967), the Natural Resources Defense Council (1970), the League of Conservation Voters (1970), the Sierra Club Legal Defense Fund (1971), Clean Water Action (1971), Greenpeace USA (1971), and the Trust for Public Land (1972). Most of those groups reported a steady increase in membership and financial support, the recession and energy crisis notwithstanding.[45] Twelve of the largest groups had a combined membership of over 4.3 million and combined budgets in excess of $48 million.[46] For these D.C.-based organizations, increasingly, the main battlegrounds were federal courtrooms and the hallways of Congress; the main weapons were scientifically, economically, and legally sophisticated policy analyses. At the same time, thousands of local groups sprang up in the early 1970s, many of them focused on passing restrictive policies at the state level.[47] Meanwhile, all the major newspapers provided extensive coverage of environmental issues, ensuring that they did not disappear altogether from the public eye. A 1975 Harris poll ranked air and water pollution just behind inflation and unemployment at the top of a list of "significant" national problems.[48]

## The Rise of Antiregulatory Conservatism

Even as a new, environmentally restrictive status quo was being established, conservatives were launching a movement that would challenge its fundamental underpinnings.[49] The timing was hardly coincidental: the nascent conservative movement was already showing signs of strength by the 1960s, and the social ferment of the latter half of that decade only fueled its development. But it was the flurry of environmental, public health, and safety laws passed in the late 1960s and early 1970s that truly galvanized conservative thinkers. Those laws also spurred a massive infusion of cash from a temporarily unified business community, as well as from conservative foundations and individual patrons. In turn, that injection of resources financed the development of a conservative policy infrastructure comprising think tanks and lobbying organizations.

Although different in their emphases, these entities were united by a political philosophy that emphasized the importance of freedom from government intervention and of efficiency in the form of unfettered markets. At the same time, a small group of committed political entrepreneurs crafted a strategy for gaining power by popularizing a public philosophy, a key element of which was hostility toward the federal government, particularly its regulatory functions, and a marked preference for private enterprise. Although environmental policy was not a central issue for many conservatives, it did preoccupy a small number of antiregulatory activists; more important, it was the preeminent concern for many of their allies in the business community.

**Generating and Disseminating Conservative Ideas**
Conservative intellectuals began to coalesce around a small number of ideas in the 1940s and 1950s.[50] But the political philosophy that underpins the contemporary conservative movement became markedly more coherent during the 1960s and 1970s in response to the liberalization of mass politics in the United States. According to George Nash, "[i]n 1945 no articulate, coordinated, self-consciously conservative intellectual force existed in the United States. There were, at most, scattered voices of protest, profoundly pessimistic about the future of their country."[51] Among the chorus of voices were the libertarians, whose main preoccupation was the threat to individual freedom posed by government. There were also traditionalists, who were appalled by the emergence during the 1930s and 1940s of a society with no clear moral standards. And there appeared around this time a third group characterized by a "militant, evangelistic anti-Communism."[52]

These factions, although they differed sharply on particular issues, gradually found common ground in their shared repugnance for the decisions of the Warren Court in the 1950s and the social ferment of the 1960s. As historian Richard Hofstadter explains, conservatives felt marginalized in America and were "determined to try to repossess it and to prevent the final destructive act of subversion."[53] They responded enthusiastically to a purposeful effort to synthesize various strands of conservative thought and broaden the audience for their ideas by William F. Buckley Jr. In 1955, Buckley launched the *National Review*, listing on its masthead prominent libertarians, traditionalists, and anti-Communists. According to journalist Sidney Blumenthal, the *National Review* was largely responsible for labeling the new movement "conservative," and thereby enabling its members to gloss over their differences and create an identity.[54] Journalist Lee Edwards concurs, noting that the *National Review* "was not a journal of opinion but a political act."[55]

Largely engineered by *National Review* editor Frank Meyer, the intellectual fusion that ensued revolved around contempt for Communism and New Deal liberalism. It rested on a veneration of markets, as well as of both their essential components—including private property, competition, decentralization, and minimal government intervention—and their underpinnings: tradition, church, and family.[56] (According to Jerome Himmelstein, among contemporary conservatives, faith in markets is rooted in the belief that American society has an organic order—harmonious and self-regulating—that is disturbed only by the misguided policies and ideas propagated by the liberal elite.[57]) Meyer's fusion resolved the tension between individualism and the community through voluntary communitarianism and faith-based organizations.[58]

Further unifying disparate factions under the conservative banner was the blizzard of federal policies enacted in the late 1960s and early 1970s. Many of the most articulate and distinguished critics of those policies were the so-called neoconservatives, former liberals who were disillusioned by the failures and unintended consequences of social welfare programs. Neoconservatives provided movement activists with analytic arguments against domestic policies they disliked on principled grounds. According to Nash, hostility toward liberalism and a determination to change politics cemented alliances among the various conservative factions, and by the early 1970s, despite philosophical differences, "most conservative intellectuals seemed content to pursue what appeared to be the commonsense middle course, veering away from paradigmatic purity."[59] A series of political and economic crises during the early and mid-1970s—international monetary jolts, a combination of high unemployment and inflation, the energy crisis, Watergate, and the end of the Vietnam War—fortified the conservative intellectual community and helped create a political context receptive to their ideas.

The *Wall Street Journal's* editorial page was one reliable outlet for popularizing the political philosophy that emerged from the conservative intellectual community in the 1970s. At that time, the *Wall Street Journal* had the largest circulation of any daily newspaper in the country and reached an extraordinarily influential audience. Its editorials became increasingly strident as the decade wore on, reflecting the rise of the acerbic Robert Bartley to editorial page editor in 1972.[60] According to journalist Blaine Harden of the *Washington Post*, under Bartley the editorial page of the *Wall Street Journal* was both "a billboard and cheering section" for conservatives. In fact, Harden said, Bartley did more than cheer; he "fine-tuned conservatism itself."[61]

But conservative intellectuals understood that if they were going to have a genuine impact on the way the nation's social problems were defined, they needed more vehicles for refining their synthesis, translating it into a public philosophy, and popularizing it. Liberals, after all, had more than a half-dozen weekly opinion magazines.[62] In response to appeals from prominent conservatives, a handful of foundations—including the Lynde and Harry Bradley, Adolph Coors, Earhart, Koch Family, Sara Scaife, Smith Richardson, and John M. Olin foundations—provided "venture capital" for the new conservative intelligentsia.[63] Although conservative foundations had limited assets relative to their liberal counterparts, they put far more emphasis on disseminating ideas and arguments in order to influence high-level policy debates.[64] To that end, they invested in publications, research centers, think tanks, academic fellowships and chairs designated for rightist scholars, campus organizations, and youth groups—in other words, in movement building, leadership development, and recruitment.[65] Many of these endeavors reflected a long-term commitment to changing the dominant public philosophy. For example, the Intercollegiate Studies Institute in Bryn Mawr, Pennsylvania, provided Weaver Fellowships to finance graduate studies for conservative students bound for academia. Another organization, Young Americans for Freedom (YAF), sought to groom future political officials; YAF had ten thousand members on five hundred campuses by the early 1980s.[66]

Particularly effective at generating and disseminating conservative ideas were a handful of newly established or rejuvenated think tanks. These organizations blurred the line between analysis and advocacy by propagating alternative analytic frameworks, policy analyses, and prescriptions, while simultaneously redefining problems and creating new policy images. The American Enterprise Institute (AEI), the first major conservative think tank, was founded in 1943 but reinvigorated in the 1970s thanks largely to an infusion of corporate and foundation funds; between 1970 and 1980, the AEI's annual budget swelled from $1 million to more than $10 million.[67] The Heritage Foundation, founded in 1973 by Paul Weyrich with $250,000 from conservative industrialists Joseph Coors and Richard Scaife, sought to promote the adoption of policies based on conservative ideas.[68] Its mantra was (and is) "We are not afraid to begin our sentences with the words 'we believe,' because we do believe in individual liberty, free enterprise, limited government, a strong national defense, and traditional American values." Moreover, "Our expert staff . . . don't just produce research. We generate solutions consistent with our beliefs and market them to the Congress, the Executive Branch, the news media and others." The Cato Institute—a libertarian think tank founded in 1977 by wealthy businessman Edward Crane—sought to "broaden the parameters of public policy debate to allow consideration of the traditional American principles of limited government, individual liberty, free markets, and peace." The Los Angeles–based Reason Foundation—created in 1978 by engineer Robert Poole, lawyer Manny Klausner, and philosopher Tibor Machan—aimed to advance "a free society by developing, applying, and promoting libertarian principles, including individual liberty, free markets, and the rule of law." The Reason Foundation's public policy center sought to promote "choice, competition, and a dynamic market economy as the foundation for human dignity and progress."[69]

With the rise of conservative think tanks came the emergence of the conservative policy expert, whose function was to reveal the biases of mainstream experts and generate policy analyses and prescriptions that would buttress efforts to promote new policy images.[70] These experts, in turn, provided the fodder for an avalanche of conservative publications— including the *American Spectator* (1967), *New Criterion* (1982), *Reason* (1968), *Regulation* (1977), *The Public Interest* (1965), and the *Conservative Digest* (1975).[71] They also testified at congressional hearings, issued reports, wrote op-eds, gave interviews to journalists, and spoke to legislative staff.[72] According to historian Donald Critchlow, "The emergence of neoconservative policy experts and the institutionalization of conservatism through think tanks brought a direct challenge to the liberal regime."[73]

### The Complicated Role of Business
Like conservative intellectuals, the U.S. business community became dramatically more cohesive and vocal in the 1970s. For decades, a small minority of businessmen had ardently opposed the New Deal policies of the 1930s and sought to squelch the nation's increasingly powerful labor unions.[74] During the 1960s and 1970s, however, the business community as a whole moved sharply to the right, partly as a result of the rising wealth and influence of anti–New Deal businessmen based in the Sunbelt, but also because of the recognition by many multinationalists—some

of whom historically were Democrats or moderate Republicans—that their goals could no longer be accomplished within the New Deal framework.[75]

The sweeping health, safety, and environmental regulations of the late 1960s and early 1970s galvanized an already disenchanted business community. As *New York Times* journalist Gladwin Hill pointed out, the new social regulations entailed a whole new level of oversight: "Not since the trust-busting days of Theodore Roosevelt [had] the force of public opinion intruded so emphatically on the business community's patterns of operation."[76] According to political scientist David Vogel, although most established businesses historically had accepted, and often encouraged, government regulation that affected individual industries, they rejected programs that "would centralize economic decision making or strengthen the authority of government over the direction of the business system as a whole."[77]

Business responded to the assault on its prerogatives, and the anticorporate rhetoric that accompanied it, by becoming more politically involved, "promoting an agenda centered on business-oriented tax cuts, opposition to economic and social regulation, reduced social welfare spending, hostility to trade union power, and the virtues of free-market economics generally."[78] That involvement took a variety of forms. To increase their political clout, businesses enhanced their organizational capacity, creating the influential Business Roundtable in 1972 and reinvigorating the U.S. Chamber of Commerce and National Association of Manufacturers.[79] They established corporate lobbying offices in Washington, D.C.: in 1971, only 175 companies had registered lobbyists; by 1978, nearly 2,000 corporate trade associations had lobbyists in the capital.[80] In addition, corporations and trade associations formed political action committees (PACs): the number of business PACs increased from 248 in 1974 to 1,100 in 1978, while the expenditures of corporate trade association PACs grew more than tenfold, from $8 million to nearly $85 million between 1972 and 1982.[81] In the late 1970s, journalist Philip Shabecoff commented that, as a result of all this activity, "After decades of reticence, the business community has quietly become the most influential lobby in Washington."[82]

Recognizing that it could not rely exclusively on "inside lobbying," the business community also waged a media campaign to improve its public image and "inform the public."[83] For example, Mobil began buying ad space on the op-ed page of the *New York Times* in 1971, later extending that practice to the *Washington Post, Boston Globe, Chicago*

*Tribune, Los Angeles Times*, and *Wall Street Journal*.[84] In addition, companies like Arco, the Sun Company, and General Electric initiated political-education programs to make employees more politically aware, in the hope that they would work as grassroots constituents in the companies' interests.[85] Political scientist John Saloma commented, "Instead of reacting to legislative and regulatory problems as they arise, business now helps to shape the evolving political debate" on issues it cares about.[86] Business also sought to enhance its image among the nation's youth. The combination of a recession and numerous programs aimed at changing students' perceptions led to a remarkable comeback in the reputation of business on campus.[87]

Although the growing clout of labor was their primary concern, many businessmen also perceived environmental policies—and particularly the Clean Air Act—as a severe threat. Automakers were especially vigorous in their complaints about the new law and pivoted rapidly from what had been a passive to a fighting stance.[88] The carmakers were dismissive of the scientific basis for EPA standards. Charles Heinem, Chrysler Corporation's chief emissions expert argued that "our citizens have been needlessly frightened," and that "frantic measures" to control auto emissions were unwarranted.[89] In 1973, the oil industry rebelled against auto emissions requirements as well, when it became clear that if catalytic converters were widely adopted, lead would have to be removed from gasoline. Most memorable were Mobil's newspaper ads, which lambasted the Clean Air Act with the headline "The $66 Billion Mistake."[90] In 1974, the American Electric Power Co. challenged the EPA's requirement that coal-fired utilities install scrubbers to remove sulfur dioxide from their smokestacks, taking out full-page ads in the *New York Times, Wall Street Journal, Washington Post, Newsweek, U.S. News & World Report, BusinessWeek*, and other publications in a campaign that cost more than $3 million.[91]

Companies complained that they would not be able to pass on the costs of air pollution control. Rather than talking publicly about reduced profits, however, they portrayed environmental requirements as a threat to the overall efficiency of the economy, raising the twin specters of lost jobs and wasted investment capital. To dramatize its position, U.S. Steel threatened to shutter a fifty-year-old plant in Duluth, Minnesota, if the state insisted on requiring it to install smoke-abatement equipment. Capitalizing on worries about an energy shortage, PPG Industries took out a full-page newspaper ad claiming that removing lead from gasoline could waste as much as one million barrels of crude per day.

An ad in the *Wall Street Journal* sponsored by Gould, an electrical and industrial products company, cleverly linked freedom and efficiency. Accompanying a frowning Statue of Liberty with a noose around her neck was the caption: "Government overregulation doesn't dampen inflation. It fuels it."[92]

In addition to enhancing their capacity to influence politics directly, businesses began giving generously to conservative organizations, convinced by the argument of conservative intellectuals that "ideas have consequences," and that business ought to fund the creation and dissemination of a procapitalist public philosophy. What was needed, according to William Baroody, president of the American Enterprise Institute, was "public attitude formation."[93] Particularly influential, by all accounts, was a memo submitted to the U.S. Chamber of Commerce by corporate lawyer Lewis Powell in August 1971, shortly before he was appointed to the Supreme Court. Powell wrote: "One of the bewildering paradoxes of our time is the extent to which the enterprise system tolerates, if not participates in, its own destruction." He urged businessmen "to recognize that the ultimate issue" was "survival of . . . the free enterprise system, and all that this means for the strength and prosperity of America and the freedom of our people." Political activity by individual corporations was necessary but not sufficient, he added. "Strength lies in organization, in careful long-range planning and implementation, in consistency of action over an indefinite period of years, in the scale of financing available only through joint effort, and in the political power available only through united action and national organizations."[94]

In retrospect, the symbiotic relationship that developed between business and antiregulatory conservatives during the 1970s is hardly surprising. The emerging conservative public philosophy disdained the liberal idea that spending, often by government, was the key to economic growth, instead positing that business investment was the crucial driver. From this perspective, government regulations that inhibit private sector investment are a problem, and government itself harmful. By contrast, the pragmatic businessman—the energetic entrepreneur who creates jobs and economic vitality—is the hero, not the villain.[95] In fact, in *Wealth and Poverty*, George Gilder argued that businessmen were motivated not by greed but by altruism; from this perspective, the market was "a measuring stick for morality that meted out rewards for people who lived virtuous lives while punishing those who violated codes of decency."[96] Furthermore, among conservative intellectuals' main goals were to expose the ideology of a "new class" of cultural elites rooted in universities and the media that was critical of business, and to articulate the cultural and economic benefits of unfettered corporate capitalism.[97]

Three books that appeared in 1978 captured these themes. In *Two Cheers for Capitalism*, neoconservative Irving Kristol argued that the "new class" of professionals and intellectuals was sapping America's entrepreneurial energies and imposing its values on the "silent majority." Similarly, in *A Time for Truth*, former treasury secretary William Simon deplored the "impecunious Ph.Ds who destroyed the economy" and praised instead the "Ph.D-less financiers who fought to save the economy."[98] Simon linked the free enterprise system to political and social freedom and described an intimate connection between individuals' pursuit of self-interest and the public interest. Following Powell, he urged corporations to sponsor the creation of a new set of institutions—a counterintelligentsia—to lead America into a new era. Michael Novak's book, *The American Vision: An Essay on the Future of Democratic Capitalism*, advised conservative activists to combat liberal social policies by emphasizing the costs they imposed on ordinary taxpayers. Novak laid out an elaborate plan for removing corporate sponsorship of liberal ideas, expressed through television programs and university grants, and creating an alternative, corporate-funded bulwark of conservative ideas. In the *Harvard Business Review*, neoconservative Norman Podhoretz urged businessmen to pay attention to the work of figures like Kristol and Novak, noting that "the very survival of private enterprise in the United States may depend on whether this newly sympathetic view of capitalism ultimately prevails in the world of ideas over traditional hostility."[99]

David Vogel contends that conservatives' "new class" doctrine "reassured business executives that their interests and those of the public were indeed identical; whatever tensions had developed between business and the American people were the artificial creation of an elitist minority."[100] Moreover, by the late 1970s, conservatives had developed an "intellectual case equating unregulated capitalism with prosperity, and big government with [economic] stagnation."[101] Think tanks like the American Enterprise Institute bolstered this argument by conducting policy analyses purporting to show that government regulation was throttling business by imposing needless costs on production.[102] Such arguments found a foothold in a period of high unemployment, rising inflation, and prolonged economic malaise. According to political scientist Joseph Peschek, by 1980, "pressing issues in the United States were framed by terms of discourse that were increasingly economic in character"; in fact, "restoring economic growth [became] the touchstone to which all government policies [had to] conform."[103] In short, although some observers attribute conservatives' ascendance to their strategic use of divisive social issues, careful historical analysis suggests that, ultimately, conservatives translated their ideological coherence into political dominance by crafting an economic message that business found appealing.[104]

All that said, the relationship between business and conservatism was often fraught: Powell made his arguments in the early 1970s, but pragmatic businessmen continued to funnel money to Democratic incumbents well into the mid-1970s, prompting some young conservatives to repudiate big business for its lack of principles.[105] Moreover, the alliance between ideological conservatives and business was complicated by the heterogeneity of the business community. The nationalists, represented by the National Association of Manufacturers and the U.S. Chamber of Commerce, were happy to receive government subsidies but were hostile to any form of "strong state" that would impinge on their entrepreneurialism. By contrast, the multinationalists continued to want a stable, predictable regulatory environment and were willing to accept considerably more government intervention in the economy as a result. Furthermore, over time, many environmental issues would pit one industry against another, or different segments of a single industry against one another, and as the 1980s wore on, rifts within the business community would become more pronounced. But at least from the mid-1970s into the early 1980s, business was unified in its opposition to environmental and other new social regulation.

### Conservatives' Electoral Strategy

Foundation and business support for the development and diffusion of conservative ideas arrived just in time to bolster a budding grassroots conservative movement whose leaders were already poised to contend for political power at the national level. According to historian Lisa McGirr, a vibrant conservative mobilization developed in the Sunbelt during the 1950s and early 1960s.[106] Nationally, an energized group of activists succeeded in getting Arizona senator Barry Goldwater nominated as the Republican candidate for president in 1964. The Goldwater nomination revealed a deep schism within the Republican Party between conservatives and traditionalist moderates, however, and many businessmen placed their bets on the politically savvy Democrat, Lyndon Johnson.

The nascent conservative movement fell briefly into disarray after Johnson defeated Goldwater in a landslide, but its adherents quickly regrouped. A few weeks after the election, a handful of political entrepreneurs formed the American Conservative Union, whose purpose was to consolidate the intellectual resources of the movement; provide leadership to existing organizations; influence public opinion in favor of conservative principles; and stimulate and direct citizen action for conservative causes, legislation, and political candidates.[107] Within three years of Goldwater's defeat, according to the conservative magazine *Rally*, "The communications, activist, and academic sectors [had] coalesced into a conservative commonwealth, with sophisticated internal communication and division of labor."[108]

As a result of this conservative mobilization, grassroots conservatives experienced some measure of electoral success during the late 1960s. Playing on the anguish of the Vietnam War and the race riots that began that spring, they helped Republicans gain forty-seven House seats in the 1966 midterm elections.[109] Two years later, they vaulted Republican Richard Nixon to the presidency. Nixon's rhetorical strategy, which presaged that of later conservative candidates, was to "create the impression that there were two Americas: the quiet, ordinary, patriotic, religious, law-abiding Many, and the noisy, elitist, amoral, disorderly, condescending Few."[110] But conservatives, many of whom had supported Nixon reluctantly, were appalled by his unprincipled concessions to political expediency—including his support for stringent new environmental laws—once in office.[111] Moreover, liberal activism surged in the late 1960s and early 1970s, with widespread campus unrest, labor strikes, and rising anti-business sentiment. In 1974, after Nixon resigned in disgrace, conservative activist Howard Phillips told the press that "[u]nder Richard Nixon, our ideological opportunity has been squandered, our loyalties have been unreciprocated, and our party's reputation for integrity has been virtually destroyed."[112] The midterm elections that year were disastrous for Republicans: they lost forty-eight seats in the House and three in the Senate.

Disgusted with the missteps of the Republican Party, in 1975, a group of neopopulist conservatives seized the reins, choosing the moniker "New Right" to distinguish themselves from the "slightly effete conservative leadership of the East Coast."[113] Journalist Lawrence Martin described the New Right as an aggressive coalition of antigovernment activists that included tax cutters, antiabortion advocates, pro-gun groups, and labor-union busters.[114] According to Richard Viguerie, a political strategist and one of the masterminds behind conservatives' political ascendance, New Right activists shared a willingness to put aside differences and work together, a commitment to put philosophy above party, and an optimism and conviction that they could win and lead.[115] As journalist Paul Martin observed:

While Democrats and Republicans stripe away at each other from entrenched positions, a third force is quietly building a political apparatus that pointedly disregards party labels. The newcomers: conservatives of widely varying backgrounds, linked by a common devotion to limited government, free enterprise and a strong national defense. Their aim: mobilize public opinion on major issues and elect conservatives in office at every level, whether they run on Republican or Democratic tickets.[116]

By the late 1970s, New Right leaders were meeting regularly to discuss the strategy and tactics by which they could "build a grass-roots conservative lobby throughout the country, elect a working majority of conservatives of both parties to Congress and, eventually, place a conservative in the White House."[117] They stressed that their aim was not merely to gain political power, but to transform the culture.[118] In mobilizing voters, New Right political entrepreneurs emulated the tactics employed by liberals but also devised original approaches. Viguerie claims to have pioneered the use of direct-mail solicitation to build a huge constituency of disaffected blue-collar workers, housewives, and others.[119] With the backing of Joseph Coors, Paul Weyrich founded the Committee for the Survival of a Free Congress in 1974 to rival the liberal National Committee for an Effective Congress. While Weyrich organized conservatives in Washington, D.C., Howard Phillips founded the Conservative Caucus, whose aim was to mobilize legislators' constituents to influence policy—or, as he explained it, to "organize discontent."[120] The National Conservative Political Action Committee (NCPAC), founded in 1975 by Terry Dolan, pioneered the use of polls and "independent expenditure" campaigns—better known today as attack ads.[121]

The federal government's decision to turn over the Panama Canal galvanized the New Right, which in turn solidified conservatives' electoral clout by involving lots of new people, enhancing the competence of campaigners, committing only to winnable campaigns, working with single-issue groups, and persuading business to spend on conservative candidates.[122] Although conservative opponents of the Panama Canal treaties were defeated in the Senate in April 1978, that loss translated into a victory at the polls in November, when many senators who had voted for the Panama Canal treaties were replaced by conservatives, both Republicans and Democrats.[123]

Despite their initial independence, New Right conservatives soon came to constitute the Republican Party's base. As early as 1976, the party's platform reflected their preferences, emphasizing local control of regulation, freedom for business, and exploitation of natural resources; it implied that environmental protection and economic growth were incompatible. New Right conservatives reinforced their dominance by creating new institutions within Congress. Political scientist John Saloma, a former moderate Republican member of Congress, described the contrast between the old Republican guard and the new conservative legislators in the Senate and the House that was evident by 1980. "Conservative organizations," he complained, "helped to recruit, fund, and elect members of Congress from their ranks who have used their offices to help build the conservative movement."[124] Conservatives developed and staffed their own organizations, such as the House Republican Study Committee, formed in the early 1970s and modeled on the Democratic Study Group. (By 1983 the committee boasted 130 of the Republican Party's 166 members.) In 1974, Carl T. Curtis, Jesse Helms, and seven other senators established a counterpart in the Senate, the conservative Steering Committee. The Senate Steering Committee succeeded in electing conservative James McClure to the number three position in the Senate (chair of the Senate Republican Conference), and installing a host of Senate committee and subcommittee chairs important to the advancement of the New Right's legislative priorities. In addition to such "formal" institutional changes, conservatives introduced a new, more confrontational political style to congressional operations in both the Senate and the House. *CQ Weekly* explained the shift by noting that many of the new legislators "arrive[d] in Washington with stronger loyalties to national conservative politics than to Congress as an institution or to the Republican Party."[125]

## Conservatives' Legal Strategy

Conservatives set out not only to capture the electoral sphere, but also to transform the judicial context. Throughout the 1950s and 1960s, environmentalists and other liberal activists had used the courts to constrain federal agencies' discretion and expand their rights. Although conservatives decried such judicial activism, many took the pragmatic view that the courts' growing role was a fact of life, and conservative views needed to be heard.[126] So, following the advice of Lewis Powell, in 1973, the California Chamber of Commerce supported the creation of the first conservative public interest law firm, the Pacific Legal Foundation (PLF).[127] The PLF's objective was "winning decisive actions in the courts of law and the court of public opinion to rescue liberty from the grasp of government power."

Shortly after the PLF opened its doors, conservative donors funded the National Legal Center for the Public Interest (NLCPI), which served as a clearinghouse and umbrella organization for the creation of more regional firms on the PLF model. By 1977, the Southeastern, Mountain States, Gulf Coast, Great Plains, Mid-Atlantic, and Capital Legal Foundations were in business. Critics suggested these firms were shills for business. But Michael Uhlmann, president of the NLCPI, rejected that charge, saying: "We articulate the defense of a system, one of whose benefits happens to be the preservation of a large degree of private decision-making."[128] Raymond Momboisse, head of the PLF's Washington, D.C. office, was blunter: "The liberal groups only represent their own selfish interests. We support broader interests, the free enterprise system and the little guy. Business can take care of itself."[129]

As political scientist Steven Teles explains, conservatives' initial efforts in the judicial realm were halting: with their regional focus, business orientation, and tendency to pursue small-bore approaches, such as filing amicus briefs, the first generation of public interest law firms was relatively ineffective.[130] In 1980, in a report to the Scaife Foundation, lawyer Michael Horowitz critiqued conservative public interest law firms, arguing that they should focus more on transforming legal culture and legal debates than on winning tactical victories, and pointed out that their close ties to business were a hindrance to doing so.[131] Despite some initial missteps, a handful of conservative legal foundations—particularly those that focused on environmental issues, including the PLF and the Mountain States Legal Foundation—flourished.[132]

Some conservative thinkers understood that if conservative plaintiffs were to succeed, litigating was not enough; the analytic framework on which they based their legal challenges needed to seem familiar and legitimate. To disseminate conservative legal reasoning among lawyers and judges, policy entrepreneur Henry Manne created the academic field of law and economics. Manne established the first Law and Economics Center at the University of Miami, and eventually such programs spread to law schools across the country. He also created a series of institutes and seminars, including an economic institute for law professors, another for congressional staffers, and a two-week course for judges inaugurated in December 1976.[133]

In 1978, Manne's center produced a book aimed at a popular audience, *The Attack on Corporate America*, which rebutted criticism of corporate America with a series of brief, easy-to-read primers on microeconomic theories of business. The authors hoped these essays would form the basis for a procapitalist public philosophy—one that stressed the importance of unfettered markets for overall efficiency. Manne's preface emphasized the need for the book, saying, "Periods of strong, even strident, anti-business and anti-corporate sentiment are not new in American political history. But we have probably not previously experienced the near hysteria that characterizes current attitudes. From those quarters of society charged with developing and disseminating ideas and social attitudes comes the view that the large corporate system is an unmitigated evil."[134] After listing a variety of charges that were being leveled against business, Manne replied: "Excessive consumerism and environmentalism and undesirable regulatory schemes of all kinds feed on such nonsense."[135] But in fact, he asserted, study after study had vindicated the workings of large corporations, capital markets, and the free-market system in general.

### The Emergence of an Antiregulatory Storyline

Although environmental regulation was not the conservative movement's primary target, many conservatives were skeptical from the outset about the environmental regulatory framework that was being constructed in the 1970s. In particular, they endorsed the view of those in industry who felt the new pollution control regulations were excessively onerous and costly, and in doing so they imparted legitimacy to those complaints. Drawing for support on an emerging analytic framework rooted in the analyses of a handful of experts, mostly economists, conservative commentators devised an alternative storyline. According to this storyline, the condition of the environment was not a serious concern. Rather, regulation—because it was inefficient and impinged on individual freedom—was the real problem. The ideal remedy was not to refine the mechanics of environmental regulation but to scale it back or eliminate it altogether.

#### Advancing Two New Analytic Frameworks
Within the environmental policy community, one critique that gained prominence during the 1970s accepted the goals of environmental policy but highlighted the inefficiency of rule-based regulation and promoted effluent and emissions charges as a more cost-effective prescription. Since

the 1960s, the idea of pollution charges had been circulating in the policy community in white papers and monographs. It had even reached the political arena: Senator William Proxmire proposed establishing effluent charges to control water pollution during the 1960s, and in 1972, President Nixon proposed a tax on sulfur dioxide emissions. But what vaulted the concept of pollution charges into the mainstream was a series of publications by economists who sought to popularize it. Articles in *The Public Interest* between 1970 and 1973 advocated effluent fees to address air and water pollution.[136] In 1975, the influential book *Pollution, Prices, and Public Policy*, by economists Allen Kneese and Charles Schultze, summarized the mainstream economic view that "the current strategy, with its reliance on detailed regulation and construction subsidies, is likely to be excessively costly and dependent for its effectiveness on an omniscience that a regulatory bureaucracy cannot be expected to possess."[137]

In 1977, the Brookings Institution published a series of lectures delivered in 1976 by Schultze—who shortly thereafter became chair of President Carter's Council on Economic Advisers—about how "command-and-control" regulation could be made more effective and efficient by using incentives (*The Public Use of Private Interest*). *Regulation* magazine published a condensed version of the lectures in its first issue, and *Harper's* published an edited version. Also in 1977, the nonprofit Resources for the Future produced a book about the value of economic incentives as a policy tool for dealing with environmental management: *Environmental Improvement Through Economic Incentives* argued that pollution charges would change the incentives facing private decision makers for the allocation and management of common-property resources, significantly reduce the demands on government bureaucrats, and create an impetus for firms to innovate.[138]

Some economists sought to advance a more fundamental critique of environmental regulation, however. This critique was rooted in a view of efficiency according to which government regulation reduces private investment and hence the productivity of the market overall. Its proponents challenged not just the means but also the ends of regulation; they recommended subjecting any proposed regulation to a rigorous, quantitative assessment of the risks being addressed and the likely costs and benefits to society of mitigating those risks. Such analyses were controversial among environmentalists for several reasons. First, it was extraordinarily difficult to calculate the benefits of environmental regulations and translate them into dollar values, while industry was inclined to overestimate their future costs. Second, these approaches replaced the worst-case-scenario analysis embodied in most environmental laws with a calculation of precisely how much harm an ecosystem or human population could tolerate before showing irreversible damage. And third, these approaches dispensed with concerns about the distribution of costs and benefits and shifted the burden of proof of harm from polluters to proponents of regulation—amounting to a return to the common-law standard that environmental statutes had replaced.[139]

One proponent of this antiregulatory view was Henrik Houthakker, a member of Nixon's Council of Economic Advisers. Houthakker advocated hard-nosed consideration of the economic costs of environmental regulations and characterized environmentalists as bent on dictating extreme solutions that were not in the public interest. In a speech to the Cleveland Business Economists Club, he compared the importance of getting more oil out of Alaska via the pipeline to losing a tiny bit of permafrost; contrasted the need for more lumber to boost housing construction with the argument made by "some of the more extreme conservationists" that "there should be no cutting on the national forests at all"; and advocated some degree of local choice about how stringent air pollution standards should be, arguing that a depressed area should be able to attract industry at the expense of air quality if the citizens of that area wanted to do so.[140]

Similarly, economist Lewis J. Perl, vice president of National Economic Research Associates, estimated that the Clean Air Act had a cost-to-benefit ratio of 13 to 1. He argued that the amendments under consideration during the mid-1970s would boost that ratio to 33.5 to 1, and pointed out that such expenditures would necessitate reordering national priorities and diverting funds from other desirable social goals.[141] Subsequently, in an op-ed for the *New York Times*, Perl urged industry to conduct economic studies of the cost of legislation and make clear to legislators what the magnitude of the costs of regulation per household or per consumer really were. Legislators should be made to see, he said, that "[a]t some level of mandated expenditures, air-pollution control legislation will increase the percentage of the population in poverty. It does so by increasing the level of expenditures required to comply with pollution legislation, thereby decreasing expenditures on productive investment."[142]

Economist Murray Weidenbaum sought to demonstrate conclusively that the overall cost of regulations greatly exceeded their benefits. In a 1975 op-ed in the *Washington Post*, he argued that regulation constituted a "hidden tax" that exacerbated inflationary pressures and fell most heavily on low-income groups. In 1978, he estimated the costs of regulation to the economy at $100 billion a year—a figure that, although based on an extremely rough calculation, gained widespread currency.[143] A year later, Weidenbaum published *The Future of Business Regulation*, a small book explicitly aimed at a popular audience that laid out the "extremely negative impacts" of regulation on the private enterprise system, including higher taxes, higher prices, job losses, the elimination of small businesses, and a reduced standard of living. In a nutshell, he argued, "[w]hen excessive government regulation of business reduces the ability of and the incentive for business to engage in technological innovation, the economy suffers a further reduction in its capability to achieve such important national objectives as greater job opportunities, rising standards of living, and an improved quality of life." As an alternative to regulatory excess, Weidenbaum offered an "ambitious agenda of voluntary steps by business, government, and private interest groups."[144]

**Crafting the Antiregulatory Storyline**
Drawing primarily on the analytic framework advanced by conservative economists, conservative opinion leaders popularized an antiregulatory storyline that challenged the environmental narrative. In this storyline, the villains were environmentalists and government bureaucrats; the victims were entrepreneurs and, by extension, ordinary Americans. The problem was burdensome regulation, which caused inflation, slowed growth, dampened innovation, crippled small business, and impeded the accumulation of capital necessary for business expansion.

Initially, the tone of the conservative challenge was mildly skeptical. For example, a February 1970 editorial on the Clean Air Act in the *Wall Street Journal* opined that "in a free economy, regulations do not necessarily lead to efficient and proper use of resources. Sounder policy would involve the establishment of incentives to cause all of society to value the threatened resource more highly." Not only was the prescription Nixon favored for addressing air pollution unlikely to work, the editorial went on to say, but the president was skirting "the larger issue looming behind the environment problem: the obvious conflict between the economic benefits and technology millions have come to enjoy and good management of the environment." Nixon's assumption "that technology can be turned to save much of what is now being destroyed, and apparently without severe social or economic consequences" struck the editorial writer as problematic. Rather, it seemed likely that "as pressures to save the environment increase and as the full depth and complexity of man's tendency to abuse his surroundings is exposed, some people, and maybe a lot of people, are going to suffer. If not because of damage to the environment, they may suffer for the loss of economic luxury and social freedom." Therefore, the writer concluded, "Surely the question is valid: To what extent should concern for the environment take priority over economic and social welfare?"[145]

It was not long, however, before conservatives began asserting more confidently that the costs of environmental regulation plainly outweighed their benefits. Demands for regulation, they asserted, were based on exaggerated science. Regulation, not environmental damage, was the more serious threat; and the newly created EPA was running amok. Citing the work of Murray Weidenbaum, columnist Irving Kristol raised questions about the costs and unintended consequences of regulation and asserted the need for "balance"—a combination that would become a staple of the conservative storyline.[146] In establishing the EPA, said Kristol, Congress "certainly never intended to give a handful of bureaucrats such immense powers. If the EPA's conception of its mission is permitted to stand, it will be the single most powerful branch of government, having far greater direct control over our individual lives than Congress, or the Executive, or state and local government." Making matters worse, "this bureaucratic usurpation of power is wedded to an utterly irresponsible use of such power." Kristol concluded that "[c]ommon sense seems to have gone by the board, as has any notion that it is the responsibility of regulators and reformers to estimate the costs and benefits of their actions." He reprised the latter theme in a 1977 op-ed entitled "The Hidden Costs of Regulation," in which he asserted: "We shall never persuade the American people to take the problem of regulation seriously until they appreciate, in the clearest possible way, what it is costing them—as stockholders, consumers, employees."[147]

Conservative critics' main target during the 1970s was the Clean Air Act, which they regarded as a prime example of regulatory excess administered by a single-minded and overbearing EPA. For instance, a July 1972 *Wall Street Journal* editorial suggested that Congress ought to relax some provisions of the act, particularly those aimed at the auto industry, "in order to achieve better balance" in the effort to improve environmental quality. The editorial urged Congress to be aware that the act "set in motion a chain of events, some of which [were] not planned or intended."[148]

Following a three-part series disparaging the Clean Air Act by staff writer Jude Wanniski, a July 1973 editorial in the *Wall Street Journal* argued that, despite an "astonishingly thin" scientific justification, car-makers were being rushed into installing catalytic converters, the oil refining industry was being forced to convert to unleaded gasoline, and dozens of cities were being forced to consider disruptive traffic control and gas rationing schemes. The editorial ridiculed the scientific basis for the EPA's actions, claiming, "As it reads its congressional mandate, EPA believes it must insure that the sickest man in Chicago can be able to stand on the busiest corner of his city on the smokiest day of the year and experience no unpleasantness from the air he breathes. . . . In other words, the EPA has strung together a series of worst-case scenarios, added in safety factors at each point, multiplied the factors together, and has come out with numbers that may not have been attained in parts of the Garden of Eden." The author welcomed a review of the EPA's ambient air quality standards by the National Academy of Sciences, which it hoped would "clarify the distinction between air standards that are absolutely necessary regardless of cost, and those that are desirable but need to be balanced against the enormous costs and cultural upheavals the current standards would require."[149]

A 1974 *Wall Street Journal* editorial railed against the EPA's efforts to prevent "significant deterioration" in air quality. "By pushing the hard decisions to the states, EPA guarantees an expansion of the bureaucratic red tape that is mother's milk to the Sierra Club and the National Clean Air Coalition," it complained. The author argued that unless the nation was "happy to do without industrial development and [was] willing to accept the economic consequences of this policy," Congress needed to revise the provision in the law that led to the Supreme Court's interpretation.[150] Similarly, a 1976 article in the *Wall Street Journal* criticizing the EPA's traffic management initiatives argued that shortly after their inception "the [EPA's] grand plans were going awry; clean air had sounded like a great idea, but the inconveniences required to achieve it sounded horrible."[151]

Conservative commentators targeted not only the federal government and its regulations but environmentalists as well, in an effort to consign them to the social and political margins. For instance, a 1972 book entitled *The Doomsday Syndrome* by John Maddox, a physicist and the editor of *Nature*, characterized environmentalists as prophets of doom who always assumed the worst. Although they identified real problems, Maddox explained, the "doomsday men" oversimplified or even ignored reality. Maddox laid particular blame at the feet of scientists who used calculated exaggeration, a technique pioneered by Rachel Carson and subsequently employed by popularizers Paul Ehrlich and Barry Commoner. Maddox, by contrast, claimed that the scale of human impact was small relative to the size of the earth; that "in economic terms, the earth's resources seem[ed] to be becoming more plentiful";[152] that human management of the environment, as measured by air quality in cities, was already improving, even without regulation; and that prosperity was an essential precursor to pollution reduction in developing countries.

*The Disaster Lobby*, a 1973 book that disparaged the Left, reserved particular venom for environmentalists. The authors, both journalists, described the 1960s and early 1970s as the Age of Unreason whose inception they dated back to the 1962 release of Rachel Carson's "impassioned, one-sided, and largely unscientific" book *Silent Spring*. The public, they claimed, "bought the foolishness of *Silent Spring* as avidly as the buxom hausfraus of Bavaria had bought the garbage of Adolf Hitler," while an overzealous news media fed the frenzy and politicians simply followed the crowd. "If any one factor could be singled out as dominant in the thinking of the Disaster people," the authors said, "it was the belief that man must subordinate his own health, his own comfort, and if necessary, his own life to the health, comfort, pleasures and lives of other animals as well as to the purity of the environment." On the one hand, they said, the Disaster Lobbyists were inveterate levelers: "They wanted everybody to own and enjoy the same things, regardless of differences in individual capabilities, regardless of differences in individual ambitions." On the other hand, they did not really believe in equality; rather, "They believed in an intellectual elite. They regarded themselves as superior in intelligence to the masses of Americans. . . . This elitism of the intelligentsia was at the very foundation of almost every major movement of the period. The ecology crusade was predicated on the right of an intellectual minority to deny to the majority the comforts and health benefits of science and technology."[153]

Neoconservative Irving Kristol echoed the charge of environmental extremism. There was, he said, considerable evidence that the environmental movement—which began with "a massive reservoir of public sympathy"—was "becoming an exercise in ideological fanaticism."[154] And in December 1977, journalist William Tucker launched a broadside against the environmental movement with an article in *Harper's* that described an attempt by Con Edison to build a hydroelectric power plant at the base of New York's Storm King Mountain. Tucker charged that, in resisting the plant, environmentalists were nothing more than aristo-crats seeking to preserve their privileges. Although they talked in terms of "ecosystems," "rare, endangered species," and "carrying capacities," Tucker asserted, their real motivation was to prevent incursions on their surroundings—a theme he expanded on in his 1982 book, *Progress and Privilege*.[155]

### The Carter Administration: Environmentalism Meets Inflation

The impact of conservative ideas was evident in the presidential election of 1976. After a campaign in which he touted many conservative themes, President Jimmy Carter narrowly defeated the incumbent, Ford. As Cart-er's political advisors read the situation, the New Deal coalition was shrinking: union members had become middle-class taxpayers, worried about the impacts of inflation on their lifestyles; farmers constituted a mere 3 percent of the population; and Jews and blacks were being inte-grated into the political mainstream.[156] Therefore, they calculated, Carter—a fiscal conservative by disposition—would have to broaden his appeal by endorsing some aspects of the antiregulatory storyline. To that end, his 1976 nomination address had been "tinged with antigovernment conservatism."[157] In it, he said: "Government has its limits and cannot solve all our problems"; he criticized the "complicated and confused and overlapping federal bureaucracy"; he praised the free enterprise system, condemned regulation, and promised minimal government intrusion into the economy; and he called for a balanced budget and for strengthening state and local government.

Despite his antiregulatory rhetoric, environmentalists were optimistic when Carter took office in January 1977. He had received an "outstand-ing" rating from the League of Conservation Voters based on his record as governor of Georgia.[158] "As far as his environmental ideas and phi-losophy go, Jimmy Carter is probably the best President this country ever had," said Brock Evans, a Sierra Club official.[159] Consistent with his proenvironmental worldview, Carter pledged early on to make natural resource conservation a priority within his administration.

To create a hospitable institutional context, Carter installed a host of officials with environmental credentials in important positions. As EPA administrator, he chose Douglas Costle. A thirty-seven-year-old lawyer, Costle had experience with environmental issues at the state and federal levels: he had been a member of the Ash Commission that recommended creation of the EPA and had served as Connecticut's commissioner for environmental protection. In deference to the mainstream economic critique of environmental regulation, Costle vowed to undertake "a major regulatory reform effort," incorporating incentives into the EPA's regulatory toolkit and improving the scientific basis for regulations. "We're past the social debate over whether it is a good thing to protect the environment," he said. "The debate now is how to do it."[160] Costle's first move, however, was to approach the OMB in hopes of working out a substantial increase in the EPA's budget, to make it more commensurate with the agency's workload.[161] In fact, the EPA was one of the few federal agencies whose funding was allowed to grow under Carter's budget for fiscal year 1979.

As secretary of the interior, Carter appointed former Idaho governor Cecil D. Andrus, who swore to manage the federal lands more protectively than his predecessors. "I am part of the environmental movement," Andrus explained, "and I intend to make Interior responsive to the movement's needs." Under his watch, Andrus added, "Policymaking will be centralized and it will be responsive to my philosophy and the philosophy of President Carter. And, our philosophies do not include allowing developers to crank up the bulldozers and run roughshod over the Public Domain."[162] Shortly into his tenure, Andrus told journalist Margot Hornblower: "We have begun to make sweeping institutional and policy changes to end the domination of the department by mining, oil, and other special interests. Our president," he added, "is canceling the blank check which once went to those who would exploit resources and pollute the environment in the name of progress. Business as usual has been put out of business."[163]

Carter also sought to reestablish a rhetorical context favorable to environmental protection. In his thirty-six-page "Environmental Message to the Congress," delivered in May 1977, he laid out a "breathtakingly broad and ambitious" environmental agenda.[164] He rejected the conservative charge that environmental regulations were unduly expensive, or that pursuing environmental quality involved painful trade-offs, saying, "I believe environmental protection is consistent with a sound economy. Previous pollution control laws have generated many more jobs than they have cost. And other environmental measures whose time has come . . . will produce still more jobs, often where they are needed most. In any event, if we ignore the care of our environment, the day will eventually come when our economy suffers for that neglect." Not surprisingly, given the recent energy crisis, the speech also revealed Carter's intention to foster energy development, including more aggressive leasing of the outer continental shelf and reform of the federal coal leasing program, while emphasizing that any new exploration and development would be done in an environmentally sound manner. Overall, however, it appeared that Carter's approach to environmental policy would be restrictive; he expressed enthusiasm for conserving large swaths of Alaskan land, for example, and he vowed to address the nation's growing concern about toxic chemicals.[165]

Despite Carter's personal commitment, the prospects for his environmental agenda were murky. By the time he took office, stagflation—the combination of rising inflation and sputtering job growth—had taken hold, and the conservative revolt against Keynesian economic ideas was gathering steam among policy analysts. The public was uncertain, negative toward government, and demoralized about the economy, with a growing number of people calling themselves conservatives and rejecting the liberal orthodoxy.[166] Although Democrats retained their majorities in the 95th Congress—they enjoyed a 292 to 143 advantage in the House, while in the Senate the distribution remained 61 to 38, with 1 Independent—many members, and particularly the 47 freshmen in the House, were skeptical of government and susceptible to vigorous lobbying by business and conservative groups.[167]

### Revising the Clean Air Act

The reauthorization battle over the Clean Air Act was among the first major tests of Carter's ability to navigate the divide between a growing antiregulatory sentiment among policy elites and his own proenvironmental worldview. In legislative hearings, representatives of automakers, factories, electric utilities, and the mining industry deplored the inefficiency of the law, telling Congress that tightening air-pollution-control standards would raise prices, contribute to inflation, and force cuts in output, throwing employees out of work.[168] Despite these criticisms, the Clean Air Act Amendments, signed in August 1977, allowed the EPA to set tighter standards for new stationary pollution sources, requiring New Source Performance Standards to be based on "the best technological system of continuous emission reduction." The amendments also prohibited new industrial plants after July 1, 1979, in any area where air quality standards had not been fully attained, unless the EPA had approved a state plan that would assure full compliance by 1982, or 1987 in the case of photochemical oxidants (the Prevention of Significant Deterioration, or PSD, provisions). After turning back a high-stakes drive by industry and labor to weaken the Clean Air Act in the Senate, Carter did ultimately accede to some of the complaints of economists, industry, and state and local officials by approving changes that relaxed several of the law's provisions. For example, the revised law extended the deadline by which states had to meet primary air quality standards to 1982. In addition, after prolonged wrangling with the auto industry and its labor unions, Congress eased auto emissions targets for nitrogen oxides (from 0.4 grams per mile to 1 gram per mile) and extended the compliance deadlines for hydrocarbon and carbon monoxide standards. Congress also set performance warranties on catalytic converters at 24,000 miles, rather than 50,000 miles, as environmentalists had demanded, and dropped stringent product-line testing and requirements for emissions checks on new cars.

As inflation worsened, Carter became more susceptible to the advice of his economic advisors and the business-oriented members of his cabinet—Treasury Secretary Michael Blumenthal, Commerce Secretary Juanita Krebs, and trade negotiator Robert Strauss—who were pressuring the EPA and Interior Department to reduce the cost of regulation to fight inflation. Alfred Kahn, the head of the Council on Wage and Price Stability and Carter's chief inflation fighter, emphasized that regulation involved trade-offs: "We can't have cleaner air and cleaner water and safer products and reduced industrial accidents while at the same time having just as much of everything else as we had before," he told the Joint Economic Committee.[169] In his October 1978 inflation message, Carter himself pronounced: "We must realize everything has a price— and that consumers eventually pick up the tab. Where regulations are essential, they must be efficient. . . . Where they are unnecessary, they should be removed."[170]

A primary target of the administration's inflation fighters was implementation of the revised Clean Air Act. In June 1978, a senior EPA official told journalists Bill Richards and Helen Dewar: "There seems to be a different set of priorities coming up with inflation elevated to a much higher status of concern than it was six months ago."[171] The impact of pressure from Carter's economic advisors on rulemaking was evident. In 1977, for example, the EPA proposed PSD rules that would have required new or modified sources to install the best-available control technology if their emissions would exceed 100 tons per year without emissions controls—a change that would have affected some 4,000 sources. William Nordhaus and Barry Bosworth of the Council on Wage and Price Stability proposed relaxing the PSD rules and warned that unless the changes were made, the rules would cost industry "tens of billions of dollars over ten years." During the first half of 1978, the two economists held meetings and exchanged memos with EPA officials. Partly as a result of their efforts, in its final rules, published in June 1978, the EPA subjected any source that would emit less than 500 tons of pollutants to a lesser degree of control, thereby cutting the number of sources affected to 1,600.[172]

The EPA also relaxed the air quality standard for ozone (or smog), changing it from 0.08 parts per million (ppm) to 0.12 ppm, in tacit recognition of the costs involved.[173] In June 1978, after reviewing evidence that showed people suffering from chronic respiratory diseases could tolerate ozone levels as high as 0.15 ppm, Costle had proposed a 0.10 standard—a level 25 percent higher than the status quo that included a "margin of safety," as required by the Clean Air Act. The EPA's science advisory board three times rejected the "criteria document" on which the 0.10 ppm standard was based, calling its risk assessments "largely speculative."[174] But an independent panel of smog experts saw no reason to relax the standard at all, citing health effects for sensitive populations at levels below 0.12 ppm. Nevertheless, Alfred Kahn and Charles Schultze, chairman of Carter's Council of Economic Advisers, pressed Costle to raise the standard to 0.12 ppm. Economists Robert Crandall and Lester Lave urged the EPA to raise it even higher, saying, "Even a relatively modest relaxation of the standard could save consumers as much as $7 billion per year." By contrast, they pointed out, "the evidence implies that smog causes temporary discomfort in some people and tends to reduce the ability to perform heavy work. But there is no suggestion of potentially disastrous consequences."[175]

In what some environmentalists regarded as the EPA's most significant rulemaking under the 1977 amendments, neither inflation nor public health was the primary consideration; instead, the victors were high-sulfur coal interests. EPA officials initially resisted pressure from Schultze and from the recently created Department of Energy to relax the New Source Performance Standards for sulfur dioxide. Schultze had argued that the proposed standards, which would mainly affect new coal-fired power plants in the West, were "unnecessary" and would require industry to spend $13 billion to $35 billion on scrubbers, even though they were burning low-sulfur coal. Nevertheless, the EPA's draft proposal set a ceiling of 1.2 pounds of sulfur per million Btus and called for sulfur dioxide emissions to be reduced across the board by 85 percent— essentially a requirement that all new facilities install scrubbers.[176] That decision reflected Carter's interest in wooing Eastern coal interests, which mine high-sulfur coal, rather than a concern for public health. White

House economists argued in favor of lowering the ceiling and permitting utilities to mix scrubbing and fuel switching (to low-sulfur coal) in a way that made sense for them. On May 25, 1979, after "one of the most intense regulatory battles of the administration," the EPA issued final rules that retained an emissions ceiling of 1.2 pounds of sulfur per million Btus, but required power plants to remove between 70 percent and 90 percent of sulfur from their emissions. This amounted to a partial-scrubbing standard that satisfied eastern coal interests but disappointed both environmentalists, who wanted a more restrictive standard, and economists who had hoped for a more flexible one.[177]

### Protecting Endangered Species

Although the main focus of conservative criticism in the early and mid-1970s was pollution control regulation, particularly the Clean Air Act, by the late 1970s some conservatives were beginning to raise questions about biodiversity conservation as well, and in particular the Endangered Species Act. From the outset, regulation under the Endangered Species Act provoked opposition. When asked in 1975 about the relatively slow pace of the act's implementation, Keith Schreiner, head of the Office of Endangered Species, pointed out that, while environmental groups were demanding faster action, the OMB was reluctant to approve ESA-related rulemaking procedures. "But money and wildlife conservation groups are not our only problem," he said. "On the other side of the fence you have many people who, for reasons of commerce, want to have the Endangered Species Act declared unconstitutional. They exert pressure too."[178]

The first rumblings of public controversy over the act concerned plans to protect the grizzly bear, which was listed in 1975, infuriating residents in northern Wyoming. Then, in late 1976, the Supreme Court upheld the Fish and Wildlife Service's decision to halt construction on an interstate highway interchange that would jeopardize the habitat of the forty remaining Mississippi sandhill cranes. A November 1976 *Wall Street Journal* editorial complained that the endangered furbish lousewort, a riverine plant, had forced the abandonment of a massive hydroelectric dam in Maine—although it acknowledged the project was a boondoggle anyway.[179] But the most visible eruption over the Endangered Species Act occurred in 1977, when the U.S. Court of Appeals for the Sixth Circuit halted construction on the Tennessee Valley Authority's Tellico Dam, which threatened the habitat of the snail darter, a tiny fish, despite the fact that the $100 million dam was nearly complete. Conservatives were aghast at what they regarded as a decision to elevate the needs of trivial creatures above those of human beings. The alarming headline of a front-page, January 1976 article in the *Wall Street Journal* asked: "Will the Protection of Animals, Plants Peril Homo Sapiens?"[180] Prompted by the proposed listings of a host of new species, the author forecast a growing number of controversies over the act.

When the law was up for reauthorization in 1978, critics depicted it as extreme and absurd. A series of editorials and op-eds ridiculed it, describing it as "neat, simple—and wrong,"[181] arguing that extinction was a natural process and that "the United States Congress has tried to outlaw evolution itself."[182] (Although extinction does occur naturally, environmentalists and their scientific allies were concerned about the unusually rapid rate of extinction caused by human activities, particularly hunting and habitat destruction.) An October 1978 *Wall Street Journal* editorial bemoaned: "It is hard to imagine how it could be made much worse. Everyone by now knows about large and sometimes useful projects subjected to expensive delays and redesigns because of an alleged threat to some organism on the endangered species list." The author raised complaints familiar to conservative activists: "Choices of what is, and isn't, an endangered species have often been capricious and unscientific, not to mention devoid of any judgment over whether a species seems worth protecting."[183]

In Congress, Republican senators James McClure of Idaho and Howard Baker of Tennessee also criticized the Endangered Species Act in familiar conservative terms: they claimed it was inflexible and should be amended to allow the balancing of environmental concerns with energy and economic concerns.[184] Robert Herbst, assistant secretary of the interior, insisted that the act *was* flexible, considering that out of 4,500 consultations only three projects had gone to court. Nevertheless, after a parade of witnesses told the Resource Protection Subcommittee of the Senate Environment and Public Works Committee that the Endangered Species Act was inflexible and cumbersome, Republican senator Jake Garn of Utah remarked, "I do not believe that any animal, no matter how worthless, ought to be allowed to halt any project, no matter how valuable. . . . I frankly don't give a damn if a 14-legged bug or the woundfin minnow live or die."[185]

Further inflaming the act's critics, in mid-June, the Supreme Court affirmed (6–3) the appeals court ruling that the Tellico Dam had to be halted to save the snail darter (*Tennessee Valley Authority v. Hill*). The Court found that Section 7 of the act provided no exceptions for projects that were already under way when the law was passed, if those projects would jeopardize a species listed as threatened or endangered. Chief Justice Warren Burger wrote the majority opinion that "the plain intent of Congress in enacting this statute was to halt and reverse the trend toward species extinction, whatever the cost." In the debate that followed, conservative members of Congress repeatedly warned that ESA-related conflicts would jeopardize important projects, increase unemployment, and stop "progress." Of course, the ruling affronted not just conservatives but members of Congress concerned about public works projects in their districts. For instance, Democratic representative Ted Risenhoover of Oklahoma remarked: "I would rather see nature lose species than for our people to lose their rights to decide their own destiny."[186]

In late 1978, Carter signed amendments to the Endangered Species Act that retained its basic structure but rendered it somewhat less restrictive. First, Congress added procedural requirements to the listing process: it imposed additional notice provisions, required local hearings, and mandated the designation of critical habitat during the listing process—all of which made listing more complex—while imposing a two-year time limit on the process. The net effect of these procedural changes was immediate: on December 10, 1979, the Fish and Wildlife Service withdrew proposals to list 1,876 species after the deadline for action on them passed; less than 5 percent of the 2,000 species proposed for listing as of November 1978 ultimately were listed.[187] According to one scientist in the Office of Endangered Species, the office was paralyzed, "afraid to take the bull by the horns because they worried what would happen politically to the Endangered Species Act itself. We have been so busy saving the Act," he added, "that we are not saving plants and animals."[188]

Second, in response to the snail-darter ruling, Congress added a provision allowing the convention of a cabinet-level Endangered Species Committee, which became known as the God Squad, comprising the secretaries of agriculture, interior, and the Army, the chair of the Council of Economic Advisers, the heads of the EPA and the National Oceanographic and Atmospheric Administration (NOAA), and a representative from the affected state. The God Squad was empowered to grant exemptions from ESA requirements for economic reasons when no "reasonable and prudent" alternative exists, when the project is of national significance, and when the benefits "clearly outweigh" those of alternative actions. Amendments to the act required immediate action by the God Squad on two specific projects. One was the Tellico Dam project. The second was the Grayrocks Dam, in Wyoming, which would back up the Laramie River, blocking the flow of water flowing into the Platte River. In addition to furnishing energy, the Grayrocks Dam, in which more than $400 million had already been invested, threatened to dry up the mating grounds of the whooping crane 275 miles downstream from the dam site. (Absent spring floods, vegetation would grow on the sandbars of the Platte, and cranes would be exposed to predators if they stopped there.) In January 1979, the God Squad voted unanimously to prohibit completion of the Tellico Dam—not because of threats to the snail darter but because the project was economically unjustified.[189] But it agreed to allow the completion of the Grayrocks Dam as long as its builders guaranteed the release of enough water to maintain adequate stream levels on the Platte to protect the whooping crane and paid $7.5 million to buy land for the birds.

**Energy Policy: Setting the Stage for the Climate Change Debate**
More central to Carter's agenda than air pollution or endangered species was ensuring a reliable domestic energy supply. Early on, the president asked his energy advisor, James Schlesinger, to develop a plan that would provide an orderly transition from an economy predicated on "cheap and abundant energy used wastefully and without regard to international and environmental imperatives to an era of more expensive energy with concomitant regard for efficiency, conservation, international and environmental concerns."[190] The resulting National Energy Plan (NEP), released in March 1977, contained 113 separate proposals but rested on four pillars: conservation and energy efficiency; reducing oil imports; balancing energy needs with environmental stewardship, even if doing so raised costs; and ensuring that energy prices reflected the true cost of fossil fuels. To promote the NEP, Carter appeared on television wearing a cardigan and depicted the fight for a coherent energy policy as "the moral equivalent of war."[191] Despite prolonged lobbying by the White House, Congress split Carter's plan into six separate bills, and approved only a fraction of them in October 1978. Included were measures to deter the production of gas-guzzling cars, discourage utilities from wasting energy, require more efficient home appliances, encourage carpooling and the production of gasohol (a mixture of gasoline and ethyl alcohol), and phase in decontrol of natural gas prices. Excluded, however, were mechanisms for raising fossil fuel prices to encourage conservation and the development of alternative fuels. The plan's reliance on higher energy prices antagonized a variety of blocs in Congress, including con-

servatives in both parties, Democrats from oil- and gas-producing states, and liberals who objected to higher energy prices as disproportionately burdensome on the poor.[192]

By 1979, the one-two punch of rising inflation and a second energy crisis instigated by the oil-producers' cartel after the Iranian revolution had strengthened the hand of Carter's economic advisors. At the same time, although Democrats had retained control of Congress in the midterm elections, the impact of the conservative storyline was unmistakable: Republicans had gained only three new Senate seats, but five prominent liberal Democrats and two moderate Republicans went down to defeat. Ten new senators were regarded as more conservative than their predecessors, while only four were regarded as more liberal. More important, as *Newsweek* noted, Republicans' "real triumph was philosophic and often vicarious—the pride of authorship in a new politics in which Democrats talk like Republicans to survive."[193] According to the article's authors, "The real message of the election returns was the ratification of a new and no longer partisan agenda for the nation—a consensus on inflation as the primary target and tax-and-spend government as the primary villain." Even Senator Charles Percy, a liberal Republican from Illinois, got on the bandwagon, saying, "We've had it with big spending. We've had it with overregulation. We've had it with inflation. We've had it with high taxes. Clearly the agenda before Congress must be the taxpayer's agenda."[194]

In this context, Carter's ambitious ideas for rationalizing the energy system—decontrolling oil prices and imposing a windfall tax on oil companies, using the revenues to fund mass transit, offset fuel expenses for low-income families, and subsidize the development of alternative energy—drew intense opposition from both Republicans and Democrats in Congress. So instead, with an eye toward the 1980 election, on July 15, 1979, Carter delivered a speech in which he outlined a series of measures whose primary aim was to enhance the energy supply. In particular, he sought ways to ease environmental restrictions on domestic energy development, infuriating environmentalists with a proposal for an Energy Mobilization Board that would have the authority to override environmental laws in the service of increasing the domestic energy supply. Although Carter's speech was well received by the public, Congress responded to his proposals at a glacial pace, eventually approving a windfall profits tax the following March and creating an Energy Security program to develop synthetic fuels in June. In the summer of 1980, the House defeated the Energy Mobilization Board 232–131, after

Republican members withdrew their support. Carter's energy policy never recovered its momentum.

### The Carter Administration's Attempts at Regulatory Reform

With Carter's inauguration came a strengthening of the EPA's enforcement programs. In one major shift, agency leaders discouraged enforcement officials from negotiating with Clean Air Act violators until litigation had begun; where litigation had been the exception, it became the rule. Overall, argues legal scholar Joel Mintz, Carter-era enforcement policy was bold and led to an expansion of the Justice Department's responsibility for environmental enforcement. Industry was resentful and criticized agency staff as ineffective bureaucrats and antibusiness zealots.[195] Yet even as it beefed up enforcement, the Carter administration sought to tamp down rising antiregulatory sentiment.

According to historian Sam Hays, however, "By the fall of 1977, those [in the White House] concerned with development had begun to get the upper hand and to call into question regulatory proposals that agencies initiated to carry out legislative enactments. . . . By the time of the energy crisis in the spring and summer of 1979 this group had obtained a commanding influence."[196] There were numerous indications of growing antipathy toward regulation. In late 1978, in hopes of adding weight to demands for deregulation, the American Enterprise Institute launched its new bimonthly magazine, *Regulation*, to disseminate critical analyses of regulatory policy; the Business Roundtable commissioned a yearlong study of the costs to forty companies of complying with the regulations of six federal agencies; and the Ford Motor Company issued a comprehensive study of the effects of regulation on its operations. In January 1979, the Senate Governmental Affairs Committee released its sixth and final volume in a two-year study of regulation. The report noted that, given the volume of discouraging news about regulation, "it is little wonder that there is a deepening public concern about the effectiveness of government programs, particularly those which attempt to regulate business activity."[197]

The Carter administration responded to the rising pressure for regulatory reform in a variety of ways. As he had during the campaign, Carter sounded conservative themes, emphasizing that he wanted to cooperate with industry, simplify federal regulation, and encourage a greater degree of local control over implementation. In his second annual address to Congress, delivered in early 1978, he declared, "Government cannot solve our problems"; in 1979, after a trip to the Midwest, he said he had been reminded that "all the legislators in the world can't fix what's wrong with America."[198] Carter also built on Ford's efforts at regulatory centralization, thereby erecting a hurdle to new rules in an effort to mitigate their inflationary impact. In March 1978, he issued Executive Order 12044, which required all federal agencies to conduct a cost-effectiveness analysis for any major proposed regulation and to evaluate alternative means of achieving its objectives. To help implement the order, he created the Regulatory Analysis Review Group, chaired by a member of the Council of Economic Advisers and composed of representatives of executive branch agencies and other agencies in the Executive Office of the President. Then, in late October 1978, he established a Regulatory Council to coordinate federal regulatory activities and help ensure regulations "do not impose excessive burdens on particular sectors of the economy."[199] According to political scientist Phillip Cooper, although economists had always been involved in the regulatory arena, these steps taken by Carter "dramatically expanded the role and influence of economics as a field in regulatory policy and the agencies that designed and implemented it."[200]

In early 1979, the White House drafted the Reform of Regulation Act, which would give federal regulatory agencies the power to suspend the law in order to conduct regulatory experiments. The aim was to ease the burden of regulation on industry and promote the use of economic incentives to achieve regulatory goals. "This is a response to the backlash against regulatory activity," explained Pete Petkas, director of the Regulatory Council. "Unless we go to Congress with concrete proposals, there will be efforts to take the teeth out of environmental, health, and safety legislation. The perception in Congress is that regulations are burdensome, and we better do something about that quickly."[201] Among the experiments the EPA hoped to launch were establishing marketable rights in pollution, allowing trade-offs between one pollutant and another, and substituting performance for technology-based standards. Other reforms included: requiring agencies to publish regulatory analyses of the economic impact of regulations, alternatives, and the most cost-effective approach; and requiring agency heads to supervise the early stages of regulation development personally, so that economic issues could be brought to the fore. Although Congress ultimately declined to pass the Reform of Regulation Act, it did approve two other regulatory reform laws in 1980: the Regulatory Flexibility Act and the Paperwork Reduction Act.

Sensitive to the political attacks his agency in particular faced, EPA administrator Costle experimented with incentive-based regulatory approaches, in an effort to "be out in front of this situation in order to control [the agency's] destiny."[202] One sign of the influence of the mainstream economic critique was a booklet issued by the EPA that characterized "command-and-control" regulation as "rigid, wasteful, and sometimes simply illogical."[203] But there were more concrete demonstrations as well. Building on the efforts of his predecessor, Russell Train, Costle expanded the agency's "offset" policy, under which new stationary pollution sources could be built in areas that did not meet air quality standards, as long as existing plants reduced their emissions by a larger amount, thereby reducing overall pollution. He enhanced the utility of the offset policy in 1979 by allowing polluters to "bank" emissions credits, which they could later use for offsets. (In practice, however, there were few trades because companies typically retained the credits to offset future expansion.) In addition, Costle instituted a bubble policy that allowed industrial plants to average emissions of a particular pollutant from different sources across entire facilities. Although the EPA had first used the bubble policy in December 1975, the courts had rejected the approach on the grounds that the agency had exceeded its regulatory authority. In early 1979, Costle promulgated a revised bubble policy that simplified compliance. He explained to skeptical environmentalists: "This policy would mean less expensive pollution control, not less pollution control."[204] In 1980, the EPA added "netting," which allowed modifying or expanding sources to escape New Source Review requirements as long as any net increase in plant-wide emissions was insignificant.[205]

In another bid to incorporate incentives into its operations, in 1979, the EPA established a practice of fining violators as much as they saved in pollution control equipment plus an amount equal to the return on capital they were able to invest by not complying with air quality standards—a carefully tailored incentive aimed at discouraging companies from delaying compliance. In deference to critics, Costle tripled the number of EPA employees whose job it was to analyze the costs of proposed rules on industry. He made other adjustments in agency operations as well, most of them aimed at allowing industry to meet their cleanup requirements at lowest cost.[206]

The efforts of the Carter administration did not appease industry or its conservative allies, whose criticisms continued unabated. As always, the EPA remained a key target. In a September 1979 piece in *National*

*Journal*'s policy forum, Richard Lesher, president of the U.S. Chamber of Commerce, argued that industry was facing heavy costs as a result of pollution control regulation—costs that were reflected in consumer prices, industries' ability to compete with foreign producers, and industry's use of capital, which was sorely needed to increase productivity and capacity. The cost to the nation, he said, was higher inflation, job losses, and waste of critically scarce energy. "As a result of rigidity at EPA and at state agencies that operate under the pressure of EPA policies," he concluded, "industry is often confronted with confusing or unreasonable regulatory requirements which are not cost effective."[207]

## Environmentalism and the Rise of Conservatism in the 1970s

In short, the 1970s was not—as some have portrayed it—an unmitigated sweep for environmentalists or the environmental storyline. According to John Quarles, "the tide of environmental reform was running strong" in the early 1970s. "No one objected that the costs might outweigh the benefits. No one argued that the goal of environmental purity had to be balanced against other essentials of national life, such as economic production and employment."[208] The EPA, Quarles contends, was widely regarded as a hero, and business viewed as the villain. But even as federal officials established a formidable set of institutions rooted in the environmental storyline, an antiregulatory alternative was emerging whose sponsors were increasingly well prepared to challenge the environmental status quo. The intractable economic downturn and its attendant anxieties imparted legitimacy to complaints about the costs of regulation by industry leaders and their conservative allies. By 1980, the young EPA was mired in litigation: as of early 1979 there were 1,809 lawsuits against federal laws, compared with 582 at the end of 1973; about 750 were against the EPA, 500 of them industry challenges.[209]

Nevertheless, by the end of 1980, environmentalism was firmly institutionalized throughout much of the U.S. government. During the 1970s, seventy federal agencies prepared more than twelve thousand environmental impact statements in conformance with NEPA, and by 1980, the EIS process had become routine.[210] Agencies within the Interior Department began implementing new mandates aimed at reducing the impact of resource extraction and conserving biological diversity. The EPA's budget (excluding construction grants for sewage treatment plants) grew substantially, rising from about $500 million in 1973 to $1.3 billion in 1980, while the number of full-time employees—most of them in the agency's ten regional offices—climbed from seven thousand in 1971 to thirteen thousand in 1980.[211] Although it increasingly factored costs into the equation, the EPA continued to make risk-averse implementation its signature. And, more often than not, the federal court system affirmed a risk-averse interpretation of that agency's new environmental mandates.

Outside of government, a full-fledged policy community began to form around environmental issues. A host of environmental advocacy groups emerged in response to incentives embedded in the new environmental laws—groups with scientific, economic, and legal expertise that could capitalize on the transparent and accessible administrative decision-making process those laws mandated. As the 1970s wore on, environmental groups continued to gain members and financial support, notwithstanding the onset of recession. In addition, journalists became attuned to environmental issues, and policy analysts in academia and think tanks busily evaluated the effectiveness of existing regulations.

As important, environmentalism became embedded in the public consciousness. A variety of polls taken in the late 1970s suggested that even as the recession deepened, support for environmental protection remained strong: a 1977 national telephone survey by Opinion Research Corporation found that 68 percent of Americans favored higher prices and taxes to protect the environment; a March 1978 Louis Harris poll showed that the public strongly opposed slowing environmental cleanup either to produce more energy (65 percent to 22 percent) or to improve the economy and create more jobs (64 percent to 22 percent).[212] In a poll conducted by the Roper Organization and Cantril Research Inc. in early 1980, 62 percent of respondents described themselves as either sympathetic to (55 percent) or active participants in (7 percent) the environmental movement; seventy-three percent said the label "environmentalists" applied to them either definitely (18 percent) or "in part" (55 percent); and only one in four rejected the label altogether.[213] Robert Cameron Mitchell of Resources for the Future analyzed twelve sets of national polls taken between 1977 and 1979 and found continued support for environmental protection regardless of cost.[214]

Environmental leaders were buoyed by these results and confident that they could withstand minor setbacks.[215] But the advances made by environmental advocates were hardly secure. Conservative critics were increasingly vocal, and a handful of polls showed support for environmentalism waning: in April 1970, 53 percent of the public believed that reducing pollution was one of the top three national problems; by 1980 that figure had declined to 24 percent. A Roper poll found that the percentage of people who believed the government had gone "too far" with environmental protection laws and regulations increased from 13 percent in 1973 to 25 percent in 1980. And whereas in 1978, 50 percent of the public indicated they would be willing to accept a slower rate of economic growth in order to protect the environment, by 1980, that figure had slipped to 27 percent.[216]

The 1980 presidential contest between incumbent President Carter and conservative Republican Ronald Reagan pitted two diametrically opposed public philosophies against one another. Over the course of the 1970s, the Republican Party had translated a pervasive feeling of estrangement and alienation into anti-big-government sentiment, in the process capturing the Christian Right, which—like its newfound allies—feared the "overweening power of the federal government" above all.[217] In November, this conservative mobilization finally bore fruit: Ronald Reagan swept into office, along with a Senate that turned Republican for the first time in twenty-five years. Although environmental issues played a minor role in the election, in 1981, conservatives found themselves in a position to execute their antiregulatory vision.

# 4

# Ronald Reagan Brings Conservatism to the White House

*By the late 1970s many experts had become convinced of the need for modest reforms that would enhance the efficacy of environmental regulations. President Reagan took office in 1981 with a far more ambitious deregulatory agenda, but he faced the same Congress that had enacted the nation's environmental statutes by large majorities and was reluctant to squander his political capital fighting over legislative reforms. Instead he focused on changing the institutional context—reorienting the agencies responsible for environmental protection—and then revamping the status quo administratively. His political appointees' low-profile challenges to restrictive regulations provoked a sharp backlash, however. Environmentalists succeeded in using the administration's assault to increase the salience of environmental concerns; in response, Congress curbed the administration's most blatant efforts to subvert recently institutionalized environmental values. The federal courts, heavily staffed with moderate appointees and constrained by the plain language of environmental statutes, also rejected most of the Reagan-era interpretations.*

*Still, the administration's efforts to weaken environmental regulations and delay action on new problems were not in vain. By declining to lead on the recently identified phenomenon of acid rain, the administration hobbled efforts to mitigate it for a decade. At the same time, by layering more onerous analytic standards on the regulatory process, the White House discouraged the adoption of restrictive rules. Meanwhile, budget cuts, personnel reorganizations, and other changes in the institutional context eroded the ability of agencies with environmental mandates to implement and enforce the rules already in place. More subtly, the anti-regulatory storyline articulated by high-level officials in the White House began to gain legitimacy among political elites. As a result, by the late 1980s, the prospects for bipartisan regulatory reform, which appeared bright when Reagan took office, had dimmed.*

## The Antiregulatory Storyline Gains Traction

During the 1970s, bipartisan criticism of economic regulation prompted deregulation of the airline, trucking, and other industries. By the early 1980s, skepticism about social regulation was running high as well, not only among conservatives but also among many moderates. As historian Theodore White pointed out, the number of social regulatory agencies had grown from twelve in 1970 to eighteen by 1980, and their budgets had increased from $1.4 billion to $7.5 billion; during the same period, he noted, the *Code of Federal Regulations* had expanded dramatically.[1] Economist George Eads and attorney Michael Fix captured the prevailing sentiment at the start of the new decade:

Federal agencies were still churning out social regulations at a furious pace, and the cost of complying with regulations, even by the calculations of its supporters, were clearly growing. Regulators seemed to lack the information they needed to regulate intelligently, yet the regulatory paperwork seemed endless. Stories of conflicting regulations plus the apparent lack of improvement in many of the problems on which so much money was being spent raised questions about whether social regulation could *ever* be made to work.[2]

A handful of scholarly books and articles published in the early 1980s translated this general discontent with burgeoning regulations into an analytic framework that, consistent with industry complaints, depicted the prescriptive environmental regulation of the 1970s as inordinately expensive, ineffective, and arbitrarily implemented. Many policy analyses focused on the Clean Air Act. For example, economists Lester Lave and Gilbert Omenn attributed most of the air quality improvements of the 1970s to a slow economy and fuel switching, rather than Clean Air Act enforcement.[3] They predicted that an expanding economy would degrade air quality markedly unless pollution control regulations became more effective. Likewise, based on a review of the available data, economist Robert Crandall argued that the approach embodied in the Clean Air Act was unduly costly while yielding uncertain benefits.[4] Other analyses yielded similar results. For example, a study commissioned by the Business Roundtable concluded that the Clean Air Act had delayed industrial modernization, slowed energy development, and imposed "substantial burdens of unnecessary costs without improving air quality."[5]

Criticism of environmental regulation was not confined to economists. Legal scholar Bruce Ackerman wrote, "No thoughtful academic would deny that we could achieve our present environmental objectives at half the price."[6] In *Going by the Book*, political scientists Eugene Bardach and Robert Kagan documented resentment among businesspeople, even those who might be ideologically inclined to support the goals of regulation, in response to the apparent arbitrariness of implementation.[7] A 1983 book by political scientist R. Shep Melnick decried the "unintended and undesirable consequences" for air pollution policy of "judicial activism."[8] Melnick concluded, "The policymaking of which the federal courts are now an integral part has produced serious inefficiency and inequities, has made rational debate and conscious political choice difficult, and has added to frustration and cynicism among participants of all stripes."[9] And former EPA deputy administrator John Quarles characterized the environmental regulatory system as unnecessarily complex, unduly rigid, and unreasonably heavy on paperwork, especially for small business.[10] He also charged that "in the environmental area, the most serious burdens on industry arise under the Clean Air Act."[11]

In some respects, the public seemed to have gotten the message that prescriptive regulation was economically damaging. In a poll taken for the Council on Environmental Quality in 1980, only 27 percent of respondents agreed that growth should be sacrificed for clean air and water, down from 58 percent in 1978.[12] According to a 1981 Harris Poll, 77 percent of Americans allowed that an important cause of lowered productivity was "excessive government regulation."[13] In a 1981 ABC News/*Washington Post* poll, 54 percent of the respondents accepted the statement that some important environmental regulations should be dropped, "so we can improve the economy."[14] And in a 1981 poll by the Opinion Research Corporation, 95 percent agreed it was a good idea to review the Clean Air Act because experience with it might indicate it needed change.[15] Poll results were not entirely consistent, however; for example, a 1980 survey by Resources for the Future found that only one in five respondents thought environmental standards should be relaxed to spur economic growth.[16] A July 1981 Gallup poll taken for *Newsweek* found that those willing to pay the extra cost of environmental protection outnumbered those unwilling to do so by 58 percent to 36 percent; and in a September 1981 *New York Times*/CBS News poll, two-thirds of respondents wanted to maintain existing laws even at a cost to economic growth.[17]

Regardless of public ambivalence, many in the environmental policy community believed the time was ripe for legislation to reform the nation's environmental regulations.[18] A growing number of experts supported requirements for more detailed analysis, particularly of the costs of regulation, and greater reliance on incentive-based mechanisms. According to Crandall and fellow economist Paul Portney, the "consensus prescription" in the policy community in 1981 was that the EPA should evaluate what it had accomplished to date, increase its staff and capabilities, spend more on monitoring and data collection, search for market solutions to replace inflexible regulatory approaches, carefully review and perhaps replace some standards set prior to 1981, and propose legislative initiatives to reduce the cost of environmental regulation without increasing environmental risk.[19] In 1982, the U.S. General Accounting Office (GAO) weighed in, concluding that an incentive-based approach to air pollution control could save 40 percent to 90 percent of control costs.

Most of these critics espoused policy prescriptions that would "rationalize" the regulatory process; they claimed to be sympathetic to environmental protection goals but skeptical of the means by which they were achieved. But others, particularly libertarians working in the recently created field of law and economics, advanced an analytic framework that prescribed eliminating most social regulations altogether. For example, a 1979 article by economist Charles Wolf in the *Journal of Law and Economics* warned that government failure might be more serious than market failure, so that before enacting any regulation one should compare the two.[20] Economist Peter Aranson argued that the best way to address pollution would be to enforce property rights through common-law litigation, and that government regulation in the form of effluent fees should be considered only when a common-law approach was impractical.[21] In his essay "Richer Is Safer," political scientist Aaron Wildavsky rejected the notion that unbridled economic growth harms the environment, suggesting instead that economic growth might advance human welfare more than regulations aimed at reducing risk.[22]

Such antiregulatory arguments were rooted in a worldview articulated most forcefully by economist Julian Simon, whose 1981 book *The Ultimate Resource* dismissed the claim that the world was entering an age of scarcity; in his view, the data supported "precisely the opposite" conclusion. "The relevant measures of scarcity—the cost of natural resources in human labor, and their prices relative to wages and to other goods—all suggest that natural resources have been becoming less scarce over the long run, right up to the present," Simon argued.[23] He forecast that natural resources would, in fact, become even cheaper and more abundant in the coming years because "[t]here is no physical or economic reason why human resourcefulness and enterprise cannot forever continue to respond to impending shortages and existing problems with new expedients that, after an adjustment period, leave us better off than before the problem arose."[24]

Conservative activists drew on both of these prescriptions, although they leaned more heavily on the latter, in elaborating their antiregulatory storyline. The most comprehensive conservative position statement on environmental regulation appeared in *Mandate for Leadership*, a 1,000-page volume produced by the Heritage Foundation in the fall of 1980 and explicitly aimed at influencing the next administration. In the foreword, Heritage Foundation president Edwin Feulner discounted efforts at bipartisanship, claiming that "pragmatism" was "the new watchword of liberals in retreat."[25] The report's chapter on regulatory reform began with a section on "The Crisis of Overregulation." In a nutshell, its diagnosis was that "[t]he extraordinary growth of government, particularly during the past decade, has brought mounting costs to society which, in turn, have added to inflationary pressures, reduced productivity, discouraged new investment, and increased bureaucrats' intrusion into everyday life." As a result, "regulation threatens to destroy the private competitive free market economy it was originally designed to protect." The chapter's author, James Hinish, contended, "The conservative's dream of doing away with government controls and abolishing federal agencies is now more generally understood and accepted by large segments of the population."[26] *Mandate*'s chapter on the EPA described the agency as a "morass of regulatory controls." Its author, Louis Cordia, offered a host of recommendations, from bringing better science to bear on regulatory decision making to requiring the EPA to conduct risk-benefit analysis on all regulatory proposals, and ensuring implementation did not impinge on economic growth and energy development. He also urged the next EPA administrator to make a special effort "to test and expand concepts of self-regulation and consensus rulemaking."[27]

Conservatives continued to denigrate the Clean Air Act in particular. In March 1981, the bipartisan National Commission on Air Quality issued a congressionally mandated review of the Clean Air Act suggesting some reforms but concluding the act had "generally worked well" to improve the nation's air quality and had not "been a major factor inhibiting energy development in the West," as both industry and conservatives had alleged.[28] Nevertheless, a *Wall Street Journal* editorial urged Congress to examine studies that would inject some "economic realism" into their deliberations on the act. The author cited not only the Business Roundtable analysis, but also projections by Murray Weidenbaum's Center for the Study of American Business at Washington University, St. Louis, which described the Clean Air Act as possibly the most expensive piece of regulatory legislation in history.[29] An April 1982 editorial in the

*Journal* argued that the initial goals of the Clean Air Act had been met. "What we are often faced with now," the author said, "are unrealistic standards that gain only a marginally cleaner atmosphere at great cost to industry, workers and car and truck buyers."[30] A December 1982 editorial chided Congress for "doing nothing . . . to stop destroying [jobs] with onerous regulations." The author focused on the Clean Air Act, "which has since 1970 diverted massive amounts of scarce capital into non-productive scrubbing equipment and the like."[31]

While conservative opinion leaders were refining an antiregulatory storyline that emphasized the shortcomings of pollution control policy, the West was roiling as a result of the Sagebrush Rebellion, a short-lived attempt to transfer hundreds of millions of acres of federal land to the states.[32] With large fractions of their land base under federal control, the western states—particularly those in the Rocky Mountain West, Intermountain West, and Western Great Plains—relied heavily on federal subsidies for ranching, logging, mining, water development, and recreation. Historically, the western congressional delegation had treated the Interior Department as a regional agency, reacting fiercely whenever land managers tried to institute nationally supported environmental protection measures.[33] In the 1970s, however, the Carter administration inflamed western commodity interests and their allies in local government by limiting grazing and off-road vehicle use on public lands, aggressively reviewing land for wilderness designation, proposing legislation to replace the permissive Mining Law of 1872 with a more restrictive leasing system, and seeking to enforce a 160-acre limit on the size of farms that could receive low-cost water from the Bureau of Reclamation.[34] Perceiving that they had lost their advantage in administrative decision making, the Sagebrush Rebels disparaged environmental protection rules as opportunities for overbearing federal bureaucrats to impose unacceptable regulatory burdens on sovereign states.[35]

The rebellion began in 1976, when the Associated California Loggers and a spinoff group, Women in Timber, undertook a concerted campaign of grassroots mobilization, working in partnership with industry; almost concurrently, Chuck Cushman organized property owners in Yosemite against federal policy on inholders.[36] But the event that officially touched off the rebellion was Nevada's passage in 1979 of a law declaring control over land within the state's borders (87 percent of the land in Nevada is federally owned).[37] Proponents framed the rebellion as a constitutional challenge; they cited the "equal footing" doctrine, first advanced in 1845, according to which newer states should be admitted to the Union under the same conditions as the original thirteen former colonies. In truth, support for transferring control over federal lands to the states was limited, but popular resentment of federal authority was broader: many westerners were aggrieved by Carter's actions—from his 55 mph speed limit to his proposed deployment of the MX missile in Utah and Nevada deserts to his attempt to cancel a slew of water projects, most of them in the West.

In the late 1970s, evidence of antienvironmental sentiment was pervasive across the West. For example, in the fall of 1976, voters in Colorado rejected every ballot measure supported by environmentalists—this in a state that four years earlier had turned down the winter Olympics on the grounds that they would damage Colorado's landscape. According to journalist Lou Cannon, "The one reliable applause-getter at the National Governor's Conference in March 1977 was a theme that would have received only scattered handclaps a few years earlier: denunciation of the environmental movement and all its works."[38] Governors who in the past had stressed "environmental preservation" and "conserving our natural resources" signaled their constituents' mood by emphasizing energy production and the need for jobs to boost sagging economies. Antipathy toward federal environmental regulations was so severe that *New York Times* journalist John Herbers claimed the West had replaced the South as the nation's most alienated region.[39]

The Sagebrush Rebellion lent a populist cast to the emerging antiregulatory storyline because it appeared to be "an authentic political movement" driven by people "who believed that federal land management policies had become overly responsive to environmental preservation values."[40] Observers point out, however, that some members of the Western business community used the uprising as "a weapon against any restrictions on the booming development of the West."[41] According to Western novelist Wallace Stegner, the main voice of the rebellion was that of a "regional elite, an economic and political oligarchy. . . . It was the voice of the united mining industry. It was the voice of the chambers of commerce, the boosters, the real estate operators, the developers."[42] Although the connections were rarely acknowledged, several prominent Sagebrush Rebels were also founders of the New Right coalition, including Republicans Orrin Hatch of Utah, James McClure of Idaho, and Paul Laxalt of Nevada. Conservative journalist Lee Edwards explains the philosophical connection between the Sagebrush Rebellion and the New Right as a matter of economic liberty, in which hardworking Americans were pitted against an oppressive federal government. He contends that, because of the environmental movement, "Descendants of those who had settled the West—ranchers and farmers—were besieged."[43]

*Mandate for Leadership*'s chapter on the Interior Department, by Robert L. Terrell, underscored the affinity between the claims of the Sagebrush Rebels and the antiregulatory storyline. Terrell began by charging that the department had been "flaccid" in its posture toward energy and minerals under Carter. Because the Carter administration's constituency was the environmental community, Terrell explained, Interior had begun to consider itself primarily a conservation agency. Terrell was particularly scathing in his depiction of the Fish and Wildlife Service, whose "inflexible purpose [had] caused [it] to take actions which [were] not in the general public interest, but in fact, seriously damage[d] the general welfare of this country's citizenry." The service, said Terrell, was using the Endangered Species Act as a cudgel to stop development. In the process, it had impeded the "prudent balancing" of the utility of federal projects with concern for endangered species.[44]

### Ronald Reagan Articulates a Conservative Public Philosophy

It was this strident antiregulatory storyline, rather than the technocratic reform ideas taking hold in the policy community, that meshed with the antigovernment public philosophy espoused by Reagan. As Theodore White explained, for three decades Republicans had watched the growth of government with dismay; they had warned of an impending disaster and had been ignored.

But by 1980 they enjoyed the counsel of a corps of intellectual outriders of a quality not entertained by their party since Theodore Roosevelt gave up the White House 72 years before. From the Hoover Institution at Stanford, Calif., to the American Enterprise of Washington, from William F. Buckley Jr. to Irving Kristol, conservative thinkers were furnishing ideas that ran counter to the liberal creed. They questioned the entire transformation of American life and government.[45]

No politician bore conservative, antigovernment ideas more enthusiastically than Reagan, White said; no one could speak about big ideas more simply.

Reagan's conservatism was optimistic about the ability of business to rescue the American economy. In stark opposition to New Deal liberalism, it reflected a belief that individuals, left to themselves, would pursue material prosperity to the benefit of society. "Reagan reminded America that government cannot create economic growth and that government generally is the enemy of economic growth," according to historian Burton Yale Pines. "Yet Reagan also taught us that there is something government can do. It can create an environment that is friendly to growth. Government can help unleash human imagination and creativity. It can encourage men and women to take economic risks and then allow them to get big rewards when they succeed." Pines goes on to note that from Reagan's perspective, the hero of economic growth is the entrepreneur, and while government cannot be an entrepreneur, it can foster entrepreneurship "by lowering taxes, by reducing government regulation and interference in the economy, and by making it easier for individuals to accumulate the money they can use for new economic enterprises."[46]

Like his views on government, Reagan's position on the environment was clear. His biographer, Lou Cannon explains that, although Reagan was an outdoorsman and nature lover, he was contemptuous of environmentalists.[47] He believed that individuals would exercise stewardship and did not need government controls to prod them. As governor of California Reagan had seemed proenvironment largely because he delegated responsibility for the issue to his Resources Director Norman (Ike) Livermore and State Parks Director William Penn Mott. But in the six-year interval between his second term as governor and his ascension to the presidency, Reagan had no environmentally oriented advisors and became increasingly close to his prodevelopment friends in business.

Although the environment was not much discussed during the presidential campaign, Reagan did make several statements that betrayed his ignorance about, or lack of concern for, environmental protection and displayed a belief that environmental regulation hampers private sector investment. Most notably, Reagan told an audience of steel- and coal-company executives and community leaders in Steubenville, Ohio, that [s]ome people "associated with the agency in Washington" had gone beyond protecting the environment in a responsible manner. "In reality," he said, "what they believe in is no growth. What they believe in is a return to a society in which there wouldn't be the need for the industrial concerns or more power plants and so forth."[48] Reagan proceeded to make the (erroneous) claim that Mount St. Helens had probably released more sulfur dioxide into the atmosphere than had been released by cars in the previous ten years. He then observed that trees and vegetation emit 93 percent of the country's nitrogen oxides—failing to add that the chemical released by vegetation is not the same as the harmful one emitted by cars and smokestacks.[49] The following day, Reagan blamed the Clean Air Act for the steel industry's woes, echoing the antiregulatory storyline that "many regulations impair the ability of industries to compete, reduce workers' real income and destroy jobs. Therefore, we must have a balanced regulatory approach in which we recognize that regulations have costs as well as benefits."[50]

On other occasions, Reagan was even more explicit in his antipathy toward "environmental extremists." He criticized EPA officials, saying: "if they had their way, you and I would have to live in rabbit holes or bird's nests."[51] The agency's actions, Reagan claimed, had raised the costs of everything Americans bought. He vowed to augment the nation's energy supply by eliminating "thousands of unnecessary regulations," particularly "cumbersome and overly stringent Clean Air Act regulations," and put the EPA in the hands of people who understood the coal industry.[52] Reagan also signaled his sympathy for western resource users when he declared in an August 1980 campaign speech: "I am a Sagebrush Rebel."

The Republican Party platform was equally forthright in its hostility toward government in general and environmental regulation in particular. The platform asserted that "at the root of most of our troubles today is the misguided and discredited philosophy of an all-powerful government ceaselessly striving to subsidize, manipulate, and control individuals." Republicans, by contrast, believed the country's well-being could be restored "through a rebirth of liberty and resurgence of private initiatives." Individuals, the platform went on to say, "can make the right decisions affecting personal or general welfare, free of pervasive and heavy-handed intrusion by the central government into the decision-making process." With respect to energy, the platform advocated a "comprehensive program of regulatory reform, improved incentives, and revision of cumbersome and overly stringent Clean Air Act regulations" as well as simplified regulation of the use of coal. Whereas the Democratic platform listed conservation as the top energy priority, the Republicans put it third, after maximizing development of fossil fuel resources and exploring alternative sources. "We reject unequivocally," the Republican platform said, "punitive gasoline and other energy taxes designed to artificially suppress energy consumption." More generally, the platform expressed the view that although environmental regulations had yielded some benefits, those improvements came at too high a cost. Only "necessary and reasonable" environmental controls should be retained, and any regulations "must be made rational . . . to accelerate private investment. We strongly affirm," it added, "that environmental protection must not become a cover for a 'no-growth' policy and a shrinking economy."

### Institutionalizing the Antiregulatory Storyline During President Reagan's First Term

The election of 1980 seemed to mark the ascension of the conservative public philosophy over New Deal liberalism. Reagan won the presidency with 50.7 percent of the popular vote, to Carter's 41 percent (Independent John Anderson garnered 6.6 percent); his Electoral College margin was an overwhelming 489 to 49. In addition, Republicans picked up 33 seats in the House of Representatives, narrowing Democrats' margin from 273–179 to 243–192. And, by winning 12 new Senate seats, the Republican Party gained control of that chamber (which went from 58–41–1 to 46–53–1) for the first time in decades. Importantly, these shifts were due largely to the election of Western conservatives. With their arrival, only about fifteen of the remaining Republicans in the Senate could be considered moderate, and most of the chamber's leaders were conservative.

Despite the ascension of conservatives, the Senate as a whole remained relatively moderate,[53] so Reagan was wary of attempting to rescind popular environmental statutes or replace them with more business-friendly ones; his legislative strategy was confined to resisting efforts to strengthen existing laws and deflecting legislation to address newly identified problems. At the same time, he sought ways to infuse antiregulatory ideas into implementation and enforcement. He hoped this approach would provoke less opposition and enable him to conserve his political capital for higher-priority concerns, such as the budget and taxes.[54] To carry out his administrative strategy, Reagan modified the policymaking context by appointing ideological conservatives, slashing agency budgets, and centralizing control over regulatory decision making. His appointees, in turn, used their discretion to reallocate the budgets and staff of their agencies, while relaxing enforcement of restrictive rules. After Congress and the courts rebuffed many of the administration's deregulatory forays, however, Reagan adopted a more conciliatory approach in hopes of ensuring his reelection.

### Reagan's Legislative Strategy: Obstructing Restrictive Laws

Rather than challenge the restrictive status quo directly, President Reagan adopted a defensive posture: the White House counteracted environmentalists' efforts to raise the salience of environmental problems by downplaying the risks to human health and the environment and shifting public attention to the cost, in terms of lost efficiency and freedom, of policies to address those risks. The Clean Air Act, due for reauthorization in 1981, presented an early opportunity for Reagan to demonstrate his antiregulatory bona fides. The positions of the participants in the debate were well established. Although united in its belief that the act was unnecessarily burdensome, industry was divided on the appropriate prescription, with some groups hoping to weaken the act and others simply trying to reduce its complexity.[55] In an opening salvo, the Business Roundtable made public its $600,000 study attacking the law and suggesting that regulations could be loosened—cutting compliance costs in half in some cases—without jeopardizing public health.[56] As it had in the 1970s, the auto industry continued to lobby hard for relaxing emissions requirements, despite numerous concessions already made by the EPA to help the industry.[57] Organized labor was divided on Clean Air Act revisions as well, depending on how changes would affect them: construction unions in the AFL-CIO supported modifying the bill, but many industrial unions in the federation opposed major changes.[58] Environmentalists were prepared to see the act streamlined, but not weakened; they pointed out that several analyses showed the societal benefits of the act clearly exceeded its costs.[59]

As controversy over the act heated up in Congress, the bipartisan National Commission on Air Quality weighed in with a March 1981 report predicting that the Clean Air Act would not hinder the nation's energy development and pointing out that the states did not have the capacity to set their own air quality standards. The commission agreed that the act should be made more effective, however. It recommended eliminating deadlines, simplifying the Prevention of Significant Deterioration rules, and raising carbon monoxide emissions standards for cars. It also recommended adding provisions to deal with acid rain.[60] Robert Stafford of Vermont, a moderate Republican who had long been an environmental champion and was chair of the Senate Environmental Public Works Committee, made clear that he would not advance legislation that weakened the act.

Initially, the administration claimed that easing air pollution rules under the Clean Air Act was a top legislative priority. Splits soon developed within the White House, however. Some presidential advisors were determined to codify cost-benefit requirements in the statutory language, rather than simply relying on an executive order that could easily be overturned. Others were more circumspect, reluctant to suggest major changes to a broadly popular law. In June 1981, the administration generated a 106-page draft, including legislative language and a detailed analysis of proposed changes, that "would have eased much of the economic and regulatory burden on industry and turned over substantial enforcement to the states."[61] The document proposed giving the states much more freedom to decide whether and how to clean up polluted air and no longer requiring the EPA to intervene in the event of an unsatisfactory plan. In addition, the draft eliminated secondary air quality standards, which protect crops, lakes, and general welfare, leaving such standards optional for states. It also did away with PSD standards altogether, except for national parks. And it dispensed with requirements to meet the lowest achievable emission reductions where air quality standards were not being met, or to offset pollution from new sources in those areas. Automobile tailpipe standards were loosened, and there was no requirement to maintain pollution control devices on cars. Nor were there mandatory penalties for violators. Mark Griffiths, associated director of environmental matters for the National Association of Manufacturers (NAM) said the proposals contained in the draft were "right in line with the things we asked for."[62]

It quickly became apparent that Congress would not adopt the administration's proposals. Representative Henry Waxman, a California Democrat and chair of the Subcommittee on Health and Environment, obtained a copy of the administration's proposal and released it to the media, saying, "This proposal is nothing less than a blueprint for the destruction of our clean air laws."[63] Waxman wrote to the president saying he could expect a "furious and acrimonious battle" over the act, and Senator Stafford said he would be "very dismayed" if the administration adhered to the position outlined in the draft.[64] Survey data suggested it would be foolhardy to stake the administration's popularity against the popularity of clean air. A Harris poll taken in June 1981 indicated that 86 percent of respondents wanted a Clean Air Act that provided protections as strong as or stronger than the existing law.[65] Louis Harris told a congressional committee in the fall of 1981 that any member of Congress who voted to weaken the Clean Air Act did so at the risk of losing his or her seat. "The desire on the part of the American people to battle pollution is one of the most overwhelming and clearest we have ever recorded in our 25 years of surveying public opinion around this country," he said.[66] President Reagan's pollster, Richard Wirthlin, told a group of Republican Senate staffers that his own findings "emphatically confirmed the Harris results."[67]

Rather than negotiate a detailed agreement with legislative leaders, in early August the administration proffered a set of eleven broad principles, several of which—adjusting deadlines "to reflect realities," raising automobile emission standards to "more reasonable" levels, retaining PSD for parks and wilderness areas only—would have made the act more permissive and slowed compliance.[68] Jerry Jasinowski, chief economist at NAM, commented: "There is not anything missing that was a major priority for us."[69] But conservatives chastised the administration for failing to make a stronger case in favor of weighing the costs of regulations against their benefits.[70] In any event, the administration did little to press its case.

Just before Congress adjourned in November 1981, Democratic representative Thomas Luken of Ohio introduced legislation that had the backing of both the administration and NAM. The bill doubled emissions limits for carbon monoxide and nitrogen oxides and relaxed inspection and maintenance rules for cars; extended deadlines for meeting national air quality standards at the discretion of the EPA administrator; and eliminated penalties for failing to submit state implementation plans while expediting the review and approval process for those plans. In early 1982, in an effort to exert pressure on Congress to pass Luken's bill, the Reagan administration rolled out a new tactic: the EPA administrator threatened to ban construction in metro areas in eleven states because they had failed to implement anti-smog programs. The EPA sent letters to governors shortly after industry lobbyists and the administration encountered setbacks in the House Energy Committee. The letters said: "In spite of our opposition to these requirements in the legislative arena, we must enforce the provisions of the Clean Air Act until it is changed."[71]

The agency's brinksmanship was not enough to break up the logjam in Congress, where regional and partisan differences continued to thwart legislative action. Exacerbating the legislative stalemate was the administration's staunch refusal to consider controls on acid-rain-causing emissions. Identified in the early 1970s, acid rain is the result of long-distance transport of sulfur dioxide and nitrogen oxides. Scientists suspected that acidic precipitation, caused primarily by tall smokestacks in the Midwest, threatened aquatic systems and forests in the Northeast. In fact, acid rain was largely the consequence of industry efforts to evade complying with the Clean Air Act, as many utilities had built tall stacks to disperse pollution rather than install scrubbers or use low-sulfur coal.[72]

By the late 1970s, environmentalists were lobbying for additional controls on sulfur dioxide and nitrogen oxide emissions from coal-fired power plants, arguing that there was a strong scientific consensus that acid rain posed a serious environmental threat. In early April 1980,

Carter's EPA administrator Doug Costle had said, "What we know and what we suspect about acid deposition tell us we are faced with a genuine and serious environmental problem."[73] The utility industry countered that it would be absurd to spend astronomical sums when cause and effect were so poorly understood. The American Electric Power Company estimated acid rain controls would prompt rate increases of more than 50 percent for residential electricity users and more than 80 percent for industrial users, while the National Coal Association—quoting figures from the United Mine Workers—claimed that more than one-third of the coal-mining labor force would be affected and $6.6 billion in income would be lost every year.[74]

In October 1981, the National Academy of Sciences released a report on the biological consequences of acid rain. Based on the evidence it reviewed, the committee concluded, "[T]he picture is disturbing enough to merit prompt tightening of restrictions on atmospheric emissions from fossil fuels and other large sources. . . . Strong measures are necessary if we are to prevent further degradation of natural ecosystems, which together support life on this planet." The panel also warned that "continued emissions of sulfur and nitrogen oxides at current or accelerated rates, in the face of clear evidence of serious hazards to human health and the biosphere, will be extremely risky from a long-term economic standpoint as well as from the standpoint of biosphere protection."[75] But the administration ignored the conclusions of that panel as well as those of a joint U.S.-Canada commission, and suppressed reports issued by EPA staffers and its own hand-picked group of scientists.[76] Instead, administration officials focused on scientific uncertainty about the causes and consequences of acid rain as a rationale for delaying action. They pressed scientists for information on the precise relationship between sources and receptors of acid rain—data that were hard to come by because other types of pollution complicated the analysis and because scientists lacked historical baseline information. Assistant EPA administrator Kathleen Bennett testified before Congress that there were still too many uncertainties about acid rain and warned Congress not to "impose any additional multibillion dollar programs without first determining with some assurance that the intended benefits will be achieved."[77]

Siding with industry, the Reagan administration also argued that the benefits of mitigating acid rain paled in comparison to the costs of regulating utilities. OMB director David Stockman captured the administration's view when he wondered, "How much are the fish worth in those 170 lakes that account for 4 percent of the lake area of New York? And does it make sense to spend billions of dollars controlling emissions from sources in Ohio and elsewhere if you're talking about a very marginal volume of dollar value, either in recreational terms or in commercial terms?"[78] Other administration officials were even more scathing. Interior secretary James Watt complained that "every year there's a money-making scare. This year it's acid rain." And James B. Edwards, Reagan's energy secretary, said: "I don't want to stop acid rain, because 99.9 percent of all rain is of an acid nature. In some areas, it's good for crops. . . . and a little acid helps to neutralize the soil."[79]

### Changing the Policymaking Context through Administrative Centralization

Critical to the Reagan administration's approach to regulatory reform was infusing every decision with rigorous cost-benefit considerations. The first step in this direction was to centralize White House control over the regulatory process. During his first two weeks in office, President Reagan instituted a moratorium on new regulations. He also created a Task Force on Regulatory Relief, staffed by the recently created Office of Information and Regulatory Affairs (OIRA) within the OMB. The task force was chaired by Vice President George H. W. Bush and made up of the secretaries of commerce, labor, and treasury, the attorney general, the OMB director, the chairman of the Council of Economic Advisers, and the president's assistant for policy development—all personnel for whom economic growth was a primary concern. According to its mandate, the task force stressed four conservative principles in its regulatory review: harnessing market incentives, reducing burdens on state and local governments, modifying regulation where social costs exceeded benefits, and streamlining regulatory procedures.[80] Explaining the task force's role, Bush said: "It came through loud and clear during the election campaign that there is too much regulation, and that this is acting as a depressant on the economy."[81]

In mid-February, Reagan issued Executive Order 12291, which required agencies to prepare a "regulatory impact analysis" (essentially a cost-benefit analysis) on any major regulation under consideration, and submit that analysis to OIRA before publicly proposing the rule. Although Carter also had required agencies to subject new rules to formal economic analysis, Reagan went considerably further in raising hurdles to new regulation: except where explicitly prohibited, his order required agencies to demonstrate that the benefits of proposed regulations outweighed the costs, and to show that their approach minimized net social

costs and maximized net social benefits.[82] Whereas Carter's review aimed
to ensure that regulations were not unduly onerous, the Reagan administration's review strongly emphasized consideration of regulatory costs
at every step and put the burden on agencies to quantify the monetary
value of proposed regulations. Reagan asked the Task Force on Regulatory Relief to oversee this review and ensure that major regulatory
proposals were not burdensome to the national economy or key industrial sectors.

In addition to emphasizing quantitative cost-benefit analysis, the task
force review process changed the policymaking context by combining
greater industry access with little transparency, thereby facilitating low-
profile challenges by antiregulatory forces. In 1981 and 1982, the task
force worked with the OMB to generate a series of "hit lists" containing
rules it hoped to "defer, revise, or rescind," based largely on suggestions
from industry or state and local governments.[83] By December 1981,
the task force had singled out for review 91 regulations, 60 percent of
which concerned health, safety, or environmental quality. Over the course
of its two-and-one-half-year existence, the task force reviewed 119
regulations, 76 of which were revised or eliminated, including 22 from
the EPA.[84] In its final report, released in August 1983, the task force
claimed the number of rules published by the federal government had
dropped by more than one-quarter, and proposed regulations had
dropped by nearly one-third, when compared with the Carter administration's record.[85]

The number of rules changed or withdrawn gives an incomplete
picture of the impact of task force/OMB review, however. According to
journalist Peter Behr, the review effected an "abrupt and historic shift of
power from the regulatory agencies and into the hands of" the OMB—a
shift that industry clearly perceived as beneficial.[86] For example, upon
receiving an advance copy of one of the task force hit lists, Bob Ragland
of the National Association of Manufacturers commented: "This continues to add credibility to the Reagan administration's commitment to
changing . . . what up until a year ago was an unchangeable attitude in
this town—that government was big brother."[87] Corporate attorney
William Warfield Ross advised his colleagues about the new accessibility
of the White House through the OMB portal:

Given the very considerable powers vested in the [OMB] director—and the fact
that the executive order is completely silent as to any restrictions on communication with OMB or the task force with respect to the review of major rules—the
practitioner should make every effort where appropriate to communicate with

the director to attempt to influence his "views" on a proposed rule in the direction of the client's preference. In the absence of any ground rules, the possible approaches are limited only by the extent of the practitioner's ingenuity or effrontery.[88]

In September 1983, John E. Daniel, former chief of staff at the EPA, testified before the House Energy and Commerce Committee's Investigations Subcommittee that the OMB had leaked proposed changes in environmental regulations to industry and had brought "tremendous pressure" on the EPA to make business-friendly changes in regulations.[89] Specifically, Daniel said, the OMB tried to dictate regulations to the agency, threatened reprisals, and urged that cost factors be built into health rules even when the law prohibited doing so.

### Changing the Context through Appointments and Budget Cuts

The EPA acceded to task force requests, often over the advice of its professional staff, because its leadership shared the antiregulatory worldview of task force members. Such ideological compatibility was not accidental; in a departure from the historic norm, Reagan sought to change the institutional context by appointing top officials who shared his beliefs. In the fall of 1980, Reagan established a transition task force on the environment headed by Dan Lufkin, a director of Columbia Picture Industries, and including such well-respected figures as former EPA administrators Russell Train and William Ruckelshaus. The group produced a detailed report that, according to Russell Peterson, head of the Council on Environmental Quality under Nixon and Ford, "sought to maintain the momentum of environmental protection while allowing for some easing of regulation and for economic incentives for pollution control."[90] Ultimately, however, the administration ignored the Lufkin report in favor of the recommendations of two key advisors—Senator Paul Laxalt, a close Reagan ally and key conservative operator in Congress, and Joseph Coors, a prominent businessman and donor to conservative causes—as well as the advice contained in the Heritage Foundation's *Mandate for Leadership*.

First and foremost, the administration selected ideological conservatives whose main qualification was loyalty to the president. James Hinish, one of the contributors to the *Mandate* volume, said the president's most important weapon against regulatory overkill was his appointment power; therefore, Hinish urged the president to make the most important qualification for appointees that they "share the general philosophy and outlook of the president."[91] According to political scientist Chester

Newland, "loyalty as ideological consistency was applied far more exten-
sively as *the* test for appointment in the Reagan administration than in
any other presidency in at least half century."[92] This strategy paid off;
there was a striking degree of homogeneity among the Reagan White
House staff, who were uniformly conservative but often lacked experience and expertise.[93] In the regulatory and natural resource management
agencies, most appointees were former employees or financial beneficiaries of the industries whose activities they were supposed to police.[94]
Even as he filled leadership positions with conservatives, Reagan cut back
the White House science advisor's office and populated it with officials
borrowed from other agencies, rather than choosing prominent figures
in science and technology.[95]

Reagan's choice for secretary of the interior, James Gaius Watt, shared
the president's principled beliefs about making natural resources available for economic use. Watt was president and founder of the Mountain
States Legal Foundation, whose purpose was "to fight in the courts those
bureaucrats and no-growth advocates who create a challenge to individual liberty and economic freedoms." According to Cannon, Watt
vowed that when he reached Washington, "We will mine more, drill
more, cut more timber to use our resources rather than simply keep them
locked up."[96] Watt deftly wove together the storyline of the Sagebrush
Rebellion with that of the New Right; for example, in a January 1982
*Saturday Evening Post* interview, he argued, "What too many people fail
to recognize is that being a good steward involves decisions on the *use*
of resources as well as the *preservation* of resources." If we don't use our
resources, he went on to say, "we unduly penalize and impoverish our
people, weaken our nation, and deny ourselves the economic base essential to good stewardship."[97] When in doubt, he would "err on the side
of public use vs. preservation."[98] In fact, Watt ridiculed environmentalists' ideas about wilderness, saying, "My concept of stewardship is to
invest in it—build a road, build a latrine, pump in running water so you
can wash dishes. Most people think if you can drive in, walk 20 yards
and pitch a tent by a stream you've had a wilderness experience. Do we
have to buy enough land so that you can go backpacking and never see
anyone else?"[99]

Reagan's emphasis on ideological fealty was realized even more fully
in the selection of Anne Gorsuch as administrator of the EPA. Gorsuch,
who had served for four years in the Colorado legislature, had little
managerial experience but was an avowed critic of environmental regulation and was deeply loyal to the president. During her confirmation

hearings, Gorsuch assured senators that she was "committed to restoring, preserving, and protecting the environmental heritage that is a critical, integral part of the legacy our children and grandchildren must inherit."[100] She emphasized, however, that policy would be determined by the president, that she favored giving the states more power, and that at the top of her list of priorities was balancing environmental protection with economic and energy considerations. Like Reagan, she was convinced that the real problem was too much government, and she looked forward to playing a key role in the administration's regulatory reform efforts.[101] She told journalist Philip Shabecoff that she was looking to reduce the "overburden" of regulation and that her emphasis would be on "voluntary participation."[102]

Other appointees boasted impressive antiregulatory credentials as well. As chief pollution officer in Ohio, James McAvoy, a member of Reagan's Council on Environmental Quality, helped crusade for relaxed air quality standards to allow the burning of soft coal. W. Ernst Minor, also on the CEQ, believed the pendulum had "swung too far toward the environment protection side" and wanted to give "industry a break to get this country moving again."[103] In the Interior Department, Robert Burford, head of the Bureau of Land Management (BLM), was a Colorado legislator who had sponsored a Sagebrush Rebellion bill to return BLM land to state and private ownership. As an Indiana state senator, James Harris, director of the Office of Surface Mining (OSM), had led Indiana to join a Supreme Court case challenging the constitutionality of the restrictive Surface Mining Conservation and Recovery Act. Steven Griles, deputy director of the OSM, had also worked to have the mining law declared unconstitutional. Carol Dinkins, the assistant attorney general for land and natural resources, was a corporate lawyer from Texas, where she had worked for clients who were challenging federal air and water pollution laws. At the EPA, John Daniel, the chief of staff, was a former lobbyist for the Johns-Manville Corporation, the leading producer of asbestos; Kathleen Bennett, assistant administrator for air, noise, and radiation, had served as a lobbyist for the Crown Zellerbach Corporation, a major paper producer; and Robert Perry, general counsel for EPA enforcement, was a former Exxon lawyer.

In addition to those in regulatory positions, Reagan's White House advisors—particularly his economic team—played a critical role in shaping and enforcing the administration's views on environmental policy. Reagan recruited Murray Weidenbaum, an avowed critic of regulation, to head his Council of Economic Advisers and appointed James

Miller, also a skeptic of regulation, to head OIRA.[104] Most outspoken, however, was David Stockman, Reagan's pick to head the OMB. Stockman was a vocal adherent of supply-side economics and a staunch conservative.[105] He had warned in his 23-page "Dunkirk memo," coauthored with Republican representative Jack Kemp of New York and issued just before the inauguration, of a "ticking regulatory time bomb." According to the memo:

During the early and mid-1970's, Congress approved more than a dozen sweeping environmental, energy and safety enabling authorities, which for all practical purposes are devoid of policy standards and criteria for cost-benefit, cost-effectiveness, and comparative risk analysis. Subsequently, McGovernite no-growth activists assumed control of most of the relevant sub-Cabinet policy posts during the Carter Administration. They have spent the past four years "tooling up" for implementation through a mind-boggling outpouring of rule-makings, interpretative guidelines, and major litigation—all heavily biased toward maximization of regulatory scope and burden. All told, there are easily in excess of $100 billion in new environmental safety and energy compliance costs scheduled for the early 1980's.[106]

Stockman urged the Reagan administration to make "strict, comprehensive and far reaching regulatory policy corrections." In fact, he argued that "a whole new mindset was needed at EPA," or else the agency "would practically shut down the economy."

A less-noticed facet of Reagan's appointment strategy involved his approach to the judiciary. Reagan began by staffing the Justice Department with energetic movement conservatives, many of them associated with the newly created Federalist Society for Law and Public Policy. Launched in 1982, the Federalist Society brought together conservative and libertarian law students, practicing lawyers, and legal scholars in on-campus seminars and forums. Formed to counter what they saw as the liberal ideological domination of law schools, the society's goal was "reordering priorities within the legal system to place a premium on individual liberty."[107] More pragmatically, it sought to advance the nomination of conservative judges and to recruit and train practitioners who could shepherd important cases through the legal system.

In addition, by contrast with his predecessors, who generally adopted a bipartisan approach to judicial selection, Reagan put into place and fine-tuned "a rigorous, ideological process for selecting federal judges."[108] Primary responsibility shifted from the Justice Department to the White House Office of Legal Policy and the White House Judicial Selection Committee. Those offices, in turn, introduced an extensive screening process for potential nominees. Abetting the administration in the Senate was Strom Thurmond, the conservative Republican chair of the Senate Judiciary Committee.

Another means Reagan used to render the policymaking context hospitable to antiregulatory ideas was cutting the budgets of agencies responsible for environmental protection. Initially, Reagan had hoped to eliminate the Council on Environmental Quality altogether. Upon discovering that doing so would require legislative authorization, he simply cut it to the bone: its annual budget went from $2.5 million in 1981 to $700,000 in 1984, while its staff fell from fifty to twelve.[109] As a result, according to political scientists Michael Kraft and Norman Vig, "for all practical purposes the council . . . ceased to exist for most of the 1980s. . . . It was barely able to produce its mandated annual report on the nation's environmental quality, running several years behind schedule with a much briefer report than those submitted in earlier years."[110] Moreover, under Reagan the CEQ adopted a very different stance than that of its predecessors. Its chair, A. Alan Hill, asserted that it would be more accessible to business. Consistent with this position, the council explained that the costs of the environmental regulation enacted in the 1970s exceeded their benefits, and called for reevaluating all environmental programs in terms of their economic costs and benefits, adding that, because history showed that resources held in common almost inevitably deteriorated, the government should turn environmental amenities over to private owners.[111]

Another target of Reagan's budget-cutting axe was the EPA. By the time Administrator Gorsuch took office in late summer of 1981, the OMB had already slashed the agency's budget by 11 percent.[112] Ironically, although Gorsuch recommended an additional 28 percent reduction for fiscal year 1982, she found herself defending the agency against the even deeper cuts sought by the OMB, which proposed shrinking the EPA to just over half the size it had been in January 1981. After taking her case to the president, Gorsuch prevailed: the EPA's fiscal year 1982 budget was "only" 29 percent below its 1981 level.[113] For fiscal year 1983, Gorsuch proposed an operating budget another 20 percent lower than her fiscal year 1982 request of $1.19 billion. Ultimately, despite efforts by Congress to restore some of its funding, the agency's total operating budget (excluding Superfund and sewage treatment funds) fell 22 percent during Reagan's first term.[114]

Particularly hard hit in the EPA's early budgets was research and development: over a two-year period, the administration proposed cutting the agency's R&D budget in half (after accounting for inflation).

Almost all the cuts affected the agency's contractual science wing, its most credible source of information. Such draconian cuts meant the agency would be unlikely to detect new problems or suggest that existing problems were more serious than originally believed; they would also facilitate industry challenges to proposed regulations on the grounds of inadequate scientific justification.[115]

For the Fish and Wildlife Service, Reagan proposed an endangered species budget of $16.5 million for 1983, a 28 percent cut from the program's 1981 level. Money for listing specifically was to be cut by 51 percent, from $4.1 million to $2 million, and state grants would be eliminated. Recovery funds would be increased by 10 percent.[116]

**Low-Profile Challenges: Reallocating Agency Budgets and Staffing**
Reagan's appointees used low-profile mechanisms like reallocating funds and laying off or transferring personnel to achieve the administration's deregulatory goals. For example, to make her lean budgets work, Gorsuch approved a Reduction-in-Force plan that involved firing 40 percent of headquarters staff and demoting or transferring many others. Once the administrator's intentions became clear, however, enough people quit that few needed to be fired; as a result, within a year, many of the agency's best professional staff had left.[117] One consequence of Gorsuch's purge, according to political scientist Marc Landy and his coauthors, was that "[t]he atmosphere of frenetic activity and organizational ambition that had characterized the EPA during the Costle years simply dissipated."[118] In an editorial in the *Washington Post*, former EPA administrator Russell Train fumed:

It is hard to imagine any business manager consciously undertaking such a personnel policy unless its purpose was to destroy the enterprise. Predictably, the result at EPA has been and will continue to be demoralization and institutional paralysis. Attrition within the agency is running at an extraordinary 2.7 percent per month or *32 percent a year*. . . . The budget and personnel cuts, unless reversed, will destroy the agency as an effective institution for many years to come.[119]

In the face of substantial cuts to Interior Department funding, Secretary Watt reoriented his budget and staffing to emphasize resource development rather than conservation. "That's how I've changed the priorities of the Department of Interior, by shifting the allocation of manpower and dollars," Watt explained.[120] Ron Arnold, an admiring conservative activist, described Watt's strategy in the following way: "[M]uch of the over-regulation and land-grabbing of past years had been done contrary to the intent of Congress in the first place. . . . And, since most of Watt's goals consisted of eliminating governmental powers rather than enlarging them, he could refuse to exercise discretionary powers and still remain true to the intent of Congress. One way to do that would be to set budgetary levels for Interior programs according to their merits as seen in terms of his policy."[121] Arnold added that, although Congress could restore some of Watt's spending cuts, in doing so they would risk being seen as big spenders in hard times.

One way that Watt effected budget cuts was to institute a moratorium on grant programs for recreation and historic preservation and on federal land acquisitions from the Land and Water Conservation Fund. He also abolished three agencies: the Water Resources Council, the Office of Water Resources, and the Heritage Conservation and Recreation Service (some of whose functions were taken over by the National Park Service). And, having endorsed cutting the budget for the Endangered Species Office in half, he forced the agency to scale back contracts for biological studies used in species listing.[122] Even as he slashed funding for biodiversity conservation, Watt recruited and promoted civil servants dedicated to natural resource development. When asked about this practice, he explained, "I will build an institutional memory that will be here for decades."[123]

### More Low-Profile Challenges: Making Implementation and Enforcement More Permissive

In addition to altering agency priorities by reallocating money and personnel, Reagan appointees employed a number of other low-profile tactics to ease the burden of environmental regulations. In the Interior Department, Secretary Watt instituted a host of policies—typically by modifying operating manuals and directives—aimed at easing access to natural resources on federal property. For example, he made almost all of the country's coastal waters available to oil and gas companies; accelerated the leasing of federal lands containing coal and reduced regulation on strip mining; transferred responsibility for maintaining federal rangelands from the Bureau of Land Management to private ranchers; and issued coal leases in environmentally sensitive areas, even though experts said the United States already had mined enough coal to satisfy the country's needs through 2000.[124] Watt's "good neighbor" policy, aimed at defusing the Sagebrush Rebellion, involved transferring a relatively small amount of land to the states but, more important, giving states and localities a greater voice in natural resource policy and making sure that federal land managers were responsive to the concerns of western resource users.

Watt also "profoundly influenced the Fish and Wildlife Service, virtually halting Endangered Species Act implementation and enforcement."[125] The agency listed only one species during Watt's first year, the Oahu tree snail, and only eleven species in 1982. According to conservation biologist Michael Scott and his coauthors, the slowdown occurred because Executive Order 12291 required listings to be justified economically.[126] (In March 1982, about sixty proposals for new listings were bottled up in cost-benefit review.[127]) Reviews by the Interior Department's solicitor and the OMB also impeded the listing program. Ronald E. Lambertson, associate director of the Fish and Wildlife Service, instructed the office to reduce by half the number of species to be considered for listing in 1981 and to concentrate on recovery of already-listed species rather than new listings.[128] Several biologists in the office told Shabecoff they were disturbed by the directive, as well as by another new policy under which all listing operations would be done by regional offices rather than in Washington, D.C. Morale in the office was low, they said, because of lack of sympathy for the endangered species program in the administration.[129]

Low-profile efforts to make implementation of the Endangered Species Act more permissive were not always successful, however. For example, the Interior Department tried to weaken the Fish and Wildlife Service's implementation of the act by redefining "harm" to an endangered species. The ESA made it illegal to "take" an endangered species. It defined "take" as "to harass, harm, pursue, hunt, shoot, wound, kill, trap, capture, collect, or attempt to engage in any such conduct." The only ambiguous word in this sequence was "harm." In 1975, the service defined "harm" as acts that kill or injure wildlife or that disrupt essential behavioral patterns, including "breeding, feeding or sheltering," adding that "significant environmental modifications or degradation which has such effects is included within the meaning of 'harm.'" A federal court in early 1981 affirmed that "harm" encompassed damage to a species' natural habitat. Within two months of the ruling, the Interior Department's associate solicitor produced a memo characterizing the definition of "harm" as "overly broad" and recommending that the service redefine "harm" to mean only "an act or omission which actually injures or kills wildlife."[130] After months of rulemaking, however, environmentalists prevailed: the

Fish and Wildlife Service ended up including as harm "significant modification or degradation" of a species' habitat, if it "kills or injures wildlife" by upsetting breeding, feeding, or sheltering patterns.[131]

Under Gorsuch, the EPA undertook some genuine reforms, building on the work that EPA staff had already initiated. For instance, as part of its accelerated lead phase-out the administration introduced an innovative policy that allowed refiners to trade the right to use lead in gas on a nationwide basis. In addition, the agency continued to experiment with emissions trading mechanisms, which it promoted as a business opportunity for brokers.[132] In April 1982, it consolidated bubbles, offsets, netting, and emissions reduction banking into a single program. Initially, the agency also broadened the bubble policy to include areas that were dirtier than the law's standards permitted—a move that alarmed environmentalists. (Previously, the bubble policy had only been employed in areas where the air exceeded national standards.) Although the D.C. Circuit struck down the administration's attempt to allow the bubble policy to be applied in areas that had not attained air quality standards (*Chevron v. NRDC*), in 1984, the Supreme Court unanimously (6-0) upheld the modification. Justice John Paul Stevens, who wrote the opinion, said the EPA's interpretation of the Clean Air Act "represent[ed] a reasonable accommodation of manifestly competing interests."[133] (Despite the Court's willingness to defer, when the EPA issued its final guidelines for trading allowances under the bubble/offset policies, it no longer allowed an overall increase in pollution and the baseline was lowered, so larger emissions reductions were required.)

But many of the agency's efforts involved low-profile efforts to undermine regulations that hampered industrial development, often at the behest of the Task Force on Regulatory Relief. Specifically, the EPA relaxed motor vehicle emissions standards for carbon monoxide to the extent permitted by Congress and changed measurement standards for hydrocarbon pollution; eliminated the requirement to install canisters on vehicles to control the release of gasoline vapors during refueling; gave manufacturers greater authority to check their own compliance with pollution controls on new cars, rather than requiring particular tests; relaxed emissions regulations for test vehicles; scaled back government audits of manufacturers to assure compliance with pollution standards; and gave companies longer advance notice of new regulations. The agency also delayed carbon monoxide and hydrocarbon emissions standards for 1984-model-year heavy-duty trucks, so catalytic converters would not be required on these vehicles; permitted a failure rate of up to 40 percent in assembly line exhaust emissions tests for light and heavy trucks, rather than the proposed limit of 10 percent; delayed selective enforcement audits to check on emissions testing of heavy-duty truck engines for two more years; and relaxed standards for nitrogen oxide emissions from heavy-duty engines.

The task force's efforts to reduce the regulatory burden imposed by the Clean Air Act did not always succeed, particularly if opponents managed to publicize them. For example, at the behest of small refiners, the task force and the OMB persuaded a reluctant EPA to relax Carter-era regulations limiting lead additives in gasoline, despite well-documented evidence of lead's damaging health effects. Specifically, the EPA proposed to postpone indefinitely an October 1982 deadline for small refiners to comply with the 0.5 grams/gallon lead standard and to exempt large refiners from the standard except for gasoline sold in cities. The plans were leaked, however, and a major outcry ensued. The public health and environmental communities reacted so strongly that Congress convened hearings at which it was disclosed that Gorsuch had told representatives of one small refinery that they did not need a waiver because the agency was planning to abolish or drastically revise the lead rules. Furthermore, agency officials had held meetings with industry officials but none with public health advocates. To the surprise of all observers, in October 1982, the EPA announced it was *tightening* the lead standards, rather than loosening them.[134]

Like Watt, Gorsuch was particularly committed to curbing what she regarded as overzealous enforcement of environmental regulations. Within three weeks of her confirmation, Gorsuch announced a reorganization that eliminated the EPA's enforcement office, dispersing its staff throughout the various program offices. Shortly thereafter, she reestablished the office with a much smaller staff. In the spring of 1982, she reorganized the enforcement office again and redefined its responsibilities. (According to policy scholar Richard Andrews, Gorsuch reorganized the enforcement office every eleven weeks during her first year.[135]) The agency's enforcement capacity was clearly diminished: between 1980 and 1982, the number of cases referred to the Justice Department declined by 50 percent, from 200 a year to 100, while the number of enforcement orders dropped by one-third.[136] Meanwhile, enforcement counsel William Sullivan told the administrators of the EPA's ten regional offices that they should not send any cases to headquarters for review until they had "explored every opportunity for settlement," adding that "[e]very case you do refer will be a black mark against you."[137] Not surprisingly,

enforcement actions by the regional offices plummeted, from 313 referrals in 1980 to 59 in 1981.[138]

Gorsuch also adopted a host of more subtle tactics, such as reducing
the dollar amount of civil penalties assessed, adopting new and more
exclusive screening criteria for identifying potential violators, declining
to test new legal or economic theories that might expand the existing
classes of violators, reducing discretion for field enforcement personnel,
relying on state and local governments and trade and professional associations instead of federal enforcers, and adopting a less threatening, more
flexible posture toward regulated entities.[139] According to legal scholar
Joel Mintz, under Gorsuch, the agency shifted from a file-first, negotiate-
later approach to a "nonconfrontational" approach that involved talking
first and filing only if it was absolutely necessary and could be cleared
with headquarters. Interviews conducted by Mintz made clear that the
Gorsuch years were devastating for enforcement at the EPA.[140]

Beyond relaxed enforcement, Gorsuch sought low-profile mechanisms
that would slow the EPA's production of new regulations and impede
efforts to address recently identified problems. She required more detailed
prepublication review by senior administrators and the agency's Science
Advisory Board of all internal and contract studies—a process that
delayed rulemaking and subjected proposed rules to scrutiny by experts
who had been selected partly based on their political beliefs. She also
channeled the EPA's declining research funds toward regulatory support,
reducing or eliminating studies of problems that EPA staff were concerned about but that were not yet regulated. More generally, under
Gorsuch, the EPA displayed an increased propensity to rely on scientific
analyses that made risk-tolerant assumptions, and often declined to regulate on the grounds that there was not yet sufficient scientific evidence.
For example, the agency adopted rules for formaldehyde and several
pesticides that permitted risks to life of 1 in 1,000. According to several
career officials, the risks accepted in those standards were far higher than
those permitted prior to the Reagan administration, when accepted risk
ranged from one in a million to 1 in 100,000; on only two occasions
were levels as low as 1 in 10,000 permitted.[141]

### Still More Low-Profile Challenges: Devolving Responsibility and Narrowing Participation

The Reagan administration found other low-profile ways to reduce the
federal regulatory burden on industry as well. Gorsuch's EPA made a
concerted effort to transfer authority for regulatory programs to the

states—in some cases continuing a trend of devolving mature programs, but in others transferring authority to states that lacked adequate capacity. Reagan's Council on Environmental Quality boasted:

by the end of 1982 state governments had been delegated enforcement responsibilities for over 95 percent of applicable National Emissions Standards for Hazardous Air Pollutants, and over 90 percent of applicable New Source Performance Standards, up from 64 percent at the beginning of the year. In addition, of the 60 state and local agencies eligible to grant and enforce new source (air) permits, 48 had been delegated full or partial authorities by the end of 1982, up from 26 at the end of 1981.[142]

At the same time, however, the administration cut back on financial aid to the states: the Congressional Budget Office reported that between 1981 and the 1984 budget request, state air grants fell 46 percent, in 1982 dollars.[143] "Such a policy," argued Richard Andrews, "could only be interpreted as a backdoor repeal of statutory responsibilities through administrative tactics."[144]

Sure, enough, the *Wall Street Journal* reported that states hard hit by federal budget cuts responded by trimming their environmental programs. Pennsylvania closed nearly half of its forty-six enforcement offices; Indiana had to cut its clean air program to the "bare bones" and "place as much of the burden upon industry" as possible. Even states in reasonable fiscal shape looked to cut costs—by reducing air quality monitoring, scaling back public participation requirements, and raising fees for environmental inspections and permits. Nevertheless, Gorsuch was determined to "make good on the idea of equal partnership" with the states by delegating 75 percent of all federal programs before the fall of 1984.[145]

Some in the Reagan administration hoped to take devolution even further, by privatizing federal lands. On the advice of budget director Stockman and Steve Hanke, a member of Reagan's Cabinet Council on Economic Affairs, in late February 1982, the president issued Executive Order 12348, establishing a Property Review Board to identify excess property owned by the federal government and facilitate its disposal. In his budget message for fiscal year 1983, Reagan endorsed the goal of moving "systematically to reduce the vast holdings of surplus land and real property, [since] some of this property is not in use and would be of greater value to society if transferred to the private sector."[146] The administration's Asset Management Program garnered overwhelmingly negative press coverage, however, and provoked a furious response by environmentalists, professional foresters, and many western politicians.

Most western resource users opposed privatization as well; they wanted not to own the resources but simply to return to the days of unfettered access.[147] John Crowell, assistant secretary of the Agriculture Department, defended the privatization initiative, saying it was "an opportunity to improve the National Forest System by disposing of land that cannot be managed efficiently."[148] But in November 1983, Congress quashed the program through a rider to the Department of the Interior Appropriations Act.

In addition to accelerating devolution, both Gorsuch and Watt narrowed participation in decision making to those most likely to agree with them. They excluded career employees from policy discussions, asked political appointees rather than careerists to produce agency reports, centralized rulemaking so that all regulatory proposals were reviewed by political appointees, and actively disparaged the work of civil servants.[149] They also cut back sharply on funding for information dissemination and eliminated support for citizen education. They made a particular point of declining to meet with environmentalists. Watt met with environmentalists once, in 1981, at which point he told them there would be no more such gatherings because "there was nothing further to discuss."[150] In early 1982, in an effort to defuse the growing hostility, presidential counselor Edwin Meese met with Russell W. Peterson of Audubon, Jay Hair of the National Wildlife Federation, and Michael McCloskey of the Sierra Club. Peterson, who took notes at the meeting, concluded: "If we needed any confirmation of the complete disrespect on the part of the President and his team for what we in the conservation and environmental movement stand for, we got it during this meeting."[151]

### The Political Response to Reagan Administration Challenges

Environmentalists did not cave in to the Reagan administration's low-profile efforts to render environmental policy more permissive. One way they sought to thwart administrative adjustments was through litigation. Not surprisingly, given the plain language of the statutes and the fact that most of the federal judiciary had been appointed by liberal or centrist presidents, the courts spurned many of the Reagan administration's regulatory relief efforts. In fact, according to Eads and Fix, the courts upheld the administration's initiatives only if they clearly extended policy changes begun by their predecessors—presumably an indication that the administration's aim was to improve regulations, not remove regulatory barriers.[152] For example, the Supreme Court ruled that the Coastal Zone Management Act did not require the federal government to consider the environmental concerns of coastal states when offering oil and gas leases for sale on the outer continental shelf (*Secretary of Interior v. California*). As a result, the Court effectively upheld Watt's proposal to lease the entire outer continental shelf to oil and gas exploration. But the federal courts blocked several other oil leasing decisions that disregarded federal environmental laws, and they rejected many of Watt's efforts to weaken surface-mining rules.[153] The courts rebuffed many of Gorsuch's low-profile challenges as well; for example, in 1984, the D.C. Circuit ruled that the EPA *did* have the authority to control emissions from vessels docked at marine facilities, saying the agency had "acted far too precipitously" in withdrawing Carter-era rules to regulate air pollution around shipping terminals (*Natural Resources Defense Council v. U.S. EPA*).[154]

Environmental groups did not rely exclusively on the courts; they seized every opportunity to publicize their concerns about low-profile maneuvering by the administration. Initially, they focused on Watt and Gorsuch, sensing that personal attacks on the popular president might backfire. In late March of 1982, however, a team of environmental groups released a thirty-five-page list of 227 charges against Reagan himself, saying they had decided to "indict" him because they had found an "across-the-board pattern of lawlessness and heedlessness with regard to the nation's natural resources unequaled since the days of the robber barons a century ago."[155] By June, even the moderate Conservation Foundation had jumped into the fray, issuing its own "State of the Environment" report, since the Council on Environmental Quality had not published one for 1981 or 1982. The report concluded that the Reagan administration had introduced a "fundamental discontinuity into natural resource and environmental policy" and broken a decade-long bipartisan consensus.[156] Environmental groups broadened their audience, targeting hunting and fishing groups on wilderness issues and public health advocates on air pollution. And they began raising money and recruiting volunteers for candidates they supported in the 1982 campaigns—targeting districts where incumbents had poor environmental records.

Other observers were also critical of the president's environmental policies. Economists, many of whom had advised the president during his transition, disparaged the administration's blunderbuss approach.[157] Dan Lufkin, a lifelong Republican who had been the chair of the president-elect's environmental task force expressed dismay at the administration's early actions, which he described as "crazy." Lufkin said the administration's plans for the Clean Air Act would "throw out the baby, tub and all . . . to create an unworkable, unenforceable, impractical, and ineffective travesty of regulation on which so much of our human and physical survival depends."[158]

Even some of the ostensible beneficiaries of laxer policies were dubious. An October 1981 *Chemical Week* article described the EPA as an agency "in disarray." An accompanying editorial entitled "We Need a Credible EPA" expressed concern about Gorsuch's management. "Legal uncertainties aside," the editorial said, "neither EPA nor industry can afford even the appearance that EPA is a captive of industry. We believe that the regulators ought to rethink some of the new procedures. And we believe that industry ought to choose to press its case in full view."[159] In the natural resource arena, moderate businesspeople were similarly disaffected; they worried that the administration's aggressiveness created uncertainty and reduced the prospects for compromise.[160] Journalist Andy Pasztor reported that business leaders and industry groups that supported deregulation feared that, in response to the Reagan administration's missteps, Congress and the courts would enact even more stringent regulations.[161]

Environmental salience campaigns, whistle-blowing by civil servants disgruntled with the actions of their political superiors, criticism by moderate businesspeople, and journalists' proenvironmental predilections, combined to ensure universally negative media coverage of the Reagan administration's low-profile efforts to render the environmental policy framework more permissive. That coverage, in turn, provoked a hostile response from the public. *New York Times*/CBS News polls showed steady growth in support for tougher environmental regulations. In September 1981, 45 percent of those surveyed agreed that "protecting the environment is so important that requirements and standards cannot be too high, and continuing environmental improvements must be made regardless of cost." In September 1982, 52 percent agreed, and by April 1983, 58 percent did.[162] A poll conducted for the Continental Group Inc. between February and March 1982 documented a persistent "environmental ethic" shared by business leaders and the unemployed, liberals and conservatives alike—all in the midst of difficult economic times.[163] A Harris poll conducted for *Business Week* in early 1983 seemed to suggest that the Sagebrush Rebellion was a chimera; Harris found that the West wanted "more and tougher federal regulation than any other part of the country."[164] "Environmentalism," Harris remarked, was one of the "sacred cows of the American public."[165] Importantly, the environment became a potent political issue in New Hampshire, a key proving ground for presidential campaigns.[166]

Congress responded to the rapidly rising salience of the Reagan administration's antiregulatory initiatives by rebuffing most of its proposals. In addition to rejecting the administration's Clean Air Act principles, in 1982, Congress easily reauthorized the Endangered Species Act for three years, overriding the administration's preference for a one-year extension and codifying restrictive regulatory interpretations the administration had previously tried to reverse.[167] In particular, Congress curbed the interior secretary's ability to delay listings and enhanced the ability of nongovernmental organizations to press for enforcement of the act by establishing strict timelines for processing petitions and completing listing decisions. (The response time on a petition was reduced from two years to one, with the possibility of a six-month extension.) Congress also specified that listing decisions be made "*solely* on the basis of the best scientific and commercial data available," thereby preventing the incursion of cost considerations. At the same time, Congress added Section 10, which authorized the creation of habitat conservation plans, voluntary agreements with landowners who set aside habitat in return for permission to "take" listed species—a mechanism its sponsors hoped would assuage the nascent concerns of private landowners about the law's inflexibility.[168]

Congress also thwarted many of the administration's low-profile deregulatory initiatives, particularly those that garnered widespread publicity. For example, on July 22, 1981, Republicans joined Democrats in appropriating $155 million for park expansion in 1982, even though Watt had asked for a moratorium on spending for new parks, preferring to redirect the money to repairing roads and hotels in existing parks.[169] A few weeks earlier, the House Interior and Insular Affairs Committee had invoked a seldom-used procedure and declared an "emergency" in order to prevent Watt from authorizing mineral development in the Bob Marshall, Scapegoat, and Great Bear Wilderness Areas in Montana. In late 1981, according to Cannon, Watt got "an even more personal rebuke" when he tried to allow oil drilling in the Washakie Wilderness outside Yellowstone National Park. Both of the state's Republican senators (one of whom Watt had worked for) and its lone Republican member of the House opposed him.[170] Then, in 1982, Congress blocked Watt's plans to open wilderness areas and wildlife refuges to oil and gas development. Congress targeted Gorsuch as well, and by early 1983, six committees and the Justice Department were investigating charges of political favoritism and corruption at the EPA. In March, Gorsuch and more than twenty other top officials resigned.

At first, Reagan dismissed criticism of his handling of the environment, charging his detractors with "environmental extremism."[171] According to Philip Shabecoff, however, during the EPA hearings the environment "captured and held the public's attention for weeks and preoccupied the Government at its highest levels."[172] As the controversy dragged on, the president's political advisors became concerned about the impact of the controversy on the 1984 election. In an effort to mitigate the political damage, Reagan appointed the highly regarded William Ruckelshaus to replace Gorsuch. While EPA employees welcomed Ruckelshaus's return, environmentalists were wary; in a letter to Vice President Bush written in June 1981, Ruckelshaus had urged major changes to the Clean Air Act to make it less restrictive, as well as the creation of a mechanism to assess the economic impact of air quality standards. In another letter to Bush, he joked that as the first EPA administrator he was "largely to blame for most of the bad things done to business by environmental regulations over the last decade."[173] In his confirmation hearings, Ruckelshaus said he planned few substantive departures from the Reagan administration's policies but rather would focus on management style.[174]

Upon reassuming the reins at the EPA, Ruckelshaus assured reporters that the Reagan administration had confused the public's wish to improve the way goals were achieved with a desire to change those goals, and he moved quickly to restore the agency's morale and credibility.[175] Among his first acts was to announce that he would not impose sanctions on localities that were out of compliance with air quality standards, as threatened by Gorsuch, unless they were making no effort to comply. Ruckelshaus also reinvigorated enforcement at the EPA. Alvin Alm, the agency's deputy administrator, began pressuring regional offices to up their enforcement levels, while Ruckelshaus concentrated on beefing up the agency's fledgling criminal enforcement program.

When Ruckelshaus pursued new policy restrictions, however, he faced firm opposition from the White House. For example, after the EPA developed a set of options for reducing emissions of sulfur dioxide and nitrogen oxides, the precursors of acid rain, the White House Office of Policy Development insisted that too little was known about the phenomenon to justify any controls. In addition, although the OMB acceded to Ruckelshaus's request for $165 million more than the original administration request for fiscal year 1984 and also approved an increase in the EPA's budget for fiscal year 1985, it gave the agency less than half of the increase Ruckelshaus sought. As a result, even though its workload had practically doubled, the agency's 1985 budget was still 10 percent lower than what it had been in the last year of the Carter administration.

Furthermore, although most observers attest that he succeeded in reinvigorating the EPA, Ruckelshaus nevertheless adhered to Reagan administration priorities. He declined to press for legislation strengthening pesticide regulation, drinking water protection, or toxic air pollutants. He perpetuated the practice established by Gorsuch of accepting higher levels of risk than had previously been deemed acceptable.[176] He proposed relaxing controls on sulfur dioxide emissions from coal-fired utilities and industrial plants by basing compliance on a thirty-day rather than a three-hour average—a change that would have allowed significantly more sulfur dioxide to be emitted.[177] In mid-January 1984, the EPA postponed tougher emissions standards for diesel cars and light trucks, giving manufacturers two extra years to reduce diesel emissions by one-third. That December, Ruckelshaus denied a petition by New York, Pennsylvania, and Maine to curb acid-rain-causing pollution from the Midwest, explaining that the petition would entail imposing new controls on sources of sulfur dioxide emissions. "Such actions," he said, "would require that a definitive and significant link be established" between sources of sulfur dioxide and the effects of acid rain.[178]

Two months earlier, the EPA had scrapped regulations to curb airborne radiation from nuclear weapons facilities, power plants, and phosphorus mines, contending the risks from airborne radioactive particles were "relatively trivial" because so few people lived near the sites. That action drew a contempt order from William Orrick, a U.S. District Court judge, who described "foot dragging by the EPA" and said the agency had ignored its "mandatory statutory duty."[179] After the 1984 election, Ruckelshaus quietly resigned, and the agency hastily issued the radiation regulations so that incoming administrator Lee Thomas would not be thrown in jail.

While Ruckelshaus struggled to right the EPA, Watt tried to defuse the controversy that surrounded him by announcing his intention to shift from development toward conservation.[180] The apparent transformation came too late, however; in October 1983, after an impolitic remark about the composition of a commission assembled to investigate his coal leasing policies, Watt tendered his resignation. Reagan promptly replaced him with William P. Clark, formerly the national security adviser. Like Reagan's other appointees, Clark was first and foremost a conservative with a strong allegiance to the president. But he contrasted sharply with Watt in terms of personal style, preferring consensus to confrontation. In an effort to mend some of the rifts opened by Watt, Clark began his tenure by calling for an end to partisanship over conservation issues and offering to make the department more accessible to environmentalists, Congress, and the media.[181] On the other hand, Clark had no experience or apparent interest in the environment; in fact, his record as an associate justice on the California Supreme Court appeared to be consistent with an antiregulatory worldview: he had participated in twelve cases involving environmental regulations, and in each case he had sided with development interests.[182]

### Reagan's Second Term: Drift and Prevention

By replacing Gorsuch and Watt, Reagan managed to defuse the issue of environmental protection.[183] As Shabecoff observed, Ruckelshaus and Clark "operated as if they had a mandate to render environmental policy harmless as a political issue, making moves largely favored by environmentalists and avoiding controversial decisions."[184] After winning the 1984 election with nearly 60 percent of the popular vote, Reagan paid scant attention to the environment during his second term. At Interior, Donald Hodel replaced Clark and persisted on the prodevelopment path established by his predecessors, albeit more quietly. EPA administrator Lee Thomas—who replaced Ruckelshaus shortly after the election— strived to maintain a cautiously proenvironmental trajectory, while conservatives in the White House sought to delay or prevent new regulations and to undermine environmentalists' legal forays. Even as it returned Reagan to the White House, however, the 1984 election brought a large number of Democratic legislators into office, and a more proenvironmental Congress reauthorized several major environmental statutes. In the process, Congress constrained Reagan appointees' discretion by increasing the scope and detail of environmental laws, adding more prescriptive mandates along with rigid implementation deadlines and "hammer" clauses for enforcement.[185]

### Low-Profile Challenges to Restrictive Policies Persist at Interior
During Reagan's second term, Donald Hodel, who had previously served as undersecretary of the interior, continued the trend begun under Watt of making public resources available for development; he simply did so in less provocative ways.[186] In fact, one Park Service official characterized

Hodel as a "Watt clone in a three-piece suit."[187] According to Watt, Hodel wrote in the book celebrating the 150th anniversary of the Interior Department, "I asked President Reagan was it proper to assume that I was to proceed under the direction you gave James Watt." And the president said, "You are."[188] Hodel acknowledged as much halfway through his tenure, telling journalists that Reagan's interior secretaries had reestablished "a basic fundamental balance" in the management of public lands and resources. "We have been maintaining the proper course and the next two years will be basically the same," he said.[189]

Hodel delighted environmentalists in 1987 with his proposal to drain the Hetch Hetchy reservoir in northern California. Moreover, endangered species listings jumped dramatically starting after Watt's departure and in response to funding increases from Congress, averaging fifty-four per year for the remainder of the Reagan administration. More commonly, though, Hodel's Interior Department emphasized resource development. He transferred water rights on Bureau of Land Management lands to ranchers, leased oil-shale lands to companies at below-market prices, and relaxed the conditions under which owners of claims to mineral rights on BLM lands could exercise those rights.[190] Like Watt, Hodel opposed expansion of the national park system and worried about "blindfolding America as to its resources potential" by closing off land and offshore areas to development.[191] Hodel also decided against providing states with a list of especially scenic vistas from national parks that should be kept free of smoke and other emissions from proposed industrial plants, on the grounds that doing so could provoke state resentment. (If the department provided states with such a list, as allowed under the Clean Air Act, they would have been required to "consider" the special value of the vista before granting a permit for an industrial development.) During the administration's final weeks, the department proposed a series of rules that could open as many as 4 million acres of national parks and other protected lands to coal mining. It also proposed accelerating and simplifying the process of transferring public resources to private developers; specifically, Interior resumed the process of transferring title to large federal oil-shale tracts in the West at a fraction of their market value, prepared rules to lower the royalty fees paid by private operators for coal mined on federal lands, and delayed issuing rules that would limit oil and gas drilling in national forests.[192]

Even as it promoted resource development, the department declined to implement restrictive biodiversity conservation measures. Consistent with the administration's governing philosophy, the Fish and Wildlife

Service delegated authority to states and deferred to development interests. For example, it allowed the state of Minnesota to set up a sport-
trapping season for the northern timberwolf, although environmentalists
successfully sued in 1985 to stop that practice. The service also turned
over management of the black-footed ferret to the Wyoming Fish and
Game Department. In another case, the Fish and Wildlife Service undermined an agreement forged during the Carter administration in which
Colorado irrigators had to replace water downstream of a dam on a
tributary of the South Platte River to avoid jeopardizing the nesting
habitat of the whooping crane. Under Reagan, the agency allowed dam
developers to show that the cranes might not need as much water as the
agency originally thought.

In September 1986, scientists met in Washington, D.C. to raise awareness of an ongoing mass extinction of species at a three-day National
Forum on Biodiversity, sponsored by the National Academy of Sciences
and the Smithsonian Institution. At the forum, nine of biology's most
respected leaders issued a statement ranking the extinction crisis as "a
threat to civilization second only to the threat of thermonuclear war"
and recognized the chief threat to biodiversity was not hunters but bulldozers. Despite growing concern about biodiversity loss within the scientific community, in late 1987, the Reagan administration reorganized
the Endangered Species Office—merging it with the Ecological Services
Division and transferring its functions to the Fish and Wildlife Service's
regional offices. Scientists in the office claimed a major reason for dismantling the Washington office was that the staff were "rather idealistic"
and had made recommendations that would impinge on political and
economic interests, whereas the regional offices would be more receptive
to local political and economic concerns.[193]

## Resisting Restrictive Policies on Acid Rain at the EPA

Whereas Hodel capitalized on public complacency to advance antiregulatory ideas at Interior, Lee Thomas, who replaced Ruckelshaus as EPA
administrator after the 1984 election, took advantage of White House
inattention to enhance the EPA's credibility and restore some measure of
its autonomy.[194] In collaboration with the Department of Justice, Thomas
both increased the level of formal enforcement activity at the agency and
took pains to publicize its numbers. After filing virtually no lawsuits in
the administration's early years, in 1985, the EPA filed a record number
of legal actions against polluters. According to Henry Habicht, assistant
attorney general for land and natural resources, in 1987, his division of

the Justice Department brought twice the number of civil suits against violators of the environmental laws as it had in its previously most active period in the 1970s. In his four years as head of the division, Habicht said, his lawyers filed more than one thousand civil cases and won more than $600 million in penalties from violators of the toxic waste cleanup law and $20 million from those found in violation of the Clean Air and Water Acts. He also reported that the division successfully pursued more than three hundred criminal cases.[195]

In addition, Thomas at times stood up for restrictive regulations. He tangled twice with the OMB in 1985—once on the asbestos ban and again on pollution controls for trucks and buses—and both times he emerged victorious, having wielded the threat of publicity to gain leverage. In February 1988, the EPA released rules on information disclosure for toxic substances, as mandated by the Resource Conservation and Recovery Act. Later that month the agency unveiled its long-awaited plan for protecting groundwater from pesticides. And in September it issued "comprehensive and stringent" rules for protecting groundwater supplies from leaks of underground storage tanks.

Most important, Thomas argued successfully for government intervention to address the buildup of atmospheric-ozone-depleting chlorofluorocarbons (CFCs). At his urging, in 1987, the administration signed the Montreal Protocol, in which thirty nations agreed to reduce their production of CFCs by 50 percent by 1998. Thomas prevailed only after a dispute in the Cabinet Council on Natural Resources, where Hodel and his allies argued for substituting adaptive measures—such as hats and sunglasses—for a CFC phase out. President Reagan settled the matter by siding with Thomas, and the EPA proceeded to issue binding restrictions on the use of CFCs and halons under the Clean Air Act. The new rules took effect on the schedule agreed to in Montreal: a freeze on all CFCs at 1986 levels starting in 1989, a 20 percent rollback in their use by 1994, and a 50 percent cut by 1999.

At the same time, Thomas took low-profile steps to avoid promulgating restrictive rules. One tactic the EPA continued to rely on was devolving responsibility to the states. For example, in June 1985, Thomas announced a "national strategy" for dealing with toxic air pollutants, in which state and local agencies would be the primary regulators. In the agency's first concrete move under the new strategy, it made decisions on two probable human carcinogens. For chromium, Thomas said it would take at least four years to issue a national standard; for acrylonitrile, the EPA planned to work with fourteen states to regulate the chemical "if necessary." S. William Becker, executive director of STAPPA/ALAPCO, an organization of state and local regulators, complained that the states had neither the expertise nor the resources to take on the regulation of air toxics; state regulators also worried that industry would engage in venue shopping for lax regulations.[196]

In a move that was controversial among scientists both within and outside the agency, the EPA adjusted its approach to assessing the risks posed by regulated substances, as a result declaring some of them less dangerous than previously believed.[197] Consistent with the administration's relatively risk-tolerant approach to standard setting, in mid-April 1988, the agency declined to adopt tougher rules for spikes in sulfur dioxide levels to protect asthmatics, saying that the existing standard was adequate to protect public health.[198] The EPA also declined to lower the ambient air quality standards for nitrogen oxides and carbon monoxide, despite evidence presented during the 1985 review of the standard that sensitive populations continued to be at high risk from these pollutants.[199]

Moreover, unlike Ruckelshaus, Thomas agreed with White House conservatives that the president should not take the lead on acid rain, despite a growing body of research indicating that it was developing into a national problem. Thomas testified before Congress that the Clean Air Act in its current form provided adequate protection and that additional controls on acid rain precursors were unnecessary. "I do not believe the current state of knowledge can sustain any judgment with respect to the level of emission reductions needed to prevent or eliminate damage," he explained.[200] He added that it would take two or three more years to complete the necessary research.

Facing a recalcitrant EPA and gridlock in Congress on the issue of acid rain, environmentalists turned to the courts, where they experienced a small measure of success. Environmentalists and the state of Pennsylvania had filed suit to challenge rules issued in 1982, charging that the EPA had not adequately met a mandate from Congress in the 1977 Clean Air Act Amendments to discourage the use of tall smokestacks.[201] In late June 1985, under court order, the EPA finalized new restrictions on the use of tall stacks. The new rule, which changed the way tall stacks affected the computer models used to determine if a source was in compliance, required many facilities to put scrubbers on their stacks or switch to low-sulfur coal. (Environmentalists' analysis of the rule showed it would not come close to achieving a 1.7-million-ton annual reduction in sulfur dioxide, as the EPA claimed.) Another lawsuit, by seven northeastern states demanding that midwestern and border states reduce their emissions of acid rain precursors, fared less well. The plaintiffs prevailed in U.S. District Court, where Judge Norma Holloway Johnson ruled in August 1985 that the EPA had unlawfully delayed responding and ordered the agency to impose emissions curbs. The EPA appealed, however, and in September 1986, the D.C. Circuit unanimously dismissed the case. The ruling focused not on scientific questions about acid rain but on the notice-and-comment requirements of rulemaking; the plaintiffs had hoped to convince the court that a letter written by Doug Costle contending that acid rain was a problem that warranted regulatory action constituted a formal agency policy that the Reagan administration had unlawfully overturned. But the judges found the EPA's actions "within the agency's discretion and not subject to judicial compulsion" (*Thomas v. New York*). Undaunted by this setback, environmentalists and the states continued to sue. In July 1987, for example, six northeastern states and five environmental groups filed yet another acid rain suit—this one charging the EPA with failing to meet a 1979 deadline for regulating emissions that cause haze in national parks.

In response to federal inactivity, states and localities in the Northeast passed their own rules to control smog and acid rain. Many state officials complained, however, that federal officials did not give them enough money or guidance to be effective. Thomas Jorling, New York State commissioner of environmental conservation, pointed out, "Pollution doesn't respect state boundaries and it is difficult if not impossible to solve these problems on a state-by-state basis."[202] In an interview shortly before he stepped down, Thomas said that having the federal government set pollution control standards and giving the states authority to carry them out was a sound concept. But, he acknowledged, in some areas, particularly in administering the Clean Air Act, "the theory isn't working in practice," and "there has to be more of a directed Federal effort."[203]

### Resisting Action on the Emerging Problem of Global Warming

By contrast with his position on acid rain, Thomas advocated precautionary action to address the recently identified problem of global warming. Scientists had been investigating a link between rising emissions of carbon dioxide and other greenhouse gases and rising global temperatures since the 1950s. During the 1970s, a small cadre of atmospheric scientists made a concerted push to draw attention to the possibility of a "runaway greenhouse effect." In response, legislators convened hearings at which scientists testified that the rise in carbon dioxide could bring worldwide disaster, and proposed bills that would fund scientific research into the issue. Following the issuance of an ominous National Academy of Sciences report in July 1977, a front-page headline in the *New York Times* alerted readers that "Scientists Fear Heavy Use of Coal May Bring Adverse Shift in Climate." Journalist Haynes Johnson wrote in the *Washington Post* that "it now appears that the levels of carbon dioxide in the atmosphere are increasing to the point that they could have a profound long-term impact on the planet, and all the life on it."[204] In 1978, Congress passed a National Climate Act, which created a National Climate Program Office within the National Oceanographic and Atmospheric Administration. After laying out the dire consequences associated with a runaway greenhouse effect, from sea-level rise and coastal flooding to shifts in precipitation patterns and agricultural disruption, Carter's Council on Environmental Quality warned before leaving office that national and international policies would have to be enacted immediately to avoid major long-term climate problems.[205]

When the Reagan administration took office, however, it marginalized the new climate program and was downright hostile toward scientists concerned about a runaway greenhouse effect. Deeming it unnecessary, the administration sought to gut funding for climate change research—a result that was averted only after the Senate, led by Tennessee Democrat Albert Gore Jr., held hearings to publicize the proposed cuts. As historian Spencer Weart explains, "Sporadic press attention to greenhouse warming . . . embarrassed the administration enough to avert the worst of the threatened budget cuts."[206] Nevertheless, the White House continued to block funding for global warming research, spending less than $50 million per year—a relatively trivial sum given the complexity of the science. At the same time, the administration adopted a risk-tolerant stance identical to the one taken on acid rain: it would be foolhardy to act in the absence of scientific certainty about the magnitude of the problem and its causes.

After the departure of their more stridently antienvironmental appointees in 1983, Reagan administration agencies became more receptive to requests for information on the likely social and economic impacts of global warming. For example, an October 1983 report released by the EPA warned that a runaway greenhouse effect would begin to manifest itself in the 1990s. The report—the first to be issued by the federal government on the threat of global warming—concluded, "A soberness and sense of urgency should underlie our response to a greenhouse warming."[207] Shortly after the EPA report, however, the National

Academy of Sciences issued a more sanguine assessment of the threat posed by global warming, based on the same data used by the EPA. President Reagan's science advisor, George A. Keyworth 3rd, praised the Academy's report and called the EPA's "unwarranted and unnecessarily alarmist."[208]

At a Senate hearing in June 1986, scientists predicted that rising concentrations of carbon dioxide in the atmosphere would have a swifter and more pronounced impact than earlier suspected. Lee Thomas said the administration might have to take political action despite the scientific uncertainty, and that the United States was committed to an active role domestically and internationally. But two other Reagan aides— William Graham, deputy director of NASA, and Alvin Trivelpiece of the Department of Energy—suggested that more research, perhaps as much as a decade's worth, was needed before acting. That year, even as concern about global environmental problems was growing, the Reagan administration reduced the United States' contribution to the United Nations Environment Programme from $10 million per year to $6.8 million. In 1987, the administration proposed reducing that amount to $4.8 million.[209]

### Using Regulatory Review and Executive Orders to Quash Restrictive Rules

Beyond resisting legislation on new environmental issues like acid rain and global warming, White House officials exploited centralized review and legal tactics to prevent the adoption of restrictive regulations. At the beginning of his second term, Reagan issued Executive Order 12498, creating a "regulatory calendar" that would "interdict the regulatory process at its start."[210] The order and its accompanying memo gave the OMB the authority to intervene in agencies' "preregulatory" activities, for example by dictating the amount and type of information they could collect. Under its new authority, the OMB wrangled with the EPA over rules requiring heavy trucks and buses to install traps for emissions of particulates from diesel and gas engines made after 1994, as well as over asbestos regulations, drinking water, and underground storage tank rules—repeatedly delaying issuance of those rules well beyond legal deadlines.[211]

Once again, Congress and the courts tempered the OMB's attacks. In 1986, the Democrat-controlled House deleted funding for the OMB's regulatory division from the fiscal year 1987 budget, forcing a showdown. The House restored the money only after the OMB adopted the

"Gramm procedures," authored by OMB director Wendy Gramm, under which the OMB agreed to provide the agency with copies of written material it received from people outside the government and advise the agency of any oral communication. The courts also limited the OMB's authority by prohibiting it from imposing cost-benefit analyses on regulations for which Congress had explicitly prohibited such tests. Moreover, in January 1986, a federal judge ruled that the OMB lacked the authority to delay the EPA's issuance of regulations beyond statutory deadlines (*Environmental Defense Fund v. Thomas*). Despite these steps, nearly one-quarter of the regulations proposed by agencies and departments across the government were changed at the behest of the OMB before they were issued.[212] During 1985 the EPA revised 74.5 percent of agency rules reviewed by the OMB; that figure was 66.2 percent in 1986, and 66.2 percent in 1987. Moreover, in cases where the EPA and the OMB disagreed, the OMB "invariably prevailed."[213] In short, seven years into the Reagan administration, OMB influence over the EPA remained substantial.

The administration did not rely exclusively on the OMB to curtail restrictive regulations; it also devised a new legal tactic: limiting environmentalists' standing to sue. In the early 1970s, the Supreme Court had broadened the definition of standing, and throughout that decade environmentalists had taken full advantage of the courts' newfound openness to press agencies for restrictive implementation of their mandates. But in 1981, Carol Dinkins, assistant attorney general in charge of the Justice Department's land and natural resources division, urged division attorneys to challenge the right of environmentalists to sue under the National Environmental Policy Act.[214] In 1987, the president bolstered Dinkins' initiative by issuing a directive to the Department of Justice stating that any staff attorney litigating a case involving the EPA and public interest groups who did not challenge the group's standing to sue would have to persuade his or her section chief to prepare a memo to the appropriate deputy attorney general explaining why not. Even if this tactic failed to prevent lawsuits, it ensured that environmental plaintiffs would have to expend their scarce resources establishing standing.[215]

The White House pursued a second court-related tactic as well: in the mid-1980s Attorney General Edwin Meese III launched an initiative that Reagan's solicitor general Charles Fried dubbed the "Takings Project." According to Fried, this group "had a specific, aggressive and . . . quite radical project in mind: to use the takings clause of the Fifth Amendment to the U.S. Constitution as a severe brake upon federal and state regulation of business and property"—an idea that was first articulated by libertarian legal scholar Richard Epstein. "The grand plan," Fried explained, "was to make the government pay compensation as for a taking of property every time regulations impinged too seriously on property rights. . . . If the government labored under so severe an obligation, there would be, to say the least, much less regulation."[216]

Takings Project lawyers drafted President Reagan's 1988 Executive Order 12630, which required that "government decision-makers evaluate carefully the effect of their administrative, regulatory, and legislative actions on constitutionally protected property rights." This order dramatically expanded the traditional concept of "taking"; for example, it said "regulations imposed on private properties that substantially affect its value or use, may constitute a taking of property" even where there is "less than a complete deprivation of all use or value." The aim, according to the administration, was to sensitize federal officials to the Fifth Amendment's prohibitions. Takings Project lawyers also focused on promoting the appointment of libertarian judges to spots on the three federal courts that control the direction of federal takings jurisprudence: the U.S. Supreme Court, the Federal Circuit Court of Appeals, and the U.S. Court of Federal Claims. As the number of conservative judges swelled—by the end of his second term, Reagan had appointed 350 federal judges, more than any other president in history—proponents anticipated that the judiciary's receptiveness to such arguments would grow.

## The Democratic Congress Passes Restrictive Legislation

In the absence of presidential leadership, the 99th Congress remained stalemated on reauthorizing the Clean Air Act, and regional divisions stymied efforts to address acid rain in particular. Even when Congress seemed close to acting, in 1988, an anticipated veto by Reagan was enough to bolster industry's position, reinforce regional divisions, and prevent forward motion. On other issues, however, Congress seized the initiative, crafting proposals that not only ran counter to the administration's philosophy but "force[d] EPA to write far more regulations, and more rapidly as well. In the process . . . they created a vast range of new regulatory mandates and allowed EPA less and less discretion to set priorities among them."[217]

In 1986, Congress approved amendments to the Superfund Act that increased funding for the program more than fivefold. After initially threatening to veto it, Reagan reluctantly signed the $9 billion reauthorization, which included a provision requiring U.S. chemical makers to inform the public about toxics stored in and routinely released into their communities. In addition, Congress renewed and strengthened the Safe Drinking Water Act by veto-proof margins of 94–0 in the Senate and 382–21 in the House, ordering the EPA to set standards for eighty-three contaminants over three years. At the behest of both environmentalists and hunters, Congress passed and Reagan signed the 1986 Emergency Wetlands Resources Act, which established an entrance fee at national wildlife refuges. Congress also inserted new soil conservation measures into the farm bill, authorized millions of acres of wilderness and a new national park in Nevada, approved a law requiring the EPA to toughen its program for removing asbestos from schools, and passed amendments to the Clean Water Act by large margins—although Reagan pocket vetoed the latter at the end of the session.

In the 1986 elections, Democrats regained control of the Senate, garnering a 55–45 advantage. Given their 258–177 majority in the House, observers anticipated a renewed focus on the environment.[218] Sure enough, the 100th Congress reauthorized the Clean Water Act after Reagan vetoed it for the second time. "In this administration, environmental protection has been given the lowest possible priority," remarked Democratic senator George J. Mitchell of Maine, a member of the conference committee on the Clean Water Act reauthorization. "The only steps taken have been grudgingly and only in response to immediate political pressure. So, we have an obligation to keep up the pressure."[219] Congress also approved amendments to the Federal Insecticide, Fungicide, and Rodenticide Act (FIFRA), requiring the EPA to reregister or cancel some fifty thousand chemical products that had been grandfathered under the original 1972 law.

Finally, after several years of delay, Congress overwhelmingly passed (399–16 in the House and 93–2 in the Senate) a five-year Endangered Species Act reauthorization. The administration supported reauthorizing the bill without changes, and Hodel made it clear that he was not a fan of the act, which he said gave a "mid-level or lower-level employee at the Fish and Wildlife Service [the power to determine] whether or not activities and projects that affect the health and safety of tens of thousands of people can go forward."[220] Despite opposing the bill on cost grounds, Reagan ultimately signed it in the fall of 1988. The revised law substantially increased funding for the endangered species program, raised fines for violations, and imposed substantial new monitoring and reporting requirements on the wildlife agencies. At the same time, legislators established a "cooperative endangered species conservation fund" to provide matching grants to states for endangered species conservation.

Also noteworthy was the signing by President Reagan of the Global Climate Protection Act in January 1988. The administration's position continued to be that, given scientific uncertainties and the costs of preventive action, it made sense to await more scientific knowledge before acting. But the new law, an amendment to the State Department Authorization Act, began by acknowledging the potential risks associated with climate change.

The Congress finds as follows: (1) There exists evidence that manmade pollution— the release of carbon dioxide, chlorofluorocarbons, methane, and other trace gases into the atmosphere—may be producing a long-term and substantial increase in the average temperature on Earth, a phenomenon known as global warming through the greenhouse effect. (2) By early in the next century, an increase in Earth temperature could (A) so alter global weather patterns as to have an effect on existing agricultural production and on the habitability of large portions of the Earth; and (B) cause thermal expansion of the oceans and partial melting of the polar ice caps and glaciers, resulting in rising sea levels.

The law required the administration to prepare a plan to stabilize the level of greenhouse gases. It gave the EPA and the State Department two years to assemble a report on the state of scientific knowledge on climate change and devise a strategy by which the United States could advance international cooperation to limit global warming. The administration also agreed to support the creation of an international scientific panel to synthesize scientific research (the Intergovernmental Panel on Climate Change, or IPCC) because—according to Weart—antienvironmentalists within the administration feared that independent scientists would make "radical environmental pronouncements" and hoped that an officially sanctioned body would be more conservative.[221]

Despite having signed the Global Climate Protection Act, the White House declined to take any other steps to signal the importance of global warming. Just before leaving office, the White House blocked plans by the Council on Environmental Quality to direct federal agencies to consider the greenhouse effect when assessing the environmental impact of any actions they took.[222] The CEQ had planned to issue a document underlining the dangers of the greenhouse effect, but presidential assistant Nancy Risque ordered the council's chairman, A. Allan Hill, not to issue the directive. She cited concerns that it would expose the government to lawsuits by environmental groups contending that past policies failed to consider greenhouse dangers.

## Antiregulatory Ideas Gain a Foothold

When it came to environmental issues, President Reagan disappointed conservatives in a variety of ways. In addition to signing the Global Climate Protection Act, between 1982 and 1988, Reagan approved forty-three wilderness bills designating more than 10 million acres of wilderness (although the administration generally opposed these bills prior to their passage). Furthermore, in direct contests between antiregulatory ideas and environmental institutions, the latter almost invariably prevailed; as a result, the Reagan administration failed to relax or eliminate any of the nation's environmental statutes.[223] In fact, during Reagan's tenure Congress succeeded in making several laws *more* restrictive. A paper prepared by analysts at the Heritage Foundation in 1988 concluded that the administration had "squandered every opportunity and perhaps made it impossible for a successor to design a Federal system to protect the environment at a cost the nation can afford to pay over the long term."[224]

The Reagan administration was more successful at changing the context for antiregulatory ideas and making existing laws more permissive through low-profile modifications. There is little debate that under Reagan fewer rules were issued and some existing rules were weakened.[225] According to the OMB, the total number of proposed rules was cut by 2,000, and the number of final rules dropped by 3,000.[226] The number of pages in the *Federal Register* fell from 87,012 in 1980 to 53,376 in 1988, after falling as low as 47,418 in 1986. Particularly effective were efforts by White House officials and agency heads to block or modify proposed regulations that would impose costs on business. The single most important tool for accomplishing this was the cost-benefit analysis, which became ubiquitous under Reagan. While many environmentally oriented federal officials acknowledged that attention to costs was appropriate, they were skeptical of the administration's neutrality, noting that little attention was given to figuring out how to calculate the benefits of regulations.[227] As one former EPA official put it, "It was a body count versus dollars spent."[228]

With respect to air pollution in particular, conservative opposition in the White House stymied efforts to update the Clean Air Act and circumscribed the EPA's ability to enact restrictive regulations under the existing law. White House conservatives also succeeded in discouraging federal efforts to address the newly identified problem of global warming.

In the realm of biodiversity conservation, under the leadership of conservatives, the Interior Department relaxed restrictions on natural resource development on federal land while devolving implementation and enforcement of the Endangered Species Act to the states, where development interests held sway.

Eight years of conservative governance had less tangible consequences as well. At the behest of officials in the Reagan administration, the total amount of money authorized by the federal government for natural resource and environmental programs fell from $17.9 billion in 1980 to between $12 billion and $15 billion for most of the 1980s (in 1994 dollars).[229] The overall impact on agencies' legitimacy was profound. As political scientist Phillip Cooper explains, thanks to budget cuts and increased responsibilities, agencies could devote less time and energy to particular cases, so errors were more likely, rendering regulatory actions more vulnerable to challenge. Legal challenges, in turn, consumed agency resources, while inflation made the available resources worth less. For deregulators, there was an added benefit: as the regulators struggled, attacks on agencies' competence became more credible.[230]

Budget cutting and reorganizing at the EPA also drove many of the agency's most talented senior staff from office. According to Richard Andrews, "In both its substance and its tactics, Reagan's deregulatory initiative caused deep and lasting damage to EPA. . . . It seriously destabilized the agency's effective functioning, and devastated its staff's professional morale. It eroded the agency's expertise, and tainted it for the first time with corruption and scandal."[231] William Drayton, a top EPA official under Carter, pointed out that it had taken a decade to build the research staff and network of research affiliates that Gorsuch decimated in the early 1980s and suggested it would take another ten years to rebuild it.[232] Similarly, journalist Bruce Ingersoll concluded, "it will take years for the EPA to repair the damage and catch up to its mandate. The continuing brain drain among its demoralized professionals won't make it any easier."[233] As Ruckelshaus put it, "It's tough being part of an agency that has developed a battered-agency syndrome."[234] Environmentally oriented Interior Department employees were also intimidated and demoralized. After Watt's tenure, Michael McCloskey of the Sierra Club warned, "It took 20 years of hard work to make the bureaucrats [at Interior] think in terms of conservation as well as development. Now they will be very cautious in the future about doing anything that looks like conservation."[235]

Reagan's appointees prolonged these effects by institutionalizing conservatism in both the EPA and the Interior Department. For example, Watt boasted that he filled the Interior Department with like-minded staff who remained in place even after appointees moved on.[236] As Stuart Eizenstat, President Carter's chief domestic policy advisor, noted at the time:

> Conservatives are in levels now that run deep in government and, unlike the people who came in with Eisenhower, Nixon and Ford who didn't have a burning ideology and saw it as their obligation to do public service, this group has a much more long-term commitment to staying and shaping government. Any administration in the future—Democratic or Republican—will have to face a bureaucracy considerably shifted to the right, and very consciously so.[237]

Reagan also stocked the judiciary with ideological conservatives. In fact, according to political scientist David M. O'Brien, the Reagan administration "had a more coherent and ambitious agenda for judicial selection than any previous administration. Indeed, judges were viewed . . . as a way to ensure the president's legacy."[238]

Moreover, although direct challenges to restrictive laws yielded few discernible policy changes, they did have some important political consequences. With its pugnacious approach, the Reagan administration shattered whatever consensus existed on regulatory reform and ushered in "a more bitter and far more partisan period of distrust and ideological trench warfare over environmental protection policy."[239] For example, according to Shabecoff, in response to Watt's confrontational demeanor, "many of his opponents became increasingly hard-line and uncompromising. The result in many instances was a strident, all-or-nothing national debate that left little room for compromise and produced two and a half years of stalemate."[240] In fact, to conservatives' chagrin, the administration's direct attacks on environmental regulation reinvigorated the environmental movement and provoked a backlash among the public. The public's concern redounded to the benefit of environmental groups, which saw immediate financial benefits: within Reagan's first year in office, contributions to eight major environmental groups were up about 20 percent;[241] between 1980 and 1985, the budgets of the Sierra Club, the National Audubon Society, and the Wilderness Society more than doubled.[242]

Finally, after being echoed for eight years, some rhetorical framings became legitimate and commonplace. These included an insistence on scientific certainty before acting, an emphasis on the cost of regulations, and the suggestion of serious trade-offs between environmental health and economic well-being. At the same time, it became more common to depict environmentalists as extremists and elitists, concerned more about their own self-interest than the public good. These accomplishments notwithstanding, conservatives certainly did not achieve the counterrevolution they had set out to foster; in fact the actions of the Reagan administration had the perverse effect of encouraging Congress to write laws that featured strict standards with deadlines and nondiscretionary penalties for noncompliance—precisely the kinds of rules that conservatives complained most bitterly about. Those statutes inflamed property and small business owners, as well as state and local government officials, thereby creating a new audience for the conservative, antiregulatory storyline. That audience, in turn, provided the impetus for the burst of antiregulatory activity that erupted in the late 1980s and early 1990s.

# 5
# Conservative Ideas Gain Ground Under George H. W. Bush

*By the time George H. W. Bush took office in January 1989, the national debt stood at $2.8 trillion, almost three times what it had been when Reagan gained the presidency. The economy was sluggish: economic globalization had taken off in the early 1980s, sending manufacturing jobs overseas and leaving a disaffected workforce; the savings-and-loan sector had been decimated by risky investments made after the industry was deregulated in the late 1970s and early 1980s. Internationally, the fall of the Berlin Wall in 1989 signaled the collapse of Communism around the world. Fed by the stalling economy and the disappearance of the Communist threat, as well as rising attention by activists and policymakers to global environmental problems, antiregulatory ideas gained momentum during the late 1980s and early 1990s. Even as a growing number of government officials and environmentalists accepted policy experts' claims about the drawbacks of the regulatory framework created in the 1970s—now routinely referred to disparagingly as "command-and-control"—and the potential efficacy of alternative policy mechanisms, conservative activists redoubled their criticisms of environmental regulation. Thanks to a proliferation of new or reinvigorated think tanks, they were able to disseminate their antiregulatory storyline even more widely than before.*

*For Bush, the resurgence of antiregulatory ideas posed a dilemma. Hoping to distance himself from Reagan's position on the environment, which appeared to be a political liability, Bush campaigned for president as an environmentalist, and early in his presidency he established a pro-environmental record. But he soon found himself caught between the demands of the environmental community and those of an increasingly strident conservative base. Within little more than a year of the election, conservatives in the White House had gained the upper hand, and by late 1991, the president had assumed a more antiregulatory posture. With*

*Democrats ascendant in Congress, the administration opted to rely on low-profile challenges to prevent regulatory action on environmental issues.[1] Those gestures were insufficient to appease a coalition of activists hostile to federal biodiversity conservation efforts that was gaining traction in the West, however. A series of antiregulatory judicial decisions seemed to bolster those dissidents' claims, setting the stage for a conservative resurgence and another round of direct challenges to environmental regulations in the mid-1990s.*

### Policy Learning about Pollution Control

By the late 1980s, it was clear to many in the business community that pollution control regulations were here to stay, and companies had begun to adjust their practices accordingly. Observers noted a shift among business as soon as it became apparent that the Reagan administration's direct challenges were provoking a proenvironmental backlash that threatened to increase the burden on industry.[2] By the mid-1980s, some businesses had embraced environmental protection in response to new regulations; pressure from customers, communities, investors, and activists;[3] and reports that companies were profiting from environmental protection.[4] According to Richard Andrews, "The cumulative impact of environmental costs, liabilities, and market opportunities produced a widespread maturation in corporate environmental management."[5] By the early 1990s, several business associations were urging "a fundamental shift in the way businesses thought about their environmental responsibilities, from reliance on end-of-pipe technology toward pollution prevention and greater efficiency throughout the entire 'life cycles' of human use of materials and energy. The driving force behind this shift was enlightened self interest, taking into account the regulatory costs both of safe waste disposal itself and of permitting and compliance requirements."[6] Companies like 3M and DuPont even began touting environmental performance in order to burnish their public image and thereby gain a competitive advantage.[7]

Recognizing that the attitudes of some businesspeople had evolved, and acutely aware of both the technical difficulties and political resistance encountered during more than a decade of implementation, many current and former agency officials from both Democratic and Republican administrations began to support reform of the nation's pollution control laws along the lines that economists and other academic critics had proposed. For example, Michael Levin, director of the EPA's regulatory reform and innovation staff from 1979 to 1988, argued in the *Wall Street Journal* that the Clean Air Act needed to be made more flexible, and insisted that "stiffer rules simply won't work."[8] Agencies lacked adequate knowledge about production processes, he explained; there were no incentives for sources to disclose information about their processes; control costs were soaring, resulting in delay and resistance; and small, diffuse sources had come to dominate the smog problem, but were not amenable to traditional regulation. Levin opined that a genuine effort to clean the air would deploy incentives to better match private interests with environmental goals and would streamline procedures. Similarly, a spring 1988 op-ed piece by Levin and two other EPA officials described an "emerging consensus" that although pollution is not a commodity, pollution control is—at least in the sense that "the cheaper and easier we make it to buy, the more we're likely to get."[9]

Some EPA officials also embraced the proposition advanced by academics that the agency's priorities were skewed and therefore its resources had been misallocated.[10] A 1987 report commissioned by EPA administrator Lee Thomas and drafted by about seventy-five career EPA officials, ranked thirty-one environmental problems according to their cancer risk, non-cancer risks, ecological effects, and welfare effects. The study showed major discrepancies between what the task force experts rated as serious risks and the major program priorities at the EPA, which—not surprisingly, given their legislative origins—were closely linked to public fears. A 1990 report conducted by the EPA's Science Advisory Board, "Reducing Risk: Setting Priorities and Strategies for Environmental Protection," also concluded the agency had neglected ecological systems by focusing on risks to human health.

In response to both these internal assessments and ongoing external criticism, the agency's practices shifted. In addition to more routinely conducting risk assessment and cost-benefit analysis, EPA staff continued to experiment with incentive-based mechanisms, nonregulatory programs, and collaborative problem solving. By the mid-1980s, for example, the EPA "had approved or was in the process of approving 50 bubbles and was following 100 others; it had also approved nearly a dozen state bubble rules, as well as several state banking rules, while dozens more of each type were in development."[11] In addition, by the late 1980s, officials had become familiar with regulatory negotiation, an approach they first tried in 1984, in hopes of shortening the time required to promulgate rules, avoiding lawsuits, and crafting "win-win" solutions. In one such negotiation, finalized in 1991, environmentalists worked with industry to forge an agreement that would reduce emissions from the coal-fired Navajo Generating Station, which produced haze over the Grand Canyon. In this case, industry and environmentalists compromised on how reliable the antipollution equipment on the power plant had to be. They settled on a rule that required a 90 percent reduction in emissions on an annual basis, rather than the original proposal of 70 percent in any given month, thereby eliminating the need to acquire a backup unit for reducing emissions. According to the EPA, the agreement resulted in a 40 percent greater improvement in visibility at a 20 percent lower cost compared with the original proposal.[12] The 1990 Negotiated Rulemaking Act codified the regulatory negotiation process.

A large fraction of the environmental community continued to be suspicious of alternatives to the traditional regulatory approach and preferred to emphasize strengthening existing rules.[13] But a growing number were willing to consider using market-based mechanisms to stimulate environmental protection. "Project 88: Harnessing Market Forces to Protect Our Environment," a transition report prepared under the auspices of Colorado senator Tim Wirth, a Democrat, and Pennsylvania senator John Heinz, a Republican, focused on using incentive-based mechanisms to achieve environmental goals. Staff from both the Conservation Foundation and the Environmental Defense Fund (EDF) participated in crafting it. Explaining his organization's contribution, EDF's executive director Fred Krupp said, "We need to make changes, but let's do it in the smartest, most efficient way."[14]

The openness of some environmentalists to new mechanisms was in part a reflection of the changes their organizations underwent in the 1980s, when the movement became bigger, wealthier, and more a part of the political mainstream. By late 1985, new and more pragmatic leaders had taken the helm of the largest Washington, D.C.-based groups; many of them spoke of the need to come to grips with the economic problems caused by environmental protection.[15] Historian Kirkpatrick Sale quotes one veteran reporter who said in early 1985, "Both sides are wearing suits and lugging laptops now, and they both talk the same 'cost benefit' and 'social risk' eco-jargon too."[16] As a result, the Washington, D.C.-based environmental groups emerged from the 99th Congress (1985–1986) with an enhanced reputation for accommodation and professionalism. This was a double-edged sword because while it facilitated the passage of legislation it alienated members of the grassroots, who disparaged them for cutting deals with legislators, accepting contributions from polluters and developers, and ignoring the plight of rural and minority communities.[17] As mainstream environmentalists moved to the center, a new generation of more militant groups arose, led by Earth First!, which appeared in the spring of 1981.[18]

## Popularizing the Antiregulatory Storyline

Even as some members of the environmental community became more pragmatic during the 1980s, the antiregulatory storyline that emerged in the late 1970s blossomed into a more vitriolic critique of environmental regulation and, increasingly, of environmentalists themselves. That criticism was motivated in part by frustration with a sagging economy: environmental regulations were a convenient scapegoat for the pain imposed by the accelerating global economic integration of the 1980s. It was also triggered by budding efforts to identify and address international environmental problems—such as the depleted ozone layer, worldwide biodiversity loss, and global warming. As the threat of Communism receded, conservatives latched onto environmentalism, which seemed to rest on an equally fundamental critique of capitalism. Doug Bandow, a senior fellow at the Cato Institute, explained: "Although the socialist dream has collapsed around the world, in America it lives on in academia and the environmental movement, where activists have proposed collectivist panaceas for a host of problems and pseudo problems."[19]

A central aim of the antiregulatory storyline propagated by conservatives in the 1980s and early 1990s was to disparage environmentalists and try to discredit their claims about the magnitude of environmental problems. Conservative activists proclaimed that environmentalists were radicals, extremists, elitists, and antihuman; and that their positions were irrational, antitechnology, anticapitalist, and antiprogress. From this perspective, environmentalists—in cahoots with the biased, liberal media, and sympathetic scientists (who wanted more research funding)—manipulated scientific evidence and used doomsday rhetoric to alarm the public in order to fill their coffers and pursue their romantic vision of a simpler, smaller world. Consequently, conservatives argued, environmental regulations focused on trivial risks, diverting attention from more serious threats while jeopardizing individual liberty and economic efficiency.

These claims were rooted in the work of a vocal cadre of academic scientists, economists, and political scientists dubious about the level of risk being regulated by the federal government. Throughout the 1980s, Philip Abelson, a physicist and the editor of *Science* magazine, questioned the EPA's risk assessments, arguing they needlessly raised public fears and wasted money on unnecessarily protective measures.[20] Other prominent academic skeptics included anthropologist Mary Douglas and political scientist Aaron Wildavsky, who depicted environmentalists as idealists who sought to root out evil in the form of technology that threatened pure nature.[21] Wildavsky's book *Searching for Safety* rejected the precautionary principle, saying: "Increasing the pool of general resources, such as wealth and knowledge, secures safety for more people than using up resources in a vain effort to protect against unperceivable, hypothetical dangers. Wealth adds to health."[22] Especially influential was a 1986 article in *Regulation* by OMB economist John Morrall III. Based on an evaluation of the costs and benefits of forty-four rules (some of which were never enacted), Morrall concluded that safety regulations are far more cost-effective than regulations that seek to reduce cancer risk by controlling emissions of chemicals.[23] In a follow-up piece, economist Ralph Keeney concluded that some expensive regulations and programs intended to save lives might actually lead to increased fatalities.[24]

Conservative popularizers echoed these themes. Building on a series of articles that had appeared in *Harper's* magazine, journalist William Tucker argued in his 1982 book *Progress and Privilege* that environmentalists were latter-day aristocrats who sought to preserve their own privileges by preventing economic growth. In *The Apocalyptics*, libertarian Edith Efron contended that the "apocalyptic movement" served as "a new conceptual mold into which one might pour one's expectations of—or yearnings for—a cataclysmic collapse of American capitalism, and the winged emergence of a Judeo-Christian egalitarian utopia from its ashes."[25] By the late 1980s, such antienvironmentalist claims had become commonplace. Writing in the *National Review*, journalist D. Keith Mano claimed: "[o]ur ecology movement is, at base, a repudiation of assertive, rational thought."[26] In *Trashing the Planet*, marine biologist and former Washington governor Dixy Lee Ray (with coauthor Lou Guzzo) charged that environmentalism contained "a strongly negative element of anti-development, anti-progress, anti-technology, anti-business, anti-established institutions, and, above all, anti-capitalism."[27] Journalist David Horowitz repeated the charge that environmentalists are radicals motivated not by "compassion for the lost soul of mankind but the hatred of human beings as they are."[28] In a scathing review of Paul and Anne Ehrlich's book *The Population Explosion* in the *National Review*, Ralph De Toledano explained that "[u]nder the banner of 'environmentalism,'" the Ehrlichs have "brought together the expatriates of Marxism and phrenology and the elitists of academe, seeking to bring life as we know it to a standstill."[29] And in a review of Christopher Manes' book *Green Rage*, Bruce Frohnen wrote that "ecoterrorists share with Marxists, as with Nazis, the disdain for mankind, which is the font of our century's ideologically inspired enormities."[30]

Conservative commentators continued to heap particular scorn on the Clean Air Act. A 1987 *Wall Street Journal* editorial characterized the act as "one of the most mindlessly utopian pieces of legislation ever enacted." After detailing problems with the law, the author said: "What this level of uncertainty tells us is that state and local officials should be responsible for deciding how best to measure local air pollution and should make the inevitable trade-offs between economic growth and environmental quality."[31] In December 1990, Jane Shaw of the Competitive Enterprise Institute complained that the recently passed Clean Air Act Amendments would "cost the economy billions each year" while producing "benefits so small as to be almost impossible to detect."[32]

During the 1980s, the antiregulatory storyline broadened to encompass natural resource management, with the claim that markets (and the clear assignment of private property rights) are better than government at conserving biological diversity. This claim had its provenance in an analytic framework, known as free-market environmentalism, devised by economists and political scientists working in the public choice tradition.[33] Economists Terry Anderson, John Baden, and Richard Stroup were among the first to articulate the tenets of free-market environmentalism; they had been influential in formulating the Reagan administration's failed privatization initiative. Proponents of free-market environmentalism rejected the notion that Congress passes environmental laws to serve the public interest, arguing instead that natural resource policy is the product of lobbying by special interest groups seeking to benefit themselves, not society. They also repudiated the idea that disinterested resource managers seek to enhance social welfare, insisting that bureaucrats respond to powerful incentives to reward rent-seeking constituencies and maximize their budgets. For instance, John Baden wrote:

The bureaucrats who . . . run the U.S. Forest Service, the National Park Service, the Bureau of Land Management, and the Bureau of Reclamation have been motivated by self-interest no less than private entrepreneurs. Their goal has been to maximize their organizations' work forces and budgets, and especially their discretionary budget authority. In collusion with elected politicians and special interests representing business and labor, the federal bureaucracies have used taxpayer funds to subsidize economic activity that would never have taken place in the absence of subsidies. Perversely, as a result of public land ownership, American taxpayers have been financing the destruction of environments they increasingly value.[34]

According to free-market environmentalists, private ownership of natural resources leads to better management because it encourages stewardship, while markets spawn innovation and prosperity, which, in turn, lead to environmental protection.[35]

## Creating and Capitalizing on New Think Tanks

In the late 1980s and early 1990s, conservative think tanks greatly enhanced their ability to popularize the antiregulatory storyline. Thanks in part to an infusion of cash from private donors, corporations, and conservative foundations, these organizations churned out materials crafted to shape the political debate by transforming policy analyses and prescriptions into more accessible problem definitions and policy images. By the mid-1980s, the Heritage Foundation was already producing more than two hundred policy papers annually—short essays designed to be consumed by busy members of Congress.[36] Heritage also held frequent roundtables for government officials and corporate executives, sponsored lecture series for young conservatives, and assembled a resource bank of scholars and policy experts to provide the media and legislators with conservative commentary.[37] Similarly, as of the mid-1980s, the American Enterprise Institute was devoting more than 20 percent of its $10 million annual budget to an outreach program that aimed to disseminate its ideas. It prepared radio and TV programs, sent out op-ed pieces by associated scholars, and provided forums to make members of Congress and White House officials aware of its latest work.

The capacity of conservative think tanks to influence policy debates increased as their numbers grew. Between 1970 and 1996, the number of independent, policy-oriented think tanks more than tripled, from fewer than 100 to roughly 305.[38] Of the 195 nationally or state-focused think tanks founded between 1976 and 1995, 55 percent were identifiably ideological. Among those that were nationally focused, nearly twice as many conservative think tanks as liberal ones opened their doors during that twenty-year period. By the mid-1990s, the conservative Heritage Foundation was Washington's largest and wealthiest think tank, with an annual budget of over $25 million.[39]

Environmental issues were a growing preoccupation for many conservative think tanks. Both Heritage and AEI produced commentary on environmental policy issues. For instance, in 1990, coinciding with the twentieth anniversary of Earth Day, Heritage issued a report on "eco-terrorism" that depicted the environmental movement as "the greatest single threat to the American economy."[40] Two libertarian organizations, the Cato Institute and the Reason Foundation, developed expertise in environmental issues as well. The 1980s also saw the emergence of several new conservative think tanks with particular interest in the environment. The Competitive Enterprise Institute, founded in 1984 by Fred L. Smith, described itself as "dedicated to free enterprise and limited government," saying, "We believe that the best solutions come from people making their own choices in a free marketplace, rather than government intervention." Another conservative think tank with particular interest in environmental issues was the Heartland Institute, based in Chicago. Also founded in 1984, the Heartland Institute's mission was to "discover, develop, and promote free-market solutions to social and economic problems," including "market-based approaches to environmental protection" and "deregulation in areas where property rights and markets do a better job than government bureaucracy."

Two think tanks devoted specifically to promoting free-market environmentalism opened their doors in the early 1980s. Founded in 1980, the Property & Environment Research Center (PERC) called itself "the nation's oldest and largest institute dedicated to improving environmental quality through property rights and markets."[41] In 1985, PERC founder John Baden resigned to create the Foundation for Research on Economics & the Environment (FREE), whose mission was to "[advance] conservation and environmental values by applying modern science and America's founding ideals to policy debates." More specifically, it sought to: "describe how incentives and voluntary cooperation can be used to protect and enhance environmental values while fostering economic prosperity; show how the application of economics and science to public policy provides insights that advance the public interest; explain the importance of secure property rights and economic freedom to the efficient and sensitive use of environmental resources; and examine the dangers of legislating 'risk free' laws."[42] Baden and his followers labeled this new paradigm, which used public choice methods to analyze natural resource management, New Resource Economics.[43]

What was distinctive about these organizations was the extent to which they aimed to influence the political debate, combined with their rapidly growing financial capacity to do so. As John Saloma observed, these new (or rejuvenated) think tanks formed "a sort of transmission belt to move ideas into politics," enabling them to "[shape] the attitudes of American voters and [alter] the context in which they consider issues."[44] Ample donations freed conservative publications from the demands of raising revenue, so they were able to distribute free copies to legislative staffers, offer free and reduced-price subscriptions to libraries, and devote time to cultivating relationships with newspaper opinion-page editors, talk show hosts, and broadcasters.[45]

As a result of this activity, the line between scholarly ideas and popular versions of those ideas became increasingly blurred. Analysts at conservative think tanks focused on recruiting credentialed associates and disseminating their work to opinion leaders, policymakers, and the public. Newly created journals attracted scholars who sought to ensure that their policy-relevant ideas and analyses would reach a broader audience. Experts affiliated with conservative think tanks did not simply produce reports; they testified at congressional hearings, issued nontechnical briefing papers, wrote op-eds, conducted interviews with the media, and talked to legislative staffers. As David Callahan explains, unlike more traditional think tanks, which produced policy papers but did little to influence the policymaking process, conservative think tanks created "a strong network of policy intellectuals who know how to advertise this research, to incorporate it into a larger story about American life and, ultimately, to use it to win national debates."[46]

In addition to investing in think tanks, conservatives enhanced their influence on environmental policy debates by increasing their media presence, which in turn extended their reach to ordinary Americans. According to Saloma, during the early 1980s, conservatives gained a national presence in the mainstream media; at the same time, they began creating their own media outlets. Two new conservative newspapers appeared in Washington, D.C., the *Washington Weekly* in 1978 and the *Washington Times* in 1982. College students founded a host of conservative campus newspapers, such as the *Yale Free Press*, the *Yale Political Monthly*, the *Harvard Salient*, and the *Dartmouth Review*. And conservative patrons funded conservative programming for PBS, such as Milton Friedman's "Free to Choose," a ten-part series that aired in 1981, and Ben Wattenberg's series "In Search of the Real America," which also ran in the early 1980s. Besides developing their own media outlets, conservatives devised an array of tactics to monitor and pressure the mainstream media. For example, Reid Irvine founded Accuracy in Media in 1969 to expose the media's "liberal bias." Ten years later, corporations founded the D.C.-based Media Institute to burnish the image of business and promote conservative perspectives in the media.

## Environmental Governance under President George H. W. Bush

Although the antiregulatory storyline was gaining momentum, it was the environmental storyline that held sway in the 1988 presidential election. As campaigning heated up during June and July, polls indicated that the national salience of environmental issues was rising rapidly, partly as a result of a prolonged drought, but also because of widespread beach closures and media coverage of global warming. Contributions to environmental groups were up, as were inquiries and offers of help. In a *New York Times*/CBS News poll conducted in July, 65 percent of respondents agreed that "protecting the environment is so important that requirements and standards cannot be too high, and continuing environmental improvements must be made regardless of cost."[47]

Aware that antiregulatory rhetoric and Reagan-era attacks on environmental protection had facilitated an environmental mobilization in key electoral states, then-Vice President Bush promised that if elected he would shift the emphasis in the White House in favor of environmental protection. "I am an environmentalist," he proclaimed in September 1988, as he derided his Democratic rival, Massachusetts governor Michael Dukakis, for failing to clean up Boston Harbor. In stark contrast to his predecessor, Bush vowed to enforce environmental laws aggressively and hold polluters accountable. With these declarations, Bush hoped to overcome the Reagan legacy, notwithstanding his own role as chairman of Reagan's Task Force on Regulatory Relief, the D+ given him by the League of Conservation Voters at the outset of the campaign, and the fact that his pick for vice president, Dan Quayle, had one of the worst environmental records in the Senate.

The Bush campaign identified six "swing" states with lots of suburban voters interested in quality-of-life issues—California, New Jersey, Ohio, Illinois, Michigan, and Missouri—and scheduled a week of environmental policy speeches in late August and early September. On August 31, Bush gave a speech at the Detroit Metropark in which he distanced himself from Reagan's controversial obstructionism and vowed to take the lead on acid rain, declaring that the "time for study alone has passed" and promising a detailed plan to cut "millions of tons of sulfur dioxide emissions by the year 2000." He also committed to end ocean dumping of garbage by 1991, prosecute illegal disposers of medical waste, and strictly enforce toxic waste laws. He pledged a program of "no net loss" of wetlands and promised to convene world leaders to discuss international environmental issues, including global warming, during his first year in office.[48]

## Modifying the Policymaking Context

Once elected, Bush took several steps to render the policymaking context more hospitable to environmental protection. Unlike Reagan, who had consistently denigrated the federal bureaucracy, Bush praised the nation's civil servants.[49] Bush also departed from Reagan-era practices by opening a dialogue with environmentalists. Even before appointing a transition team, he and his White House counsel, C. Boyden Gray, met with representatives of thirty environmental groups, who submitted a "Blueprint for the Environment" listing more than seven hundred recommendations. "It's night and day," said Jay Hair, president of the National Wildlife Federation, after the meeting.[50]

In addition to cultivating new allies, Bush articulated "a new environmental philosophy" that consisted of five objectives: (1) to harness the power of the marketplace, (2) to encourage local initiatives, (3) to emphasize prevention instead of just cleanup, (4) to foster international cooperation, and (5) to ensure strict enforcement[51]—a set of principles that was more consistent with the mainstream critique of environmental regulations than with the antiregulatory storyline. He also reinvigorated the Council on Environmental Quality, appointing as its chair the widely respected Michael Deland, formerly of the EPA New England regional office and considered one of the best administrators of the Reagan era.

In December 1988, Bush delighted environmentalists by nominating for EPA administrator William K. Reilly, a moderate consensus builder who was president of the World Wildlife Fund and the Conservation Foundation. At his confirmation hearing, Reilly promised to strengthen enforcement of environmental laws and made clear the administration was committed to a long-overdue reauthorization of the Clean Air Act. He also called for reductions in greenhouse gas emissions and faster, deeper cuts in ozone-depleting chlorofluorocarbons, predicting the Bush administration would take an active role in international environmental issues. "We are at an historic moment, characterized by urgency and opportunity," Reilly told the Senate Environmental and Public Works Committee.[52] Consistent with the mainstream critique, even as he pledged "vigorous and aggressive enforcement of the environmental laws," he also asserted that it was time to usher in "an era marked by reconciliation of interests by imaginative solutions arrived at through cooperation and consensus, by the resolve to listen and work out differences."[53] He argued that "strong environmental protection and strong economic development [were] fully compatible," adding, "The kind of economic growth we want is the kind that doesn't shorten our breath. It is the kind that can be sustained."[54]

Bush's appointees to other high-level positions at the EPA also marked a sharp contrast with their Reagan-era counterparts. Reilly created a new top-level post to handle international environmental issues and filled it with an experienced environmental lawyer, Timothy B. Atkeson. Also selected were Hank Habicht, the top environmental lawyer for the Department of Justice from 1983 to 1987, as deputy administrator, and William Rosenberg, an Ann Arbor real estate investor with a passion for environmental issues, to head the office for air and radiation.

On the other hand, Bush's appointees in charge of biodiversity conservation were similar to those who served during the latter part of the Reagan administration. As secretary of the interior, Bush appointed former New Mexico congressman Manuel Lujan, whom many observers described as affable and nonideological. "He didn't care," according one environmentalist. "He didn't really have an agenda."[55] But Lujan's environmental record in Congress was distinctly prodevelopment: a consistent supporter of resource extraction, he had received a score of 13 percent in 1988 from the League of Conservation Voters, compared with a House average of 54 percent; his LCV score for 1985–1986 was 16 percent; and in the four preceding years he averaged 19 percent.[56] By contrast, the U.S. Chamber of Commerce gave him an 80 percent pro-business rating based on its analysis of his voting record.[57] At his confirmation hearings, Lujan described his position in the following way: "President Bush and I are committed to protecting and enhancing the nation's natural resources, as well as proceeding with their environmentally sound development. We believe that development of our most promising domestic resources is called for, because continued development is essential to the national security and economic well-being of the United States."[58]

The Interior Department was staffed largely by Reagan-administration holdovers, and Bush's appointees did little to counteract their prodevelopment tendencies. For example, the new Bureau of Land Management director, Cy Jamieson, had worked for Secretary Watt and served as an aide to Montana Republican Ron Marlenee, who had one of the worst environmental records in the House. During that time, Jamison had been known as an ally of ranchers, oilmen, timber interests, and miners. The new director of the National Park Service, James Ridenour, was a former Republican Party fund-raiser who, as head of Indiana's Department of Natural Resources had routinely favored commercial development.[59]

Bush's budget proposals also sent mixed messages about the value of environmental protection. Although the text of the Bush budget for fiscal year 1989 was proenvironmental in tone, it allocated little more for environmental protection than what Reagan had proposed for that fiscal year.[60] In early 1990, Bush sent Congress a $1.23 trillion budget for fiscal year 1991 that again reflected minimal changes from the previous year. The budget did increase overall spending for environmental protection by about $2 billion, however, including a large increase in funding for global climate change research; much of the remainder was earmarked for cleaning up federal weapons facilities. The EPA's operating budget was slated to rise by 12 percent, while the Interior Department's budget was set to increase slightly, by about 2.8 percent. Bush proposed modest increases for both the EPA and the Interior Department for fiscal year 1992. An increase of 8 percent in the EPA's operating budget, to $2.5 billion, reflected dramatically increased responsibilities associated with implementing the Clean Air Act of 1990.[61] But Alvin Alm, who served as the EPA's deputy administrator from 1983 to 1985, pointed out that, although the agency's budget increased under Bush, the gap between its legislative mandates and its budget continued to grow. (In fact, because of the cuts under Reagan, the agency's operating budget was only slightly higher in fiscal year 1992 than it had been in fiscal year 1979.)[62] The administration's fiscal year 1992 proposal raised Interior's budget marginally, from $8.5 billion to $8.7 billion, but that included an increase in spending for endangered species protection of $5 million, to $37.6 million. (Congress allocated even more to the portion of the Fish and Wildlife Service budget devoted to endangered species; as a result, it grew from $18.8 million in fiscal year 1988 to $42.3 million in fiscal year 1992.) The 1992 budget also included a 24 percent increase in spending for climate change research, pushing that figure to $1.2 billion spread among several agencies.[63]

### Low-Profile Challenges to the Endangered Species Act

Early in the Bush administration, Lujan's Interior Department seemed disinclined to challenge environmentally restrictive rules; in fact, in many respects the department adopted a relatively proenvironmental approach. In terms of governing style, Lujan presented a marked contrast with his Reagan-era predecessors. He met regularly with environmentalists and frequently talked about "stewardship" and the need to develop resources in an "environmentally sound manner";[64] his openness and lack of ideological fervor raised morale within the Interior Department agencies. Moreover, on occasion the department seemed to heed environmentalists' concerns. For example, the Bureau of Land Management launched an initiative to restore streams and stream banks damaged by overgrazing; it also canceled a popular motorcycle race in southern California, citing concern about the rare desert tortoise. In addition, to the delight of environmentalists, during Bush's first two years the Fish and Wildlife Service added plants and animals to the endangered species at an annual rate faster than any president since Richard Nixon.

Interior remained closely tied to the traditional western economic interests of ranching, mining, logging, and oil and gas development, however. Lujan stumped relentlessly for oil development on the outer continental shelf and in the Arctic National Wildlife Refuge; in addition, under Lujan, Interior officials opposed legislation to expand wilderness areas, defended the archaic Mining Law of 1872, and fought efforts to raise grazing fees on federal lands. Lujan raised environmentalists' hackles when he casually observed that he tended to think of Bureau of Land Management land as "a place with a lot of grass for cows."[65] He also infuriated them with his maladroit handling of the Exxon Valdez oil spill in March 1989; after an oil tanker ran aground, spilling hundreds of thousands of barrels of crude oil in Alaska's pristine Prince William Sound, Lujan waited a month before visiting the area for a whirlwind tour. "It looks like it will be a big job to clean it up," he told reporters. "I was expecting something like this. I'd read about it and seen it on TV."[66]

One major test of Lujan's commitment to biodiversity conservation arose in 1990. Two years earlier, lobbyists from the University of Arizona had secured passage of a rider to a conservation bill that ordered the Forest Service to allow construction of three telescopes atop Mount Graham, in Colorado's Coronado National Forest. The 10,700-foot peak, a lush fragment of the Rocky Mountains surrounded by desert, harbored animals found nowhere else in the world, including the endangered Mount Graham red squirrel. In June 1990, after the Ninth Circuit lifted a lower-court ban on construction of the observatory, two House subcommittees held hearings on the issue. At those hearings, James Duffus III, natural resources director of the General Accounting Office (GAO), questioned the validity of a 1988 study by the Fish and Wildlife Service, which had concluded that building a seven-telescope observatory would not jeopardize the continued existence of the endangered squirrel. In making its decision, the service's regional director had ignored the concerns of his own biologists, relying instead on his own view that the university's interest in a "world-class" facility outweighed risks to the squirrel. Duffus pointed out that the squirrel's status had become even more precarious between 1988 and 1990, probably because of reductions in spruce and fir tree cones, the squirrel's main food source. Yet Lujan was dismissive and cited the red squirrel as a prime example of overkill by the Endangered Species Act. "No one's told me the difference between a red squirrel, a black one or a brown one," he complained.[67] Despite Lujan's reservations, after two biologists testified that they had been directed to conclude the telescopes would not harm the squirrel, the Fish and Wildlife Service reopened biological studies on the mountaintop. The service ultimately advised scrapping the project—a recommendation the Forest Service disregarded. (In August 1990, the Forest Service issued permits, and in October work on the project began.)

An even more severe test of Lujan's principles involved the controversy that erupted in the late 1980s surrounding the northern spotted owl. Concerns about the owl had arisen early in the Reagan administration, when scientists and environmentalists began pressing the Pacific Northwest offices of the Forest Service and Bureau of Land Management to set aside habitat preserves for the tiny raptor. The owl was one of about a hundred species whose survival was linked to the health of the old-growth forest in the Pacific Northwest. Once, that forest had covered 25 million acres; logging had destroyed all but 2.3 million acres, less than half of which was permanently protected in parks and wilderness areas. The remaining 1.2 million acres of unprotected forest would be cut in the next fifteen to twenty years, if logging continued at its current rate.

Although the agencies' governing statutes required them to conserve native biodiversity, throughout the 1980s, they designated only minimally protective set-asides for the owl, while facilitating record timber harvests from region's forests.[68] For its part, the Fish and Wildlife Service declined to list the owl as endangered, thereby undermining environmentalists' legal position. The tide began to turn, however, when federal judges in Washington and Oregon issued injunctions preventing the agencies from logging until they had developed adequate plans to safeguard the owl, as required by the National Forest Management Act and the Federal Land Policy and Management Act. Then, in late 1988, Federal District Court judge Thomas Zilly ruled that the Fish and Wildlife Service had acted in an "arbitrary and capricious" manner in failing to list the owl, and gave the agency until May 1, 1989 to review its decision (*Northern Spotted Owl v. Manuel Lujan*). While that case was pending, a review of the listing process by the GAO released in February 1989, found that, under Reagan, political appointees had "substantively changed the body of scientific evidence" with the effect of "changing the report from one that emphasized the dangers facing the owl to one that could more easily support denying the listing petition."[69] In spring 1989, the Fish and Wildlife Service reversed itself and announced that it would designate the owl as "threatened," thereby making it illegal to destroy spotted owls or their habitat. (The formal listing occurred in June 1990.)

Buffeted by a series of unfavorable judicial rulings, the Forest Service and BLM were paralyzed, and the spotted owl became front-page news. With the issue's rising salience came highly visible efforts to resolve it. Several congressional committees debated measures to resolve the controversy but were unable to reach agreement. Meanwhile, an interagency scientific committee led by Forest Service biologist Jack Ward Thomas prepared a plan that would reduce logging on federal lands in the Pacific Northwest by 50 percent and create a network of habitat conservation areas—measures that Thomas described as the minimum necessary to save the owl. The Fish and Wildlife Service endorsed the Thomas Committee report, which it described as "the most comprehensive and in-depth analysis of the data available."[70]

Although the Forest Service favored adhering to the Thomas Committee's strategy, Secretary Lujan demurred. Instead, he took a series of low-profile steps to minimize restrictions on logging. First, shortly after the Fish and Wildlife Service formally listed the owl, Lujan announced the formation of a new task force to devise a comprehensive proposal to protect the bird while pursuing maximum timber harvests on federal land. In the meantime, he endorsed a much higher logging rate on BLM land than the Thomas Committee had recommended. In September, with Lujan's backing, the administration released what it called a "balanced" proposal: a reduction in the 1991 timber harvest of only 20 percent, along with a provision to exempt Forest Service and BLM timber sales from all environmental restrictions.[71] (Congress rejected that proposal, which did not pass legal muster.)

In early February 1991, Lujan appointed another task force—this one charged with drafting a long-term recovery plan for the owl, in parallel with the Fish and Wildlife Service's team already creating such a plan. Three months later, the service proposed designating 11.6 million acres as critical habitat for the owl, including 3 million acres of private land. Lujan immediately responded with an alternative that would allot less than 5 million acres—not enough to support a sustainable population of spotted owls, but sufficient to save some regional timber jobs.

In late September, still seeking to circumvent the restrictions of the Endangered Species Act, Lujan convened the cabinet-level Endangered

Species Committee known as the God Squad and gave it six months to decide whether to grant an exemption from the act for forty-four timber sales covering about 4,570 acres of BLM land in Oregon. (The Fish and Wildlife Service had halted the timber sales because they would jeopardize the owl.) At the opening of the panel's deliberations, Lujan said, "My job is to protect these species, but by the same token I must make available to the American people these natural resources."[72] Eight months later, the God Squad voted to exempt only thirteen of the forty-four sales, and only on the condition that the BLM devise a long-term forest management plan. Portland District Court judge Helen Frye blocked the sales until the agency submitted a credible plan to protect the owl.

In May 1992, the Fish and Wildlife Service issued its draft recovery plan, which would restrict logging in 196 conservation zones covering 7.5 million acres of federal land. (Some two million of those acres were already protected in wilderness or parks, so the new protections covered about 5.4 million acres). Lujan simultaneously proposed an amendment to the Endangered Species Act devised by his task force that would bar logging on only 2.8 million acres.[73] Lujan's "preservation" plan left whole portions of the owl's range unprotected, thereby saving an estimated 17,000 jobs, but also gave the owl only a fifty-fifty chance of surviving the next one hundred years. The Interior Department acknowledged in a report that accompanied the proposed amendment that, if enacted, it would virtually ensure that the owl would eventually disappear over much of its range.

Even as he sought ways to minimize the impact of the Endangered Species Act through low-profile measures, Lujan repeatedly urged Congress to modify the act to enable the wildlife agencies to include economic considerations in listing decisions—so that protection of animals and plants could be balanced against the benefits to society of development.[74] In an interview given on May 10, 1990, with the *Denver Post*, Lujan said the Endangered Species Act was "just too tough an act, I think. We've got to change it."[75] When making the case for reform, Lujan repeatedly expressed skepticism about the need to "save every subspecies."[76] Consistent with the antiregulatory storyline, he pitted endangered species protection against economic well-being, particularly jobs. For instance, in 1991, with a 1992 reauthorization deadline looming, Lujan's spokesman, Steven Goldstein, said of the act, "Times are different now, and it's not just some abstract law. It's one thing for you or I to say we must protect species at any cost. But what if the cost is your father's job?"[77] And in May 1992, Goldstein declared, "At some point, Congress has to step up to the plate and determine whether the loss of 32,000 jobs [due to owl protection] is too high a price."[78]

## On Air Pollution, a Struggle between Antiregulatory and Proenvironmental Ideas

Unlike Lujan, Bill Reilly was a genuine environmentalist who garnered near-universal admiration among the career staff at the EPA.[79] Reilly not only declined to challenge the environmentally restrictive status quo; he actively promoted additional protections, and boasted several early victories. He succeeded in persuading Bush to support a worldwide phase-out of chlorofluorocarbons, after European nations announced they would stop using the chemicals and the world's largest manufacturer (DuPont) said it would stop making them. In 1989, he issued standards for benzene, a toxic air pollutant. In early 1991, he endorsed a proposal negotiated by stakeholders that required the Navajo Generating Station in Arizona to install pollution control equipment to reduce haze over the Grand Canyon—the first time the EPA had invoked the Clean Air Act to improve visibility.[80] Under Reilly, the EPA also strengthened enforcement of toxic waste laws over industry complaints; banned dangerous pesticides, antagonizing agribusiness; instituted a gradual ban on asbestos, a carcinogen, despite longstanding OMB resistance; and infuriated development interests by blocking plans to build the $1 billion Two Forks Dam in an environmentally sensitive Colorado watershed.

Reilly beefed up the EPA's enforcement as well. Between 1989 and 1992, the agency's enforcement budget increased by more than 70 percent.[81] In addition, James Strock, assistant administrator for enforcement and compliance monitoring, sought to make enforcement more effective by bolstering the authority of headquarters vis-à-vis the regional offices. He emphasized multimedia enforcement and improved communication of the agency's goals and achievements to the public. Under Strock, the agency boasted of record-setting levels of indictments, convictions, and prison sentences. For example, in 1989, the agency touted 364 referrals to the Department of Justice and more than 4,000 enforcement actions. Compared with the previous year, the Justice Department experienced a 70 percent increase in the number of pleas and convictions obtained, an 80 percent rise in the value of assessed criminal fines, and a 35 percent increase in jail time imposed.[82]

At the same time, Reilly sought to reorder agency priorities to respond to criticisms that had dogged the agency; in particular, he ordered the program and regional offices to submit risk-based budget proposals and directed the enforcement staff to use risk as a basis for deciding which cases to pursue.[83] Yet, despite his receptiveness to the mainstream critique, Reilly faced stiff and growing opposition from conservatives in the administration. Particularly influential on the antiregulatory side were White House chief of staff John Sununu and OMB director Richard Darman, both of whom regarded environmental protection as a fad and an undue burden on industry. Also aligned against Reilly were Michael J. Boskin, head of the Council of Economic Advisers, and Roger B. Porter, Bush's domestic policy advisor.

Within a few months of taking office, Reilly found himself embroiled in a "bruising internal debate."[84] Shortly after his inauguration, the president had set out to fulfill his campaign promise on acid rain by convening a task force to develop a set of proposals for reauthorizing the Clean Air Act. The group's initial package targeted three problems that were a top priority for environmentalists. First, it aimed to reduce urban air pollution so that by 1995 all but twenty cities would meet national ambient air quality standards for ozone, and all cities would meet the standards within twenty years. It would achieve this goal primarily by both switching to cleaner-burning auto fuels in the most heavily polluted areas and tightening tailpipe emissions standards for carbon monoxide and hydrocarbons. Second, the proposal sought to reduce airborne toxics by 75 percent to 90 percent by 2000 by requiring industry to install the maximum achievable control technology (MACT). Third—and most important politically—the plan aimed to cut acid rain in half by capping sulfur dioxide emissions at 10 million tons below current levels and distributing "allowances" among utilities, who could sell them if they reduced their emissions below allowed levels. (The acid rain package also reduced emissions of nitrogen oxides, another acid-rain precursor, by 2 million tons.) In addition to these measures, the Bush proposal added stiff new penalties, including criminal sanctions, for violators.

If enacted, the administration's cap-and-trade policy would mark the first legislative adoption of a major market-based mechanism for environmental protection. It therefore promised to win the backing of moderate Republicans who supported environmental protection but were critical of prescriptive regulations. Nevertheless, in a series of meetings of the White House Domestic Policy Council, Reilly had to defend the proposal against several cabinet secretaries and department heads who favored doing much less. For example, Darman castigated the blueprint as too costly to industry and demanded the task force come up with cheaper measures. He advocated a least-cost option that would cut only 7 million to 8 million tons of sulfur dioxide, for example, but Reilly worried that figure would not be credible to environmentalists and so would be dead on arrival in Congress. In addition, Reilly favored requiring automakers to cut tailpipe emissions by one-third, extend the durability of pollution control devices, and install canisters to prevent the escape of hydrocarbons during refueling. But Sununu, Boskin, and others preferred setting an overall emissions reduction schedule for cars and letting automakers choose the strategy for attaining it.[85]

Bush ultimately sided with Reilly on most measures, but the final proposal sent to Congress was weaker than the original. For example, the initial proposal called for requiring companies to control toxic air pollutants with the "best technology currently available." The final proposal called for reducing emissions to levels "typically achieved by the best-performing similar sources taking into account energy, environmental, and economic impact and other costs," language that "open[ed] the door for selective enforcement."[86] On acid rain, the nitrogen oxide reduction was based on levels projected for the year 2000, rather than 1980, a change that allowed emissions to increase as much as three million tons before reaching a cut of two million tons in 2000. On auto emissions, instead of requiring all automobiles to cut 40 percent of hydrocarbons, the final proposal allowed the industry to achieve an average 40 percent reduction among new cars.[87] At the behest of White House conservatives, the Bush plan also proposed to eliminate two points of EPA leverage: the automatic ban on new construction for states that fail to develop state implementation plans, and the requirement that EPA impose its own plan if states fail to do so.

Although he made some concessions, Reilly also demonstrated his willingness to stand on principle. When he realized that trying to reach consensus would not work, Reilly ordered the EPA to refine its research and sharpen its debating points. Then, in the midst of the negotiations, Sununu promised Representative Michael Oxley of Ohio that he would furnish new data that would help midwestern utilities. The White House promptly began to develop data that EPA officials feared would be used to justify weaker acid rain controls and derail the legislative package. Reilly responded by leaving town; he could not be reached to write a letter from EPA backing the new calculations, so negotiations ultimately proceeded without the information. Reilly also headed off backsliding by Sununu on the 10-million-ton reduction in sulfur dioxide emissions by leaking news of the plans to an environmental group.[88] These fights with Darman and others over the Clean Air Act were costly for Reilly, who was pigeonholed by his more conservative colleagues as an environmental zealot.

It took months of arduous, closed-door negotiating sessions for the president's proposal to wend its way through the 101st Congress. Finally, in March 1990, Senate leaders and the Bush administration unveiled a compromise bill. In April, the Senate held its first vote on the Clean Air Act in thirteen years: 89–11 in favor of the revised bill. Shortly thereafter, the House Energy and Commerce Committee voted (39–4) to send its own version of the bill to the floor. In late October, the House-Senate conference reached accords on toxics and acid rain, after fourteen weeks of negotiation. Both chambers then passed the final bill, 401–25 in the House and 89–10 in the Senate, and in mid-November the president signed it into law. Reflecting ongoing congressional concern about the possibility of permissive implementation by the executive branch, the legislation was filled with specific requirements and timetables that sharply limited the EPA's discretion.

**Antiregulatory Ideas Prevail on Climate Change**
The passage of the Clean Air Act Amendments was a major environmental accomplishment; it was also the administration's last major attempt to make the status quo more restrictive.[89] Even before then, with recession setting in, Sununu and Darman were gaining the upper hand. For instance, in February 1990, Sununu overruled Reilly, White House science advisor D. Alan Bromley, and two other cabinet members when he persuaded Bush to tone down a speech delivered to the recently created Intergovernmental Panel on Climate Change on the dangers of global warming. In his speech, Bush referred to the "uncertainty" of climate change projections and emphasized the need for "reconciling of environmental protections to the continued benefits of economic development."[90] Acknowledging the dispute over his role on a television news show, Sununu said he was merely preventing efforts by "faceless bureaucrats on the environmental side to try and create a policy in this country that cuts off our use of coal, oil and natural gas."[91]

Sununu's aggressiveness on global warming was critical because it was rapidly becoming environmentalists' top concern, and because initially it had appeared that Bush would act to curb greenhouse gas emissions. In the unusually hot, dry, and smoggy summer of 1988, Dr. James Hansen, an atmospheric physicist at NASA and director of the Goddard Institute for Space Studies, had drawn attention to the issue by testifying before a Senate subcommittee that human-induced global warming was imminent and that there was sufficient evidence to warrant government action. Hansens's testimony spawned a flurry of media coverage, with reporters noting that the warmest years on record had occurred in the 1980s. According to journalist John Noble Wilford, Hansen "sounded the alarm with such authority and force that the issue of an overheating world . . . suddenly moved to the forefront of public concern."[92] A draft EPA report released in October 1988 reinforced Hansen's message, forecasting environmental havoc in the United States as a result of global warming.

During the presidential campaign, Bush had suggested he would follow Hansen's advice, saying, "Those who think we are powerless to do anything about the 'greenhouse effect' are forgetting about the 'White House effect.' As President, I intend to do something about it." He had pledged to convene a global conference on the environment at the White House during his first year in office. And, he had vowed, "we will act."[93] On January 5, 1989, the National Academy of Sciences urged President-elect Bush to put global warming high on his agenda because "the future welfare of human society" was at risk.[94] Five days into his tenure as Bush's secretary of state, James Baker III told reporters, "We face the prospect of being trapped on a boat that we have irreparably damaged— not by the cataclysm of war, but by the slow neglect of a vessel we believed to be impervious to our abuse." With respect to global warming in particular, Baker said, "The political ecology is now ripe for action. . . .We can probably not afford to wait until all of the scientific uncertainties have been resolved before we do act."[95] In March, EPA administrator Reilly told a Senate subcommittee that "very large reductions" in emissions would be necessary to stabilize carbon dioxide levels in the atmosphere.[96]

It soon became apparent, however, that the administration would deflect efforts to raise the salience of climate change or to take legislative or administrative steps to address it. In May 1989, the media disclosed that the OMB had ordered Hansen to change his upcoming testimony about global warming before the Senate Subcommittee on Science, Technology and Space.[97] In particular, the OMB had softened Hansen's conclusion that computer projections of climatic changes caused by carbon dioxide and other greenhouse gases would cause substantial temperature increases, drought, severe storms, and other stresses on the earth's biological systems. Among the edits was a statement at the end of his testimony cautioning that the relative contribution of humans and natural processes to changing climate patterns "remains scientifically unknown."[98] In the wake of this revelation, President Bush promised to host a "global workshop" to prepare for negotiations on an international treaty; he also moved to increase funding for climate change research. On August 31, the White House released details of an interagency program, the U.S. Global Change Research Program, whose aim was to gain a "predictive understanding of the interactive physical, geological, chemical, biological, and social processes that regulate the Earth system."[99] The administration proposed spending $191 million on global change research in fiscal year 1990, an increase of 43 percent over 1989.[100]

Pressed by Reilly, in the spring of 1990, the president convened an international conference on global warming, despite the opposition of Sununu, Bromley, and Darman. In advance of the meeting, almost half the members of the National Academy of Sciences, including forty-nine Nobel prizewinners, appealed to Bush to take the threat of global warming seriously and begin immediately to curb greenhouse gas emissions. In their appeal, the scientists said, "Global warming has emerged as the most serious environmental threat of the 21st century. There is broad agreement within the scientific community that amplification of the Earth's natural greenhouse effect by the buildup of various gases introduced by human activity has the potential to produce dramatic changes in climate."[101] Then, in mid-April, on the eve of the conference, the IPCC released its first draft report, according to which it was a "virtual certainty" that the earth's temperature would rise substantially over the next hundred years.[102]

At the conference, however, administration officials refused to acknowledge that the risks of global warming were sufficiently clear to merit immediate action. "What we need are facts," Bush stated in his remarks opening the two-day meeting.[103] He also warned against taking steps to reduce emissions if doing so would harm the economy. To justify his position, Bush relied heavily on a paper issued by the conservative George C. Marshall Institute titled "Scientific Perspectives on the Greenhouse Problem," which downplayed the scientific consensus on climate change and concluded that it would be premature to impose policies to reduce greenhouse gas emissions. Taking a page from Reagan's acid rain playbook, Bush emphasized the need for more research. To the consternation of the meeting's European participants, administration officials monopolized the remainder of the agenda in an effort to mute opposition to Bush's stance. They adhered closely to a primer prepared for the U.S. delegation that urged delegates to avoid debating the reality of climate change. "A better approach is to raise the many uncertainties that need to be better understood on this issue," the document advised.[104]

Shortly after the White House meeting, in a startling juxtaposition, the American Assembly—a forum founded by Dwight D. Eisenhower when he was president of Columbia University—brought together seventy-six leading scientists, economists, business executives, political scientists, politicians, international officials, and environmentalists from nineteen countries to talk about the environment. After four days of debate the participants concluded that the danger of global warming was so severe that the United States should take immediate action to lessen it.[105] The following month, the IPCC released the final version of its first report, warning that unless carbon dioxide and other greenhouse gases were immediately cut by 60 percent, global temperatures would rise sharply during the twenty-first century, with unforeseeable consequences for humanity. Breaking with the Bush administration, Prime Minister Margaret Thatcher vowed to reduce the projected growth of Britain's carbon dioxide emissions enough to stabilize them at 1990 levels by 2005.[106]

### The Competitiveness Council's Low-Profile Challenges to Clean Air Act Implementation

A second indication that the antiregulatory faction within the administration was ascendant was the prominent role taken by the Council on Competitiveness. Bush established the council in 1989 "to make sure regulations fulfill the statute with a minimal amount of economic impact." He later clarified that the council was to implement two Reagan-era executive orders—12291 and 12498—aimed at reducing the burden of regulations. The council was headed by Vice President Quayle, a self-proclaimed "zealot" on the subject of deregulation,[107] and composed of Darman, Meese, Sununu, and Boskin, as well as Robert Mosbacher and Michael Brady, the secretaries of commerce and treasury, respectively. Although the council was quiescent for much of the first year of Bush's term, business complaints about regulatory backsliding spurred it to action in mid-1990. In late June Quayle hired libertarian Allan B. Hubbard to serve as the council's executive director. Hubbard in turn selected David McIntosh, another ardent free marketeer, as his deputy. As McIntosh characterized the council's role, "What we are trying to do, to the extent possible, is looking at issues and deciding what to do based on a rational, objective view of the facts." McIntosh saw as his mission "[changing] the debate about how we get the most environmental protection for the limited resources this society can spend on it."[108]

By late 1990, the competitiveness council was in full swing, seeking to head off regulations before they took effect. In its first major regulatory action, it forced the EPA to withdraw an ambitious trash recycling initiative that would have required the owners and operators of municipal incinerators to recycle one-quarter of recyclable items that release toxic substances when burned—a rule the council criticized as unduly burdensome. The council subsequently directed the EPA to drop plans to ban the incineration of lead car batteries, which it said "did not meet the benefit/cost requirements of regulatory policy."[109] (In mid-July 1992, the D.C. Circuit ruled that the EPA had to review its decision to allow the incineration of lead batteries. After a review, the EPA stuck with its decision to forgo the ban.) The council also sought (ultimately unsuccessfully) to narrow the definition of wetlands that garner federal protection because, according to a White House aide, previous wetlands protection had gone too far in blocking development and denying land-owners their rights to develop their land, and the rules' implications for private property and the environment were too important to be left to bureaucrats.[110]

The council focused most heavily on softening the impact of the Clean Air Act Amendments, delaying the issuance of regulations and using the rulemaking process to achieve exemptions or favorable terms for indus-try that had been rejected by Congress. The EPA did manage to issue some restrictive rules without interference from the council, particularly when those rules did not provoke the ire of industry. For example, in July 1992, the EPA announced plans to require the nation's smoggiest areas to toughen automobile emissions inspections by using high-tech tests that would fail more cars. The new rules garnered the support not only of environmentalists but also of automakers and oil companies, neither of which would bear the costs. But most of the rules developed to implement the new law had to run the council gauntlet. By late 1991, the council had sent the EPA about one hundred changes to proposed Clean Air Act regulations, many of them taken verbatim from industry documents. For example, the Motor Vehicle Manufacturers Association had asked the agency to add a passage to one rule saying that it would not enforce the act for just any violation, but only if a company's action was "endangering or causing damage to public health or the environ-ment." The EPA originally had rejected this language because it would complicate enforcement of some violations, but the council reinserted the phrase.[111]

Other proposed changes in Clean Air Act rules also reflected industry intent. For instance, when Congress was marking up the Clean Air Act Amendments, industry had requested the flexibility to exceed limits on emissions of toxic air pollutants specified in their permits without going through the time-consuming process of obtaining new permits. Congress firmly rejected this notion, instead specifying in unusual detail the requirements for changing emissions limits in a permit, including a lengthy public review. Initially, the EPA adhered to the legislative blueprint, but on April 6, 1991, the competitiveness council returned to the agency a set of suggested modifications that conformed to the desires of industry lobbyists. In place of a three-and-a-half-page section drafted by the EPA, the council inserted paragraphs allowing polluters to exceed their permit levels by up to 80,000 pounds annually, as long as they notified the relevant state government seven days in advance. The state would then have twenty-eight days to approve or disapprove the notification. If alerted by the state, the EPA would have seventeen days to weigh in.[112] In mid-May 1992, after a protracted internal struggle, President Bush overruled the EPA and backed the council. The final rule, issued a month later, allowed a company to increase its emissions by up to 490,000 pounds with no public notification required, albeit with a modification that gave the EPA forty-five days and a state government ninety days to reject such "minor" permit changes. Reilly agreed to implement the rule reluctantly, only after the Justice Department rendered a formal opinion supporting its legality.[113]

Several other council proposals prevailed as well, including one that adopted industry's preferred definition of a pollution "source." In drawing up the Clean Air Act Amendments, Congress decided to order chemical plants, coke ovens, and oil refineries to cut their toxic air emissions by as much as 98 percent by 1995. To encourage industry to achieve the act's objectives more rapidly, Congress offered an inducement: pollution sources that reduced emissions by 90 percent by 1994, a year before the deadline, would have six additional years to reach the full cutbacks required. The act did not define the term "source," however, leaving it to the EPA to determine what, exactly, would have to be cut 90 percent to earn the early reduction credit. The only guidance Congress provided was a speech by an author of the legislation, Republican Dave Durenberger of Minnesota, who said on the Senate floor that the most logical definition of a "source" was an entire production unit. As the rules for this provision were being written, however, chemical and oil companies lobbied for "flexibility" to define emissions sources. Specifically, they wanted to add up reductions from small, unrelated parts of a plant and transfer the credit to other parts. Eventually, as reflected in the proposed rule published May 31, 1991, the council (along with those in the EPA who favored the broader definition) prevailed—a result Senator Durenberger called a "pollution extension for business as usual."[114]

Another council proposal enabled industry to evade requirements to install state-of-the-art pollution control devices when undertaking plant overhauls. When Congress was crafting the acid rain provisions of the Clean Air Act, industry lobbyists had expressed concern that, if a plant installed a scrubber, the remodeling process could constitute a "physical change" that would require a plant-wide review of emissions. Such a review could trigger a requirement to install additional pollution control devices—a result that industry argued would constitute "double jeopardy." On the other side, some members of Congress worried that plants would take advantage of scrubber installation to undertake more extensive modifications that would result in increases of other pollutants, such as nitrogen oxides. The administration proposed a solution that would have shielded most utilities from the review process, but Congress rejected it as inconsistent with the intent of the law and left the issue to the EPA to resolve. During rulemaking, the EPA suggested a slight modification of the trigger formula, but the Edison Electric Institute, the utilities' trade association, objected and demanded a "blanket pollution control exclusion" for all power plants that installed scrubbers. In response, several White House officials crafted a rule that was essentially the same one the administration had proposed (and Congress had rejected) during the legislative process. According to Democratic representative Henry Waxman of California, the new formula virtually guaranteed that no new emissions review would be triggered.[115]

Yet another council proposal concerned the emissions figure to use in the event a sulfur dioxide monitor was broken or shut down for maintenance. The EPA had proposed to assume a level equivalent to the highest recorded level in a previously monitored period, thereby creating an incentive to keep monitors at maximum use. Industry opposed the proposal, however, and demanded a less stringent approach. An October 1991 council meeting yielded a major concession by allowing utilities to replace missing data with an amount equal to 90 percent of past peak emissions.[116]

Importantly, the council's efforts to delay or mitigate the impact of EPA rulemaking were nearly undetectable. The council intervened prior to the publication of rules and left "no fingerprints." In addition, there was a tacit "no appeals" rule, according to which cabinet officials would not appeal a council decision to the president.[117] Environmentalists tried to raise the visibility of council actions by issuing critical reports that they hoped would garner adverse publicity and, perhaps, provoke congressional hearings. For instance, in 1991, OMB Watch released "All the Vice President's Men," which sought to document the council's activities. In late 1991, Jessica Mathews, vice president of the World Resources Institute, wrote in the *Washington Post* that if the council's decisions were allowed to stand, they would "demolish much of the Clean Air Act." She went on to allege that "the council provides a back door for industry to win policies explicitly rejected by Congress and by government agencies in public proceedings."[118] Journalists repeatedly raised questions about the council's activities as well. But these reports rarely made the front page, and it was difficult to get the public interested in such arcane and seemingly trivial issues.

When challenged, the council defended its actions in terms consistent with the antiregulatory storyline. A fact sheet issued by the council explained, "The council oversees the OMB review process to ensure that federal regulations do not place unnecessary burdens on businesses, and that the benefits outweigh the costs."[119] The council conducted its business in secret because, according to spokesman Jeff Nesbitt, to do otherwise would have inhibited the free flow of discussion. Nesbitt said the council usually heard from business groups because "it is primarily the businesses in the country that see [the effect of a regulation] first."[120]

Eventually, following an exposé in the *Washington Post*, a series of congressional inquiries succeeded in raising the salience of the council's activities. In a closed-door session of a House appropriations subcommittee in June 1992, Democrat David E. Skaggs of Colorado offered an amendment to eliminate the staff budget for the council and prohibit congressionally appropriated funds from being used to support council business. On November 25, 1992, environmentalists reached a settlement with the Bush administration over delays in implementing the Clean Air Act Amendments. The agreement put the EPA on a schedule to issue fifteen air quality regulations under the supervision of the Federal District Court in Washington, D.C. over eighteen months. Although the settlement demonstrated that the public could fight back against the kind of regulatory delay tactics employed by the OMB and the council, it did little to counteract the industry-friendly rule changes already finalized.

### The Principles behind the Administration's Antiregulatory Stance

The Council on Competitiveness embodied the views of Vice President Quayle, who articulated his principled beliefs in a *Washington Post* op-ed:

In the early 1970s, my grandfather wrote an editorial that appeared in major newspapers across the country. It was titled, "Will the Federal Bureaucracy Destroy Individual Freedom in America?" So far, the answer to my grandfather's question is "no." As long as George Bush is president and as long as his Competitiveness Council does its job, the answer will continue to be "no." But major elements of the Washington establishment continue to believe that big government is the solution to our economic ills, not the cause of them. The iron triangle—the seemingly permanent clique of special interests, Hill staff and faceless bureaucrats—is now energized to stop the Competitiveness Council from demanding a serious review of the impact of regulation on our economic productivity. In recent weeks, the iron triangle has joined with its media friends to attack the council on every front as the source of all evil. In fact, the council is simply protecting America's greatness from over-zealous regulators.[121]

Quayle went on to say that, although the administration wanted to protect the safety, welfare, and health of American citizens, it was also important to remember that "the unnecessary red tape and needless litigation add nothing to the gross national product. In fact, excessive regulation simply serves to throw people out of work, lower production, reduce consumer choices, cause economic stagnation and erode our standard of living." He concluded by noting, "My outlook is similar to Thomas Jefferson's: The less regulation, the better. The strength of America lies not with government, or regulations or the iron triangle. It lies in the spirit of the American people and their ability to compete, create, innovate and generate opportunities. With this heritage, we've developed the most prosperous nation the world has ever known."

Whereas Quayle's conservatism was apparent, it was more difficult to discern President Bush's principled beliefs on environmental regulation in the midst of the tussles at the White House. In his first Economic Report to Congress, Bush said, "In some cases, well-designed regulation can serve the public interests." At speeches delivered in North Dakota and Montana in 1989, Bush spoke convincingly in favor of environmental protection. For example, he praised Montana's conservation ethic, saying, "Montanans have made a decision never to let environmental exploitation go unchecked. We can have a strong ecology and a strong economy, and that is what I am committed to." He proceeded to argue that environmental protection was a global issue about which the nations of the world must make common cause. He pledged the United States would take the lead internationally and touted the Montreal Protocol, which banned the release of chlorofluorocarbons into the atmosphere by 2000. In closing, he said, "Montanans know more than most . . . how vital it is for us to accept our responsibilities, our stewardship of the environment in Montana, across America, and around the world. We hold this land in trust for the generations that come after. The air and the Earth are riches we simply cannot squander."

Many of Bush's actions were consistent with this rhetoric. He not only facilitated the passage of the Clean Air Act Amendments, he also approved substantial increases in the EPA's budget and added more than $100 million to the federal budget for acquiring parks and wildlife refuges; established a ten-year moratorium on drilling for oil off the coasts of New England, southern Florida, and California; signed the Federal Facilities Compliance Act of 1992, which required states and the EPA to impose the same requirements on federal facilities as they did on the private sector; authorized the Department of Energy and Pentagon to spend nearly $7 billion for cleaning up toxic chemicals and radioactive contamination from weapons production; launched an initiative to plant one billion trees per year; and signed treaties banning ivory trading, eliminating large-scale drift-net fishing, and protecting Antarctica. At least initially, Bush supported stringent enforcement of environmental laws as well. His Department of Justice claimed to have secured more indictments, convictions, fines, and jail sentences in 1989 than in any other recent year.[122] And in late 1990, the EPA and OSHA announced a joint crackdown on businesses that violated federal environmental and safety laws.[123]

When it came to implementing the Clean Air Act, however, Bush tended to side with his vice president and the conservative members of his cabinet. On energy, Bush's record was also consistent with an anti-regulatory philosophy. His National Energy Strategy, released in 1991, promoted oil development in the Arctic National Wildlife Refuge while supporting only modest energy conservation measures. His administration strongly opposed raising fuel efficiency standards for automobiles, echoing the automakers' claims that doing so would cost thousands of jobs and eliminate family-sized cars in favor of unsafe compacts. (In September 1990, the Senate killed a measure that would have required cars to get 40 miles per gallon by 2001, after a lobbying blitz by the administration and the auto industry reversed what days earlier had been a sizable majority (68–28) in favor of the measure). In mid-March 1991, the League of Conservation Voters "reluctantly" gave Bush a midterm grade of "D," saying he had not lived up to his promise to be the environmental president.

Some observers believed the president genuinely sought "balance," and his decisions were the result of a thoughtful assessment; others suspected Bush wanted to do the "right" thing but worried about alienating business and his Republican allies.[124] "Looking at the record, you see he cares," Brooks Yeager, the Washington legislative director for the National Audubon Society, told journalist Keith Schneider. "You also get a sense that he could be much better than he is, that he could carve a niche for himself. But he seems paralyzed at times. In the large problem areas where taking action requires facing down the conservative elements of his constituency, he's been much more hesitant."[125] A prime example of this ambivalence was Bush's response to the issue of the spotted owl. At a 1990 Republican fundraiser in Oregon, he drew cheers when he said, "I reject those who would ignore the economic consequences of the spotted owl decision. The jobs of many thousands of Oregonians and whole communities are at stake." But in the next breath he added, "I also think we ought to reject those who do not recognize their obligation to protect our delicate ecosystem." In conclusion, he said, "Common sense tells us to find a needed balance."[126]

**Articulating Antiregulatory Ideas in Advance of the 1992 Election**
As the 1992 election approached, the president's antiregulatory tone grew more strident, suggesting that electoral calculations rather than conviction played the primary role in his conversion. In his State of the Union address in January 1992, Bush announced a ninety-day review of all existing regulations and a moratorium on new rules, which he extended indefinitely in April. "This is an attempt to see if there are some areas in which unnecessary bureaucratic red tape that's a barrier to business formation, expansion, and job creation can be reduced or eliminated," explained Michael Boskin.[127] Much of the moratorium's impact fell on environmental rules: the administration halted the listing of rare plants and animals under the Endangered Species Act, delayed rules to carry out the Clean Air Act, restricted the ability of environmentalists to block logging in national forests, and limited the liability of banks and other lenders for the cost of cleaning up toxic waste.[128]

More backtracking on regulation followed. In March, the administration jettisoned a proposal to require carmakers to install vapor recovery canisters to capture gasoline fumes.[129] In mid-May, President Bush decided to allow companies to increase their toxic air pollution emissions without notifying the public. Then, in early August 1992, the EPA announced it would not tighten the primary ozone air quality standard. The decision came almost seven years after the statutory deadline for review of the standard, and EPA officials acknowledged it did not incorporate the latest research on health effects, which had prompted many experts to demand more stringent limits.[130] (Since 1988, researchers had found that healthy people exposed to ozone in laboratories for several hours lost 40 percent of their lung power and had more severe reactions when exposed to ozone in fresh air. Animal studies showed that chronic, long-term exposure to ozone caused lung scarring similar to that caused by cigarette smoking.)

In late October, with the election imminent, journalist Michael Weiss-kopf reported that the administration was quietly planning to weaken the Prevention of Significant Deterioration provision of the Clean Air Act.[131] Under the status quo, industry was required to install state-of-the-art controls on new plants in unpolluted areas. In 1987, the EPA had imposed a "top-down" standard, under which a company could avoid installing the best-available control technology only if it could demonstrate it could not do so for technical or economic reasons. Now, however, the Bush administration was proposing to allow companies to choose their preferred technology and simply explain how their choice was "consistent" with legal requirements. According to a memo from the Pacific Northwest region to the office of deputy administrator Rosenberg, the revisions would "weaken, not improve, the effectiveness" of efforts to preserve unpolluted areas by forcing "permitting authorities to make less stringent [technology] determinations."[132] Michael Weisskopf noted that the administration intended to delay announcing the plan, which was crafted by the White House Counsel's office and the Council of Economic Advisers, until after the election, to shield the president from criticism by environmentalists.

One White House official explained the administration's shift toward a more permissive stance by saying, "What's driving this is simply that too much regulation does have the effect of decreasing economic growth and lowering the number of jobs."[133] "The president has always been in favor of protecting the environment in a way that is compatible with growth," argued David McIntosh, executive director of the Council on Competitiveness. "What you are seeing is a series of decisions that focused on the economic growth side of the balance."[134]

The administration did not abandon environmental protection altogether. On chlorofluorocarbons, the Bush administration continued the transformation, begun under Reagan, from a permissive to a more restrictive position. In late June 1990, after a last-minute concession by the United States to provide technological help to developing countries, most of the world's nations agreed to halt the production of chemicals that destroy the ozone layer by the end of the twentieth century. Then, in February 1992, Bush surprised environmentalists by supporting a unanimous Senate amendment to the energy bill that would phase out CFCs even more quickly. Only three months earlier, three Republicans senators, on behalf of the White House, had prevented such a measure from reaching the floor.[135] But with Sununu gone, Reilly engineered a White House reversal by pointing to new scientific data that portrayed the ozone situation as more serious that previously believed.[136] Bush proceeded to direct U.S. manufacturers to halt virtually all production of CFCs by December 31, 1995. The policy, authorized under a provision of the Clean Air Act, took immediate effect. (It is noteworthy that the industry coalition, the Alliance for Responsible CFC Policy, supported the move toward greater restrictiveness.)

In most respects, however, conservatives dominated the White House position on international environmental affairs. Throughout a series of meetings leading up to the United Nations' Earth Summit in Rio in June 1992, the United States strongly opposed the adoption of concrete targets and timetables for stabilizing carbon dioxide levels, insisting that more conclusive evidence was necessary before the United States would restrict the use of fossil fuels. At a meeting in Chantilly, Virginia, in early February 1991, the Bush administration acknowledged for the first time in an international setting that global warming was a problem. The U.S. delegates proposed no new steps, however, saying they believed measures the United States had already taken would be sufficient. The main components of this strategy were the chlorofluorocarbon reductions agreed to in the Montreal Protocol and its successor, as well as a handful of energy efficiency provisions in the president's long-awaited National Energy Strategy. Ironically, the OMB had deleted at least four sections of the administration's proposed energy bill that would have created incentives for energy conservation before circulating it to cabinet departments for comments. The White House had rejected other conservation-promoting options drafted by the Department of Energy before the bill was ever written, including higher automotive fuel-efficiency standards, higher taxes, and requirements that employers charge workers for parking. Administration officials explained that its free-market, anti-tax philosophy accounted for the last-minute deletion of conservation measures and the emphasis in the bill on energy production.[137] (The bill did contain voluntary programs to encourage enhanced building energy efficiency, the removal of gas-guzzling cars from the road, and reductions in energy consumption in public housing.)

As the Rio summit approached, Bush continued to emphasize that his priority was protecting American jobs. In March 1992, he threatened to boycott the conference, presumably in hopes of wringing concessions favorable to the United States. Despite an internal analysis produced by a four-agency working group showing the United States could achieve significant reductions in greenhouse gas emissions by 2000 with little economic dislocation, throughout the spring the administration held fast to its position that it could not support concrete targets or timetables.[138] In Rio, the administration demanded and won a weakened version of the climate change treaty, on the grounds that limiting carbon dioxide emissions would hamper economic growth.[139] The administration pointed out that no one had definitively proved that greenhouse gases were warming the globe, while economic studies suggested that cutting carbon dioxide would reduce economic output. Having eliminated language requiring the United States to cap its carbon dioxide emissions at 1990 levels by 2000, Bush signed (and the Senate ratified) the Framework Convention on Climate Change (FCCC), the primary goal of which was the "stabilization of greenhouse gas concentrations in the atmosphere at a level that would prevent dangerous anthropogenic [human] interference with the climate system"; he made clear, however, that he did not intend to mandate emissions reductions.[140]

Moreover, Bush declined to sign the Convention on Biological Diversity, saying it was fundamentally flawed because it would impose royalties on American companies that derived drugs or other substances from species found in developing countries, and therefore would discourage research and innovation. According to the State Department, the United States was also concerned that the treaty attempted to regulate the safety of genetically engineered products that would be used in developing countries and was worried about how money to implement the treaty would be disbursed. The decision not to sign the treaty despite support for it by Bill Reilly, assistant secretary of state for the environment Curtis Bohlen, and many biologists—was based on a memo written by David McIntosh arguing that the economic harm from signing the treaty would substantially outweigh the benefits.[141] Bush insisted that in rejecting the treaty he was "fighting for balance" between environmental needs and the health of the economy. "We cannot accept standards that are not based on the soundest of science," he said, "and we cannot shut down the lives of thousands of Americans by going to extremes" on behalf of the environment.[142]

Seeking to counter foreign and domestic criticism of his refusal to sign the biodiversity treaty, the president paired that announcement with a statement that the United States would increase its aid to developing countries to help conserve the world's forests from $120 million to $270 million. Bush also responded to his critics, saying, "I came to this office committed to extend America's record of environmental leadership, and I've worked to do so in a way that is compatible with economic growth because this balance is absolutely essential, and because these are twin goals, not mutually exclusive objects."[143] The forest plan did not go over well in Rio, however; developing countries that were the targets of the plan complained it was an effort to control them. Ultimately, negotiators could only agree on a voluntary set of principles for preserving the world's forests.

The antiregulatory storyline became ascendant in the White House as environmentalism was losing its salience among the public. A series of focusing events in 1988 and early 1989 had raised the visibility of environmental issues, starting with the testimony of James Hansen in the summer of 1988 and culminating in the Exxon Valdez oil spill in March 1989. In the spring of 1990, journalist Richard Berke reported that the environment, "once dismissed as a fringe cause by many politicians, had reached the forefront of American politics, with candidates for one public office after another proclaiming themselves environmentalists."[144] According to a 1990 Gallup poll, 76 percent of Americans called themselves environmentalists.[145] A *Washington Post* poll of 1,016 adults in March 1990 found that 73 percent believed the environment had gotten worse since 1970, and 57 percent described the situation as a crisis.[146] Eighty-four percent of Americans told pollsters for the *New York Times/ CBS News* that pollution was a serious national problem that was worsening; 74 percent said that protecting the environment was so important that "requirements and standards cannot be too high and that environmental improvements must be made regardless of cost." (By contrast, in 1981, 45 percent said they held that belief.)[147]

By 1992, however, the environment had faded as a public issue in the face of persistent economic woes.[148] While national opinion polls showed the environment ranked lower on people's priority lists, industry was becoming more vocal. For example, after a period of quiescence following the Valdez oil spill, by late 1991, the oil industry was back on the offensive, loudly denouncing environmental restrictions.[149] The meteoric rise in membership and contributions of mainstream environmental groups had been arrested. According to some top White

House environmental aides, Bush was emboldened by environmentalists' setbacks.[150]

In adopting the antiregulatory storyline, the White House was also trying to shore up support among the timber, mining, coal, and agricultural groups that anchored Republicans' western conservative constituency. Campaigning for reelection in the Pacific Northwest, Bush decried "environmental extremists" and vowed to amend the Endangered Species Act. "It's time to make people more important than owls," he said. "I know that you—you who have chosen to live in these woods—respect and revere these forests as others never can. And you resent the implication that earning your livelihood here—with sound management of the forest—makes you less of a conservationist than the city dweller or the suburbanite."[151] The act, Bush told his audience, was being used by people with "extreme views," was "broken," and should "give greater consideration to jobs, families, and communities."[152] In another speech, Bush called the act "a sword aimed at the jobs, families, and communities of entire regions like the Northwest."[153]

Bush's gestures toward conservatives in the West were not confined to rhetoric. In March 1992, the administration sided with the coal industry in a lawsuit that industry hoped would weaken strip-mining regulations. In April, with Bush's endorsement, the Interior Department announced that oil and gas drilling, logging, grazing, and other uses of the public land would proceed while appeals of agencies' decisions were under review by the department's Board of Land Appeals—all part of a broader effort to insulate natural resource industries from citizen appeals and administrative challenges to activities on federal land.[154] Secretary Lujan justified these moves by saying that useful projects on public lands were being delayed indefinitely by opponents who did nothing more than mail in criticisms, automatically initiating long reviews of the agency's decisions.[155]

Lujan told Keith Schneider he was bringing "the plight of the Western constituency to the White House," saying, "People who live in the West look at the land in a different way than people east of the Mississippi River. Land is our heritage to use and not just lock up and put away, where only backpackers can go. I have been telling the White House staff that our constituency, the conservative Republican constituency, is not pleased at being ignored."[156] "That portion of our constituency— grazing interests, oil interests, mining interests—is up in arms," Lujan explained. "They believe we've gotten too green."[157] Like other members of the administration, Lujan believed Bush should heed his conservative constituency because environmentalists would never praise the administration, no matter what it did.

## People First!: Conservatives Mobilize Against Biodiversity Conservation

More fundamentally, with this combination of regulatory laxity and a more bellicose tone, Bush was responding to the emergence during the late 1980s and early 1990s of several powerful strains of antiregulatory activism: the "wise use" movement, the county supremacy movement, and the property rights movement. The claims made by these factions added a populist dimension to the antiregulatory storyline: tapping into the powerful American dread of tyranny, policy entrepreneurs warned that the federal government, backed by the demands of elitist environmentalists, was trampling on the rights of hardworking Americans. The movements also furnished foot soldiers, broadening the reach of antiregulatory ideas that previously had been confined primarily to the realm of business leaders and policy intellectuals.

The wise use movement rekindled the embers of the Sagebrush Rebellion. James Watt had temporarily quelled that movement. But as popular support for environmentalism climbed in reaction to Reagan-era challenges, land management agencies began responding to the demands of a preservation-oriented constituency, and western anger once again began to bubble up. After percolating for several years, the wise use movement formally declared itself in 1989, at a meeting in Reno, Nevada. At that meeting, policy entrepreneurs Ron Arnold and Alan Gottlieb formulated "The Wise Use Agenda," a list of twenty-five goals that included substantially curtailing the Endangered Species Act to eliminate protection for "non-adaptive species such as the California condor and endemic species lacking the vigor to spread in range" and opening up most public lands to mineral and energy production and off-road vehicle use.[158] Although the movement initially comprised a congeries of local groups that were only loosely affiliated, a small number of umbrella organizations—such as the Alliance for America, the Center for the Defense of Free Enterprise, the Blue Ribbon Coalition, the Western States Public Lands Coalition, and People for the West!—sought to establish a network among local organizations with similar goals.[159]

Wise use leaders voiced claims familiar to adherents of the antiregulatory storyline: they vilified the federal government, which they characterized as being in cahoots with environmentalists. For example, according to rancher Wayne Hage, one of the most vocal spokesmen for the wise use movement, "The West struggles under onerous federal enactments lobbied into existence by environmental groups funded largely by eastern capitalists and their corporate foundations."[160] Pamela Neal, executive director of the Public Lands Council, which represented 31,000 cattle and sheep ranchers, argued, "It was free enterprise and private property rights that created America and made this nation great. Instead of protecting independence, the government is making us servants of an environmental movement that I can only liken to socialism."[161]

Movement leaders also disparaged environmentalists as being well outside the mainstream. For instance, Ron Arnold described environmentalists as "part of an elite, part of the Harvard Yard crowd in three-piece suits and expensive shoes that is destroying the middle class."[162] Arnold told his followers, "Environmentalism is the new paganism. It is evil. And we intend to destroy it. . . . We will not allow our right to own property and use nature's resources for the benefit of mankind to be stripped from us by a bunch of eco-fascists. . . . If property rights are lost, our liberty is lost. No one should be allowed to tell a man what he can and cannot do on his land."[163] According to Arnold and Gottlieb, the real environmentalists were "the farmers and ranchers who have been stewards of the land for generations, the miners and loggers and oil drillers who built our civilization by working in the environment every day, the property owners and technicians and professionals who provided all the material basis of our existence."[164]

The wise use movement gained momentum in the early 1990s, driven in part by globalization and automation, both of which had eroded employment and payrolls in the natural resource industries of the West. In Montana, for example, total employment in the lumber and wood products industries declined by roughly 15 percent during the 1980s, while employment in oil and gas exploration fell 45 percent; as a result, Montanans' real income in nonagriculture resource industries was 30 percent lower in 1990 than it had been in 1979.[165] Capitalizing on these economic realities, promotional literature for People for the West—which doubled its Montana membership to 1,000 between March and September of 1992—exhorted followers, "Don't allow Congress to lock us out of all 730 million acres of public lands. . . . People will lose jobs, rural communities will become ghost towns, education for our children will suffer, and state and local governments will forfeit critical income for police, fire protection, roads, and social services."[166] Critics of the movement, such as state AFL-CIO executive secretary Don Judge, characterized it as "an effort to pit workers against the environment, instead of an effort to promote responsible economic development and appropriate use of our natural resources . . . They're trying to make political hay out of the economic fears of job dislocation and community instability."[167]

The county supremacy movement, a related initiative that emerged in the early 1990s, sought local control of federal lands. The movement, which took hold primarily among state and county officials, rested on three legal theories. First, proponents contended that the federal government's authority extended only to land it legally owned, as described in Article 1, Section 8 of the Constitution—that is, land within Washington, D.C., defense facilities, and other "needful" buildings. Second, according to the "equal footing" doctrine upon which state governments assumed control of land within their borders, the federal government was supposed to hold newly acquired land temporarily, not in long-term reservations of parks and forests; the understanding, county supremacists insisted, was that the federal government would eventually return such land to the states. Third, they argued, the National Environmental Policy Act called on the federal government to cooperate with state and local governments to "preserve important historic, cultural, and natural aspects of our natural heritage." Natural resource extraction and use, they maintained, was part of western "custom and culture."

The first effort to institutionalize these legal theories was the Interim Land Use Policy Plan of Catron County, New Mexico. Adopted in 1991, this ordinance mandated that federal managers "shall comply with" the county's land-use plan or face prosecution; it sought "to protect the custom and culture of County citizens through protection of private property rights."[168] Subsequently, Nye County, Nevada went even further, declaring that the State of Nevada, not the federal government, owned the public lands within its boundaries. The courts uniformly rejected the tenets of the county supremacy movement, however. In one closely watched case decided in 1996, the Idaho Supreme Court struck down an ordinance similar to Catron County's as unconstitutional because of the preemption doctrine, according to which federal laws supersede state laws and constitutions (*Boundary Backpackers v. Boundary County*.) In another, the U.S. District Court for Nevada rejected Nye County's equal footing claim and declared the county's resolutions invalid (*U.S. v. Nye County, Nevada*).

Whereas the wise use and county supremacy movements were rooted in the West, the property rights movement was national in scope and fed primarily on resentment toward the Endangered Species Act and regulation of wetlands under the Clean Water Act. It, too, picked up steam in the late 1980s, as more species were listed and regulated interests began to feel the full effect of federal restrictions.[169] Another impetus was the Bush administration's 1989 wetlands manual, which "brought people out of the woodwork," according to Margaret Ann Reigle, founder of the Fairness to Land Owners Committee based in Cambridge, Maryland.[170] Clearly identifying victims and villains, Reigle complained that land-use regulations gave bureaucrats "a license to steal the life savings of mom-and-pop landowners."[171] According to Reigle, "It's a national crisis: landowners, and I mean moms and pops, not oil companies and miners, are being abused by restrictions that no longer make sense. Their lives have been devastated and their land is being held hostage by these laws."[172] In 1995, Nancie Marzulla, president of the Washington, D.C.-based nonprofit Defenders of Property Rights, testified before the Senate Judiciary Committee, "Today, environmental regulations destroy property rights on an unprecedented scale. Regulations designed to protect coastal zone areas, wetlands, and endangered species habitats, among others, leave many owners stripped of all but bare title to their property."[173] The fundamental principle underpinning the property rights movement was that property rights are paramount and inviolate. Advocates' preferred prescription drew on the idea of "regulatory takings" developed by legal scholar Richard Epstein, according to which property owners must be compensated when government regulations devalue their land.

By the mid-1990s, there were some six hundred local property rights groups spread across the United States. Chuck Cushman, head of the American Land Rights Association, was the policy entrepreneur who organized those groups into a coherent movement. Portraying himself as leading a holy crusade against environmentalists, Cushman unified the disparate grievances of landowners; he created a common enemy, characterizing environmentalism as "a new pagan religion" whose members "worship trees and animals and sacrifice people."[174] His own organization, the National Inholders Association, defended the rights of those who owned land within the boundaries of national parks. But he also forged alliances with other groups, such as the Defenders of Property Rights, which aimed to bring about a sea change in property rights law through strategically filed lawsuits and groundbreaking property rights legislation."[175]

One tactic employed by property rights activists was to try to pass state legislation that required regulators to consider the effects of new regulation on property owners. All fifty states debated such measures in the early 1990s, and by the end of 1995, eighteen states had passed some form of "takings" legislation. Most required state governments to conduct a takings impact assessment before proposing regulatory action, but some also included compensation provisions. Property rights activism made inroads at the federal level as well, as conservative members of Congress from both parties began attaching takings provisions to legislation, albeit without success. In 1991, Democratic representative Jimmy Hayes of Louisiana recruited 170 cosponsors for a proposed revision to the Clean Water Act that would allow all but the most ecologically valuable wetlands to be developed and would require the government to compensate owners who were prevented from using their land. The Senate version of the five-year, $100 billion transportation bill debated in November 1991 contained an amendment that would have codified Reagan's 1988 executive order by directing federal agencies to conduct takings assessments of proposed regulatory actions. Republican senator Alan Simpson of Wyoming justified the amendment, saying, "Today, particularly in the West because we are such close neighbors to public lands, we are seeing this mentality of conservation or environmental protection at any cost sweep across the federal boundaries of public lands and out onto our private lands. Some folks, in and out of Congress and the federal government, feel it is their right, indeed their duty and civic responsibility, to mandate just what actions will and won't occur on private lands in order to protect environmental qualities."[176]

The Endangered Species Act was a favorite target of wise use and property rights activists, who regarded excessive government regulation rather than species extinction as the central problem. As Troy Mader, an official with the Abundant Wildlife Society, told journalist H. Jane Lehman, the Endangered Species Act "has become the most effective tool of nature worshipers to lock up vast areas and deprive people of their individual property rights."[177] A series of ESA-related actions particularly inflamed movement activists. First, in 1989, protection of the endangered kangaroo rat slowed development in the rapidly growing city of Riverside, California. The following year, the National Park Service enraged ranchers by promoting the idea of reintroducing wolves into Yellowstone National Park. Then, in 1991, the listing of the delta smelt, a tiny fish, threatened to undermine the water rights of agribusinesses in California; the designation of the Snake River sockeye salmon as endangered jeopardized power generation in the Pacific Northwest; and the requirement that fishermen install devices to protect endangered sea turtles rocked the shrimp-fishing industry in the Gulf of Mexico.[178] High-profile controversies notwithstanding, two studies released in the early 1990s suggested that, to date, the Endangered Species Act had actually impeded very few projects.[179]

Undeterred by the statistical evidence, anti-ESA advocates proffered horror stories in an effort to tarnish the image of the act. These anecdotes typically involved a sympathetic individual trying to do something benign on his or her land, and encountering a maze of bureaucratic rules and being punished for failing to comply with them. One often-repeated tale began on a snowy September night, when Montana rancher John Shuler thought he saw a grizzly bear outside his house. Grabbing his rifle, Shuler raced outside to find three bears devouring his sheep herd. When he fired a warning shot in the air, a fourth bear emerged and turned to attack him. Fearing for his life, Shuler shot and killed the bear, thereby taking an endangered species, a crime for which the EPA fined him $4,000.[180] A second story featured Taiwanese immigrant Taung-Min Lin, who bought a 723-acre parcel of California scrub land in 1990 and began to farm it. As it turned out, his land was home to three endangered species: the Tipton kangaroo rat, the blunt-nosed leopard lizard, and the San Joaquin kit fox. According to legend, in February 1994, state and federal agents raided Lin's farm, carted off his tractor, and filed criminal charges against him for violating the Endangered Species Act.[181]

Property rights activists were particularly infuriated by efforts to protect the northern spotted owl. Bill Moshofsky, vice president of Oregonians in Action, told journalist Keith Schneider, "The Endangered Species Act leaves economic considerations, human considerations, jobs and common sense out of the loop. The sense people have here is that this was a manufactured crisis in order for preservationists to achieve their objective, which was to stop harvesting trees."[182] Laer Pearce, of the Southern California Homebuilders Association, lodged a similar complaint. "Frankly," he said, "the Endangered Species Act is used as a no-growth act, as well as a species preservation act."[183]

In addition to inflaming grassroots activists, the Endangered Species Act occasionally earned the wrath of conservative commentators, who disparaged the science on which the act was based. For example, a 1992 article in *Reason* magazine began with three anecdotes about people who could not do what they wanted on their land because of endangered species. It made the point that "[i]n these and many other cases, the Endangered Species Act has halted the plans and dreams of many thousands of ordinary Americans." Citing critiques by Julian Simon and Aaron Wildavsky of scientists' assessments of species extinction, the author went on to assert that the Endangered Species Act was "sacro-sanct because environmentalists and their friends inside the Beltway have convinced almost everyone that massive species extinction is occurring, that it threatens to destroy entire ecosystems, and that only the extreme measures legislated by the act can prevent an ecological catastrophe. The problem is that none of these assertions is supported by hard facts." Death and extinction, he added, are natural processes; attempting to preserve every species is "to try to end the process of evolution." In fact, he asserted, endangered species protection is driven by values, not science: environmentalists are trying to stop the clock. In the process, they are jeopardizing things that human beings value, such as "jobs, housing, privacy, and the freedom to do what we want when we want with what we own."[184]

Free market environmentalism—with its emphasis on property rights and commerce as mechanisms for environmental protection—provided an important policy-analytic foundation for ESA-reform activism. In a piece that appeared in the *Cato Journal* in 1981, Robert J. Smith asked why some species, such as the Atwater's greater prairie chicken, were going extinct, while others—including the Rhode Island Red, the Leghorn, and the Barred Rock—were not. He concluded that "[i]n all of these cases, it is clear that the problem of overexploitation or overharvesting is a result of the resources being under public rather than private owner-ship. . . . Wherever we have public ownership we find overuse, waste, and extinction; but private ownership results in sustained-yield use and preservation." In other words, according to Smith:

The problems of environmental degradation, overexploitation of natural resources, and depletion of wildlife all derive from their existence as common property resources. Wherever we find an approach to the extension of private property rights . . ., we find superior results. Wherever we have exclusive private ownership, whether it is organized around a profit-seeking or nonprofit undertaking, there are incentives for the private owners to preserve the resource. Self-interest drives the private property owners to careful management and protection of their resource.[185]

Ten years later, Ike Sugg made a similar point in the *Wall Street Journal*, where he pointed out that game ranches in Africa and North Texas had saved a host of rare species from extinction. The problem, he explained, was not putting a price on species; it was failing to privatize them. By contrast, listing a species as endangered has the perverse effect of discouraging its conservation by making it hard to sell, propagate, or otherwise handle. According to Sugg, "Those with an economic stake in a natural resource have every reason to conserve and care for it. With wildlife, the pursuit of profit motivates the rancher to maximize that which is valuable, which means increasing wildlife numbers. It means preserving the genetic purity of the species, from which its value is often derived. And it means taking care of the land—a collateral ecological benefit."[186] (Environmentalists and biologists pointed out that the vast majority of species have little or no economic value, and the main cause of extinction is habitat loss, so these prescriptions were unlikely to have wide application.)

## Antiregulatory Ideas Make Progress in the Courts

In addition to churning out policy analyses and popularizing alternative problem definitions and policy images that would enable them to challenge environmental laws in Congress, conservatives sought to achieve their antiregulatory goals through litigation. During the Bush administration, these tactics began to bear fruit. The courts had resisted incursions on the environmentally restrictive status quo by White House officials and agency officials during much of the Reagan administration. After nearly twelve years of conservative appointments, however, environmental groups could no longer count on the courts to be reliably friendly venues.[187] Between 1981 and 1988, Reagan appointed three of nine Supreme Court justices and 47 percent of all judges sitting on federal district and appeals courts. Of the 714 district, appellate, and Supreme Court judges on the federal bench in 1992, more than half were appointed by Reagan or Bush.[188] According to legal scholar William Kovacic, judges appointed by Reagan were more inclined than those appointed by Carter to adopt positions that either narrowed the application of existing pollution abatement requirements or discouraged the recognition of new obligations.[189] Moreover, differences in Carter and Reagan appointees' voting behavior were most pronounced in the D.C. Circuit, which—after the Supreme Court—is the most important venue for environmental policymaking. In the late 1980s and early 1990s, those judges began ruling with greater frequency than before against restrictive interpretations of environmental laws. Although they did not strike down broadly popular laws, they did weaken the tools available to environmentalists and deter aggressive implementation and enforcement by regulatory agencies.

Some conservatives were encouraged by what they regarded as the increasing willingness of judges to compel federal agencies to engage in cost-benefit analysis or risk balancing, even in the absence of a statutory mandate to do so. In the 1980s, after a decade of scrutinizing agency procedures using a "hard look" standard of judicial review, the courts began to adopt a more deferential posture toward agency decisions. According to conservative legal scholar Michael Greve, however, in the early 1990s, the D. C. Circuit adopted a third standard: "substantive review," in which judges engage in a probing analysis of the results of agency rulemaking.[190] According to Greve, this kind of review relies not on hewing to the statutory language or trying to discern legislative intent, but instead imputes to Congress a willingness to consider trade-offs between environmental and other objectives. For instance, in February 1992, the D.C. Circuit required the Department of Transportation to reconsider its 1990 fuel economy standards for cars in response to an argument by two conservative organizations—the Competitive Enterprise Institute and Consumer Alert—that the agency had to evaluate risk trade-offs; in particular, it had to consider the possibility that lighter, smaller cars were unsafe (*CEI and Consumer Alert v. NHTSA*). Although a handful of decisions rendered in the 1990s seemed to support Greve's claims, overall, there is little evidence that "substantive review" became the norm.

A more promising development for conservatives was the Supreme Court's propensity to deny environmental litigants standing to sue, thereby curbing the citizen suits that form the backbone of environmental law in the contemporary era.[191] In the 1990 case, *Lujan v. National Wildlife Federation*, the Supreme Court refused (5–4) to allow the National Wildlife Federation to challenge a decision by the Bureau of Land Management to open up a tract of public land to development. In his opinion for the court, Justice Antonin Scalia wrote that the two federation members who filed the complaint had not demonstrated any specific injury, beyond asserting that they had recreational and aesthetic interests in the land under consideration. Two years later, in *Lujan v. Defenders of Wildlife* (1992), the Court rejected (7–2) environmentalists' standing claim on the grounds that the plaintiffs would not suffer a "redressable" injury as a result of an Interior Department decision to forgo review of a U.S. government decision to fund two large overseas development projects.[192] Under the Endangered Species Act, federal agencies must consult with the wildlife agencies to make sure their actions are not likely to jeopardize endangered or threatened species, or destroy their habitats. A 1978 rule extended the scope of review to agency actions overseas. In 1986, however, the Interior Department reversed its position and announced that the law did *not* apply to U.S.-funded projects overseas. The district court struck down the Reagan-era regulation, and the Eighth Circuit affirmed that decision. But Justice Scalia, who authored the opinion for the court, said that just because the Endangered Species Act contains a citizen suit provision, that fact does not mean any person can sue to force the government to comply with required procedures. Rather, individuals must prove they have suffered concrete, imminent, and individualized harm as a result of the procedural violation.

The federal courts also proved to be critical venues for validating property rights claims during the late 1980s and early 1990s. A series of cases decided by the Supreme Court lent support to activists' "regulatory takings" claims. In *First English Evangelical Church v. County of Los Angeles* (1987), Los Angeles County had barred the First English Evangelical Church from rebuilding a summer camp after a flood on land it owned because the buildings would have violated a county flood control ordinance. The Court ruled (6–3) that if there had been a taking as a result of regulation, even if the rule was subsequently withdrawn, then compensation would have been required. That same year, in *Nollan v. California Coastal Commission*, the Court ruled that the coastal commission would have to compensate the Nollans if it required them to donate a portion of their land to the state as a public easement—a condition the commission had imposed in exchange for granting the family permission to replace their bungalow with a three-bedroom house. In this case, the Court specified that an "essential nexus" must exist between the end advanced and the conditions imposed by a regulation; otherwise, wrote Justice Scalia, the regulation is "an out-and-out plan of extortion." (In the same session, however, the Supreme Court ruled in *Keystone Bituminous Coal Association v. DeBenedictus* that regulation by the State of Pennsylvania did not cause a regulatory taking because it advanced a "legitimate state interest" and did not deprive the property owner of all economically viable use.)

Five years later, in *Lucas v. South Carolina Coastal Commission* (1992), the Court devised a new takings test and then remanded the case to the South Carolina Supreme Court, requiring it to apply the new test to the facts of the case. Following this directive, the state supreme court ultimately ruled there *had* been a taking and required the state to compensate David Lucas, whose land had been rendered completely "valueless" by the recently adopted Beachfront Management Act. The Supreme Court's ruling in this case implied that if a new law imposes restrictions that render a property valueless after the property is purchased, owners are entitled to payment.

Even more hospitable to regulatory takings claims was the U.S. Court of Federal Claims. In the early 1990s, developers, timber companies, farmers, and others filed a record number of suits in the court of claims, arguing that environmental regulations had restricted their rights to use their own property, amounting to a constitutional taking.[193] The nearly two hundred takings lawsuits pending in the claims court in 1992 included cases in which the government had required property owners to clean up toxic wastes, regulated grazing and water rights, bought land for national parks, restricted mining, and set aside land to protect wetlands. On several occasions, the claims court and the U.S. Court of Appeals for the Federal Circuit, which hears appeals from this particular court, found that landowners affected by environmental regulations were entitled to compensation.

In *Florida Rock Industry v. United States*, for example, claims court judge Loren A. Smith awarded Florida Rock slightly more than $1 million plus interest because the Army Corps of Engineers had refused to grant the company a permit to extract limestone from the South Florida Everglades. Judge Smith found a taking even though Florida Rock had received offers for the property that would have allowed it to recover more than twice the purchase price. (In 1994, the appeals court affirmed the "partial taking" in this case.) In a second case, *Loveladies Harbor, Inc. v. United States*, the corps had barred a development company in Long Beach, New Jersey, from building houses on 12.5 acres of low-lying beachfront property, the last undeveloped portion of a 250-acre parcel the company bought in 1956 for $300,000. In 1990, Judge Smith awarded the company $2.68 million plus interest because he viewed the wetland protection restrictions as a taking of private property. Again, the appeals court affirmed his ruling.

In late 1991, in the largest judgment of its kind and the strongest legal challenge ever to the Interior Department's authority to regulate strip mining, the claims court directed the government to pay a coal company in Wyoming more than $150 million because the Interior Department had barred mining in a protected area near the Tongue River (*Whitney Benefits Inc. v. U.S.*). In the spring of 1994, the Federal Circuit affirmed the claims court's judgment and ruled that the company was entitled to compound interest, so the judgment grew to $250 million. (The government appealed the ruling to the Supreme Court, which declined to hear the case.)

Conservatives were ebullient about their successes in the claims court system, which had been reinvigorated by a reorganization in the early 1980s.[194] Between them, Reagan and Bush had appointed twelve of the court's sixteen judges; Reagan had renominated the other four judges after the court's reorganization. As Clint Bolick, president of the conservative Institute for Justice explained, "The Claims Court is a place where the Reagan and Bush Administration have been able to place top-notch conservative judges without getting much attention. That is the result of liberals being somewhat asleep at the switch and the Administrations' being extremely sophisticated in their selection and placement of judges."[195] In particular, they credited Judge Smith with "transforming the claims court into a haven for defending the sanctity of property rights."[196]

Taken together, the takings cases of the late 1980s and early 1990s established clear limitations on government's regulatory authority. They also increased the burden on regulators to provide detailed analysis in support of their judgments. Perhaps more important, although property rights advocates' victories in federal court were circumscribed, they intimidated state and local officials, especially because they seemed to reinforce ongoing efforts to pass state takings laws.

## Environmental Protection Atrophies under George H. W. Bush

During the 1980s and early 1990s, some environmentalists accepted the mainstream critique of the existing regulatory framework—either because they were convinced by it, or because they wanted to stave off a backlash, or some combination of the two. At the same time, the antiregulatory storyline gained momentum. Especially commonplace were assertions about the elitism and irrationality of environmentalism; the need for a more rational (less moralistic), "fact-based" approach to environmental protection; and the beneficial effects of relying on the private sector, rather than government, to provide environmental amenities.[197]

Even as proponents of the antiregulatory storyline were becoming more strident, President Bush initially sought to rehabilitate a restrictive approach to environmental protection, particularly in the area of pollution control. As a result, after declining under Reagan, the pace of regulation picked up again under Bush: nearly 4,900 federal regulations were being written as of December 1991, compared with 4,000 at any given time during the Reagan years; also rising were the number of entries in the *Federal Register*, the number of employees working in the regulatory agencies, and the costs of administering regulations.[198] Similarly, after falling during the 1980s, the amount of money authorized by the federal government for natural resource and environmental programs rose to about $17 billion in 1994 dollars for fiscal year 1993—about what it had been before Reagan took office.[199] (As environmentalists pointed out, however, that increase was not commensurate with the growth in agencies' statutory responsibilities between 1981 and 1992.) Most visible of all was the president's sponsorship of the Clean Air Act Amendments, which passed in 1990 after a decade of delay.

After passing the Clean Air Act Amendments, however, the Bush administration rarely pressed to make air pollution controls more restrictive, despite evidence of growing hazards. One former EPA official characterized the Bush years as a period of "benign neglect."[200] Bill Reilly's effective management and his efforts to restore the EPA's reputation for integrity and independence raised morale at the agency, but he was a White House outsider and often lost important battles with the president's conservative advisors, who consistently sought to delay or relax implementation of the Clean Air Act. The president was even more disengaged with respect to biodiversity conservation, and drift was apparent in that realm as well. Bush was unwilling or unable to resolve the major conservation issue of his presidency, the dilemma over protecting the spotted owl, so it was left to the next president. He was also increasingly loath to antagonize western resource users, who resented environmental restrictions.

In July 1991, Bush created the President's Commission on Environmental Quality. He named twenty-five top business and environmental leaders to the panel. His ostensible aim was to spur innovation and cooperation between environmentalists and business, with the ultimate goal of fostering nonregulatory solutions. Conservatives dismissed the panel, and most environmentalists viewed its formation as a public relations move. The president's other efforts to "balance" the competing demands of environmentalists and their critics also drew conservative ire. In the *National Review*, Warren Brookes argued that Reagan stimulated the economy by unleashing entrepreneurialism and risk taking, but the Bush administration was tamping it down with his timidity and his conciliatory approach to policymaking. "Nowhere is the threat to risk-taking from rising statism greater," warned Brookes, "than in the Bush administration's attempt to appease the 'killer watermelons' of the environmental movement (green on the outside, politically pink on the inside) with a furious regulatory assault on insignificant dangers to health and the environment."[201] For conservatives, the one bright spot was the courts, where their ideas seemed to be making slow but steady inroads, thanks to a carefully calculated effort to transform the judicial landscape by filing cases in unsettled areas of the law, popularizing conservative legal arguments, and getting allies appointed to the federal court.

Clearly, to complete the job a direct challenge to the regulatory status quo would be required. The energy for that challenge would come from the West, where a fiercely antiregulatory movement was brewing. According to political scientist Jacqueline Vaughn Switzer, the link between policy entrepreneurs in the conservative movement and activists in the wise use and property rights movements was both ideological and pragmatic; conservative think tanks and legal foundations provided analytical ballast, while grassroots activism provided political legitimacy for antiregulatory ideas.[202] Both entities had strong industry backing because they espoused the virtues of corporate capitalism. The result of this three-way alliance was a potent surge of support for conservative Republicans that enabled the party to take control of the House of Representatives in 1994, for the first time in decades. Not long after President Clinton took office, newly elected conservatives would draw heavily on the antiregulatory storyline to launch a major series of challenges to U.S. environmental regulations since the environmental era began—this time in the legislative arena.

# 6

# Bill Clinton Confronts a Conservative Congress

By the time William Jefferson Clinton took office in January 1993, there was a clear and significant divide on environmental issues among the nation's political elites. On the one hand, environmentalists began the 1990s "never stronger or more confident."[1] They experienced huge membership and budget increases in the 1980s, and there was a massive Earth Day celebration in 1990.[2] After briefly receding in salience in 1991, environmental protection was a prominent theme in the 1992 presidential campaign, particularly in the Pacific Northwest, where the spotted owl issue continued to fester. Clinton's selection of running mate Tennessee senator Al Gore, a well-known environmentalist, clearly reflected Democrats' efforts to claim the environmental mantle. As November neared, the Bush campaign retreated from its aggressive antiregulatory stance, fearing that it would backfire at the polls.

On the other hand, throughout the late 1980s and early 1990s, conservative think tanks disseminated an analytic framework that comprehensively dismissed pollution control regulation, and grassroots activists developed a complementary storyline disparaging federal efforts at biodiversity conservation. Bolstering this backlash was rising frustration among municipal officials about the costs of implementing environmental rules.[3] The result was increasing polarization around environmental protection. As a New York Times editorial observed in 1993, "No issue inspires more heat and hyperbole. No country spends more money . . . and imposes more regulation to keep itself clean. But money and laws have not achieved consensus. America is swarming with green activists—and with critics who believe that the cleanliness crusade exacts too great a toll in jobs and economic growth."[4]

This polarization curtailed the Clinton administration's ability to move policy in a restrictive direction. Clinton sought to change the policymaking context with rhetoric that emphasized the compatibility of *environmental health and economic well-being. He also appointed a clutch of dyed-in-the-wool environmentalists to administer the federal institutions with jurisdiction over the environment. But those appointees found their discretion circumscribed by a group of emboldened and well-organized conservatives, whose influence on administrative decision making was enhanced by their increasing representation and clout in two other venues. By the 1990s, after twelve years of Republican appointments, the federal courts—which previously had favored precautionary interpretations of environmental law—were more hospitable to antiregulatory ideas. The conservative mobilization had also paid off in Congress, where a newly installed Republican leadership launched a series of direct attacks on environmental regulation. When those challenges were repudiated, conservatives tried to undermine protective measures more covertly, through legislative riders.*

*Conservatives' antiregulatory policy initiatives played out in different ways on the issues of air pollution control, endangered species conservation, and climate change. Direct challenges to the Clean Air Act were not only rebuffed but, as in the 1980s, prompted a proenvironmental mobilization. EPA administrator Carol Browner both facilitated and capitalized on the increased salience of air pollution to advance a risk-averse agenda, and the best conservatives could do was slow its progress. Conservative challenges to endangered species conservation were more effective: in hopes of blunting attacks on the Endangered Species Act, Bruce Babbitt, the secretary of the interior, adopted a conciliatory posture, promoting approaches that involved collaborating with and providing incentives to landowners and developers. Most effective of all, though, were conservatives' efforts to prevent action on climate change. With the help of Democrats from coal-dependent states, they stymied White House plans to ratify the world's first international agreement on climate change, the Kyoto Protocol, in the Senate; forced Clinton to propose only voluntary greenhouse gas emissions control measures; and restrained agencies' efforts to pursue the treaty's goals through administrative actions.*

## Creating a Proenvironmental Context, with an Antiregulatory Twist

The new president gave conservatives ample reason to fear that more stringent environmental regulations were imminent. Most galling to conservatives, Vice President Al Gore was the author of *Earth in the Balance*, a manifesto decrying humans' environmental impact and calling for drastic action to remediate it. Also worrisome, the Clinton/Gore team had made a host of ambitious campaign promises, from raising the corporate average fuel economy standards for cars, encouraging mass transit, and funding the development of renewable energy to providing new incentives for recycling, passing a revised Clean Water Act with standards for nonpoint sources, preserving the Arctic National Wildlife Refuge from oil and gas exploration, and limiting carbon dioxide emissions.[5]

Conservative concerns were borne out when, upon taking office, Clinton appointed proenvironmental agency heads. For the post of EPA administrator, Clinton nominated Carol Browner, who as the chief of the Florida Department of Environmental Regulation had earned a reputation among some business leaders as "hard-nosed," "unrealistic," and "way too intense."[6] Assisting Browner were a host of other environmentally oriented assistant administrators: for water, Robert Perciasepe, formerly Maryland's secretary of the environment; pediatrician and epidemiologist Lynn Goldman for toxics and pesticides; Mary Nichols, who had held a variety of environmental positions in California, for air and radiation; and former Sierra Club activist David Gardiner for policy, planning and evaluation.

Conservatives also found little to admire in the selection of Bruce Babbitt as interior secretary. Babbitt, a former governor of Arizona, was president of the League of Conservation Voters. A host of other Interior Department appointees had strong ties to the environmental movement as well: George Frampton Jr., former president of the Wilderness Society, as assistant secretary for fish and wildlife and parks; Bonnie Cohen, senior vice president of the National Trust for Historic Preservation, as assistant secretary for policy, management and budget; Elizabeth Rieke, director of the Arizona Department of Water Resources, as assistant secretary for water and science; Jim Baca, an environmentally oriented New Mexico land commissioner, as head of the Bureau of Land Management; and Mollie Beattie, who had held several natural resource management positions in Vermont, as director of the Fish and Wildlife Service.

In addition to making proenvironmental appointments, Clinton used the budget to enhance the prospects for restrictive policies. Although he sought to reduce spending for the environment and natural resources by 5 percent for fiscal year 1994 as part of an overall budget-cutting effort, the president nevertheless requested increases in the budgets of both the Interior Department and the EPA. His proposal increased the Interior Department's budget by 6 percent, to $9.5 billion, including a 20 percent increase in the allotment for the Fish and Wildlife Service. The EPA's budget, including stimulus funds, was slated to grow 6 percent over its 1993 level, to $7.3 billion. In addition, as part of the budget, Clinton proposed raising fees for grazing, logging, and mining on public lands. He quickly dropped the idea, however, after western members of Congress threatened to sink his entire economic agenda.

Clinton also relaxed the centralized control over regulatory policy that had begun under Carter and tightened under Bush and Reagan. He abolished Bush's Council on Competitiveness and, in late September 1993, replaced executive orders 12291 (cost-benefit) and 12498 (regulatory takings) with Executive Order 12866. The new order limited reviews by OMB's Office of Information and Regulatory Affairs to "significant regulatory actions" (those expected to have an annual effect on the economy of $100 million or more). It further moderated the OMB review process by requiring agencies to assess the costs and benefits of proposed regulations, but to maximize net benefits only if the statute did not require another approach. It increased transparency by requiring OIRA and the agencies to publicly identify substantive changes made during OIRA's review, requiring OIRA to disclose all documents exchanged with the agency during the review process and forcing industries that argued against regulations to put their views on record.[7] Finally, according to one former EPA official, the Clinton administration was far more interested than previous administrations in identifying and quantifying the *benefits* of environmental regulation and their impacts on sensitive subpopulations.[8]

Even as he rendered the institutional context more hospitable to environmental restrictions, Clinton assured the public that he was receptive to antiregulatory ideas. Upon taking office he made eliminating the budget deficit—which stood at 4.7 percent of GDP, up from 2.8 percent of GDP in 1989—his top priority.[9] To the dismay of many environmentalists, Clinton proposed to demonstrate his commitment to budget cutting by abolishing the Council on Environmental Quality and transferring its duties to the EPA.[10] (He promised to compensate for eliminating the council by elevating the EPA to a cabinet-level department.) When some lawmakers balked, saying the EPA would not be able to ensure that other agencies pursued environmentally sound policies, the White House agreed to retain the council, but cut its staff to three and its annual budget from $2.5 million at the end of Bush's tenure to $375,000 for fiscal year 1994.[11]

In addition, shortly after taking office, Clinton issued Executive Order 12839, which required each agency with over one hundred employees to eliminate no less than 4 percent of its civilian personnel positions over three fiscal years.[12] In September 1993, he issued Executive Order 12861, which required all civilian departments and agencies to review their internal management rules and scrap obsolete ones, in order to achieve a 50 percent reduction in regulation within three years. And he tasked Vice President Gore with "reinventing" the federal regulatory apparatus. In justifying this National Performance Review, the administration tapped antiregulatory themes, saying the existing system "makes it hard for our civil servants to do what we pay them for, and frustrates taxpayers who rightfully expect their money's worth." For his part, Gore promised to make the bureaucracy more efficient, by "replac[ing] regulations with incentives" and "search[ing] for market, not administrative solutions."[13]

Clinton's efforts at reframing and repositioning were mirrored in the 1992 Democratic platform, which blatantly co-opted conservative language. It "reject[ed] both the do-nothing government of the last 12 years as well as the big government theory that says we can hamstring business and tax and spend our way to prosperity." Instead, the platform went on to say, "we offer a third way." Strikingly, the platform asserted, "We honor business as a noble endeavor." Echoing the Republican platforms of prior years, it also demanded a restoration of "basic American values," including a greater emphasis on "work, family and individual responsibility."[15]

In the environmental realm, Clinton fostered a rhetorical context compatible with the mainstream critique. A political pragmatist, Clinton was inclined to worry that complex regulations deterred business, and that incentives might achieve better results at lower costs. To garner support from the political center, he sought to reposition himself as a New Democrat—as opposed to a proregulation, antibusiness (or New Deal) Democrat. In 1993, the Progressive Policy Institute—emulating the Heritage Foundation's 1981 *Mandate for Leadership*—released a volume entitled *Mandate for Change* that outlined the ideas of the New Democrats and cited Clinton as a prominent example. The theme was that Democrats needed to move beyond the traditional prescriptions of left and right. For example, economist Robert Stavins and energy analyst Thomas Grumbly argued for eschewing command-and-control regulations in favor of market-based approaches. "Now," they argued, "in an era of new environmental challenges and heightened sensitivity to regulatory compliance burdens, market forces can offer in many circumstances a more powerful, far-reaching, efficient, and democratic tool than centralized regulations for protecting the environment."[14] Among the benefits of this approach, according to Stavins and Grumbly, was that it would focus the public debate on efficiency, rather than values.

At the same time, Clinton sought to revive the notion that economic well-being and environmental quality were not in tension but were, in fact, complementary. The administration's environmental transition report asserted that bold environmental protection measures were compatible with long-term economic growth and were, in fact, necessary to a sustainable economy.[16] In an Earth Day speech delivered in April 1993, Clinton pronounced, "We think you can't have a healthy economy without a healthy environment. We need not choose between breathing clean air and bringing home secure paychecks." Following Gore, Clinton insisted that a harmonious relationship between the environment and the economy could be achieved through entrepreneurialism and the development of new technology.

### Conservatives Step Up the War of Ideas

Conservatives were not assuaged by Clinton's articulation of views that were anathema to many environmentalists; in fact, the ascension of Clinton and Gore further galvanized the members of an already agitated conservative movement by giving them a common enemy. The volume of publications and events issuing from conservative outlets grew dramatically during the Clinton years. Many conservative think tanks more than doubled their budgets between 1992 and 1996, and their revenues continued to grow as the decade progressed, with much of the money coming from corporations and businesspeople. The budget of the Competitive Enterprise Institute, for example, went from $500,000 in 1990 to $2.5 million in 1996.[17] Reflecting on these trends, commentator David Callahan argued that the influence of these organizations, though hard to quantify, was undeniable. "Most impressive," he said, "is the way in which conservative policy entrepreneurs have been so skilled and invested so heavily in marketing their grand story of American politics to the media. If national politics can be seen largely as a contest of broad frameworks, there is little question that conservatives have won this game in recent years."[18]

While environmentalists continued to emphasize the seriousness of environmental problems, conservative think tanks supported authors who that sought to discredit those claims and impugn the motives of those who made them.[19] For example, in *Science Under Siege*, a book funded by the conservative Sarah Scaife and W. H. Brady Foundations, writer Michael Fumento argued that environmentalists routinely exaggerate the risks posed by technology and modern life, resulting in irrational public policies.[20] Similarly, in *Apocalypse Not*, published by the Cato Institute, business professor Ben Bolch and chemist Harold Lyons complained that environmentalists ignore relative risks and foment hysteria among an ill-informed public. They observed that "the people who reside in the market-oriented economies of the West enjoy a cleaner and safer environment than ever experienced in modern history."[21] Fred L. Smith, president and founder of the Competitive Enterprise Institute, charged that "[t]he taste for zero risk is one in which only the richest and most advanced societies can indulge. . . . We are no longer content to take the bitter of uncertainty with the sweet of progress; instead, we insist on having the sweet only and rely on government to protect us in advance from the bitter."[22] The volume *Environmental Politics: Public Costs, Private Rewards*, edited by Fred L. Smith and Michael Greve, executive director of the Center for Individual Rights, sought to debunk the "public interest view" of environmental policy by showing that "[f]ar more often than is commonly realized, the purpose and effect of environmental policy is to serve narrow political and economic objectives, *not* environmental objectives."[23]

In his 1992 book *The Way Things Ought to Be*, conservative commentator Rush Limbaugh laid out a public philosophy that incorporated all the elements of the antiregulatory storyline. Limbaugh labeled environmental leaders "socialists and enviro-religious fanatics" and ridiculed the "presumptuous" idea that humans could destroy the planet. "With the collapse of Marxism," he wrote, "environmentalism has become the new refuge of socialist thinking. The environment is a great way to advance a political agenda that favors central planning and an intrusive government. . . . Actually, it is a modern form of pantheism, where nature is divine. This group wants to preserve the earth at all costs, even if it means that much of the Third World will be forever condemned to poverty." Regardless of which perspective they have, he added, "a common characteristic of those in the radical environmental movement is the belief that private property rights will have to be severely curbed in this country." What they really want, he said, is "to attack our way of life. Their primary enemy: capitalism."[24]

Limbaugh also disparaged the "vocal, ideological, agenda-armed scientists" who raise alarms about environmental problems and propagate "junk science" in hopes of garnering more research funding. He urged readers not to treat scientists with deference, saying, "I refuse to let scientific elitism prevent me from asking commonsense questions that are skeptical of their 'findings.'" (For scientific advice on the environment, Limbaugh relied on *Trashing the Planet*, by Dixy Lee Ray and Lou Guzzo.) Drawing on the antiregulatory storyline, Limbaugh argued that "The key to cleaning up our environment is unfettered free enterprise, our system of reward." By contrast, "When no one owns private property, there is no incentive to keep it clean and pure because no one has a stake in keeping up its value." He concluded, "My friends, the earth is a remarkable creation and is capable of great rejuvenation. We can't destroy it. It can fix itself. We shouldn't go out of our way to do damage, but neither should we buy into the hysteria and monomania which preaches, in essence, that we don't belong here. We have a right to use the earth to make our lives better."[25]

Limbaugh and other conservatives were particularly aggrieved by steps the federal government had taken to phase out chlorofluorocarbons. In 1992 and 1993, after Bush accelerated the CFC phaseout, the *Wall Street Journal*, the *National Review*, and *Omni* magazine published articles portraying ozone depletion as a politically motivated scam. Dixy Lee Ray devoted a chapter to ozone depletion in *Trashing the Planet*, in which she cited two main sources: physicist S. Fred Singer and Rogelio Maduro, who had a bachelors degree in geology. Maduro argued (incorrectly) that natural sources of chlorine in the stratosphere dwarfed the contribution from man-made CFCs.[26] Singer dismissed Maduro's argument but took the position that the ozone-depletion problem was not serious enough to warrant a federal response. Other skeptics pointed out that the dramatic ozone loss forecast by scientists in early 1992 had not materialized. Previewing the tactics they would use to challenge climate change science, a slew of editorials and articles in the conservative press questioned the motives of the researchers who had sounded the alarm.

In the mid-1990s, as the political controversy over the environment heated up, a raft of books emerged—including works by journalists Gregg Easterbrook and Ronald Bailey—that purported to set the record straight on the environment. In the tradition of economist Julian Simon, they claimed to approach the issue armed with facts, rational thinking, and optimism.[27] In *The True State of the Planet*, a Competitive Enterprise Institute project, Bailey argued that "many of the looming threats predicted in the early days of the environmental movement turned out to be exaggerated." As a result, "Resources are being poured into areas that pose little harm to either the natural world or to human beings, while other more critical problems receive relatively little attention." History, Bailey wrote, had shown that "environmental improvement depends on rapid economic progress"[28]

Geologist James Dunn and engineer John Kinney portrayed their book, *Conservative Environmentalism,* as "an adventure to see where facts and a positive attitude can lead us." They shunned the label "environmentalist," because they did not want to be associated with members of "'the environmental cult or religion' with all its accompanying irrationality." Natural resources are not finite but inexhaustible, they asserted, because *"technology creates resources."* In fact, "Industrial nations are expanding their forests, increasing many wildlife populations, improving soil productivity, enhancing water resources, and increasing biodiversity." Dunn and Kinney concluded that America's government should not discourage production of wealth or technological change. Instead, "America must massively reduce environmental laws and resultant regulations pertaining to both humans and nature," and management of the environment should be in the hands of trained professionals who have "no political agenda except that they feel people are more important than nature."[29]

Some conservative-leaning economists sought to create a favorable image for a set of environmental policies that they believed would enhance the efficiency of the regulatory system. For example, two monographs issued by the American Enterprise Institute in conjunction with the Brookings Institution proffered a blueprint for environmental policy reforms. The first, *An Agenda for Federal Regulatory Reform,* argued that the regulatory burden on business had grown dramatically and needed repair. "More intelligent policies," the authors averred, "could achieve the same goals at much less cost or more ambitious goals at the same cost."[30] The authors proposed a set of now-familiar principles that emphasized protecting the economic well-being of consumers and producers, including: requiring extensive and transparent use of cost-benefit analysis; allowing the OMB to review existing and not just proposed regulations; and enabling the courts to use a benefit-cost standard in judicial review, even if the statute did not require such balancing. The second pamphlet, entitled *Improving Regulatory Accountability,* advocated a requirement that the federal government produce a full accounting of the costs and benefits of federal regulations. The authors' ostensible purpose was to make "an arcane, unsystematic process more transparent and systematic," with the ultimate goal of producing "more effective and less burdensome regulations."[31]

But Fred L. Smith and other libertarians rejected both greater reliance on market-based regulatory tools—such as emissions fees and tradable permits—and what they labeled managerial reforms—such as scientific peer review, improved risk assessment, and better interagency coordination. Both types of reforms, Smith contended, would perpetuate biased risk selection and inefficient regulation and so were second-best solutions. The most efficient prescription, he argued, would be to produce environmental benefits by establishing new property rights and relying on private, voluntary arrangements. In the rare event of market failure, the common law of torts and contracts would provide an adequate remedy. As Smith explained, the basic premise of free-market environmentalism is that "[m]yriads of voluntary transactions register private risk preferences and tolerances far more accurately than even the most informed and open public process." In fact, he added, "Rather than viewing the world in terms of market failure, we should view the problem of externalities as a *failure to permit markets* and create markets where they do not yet—or no longer—exist."[32] Smith and other proponents of free-market environmentalism were convinced that "[a] world of voluntary arrangements may not be perfect, but it is the best solution to our ecological problems. Only under a system where resources are privately held will people have the ability to express their environmental values accurately."[33]

One legal shift and a pair of media innovations enhanced the ability of conservative activists to propagate an antiregulatory storyline that drew on both critiques. The legal shift was the 1987 repeal of the fairness doctrine in broadcast regulation, which had required that equal time be allotted to all sides in any discussion of controversial issues. This change paved the way for explicitly ideological television programming. In the late 1980s and early 1990s, new technology—particularly the satellite dish and the Internet—facilitated the emergence of national talk radio, and, in turn, political shows. The creation of the World Wide Web in the early 1990s further enabled the rapid dissemination of ideas and opinions to new audiences.[34]

New outlets allowed experts and activists to reach an even broader audience than they had through the traditional conservative media, such as the *Wall Street Journal* editorial page. For example, shortly after its inception in 1988, *The Rush Limbaugh Show* became the top-rated political radio program in the country, and that popularity soon translated into political influence. In fact, according to Republican House majority leader Tom DeLay, strategist Richard Viguerie, and members of the congressional freshman class, Limbaugh played a major role in the Republican takeover of the House in 1994.[35] (The freshman class of Republicans made Limbaugh an honorary member.) Fox News experienced a meteoric rise in popularity during the latter half of the 1990s: available to seventeen million homes when it was launched in 1996, by 2000, Fox was available in more than fifty-four million households.[36] Although both talk radio and cable TV were available to everyone, liberals were much slower to capitalize.

According to communication scholars Kathleen Hall Jamieson and Joseph Capella, Fox News and conservative talk shows like Limbaugh's "constitute important venues for reinforcing the tenets and values of Reagan conservatism." By charging the mainstream media with employing a double standard, these outlets "marginalize mainstream media and minimize their effects," while "insulat[ing] their audiences from persuasion by Democrats by building up a body of opinion and evidence that makes Democratic views seem alien and unpalatable."[37] Political scientist Markus Prior attributes the increasing polarization in the United States during the 1990s to this shift to a "high-choice media environment." According to Prior, "the spread of cable and the Internet increased partisan polarization among voters by changing the composition of the voting public because less partisan entertainment-seekers [dropped] out, while more partisan new fans [voted] even more reliably than before."[38]

## A Conservative Congress Challenges Environmental Restrictions

Agitation by conservative advocates emboldened conservatives in Congress, where Clinton faced growing resistance. By the early 1990s, Congress had undergone a profound transformation—from the one Reagan encountered, in which a bipartisan majority supported the environmental framework of the 1970s, to one in which the two parties were increasingly polarized on many issues, including the environment. During the 1970s, scores of Senate Democrats by the League of Conservation Voters were about 20 percentage points higher than those of Senate Republicans. But the average scores of Democrats and Republicans largely rose and fell in tandem until the early 1990s, when they began to diverge widely. The pattern in the House was similar (see Figures 6.1 and 6.2).[39] By 1993, Republicans' average LCV score in both the House and Senate was 19 percent, while Democrats averaged 75 percent in the Senate and 68 percent in the House.[40]

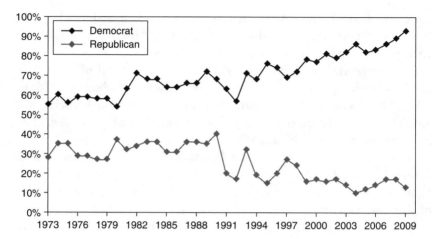

**Figure 6.1**
League of Conservation Voters Scores, House of Representatives

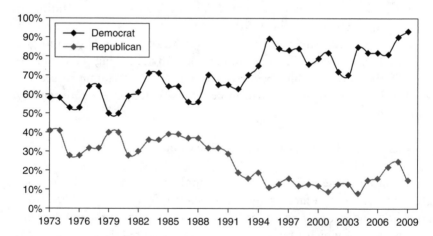

**Figure 6.2**
League of Conservation Voters Scores, Senate

**Layering Analytic Requirements on Top of Restrictive Policies**

Although polarization was already well under way in 1993, interest in measures designed to curb regulation was not limited to conservatives or even to Republicans. Several prominent Democratic senators promoted regulatory reform during the first session of the 103rd Congress. Democratic senator Mike Synar of Oklahoma, who routinely garnered high LCV scores, said that while the benefits of many environmental programs were not apparent, the "costs [were] out of sight."[41] Although he did not embrace all the managerial reforms endorsed by many economists, Synar perceived an opportunity in the impending revision of four major environmental statutes to "rationalize" the regulatory framework by incorporating three mechanisms that had gained traction in the environmental policy community. These were: requirements that agencies consider the cost of a regulation before issuing it, increased spending on more serious problems and reduced spending on less significant ones, and more flexibility for businesses and municipalities. In March 1993, Montana senator Max Baucus, the Democratic chair of the Environment and Public Works Committee, held hearings to flesh out the prospects for a more comprehensive and effective approach to environmental protection that would incorporate some of these reforms. And New York senator Daniel Patrick Moynihan, a Democrat who in 1996 would receive a 100 percent LCV score, introduced a bill that required federal regulators to amass stronger scientific proof and convene expert panels to review environmental rules before issuing them.[42]

By 1994, however, the debate had become more rancorous and partisan in the House, and reform-minded Democrats in both chambers retreated, suspicious that proposals for new analytic requirements were a cover for conservative efforts to slow or prevent new regulations. After gaining approval by the Senate the year before, in early 1994, a bill to elevate the EPA to cabinet status was defeated on the House floor by a vote of 227 to 191. Conservatives in both parties refused to debate the bill unless votes were scheduled on an amendment written by Democratic senator Bennett Johnston of Louisiana that called for a specific estimate of the risk to public health and safety meant to be controlled by any environmental regulation, and a comparison of the risk addressed by the regulation to other risks faced by the public. (The amendment was ruled out of order under House procedures.) Senator Baucus—one of the ninety-five senators who had voted to add a risk-assessment provision to the EPA bill in 1993—had second thoughts in 1994. "Face it," he said.

"Some people are using these legitimate questions about costs and benefits to gut our hard-won environmental protections."[43]

In fact, with distrust over proponents' motives increasing, efforts to attach cost-benefit or risk-assessment requirements, regulatory takings rules, and limits on unfunded mandates appeared likely to sink every major environmental law up for reauthorization in 1994—including the Clean Water Act, the Safe Drinking Water Act, the Endangered Species Act, the Mining Law of 1892, the Resource Conservation and Recovery Act, the Comprehensive Environmental Response, Compensation, and Liability Act (CERCLA; better known as the Superfund law), the Magnuson-Stevens Fishery Conservation and Management Act, and the Federal Insecticide, Fungicide and Rodenticide Act. Conservative legislators, such as California Republican Richard Pombo, defended the amendments as efficiency measures, saying they were intended to add "some common sense to the standard operating procedure of the Federal Government and to ease the burden of excessive regulation."[44] But pro-environvironmental legislators hesitated to open up laws for debate, fearful that they would be eviscerated. For his part, President Clinton declined to expend political capital fending off amendments to bills that were not at the core of his agenda. As a result, the environmental lobby was compelled to beat a tactical retreat. Jim Maddy, president of the LCV, said the best environmentalists could hope for was to prevent the 103rd Congress from weakening major laws.[45]

Then, two years into Clinton's presidency, Republicans took over both houses of Congress for the first time in thirty years. They were swept into power by a vocal conservative movement that had mobilized opponents of Clinton's efforts at health care reform and gun control. Many newly elected legislators had signed the Contract with America, a list of actions drawn up by the House Republican leadership and widely promoted by House minority whip Newt Gingrich to "rationalize" the federal government. The contract did not mention the word "environment" specifically, but it contained three commandments that had major implications for the implementation of environment policy: first, regulations should be imposed only after explicit consideration of whether the health risks justify their costs; second, property owners should be compensated if the value of their property is diminished by regulations that restrict its use; and third, the federal government should not impose costly burdens on state and local governments without funding those obligations.

After the election, Republicans had a 230–204 majority in the House (plus one Independent) and a 52–48 majority in the Senate. (The gap in the Senate widened to 54–46 after two conservative Democrats switched parties, and then fell back to 53–47 when Oregon Democrat Ron Wyden replaced Republican Robert Packwood in late 1995.) The Republican takeover owed much of its success to voters in the West.[46] There, Republican politicians had capitalized on the hostility emanating from the wise use and county supremacy movements. When the Clinton administration tried to phase out government subsidies for mining, logging, and grazing on federal land in early 1993, Republicans had labeled the effort a "war on the West"—a slogan that moved quickly to bumper stickers and became a rallying cry in the 1994 election campaigns.[47] The expression capitalized on polls that, although they showed overwhelming support for environmental set-asides in the West, also revealed a "ferocious fear of government in all its forms of regulation, from banning handguns to restricting off-road vehicles."[48]

The new class of Republican legislators was extraordinarily homogeneous on environmental issues: nearly half of the 73 members of the House freshman class received a zero rating from the League of Conservation Voters in 1995; the average LCV score for the class was 12.[49] As a result of this infusion of conservative Republicans, in 1995, the number of zero LCV scores in both chambers reached a record high of 135, compared with only 2 in 1993.[50] The disparity between the two parties was greater than ever before: House Republicans' average score was 15, while Democrats averaged 76; in the Senate, Republicans' average score was 11, while Democrats averaged 89. A 1995 statement by Republican representative Thomas J. Bliley Jr. of Virginia exemplified the attitude of many in the new Congress. "The American people sent us a message in November, loud and clear: Tame this regulatory beast! Our constituents want us to break the Feds' stranglehold on our economy and to get them out of decisions that are best left to the individual."[51]

Hoping to improve the prospects for their antiregulatory agenda, the Republican leadership appointed westerners sympathetic to the wise use and property rights movements to chairmanships of the major environmental committees. In the Senate, Alaskan Frank Murkowski took over the Natural Resources Committee, and Jim Hansen of Utah gained control of the National Parks, Forests and Lands Subcommittee. Environmentalists' only hope in the Senate lay with moderate Republican John Chafee of Rhode Island, who took over the Environment and Public Works Committee and had a lifetime LCV score of 90. In the House, Republican Don Young of Alaska became chair of the Natural Resources Committee; his first act was to drop the word "Natural" from the committee's title. The deeply antiregulatory Bliley of Virginia took over the Commerce Committee. And Tom DeLay of Texas, a vocal critic of the Endangered Species Act, became House majority whip. In addition, the leadership abolished a committee with a penchant for restrictive rules—the House Merchant Marine and Fisheries Committee—and created a new entity whose purpose was to scrutinize environmental regulations: the Subcommittee for Economic Growth, Natural Resources, and Regulatory Relief. Heading the subcommittee was David McIntosh, an Indiana freshman who had previously directed Dan Quayle's Council on Competitiveness.

Operating from their new leadership positions, the members of the Alaskan delegation were particularly unified and effective in promoting development of natural resources. They were unabashed about using tactics such as writing letters to the Forest Service and the Justice Department demanding to know which of their employees had previously worked for advocacy groups bringing suits under the Endangered Species Act. Adhering to the antiregulatory storyline, they derided environmentalists as self-interested extremists: "They are Communists," Mr. Young said. "They believe in the communal ownership of all natural resources, including the land. And they believe that every community that lives off the land should also be owned by the government. That is their ultimate goal."[52] From Murkowski's perspective, "The cause [for environmentalists] is membership; the cause is dollars."[53]

In addition to revamping the institutional context, the conservative leadership sought to inject the antiregulatory storyline into the legislative debate with strategically crafted language. As Republicans prepared to take control of Congress in 1995, House Speaker-to-be Newt Gingrich enlisted conservative psychotherapist and management guru Morris Schechtman to help Republicans reframe their social agenda to avoid appearing insensitive. Schechtman explained to GOP lawmakers that they needed to "frame this switch without looking barbaric, which liberals call anyone who holds people responsible," and to persuade people that what Democrats characterized as a compassionate government was actually oppressive. For Schechtman, regulation of business fell under the rubric of caretaking, which made the intervenor feel better, not the recipient.[54]

At the start of the 1995 session, House Republicans declared their intention to rewrite the Superfund act, the Clean Water Act, the Safe Drinking Water Act, the Endangered Species Act, and parts of the Clean Air Act of 1990. Justifying their determination with an efficiency rationale, Gingrich said the policies of the past twenty years or more "have been absurdly expensive, created far more resistance than was necessary and misallocated resources on emotional and public relations grounds without regard to either scientific, engineering or economic rationality."[55] Conservatives' allies in think tanks and the business community were confident about their prospects. "The notion of a regulatory reform revolution is not overstated at all," said Jerry Jasinowski, president of the National Association of Manufacturers. "The center of gravity has moved to the right and ideas that were dismissed before are now more acceptable. We've never had anything of this magnitude and muscle."[56] "Americans believe Washington has gone too far in regulating and they want to turn the clock and the paperwork back," argued Republican pollster Frank Luntz.[57] William Niskanen, an economist with the Cato Institute, urged Republicans to use their newfound clout to rein in the "Nanny State."[58]

To create some breathing space for their reform efforts, in late 1994, Representatives DeLay and McIntosh and Republican senators Don Nickles of Oklahoma, Christopher Bond of Missouri, and Kay Bailey Hutchison of Texas introduced the Regulatory Transition Act of 1995, legislation that would place a thirteen-month moratorium on executive-branch regulatory activities.[59] Representative DeLay also created an ad hoc group named Project Relief, comprising 350 industry members who worked closely with legislative staff to craft and defend the regulatory moratorium. Turning to business for advice on this matter made sense, DeLay explained, because "they have the expertise."[60] Although it passed easily in the House (276–146), the moratorium faced stiff opposition in the more moderate Senate, where it ultimately died.

Undaunted, in early 1995, Republican lawmakers crafted a comprehensive reform that, although it did not challenge existing environmental laws directly, layered new analytic requirements on top of those laws. The main vehicle for implementing these regulatory reforms, introduced in the House in early 1995, was the Job Creation and Wage Enhancement Act of 1995 (H.R. 9). About half of the act's provisions aimed to stimulate the economy by providing tax breaks to individuals and investors; the remaining provisions intended to reduce the regulatory burden on businesses and individuals by substituting economic calculations for health and safety considerations. The act's provisions increased the ability of groups affected by regulations to challenge them, even before they were formal proposals; required risk-assessment and cost-benefit analyses in the initial phase of drafting a regulation, and subjected those analyses to review by outside experts and to legal challenge; created a regulatory "budget"—a specific ceiling on the cost of complying with all federal regulations—that would be capped below its current level; limited the government's ability to collect data or require public information disclosure; made it impossible for regulators to carry out unannounced inspections; and capped the level of programs the federal government could require state and local governments to implement without providing funding.[61]

In defending the bill, supporters echoed the antiregulatory rationale. "Current federal policies threaten the competitiveness of American business, stifle entrepreneurial activity and suppress economic growth and job creation," the House sponsors explained.[62] The EPA, which Gingrich called "the biggest job-killing agency in inner-city America," was a clear target of the legislation.[63] In February, after the Commerce Committee passed Title III of H.R. 9, an ebullient representative Bliley declared, "We took the first steps toward bringing the Federal regulatory monster under control."[64] In early March, the full House voted 277 to 141 in favor of H.R. 9. To dramatize the occasion, the bill's sponsors, flanked by representatives of major business groups, snipped a ribbon of red tape from a mock-up of the Statue of Liberty.[65]

But in the Senate—which was only narrowly controlled by Republicans, four of whom were moderate New Englanders with LCV scores in the 50s and 60s—there was markedly less enthusiasm for the kinds of far-reaching managerial reforms advocated by their House colleagues.[66] Kansas Republican Robert Dole, the Senate majority leader (and presidential aspirant), defended his companion to the House regulatory reform bill, S. 343, which was crafted largely by experts from the Heritage Foundation and the American Enterprise Institute with input from industry lobbyists. "Last November," Dole said, "the American people sent us a message.... Stop micromanaging our lives through burdensome and costly regulations."[67] The Senate Judiciary Committee proceeded to rubber-stamp the legislation in April, after Dole advanced it without formal debate or a vote. Ultimately, however, S. 343 failed on three consecutive cloture votes, even though a broad coalition of industries made it their highest priority and pushed for the most far-reaching version possible.

Proponents of deregulation chastised their colleagues for opposing the bill, charging them with disregarding the economic burden of complying with federal rules and ignoring popular opinion. "Most Americans are tired of big government and want Congress to use some common sense," complained Republican senators Orrin Hatch of Utah and John Kyl of

Arizona.[68] Nevertheless, a more modest regulatory reform bill approved by the Senate Governmental Affairs Committee failed as well, this time thanks to opposition from conservative Republicans. That bill, sponsored by Democrat John Glenn, also emphasized cost-benefit analysis but put many fewer hurdles in the way of new regulations. The Senate did, however, approve the Congressional Review Act, which enabled Congress to review and, if it chose, reject new rules within sixty legislative days of their issuance—a move supporters hoped would put a damper on the pace of rulemaking.

**Trying a Lower-Profile Approach: Appropriations Riders**
Upon encountering resistance in the Senate, House Republican leaders resorted to more arcane mechanisms for achieving their antiregulatory goals. They began using the appropriations process to cut the funding for environmental agencies and for activities within those agencies that they viewed as particularly onerous for business. For instance, the House proposed to slash the EPA's annual budget to $4.9 billion in 1996, a reduction of $2.3 billion from its 1995 spending level and the largest cut suggested for any major federal agency. Riders attached to the House budget proposal also targeted specific programs. One rider eliminated the agency's capacity to enforce its trip reduction and vehicle inspection programs; another blocked the imposition of "maximum available control technology" rules on the toxic emissions of oil refineries; a third prevented the EPA from extending requirements for risk management plans imposed on the chemical industry by the Clean Air Act Amendments of 1990.

Budget riders were not limited to the EPA. Conservatives also attached provisions to natural resource agencies' budgets that would open the Arctic National Wildlife Refuge to oil and gas exploration, prevent the administration from implementing the Endangered Species Act while Congress worked on a rewrite of the law, short-circuit a comprehensive study of the Columbia River basin and northern Rocky Mountain region, and require the Forest Service to dramatically increase commercial logging in Alaska's Tongass National Forest. As David McIntosh, who helped compile the list of riders, explained, "The laws would remain on the books, but there would be no money to carry them out. It's a signal to the agencies to stop wasting time on these regulations."[69] According to Scott Hodge, a budget expert at the conservative Heritage Foundation, "This route isn't only faster, but less incendiary. It's as good as repealing [the rules] altogether."[70]

Environmentalists' response to these low-profile challenges was to publicize them, in hopes of activating proenvironmental voters. A raft of public opinion polls strongly supported environmentalists' expectation that if they shone light on the riders they would garner public support for removing them. According to a 1994 poll by the League of Conservation Voters, 83 percent of those who voted in the 1994 elections described themselves as "an environmentalist," while almost 40 percent called themselves "strong or very strong environmentalists."[71] In the same poll, when asked to choose among three viewpoints, only 15 percent said that environmental protection costs jobs and growth; 17 percent said that environmental protection should be postponed until we can better afford it; and 51 percent chose the statement: "tough" environmental policies foster jobs and economic growth.[72] Similarly, a January 1995 *Time*/CNN poll found that 55 percent of respondents would increase government spending on the environment, 27 percent would keep it the same, and only 16 percent would decrease it.[73] Other polls revealed strong support for environmental protection even among suburban Republicans and blue-collar white males.

A few surveys suggested that conservative appeals were causing greater skepticism among the public about environmental regulation. For example, a 1995 Roper poll for Times Mirror Magazines found that for the first time in four years, less than a majority (43 percent) said environmental regulations did not go far enough. A year earlier, that figure had been 53 percent, and in 1992, it was 63 percent.[74] But in general, the favorable numbers for the environment persisted in the face of the conservative onslaught. An ABC/*Washington Post* survey taken in the spring of 1995 asked, "Generally speaking, do you think the federal government has gone too far or not far enough to protect the environment?" Seventy percent said "not far enough," while only 17 percent said "too far"—attitudes that cut across partisan and ideological lines.[75] In a survey conducted by the Mellman Group that summer, 62 percent of respondents said Congress's priority should be to do more to protect the environment, while only 29 percent said Congress should reduce regulations.[76] And an NBC/*Wall Street Journal* poll conducted in July found that 79 percent of respondents wanted environmental laws maintained or strengthened, while a Louis Harris poll in August found that 60 percent of respondents opposed reducing the powers of the EPA.[77] Even a survey conducted by the Superfund Reform Coalition, a business organization, found strong backing for federal environmental laws: only 21 percent of respondents said environmental laws had gone too far, whereas

36 percent said they had not gone far enough. Even among GOP respondents, 77 percent of whom said there was too much regulation, only 30 percent thought environmental laws were too stringent.[78]

Environmentalists used e-mail, direct mail, fax, and the Internet to tap into this reservoir of support, capitalizing on the twenty-fifth anniversary of Earth Day. They also forged alliances with religious organizations, hunting and fishing groups, and other traditionally Republican constituencies. The major environmental groups and a handful of foundations pooled their resources to create the Environmental Information Center, an organization that could rebut the anecdotes being disseminated by conservatives to support deregulation. The mobilization campaign worked: letters and phone calls in favor of preserving existing laws poured into legislators' offices.

Despite the popular mobilization by environmentalists, conservatives pressed ahead, and in late fall, House and Senate negotiators completed work on spending bills that dramatically reduced the federal role in pollution control and cut deeply into federal biodiversity conservation programs while expanding the prospects for development on public lands. The Interior bill shaved the department's spending for the 1996 fiscal year by 8 percent from its fiscal year 1995 level, to $6 billion, and included numerous riders that favored natural resource development over conservation. The EPA budget for fiscal year 1996 was $5.7 billion, a reduction of 14 percent from the previous year and $1.7 billion less than what President Clinton had requested. It singled out enforcement for among the biggest cuts (from $395 million to $314 million).[79]

Originally, the EPA budget also featured seventeen riders that prohibited the agency from spending money on a host of activities, many of them related to Clean Air Act implementation. Some House Republicans wavered in response to constituency pressure. In a rapid series of votes taken over the summer, the House voted (212–206) first to strip the riders from the bill, with fifty-one Republicans defecting, and then—following intense lobbying by the Republican leadership—to restore them (210–210). The Senate appeared disinclined to approve the riders, however, and Clinton vowed to veto the bill if they were not removed. So on November 2, the House again deleted them, this time by a vote of 227–194.

Clinton's veto threat marked a tactical repositioning by the White House. Early on, Clinton had responded to the Republican assault by trying to placate his adversaries and pledging to "work with Congress to simplify onerous regulations."[80] In mid-March of 1995, shortly after the House passed H.R. 9, the Clinton administration tried to blunt the impetus behind the bill by announcing a package of administrative reforms aimed at easing regulatory burdens, particularly on small business. The rule changes included: (1) broadening the so-called emissions exchange program, which allows companies that exceed their emissions reduction requirements to sell credit for the excess to companies unable to meet the goals, by increasing the types of pollutants covered by the exchange program and expanding it to include water pollution emissions; (2) reducing by 25 percent the amount of paperwork companies are required to submit to the EPA; (3) consolidating federal air pollution requirements into one rule; and (4) establishing a pilot project that would allow certain plants, industries, or cities to bypass federal environmental rules and devise their own plans for reducing emissions.

According to *New York Times* journalist John Cushman Jr., the package was "a central part of the White House strategy for fending off a campaign by congressional Republicans to roll back Federal rules governing health, safety and the environment."[81] Cushman added that ordinarily such arcane modifications do not get much press, but the White House generated a blizzard of publicity for its changes, in hopes that they would stymie legislative initiatives with more draconian aims. Clinton, adopting language traditionally associated with conservatives, said "[c]ompliance, not punishment, should be our objective."[82] In June, with the debate over regulatory reform legislation raging in the Senate, the administration announced yet another set of programs to help small businesses comply with regulations.

In response to the Clinton administration's business-friendly initiatives, some industry lobbyists scaled back their campaign for new legislation that would limit the EPA's power to enforce environmental laws. Not all businesspeople were convinced, however; for example, Karen Kerrigan, president of the Washington advocacy group the Small Business Survival Committee, said the president's proposal on behalf of small business "just doesn't stack up to what Congress is doing right now. It looks like a hastily put-together defensive plan, as opposed to a well-thought-out plan that means less regulation on small business."[83] Some business groups continued to push for deregulatory legislation covertly, by tempering their antiregulatory message while simultaneously promoting probusiness senators to fill vacant seats. Similarly, Clinton's gestures did little to defuse conservatives' anger. Senator Dole said that while the president's attempts to ease compliance burdens represented a "welcome first step," administrative activity was "no substitute for eliminating unnecessary regulations that stifle productivity, innovation and individ-ual initiative."[84]

In the summer of 1995, as the budget riders gained salience, Clinton became more combative—especially after pollster Dick Morris arrived in the White House wielding surveys showing that even among antiregu-latory conservative Republicans there was a firmly held belief that envi-ronmental regulations should be strengthened, not weakened.[85] In early August, Clinton gave a White House press conference in which he deplored Republicans' "sneak attack" on the environment; later that month, after the House passed its rider-laden spending bills, Clinton issued another broadside against Republicans for "allowing lobbyists to rewrite our environmental laws. . . . This bill would effectively end Federal enforcement of the Clean Water Act and the Clean Air Act," Clinton warned. "It would be bad for our children, our health and our environment." He concluded, "Don't worry. We'll make common sense reforms, but the minute this polluter's protection act hits my desk, I will veto it."[86] True to his word, in mid-December, Clinton vetoed both the Interior and EPA budget bills for fiscal year 1996, causing a partial shutdown of the federal government.

## Conservatives Reframe Their Position
On balance, the first session of the 104th Congress was a bust for con-servatives, at least with respect to pollution control regulation. After a prolonged series of negotiations, in the spring of 1996, the EPA's budget stood at $6.5 billion—$500 million less than its pre-rescission level, but $750 million more than the level vetoed by the president.[87] On the other hand, the Interior Department's fiscal year 1996 budget was 12 percent below Clinton's budget proposal, and funding for the endangered species program, in particular, was 38 percent lower than what Clinton had requested. The one major antienvironmental rider that survived the budget fight was a timber salvage provision that greatly expanded logging of dead and dying timber in national forests.[88] Environmentalists feared—rightly, as it turned out—that rider would be used to open up previously off-limits stands of old-growth forest in the Pacific Northwest. The other area where conservatives prevailed was climate change. They were able to reduce funding for energy efficiency measures and for steps to avoid emissions of greenhouse gases, as well as for programs to encourage the development of low-carbon technologies. Furthermore, in another low-profile maneuver, conservatives resurrected several antienvironmental measures in the House-Senate conference report accompanying the

legislation. (Although conference reports are not legally binding, they provide guidance to the agencies and can prove useful in court challenges, as evidence of legislative intent.)

As a result of the highly publicized budget fracas, Republican leaders became sufficiently concerned about the party's image to send out a tip sheet to help members counteract "the environmentalist lobby and their extremist friends in the eco-terrorist underworld" who "have been working overtime to define Republicans and their agenda as antienvironment, pro-polluter and hostile to the survival of every cuddly critter roaming God's green earth."[89] The manual urged Republicans to insulate themselves from attacks by "green extremists" by participating in tree plantings, highway cleanup campaigns, and Earth Day celebrations. By January 1996, Republicans were beginning to back away from confrontation on environmental issues, particularly after hearing from core constituencies—including hunters, fishers, evangelicals, and some members of the business community—who advised their allies in Congress to scale back their reforms.[90] In the third week of January, thirty moderate House Republicans led by Sherwood Boehlert of New York and Wayne Gilchrest of Maryland wrote Speaker Gingrich to complain that the party had "taken a beating. . .over missteps in environmental policy" and to ask for a mid-course correction.[91]

Some conservatives insisted that the main problem was that Republicans simply had not done enough to communicate their views. For instance, based on his own polling results, Frank Luntz concluded that "[t]hose who wish to reduce regulatory red tape affecting the environment have not been effective in their communication effort."[92] At the same time, he conceded, "The public may not like or admire regulations, may not think more are necessary, but puts environmental protection as a higher priority than cutting regulations."[93] GOP pollster Linda DiVall concurred: "Attacking the [EPA] is a nonstarter," she warned. "Republicans should be . . . emphasizing the safeguarding of reasonable and balanced environmental protection done in a more efficient manner."[94]

For its part, the Clinton administration capitalized on Republicans' retreat to turn the tables, portraying the conservative position as radical and extreme. As one former Clinton administration official explained, the Gingrich attack "actually strengthened [the EPA], made it more popular. . . . They so overshot that we could use that to galvanize the public. We were more credible."[95] At the same time, reflecting the potency of the mainstream critique, the administration took pains to distinguish itself from the much-maligned environmentalists. The president emphasized that his administration sought "common sense" solutions to environmental issues and was open to innovative policy ideas. "I truly believe," said the head of the White House Council on Environmental Quality, Katie McGinty, "that [President Clinton] will go down in history for having put in place a new generation of environmentalism, based on cooperation not confrontation: defining and securing the common ground, defining the common interest, not the special interest."[96]

On Earth Day 1995, Vice President Al Gore also signaled the influence of the mainstream critique on environmentalists' thinking when he opined in the *New York Times* that environmental protection would need to be reinvented if the country was going to make further gains. "What have we learned?" he asked. "First, collaborative processes work better than adversarial ones. Second, flexibility works better than one-size-fits-all dictates. Third, Washington doesn't have all the answers, and we should shift some responsibilities from central bureaucracies to local communities. Fourth, pollution is often a sign of economic inefficiency, and you can make money by preventing it."[97]

Unimpressed by the Clinton/Gore rhetoric and unmoved by the exhortations of moderate Republicans to consider the popularity of environmental laws, in March 1996, House conservatives proposed another regulatory reform bill that revealed their ongoing determination to weaken the implementation of environmental (and other) rules. Within a few days, however, Republican leaders asked the party's moderates and conservatives to collaborate on a less sweeping version of regulatory reform.[98] This was a tactical shift; conservative leaders remained convinced that they had a communication problem, rather than a set of beliefs that were repugnant to the majority of Americans. "We don't want to put our members out there one more time taking a vote that the environmental extremists can twist and turn in campaign ads," Tom DeLay told journalists.[99]

In a last-ditch effort to resuscitate regulatory reform, in mid-April 1996, a group of economists published a defense of cost-benefit analysis in government rulemaking in *Science* magazine.[100] Not long thereafter, the Center for Innovation and the Environment, an arm of the Democratic Leadership Council, called for a "second generation of environmental protection" that acknowledged costs. Meanwhile, Gingrich tried to reframe the conservative position, calling for a "new environmentalism" that focused on means rather than ends and strongly resembled the storyline favored by the Clinton administration, as well as a growing cadre of academics and policy analysts. While continuing to disparage bureaucrats and environmentalists, Gingrich advocated pursuing higher levels of environmental protection but doing so more nimbly and efficiently than the regulation of the 1970s. Such an approach, he said, would be built on cooperation, not confrontation, favor incentives rather than punishment, encourage rapid adoption of new technologies, and encourage a search for innovative solutions from communities.[101] In early May, House Republicans issued a new set of guidelines for their future environmental proposals. The accompanying statement said Republicans would offer "common sense, flexible and effective approaches that build on consensus, private property ownership, free enterprise, local control, sound scientific evidence and the latest technology."[102]

Although Gingrich was chastened by the repudiation conservatives faced in the 104th Congress, others kept up the rhetorical attacks. For example, in the spring of 1996, after environmentalists had beaten back Republican reform efforts, Idaho Republican Helen Chenoweth gave a long speech on the floor of the House attacking environmentalists. "There is increasing evidence of a Government-sponsored religion in America," she said. "This religion, a cloudy mixture of New Age mysticism, Native American folklore and primitive earth worship— pantheism—is being promoted and enforced by the Clinton Administration in violation of our rights and jobs."[103] For the most part, though, in advance of the 1996 elections conservative Republicans scrambled to repair their environmental image, even as environmentalists made electoral hay out of their records and targeted them for defeat. Gingrich urged his troops to curb talk of the "war on the West" and instead show up at tree-planting photo ops.[104]

Ultimately, the 104th Congress acted only on the elements of conservatives' regulatory reform package that had substantial bipartisan support. In the spring of 1996, President Clinton signed the Small Business Regulatory Enforcement Fairness Act, which gave small businesses more flexibility in complying with regulation. (It also contained the Congressional Review Act.) A second and little-noticed law, the Regulatory Accounting Act, required the executive branch to produce an annual report for Congress estimating the total benefits and costs of all federal regulations. It also required the OMB to report public suggestions to correct any part of any regulatory program that is "inefficient, ineffective, or not a sound use of the nation's resources." According to conservative commentator John Shanahan, "Few observers even noted its passage, yet it will modestly advance efforts to curb regulatory excess."[105]

Moreover, to the surprise of many observers, the 1996 session actually yielded a handful of environmentally restrictive laws, as some conservatives sought to reposition themselves in advance of the elections. One major new piece of legislation was the Food Quality Protection Act of 1996 (FQPA), which gave the EPA more authority over common agricultural chemicals and required the agency to consider the risks of neurological damage to children from pesticide exposure, as well as the aggregate risk from different sources and the cumulative effects of pesticides that act in a similar manner.[106] The FQPA received overwhelming bipartisan support—it passed by voice vote in the Senate and by 417–0 in the House under a suspension of the rules. In part, this was a result of its timing: in late summer, when it passed, Republican leaders were desperately seeking political victories in a gridlocked Congress, and rank-and-file GOP members wanted to help the business and agricultural communities without antagonizing environmentalists.[107]

In addition, the conditions were ripe for a compromise because two court rulings had created a status quo that was regarded by all sides as untenable. For decades the Delaney clause of the 1956 Food, Drug and Cosmetic Act had prohibited the presence in food of any chemical that was a suspected carcinogen. Following the development of technologies capable of detecting minute amounts of chemicals, the EPA had proposed a standard of "negligible" (*de minimis*) risk for processed foods, thereby enabling toxic pesticides to remain in use. In 1992, however, the Ninth Circuit struck down the EPA's interpretation of the Delaney clause. That ruling forced the agency to begin canceling pesticide registrations. In early February 1993, the EPA released a list of thirty-five widely used agricultural chemicals that could be prohibited under the decision, creating alarm among agribusinesses. Carol Browner immediately pledged to work with Congress, consumer, and industry groups to develop an appropriate response to the appeals court ruling. The result, after several years of negotiation, was the FQPA.

The 104th Congress also reauthorized the Magnuson-Stevens Act (also known as the Sustainable Fisheries Act), thereby strengthening regional efforts to address overfishing, with large, bipartisan majorities: 388–7 in the House and 100–0 in the Senate. It updated the Safe Drinking Water Act by easing some requirements for small-town drinking water systems and requiring cost-benefit analysis, but not binding the agency to its results. And it approved several environmental measures that were not primarily regulatory. One, the Farm Bill, renewed several environmentally beneficial programs, including the Conservation Reserve Program. A second, the Water Resources Bill, authorized cleanup and restoration activities in the Great Lakes, the Chesapeake Bay, and the

Everglades. More controversial legislation aimed at strengthening or updating environmental regulation failed, however: bills to reauthorize the Clean Water Act and the Superfund act died, as did legislation to reform the Mining Law of 1872, curb factory-farm pollution, cut power plant emissions, and reduce sprawl.

Buoyed in part by his defense of the nation's environmental laws, Clinton won reelection handily in November 1996. At the same time, the partisan balance in Congress shifted marginally: Democrats netted eight seats in the House, shrinking the Republican advantage to twenty-two, while losing two more seats in the Senate, increasing Republicans' majority there to 55–45. The change in the Senate was significant but did not give Republicans enough votes to prevent a filibuster by the minority; moreover, a handful of moderate, proenvironmental Republicans retained their seats. Furthermore, surveys suggested the perception that Republicans did not care about the environment had cost the party dearly. So many in the GOP began reframing their positions.[108] In 1998, some Republicans, including Gingrich, formed a group that aimed to promote market-based solutions to environmental problems called the Coalition of Republican Environmental Advocates (also known, confusingly, as the Council of Republicans for Environmental Advocacy). Although two-thirds of its members had LCV scores of zero, Gingrich explained the group's approach by caricaturing its adversaries, saying, "The Al Gore, left-wing environmental model is a centralized, bureaucratized, litigious, adversarial, anti-technology model. Let's create a conservationist, common-sense, practical, high-tech environmental model."[109] Many conservatives remained determined to pursue more substantial reforms, however, and Representative McIntosh predicted, "Rather than one big regulatory reform law, you'll see a series of free-standing initiatives, restrictions through the appropriations process and stricter oversight."[110]

In fact, after a brief pause, conservative legislators renewed their low-profile attacks on environmental restrictions, attaching riders to spending bills, most of them aimed at curbing federal biodiversity conservation efforts. For example, they added provisions to the 1997 Interior Department appropriations bill that perpetuated subsidized road building and erected barriers against efforts to reduce timber sales in some national forests.[111] In July 1998, conservatives added dozens of riders to EPA and Interior Department appropriations bills, including measures prohibiting the EPA from spending any money to reduce greenhouse gas emissions;

increasing logging in Tongass National Forest; preventing the Park Service from phasing out commercial fishing in Glacier Bay National Park; requiring congressional approval for any changes in the operation of any dam in the Columbia River watershed; authorizing new road construction through Alaska's Chugach National Forest and Izembek National Wildlife Refuge; and delaying national forest, grazing, and mining policy reforms. In 1999, antienvironmental riders were back in force: attached to the fiscal year 2000 appropriations bills were measures to allow more logging, mining, and road building in national forests; relax restrictions on dumping of mining debris on public lands or into streams; shelve environmental restrictions on grazing; make it easier to develop wetlands; bar stricter fuel efficiency standards for SUVs; delay rules requiring oil companies to pay royalties they owed; and prohibit the issuance of new regulations to limit greenhouse gas emissions.

Although congressional Republicans agreed to eliminate or change most of the riders during budget negotiations, the relentless low-profile attacks limited the adoption of environmentally restrictive practices, particularly by the agencies responsible for biodiversity conservation. They achieved more subtle results as well. With a few exceptions, these attacks deterred environmentalists from trying to pass or renew restrictive legislation, diverting their energies from building support for such initiatives to defending and consolidating past gains. The strident challenges also influenced the behavior of executive branch officials. To fend off the conservative assault, the administration assured business it was listening to complaints about excessive regulation, trying to bring greater openness to the process and replace a penalty-based model of enforcement with one emphasizing greater government-industry collaboration. Sounding very much like his conservative predecessors, in a 1995 speech in Baltimore, Clinton assured the audience that his administration had done "more than anybody in 25 years to try to streamline regulation, reduce the burden of excessive regulation, and get rid of dumb rules that don't make sense."[112] In a 1995 op-ed, Clinton's OIRA administrator, Sally Katzen, boasted, "In the past two-and-a-half years, Mr. Clinton has cut red tape, reduced the regulatory burden on small business, devolved authority to states and localities, and made federal rules less intrusive— all without jeopardizing the environment or the health and safety of Americans."[113] In 1997, the White House claimed its "reinventing government" program had eliminated sixteen thousand pages of superfluous rules from the Code of Federal Regulations.[114]

### Making Air-Pollution-Control Policy More Restrictive, While Adding Flexibility

Even as the president sought to demonstrate his antiregulatory credentials, EPA administrator Carol Browner responded to the conservative assault by bolstering her defense of restrictive pollution control regulation. She seized on the attacks to expose conservatives' antienvironmental motivation. For example, she countered the amendment to the bill elevating the EPA to cabinet level that would have required a risk assessment for all proposed regulations by saying, "in many instances, risk assessment has become a code word for those who want to weaken our efforts to protect public health and the environment."[115] In late February 1995, after Republicans overwhelmingly approved their regulatory reform bill, H.R. 9, Browner complained, "This legislation is not a reform, it is a full frontal assault on protecting public health and the environment."[116]

#### Restrictive Implementation and Enforcement of the Clean Air Act

Confident that pollution control was widely salient, rather than bowing to conservative pressure, Browner stepped up the EPA's enforcement activities. In fiscal year 1993, the agency undertook 2,110 new enforcement actions against polluters, compared with 1,935 in 1992 and 1,755 in 1991. The agency also assessed $115.1 million in civil penalties, including a record $85.9 million in judicial fines and $29.2 million in administrative assessments. In fiscal year 1994, even as the enforcement program was being restructured, the agency initiated the highest number of enforcement actions and collected the highest total dollar amount of penalties in its history.[117] In December 1996, Browner announced the EPA would crack down on states that were not enforcing environmental regulations. "[L]ately we have seen a number of states that are emboldened by the anti-environmental sentiment that began here in Congress, and they are retreating from their commitment to enforce the laws," said Browner. "We are fighting the same fight that we fought over the Contract With America, but unfortunately the battle has moved down to the states."[118] A few months later, Browner withdrew a plan to give the states more flexibility in implementing environmental rules after states resisted the requirement that innovation would have to achieve superior environmental results.[119]

Under Browner, the EPA also began strictly enforcing the Clean Air Act's New Source Review (NSR) rules, long a bone of contention between the agency and the nation's utilities. The NSR rules, created pursuant to the 1977 amendments, required old coal-fired power plants—which had been grandfathered under the 1970 Clean Air Act—to install pollution control equipment when making major renovations to their facilities.[120] (Originally, Congress had expected the aging plants would be retired; the NSR rules were a response to the recognition that many of the old plants were being upgraded and kept in service.) In the early 1980s, industry challenged the NSR rules in court, and the Reagan administration negotiated a settlement that called for the EPA to rewrite the rules. The agency struggled to do so, however, encountering resistance from both environmentalists and its own legal staff.

Under George H. W. Bush, the EPA finally revised the NSR rules, prompting the Wisconsin Electric Power Co. (WEPCo) to sue the agency. In January 1990, the Seventh Circuit Court of Appeals ruled that WEPCo's upgrades had gone beyond routine maintenance, as the EPA alleged, but also that the agency's standards for determining when a source had to upgrade its pollution control equipment were too stringent (*Wisconsin Electric Power Co. v. Reilly*). Following that decision, the agency issued the so-called WEPCo guidance documents, which explained how to implement the NSR rules for the electric utility industry in a flexible manner. The agency also wrote a new rule in 1992 that replaced the EPA's formula for utilities. Rather than comparing baseline emissions to "potential" (but seldom achieved) emissions, regulators would make a less rigid comparison to future actual emissions. At the same time, the EPA began gathering data showing that utilities' actual emissions after they performed maintenance were higher than their projected emissions—data that formed the basis for subsequent lawsuits.

Meanwhile, throughout the 1980s and into the 1990s, utilities made major repairs to their plants but characterized them as "routine maintenance" so that they could avoid having to install pollution control devices. In November 1996, the EPA began examining these practices as part of its new sector-based enforcement program.[121] After the EPA assembled evidence—based on utilities' own data—that companies had systematically evaded the law, Browner tried to reach a compromise with the industry. But utilities' lawyers were intransigent, and in late 1999, the Justice Department announced it was filing suit against seven of the nation's largest utilities on the grounds that they had made major modifications that increased emissions at fifty coal-fired power plants without obtaining permits or installing pollution control devices. The EPA also sent administrative orders to the federally owned Tennessee Valley Authority.

In December 2000, Tampa Electric settled the first NSR suit, agreeing to pay a $3.5 million civil penalty, install permanent emissions control equipment, and spend between $10 million and $11 million on environmentally beneficial projects in the region. A year later, Cinergy signed an Agreement on Principle to spend $1.4 billion on pollution control equipment and to pay an $8.5 million civil fine; shortly thereafter, Virginia Power pledged to spend $1.2 billion to reduce its nitrogen oxide and sulfur dioxide emissions by about 70 percent, as well as to pay $13.9 million for environmental projects and $5.3 million in civil fines. Other utilities stalled, however, and began supporting George W. Bush's campaign for the presidency, hoping that a conservative in the White House would be friendlier to their position.

A more controversial effort to make the status quo more restrictive was Browner's decision in late 1996 to propose new ambient air quality standards for small particulates (soot) and ground-level ozone (smog).[122] The EPA issued draft standards in November 1996, after a successful lawsuit filed by the American Lung Association that argued the EPA was ignoring new scientific evidence about the harmful impacts of small particulates. Based on a review of 185 studies, the EPA issued a new ozone standard that called for concentrations not to exceed 84 parts per billion (ppb) over an eight-hour period (compared to the existing standard of 120 ppb over a one-hour period). The new standard for fine particulates (2.5 microns in diameter), based on a review of 86 studies, called for daily averages not to exceed 65 micrograms per cubic meter of air, and for annual averages no higher than 15 micrograms per cubic meter. To soften the blow, the agency advanced a three-step implementation strategy that involved (1) revising the air quality standards for ozone and small particulates, (2) negotiating an extended implementation timeline with the OMB, and (3) issuing a call to twenty-two eastern states to reduce their smog-causing nitrogen oxide emissions through their state implementation plans.[123]

Conservatives and their industry allies were appalled by the new standards, which promised to impose significant costs on business. In an effort to prevent them from taking effect, conservative critics challenged them publicly, claiming they were based on inadequate science,[124] and predicting they would cost billions of dollars while providing no real public health benefit—and in some cases inflicting harm.[125] (By contrast, the EPA's analyses suggested that the benefits of the reductions would outweigh the costs by a substantial margin.) In the spring of 1996, after the EPA began circulating its draft proposal, more than five hundred companies and trade associations representing automakers, electric utilities, oil companies, and large manufacturers calling themselves the Air Quality Standards Coalition joined forces to lobby against the restrictive standards. Jerry Jasinowski, president of the National Association of Manufacturers, charged the standards would throw hundreds of communities out of compliance and cost business and local governments tens of billions of dollars in exchange for unproven health and environmental benefits.[126] "The administration has chosen to put a political agenda ahead of either sound science or economic growth," said Jasinowski.[127] "The EPA's proposal isn't based on sound scientific research," complained Owen Drey, an environmental specialist at the association. "The . . . new, more stringent standards . . . will have a chilling effect on economic growth in this country."[128] The coalition also argued that the new rules would victimize small businesses and individuals. "EPA has already forced industry to do almost everything they can do, so what comes next is mom-and-pop businesses, dry cleaners, bakers," said Drey. "You'll see strategies directed at the voters, like forced carpooling and restrictions on charcoal grills and wood-burning fireplaces."[129] Criticism came from within the White House as well; Clinton's OMB and Council of Economic Advisers both questioned the rationale for tightening the standards.

In response to internal and external concerns, the White House subjected Browner's smog and soot proposals to a grueling review by the National Economic Council, the OMB, and the Council on Environmental Quality. As the review progressed, the industry coalition splintered, with oil companies arguing for maintaining the status quo, electric utilities asking to postpone the rules while they dealt with deregulation, and chemical companies offering to settle for a stricter interim standards that could be adjusted based on the results of additional research.[130] Finally, President Clinton settled the matter by overruling the objections of the administration's economists and coming out in favor of the rules. "I approved some very strong new regulations today that will be somewhat controversial, but I think kids ought to be healthy," he announced.[131] In early 1998, the EPA released its plan to require power plants in twenty-two states east of the Mississippi, as well as those in the District of Columbia, to reduce their nitrogen oxide emissions by up to 85 percent over ten years.

Meanwhile, though, in a last-ditch effort to prevent the smog and soot standards from taking effect, the American Trucking Associations filed suit to block them. While the air quality standards worked their way through the courts, congressional Republicans remained aloof. Although conservatives, such as Oklahoma senator James Inhofe, advocated killing the rules outright through the recently created Congressional Review Act process, others opposed expending political capital on the issue given the disastrous results of their recent legislative forays and the popularity of air-pollution-control regulations. Instead, the Republicans let Democrat John Dingell of Michigan—who was concerned about the rules' impact on his state's struggling manufacturing sector—take the lead in opposing them. (Other Rust Belt Democrats weighed in against the rules as well; more than ninety of them appealed to the president after heavy lobbying by industry. Also vocal were Democratic mayors Richard Daley of Chicago and Dennis Archer of Detroit.)

To conservatives' delight, in May 1999, the D.C. Circuit threw out the air quality standards, ruling in part that the EPA's actions were arbitrary and capricious, but also citing the rarely invoked "nondelegation" doctrine to argue that the EPA had exceeded its authority in setting the standards (*American Trucking Associations v. Browner* and *Browner v. American Trucking Associations*). A second ruling, issued two weeks later, suspended implementation of the rule requiring twenty-two states and the District of Columbia to submit plans for restricting nitrogen oxide emissions. Conservatives' triumph was short-lived, however. In June 2000, the D.C. Circuit lifted the appeals court order that had kept the EPA from enforcing the twenty-two-state rule. Then, in 2001, the Supreme Court overturned the ruling on air quality standards (*Whitman v. American Trucking Associations*). The Court's unanimous decision marked a major triumph for environmentalists. Written by Justice Scalia, it rejected both the nondelegation doctrine arguments and the claim that the EPA should consider cost in setting ambient air quality standards for criteria pollutants. In March 2002, on remand, the appeals court ruled 3–0 that the EPA could proceed with ozone and particulate regulations and further found that the administrative record supported the 1997 standards (in other words, the agency's assessment of the relevant science was *not* arbitrary and capricious).

## Selectively Increasing Flexibility at the EPA

Even as she defended her agency's right to enforce air-pollution-control measures strictly, Browner made a concerted effort to demonstrate her flexibility and willingness to work with industry, saying she had learned that encouraging business compliance with incentives was better than "command-and-control" coercion. In March of 1993, shortly after taking office, Browner visited Detroit in an effort to demonstrate that she would "cooperate" with industry and make federal regulations more business-friendly.[132] "What concerns me," she told journalist Hobart Rowen, "is that there is a growing anti-environmental movement out there, and we who believe so strongly in the need to protect the environment need to listen to what they're saying." The reason, she said, was "[t]here is some truth to it. The process by which we achieve protection is without flexibility in many instances. And it is not user-friendly." Browner made clear that she was "not open to changing the standards that are necessary to protect the public," but was "absolutely open to flexibility in how we meet those standards."[133]

According to Jon Cannon, former EPA general counsel, the watchwords of Browner's regulatory reinvention were "collaboration," "cooperation," "bargaining," "partnerships," and "negotiation."[134] Cannon contends the agency's political leaders hoped that repositioning would take the initiative for reform away from Congress by blunting the drive for deeper changes. But many other former EPA officials say that Browner adopted new approaches out of conviction as well; she had come to believe that alternative mechanisms could be more effective than prescriptive regulation in particular circumstances, and that some businesses were prepared to go beyond the existing standards if given the proper incentives.[135]

One way Browner made good on her rhetoric was by creating schemes to simplify pollution control rules and make them more flexible. Backed by a study jointly conducted by Amoco and the EPA, which found that federal regulation had forced a Yorktown refinery to mitigate relatively minor pollution threats at major expense while more important problems were overlooked, the agency began examining environmental rules to eliminate overlapping and conflicting mandates. In mid-July 1994, Browner unveiled the Common Sense Initiative, which had three goals: to eliminate the problems that arise when regulators focus narrowly on single media, such as air, water, or land; to replace the traditionally reactive, crisis-driven approach with a more proactive one; and to transform the adversarial decision-making process into a more collaborative one. The program affected six major industries that together accounted for 15 percent of U.S. gross national product and one-eighth of all toxic emissions reported to the EPA.[136]

Then, in early 1995, Browner introduced Project XL, a program that allowed companies to devise their own methods of reducing pollution. The program waived some specific regulatory requirements, as long as the participating companies produced superior overall results. By early 1996, ten major companies, including IBM and Intel, as well as two federal agencies had enrolled in Project XL.[137] Environmentalists' reactions to the voluntary program were mixed: while some regarded it as progressive, others saw it as a hasty response to conservatives' antiregulatory initiatives.[138] They were concerned that flexibility would benefit industry, which would have the time and resources to figure out ways to take advantage of it. For their part, some EPA officials found environmentalists unduly rigid in their opposition to innovation, noting that the agency's authorizing statutes sharply limited its ability to reward companies that exceeded regulatory standards.[139]

In another attempt to stem the attacks coming from Congress, the states, and the business community, the EPA funded four information centers to help small businesses comply with regulations and offered small businesses limited amnesty if they volunteered to get help in complying with air quality regulations. In 1996, Browner—taking a page from the conservative playbook—boasted that the agency had eliminated fourteen hundred pages of obsolete rules, reduced the time industry spent on paperwork to comply with federal environmental rules by ten million hours, and initiated a campaign to streamline another 70 percent of the agency's regulations.[140] EPA officials insisted they were still enforcing Clean Air Act rules but were simply being more flexible. "We tried to give state officials as much flexibility as possible in reaching the goals set under the act," Browner said, "but we did not relax a single standard for improving air quality."[141] She acknowledged that EPA officials were trying to avoid a showdown with the act's critics in Congress.

There were many other signs of flexibility at the EPA as well. In early March 1994, the EPA issued the Chemical Manufacturing Rule requiring chemical plants to cut their toxic air emissions by 88 percent. The chemical industry, which worked with the EPA to formulate the new rule, applauded it, while some environmentalists complained it was too flexible.[142] Also in 1994, the EPA began brokering a deal between the twelve Northeast states and the auto industry, after the states decided to adopt California's strict standards for tailpipe emissions. In hopes of deflecting that plan, which promised to be costly and complicated for them, the automakers offered to build a "49-state car," whose emissions would be lower than required by the federal government but higher than California's standards. In 1997, after three years of negotiation, the EPA established a legal framework to make a voluntary agreement between the states and the car companies enforceable.[143] (In the final deal, four of the original twelve states retained the right to choose between the California standard and the standard that applied to the other forty-five states.)

In another sign of flexibility, in 1995, the EPA relaxed rules on state auto emissions inspections to make them less burdensome for car owners,

after several members of Congress threatened to modify the auto pollution provisions of the Clean Air Act if the EPA did not back off.[144] In
addition, the EPA scrapped proposed Clean Air Act rules requiring
employers to set up carpools for employees in areas afflicted with severe
pollution. Instead, in October 2000, the agency announced it was teaming
up with employers and local governments to offer incentives to lure
commuters out of their cars.[145] And finally, the EPA sought to soften its
reversal of a permissive Bush administration rule. In July 1994, the
agency overturned one of the biggest concessions that President Bush had
granted industry with respect to enforcement of the Clean Air Act: easing
the rules under which industries could expand their operations, even if
the expansion resulted in higher levels of pollution than allowed by their
permits. By June 2000, however, the EPA was working on a policy that
would encourage states to issue "smart permits" that would enable companies to avoid seeking new permits every time they changed processes
or expanded their facilities.[146]

More generally, thanks to a combination of budget cuts, criticism from
congressional conservatives and industry, and pressure from the administration to cut red tape, the EPA was increasingly inclined to compromise with regulated industries. In some cases, agency officials declined
to inspect facilities or enforce restrictive rules, reversed longstanding
policies, or abandoned restrictive proposals for more flexible ones. "Some
agencies now are hesitant to push regulations that will encounter stiff
political resistance," Edward Hudgins, director of regulatory studies for
the libertarian Cato Institute, commented approvingly. "Some businesses
see an opportunity to challenge certain rules and establish more lenient,
implicit rules that are followed by an agency but not necessarily stated
in writing," he added.[147] Representative McIntosh also believed the steps
the agencies were taking were in the right direction. "I do think we have
changed the culture," he said. "The agencies are being much more reasonable with the public."[148]

### Saving the Endangered Species Act by Making It More Permissive

Whereas conservative influence on the Clean Air Act was limited to
slowing the imposition of stringent new rules and encouraging flexibility
in implementation and enforcement, their impact on the Endangered
Species Act was more substantial. Secretary Babbitt was an ardent proponent not just of biodiversity conservation but of ecological restoration.[149] For example, he promoted dam removal in the name of river
restoration; he also sponsored the Interior Department's participation in

the Everglades restoration led by the Army Corps of Engineers. Under his watch, the Fish and Wildlife reintroduced wolves to Yellowstone National Park, bringing to fruition a plan that had been in the works since the Reagan administration. And in July 2000, after a four-year consensus-building process, the service proposed to reintroduce grizzly bears to Idaho's Selway-Bitterroot Wilderness and part of the Frank Church River of No Return Wilderness. Yet, despite his passion for conservation and restoration, Babbitt was reluctant to unsheathe the regulatory provisions of the Endangered Species Act. Instead, he adopted a permissive stance that relied on inducements rather than coercion, in hopes of subduing the wrath of landowners and resource users, and thereby preventing an attack on the law by hostile legislators.

**Conservatives Tarnish the Image of the Endangered Species Act**
The Endangered Species Act enjoyed widespread support in the early 1990s. A poll conducted by the National Audubon Society and the Nature Conservancy in early 1992 showed that 66 percent of voters supported the act. Forty-eight percent said they were more sympathetic to the goal of protecting wildlife than jobs, while only 29 percent expressed more concern about the economy. Another poll, conducted for the Defenders of Wildlife by Democratic pollster Celinda Lake, showed that three-quarters of voters—including two-thirds in the Pacific states— supported the act. In addition, 78 percent of those asked said they would favor making violators pay fines, and 73 percent said they would support funding for ecosystem conservation.[150]

Unmoved by the law's apparent popularity, by the early 1990s, conservative commentators were routinely challenging the notion that species endangerment was a serious problem and were deriding the Endangered Species Act as a solution. A 1993 article by Ike Sugg of the Competitive Enterprise Institute charged that the claim of spotted owls' dependence on old growth was "as specious as the contention that environmentalists want to preserve old growth forests merely 'to save owls.'" The truth, Sugg charged, was that environmentalists were acting on behalf of "a vague and vast 'intrinsic value' in nature that (in their view) must be preserved at all costs, even if they must sacrifice the material interests and well-being of others." Meanwhile, he added, the Endangered Species Act creates perverse incentives that punish those who are stewards and promotes rapid deforestation.[151] Conservative columnist David Gelertner was similarly offended by efforts to protect the kangaroo rat, which he claimed had prevented homeowners in Southern California from building firebreaks around their houses. The nub of the issue, said Gelertner, was that what environmentalists see as hubris—the human drive to build where building is difficult—their opponents see as "the essential human enterprise, inspiring and noble."[152]

In May 1993, an op-ed piece in the *New York Times* by Julian Simon and Aaron Wildavsky accused scientists of hysteria when they warned of an impending wave of species extinctions. "Both of us," wrote Simon and Wildavsky, "have documented the complete absence of evidence for the claim that the extinction of species is going up rapidly—or going up at all."[153] Several prominent biologists responded with letters objecting vociferously to this assertion. They cited abundant evidence of rising species extinctions but also pointed out how many species were likely to go extinct if current trends continued. Ecologist David Wilcove and lawyer Michael Bean identified the central disagreement when they asked, "Must we wait until the roster of extinct species has grown so that the losses are apparent even to office-bound skeptics before sounding an alarm?"[154]

Even ostensibly moderate commentators disparaged the Endangered Species Act. For example, journalist Gregg Easterbrook challenged the science underpinning efforts to protect the spotted owl, suggesting that scientists and environmentalists who portrayed the spotted owl as fragile, unable to withstand the slightest variation in its habitat, were exaggerating. Species that cannot withstand change usually perish anyway, he pointed out, and in fact the owl probably is not that fragile—that is just typical "doomsday thinking." He concluded, "If it is eventually understood that affluent environmentalists with white-collar sinecure destroyed thousands of desirable skilled-labor jobs in order to satisfy an ideology and boost the returns on fund-raising drives, a long-lasting political backlash against environmentalism will set in."[155] In the pages of the *Atlantic*, journalists Charles Mann and Mark Plummer rued the irrationality of endangered species protection and its inequitable impacts on landowners. They concluded that compromises between developers and officials charged with conserving endangered species offered one path through the impasse created by enforcing the Endangered Species Act.[156]

While conservative writers sought to undermine the Endangered Species Act, wise use and property rights activists pressed Congress to adopt "takings" legislation, in which the primary mechanism for conserving endangered species is financial compensation for landowners whose economic use of their property is restricted by regulatory requirements. By the time President Clinton took office, Congress had already considered and rejected a variety of "takings" provisions. In 1993, however, after the House again repudiated such a measure, conservative Democrat Billy Tauzin of Louisiana warned ominously that although he and his allies had lost a round, there was going to be "a real war in this chamber over what kind of balance we want to strike between environmental protection and the protection of human beings on their property."[157]

The image of a pitched battle was apt. Although the Clinton Justice Department moved quickly (and successfully) to quash the county supremacy movement in the courts, its message inspired many in the rural West to action. The October 23, 1995, cover story of *Time* magazine reported on a spate of confrontations between citizens and federal employees in the West, in which movement sympathizers engaged in a variety of hostile acts, including illegal road openings and livestock trespasses. In one such episode, in Nye County, Nevada, on July 4, 1994, county commissioner Dick Carver—brandishing a copy of the U.S. Constitution—bulldozed a weather-damaged Forest Service logging road while an armed crowd cheered him on. "All it would have taken was for [the forest ranger] to draw a weapon," Carver later bragged, "and 50 people with sidearms would have drilled him."[158]

There were other threats and violent incidents as well: pipe bombs were found in the Gila Wilderness in New Mexico; an unknown assailant fired shots at a Forest Service biologist in California; and in Carson City, Nevada, a bomb destroyed the family van of a forest ranger while it was parked in his driveway.[159] According to other reports, a Clark County, Nevada, rancher who had violated his grazing permit threatened to shoot any government employee who approached him on his property; and a miner in Clark County who refused to pay mining fees confronted inspectors with a firearm when they tried to check his property.[160] After a string of such incidents, the agencies adopted buddy-system travel policies.

Environmentalists were also targets. A Greenpeace activist had her home firebombed, and two organizers for Earth First! were badly injured when a bomb went off in their car in California. In November 1994, at a public hearing in Everett, Washington, an Audubon Society activist was threatened by two men who fashioned a noose with a sign that said, "This message is for you." In March 1995, in Corvallis, Oregon, United States Militia Association leader Samuel Sherwood warned there would be "blood in the streets" if a judge enforced the Endangered Species Act in the national forests of the Pacific Northwest.[161]

Some individuals set their sights on endangered species themselves. In 1992, journalist Maura Dolan reported, "Private landowners across the United States are quietly waging an underground war against endangered species, killing them off or destroying their native surroundings to avoid costly government restrictions for their protection."[162] One federal agent lamented to Dolan that ranchers were dealing with listed predators like wolves and grizzly bears by "shooting, shoveling, and shutting up." In California, farmers stopped rotating crops to prevent endangered kangaroo rats from moving onto fallow fields. Endangered sea turtles washed up on beaches in the Gulf of Mexico, their throats slashed—presumably by shrimpers angry about being required to install turtle excluder devices on their nets. The Fish and Wildlife Service's enforcement capacity was completely inadequate to deal with these transgressions; it was difficult to catch violators and even more so to convict them.

### Direct Challenges to the Endangered Species Act

Fueled by controversy and buoyed by the Republican takeover in Congress in 1994, efforts to pass "takings" legislation proliferated and proponents became more vociferous. In early March 1995, the House passed (277–148) the Private Property Protection Act, which made property owners eligible to receive compensation for a reduction in the value of their property of 20 percent or more resulting from government restrictions under the Endangered Species Act, Clean Water Act, or Food Security Act. To meet the terms of the act, within ninety days of receiving notice of a final government action, a property owner would have to submit a written request for compensation. Within 180 days of receiving that request, the agency would have to compensate the owner for the difference between the market value of the property absent regulation and the market value of the property if the regulation were implemented. If federal action reduced the property's value by 50 percent or more, the landowner could insist that the government buy it. Most commentators believed that such a measure, if passed, would dramatically reduce the government's propensity to regulate.

During the same legislative session, the Senate contemplated the Omnibus Property Rights Act of 1995 (S. 605), which was even bolder than the House bill. It allowed landowners to demand compensation plus attorneys fees and costs if (1) the market value of their property was reduced by 33 percent or more, (2) regulatory action did not substantially advance the "stated government purpose" of the regulation, and (3) owners were told they had to give up certain ownership rights to get a federal permit to use their own property.[163] Ultimately, however, S. 605 was buried by an unlikely alliance of progressives and cultural conservatives worried that the law would limit municipalities' ability to pass local ordinances prohibiting the sale of pornography.

Having failed to pass a property rights measure in the 104th Congress, midway through the 105th, in October 1997, both the House and Senate Judiciary Committees again took up the cause. This time the bills took a slightly different tack: they gave landowners new avenues for legal challenges to rules that developers considered "taking," by expanding the authority of the federal claims court and allowing developers to shift zoning disputes from localities to federal court.[164] "We all know that every day in America, private property is being taken without just compensation," Republican senator Phil Gramm of Texas explained. "We all know in the name of endangered species, in the name of wetlands, in the name of numerous other public purposes, that private property is being trampled on."[165] The House version of the property rights bill passed easily in 1997, but in mid-July 1998, the Senate killed the companion bill by a vote of 52–42, despite strong support among Republican leaders.

In addition to backing generic takings legislation, conservative members of Congress targeted the Endangered Species Act itself. In the 103rd Congress, Democrats and moderate Republicans expressed their willingness to reform the act, which was due for reauthorization. In 1993, Representative Gerry Studds of Massachusetts, the Democratic chair of the Merchant Marine and Fisheries Committee (which was abolished by the Republicans in 1995), held hearings on reauthorizing the act, after which he proposed a bill that would create incentives for property owners to conserve species and would improve cooperation between the wildlife agencies and the states, two principles that were important to conservatives. At the same time, Studds' bill more than doubled annual spending on endangered species conservation, to $120 million; required recovery plans to be issued within a year of a species' listing; and allowed citizens to file suit to protect listed species without waiting sixty days, as was required at the time. In the Senate, the Democratic chair of the Environment and Public Works Committee, Max Baucus of Montana, and ranking Republican John Chafee introduced a bill that largely mirrored Studds' bill. But environmentalists were leery of opening up discussion of the bill, and its sponsors soon retreated from the fray. One environmental activist justified this defensiveness, saying, "as soon as you tried to do anything, the development interests and mining interests and timber interests and drilling interests would come roaring in. Their allies would offer amendments that were very dangerous. John Chafee took the bill off the floor rather than see it weakened."[166]

For their part, having propagated a steady stream of criticism of the act during the early 1990s, conservative activists mobilized to press for much more substantial Endangered Species Act reforms. In 1994, property rights activist Chuck Cushman formed the Grassroots ESA Coalition (GESAC), an umbrella group comprising about 250 organizations with a combined four million members. The group's mission statement asserted, "The old law failed because it is based on flawed ideas. It is founded on regulation and punishment. . . . It is a bureaucratic machine and its fruits are paperwork and court cases and fines—not conserved and recovered endangered species." The coalition, by contrast, favored an approach that "works for wildlife, not one that works against people."[167] GESAC promoted reform of the Endangered Species Act based on three principles long advocated by conservative experts: (1) primary responsibility for conservation of plants and animals should be reserved for the states; (2) federal conservation efforts should rely entirely on voluntary, incentive-based programs aimed at private property owners; and (3) federal conservation efforts should encourage conservation through commerce. Additional principles promoted by GESAC included ensuring that federal conservation efforts were "based on sound science"—an apparently benign requirement that would, in practice, shift the burden of proof for protection to environmentalists; giving priority to "taxonomically unique and genetically complex and more economically and ecologically valuable animals and plants," another measure that would curb protection; and limiting federal prohibitions on actions intended to kill or physically injure a listed vertebrate species, with the exception of uses—such as trophy hunting and exotic pet collection—that (presumably) create incentives and funding for an animal's conservation.

GESAC was encouraged when, early in the 1995 legislative session, the Senate Republican Regulatory Relief Task Force put the Endangered Species Act at the top of its "Top Ten Worst-Case Regulations." Slade Gorton of Washington laid down the first marker in the Senate. He had worked closely with representatives of the mining, ranching, timber, and utility industries to craft a bill that abolished fines or imprisonment for those who destroy the habitat of endangered species, and eliminated the law's objective of conserving "the ecosystems upon which endangered species and threatened species depend."[168] Gorton's bill also allowed the secretary of the interior to decide when, how, and whether to save a species, replacing the requirement that such a decision be based strictly on the best available science. Explaining this shift, Gorton sought to highlight the possibility of short-term economic costs associated with Endangered Species Act implementation, pointing out that under his bill, the interior secretary could ask, "Is this species so important that a single person should lose their job over it?"[169]

In devising their revisions to the Endangered Species Act, House Republicans led by Alaskan Don Young and Richard Pombo—a California rancher who ran his own wise use group before gaining a position in Congress—adopted the even more permissive approach favored by GESAC. In the Young-Pombo bill, the states would have primary responsibility for conserving animals and plants; federal conservation efforts would rely entirely on voluntary, incentive-based programs; and the federal government would encourage conservation through commerce—a combination most federal biologists regarded as devastating to biodiversity conservation.[170] The federal government would finance this nonregulatory approach by selling federal land to ranchers and the timber industry. The bill would narrow the scope of the Endangered Species Act in other ways as well. For example, federal officials would be able to simply forbid killing an endangered species without protecting its habitat, if they deemed the costs of doing so too great. The bill emphasized species protection in wilderness areas and national parks, while limiting conservation requirements on national forest and Bureau of Land Management property.

In May 1995, a panel assembled by the National Academy of Sciences concluded that the much-maligned Endangered Species Act was a "critically important" and successfully used tool for conserving biological diversity, and recommended the law's protections for habitat be *strengthened*.[171] Then, in an effort to rebut charges that the law was ineffective, in October 1995, the Clinton administration released a report demonstrating the law was saving hundreds of plant and animal species at relatively little cost.[172] Despite these analyses, as well as fierce lobbying on behalf of the act by scientists, in October 1995, the House Resources Committee approved a rewrite of the Endangered Species Act sponsored by Pombo and Young. In an effort to improve the prospects for his bill, Young sought to highlight the act's economic impacts by convening hearings that showcased the hardships of property owners and "ordinary people." "Eventually," he predicted, "the working class, the poorer people, will realize that [the Endangered Species Act] is saving crickets over saving babies."[173] The Young-Pombo bill did not receive serious consideration in the Senate, however. To the chagrin of many conservatives, it was killed in part by the mobilization of evangelicals, who waged a $1 million campaign to save the Endangered Species Act. In it, they portrayed the act as "the Noah's ark of our day" and accused "Congress and special interests" of "trying to sink it."[174]

**Making Implementation of the Endangered Species Act More Permissive**
In addition to pressing for legislative reform, conservative activists challenged restrictive implementation of the Endangered Species Act through litigation. In the decade's most important ESA-related suit, a consortium of logging interests led by the American Forest and Paper Association challenged the Fish and Wildlife Service's definition of "harm" to a species. (Since 1981, the service had defined "harm" as any action that "may include significant habitat modification or degradation where it actually kills or injures wildlife by significantly impairing essential behavioral patterns, including breeding, feeding, or sheltering.") The case, *Babbitt v. Sweet Home Chapter of Communities for a Greater Oregon*, went all the way to the Supreme Court, which in June 1995 upheld (6–3) the agency's restrictive interpretation of the statute. Writing for the majority, Justice John Paul Stevens reasoned that unless "harm" was taken to mean more than direct physical action to hurt an animal, it would be superfluous, having no meaning beyond that of the other words in the list. Stevens also referred to the act's stated purpose, "to provide a means whereby the ecosystems upon which the endangered species and threatened species may be conserved."[175]

In other cases, however, wise use activists were more successful at forcing the wildlife agencies to implement the act more permissively. In 1996, for example, the Court of Appeals for the Tenth Circuit ruled that the Fish and Wildlife Service failed to comply with National Environmental Policy Act by declining to prepare an environmental impact statement when designating critical habitat for the loach minnow and the spikedace, two endangered fish (*Catron County Board of Commissioners v. U.S. Fish and Wildlife Service*). This ruling added to the analytic burden facing the agencies, thereby slowing the designation of critical habitat. A year later, in *Bennett v. Spear*, Oregon ranchers and irrigation districts convinced the Supreme Court that they had legal standing to challenge a jeopardy determination under the Endangered Species Act, even though their interests were primarily economic, not environmental. Although environmentalists did not file briefs in support of the government in the case, because they welcomed a judicial expansion of standing, legal scholar J. B. Ruhl points out that this case marked a significant change in fortune for them.[176] In his opinion for the Court, Justice Scalia wrote that there was no basis for concluding that the act's citizen suit provision applied only to "underenforcement" and not to "overenforcement" of the law. Scalia explained that the requirement to use the "best scientific . . . data available" was intended "to ensure that the ESA not be implemented haphazardly, on the basis of speculation. . . [and] to avoid needless economic dislocation produced by agency officials zealously but unintelligently pursuing their environmental objectives."

Litigation aimed at making the Endangered Species Act more permissive, combined with continuous demands for "takings" legislation and Endangered Species Act reform, shaped the behavior of those responsible for implementing the act, who feared it was vulnerable to serious curtailment. In the early 1990s, a handful of environmental groups had begun to enforce the act using litigation; in response to three large lawsuits, the Fish and Wildlife Service agreed to list 237 species between 1991 and 1995.[177] Those increased listings, in turn, dramatically expanded the reach of the law and placed a heavy burden on regional offices, which were not set up to operate as permit-granting enterprises for property owners seeking to conduct activities that might harm species.[178] In hopes of defusing conservatives' anger over new listings secretary, while also restoring the service's autonomy, Babbitt sought to limit the ability of environmental organizations to force the Fish and Wildlife Service to list species. In the wake of the moratorium placed on listings by Congress in 1995, the Interior Department requested *less* money for listing activities in fiscal year 1997 than had been allocated in the previous fiscal year: $7.483 million versus $8.157 million. Congress responded by appropriating only $5 million.[179] In addition, Congress acquiesced to the department's requests that it sharply limit the budget for critical habitat designations for fiscal years 1997, 1998, and 1999.[180]

Babbitt took a series of additional steps to both regain control over Endangered Species Act implementation and placate critics. He developed a set of administrative policies that curbed petitions and lawsuits by nongovernmental organizations, thereby easing the pressure for new listings. Most important, in late 1995, the Interior Department issued a policy prohibiting petitions to list species already on the candidate list; therefore, the agency was no longer obliged to process a "second" petition according to a statutory timetable. Then, in 1997, the Fish and Wildlife Service began employing a rarely used statutory provision to claim that it was "not practicable" to issue findings on petitions within ninety days. The consequences were readily apparent: in 1996, the wildlife agencies listed thirty-one species in response to petitions without being sued; between 1997 and 2003, they listed a total of only six species in this fashion. Because they accepted so few listing petitions, few enforceable deadlines were established, and few new lawsuits could be filed. The agencies also "dramatically reduced the number of species listed at their discretion. In 1996, [they] listed 40 species through that pathway. Between 1997 and 2000, they listed 11."[181]

Concerns about the prospect of a legislative rollback of the Endangered Species Act also made federal officials more receptive to landowner-friendly prescriptions, which themselves arose out of a combination of learning from experience and aversion to conflict. At the beginning of his tenure, Babbitt was saddled with resolving the spotted owl controversy that had plagued the Bush administration. To resolve that conflict, President Clinton convened a "timber summit" in the Pacific Northwest in April 1993, at which he urged environmentalists, scientists, representatives of the timber industry, and government officials to reach a consensus about how to break the impasse over protecting the owl. He promised the upshot would be a "balanced and comprehensive long-term policy" that would be "scientifically sound, ecologically credible and legally responsible."[182] Three months later, the administration released its Northwest Forest Plan, which allowed for timber harvests of only 1.2 billion board feet (bbf) per year from old-growth forests, down from a high of more than 5 bbf in 1987 and 1988, while setting aside about 7.4 million acres in protected reserves. (The allowable harvest was reduced slightly, to 1.1 bbf, a few months later.) The plan also provided $1.2 billion over five years to assist displaced timber workers. It took effect in early 1995, after getting approval from Seattle District Court judge William Dwyer, who had halted most of the logging in the region four years earlier.

While the Northwest Forest Plan was being prepared, Babbitt announced he would launch a major policy shift to minimize contention resulting from "repeated eleventh-hour listings" and therefore avert "national train wrecks" like the one over the spotted owl. "Everyone agrees," Babbitt told the House Natural Resources Committee in February 1993, "we're going to need to revisit the concepts of the Endangered Species Act" and determine "if we can't find some way to look at ecosystems on a multispecies basis" in order to "take reasonable steps" to "deal with the economic tradeoffs" before a crisis erupts. If we behave proactively, he argued, we have more "flexibility to manage the problem."[183] Babbitt proposed conducting a national scientific assessment of the nation's biological diversity that would lay the groundwork for negotiated settlements with landowners. To create this map, he wanted to establish a National Biological Survey (NBS), analogous to the U.S. Geological Survey, that would consolidate the Interior Department's biological research in a single agency. Babbitt initially established the NBS through administrative action, but conservatives in the 104th Congress raised fears that it would trample on private property rights. Ultimately, it was renamed the Biological Resources Division and moved into the Geological Survey, and its purview was sharply curtailed.

Despite this setback, Babbitt continued to seek ways to advance conservation without inflaming the opposition. In the spring of 1995, as efforts to gut the Endangered Species Act gathered steam in Congress, Babbitt proposed a set of modest administrative changes to the act. Specifically, he proposed exempting from regulation activities on small plots of land (less than five acres, a delineation that covered 95 percent of all homes in the country), giving more power to state governments to carry out the law, and requiring future listing decisions to be supported by independent peer reviews. In addition, Secretary Babbitt and James Baker, undersecretary of commerce, laid out ten principles to guide Endangered Species Act implementation. The principles—most of which would make the law more permissive—were designed to minimize the impact of the act on landowners, grant more authority to state and local governments, require greater scientific scrutiny of endangered species decisions, and make Endangered Species Act implementation more "efficient."[184] Baker insisted that following the principles would yield a "more balanced and practical approach" to the task of conserving biological diversity. "With these changes," he said, "we are signifying our commitment to making the act work for the human species as well."[185]

Consistent with these principles, Babbitt introduced several voluntary programs through which private landowners could undertake conservation activities in return for regulatory relief. One such mechanism was the candidate conservation agreement, which allows landowners to address the needs of species that are candidates for listing on the condition that they will not be subject to future regulatory obligations if the species is subsequently listed. Another novel mechanism was the safe harbor agreement, in which landowners who improve habitat for endangered species on their property receive assurances that they will not be subject to penalties or additional land-use restrictions if they later undo the improvements and restore their property to "baseline" conditions.

Most prominently, Babbitt promoted the development of habitat conservation plans (HCPs), which allow landowners to develop some of their property in exchange for conserving prime habitat for endangered species. Preparation of an HCP enables landowners to avoid the Endangered Species Act prohibition on "take" of listed species. Landowners receive an "incidental take permit" if the Fish and Wildlife Service finds the impacts will be minimized and mitigated "to the maximum extent practicable" and the taking would not "appreciably reduce the likelihood of the survival and recovery of a listed species." Created by legislation in 1982, the HCP mechanism was rarely employed before 1993 (only fourteen HCPs were approved between 1982 and 1992). The number of HCPs rose dramatically in 1994, however, after Babbitt introduced the No Surprises policy, which freed landowners from additional obligations once an agreement was approved by the Fish and Wildlife Service.

When the administration codified No Surprises in a formal rule and invited public comment, it received over 750 letters in opposition and only 50 in favor. Subsequently, a series of studies revealed flaws in the HCP process. In 1997, 167 prominent scientists wrote a letter to Congress expressing concerns about the No Surprises policy, arguing it did "not reflect ecological reality and reject[ed] the best scientific knowledge and judgment of our era."[186] Nevertheless, in 1998, the administration finalized the No Surprises Rule, and in 1999, promulgated the Permit Revocation Rule, according to which an incidental take permit may not be revoked unless continuation puts a listed species in jeopardy of extinction—another mechanism adding certainty for landowners. In an effort to quell the complaints of scientists and environmentalists, between 1999 and 2000, the Interior Department responded to the five main issues raised in critical studies and comments with a series of clarifications to the guidance for issuing HCPs. Still, some environmentalists worried that its flexibility made HCPs vulnerable to abuse by people with different motivations.[187] By the end of 2000, more than 330 HCPs had been approved and another 200 were under development or pending approval.[188]

According to assistant secretary George Frampton, the idea behind the Interior Department's incentive-based programs was to "change the Endangered Species Act from a regulatory program to more of a cooperative program with state and local governments and private landowners."[189] Karen Donovan, a development lawyer, commented approvingly that "[a]t a time when the ESA was under attack, the no-surprises policy and the HCP program it facilitated gave rise to a constituency of regulated entities willing to acknowledge that it is possible to balance conservation with development and resource use."[190] For his part, Babbitt perceived his reforms not just as a way to defuse attacks on the law, but also as efforts to use the law creatively to enhance biodiversity.[191]

Some environmentalists were skeptical, however. Many supported the focus on conserving habitat rather than individual species, a move that reflected the concerns of biologists. But others worried that HCPs, as they were being implemented, would benefit developers more than species. For example, attorney John Kostyack charged that implementation of the Endangered Species Act by the Clinton administration had "radically changed how the ESA is administered . . . from a system of regulation by citizen enforcement toward a system of largely closed-door negotiations between agencies and regulated interests, with little meaningful public involvement."[192] He claimed that the administration had seriously weakened safeguards for listed species that were key features of the 1982 amendments creating the HCP concept.

Not all environmentalists were critical of Babbitt's innovation. In 1992, conservation biologist Michael O'Connell noted with alarm the rising number of legislative attacks on the Endangered Species Act, as well as the growing number of meetings being held across the country to discuss anti-ESA strategy. He pointed out that the law's supporters were struggling to defend it against "rapidly organizing opposition."[193] Similarly, although skeptical of compensating landowners who were simply complying with the law, Rodger Schlickeissen, CEO of Defenders of Wildlife, was "all for creating positive incentives to reward landowners who go beyond what the law requires."[194] Michael Bean, a lawyer with the Environmental Defense Fund who helped design the new policies, had learned from experience that some of the criticism of the Endangered Species Act was justified.[195] In a series of articles, Bean noted that the great majority of endangered species occur on privately owned land, and that efforts to conserve species on private land had not been very successful.[196] "[C]onflicts—or perceived conflicts—between species conservation and the interests of private landowners are increasingly common," he wrote, "and have provided much of the fodder for a recent backlash against not just the ESA, but environmental regulations and programs in general."[197] That backlash, he went on, was imperiling information-gathering efforts on which conservation must be based, and impeding cooperation between government and landowners. Such conflicts might be an acceptable cost if the result was excellent conservation, but the evidence suggested that the conservation gains associated with Endangered Species Act regulations were not substantial. Furthermore, there was some evidence that landowners were acting preemptively to destroy endangered species on their land before they could be catalogued and protected. Absent legislation providing positive incentives, the only option was to use the act's provisions creatively to conserve habitat, as Babbitt was doing.

In an effort to codify in legislation some of the changes Babbitt was making, in the 105th Congress (1997–1998), Senate Republicans John Chafee of Rhode Island and Dirk Kempthorne of Idaho, in collaboration with Democrats Max Baucus of Montana and Harry Reid of Nevada, circulated the Endangered Species Recovery Act, which put a congressional stamp of approval on Babbitt's No Surprises policy, created incentives for landowners to conserve habitat, and required economic impact analyses as part of the listing process. Like Babbitt's administrative innovations, the bill divided environmentalists into pragmatists and idealists. While the Nature Conservancy and Environmental Defense Fund supported it, the Native Forest Council of Eugene, Oregon, and Defenders of Wildlife condemned it as an "immoral tool of compromise."[198] Prominent scientists representing eleven scientific societies published a full-page ad in the *New York Times* in February 1998 condemning it. According to the scientists, by supporting compromises such as HCPs, the bill facilitated species extinction; "no private or public agency action," they wrote, "should negatively modify habitat occupied by a threatened, endangered, or candidate species." At the same time, property rights advocates opposed the bill because it did not go far enough and, in particular, did not guarantee compensation for regulatory takings under the act.

In an effort to bolster support for Kempthorne's bill while fending off more drastic reforms, in May 1998, Babbitt announced plans to remove twenty-nine formerly threatened plants and animals from the endangered list, declaring them fully or partly recovered. Among the species targeted for removal was the gray wolf, whose protection had particularly infuriated ranchers in the West. In the end, however, the Senate majority leader refused to bring the bill to the floor. Although proponents hoped to attach the measure to the omnibus spending bill, thereby rewriting the Endangered Species Act without a separate vote in the House or Senate, House conservatives managed to prevent this as well. For the bill's proponents, its fate was a prime example of how polarization in Congress impeded the adoption of meaningful reform.

## Preventing Action to Address Climate Change

While environmentalists remained deeply concerned about controlling air pollution and conserving biodiversity, the issue on which they focused increasingly during the 1990s was climate change. A series of reports released by the prestigious Intergovernmental Panel on Climate Change expressed growing confidence that human activities were altering the global climate, with potentially devastating impacts on the earth's biophysical systems. Even as environmentalists issued dire warnings about the likely environmental consequences of greenhouse gas emissions, however, conservative activists advanced an alternative definition of the problem. They claimed that climate change was not a serious concern, while criticizing proposals to curb greenhouse gas emissions as economically devastating. Initially it appeared as though President Clinton would take bold steps to reduce the nation's greenhouse gas emissions. But the administration soon retreated in the face of a staunch defense of the permissive status quo by conservative members of Congress and their industry allies, as well as skepticism among the president's own economic advisors.

### Conservatives Redefine the Problem of Climate Change
Although they decried claims about the hazards of air pollution and the perils facing species, conservatives reserved their most biting commentary for climate change. They brought all the elements of the antiregulatory storyline to bear in an effort to discredit the thesis that human-caused greenhouse gas emissions, as well as widespread deforestation, were causing potentially catastrophic changes in the global climate. First and foremost, conservatives rejected the notion that global warming was an impending crisis. To support their position, they marshaled arguments by contrarian scientists that the science supporting the theory of climate change was highly uncertain. They asserted that scientists knew little about the critical interaction between the ocean and the atmosphere; the impact of sulfate aerosols and clouds on climate was poorly understood; the natural variability of the climate dwarfed the observed warming to date; and the global circulation models on which climate forecasts were based were driven by unverifiable assumptions. In the 1995 volume *The True State of the Planet*, geographer Robert Balling Jr. purported to

deconstruct the science on which claims about climate change rested, concluding, "The scientific evidence argues against the existence of a greenhouse crisis, against the notion that realistic policies could achieve any meaningful climate impact, and against the claim we must act now if we are able to reduce the greenhouse threat."[199] Similarly, conservative columnist Warren Brookes charged, "As bad as the Clean Air Act is . . ., the most insane threat to our way of life is the alleged 'crisis' of climate change, whose scarier scenarios are fading before the cold light of factual dissent even as the [George H. W.] Bush Administration signs on to a program of worldwide [carbon dioxide] control."[200]

Invariably, the villains in conservatives' definition of the problem were environmentalists, who exaggerated the seriousness of the threat in an effort to scare their victims (the American public) into giving them control over the government. Ben Bolch and Harold Lyons cautioned that "the prevention of any possible greenhouse effect will require a degree of bureaucratic control over economic affairs previously unknown in the West"—which they asserted was precisely the aim of the "eco-socialists" who advocated the prevention of global warming.[201] In the same vein, S. Fred Singer claimed that warnings about climate change were part of a larger, coordinated effort to "establish international controls over industrial processes and business operations."[202]

Second, conservatives denigrated solutions to global warming that involved pricing or limiting carbon, arguing that such measures would cripple the U.S. economy, particularly if developing nations—which accounted for a growing fraction of the world's greenhouse gas emissions—were allowed to continue building coal-fired power plants without controls. Writing in the *National Review*, conservative writer Jane Shaw and economist Richard Stroup raised concerns that curbing greenhouse gas emissions "would give government greater power, would force people to make large sacrifices, and would probably limit innovation." They argued, "The most effective thing that we can do to cope with climate change is to allow progress to continue. . . . Human progress is exactly what enabled people to cope with catastrophes in the past and it can continue to do so." They concluded, "As scientific understanding of the global atmosphere improves, our ability to make well-informed policy decisions should improve too. Let's hope that those decisions take into account the resilience that comes from freedom and material progress."[203]

Likewise, Wilfred Beckerman, a research fellow with the Independent Institute, and fellow conservative Jesse Malkin argued that any charge that we are being unfair to the future is a red herring because economic growth and technological development will take care of future generations. In short, "global warming may be a problem, but it is no cause for undue alarm or drastic action. . . . It does not justify diverting vast amounts of time, energy, and funds from more urgent environmental problems, particularly those in developing countries. Nor does it justify a massive diversion of resources from high-yield projects in the private sector."[204] The heroes in this conservative narrative were businesspeople, particularly the purveyors of cheap energy, who enabled the productive economy that furnished ordinary Americans with jobs and inexpensive products, and hence a high standard of living.

Some conservatives added a twist: they suggested that if global warming *was* happening it would probably *benefit* the United States; in any case it could not be stopped, so there was no point in expending resources, except perhaps on adaptation. The most prominent proponent of this view, economist Thomas Gale Moore, pointed out in the *Public Interest* that service industries, the foundation of the modern U.S. economy, could prosper in a warm climate as well as in a cold one. Moreover, he argued, higher temperatures combined with more carbon dioxide in the atmosphere would enhance plant and crop growth, thereby providing more food for the burgeoning global population.[205]

Like their conservative allies, industry—particularly the fossil fuel trade associations that represented those implicated as villains in environmentalists' definition of the climate change problem—reviled efforts to stabilize carbon dioxide emissions. John Knebel, president of the American Mining Congress, charged that the proposed United Nations treaty to coordinate action on climate change not only ignored scientific and economic realities, but also "opened the door for people like Rep. Waxman and Sen. Gore to demand that other countries dictate to our nation what determines an appropriate level of economic activity." Richard Lawson, president of the National Coal Association, argued that domestic legislation "would serve only to exacerbate U.S. dependence on foreign energy sources, reduce economic activity and increase unemployment." The Edison Electric Institute issued a statement arguing the law "would impose great economic costs for minimal environmental benefits."[206] Thomas Donohue of the U.S. Chamber of Commerce warned that "if the U.S. negotiators were looking for a way to mess up the world's most prosperous and productive economy, this is the way to do it."[207]

Leaving nothing to chance, industry poured resources into lobbying campaigns to persuade politicians. In 1991, the year before the United Nations Earth Summit in Rio de Janeiro, Brazil, a group of utility and coal companies led by the Western Fuels Association created the Information Council on the Environment (ICE), whose aim was to "reposition global warming as theory rather than fact."[208] The campaign, devised by the polling firm Cambridge Reports, targeted "older, less-educated men" and "young, low-income women" in electoral districts that got their electricity from coal and, ideally, had a member of Congress on the House Energy Committee. ICE involved promoting the views of prominent scientific contrarians Patrick Michaels, Robert Balling, and Sherwood B. Idso by staging public appearances, placing op-ed pieces, and setting up newspaper interviews. The ICE campaign was just getting under way when environmentalists leaked it to the *New York Times*. It disbanded after receiving a wave of adverse publicity.[209] Whereas ICE sought to discredit climate science, the Global Climate Coalition (GCC), launched in 1989 by fifty-four industry and trade-association members, focused on disparaging climate-change policies—probably because, as *New York Times* reporter Andrew Revkin revealed in April 2009, the GCC's own scientific and technical experts advised them that the scientific support for the role of greenhouse gases in causing climate change was irrefutable.[210]

Although cautious about producing their own anti-science campaigns, threatened industries generously funded conservative efforts to discredit environmentalists' climate change narrative. During the 1990s, a host of new organizations began propagating the antiregulatory definition of the climate change problem. Prominent among these was the Science and Environmental Policy Project (SEPP), directed by S. Fred Singer. SEPP worked furiously to undermine confidence in climate change science, even as the global scientific consensus about global warming strengthened. In 1995, two reports—one by the EPA and the other by the IPCC—expressed broad agreement among scientists that human activity was changing the climate and that governments ought to take steps to avert some of the consequences. That same year, SEPP sponsored the Leipzig Declaration, a manifesto aimed at countering the mainstream view of climate change. Ostensibly signed by eighty scientists and twenty-five meteorologists, the declaration asserted (falsely), "There does not exist today a general scientific consensus about the importance of greenhouse warming from rising levels of carbon dioxide. On the contrary, most scientists now accept the fact that actual observations from earth satellites show no climate warming whatsoever."[211]

In 1998, SEPP helped to circulate the so-called Oregon Petition written by physicist Frederick Seitz, a former president of the National Academy of Sciences. The petition urged the United States to reject the Kyoto Protocol because "proposed limits on greenhouse gases would harm the environment, hinder the advance of science and technology, and damage the health and welfare of mankind." In any case, the petition added, the protocol was unwarranted because there was no convincing evidence "that human release of . . . greenhouse gases is causing or will, in the foreseeable future, cause catastrophic heating of the Earth's atmosphere and disruption of the Earth's climate." In fact, it noted, "there is substantial scientific evidence that increases in atmospheric carbon dioxide produce many beneficial effects upon the natural plant and animal environments of the Earth."[212] The article that accompanied the petition, was in a format and typeface identical to the one used by the academy for its journal, *Proceedings of the National Academy of Sciences*; a cover letter from Seitz identified him as a past president of the academy. (The academy immediately disassociated itself from the statement and petition.)

During the 1990s, conservatives increasingly capitalized on the Web, which provided a relatively inexpensive means of disseminating their definition of the climate change problem as inconsequential and their negative image of policies to address it. One web-based organization, Citizens for a Sound Economy, warned that imposing regulation to curb greenhouse gas emissions could cost 4.9 million jobs. Another, the Cooler Heads Coalition, backed by conservative and libertarian advocacy groups, offered ways to educate children about the environment: "Explain to them that at the time dinosaurs lived, the atmosphere had carbon-dioxide levels that were at least five times greater than what we now have, and that these high levels of carbon dioxide contributed to the rich vegetation," the group's Web site suggested. A third organization, the Advancement of Sound Science Coalition, hosted a Web site called the Junk Science Home Page, where it posted an essay that explained, "As far as agriculture is concerned, a modest warming is bound to be beneficial for several reasons. The increase would register largely as warmer nighttime and winter temperatures, leading to fewer frosts and longer growing seasons, while increased carbon dioxide will stimulate plant growth and lessen the plants' need for water."[213]

In addition to sponsoring Web sites, conservative think tanks published a slew of books—such as Patrick Michaels' *Sound and Fury: The Science and Politics of Global Warming* (Cato Institute, 1992), Robert C. Balling's *The Heated Debate: Greenhouse Predictions Versus Climate Reality* (Pacific Research Institute for Public Policy, 1992), *Hot Talk, Cold Science: Climate Change's Unfinished Debate* (The Independent Institute, 1997) by S. Fred Singer and Frederick Seitz, and Thomas Gale Moore's *Climate of Fear: Why We Shouldn't Worry About Global Warming* (Cato Institute, 1998)—all aimed at furnishing detailed, if inaccurate, rebuttals of the case for climate change policies. They also issued briefing pamphlets for candidates, sponsored policy forums, held press conferences, and delivered testimony at congressional hearings.

Numerous studies suggest that the industry-funded conservative challenge to climate change policy affected both media coverage of the issue and public opinion. For example, based on a content analysis of prestige-press coverage of global warming between 1988 and 2002, Maxwell and Jules Boykoff found a significant divergence between scientific and popular discourse. In 1988 and 1989, most of the media coverage emphasized man-made contributions to global warming, mirroring the scientific discourse of the time. By the release of the first assessment by the IPCC in 1990, however, coverage had shifted to "balanced" accounts that gave equal time to the views of scientific contrarians.[214]

Public opinion followed a similar pattern. In the late 1980s, public opinion polls showed a dramatic rise in public concern about climate change. For instance, a poll conducted for the Union of Concerned Scientists by the chief pollster for the Bush/Quayle campaign in November 1989 found that about 80 percent of respondents were aware of global warming, compared to 58 percent in 1988.[215] In a 1990 Gallup poll, 30 percent of respondents said they worried "a great deal" about global warming or the greenhouse effect;[216] another 1990 poll found that 72 percent of respondents wanted the United States to lead the fight against global warming. By 1991, however, as media coverage shifted to debates over the seriousness of the problem and the costs of addressing it, polls showed the public becoming less concerned about the issue.[217] Whereas a January 1992 Gallup poll found that 61 percent of Americans thought the effects of global warming had already begun to be felt, by 1997, only 41 percent agreed with that assessment. Writing for the Gallup Poll On-Line, David Moore contended that the key to public opinion was public perception about what most scientists thought; 42 percent said scientists mostly believed global warming was a serious threat, while 44 percent said scientists were mostly divided on the issue. Maxwell and Jules Boykoff likewise concluded that "scientific uncertainty has been the key ingredient inserted into the debates regarding action, often in order to inspire inaction."[218]

### Permissive Climate Change Governance

Early on, the Clinton administration appeared poised to act boldly to curb greenhouse gas emissions: the president promised in his first Earth Day speech to convert energy consumption in the United States from fossil fuels to clean-burning and renewable sources. Specifically, he vowed to reduce greenhouse gas emissions to 1990 levels by 2000. At the same time, Clinton's speech reflected the influence of antiregulatory ideas: the president instructed his administration to "prepare a cost-effective plan . . . This must be a clarion call, not for more bureaucracy or regulation or unnecessary costs, but instead for American ingenuity and creativity, to produce the best and most energy-efficient technology." This formulation was the product of sharp disagreement within his administration, with Gore pressing Clinton to fulfill his campaign promise to address climate change and Energy Department Secretary Hazel O'Leary and Treasury Secretary Lloyd Bentsen expressing concern about the impact of emissions limits on industry.[219]

In short order, Congress dampened Clinton's momentum by quashing the administration's first climate-related initiative, a tax on the energy content of fuels measured in British thermal units, or Btus. Proposed at the behest of Vice President Gore, the Btu tax would have levied a fee on fossil fuels, hydroelectric, and nuclear power, with an additional charge for petroleum products. Environmentalists had hoped to amass support for the tax by linking interest in both checking carbon dioxide emissions and reducing the nation's dependence on foreign oil with pressing concern about reducing the deficit.[220] The measure narrowly passed in the House (219–213), after President Clinton threw his weight behind it. But lobbyists for the coal and oil industries promptly sprang into action. They conducted an intense public relations campaign to pressure key Democrats on the Senate Finance Committee by persuading their constituents that the Btu tax would hurt consumers, particularly those with lower incomes, hamper American competitiveness, and drain the economy.[221] Gore argued passionately for trying to save the tax, which had already been gutted by changes made to assuage various interests, but Clinton abandoned it in order to save his overall economic plan.[222]

As journalist Eric Pooley points out, the campaign against the Btu tax was successful in several respects: the tax died; those who had voted for it in the House paid for it in the next election; and many observers concluded that a carbon tax was politically infeasible.[223]

After the demise of the Btu tax, infighting erupted once again between Vice President Gore and his camp, who wanted to press for tough measures to mitigate global warming, and the president's more conservative economic advisors, particularly Lawrence Summers, deputy secretary of the treasury, and Janet Yellen, chair of the Council of Economic Advisers. So it was not entirely surprising when, on October 19, 1993, the president unveiled a Climate Change Action Plan that consisted exclusively of voluntary measures: fifty initiatives that would ostensibly reduce the nation's greenhouse gas emissions to 1990 levels by 2000, a reduction of one hundred million metric tons per year. The plan called for $1.9 billion in federal spending, most of it redirected from existing programs, that would in theory stimulate $60 billion in private sector investment.[224] Industry leaders immediately praised the plan's flexibility.[225] But environmental groups, even those that generally support incentive-based policies, like the Environmental Defense Fund, were critical, pointing out that the plan did not provide strong incentives or backup measures if voluntary steps proved inadequate.

Upon taking control of Congress in 1995, House Republicans used their power to obstruct efforts to limit U.S. greenhouse gas emissions. They lost no time in convening hearings aimed at discrediting the science behind climate change and other global environmental problems. Republican Dana Rohrabacher of California announced in February 1995 that the Subcommittee on Energy and the Environment would investigate "charges that political pressure was put on people making scientific decisions" about ozone depletion and climate change.[226] At the hearings themselves, "witnesses alleged that the scientific community and environmental activists had systematically exaggerated the gravity of these issues to the public, the media, and policymakers and had ignored, even actively suppressed, contrary scientific data and views."[227]

Despite the activism of conservatives in Congress, the Clinton administration continued to work with other nations during a two-year series of international meetings whose goal was to flesh out a climate change treaty that could be signed in Kyoto, Japan in December 1997. In mid-July 1996, Timothy Wirth, undersecretary of state for global affairs, called for the international community to set a "realistic, verifiable and binding medium-term emissions target," saying the scientific evidence for climate change "cannot be ignored and is increasingly compelling."[228] The notion that the United States would sign on to a binding commitment spurred a massive response from the fossil fuel industry, however, and industry groups began contacting the president directly, launching new public relations campaigns, and mobilizing their members. For example, the Western Fuels Association provided "rapid response to the spurious reports that try to create . . . a phony picture of increasing weather catastrophes caused by emissions."[229] As the Kyoto negotiations neared, the Global Climate Coalition launched a $13 million ad campaign warning that policies to address global warming would prompt job losses and economic dislocation.[230] One GCC ad warned television viewers, "Strict reductions in greenhouse gases would have catastrophic economic consequences, endangering the lifestyle of every American. Gasoline would shoot up by fifty cents or more a gallon; heating and electricity bills would soar, while higher energy costs would raise the price of almost everything Americans buy. The livelihood of thousands of coal miners, auto-workers, and others employed in energy-related fields was on the line."[231]

The mobilization by industry and their conservative allies appeared to pay off: in late July 1997, the Senate voted 95–0 on a resolution against any treaty that did not require developing nations to control their emissions or that would impose "serious harm" on the U.S. economy. Supporters of a climate change treaty, including Democratic senators John Kerry of Massachusetts and Joseph Lieberman of Connecticut, believed that a unanimous vote could not possibly be taken as a referendum against *any* treaty. But, in fact, the resolution was widely interpreted as a sign that the Senate was monolithically opposed to action on climate change.[232] The Senate's action was particularly striking, given that six years earlier the chamber had approved by a vote of 87–11 a nonbinding resolution calling on President Bush George H. W. Bush to take a leadership role on global warming at the Rio Earth Summit.[233]

The anti-Kyoto mobilization bore fruit in other respects as well. Despite the fact that U.S. emissions were continuing to rise under his 1993 plan, thanks to vigorous economic growth and low fuel prices, Clinton continued to pursue a voluntary approach to curbing greenhouse gas emissions. In October 1997, in an effort to demonstrate the United States' commitment, he pledged to "harness the power of the free market" to cut U.S. emissions to 1990 levels between 2008 and 2012 through tax incentives and research subsidies for clean energy and conservation.[234] He proposed to begin with a five-year, $6.3 billion program of tax credits for companies that invested in energy-saving technologies, along with government spending on energy research. He also proposed a set of incentive-based programs in which companies would earn credit if they reduced their greenhouse gas emissions or helped firms in other countries to do so. These credits could then be sold to other firms in the United States or abroad. The weakness of Clinton's proposals reflected not only the political uncertainty created by vigorous political opposition, but also the competing advice he was receiving from his advisors. Wirth, who left his post after the Kyoto talks, and White House environmental advisor Katie McGinty both advocated an aggressive greenhouse-gas-reduction plan. But Clinton scaled back that plan incrementally as he listened to warnings of his senior economic advisors.[235] The disagreements within the White House revolved around the desirability of raising the cost of energy to stimulate technological development, and the reliability of predictions of how markets would respond to new regulations.[236]

Clinton's goals were modest relative to those proposed by the European nations (15 percent below 1990 levels by 2010) and even Japan (5 percent below 1990 levels by 2010). Nevertheless, conservatives in Congress lost little time in denouncing the administration's plan as an economic disaster. The House majority whip Tom DeLay said, "Before we do anything that hurts children, hurts our nation's competitiveness, hurts the taxpayers and hurts economic growth, we need to know all the facts."[237] Representative Bliley, chair of the House Commerce Committee, was equally negative. "What the president is proposing," he said, "is unilateral disarmament by the United States. The result will be a treaty that isn't global and which won't work, and that ultimately will cost American jobs and raise American taxes."[238] Representative James Sensenbrenner of Wisconsin agreed. "The Clinton-Gore climate plan threatens the quality of life for all Americans," he said. Its restrictions would "result in higher energy prices for working Americans and send U.S. jobs overseas."[239]

Opposition to the Kyoto Protocol mounted—not just among conservatives and industry groups but also among Democrats from coal-dependent states, as well as from unions representing coal miners and auto workers, which feared layoffs. But it was conservative Republicans who took the most vocal aim at the treaty, parroting the antiregulatory depiction of the agreement. Journalist Ron Elving described Republicans as competing to see who could forecast the direst consequences of Kyoto.[240] For example, Senator Chuck Hagel echoed the concerns of Gail McDonald, president of the Global Climate Coalition, who said meeting the protocol's emissions reduction goals would require restrictions on energy use and "result in devastating job losses and skyrocketing energy prices."[241] "Protecting our environment is an honorable goal," said Representative Bill Paxon, a fast-rising Republican star from New York. "But we must ask ourselves an equally important question: 'Can we afford to destroy our children's economic future in the process?'"[242]

To the dismay of treaty opponents, after a last-minute appearance by Gore, U.S. negotiators in Kyoto agreed to a protocol that committed the United States to reducing its emissions 7 percent below 1990 levels between 2008 and 2012, while declining to impose binding reductions on developing countries. (The European Union agreed to cut its emissions by 8 percent, Japan by 6 percent.) The treaty was designed to take effect when ratified by at least fifty-five countries representing 55 percent of total emissions by industrialized countries. But domestic opponents were determined to prevent the treaty from being signed by the president or ratified by the Senate. Fresh from their victory on health care, conservatives set out to frame the Kyoto Protocol in the minds of Americans as a looming economic catastrophe. Steve Forbes, a Republican presidential candidate, called the protocol "an unprecedented government seizure of American freedom and sovereignty." Audrey Mullen, executive director of Americans for Tax Reform, said, "Al Gore would prefer to stick working-class America with a big tax increase and stick America with lost jobs or seek the approval of his liberal environmentalist tree-hugging friends."[243] In a hearing on June 4, 1998, before the Energy and Natural Resources Committee, Senator Murkowski remained stubbornly opposed to mandatory greenhouse gas reductions. "We are talking about profoundly altering the economic destiny of this country. We are talking about severe disruptions to the energy sector of our economy," he said.[244] Senator Hagel insisted, "The science is at best uncertain. And we don't know all the economic consequences, although what we do know is devastating."[245]

Conservative legislators were determined not only to block ratification of the Kyoto Protocol but also to prevent the administration from using its discretion to implement the terms of the treaty. To that end, they adopted the low-profile tactic of attaching riders to budget legislation that prohibited spending on climate-related activities. For example, in addition to cutting spending on climate change research, the House version of the EPA appropriations bill for fiscal year 1999 prevented the administration from spending money to "develop, propose or issue regulations, decrees or orders for the purpose of implementation, or in contemplation of implementation, of the Kyoto Protocol."[246] The bill's committee report also included language directing the EPA to "refrain from conducting educational outreach or informational seminars on policies underlying the Kyoto Protocol" unless the treaty was ratified by the Senate.[247] Defending the amendment, Representative Joe Knollenberg of Michigan succinctly reiterated the objections of the conservative-industry coalition, "The Kyoto Treaty is unfair. It's based on immature science. And it would have a chilling effect on the American economy."[248] The omnibus spending bill, finalized in late October 1998, prohibited spending to implement the Kyoto Protocol and reduced the $1.29 billion requested by the White House for energy-efficiency and renewable-energy initiatives to $1 billion, although it did not contain the prohibition on climate-related outreach and education.

Ignoring his critics, in mid-November 1998, President Clinton signed the Kyoto Protocol, a largely symbolic move aimed at giving a boost to negotiators in Buenos Aires, who were struggling to work out the details of the treaty's implementation.[249] Although he declined to submit it for ratification, Clinton's decision to sign the treaty set off another furious round of negative commentary. Republican Larry Craig of Idaho commented, "By signing such an agreement, it will be the first time in history that an American president has allowed foreign interests to control and limit the growth of the U.S. economy."[250] On May 20, 1999, the House and Senate held a rare joint hearing to review the administration's budget request for climate change activities, and conservative lawmakers again seized the opportunity to disparage the Kyoto Protocol. That summer, the Republican Congress approved bills covering fiscal year 2000 appropriations for Interior, EPA, Commerce, Justice, and State that prohibited spending to implement the treaty. Frustrated, Clinton resorted to low-profile tactics of his own: in June 1999, he issued an executive order requiring the federal government to cut its greenhouse gas emissions by 30 percent.[251]

## Conservative Ideas Advance in the Courts

Even as conservative lawmakers were wrangling with the Clinton administration, their allies in the federal courts were providing the movement with a slow but steady series of victories on several important matters of principle. For example, during the 1990s, conservatives saw progress in the courts' interpretation of the Fifth Amendment's "takings" clause, an area in which there was relatively little "settled law" to circumscribe judges' decisions.[252] In *Dolan v. City of Tigard* (1994), the owner of a plumbing and electrical supply store in Tigard, Oregon, sought to expand her store and pave its parking lot. The city granted approval on the condition that she dedicate a portion of her land to a bike-and-pedestrian path that ran behind her store. A five-to-four majority of the Supreme Court found the city's requirements to be an uncompensated taking of Dolan's property. The Court explained that zoning officials could impose exactions on property owners only if they were related to the proposed development and were "roughly proportional" to any harms that development may cause. Legal scholar Rosemary O'Leary argues that the implications of the court's doctrine in *Dolan* were "profound."[253] She notes that the ruling was likely to dampen local regulatory activity because it imposed the burden of proof on strapped local governments to conduct detailed analyses demonstrating that proposed regulatory actions were justified.

Six years later, a ruling by the Ninth Circuit Court of Appeals in *Tahoe-Sierra Preservation Council, Inc. v. Tahoe Regional Planning Agency*, clarified the limits of regulatory takings jurisprudence. Between 1981 and 1984, the Tahoe Regional Planning Agency had imposed two development moratoria to give community planners time to formulate a comprehensive plan for the Lake Tahoe area. The council, a consortium of real estate owners, argued that the moratoria deprived property owners of gains they would have made from developing their land, so they were entitled to compensation. The planning agency responded that the temporary measure, by definition, did not deprive property owners of all their land value and so did not require compensation. The Ninth Circuit ruled in favor of the planning agency, and in 2002, by a vote of six to three, the Supreme Court upheld the Ninth Circuit ruling. Justice John Paul Stevens, writing for the majority, held that whether a taking has occurred depends on a mix of considerations: landowners' expectations, actual impact, the public interest, and the reasons for the moratorium. He added that imposing a categorical rule that any deprivation of all economic use, no matter how brief, constitutes a compensable taking would impose unreasonable financial obligations on government for normal delays in processing land-use applications.[254]

Thanks to a series of rulings, environmentalists' access to the courts continued to decline during the 1990s. Although neither the Supreme Court nor the lower courts invalidated citizen suit provisions, they continued to raise the bar for standing to sue. As a result, according to both sides, environmental groups lost much of their influence.[255] In 1997, the

Third Circuit Court of Appeals ruled that citizens living along a river in New Jersey lacked standing under the Clean Water Act to sue a chemical company for polluting the river because, although the company had 150 Clean Water Act violations, the plaintiffs could not show that the upstream discharges had caused downstream harm (*Public Interest Research Group of New Jersey v. Magnesium Elektron, Inc.*). The following year, in *Steel Company v. Citizens for a Better Environment*, the Supreme Court held (6–3) that citizens living near an industrial plant in Illinois lacked standing to challenge the company's failure to file reports documenting the use and storage of hazardous chemicals. The rationale for denying standing in this case was that any fine would go to the government, and the injunctive relief sought could not correct a past injury. (The company began reporting its emissions upon receiving notice of the plaintiffs' intent to sue.) Legal scholars John Echeverria and Jon Zeidler suggest this evolution in standing was the result of an "unusually focused and determined effort at jurisprudential reform" by Justice Scalia.[256]

Like their victories on regulatory takings, conservatives' triumph on standing was circumscribed in 2000, when the Supreme Court definitively reversed the Fourth Circuit Court of Appeals' decision in *Friends of the Earth v. Laidlaw*. In 1998, the Fourth Circuit denied standing to Friends of the Earth in its suit against Laidlaw Environmental Services, a hazardous waste operator, for some two thousand violations of its Clean Water Act permit. This ruling overturned the district court, which found that Laidlaw had violated its permit under the Clean Water Act, and a consortium of environmental groups was entitled to civil penalties that would be paid to the federal government. By a 7–2 majority, the Supreme Court reversed the Fourth Circuit's decision on two grounds: first, individual members of the environmental groups lived near the affected river; second, the environmentalists had argued convincingly that civil penalties would deter future violations, and would therefore both address existing injuries and prevent future ones. Subsequent lower-court decisions have hewed to the standard established in *Laidlaw*.

To some extent, the antiregulatory rulings of the 1990s were a product of activists' efforts to purvey an analytic framework that conservative lawyers and judges could draw on in arguing and deciding environmental cases. Throughout the 1990s, conservative public interest law firms posted a steady stream of briefing papers on their Web sites. In addition, a handful of conservative organizations offered seminars on free-market environmentalism, usually at resorts in the West. For example, in 1992, the Montana-based Foundation for Research on Economics and

Environment began hosting all-expense-paid seminars for judges on property rights and the environment .[257] Between 1992 and 1998, according to a 2000 report by the Community Rights Counsel, a liberal public interest law firm, more than 230 federal judges took one or more trips to resort locations for legal seminars paid for by corporations and foundations with an interest in federal litigation on environmental topics.[258] Those seminars made two central points: the market should be relied on to protect the environment, and the "takings" clause of the Constitution should be interpreted to prohibit rules against development in environmentally sensitive places. Federal appeals court judge Abner Mikva points out that judges who attended the seminars wrote ten of the most important rulings of the 1990s curbing federal environmental protections.[259]

Although conservative observers argued that the shift in judicial opinions on takings and standing during the 1990s evinced a "learning process that transcends partisan political considerations,"[260] a spate of systematic empirical studies conducted in the late 1990s suggest instead that the preponderance of conservative judges on the bench explained the result.[261] For most of the Clinton era, the partisan balance worked in favor of conservatives: by the time George H. W. Bush left office, 80 percent of all federal judges were Republican appointees, as were two-thirds of the members of the appellate bench, and Republican appointees dominated all thirteen courts of appeals. During Clinton's tenure the balance slowly shifted, however, and by the time Clinton left office in early 2001, only 42 percent of the appeals court judges had been appointed by Republicans, while 44 percent had been appointed by Democrats, and 14 percent were vacant. Republican appointees still dominated eight of the thirteen courts of appeals, but several of them only narrowly. Eight years of appointments by the Clinton administration meant that conservatives' judicial victories were unlikely to be sustained in the 2000s. Furthermore, judicial victories by environmentalists during the 1990s—such as the 6–3 Supreme Court decision in *Babbitt v. Sweet Home Chapter of Communities for a Greater Oregon*—made clear that precedent and statutory language continued to circumscribe judges' discretion, whatever their ideological predilections.

### Clinton's Compromises Fail to Quell Dissent

The Clinton era saw the ascendance of conservatives in Congress who sought to reduce the impact of regulation on the private sector, even if doing so weakened environmental protection. As in the 1980s, however, direct attacks on existing environmental laws backfired; in fact, they emboldened President Clinton, whose resistance in turn bolstered his popularity. When their direct challenges were rebuffed, conservative legislators adopted a low-profile approach, while reframing their position as a "new environmentalism." Ultimately, conservatives' impact on environmental policy during the 1990s was a mixed bag. On the one hand, industry and their conservative allies were able to do little more than slow the imposition of restrictive air-pollution-control rules. On the other hand, Carol Browner's EPA adopted a host of industry-friendly practices, at least partly in an effort to blunt criticism of regulation. Moreover, conservatives succeeded in discouraging the enforcement of the Endangered Species Act, instead prompting more flexible, developer-friendly implementation. Conservatives' most notable policy triumph, however, was their effectiveness—in concert with industry—at creating doubts about environmentalists' definition of the climate change problem and tarnishing the image of environmentalists' preferred solution (mandatory emissions limits). Both of these successes helped to prevent the enactment of policies to curb greenhouse gas emissions.

After spending most of the decade fending off conservative attacks, the president and his appointees took several bold steps that put conservatives back on the defensive as the Clinton administration drew to a close. The EPA issued a series of restrictive air pollution rules that had long been in the pipeline, including rules designed to curb emissions from diesel engines and remove sulfur from diesel fuel. The EPA also designated mercury as a hazardous air pollutant, thereby setting the stage for requiring mercury emitters—mostly coal-fired power plants—to install the "maximum achievable control technology" (MACT). Other pollution control rules issued in late 2000 included an executive order lowering the acceptable level of arsenic in drinking water from 50 parts per billion (ppb) to 10 ppb, restrictions on the use of several common pesticides, and a requirement that General Electric clean up toxic sediment in the Hudson River.

Urged on by Secretary Babbitt, Clinton acted aggressively on biodiversity conservation as well, in hopes of cementing his legacy. Employing his power under the Antiquities Act of 1906, Clinton set aside over 3 million acres in twenty-one national monuments across the lower forty-eight states—more than any other president in history. As former Interior Department solicitor John Leshy points out, much of that land was put under the jurisdiction of the Bureau of Land Management—a shrewd tactic aimed at moving that agency in a more conservation-oriented direction.[262] Clinton's Interior Department also issued a final rule banning snowmobiles in Yellowstone and Grand Teton National Parks and prohibiting new road construction on 58.5 million acres of undisturbed wilderness in national forests. Finally, the Interior Department issued a regulation that established requirements for cleaning up and restoring mining sites and gave the interior secretary the authority to deny a permit on the grounds that mining could cause irreversible environmental harm.

The business community did not take this flurry of regulatory activity lying down. They complained bitterly about Clinton's "midnight regulations" and lobbied their allies in Congress to use appropriations riders to stop or delay them.[263] "There are more legal meters running in this town preparing to fight anti-business regs in the closing days of the Clinton administration than there are attorneys in Florida," said U.S. Chamber of Commerce spokesman Frank Coleman.[264] Similarly, the administration's land-conservation initiatives fueled outrage in the West, where antagonism toward the federal government continued to simmer.

Although the surge of proenvironmental activity late in the administration's tenure infuriated industry and its conservative allies, conservative activism throughout the decade was nevertheless effective. It helped cement a major rhetorical shift. A growing number of commentators criticized the environmental movement, echoing conservative charges that its scare tactics were excessive.[265] Moreover, throughout the 1990s, policy analysts of various stripes proffered critiques of the paradigm embodied by the environmental laws and regulations of the 1970s. Adopting the disparaging term coined by economists, they argued that "command-and-control" regulation had served its purposes, but was ill-suited to deal with the economic and environmental challenges of the twenty-first century. Analysts pointed out that many prescriptive regulations had unintended consequences, and they endorsed reforms such as market-based mechanisms, performance-based regulation, more flexible and streamlined regulatory schemes, community-based conservation, and collaborative problem solving.[266] According to Paul Portney, an economist with Resources for the Future, by the late 1990s, the notion of using incentive-based approaches rather than prescriptive rules had achieved widespread acceptance. "Gone are the days when charges of 'license to pollute' were rife," he argued. "Now those active in both the environmental advocacy and the regulatory community talk approvingly of and are concerned about developing least-cost approaches."[267]

Environmentalists themselves were contrite, acknowledging that they had failed to build bridges to farmers, landowners, and municipal officials who complained about the burden of environmental laws. The mainstream groups were even in trouble with sympathizers: in becoming professionalized, they had become "corporate"; in seeking the support of foundations, they had lost touch with the priorities of the grassroots. On the twenty-fifth anniversary of Earth Day, the *New York Times'* Keith Schneider claimed that "the cracking sound heard across the country is more than the breaking up of old notions about environmental protection. It is also a shattering of the dominance that large conservation groups have exerted over America's environmental priorities and laws."[268] Representatives of many environmental groups embraced the notion that they needed to evolve—partly because they were persuaded by the mainstream critique, but also in response to the political backlash fomented by conservatives.

Perhaps the clearest illustration of the convergence on the need for reform was the Enterprise for the Environment (E4E) initiative led by Karl Hausker and former EPA administrator Bill Ruckelshaus. The final E4E report, released in January 1998, was the product of a two-year, bipartisan consensus-building process that included environmentalists, industry leaders, and policymakers. The group recommended that policymakers adapt and adjust policies based on up-to-date scientific information; replace a standards-based system with one that offered flexibility of means coupled with clarity of responsibility, accountability for performance, and transparency of results; rely on a broad set of policy tools, including economic incentives and information disclosure; and promote collaborative problem solving. As policy scholar Cary Coglianese observed, however, the E4E consensus was extremely vague, and agreement broke down on specifics.[269]

More generally, apparent agreement among antiregulatory conservatives and environmentalists on procedural principles concealed fundamental differences in motives. Whereas environmentalists hoped that collaborative decision making would facilitate agreement on a risk-averse approach—because short-term economic interests would be transformed into long-term, collective interests through deliberation—conservatives regarded it as a way to enhance the influence of the regulated community on policy. For environmentalists, focusing on the most serious risks entailed devoting more resources to global and ecological threats, such as climate change and biodiversity loss. But conservatives anticipated that rigorous risk assessments would lead to reductions in regulatory expenditures for all environmental hazards. Environmentalists believed that reliance on "sound science" would lead to precautionary results, whereas conservatives hoped that engaging in "sound science" would involve relying exclusively on data, rather than models, and requiring proof of harm, and would therefore delay the day of reckoning. Environmentalists expected that information disclosure requirements would be accompanied by high performance standards, whereas conservatives regarded information disclosure as a substitute for regulatory requirements. More broadly, when environmentalists talked about the compatibility of economic and environmental health, they envisioned an economy powered by alternative fuels and environmentally oriented businesses. By contrast, conservatives asserted that a marketplace freed of cumbersome regulations would produce optimal results, including adequate levels of environmental protection.

Despite these underlying differences, during the Bush-Gore race of 2000, both sides converged on language that polled well: balance, common sense, and no trade-off between environmental and economic health. Both candidates claimed to favor science-based policies, and each labeled the other an extremist. Such linguistic similarities notwithstanding, it was clear that the two candidates had strikingly different philosophies about the role of the federal government in the market. Knowledgeable observers therefore expected the outcome of the Bush-Gore race to have a major impact on environmental regulations. Angela Antonelli, director of economic policy for the Heritage Foundation, was confident that "a Bush administration [was] not about to embrace the belief that agencies should be left to their own devices to shape regulatory policy." Bruce Josten, executive vice president of the U.S. Chamber of Commerce expected a Bush administration to be more flexible than a Gore administration. And Michael Baroody, senior vice president of the National Association of Manufacturers, anticipated a Republican victory would bring "a healthier dose of skepticism about the ability of federal agencies to solve every problem with a new regulation."[270]

# 7

## George W. Bush Advances Conservatives' Antiregulatory Agenda

*The eight-year George W. Bush presidency constituted the most prolonged opportunity for conservatives to challenge the environmental status quo. Learning from the mistakes of their predecessors, during the Bush era conservative politicians eschewed frontal attacks in favor of a more sophisticated, two-pronged campaign. First, they couched their legislative proposals in environmentally friendly language, thereby transforming them into low-profile challenges. Second, they employed a variety of other low-profile administrative techniques, such as proposing permissive new rules; altering key words within existing rules; changing guidelines and otherwise adjusting the interpretation of those rules, or making procedural changes that altered their implementation or enforcement; and declining to contest development-friendly judicial rulings or settling lawsuits on terms favorable to industry. The administration enhanced the effectiveness of these maneuvers by exerting extraordinarily tight control over the information used to support decisions, particularly with respect to science. According to journalist Andrew Revkin, to an unprecedented degree, under Bush "[s]cientists were essentially locked out of important internal White House debates; candidates for advisory panels were asked about their politics as well as their scientific work; and the White House exerted broad control over how scientific findings were to be presented in public reports or news releases."[1]*

*Initially, the Bush administration's efforts to relax environmental regulations garnered extensive media coverage. Democrats made a point of highlighting the administration's environmental decisions,[2] and several journalists focused on its low-profile actions as well. Their combined efforts helped to create the widespread belief among the public that the Bush White House was catering to industry at the expense of the environment. After the terrorist attacks of September 11, 2001, however, security-related issues dominated the headlines, and environmentalists—*

*fearing to appear unpatriotic or unconcerned about national security—*
*were reluctant to criticize the president publicly. As a result, political*
*appointees were able to shape the implementation of environmental laws*
*in ways that reduced the regulatory burden on industry and landowners.*
*They were more successful at influencing regulations affecting endan-*
*gered species conservation than those affecting air pollution control—*
*although in both cases, the courts ultimately limited the administration's*
*most aggressive challenges. But their greatest achievement was preventing*
*the enactment of restrictive policies to curb greenhouse gas emissions.*

### George W. Bush's Rhetoric on the Environment

Although relatively silent on the environment early in the campaign, when he did speak on the issue candidate Bush did not disparage environmental protection but rather articulated a storyline consistent with the mainstream critique of environmental regulation. For example, in an interview with the *New York Times*, Bush focused on process rather than goals, arguing that the best way to achieve clean air and water was "to work with local jurisdictions using market-based solutions and not try to sue our way or regulate our way to clean air and clean water."[3] With respect to biodiversity, Bush promised full funding for the Land and Water Conservation Fund, which provides money for acquiring and protecting sensitive property; he also vowed to increase funding for national parks.[4] At the same time, he emphasized the importance of reducing federal red tape and enhancing the ability of states and localities to devise their own solutions. In a speech delivered in June 2000, for instance, he criticized the Clinton-Gore administration for using too much federal muscle and providing too little local flexibility in land conservation. Tapping into western resentment of Clinton's national monument designations, Bush told his audience:

We have a national consensus about the importance of conservation, but critical problems arise when leaders reject partnership, when they rely solely on the power of Washington and the regulations and penalties and dictation from afar. Unfortunately, this is exactly what we have seen for the last seven years. We've seen millions of acres of land declared off limits and designated as national monuments just like that, with no real public involvement, no regard for the people affected by these decrees.[5]

Both Bush and his opponent, Vice President Al Gore, defined the nation's energy problem primarily in terms of reducing dependence on foreign oil rather than addressing climate change, recognizing that the former was a more widely held concern. But whereas Gore proposed investing billions in tax breaks for conservation and spending to develop renewable energy technologies, Bush laid out an energy plan that called for more domestic production, including opening the Arctic National Wildlife Refuge (ANWR) to oil and gas drilling—policies that he characterized as a remedy for high energy prices.[6] On climate change specifically, Bush initially equivocated, saying not enough was known about the problem to act and that, in any case, there was no economically viable solution. But in a speech delivered in Michigan, as well as in an energy policy paper released in late September 2000, he committed to mandatory cuts in the nation's carbon dioxide emissions as part of a strategy to control several air pollutants simultaneously.[7]

Within a few months of taking office, Bush's approach to environmental policymaking crystallized. Shortly after his inauguration, Bush said he was "deeply concerned" that California's power crisis was spreading, and he vowed to make it easier for companies to exploit and transport oil and gas for electricity production.[8] The president said he would move "boldly and swiftly" to enact a plan that included drilling in ANWR and granting waivers to states seeking to run power plants at full capacity—even if doing so violated air quality standards.[9] In his first address on the environment, delivered on May 30, 2001, the president expressed support for environmental protection, saying, "Our duty is to use the land well and sometimes not to use it at all. This is our responsibility as citizens, but more than that, it is our calling as stewards of the Earth. Good stewardship of the environment is not just a personal responsibility, it is a public value. Americans are united in the belief that we must preserve our natural heritage and safeguard the land around us." In the same speech, however, he made clear that he intended to reduce the burden of environmental regulation on business, increase domestic fossil fuel and nuclear production, and devolve responsibility for implementing and enforcing environmental regulation to the states.

In subsequent statements, administration officials avoided language that would appear antienvironmental, instead choosing more conciliatory terms that emphasized individual stewardship, partnership with the private sector, and compatibility between environmental health and economic growth. For example, White House spokesman Scott McClellan explained, "The president believes economic growth and environmental protection can go hand in hand, and it doesn't have to be a zero-sum game."[10] James Connaughton, chair of the Council on Environmental Quality, adopted the vague but positive language of sustainability, describing the Bush administration's approach as "balancing the environmental equation with the natural resource equation, the social equation and the economic equation."[11] In his 2003 State of the Union address, Bush took a page from Al Gore's book, declaring, "In this century, the greatest environmental progress will come about, not through endless lawsuits or command and control regulations but through technology and innovation." A White House memo issued prior to the 2004 election summarized the administration's position as: (1) focusing on results, (2) employing the best available science and data, (3) encouraging innovation and the development of new technology, (4) building an ethic of stewardship and personal responsibility, and (5) exploring nonfederal opportunities for environmental improvement.

In their choices of words, administration officials were adhering closely to the advice of pollster Frank Luntz, who—in light of the debacle of the mid-1990s—urged Republicans to soften their antienvironmental language and mimic the mainstream critique, not the more strident antiregulatory storyline. In particular, in a sixteen-page memo Luntz encouraged Republicans to emphasize that their gripe was not with environmental goals but with the means used to achieve them.[12] "If we suggest the choice is between environmental protection and deregulation, the environment will win consistently," Luntz wrote. Instead, he suggested, you should argue that "Republicans have a better approach to solving environmental challenges, not that the environment is not a significant issue." Luntz pointed out that if President Bush characterized his initiatives as environmentally friendly, journalists would be compelled to portray them as such, or risk sounding biased. He advocated using the term "climate change" instead of "global warming" because the former sounds more controllable and less emotional. Similarly, he recommended characterizing oneself as a "conservationist" because that term conveys a "moderate, reasoned, common sense position," whereas "environmentalist" has the "connotation of extremism." Luntz also advised Republicans to employ words and phrases like "balance," "safe and healthy," and "common sense."[13]

## Creating an Antiregulatory Context through Appointments, Budgets, and Regulatory Centralization

Moderate environmental language notwithstanding, upon taking office, the Bush administration moved quickly to establish its antiregulatory bona fides. On January 20, 2001, the president put a hold on all the "midnight regulations" and executive orders issued in the final months of the Clinton administration, dismissing them as hastily assembled and ill-considered (although most had been in the works for years).[14] Shortly thereafter, the administration suspended some of the most restrictive Clinton-era rules in order to reduce the regulatory burden on industry and resource-development interests. Next, the president used appointments, budget requests, and centralized oversight to render the institutional context more hospitable to a permissive regulatory approach.

**Choosing Experienced Conservative Appointees**
Like Reagan, Bush understood the importance of appointing officials who shared his antiregulatory worldview. Unlike Reagan, Bush had access to a pool of people who were relatively experienced in environmental matters—albeit a pool mostly comprising industry lawyers and lobbyists, as well as staff from conservative think tanks. In addition to choosing sympathetic agency heads, Bush selected conservative deputy secretaries and assistant administrators who understood the arcane details of rulemaking because they had worked to change the rules on behalf of their industry clients.[15] Those appointees, in turn, exerted an extraordinary amount of influence by taking personal responsibility for policy decisions, even in agencies that historically had been decentralized.[16]

Bush's choice for EPA administrator was Christine Todd Whitman. Considered a moderate Republican, Whitman exhibited a marked propensity for business-friendly environmental policymaking during most of her tenure as governor of New Jersey. After pledging at her inauguration that the state would be "open for business," she cut New Jersey's environmental protection budget by about 30 percent, while eliminating more than two hundred positions from the Department of Environmental Protection (DEP). She relaxed enforcement of pollution control regulations, reducing inspections and promoting voluntary compliance and cooperation; as a result, there was an 80 percent drop in fines and environmental penalties collected during her seven-year reign. She abolished New Jersey's environmental prosecutor's office, created by her predecessor, Governor Florio, and replaced its public advocate with a business ombudsman. Whitman also streamlined the state permitting process for developers, eliminated more than one hundred water-quality-monitoring stations, removed more than one thousand chemicals from the state's right-to-know list, and signed an executive order rolling back most of the state regulations that were stricter than their federal counterparts.

As her term wore on, however, the economy strengthened, and public support for environmental protection gathered force. In response,

Whitman shifted direction. She took steps to curb ocean dumping and conserve open space, reduce water pollution, and speed the cleanup of toxic waste sites. She also endorsed federal New Source Review lawsuits aimed at forcing midwestern power plants to curb their emissions, and she stuck by an emissions-testing program for automobiles despite a difficult implementation process. She eventually restored funding for the DEP as well—although the agency's budget did not return to 1994 levels until 2000.[17]

At the press conference announcing Whitman's nomination, both she and President Bush emphasized the importance of striking a "balance" between economic growth and environmental protection.[18] Then, during her confirmation hearings, Whitman hit several notes that were familiar to proponents of the mainstream critique: she vowed to give the states more latitude in enforcing federal pollution control rules, said that environmental regulations should be subject to strict cost-benefit tests, and promised to move beyond the "command-and-control" mode of environmental protection. She also called for a "new era of cooperation" among government, business, and environmentalists. At a meeting of the Business Roundtable early in her tenure, Whitman told executives, "When the president says he wants to look at government as a partnership" with private enterprise, "he really means it."[19] Finally, when asked directly about the relationship between the economy and the environment, she echoed the president's emphasis on reforming means rather than ends, saying, "No longer do we debate about whether we need to protect our environment. Instead, we discuss how we can keep America green while keeping our economy growing."[20]

Whitman soon ran afoul of powerful conservatives in the White House, however, particularly the vice president. After she resigned on May 21, 2003, the *Wall Street Journal* opined that the EPA needed a head who articulated an antiregulatory storyline, someone who:

refuses to cede the terms of environmental debate to the Sierra Club and other Big Government greens. That person could talk about all of the environmental progress that's been made over the past 30 years. He or she could also explain the virtues of free-market environmentalism, which prizes individual and community stewardship over regulation, recognizes private property rights as a way to protect land, and knows that growth and prosperity are the best insurance for a healthy environment. . . . With so much of the U.S. economy now hostage to assorted environmental regulation, the costs are also growing. Democrats are going to attack Mr. Bush's environmental record no matter what he does, so he might as well pick an EPA spokesman who can fight back on the merits. Republicans learned how to change the welfare debate to compassion from dependency, and the education debate to accountability from spending. Why not the same for the environment?[21]

Whitman's replacement, Michael O. Leavitt, was a three-term Republican governor of Utah who had a reputation as a consensus builder but also a critic of regulation. Under Leavitt's leadership, Utah had tied for last as the state with the worst enforcement record and ranked second-to-last for both air quality and toxic releases.[22] Leavitt characterized the Bush administration's philosophy in the following way: "There is no environmental progress without economic prosperity. Once our competitiveness erodes, our capacity to make environmental gains is gone."[23] He described his own environmental views as in the "productive middle" and depicted his environmental critics as "extremists."[24] According to one career EPA official, with the 2004 election in sight, Leavitt's main charge from the White House seemed to be "just don't get us into the news."[25] Shortly after the election, Bush moved Leavitt to Health and Human Services and replaced him with Stephen L. Johnson, a scientist and twenty-year EPA veteran. Johnson, who had been serving as assistant administrator for the Office of Prevention, Pesticides and Toxic Substances, received a warm welcome from Republicans, Democrats, and many environmentalists—although the honeymoon did not last.

Below the level of administrator, the president appointed several other EPA officials who had experience with the regulatory process but were receptive to the arguments of business lobbyists who claimed that regulation impeded their companies' ability to create jobs and provide Americans with low-priced products and services. According to Thomas J. Donohue, president and chief executive of the U.S. Chamber of Commerce, "Under Clinton, some of the regulatory agencies had a view that they didn't trust business.... The Bush guys have more of an understanding of the effect of regulation on the business community and on the economy."[26] For example, Linda J. Fisher, the agency's deputy administrator, had most recently headed the government affairs office at Monsanto; prior to that, she worked in the EPA under Reagan and George H. W. Bush. Jeffrey Holmstead, the assistant administrator for air and radiation, was a lawyer and former lobbyist for the Alliance for Constructive Air Policy, an electric utility trade group that sought to relax the Clean Air Act.

Bush's nominee for interior secretary, Gale Norton, was far more to conservatives' liking than Whitman. Norton was a protégé of James Watt. She began her legal career at the conservative Mountain States Legal Foundation in 1978 and—after a short stint in the federal government—went on to become the attorney general for Colorado and then a lawyer in private practice. She was committed to developing public lands and drilling for oil and gas in Alaska, and she believed fervently that states and localities should have more control over the land within their borders. A longtime critic of the federal government's role in enforcing environmental standards, she had disparaged the Endangered Species Act and denied the existence of a scientific consensus on global warming. "The appointment of Gale Norton is a throwing down of the gauntlet against the constituency who believes that the federal government needs to lock up more land from further economic exploitation," proclaimed Jerry Taylor, director of natural resource policy at the Cato Institute.[27] In her confirmation hearings, however, Norton placated her critics by disavowing many of her earlier positions. Employing the moderate rhetoric recommended by Luntz, she said she would try to develop a "collaborative partnership" with local governments and residents, and she emphasized her desire to "balance" environmental protection with energy production.[28] Norton also explained that while she disagreed with how some laws were structured, she "[didn't] necessarily disagree with the goal."[29]

Norton relied heavily on her assistant secretary of policy, management and budget, Lynn Scarlett. A former president of the libertarian Reason Foundation, Scarlett articulated her political philosophy in a piece called "The New Environmentalism," in which—after positing her deep commitment to environmental quality—she asserted, "Evidence suggests that wealthier societies have generally higher living standards, lower pollution levels, longer life spans and higher quality environmental amenities." Traditional environmentalism, she continued, assumes that planners have all the answers and ignores local experience; it fails to appreciate the power of incentives to change behavior and links the market to environmental degradation. "But there is a better vision," she concluded, "one that underscores the importance of personal accountability, flexibility, diversity and decentralization."[30]

Other appointees to the Interior Department also had conservative credentials, although most had stronger ties to industry. For the department's number-two position, Bush chose J. Steven Griles, who—after working in the Interior Department under Reagan—had been a coal-industry executive and then a lobbyist for coal, oil, and utility companies. Griles made no secret of his view that environmental regulations should be relaxed and public resources developed. (After Griles resigned in December 2004, Scarlett moved into his position, where she remained until early 2009.) As the department's chief lawyer, Bush selected William

Myers III, formerly a lobbyist for the National Cattlemen's Beef Association. To the post of assistant secretary for water and science, he appointed Bennett Raley, a lawyer who had long worked for large mining, landowning, and irrigation interests. Rebecca Watson, a mining lobbyist, became assistant secretary of land and minerals management. Besides Scarlett, H. Craig Manson, who became assistant secretary for fish, wildlife, and parks, was the lone Interior appointee without an industry lobbying background; he had been a judge and, prior to that, general counsel for the California Department of Fish and Game.

Overall, conservatives applauded the administration's choices for the Interior Department. Michael Hardiman, director of the American Conservative Union, said, "After eight years of the extremist, anti-people, anti-access policies of the Clinton administration and its overzealous application of the Endangered Species Act and the shutdown of recreational access to public lands as well as the commercial access, we're now going to have more of a balance."[31] Bush earned conservative approbation for his other environmental appointments as well. To serve as chair of the Council on Environmental Quality, he selected James L. Connaughton, a D.C. lawyer who had spent the previous decade representing corporations and trade groups on environmental issues. Connaughton was skeptical about government regulation as a means to solve environmental problems and preferred to rely on personal stewardship and technological innovation. At the same time, he regarded himself as a mediator whose role was to reconcile competing factions.[32] As assistant attorney general for the environment at the Department of Justice, Bush nominated Thomas Sansonetti, a Wyoming lawyer who specialized in minerals and energy and was a member of the conservative Federalist Society. And to head the Department of Energy, Bush chose Spencer Abraham, a former congressman from Michigan who had proposed abolishing the Energy Department.

The president's choice to head the Office of Information and Regulatory Affairs reflected political learning. Although the administration intended to use OIRA to constrain regulatory policymaking, it took pains to avoid the appearance of returning to the Reagan era. To that end, Bush appointed John D. Graham, an academic who managed to be responsive to industry's concerns about regulation without sounding overtly ideological. During his sixteen-year career at the Harvard School of Public Health, Graham had founded the Center for Risk Analysis, where he established a reputation for criticizing restrictive regulation as wasteful and often dangerous, and for advocating the ubiquitous use of cost-benefit analysis and comparative risk assessment. In op-eds and congressional testimony, Graham famously argued that the federal government, by spending money on the wrong priorities, caused sixty thousand deaths each year—committing "a shocking display of statistical murder." In a 1996 speech at the Heritage Foundation, he told the audience that "environmental regulations should be depicted as an incredible intervention in the operation of society."[33] During his confirmation hearing, however, Graham was more circumspect, emphasizing his "rationality" and telling the Senate he would hire more scientists for the regulatory review office, solicit public input on rules, and push agencies to adopt a "science-based approach to regulation that weighs a rule's costs as well as its benefits."[34]

### Shrinking Budgets and Centralizing Regulatory Review

As his predecessors had, President Bush sought to use not only appointments but also the budget and centralized regulatory review to staunch the flow of new regulations and ensure that rules that did make it through the procedural gauntlet intruded minimally on the operations of industry and resource extraction. The administration's first budget proposal, released on April 10, 2001, called for an 8 percent decrease in funding for natural resource and environmental programs, despite proposing a 4 percent increase in domestic discretionary spending overall. The president proposed cutting the EPA's budget by 6.4 percent, including a 9 percent reduction in enforcement staff and a 7 percent reduction in funding for research and development. The Interior Department faced a 3.5 percent cut, including a 20 percent reduction in the budget of the U.S. Geological Survey—although the allotment to the Bureau of Land Management for oil, gas, and coal exploration was slated to grow by 19 percent.[35] The administration also proposed shaving 10 percent off the Department of Energy's budget, including a 50 percent cut in funding for renewable energy. Congress did not approve the president's proposed cuts, however, nor did it approve similar cuts in Bush's budgets for fiscal years 2003 and 2004, instead increasing the EPA's budget and raising spending for other environmental programs as well. The administration's budget-cutting proposals met with greater success after the 2004 election.

Bush's efforts to use centralized review to constrain regulatory activity yielded more immediate results. Although the OMB was extremely active, the administration took pains to avoid appearing excessively business-friendly. Officials emphasized that regulation hurt consumers and insisted they were prescribing "smarter regulation," which often amounted to regulatory relief in practice.[36] According to OMB chief Mitch Daniels, the new administration intended to revamp the image of regulation, replacing the custom of regarding strong regulation as protecting consumers with one in which weaker regulation was seen as consumer-friendly. Daniels told journalist Amy Goldstein, "This is all about consumers and how much they should be charged for the protection a given regulation purports to provide. . . . We're in favor of wise regulation, not no regulation. I view this very much as a consumer protection assignment."[37]

In an effort to enhance OIRA's legitimacy, John Graham took steps to make that office's regulatory review process more transparent by opening up its records to the public and meeting with activists, not just businesspeople. Still, most of his efforts were directed at reducing the regulatory burden on industry, from issuing "prompt letters" that urged agencies to rewrite what he regarded as onerous regulations to working closely with regulatory officials early in the regulation-writing process to ensure that their proposals balanced costs and benefits. As one former EPA official explained, the process was unusually covert. "Before . . . we'd send things over to OMB, and they'd have a certain amount of time and would make formal comments. With this administration, that didn't happen. We were told to send [a proposed rule] over informally, and they'd decide whether we could submit it formally, but only after we'd made some changes. This way, they could rewrite a lot of it, but make it look like it was the agency, thereby keeping their hands clean."[38] Furthermore, instead of hiring only statisticians and lawyers, Graham hired career-level staff with expertise in engineering, epidemiology, toxicology, and biology, thereby enhancing OIRA's ability to challenge regulations on grounds other than cost.[39]

To expedite efforts to ease the regulatory burden on industry, Graham solicited complaints from industry. Early on, he asked Barbara Kahlow, a Republican congressional aide, to convene lobbyists who could identify and rank regulations that business found overly burdensome. Kahlow, in turn, created a chart listing 57 rules the business community wanted to target for "sunset review."[40] Of the 576 nominations received during the administration's first four years, most of them from business groups, 135 (about one-quarter) were actually revised in proposals or in final rules.[41] The GAO—which reviewed 85 health, safety, and environmental rules that were changed, returned, or withdrawn between July 1, 2002 and June 2, 2003—found that OIRA review significantly affected 25 of those, and that the EPA's rules were the most dramatically changed (14 of the 17 changed rules were the EPA's). The GAO concluded that many of OIRA's actions appeared to have been prompted by concerns about the cost of the regulatory options.[42] In the spring of 2004, Graham boasted to the Senate Small Business and Entrepreneurship Committee, "this administration has slowed the growth of burdensome new rules by at least 75 percent when compared to the previous administration, while still moving forward with crucial safeguards."[43] The following year, under a new White House initiative, the OMB reviewed 76 regulations—out of 189 requests received—because they were too costly, too time consuming, or unnecessary. Half of the 76 were EPA regulations.[44]

While OMB review could provide short-term relief, Graham was especially preoccupied with permanently overhauling the way federal agencies wrote regulations. Over the course of his five-year tenure, he issued wide-ranging edicts on the quality of information employed in the regulatory process, cost-benefit analysis, and scientific peer review. (After the National Academy of Sciences released an unsolicited critique of Graham's September 2003 peer-review guidance, the OMB modified it to accommodate their concerns.) Graham also put forward a new way of valuing life that would have reduced the benefits of environmental, health, and safety regulations. For years, the EPA had estimated the value of human life in its cost-benefit analyses as the lifetime differential in wages between more and less hazardous jobs—about $6 million. Graham adopted a lower figure ($3.7 million) based on a British estimate of people's willingness to pay for increased safety, even though willingness-to-pay surveys are widely recognized as generating conservative estimates. Graham suggested the EPA use an even lower figure ($2.3 million) for the elderly, based on international studies suggesting that elderly people were less inclined to spend money to avoid risks than younger people. Graham's proposal generated a furious backlash among environmentalists, however, and the EPA declined to adopt it.

Capping his tenure, just before leaving OIRA in early 2006, Graham issued a twenty-six-page document (the Risk Assessment Bulletin) laying out guidance on how agencies should conduct risk assessment and broadening the circumstances under which such analyses should be done. According to journalist Colin Macilwain, "Both critics and supporters agreed that the document was the crowning achievement of Graham's long march to regulatory reform."[45] The U.S. Chamber of Commerce and several industry associations expressed strong support for the proposal. But the OMB backed off after a National Academy of Sciences panel derided the plan as "too simplistic" and "fundamentally flawed."[46]

According to the panel, the OMB had erred in calling for evidence of adverse health effects before regulating, when public health needs might be better served by regulations that reduce risks before damages occur. In 2007, the OMB issued a memo containing "Updated Principles for Risk Analysis" that laid out what it said were generally accepted principles for assessing risk. The revised document retained an emphasis on cost-benefit analysis and quantification, but was considerably more moderate in tone than its predecessor.[47]

Critical to OIRA's efforts to rein in regulation was the Data Quality Act, a little-noticed law signed in the waning days of the Clinton administration.[48] The Data Quality Act charged the OMB with "ensuring and maximizing the quality, objectivity, utility and integrity" of scientific information and statistics disseminated by government agencies. Jim Tozzi, formerly an OMB official and the cofounder of the Center for Regulatory Effectiveness, hoped the act would enable critics of regulation to build more convincing cases showing that an agency had been arbitrary and capricious in its use of data—a tactic that had failed in the past.[49] Observers agreed that the law was most likely to be of value to critics of regulation because, while agencies typically use a weight-of-the-evidence standard, the Data Quality Act focuses on individual studies, each of which is vulnerable to criticism. Writing in the *Administrative Law Review*, lawyer James T. O'Reilly suggested "A prudent opponent of lawmaking will challenge the data accuracy first, before the notice of proposed rulemaking appears, so that the agency must be prepared to defend itself twice."[50] William L. Kovacs, vice president for environment, technology and regulatory affairs at the U.S. Chamber of Commerce concurred, saying, "This is the biggest sleeper there is in the regulatory area and will have an impact so far beyond anything people can imagine."[51]

In August 2004, the *Washington Post* reported that after the rules for implementing the Data Quality Act were finalized in February 2002, Bush's OMB began using it as "a potent tool for companies seeking to beat back regulation."[52] A *Post* analysis of government records indicated that, as expected, in the first twenty months after the act was fully implemented it was used predominantly by industry. Setting aside the numerous petitions filed to correct narrow typographical or factual errors in government publications or Web sites, the analysis identified thirty-nine petitions with potentially broad economic, policy or regulatory impact. Of those, thirty-two were filed by regulated industries, business, or trade organizations or their lobbyists, while only seven were filed by

environmental or citizen groups. Although agencies initially resisted challenges to their regulations, Graham acknowledged that petitioners were
becoming more innovative in their use of the act, and were homing in
on agencies whose missions involved protecting the environment and
public health.[53]

Beyond intensifying regulatory review, President Bush sought to
"streamline" the environmental reviews required by the National Environmental Policy Act. According to journalist Margaret Kriz, the administration worked "quietly but systematically" to make NEPA less of an
impediment to logging in national forests, building transportation projects, and developing energy resources on public lands. Meanwhile, the
Council on Environmental Quality, which has jurisdiction over NEPA,
created an interagency task force to "update" the NEPA process. The
federal courts routinely blocked efforts to weaken NEPA, however. A
study by the Vermont Law School and Defenders of Wildlife found that
during Bush's first two years, his administration was involved in ninety-
four lawsuits in which it tried to short-circuit NEPA. In seventy-three of
those cases, a federal judge ruled against the administration. By contrast,
in the seventy-eight lawsuits in which the administration defended NEPA,
it had a 96 percent success rate.[54]

In a final effort to rein in agencies that were engaging in what he
regarded as excessive regulation, in January 2007, President Bush issued
an executive order that extended a cost-benefit requirement to regulatory
guidance when the impact of that guidance was likely to be significant.
The order also required agencies to provide written rationales for regulation and to designate political appointees as their regulatory policy
officers. Economists Robert Hahn and Robert Litan commented approvingly that the order "could have far-reaching consequences for how the
government weighs the costs and benefits of regulatory activity."[55]
William Kovacs of the U.S. Chamber of Commerce also hailed the initiative, saying, "This is the most serious attempt by any chief executive to
get control over the regulatory process, which spews out thousands of
regulations a year. Because of the executive order, regulations will be less
onerous and more reasonable. Federal officials will have to pay more
attention to the costs imposed on business, state and local governments,
and society."[56]

## Conservatives Gain Clout in Congress

At first, Congress offered some resistance to Bush's deregulatory push.
Although the Republicans gained control of Congress in the 2000 elec-

tion, their margins were extremely thin. The House was split 221 to 211, with Republicans holding a slim majority. The Senate was evenly divided, with Vice President Dick Cheney serving as the tie breaker. Shortly after the election, however, Senator Jim Jeffords of Vermont left the Republican Party to become an Independent, and the Democrats regained control of the Senate.[57] In a series of early votes a bipartisan majority blocked administration plans for oil and gas exploration in the eastern Gulf of Mexico and in national monument lands; upheld Clinton-era hardrock mining reforms that Bush had suspended; and restored millions of dollars for land protection, as well as energy conservation and alternative fuels research, that the president had tried to cut from the federal budget.

After the terrorist attacks of September 11, 2001, however, Congress was more inclined to support the president's agenda. House and Senate negotiators included in the Interior Department's fiscal year 2002 appropriations bill provisions to scrap Babbitt's hardrock mining regulations, circumvent a federal court ruling limiting the number of cruise ships allowed to visit Alaska's Glacier Bay, and allow increased logging in some national forests. In late 2001, Congress approved Bush's Small Business Liability Relief and Brownfields Revitalization Act, which appropriated $200 million for cleaning up contaminated sites while protecting small businesses and property owners from liability. (This law, which the president had promised to support during the campaign, was widely popular.)

Then, in the 2002 election, Republicans expanded their majority in the House (229–205) and regained the majority in the Senate (51–48). As a result, conservatives attained crucial leadership positions in both chambers. James Inhofe of Oklahoma, a former real estate developer, took over the Senate Environment and Public Works Committee, while Pete Domenici of New Mexico, a long-time proponent of development on federal land, assumed control of the Energy and Natural Resources Committee. In the House, Richard Pombo—a California rancher and cofounder of a wise use group—took over the chairmanship of the Committee on Resources. Conservative climate change skeptic Joe Barton of Texas assumed control of the Energy and Commerce Committee.

Reflecting the GOP's momentum, in 2003, the 108th Congress passed the Healthy Forests Restoration Act, which environmentalists strongly opposed. The new law allowed timber companies to thin national forests, limited litigation by environmental groups, and eased NEPA requirements for timber projects that federal officials deemed necessary to prevent fires. The Bush administration and its allies in Congress defined the problem of forest health as one in which endless administrative appeals served not as important safeguards for the public interest but as obstacles to necessary action. By preventing efforts to thin overgrown forests, they claimed, appeals and litigation had precipitated a crisis of alarming proportions, as evidenced by rampant western wildfires and insect infestation across the West.[58] Enabling more logging, they argued, would reduce fuel buildup and help restore damaged forests. Limiting appeals of Forest Service decisions was a "common sense" way to make the forest management process more efficient. By naming the law the Healthy Forests Restoration Act, the administration disarmed environmentalists and their allies, who tried in vain to alert the public about the bill's potential to open up forests to widespread logging.

The 2004 elections, which gave the GOP more seats in both the House and the Senate, further emboldened conservatives. The Republican Congress and the Bush administration vowed to move ahead with an ambitious environmental agenda that included revamping the Clean Air and Endangered Species Acts, and reviving an energy bill that would promote domestic production. Although environmental issues had played virtually no role in the election, EPA administrator Leavitt insisted, "The election is a validation of our philosophy and agenda."[59] Charles Wehland, a lawyer who represented clients like the OGE Energy Corporation and the Great Lakes Chemical Corporation, predicted, "What you're going to see is an administration focused on setting broad goals and then letting states and companies and individuals work to achieve those, within an economic framework."[60] For their part, environmentalists fully expected to spend the 109th Congress playing defense. Although the 2006 elections returned control to the Democrats, few environmentalists believed a proenvironmental agenda would emerge because the majorities in both chambers were so narrow.[61]

### Drifting on Air Pollution Control

Despite its antiregulatory disposition, the Bush administration retained several major air-pollution-control rules finalized in the waning days of the Clinton era. It did so in part because Whitman supported a tough approach to air pollution, and the courts made clear they would adhere to a restrictive interpretation of the law, but also because repealing popular rules already in place would have entailed embarking on a lengthy and controversial rulemaking process. On the other hand, there was little appetite in the White House for additional regulations, and Vice President Cheney was determined to roll back Clean Air Act rules that impeded electricity production by coal-fired utilities. Well aware that previous efforts to challenge the status quo directly had failed spectacularly, and stung by the harsh criticism that accompanied its early action on several other Clinton-era environmental rules, the administration adopted a novel approach: it challenged the Clean Air Act directly, but characterized its proposed reforms as environmental improvements.

Environmentalists succeeded in undermining the Bush administration's credibility, however, and their allies in Congress refused to support changes to the Clean Air Act. At the same time, the federal courts repeatedly blocked efforts to promulgate rules that weakened implementation of the law. So the administration was forced to rely on low-profile challenges, primarily relaxed enforcement and flexible implementation of existing rules, to achieve its goal of reducing the regulatory burden on the nation's electric utilities. The administration relied on more subtle mechanisms as well. The White House pressed EPA staff to focus on the cost of regulations to industry, regardless of statutory requirements to consider only public health. In addition, EPA appointees populated scientific advisory panels with industry-friendly experts. They also limited public access to federal information on industrial pollution, while easing requirements on companies to provide data about their air and water emissions.[62] And in late 2006, the EPA instituted yet another process designed to enhance the influence of policymakers and industry groups vis-à-vis scientists. Under the new arrangement, from the outset, reviews of the science for air quality standards would involve both agency scientists and political officials, rather than scientists exclusively. Furthermore, the agency's scientific advisory committee would comment on agency decisions at the same time as the public, during the review-and-comment period.[63]

### Endorsing Restrictive Air-Pollution-Control Rules

A series of Supreme Court decisions early in Bush's first term limited the EPA's autonomy by making it clear that, regardless of individual judges' ideologies, the federal judiciary was inclined to affirm a stringent interpretation of the Clean Air Act. In late February 2001, the Supreme Court overturned two appeals-court rulings that conservatives had celebrated during the Clinton era. The Court unanimously rejected arguments that the Clean Air Act requires the EPA to take the costs of regulating into account in setting air quality standards (*Whitman v. American Trucking Associations*). It also overturned a ruling by the D.C. Circuit that had invalidated Carol Browner's standards for ozone and small particulates based on the nondelegation doctrine. Then, on March 5, 2001, the

Supreme Court handed environmentalists a third Clean Air Act victory by declining to hear three cases (*Appalachian Power Co. v. EPA*, *Michigan v. EPA*, and *Ohio v. EPA*) in which power companies had challenged Clinton-era regulations on nitrogen oxide emissions that drift northeast from twenty-two states in the Southeast and Midwest.

Faced with the welter of scientific support amassed under the Clinton administration, as well as the courts' propensity to uphold restrictive regulation under the Clean Air Act, the EPA decided to finalize a slew of Clinton-era air pollution regulations. For instance, in June 2001, the EPA issued rules prepared under Clinton that required coal-fired power plants that cause haze in national parks and wilderness areas to install the best available retrofit technology. Given the overwhelming popularity of the national parks, the Bush administration felt compelled to move forward with the rules, which called for improving visibility in the parks by 15 percent per decade and achieving "pristine" air quality by 2064.

Whitman also finalized restrictions on diesel emissions from trucks and buses, despite heavy lobbying from the oil and trucking industries. The on-road diesel rule required manufacturers of heavy trucks and buses to reduce diesel emissions by more than 90 percent, to 15 parts per million, and refiners to reduce the sulfur content of diesel fuel by 97 percent. Some members of Congress supported truck manufacturers by seeking to delay the standard for trucks and buses, pitting a coalition of powerful House Republicans against the administration.[64] But the EPA held fast, and in May 2002, the D.C. Circuit unanimously upheld the diesel rule against an industry challenge. The Bush administration got little credit for issuing the diesel rule, however, because it declined to publicize its decision.[65]

Shortly thereafter, under a court-ordered deadline, in September 2002, the EPA endorsed rules—also devised by the Clinton administration—for several types of off-road diesel engines, such as snowmobile engines. As a result of OMB intervention, the final regulations were slightly less restrictive than the original proposal. Nevertheless, they were sweeping: they called for a 70 percent reduction in hydrocarbons and a 30 percent reduction in carbon monoxide by 2012. The agency estimated its standards would be achieved by the use of four-stroke engines in 70 percent of all new snowmobiles by 2012. It further claimed that broader adoption of four-stroke engines would not be possible because of resource constraints on manufacturers. Environmentalists sued, however, arguing that the 70 percent goal was not aggressive enough. And in early June 2004, the D.C. Circuit blocked the proposed standards, saying the EPA had not furnished an adequate rationale for assuming they could not be met for more than 70 percent of snowmobiles, despite the availability of much cleaner technology (*Bluewater Network v. EPA*).

The following spring, the EPA proposed rules for diesel fuel that would cut particulate and ozone-forming emissions from bulldozers, tractors, boats, and off-road vehicles by more than 90 percent. Justifying the agency's decision, OIRA's Graham explained that the rules, which were finalized in May 2004, were consistent with cost-benefit analyses showing the potential costs to industry were outweighed by long-term economic and public health benefits. Contrary to the administration's perception that it would never get credit from environmentalists, Richard Kassel, a senior attorney and diesel specialist for the Natural Resources Defense Council, called the new rule "the biggest public health step" since the United States removed the lead from gasoline in the 1980s.[66] "The administration has hit a home run," exclaimed Fred Krupp, president of the Environmental Defense Fund. [67]

More diesel rules followed in the administration's second term. In late June 2005, the EPA proposed regulations aimed at curbing emissions from stationary diesel engines, such as backup generators. In March 2006, the EPA announced a plan for new standards for lawnmowers that would cut emissions and save gas. And in mid-March 2008, the EPA announced tough rules governing emissions from the diesel engines of trains and small ships (although they made a major exception for cargo liners, tankers, and cruise ships), again winning praise from environmentalists.[68] Finally, in mid-October 2008, the EPA tightened the regulatory limit on airborne lead for the first time in thirty years. The standard was lowered tenfold, from 1.5 micrograms per cubic meter of air to 0.15 micrograms per cubic meter of air, consistent with the recommendations of both EPA staff and the agency's Clean Air Scientific Advisory Committee.[69]

### Trying to Make New Source Review More Permissive

Although Whitman and her successors made improving air quality a priority, they ran into difficulty when that aim conflicted with the White House goals of relieving the regulatory burden on the utility industry and increasing the domestic energy supply. These objectives met head-to-head in the New Source Review rules that require stationary sources to install state-of-the-art pollution control equipment when they make substantial renovations to their operations. Utilities had complained strenuously that the Clinton administration's stringent interpretation of

NSR impeded their ability to perform maintenance and improve efficiency. By the time President Bush took office, the Department of Justice had filed suit against eleven utilities, as well as two non-utilities, and the EPA was investigating possible violations at more than one hundred additional power plants and oil refineries.[70] As journalist John Fialka pointed out, the NSR rule offered the Bush administration a rare opportunity to provide substantial regulatory relief without congressional action.[71]

The administration's position on NSR was heavily influenced by the National Energy Policy Development Group, a task force convened by the president in early 2001 and chaired by Vice President Dick Cheney. From the outset, the energy task force focused on expanding the nation's energy supply, while targeting environmental regulations as a primary impediment. (When formulating its strategy, the task force consulted almost exclusive with representatives of the electric utility and the energy industries.) Therefore, it considered a variety of measures to relax regulations that constrained energy generation, including: easing clean air rules for coal-fired power plants, loosening federal standards on river flows that protect fish but impinge on hydropower production, giving refiners relief from the diversity of antipollution standards in different states, allowing states to control drilling rights on some federal lands, and opening the Arctic National Wildlife Refuge to oil and gas exploration.[72] According to Jeremy Symons, a former advisor on climate policy at the EPA, the Department of Energy resisted any efforts to include energy conservation in the task force plan. For his part, Vice President Cheney said conservation might be a "personal virtue" but was not "a sufficient basis for a sound, comprehensive energy policy."[73] The issue came to a head at a cabinet-level meeting hosted by Cheney in early April 2001, in which energy secretary Abraham prevailed over Whitman, who had recommended a national goal for energy efficiency. (The plan ultimately did contain $6.3 billion over ten years for efficiency and conservation—although $5 billion of that was for the development of hydrogen fuel-cell cars.)

On May 16, 2001, the task force issued a 163-page report laying out the Bush administration's national energy policy. The premise of the report was that "America in the year 2001 faces the most serious energy shortage since the oil embargoes of the 1970s." Without action, it continued, projected energy shortfalls "will inevitably undermine our economy, standard of living, and our national security." As journalist

Douglas Jehl pointed out, the proposal, with its bullish tone, flipped the question from "why drill?" to "why not?"[74] The most serious of the report's 105 policy recommendations, most of which could be implemented without congressional approval, made clear the administration viewed increasing supply and improving the infrastructure of fossil fuels and nuclear power as overwhelming priorities. The plan was silent on the issue of climate change.

In justifying the administration's approach, the White House seized on the California blackouts of 2000 and 2001 to suggest the United States faced an energy crisis that necessitated an immediate and serious response. In addition, both the president and vice president echoed conservative claims that regulatory hurdles and delays were stifling investment in new facilities and rendering energy markets vulnerable to disruption. (Ironically, even as the Bush administration sought to relax regulations, the energy industry was already ramping up, responding to high energy prices with investments in power plants, gas pipelines, and new oil wells.[75]) Upon reading these comments, former interior secretary James Watt told journalist Mike Soraghan of the *Denver Post*, "Everything Cheney's saying, everything the president's saying—they're saying exactly what we were saying 20 years ago, precisely. Twenty years later, it sounds like they've just dusted off the old work."[76] Although many environmentalists agreed with this assessment, there were two crucial differences. First, twenty years of conservative dominance had created a rhetorical context that was more hospitable to claims of government inefficiency and ineffectiveness. Second, the Bush administration was more judicious in its language than Watt had been. Bush was careful to couch his energy plan in proenvironmental terms. He assured listeners that whenever the administration sought new places to drill, they would be "mindful of the environment."[77]

President Bush acted quickly and unilaterally to implement the recommendations of the energy task force, issuing two executive orders—one requiring federal agencies to conduct an "energy impact statement" for any major new regulation, and a second directing federal agencies to expedite energy projects on federal lands. In addition, at the urging of the task force, Bush gave the EPA and the Energy Department ninety days to review the impact of NSR rules on electricity-generation capacity and come up with ways to make them less onerous. He also directed the Department of Justice to assess the legal basis for pending Clinton-era NSR lawsuits against coal-fired power plants.

Despite pressure from the White House, EPA officials were reluctant to reexamine the NSR program or pull back on enforcement. In May 2001, less than two weeks before the task force report was released, Whitman had sent a two-page memo to Vice President Cheney, who was pushing the utility industry position. "As we discussed," she wrote, "the real issue for industry is the [NSR] enforcement cases. We will pay a terrible political price if we undercut or walk away from the enforcement cases; it will be hard to refute the charge that we are deciding not to enforce the Clean Air Act."[78] As the EPA and the Energy Department were drafting their recommendations on the NSR rules, environmentalists tried to draw public attention to the issue by releasing a study titled *Power to Kill*, which documented a host of health problems and premature deaths that result from the emissions of coal-burning power plants. In early January 1992, Senators Jeffords and Patrick Leahy of Vermont held hearings on NSR at which attorneys general from six states came to D.C. to protest the changes being contemplated by the administration. But Cheney and the Energy Department prevailed, and by February 2002, it was clear that the White House was leaning toward endorsing a relaxation of the NSR rules.[79] Comments by the EPA on the draft report to the president were telling. "The current draft report is highly biased and loaded with emotionally charged code words," they wrote. EPA officials described the report's NSR proposals as "a prelude to recommendations to vitiate" the program and the report as a whole as dominated by industry concerns.[80]

In late February, Eric Schaeffer, EPA's director of regulatory enforcement, quit the agency in disgust, saying he was "fighting a White House that seems determined to weaken the rules we are trying to enforce."[81] According to Schaeffer, signals that the White House would relax the rules had already undermined his ability to file NSR lawsuits and win settlements; two companies (Cinergy and Dominion) had refused to sign consent decrees that they had agreed to fifteen months earlier, and others had walked away from the bargaining table. "The momentum we obtained with agreements announced earlier has stopped," Schaeffer wrote to Whitman, "and we have filed no new lawsuits against utility companies since this administration took office. We obviously cannot settle cases with defendants who think we are still rewriting the law."[82]

In mid-June 2002, bowing to the recommendations of the EPA/Energy Department panel, the EPA proposed NSR revisions that would give industrial facilities more leeway in modernizing their plants without having to install new pollution control equipment. Under the new rule, an industry source could make modifications that increased emissions without triggering NSR review, as long as the source did not exceed a facility-wide pollution cap—the so-called plantwide applicability limit. The new rule also enabled all companies, not just utilities, to compare baseline emissions with actual plant emissions, rather than estimated (and seldom achieved) potential emissions if the plant were run at full capacity; gave companies that voluntarily installed state-of-the-art pollution controls wide latitude to update equipment without seeking a new permit; and, most controversially, dropped requirements that plants update pollution control equipment if they already had done so within the past ten years (the "clean unit exemption").[83]

In announcing the new rule, Whitman employed an industry talking point, saying that disputes over NSR rules had "deterred companies from implementing projects that would increase energy efficiency and decrease air pollution."[84] In August 2002, while the rule package was undergoing OMB review, forty-four senators sent a letter to the White House asking it to postpone plans to ease enforcement of NSR—another effort to raise the issue's salience. Unpersuaded, the EPA formally released the proposed rule in mid-November, converting an already low-profile action into an even more covert one by announcing the change after the midterm elections, in a low-key press conference, with no cameras allowed. Immediately after the EPA issued the final rule, on New Year's Eve, a group of state and local attorneys general led by Eliot Spitzer of New York filed a legal challenge.

Throughout the spring of 2003, the EPA and the Department of Energy wrestled with the most critical matter of all for coal- and oil-fired electric utilities: where the line would be drawn between "routine maintenance" and the significant overhauls that would trigger NSR. Finally, in late August 2003, acting EPA administrator Marianne Horinko released the much-anticipated definition of routine maintenance. Under the new definition, a utility or industrial facility could repair, replace, or upgrade production equipment without triggering new pollution controls if the cost of parts and repairs did not exceed 20 percent of the cost of replacing the plant's essential production equipment. Such repairs would be considered routine maintenance even if the renovation increased emissions. Again, administration officials justified their permissive approach by saying it provided more regulatory certainty and clarity, and enabled facilities to make improvements that would enhance efficiency. Thomas Kuhn of the Edison Electric Institute hailed the decision, saying it would "lift a major cloud of uncertainty, boosting our efforts to provide affordable, reliable electric service and cleaner air."[85]

Environmentalists continued to insist that the Bush administration's rule changes would increase pollution, however, and two studies released in October 2003 supported this contention. An analysis by the Environmental Integrity Project and the Council of State Governments/Eastern Regional Conference found that the rule changes finalized in late 2002 could lead to almost 1.4 million tons more air pollution in twelve states, as a result of changes in emissions baseline calculations.[86] A second study, by the GAO, found that the 20-percent rule would jeopardize Clinton-era NSR lawsuits, while the earlier rule changes would provide "less assurance that [the public] will have notice of, and information about, company plans to modify facilities in ways that affect emissions, as well as less opportunity to provide input on these changes and verify they will not increase emissions."[87] Twelve states and several major cities sued to block the routine-maintenance rule on the grounds that it would increase air pollution. But during a tour of Detroit Edison's Monroe Power Plant, Bush defended the change, saying, "The old regulations on the books made it difficult to either protect the environment or grow the economy." Elaborating, he explained, "Regulations intended to enhance air quality made it really difficult for companies to do that which is necessary, to not only produce more energy, but to do it in a cleaner way." And perhaps most succinctly, "We simplified the rules. . . . We trust the people in this plant to make the right decisions."[88]

At first, while the administration was revising the NSR rules, it continued enforcing established cases. In January 2002, the Justice Department released its long-awaited review, which concluded that the EPA was justified in pursuing NSR cases against coal-fired utilities, oil refineries, and other industrial plants. By summer 2003, the Justice Department and the EPA had settled five Clinton-era NSR suits; in each instance, the utility agreed to install state-of-the-art pollution controls and pay substantial penalties.[89] Although the Bush administration had not initiated any new lawsuits, it took full credit for the settlements when touting its enforcement record. But in early November 2003, after the routine-maintenance rule was finalized, J. P. Suarez, the EPA's assistant administrator in the Office of Enforcement and Compliance Assurance, ordered agency staff *not* to pursue additional NSR enforcement cases unless a facility was in violation under the Bush administration's new interpretation of the law. Suarez confirmed that, in light of the rule change, the administration would close pending investigations of seventy power plants and consider dropping thirteen cases against utilities that had been referred to the Justice Department for action. Two months later, Suarez resigned. He said the 20-percent threshold was excessive and would "eviscerate" the agency's enforcement program for utilities," adding that "the goal of NSR reform was to prevent any enforcement case from going forward."[90] In the interim, two more top EPA enforcement officials—Bruce Buckheit and Rich Biondi— stepped down.

In early February 2004, shortly after the D.C. Circuit temporarily blocked the routine-maintenance rule from taking effect, EPA adminis- trator Leavitt abruptly adopted a tougher enforcement posture, warning the utility industry to begin cleaning up its plants and saying that new lawsuits were in the works.[91] Some observers attributed this pivot to Bush administration efforts to establish its environmental credentials in advance of the 2004 election. That suspicion was confirmed in early 2005, when the Justice Department's Tom Sansonetti made clear that he was not actually planning any new lawsuits against the utility industry.[92] In the intervening period, the EPA brought only four enforcement actions, and only one that involved alleged violations under the old NSR inter- pretation, despite the fact that staff had compiled cases against twenty- two utilities.[93] In late September 2004, Nikki Tinsley, the EPA inspector general, concluded that Bush's NSR reforms—particularly the 20-percent capital spending threshold for utilities—had, in fact, "seriously ham- pered" the agency's efforts to prosecute or settle existing cases and stymied the development of new ones.[94]

Complicating matters, various courts reacted differently to the Bush administration's rule changes, issuing contradictory decisions in suits filed by states, environmentalists, and the Clinton administration. In mid-March 2005, Ohio Edison finalized a $1.1 billion settlement with the EPA after a district court judge (in August 2003) ruled in favor of the Clinton administration's interpretation of the NSR rules.[95] But two cases decided in June created confusion. The Fourth Circuit Court of Appeals ruled unanimously in favor of Duke Energy, upholding the dis- trict court, which had adopted the industry's view that NSR exemptions could be given if a modification did not increase a plant's *hourly* emission rates (*United States v. Duke Energy Corp.*). (The EPA gave NSR exemp- tions only if a modification did not increase a plant's *annual* emission rates.) And the D.C. Circuit upheld two of the Bush administration's December 2002 NSR reforms while remanding three as "impermissible interpretations" of the Clean Air Act. (The 2002 rule changes were less controversial than the routine-maintenance definition issued in the summer of 2003.) Confusing matters even further, in early September a federal district court judge in Indianapolis ruled against Cinergy in an NSR case.

In hopes of eliminating some of the uncertainty caused by inconsistent court rulings, in October 2005 (on the Friday before Columbus Day weekend), the administration released its proposal for a third NSR rule. This one offered three new triggers for NSR; most important, it adopted the position of the utility industry that NSR should apply only if a plant modification leads to an increase in *hourly* emissions. EPA administrator Stephen Johnson vowed that the agency would not bring an enforcement case unless a company violated the hourly test. In fact, a memo sent by Marcus Peacock in mid-October 2005 argued that the government's enforcement policy should reflect all three of Bush's major regulatory changes to NSR.

Despite the administration's low-profile efforts to modify NSR in favor of utilities, momentum in the courts eventually shifted decisively in favor of environmentalists. In March 2006, the D.C. Circuit unanimously vacated the NSR rule change that defined routine maintenance as any activity amounting to less than 20 percent of a plant's value, noting that it was "contrary to the plain language of . . . the [Clean Air] Act" (*State of New York et al. v. EPA*). Judge Judith Rogers wrote, "Only in a Humpty Dumpty world would Congress be required to use superfluous words while an agency could ignore an expansive word that Congress did use." The court denied the Bush administration's request for a rehearing in July 2006, and the Supreme Court declined to take the case.

Then, in mid-August 2006, the Seventh Circuit Court of Appeals unanimously upheld the district court's ruling in the Cinergy case (*U.S. v. Cinergy Corp.*). The nine-page decision written by Judge Richard Posner found that Cinergy's interpretation of NSR did not conform to the meaning of the Clean Air Act and would "distort the choice between rebuilding an old plant and replacing it with a new one." And finally, in the spring of 2007, in *Environmental Defense et al. v. Duke Energy Corp*, the Supreme Court dealt the Bush administration's interpretation of NSR a third blow: it unanimously overturned the Fourth Circuit Court of Appeals, holding that the same word used in different parts of a statute may have different meanings and may therefore be implemented differently. In others words, the Court ruled that the EPA is entitled (though not obligated) to apply the hourly-rate criterion when administering New

Source Performance Standards but may adhere to the annual-rate criterion under NSR.[96]

After the Supreme Court ruling in the *Duke Energy* case, utilities began settling lawsuits originally brought by the Clinton administration in 1999 but long delayed by the Bush administration's wavering. That trend culminated in early October 2007, when American Electric Power—the nation's largest coal-burning utility—agreed to pay a $15 million civil penalty, spend $60 million on environmental mitigation projects, and install $4.6 billion worth of pollution control devices at sixteen power plants in the Midwest and mid-Atlantic.[97] Although the EPA joined the legal settlement, it included language indicating the administration did not intend to take enforcement against American Electric Power for the same kind of Clean Air Act violations in the future.

### Clear Skies and the Clean Air Interstate Rule

Even as it struggled to provide relief to utilities by modifying NSR implementation and enforcement, the Bush administration hoped to obviate the need for those adjustments in the long run through legislative changes to the Clean Air Act. During the presidential campaign, Bush had outlined a legislative plan to reform the Clean Air Act by instituting a multipollutant cap-and-trade system. That approach originally emerged during the Clinton administration in meetings between Vice President Gore and industry representatives, who had volunteered to make steep cuts in emissions of sulfur dioxide, nitrogen oxides, and mercury in exchange for several years of regulatory certainty.

On Earth Day 2002, President Bush and Administrator Whitman held a press conference in the Adirondacks to tout the administration's multipollutant strategy, labeling it the "Clear Skies" initiative. By 2010, they promised, Clear Skies would cut sulfur dioxide emissions from coal-fired power plants from 11 million tons to 4.5 million tons, nitrogen oxides from 4.1 million tons to 2.1 million tons, and mercury from 48 tons to 26 tons. By 2018, annual emissions of nitrogen oxides would fall to 1.7 million tons, sulfur dioxide to 3 million tons, and mercury to 15 tons. Clear Skies would achieve these reductions through a cap-and-trade system that would replace the existing approach of requiring plant-by-plant permitting and mandatory installation of pollution control technology. At the same time, it would simplify the regulatory environment for utilities and provide them with regulatory certainty in a variety of ways. It would prevent downwind states from petitioning the EPA to impose curbs on upwind states that kept them from meeting their own cleanup deadlines. It would also eliminate the Regional Haze Rule, as well as rules forcing individual utilities to reduce nitrogen oxides that cross state lines. Most important to utilities, it would exempt old plants from NSR and phase out source-by-source mercury controls.

Environmentalists pointed out that, its name notwithstanding, Clear Skies represented a retreat from the status quo because existing Clean Air Act rules, if strictly enforced, would achieve larger emissions reductions. They noted that, at a briefing for the Edison Electric Institute in September 2001, the EPA had acknowledged that nitrogen oxides could be cut as much as 75 percent, to 1.25 million tons, in ten years under existing Clean Air Act rules. By contrast, Clear Skies would take more than fifteen years to cap nitrogen oxides at 1.7 million tons. Sulfur dioxide could be reduced to 2 million tons under existing rules, while the president's plan called for a sulfur dioxide cap of 3 million tons. In December, the EPA estimated that mercury would be cut to 5.5 tons under the existing Clean Air Act, whereas Clear Skies would reduce mercury emissions only to 15 tons by 2018.[98] Moreover, environmentalists pointed out, the EPA had originally put forward a more restrictive proposal than the one embodied in Clear Skies, the so-called straw proposal, but the White House rejected it in favor of an alternative that would achieve less pollution reduction. Acknowledging that the agency had considered a more stringent alternative, Jeffrey Holmstead explained, "we talked with people in the power sector and union folks, and we were convinced it was not feasible."[99]

Whatever its merits, the Clear Skies Act foundered in the 108th Congress. Prodded by the president's call for action during his State of the Union address, in late January 2003, Senator Inhofe, the newly ascendant chair of the Environment and Public Works Committee, began marking up the bill. Major utilities quickly lined up behind the plan because it would stabilize regulations for ten to fifteen years. Clear Skies' prospects were complicated, however, by the fact that, although some utilities were interested in the concept, the coal-mining industry staunchly opposed it, as did carmakers, who worried they would be the next target of restrictive regulations. Moreover, by mid-July a competitor to Clear Skies was gaining bipartisan support. Written by Democratic senator Thomas Carper of Delaware and cosponsored by three prominent Republicans, the alternative bill imposed tougher emissions limits that would be achieved sooner, while also regulating carbon dioxide.

Most observers regarded the Carper bill as a compromise between Clear Skies and the much more stringent Clean Power Act authored by

Independent James Jeffords and Connecticut Democrat Joe Lieberman. The latter boasted the fastest timetable, achieved the largest emissions reductions, and called for all electric generating units forty years or older to be retired if they did not install the best-available pollution control technology.[100] In early July 2003, the *Washington Post* revealed that the EPA had prepared an analysis showing that Carper's bill would generate $50 billion per year more in health benefits than Clear Skies, and that Clear Skies would lead to 17,800 more premature deaths by 2020.[101] The analysis also suggested that the carbon dioxide reduction measures in Carper's bill would impose only a minimal cost on the economy. The EPA had withheld this information, however, telling Carper only that his bill would cut emissions of sulfur dioxide, nitrogen oxides, and mercury faster than the president's bill. In response to the revelations, Holmstead defended Clear Skies as the superior alternative "from a public policy perspective," because it took into account the economic and energy-security effects of emissions reductions.[102]

After Republicans increased their margins in both chambers in the 2004 elections, supporters hoped that the 109th Congress would finally pass Clear Skies, and Senator Inhofe expressed his determination to do so. White House lobbying intensified, as did pressure from industry supporters. But opponents had a variety of institutional weapons with which to resist change. The makeup of the Environment and Public Works Committee appeared likely to foil Inhofe's efforts, since moderate Republican Lincoln Chafee of Rhode Island was inclined to vote with the Democrats in opposition, mainly because the bill lacked a carbon dioxide provision. If a committee vote ended in a tie, the Senate majority leader, Bill Frist of Tennessee, could move the bill directly to the floor, but there Senate Democrats could filibuster it.

Bolstering the opposition, in early December the Congressional Research Service issued a report showing that the EPA's analysis had been unfairly skewed to favor Clear Skies over the two competing proposals by exaggerating the costs and underestimating the benefits of more stringent pollution controls. Then, dealing another blow to Clear Skies, in mid-January 2005, the National Academy of Sciences released an analysis showing that it would likely allow higher emissions levels at individual utility plants than enforcement of existing NSR provisions—just as environmentalists had claimed. Unmoved by these threats to his administration's credibility, President Bush again called on Congress to pass Clear Skies during his 2005 State of the Union address, saying it would make America "more secure and less dependent on foreign energy." But on March 9, after a flurry of lobbying by both sides, the deadlocked Environment and Public Works Committee snuffed the bill with a 9–9 vote.

With Clear Skies stalled, the administration proposed to institute an expanded cap-and-trade system for sulfur dioxide and nitrogen oxides in low-profile fashion.[103] Under the administration's Clean Air Interstate Rule (CAIR), which would take full effect in 2015, nitrogen oxide emissions from power plants would fall 60 percent from 2003 levels, and sulfur dioxide emissions would fall more than 70 percent. Each state would devise measures to curb emissions affecting downwind states but could also achieve those reductions through a regional cap-and-trade system. Like Clear Skies, CAIR extended Clean Air Act' deadlines for meeting air quality standards; unlike Clear Skies, CAIR applied only to the twenty-eight states east of the Mississippi and to Washington, D.C., where transboundary air pollution was a particularly severe problem. Also unlike Clear Skies, CAIR offered no regulatory relief for industry; it did not repeal NSR, eliminate the right of downwind states to petition the EPA for help, or roll back the Regional Haze Rule.

Although industry preferred the certainty and breadth of Clear Skies to CAIR, it generally endorsed the proposed rule. For example, the National Association of Manufacturers praised it as "the best available regulatory alternative" to Clear Skies.[104] "Cost-effective, and effective, are reasonable ways to describe the Bush administration's clean-air policy," said industry lobbyist Scott Segal.[105] There were, however, strenuous disputes within the utility industry over how emissions credits should be allocated. One approach would allocate credits only to electricity generators that used fossil fuels, while another would give credits to all generators, including those that relied on hydroelectric, nuclear, and other fuel sources.

After considerable delay—the administration proposed CAIR in 2003 but was reluctant to adopt it as long as Clear Skies remained viable— CAIR was finalized on March 10, 2005, by the recently confirmed EPA administrator Stephen Johnson. In July 2006, the National Academy of Sciences concluded that CAIR would be about as effective at cutting overall pollution as NSR enforcement—although its impacts would be more variable because NSR applied to all sources while CAIR allowed some sources to avoid emissions reductions.[106] On July 11, 2008, however, the D.C. Circuit struck down the new rule in response to an industry appeal (*North Carolina v. EPA*). The court asserted that CAIR—which the *Washington Post* called the administration's "single boldest move in favor of clean air"[107]—was "fundamentally flawed." The judges added that "no amount of tinkering with the rule or revising of the explanations will transform CAIR, as written, into an acceptable rule." Entergy and Duke Energy, two of the plaintiffs in the case, emphasized that they did not want the entire rule thrown out and had contested only the portion of the rule that allocated pollution allowances among utilities. Upon rehearing the case, on December 23, the court affirmed its earlier decision, but agreed to leave CAIR in place until the EPA issued new rules to replace it. That task would fall to the next administration.

### The Clean Air Mercury Rule

One of the most controversial aspects of Clear Skies was its treatment of mercury, a potent neurotoxin emitted during coal combustion.[108] A Clinton-era regulatory finding, issued in December 2000, designated mercury as a hazardous air pollutant. That finding triggered a requirement that the EPA issue standards for coal-fired power plants that would sharply reduce their emissions of mercury and other toxic pollutants by requiring them to install the "maximum achievable control technology" (MACT) by 2007. Facing a court-ordered deadline, and with Clear Skies in limbo, the administration began preparing its own Clean Air Mercury Rule. As part of its proposal, in early 2004, the Bush administration moved to downgrade mercury's "hazardous" designation—an apparently minor change that in effect gave utilities ten additional years to implement the most costly controls. The administration also proposed substituting a cap-and-trade program for the MACT standard. Overall, the Clean Air Mercury Rule would cut mercury emissions from 48 tons annually to 34 tons by 2010 and 15 tons—nearly 70 percent—by 2018. (By contrast, the Clinton administration's MACT rule would have cut emissions 90 percent by 2008, a goal Bush administration officials decried as infeasible.[109]) The Bush administration chose its 2010 goal after seeing an EPA analysis showing that, by installing equipment to reduce sulfur dioxide and nitrogen oxide emissions, power plants could get a 46 percent reduction in mercury as a "co-benefit." Mike Leavitt, who was the EPA administrator when the new rule was proposed, characterized it as an efficient compromise that would reduce mercury emissions in a way that did not place a financial burden on utility companies.[110]

The EPA announced its proposal after dismantling a stakeholder task force that had concluded that all coal- and oil-fired power plants should be required to install MACT to reduce mercury and other hazardous pollutants. According to an industry lawyer who had been on the task force, "People in the industry never expected EPA to go in that direction of a mercury trading program. . . . It's something they liked, but [executives] thought the MACT standard was on the table, and they were resigned to that."[111] Jeffrey Holmstead engineered this regulatory reversal. In early 2004, the *Washington Post* reported that in formulating its new mercury rules the EPA had adopted some industry recommendations verbatim. In one instance, the language of the administration's proposed rule repeated word for word a report issued by West Associates, a consulting group funded by western power companies. At least a dozen paragraphs were lifted from suggestions sent to federal officials by Latham & Watkins, Holmstead's former employer, on behalf of the utility industry.[112]

In recommending a cap-and-trade approach, the administration dismissed environmentalists' contention that mercury's impacts were substantially local, despite a decade-long study by the EPA and the U.S. Geological Survey showing that tough regulations of airborne mercury have a profound and almost immediate effect on the levels of mercury in the local environment and in the food chain.[113] The White House also rebuffed a request by ten House Republicans, led by Sherwood Boehlert of New York, to include additional safeguards against local mercury hot spots. Furthermore, while working with the EPA to craft the proposal, White House staff members played down the toxic effects of mercury. Although they did not actually distort information, drawn mostly from a 2000 report by the National Academy of Sciences, they minimized health risks in any area where there could be disagreement, choosing risk-tolerant interpretations of the science where possible.[114] Nevertheless, EPA and White House officials insisted their approach was "greener" than the MACT approach. In the long run, they said, it would encourage development of new mercury-removal technologies, offer utilities economic incentives to continuously remove mercury emissions, and cover emissions from new plants—familiar reasons for adopting market-based approaches.

Once again, the EPA came under fire from environmentalists for failing to properly analyze the impacts of its proposed rule. (The EPA had declined to conduct its own analysis, instead publishing four analyses that reached divergent conclusions, all done by outside groups.) Two investigations vindicated environmentalists. In February 2005, the EPA's inspector general reported that Holmstead and other top officials had instructed their staffs to develop a mercury standard that would yield annual reductions comparable to what the electric utilities could meet through CAIR or Clear Skies[115] In a report issued the same month, the GAO pointed out that the agency had failed to conduct a complete economic analysis, did not examine all the regulatory alternatives in a consistent manner, and declined to quantify the public health benefits of lower mercury emissions[116]

Despite environmentalists' efforts to draw attention to these reports, on March 15, 2005, the EPA finalized the Clean Air Mercury Rule. EPA modeling suggested the rule, coupled with CAIR, would actually lower mercury emissions only to 31 tons in 2010, 28 tons in 2015, and 24 tons by 2020—considerably smaller reductions than required. (The difference between the caps and actual emissions was caused by a provision allowing utilities to "bank" extra emissions credits in Phase I and spend them in Phase II.) Nevertheless, the administration defended its approach as the most efficient way to reduce health risks from mercury without disrupting the nation's ability to use coal. Nine states sued the agency, however, and in early February 2008, the D.C. Circuit ruled that the EPA had ignored the Clean Air Act by failing to require deep and timely reductions in mercury emissions from coal-fired power plants (*State of New Jersey et al. v. Environmental Protection Agency*). The court's critique of the EPA's decision was pointed; it likened the EPA to "the capricious Queen of Hearts in Alice's Adventures in Wonderland," saying the agency had (once again) "substituted its desires for the 'plain text of the law.'" In May, the court unanimously declined requests by the EPA and industry groups to rehear the case.

### Ozone, Small Particulates, and Air Quality in Pristine Areas

In a series of additional low-profile steps aimed at making Clean Air Act implementation more permissive, the Bush administration adopted a similarly risk-tolerant approach—one less concerned with an ample margin of safety than with efficiency. For example, in mid-March 2008, after a new scientific review, the EPA proposed to tighten the primary standard for ground-level ozone to 75 parts per billion (ppb) over an eight-hour period. Although more stringent than the previous standard, 75 ppb was less protective than the standard sought by public health advocates, who were pushing for 60 ppb; it also ignored the unanimous advice of the EPA's Clean Air Scientific Advisory Committee to limit ozone concentrations to no more than 70 ppb.

Furthermore, after a last-minute intervention by the president, the EPA weakened its secondary ozone standard, setting it at the same level as the primary standard. Originally, the EPA had set a lower seasonal limit (the secondary, public welfare standard) to protect wildlife, parks, and farmland. After reviewing the EPA's proposal, the OMB's Susan Dudley had urged the agency to consider the impacts of cutting ozone further on "economic values and on personal comfort and well-being." Chafing at the OMB's insistence on regulatory laxity, 'Marcus Peacock responded in a memo that "EPA is not aware of any information that ozone has beneficial effects on economic values or on personal comfort and well being."[117] But a direct order from the president to adopt the more permissive standard prompted "a scramble by administration officials to rewrite the regulations to avoid a conflict with past EPA statements on the harm caused by ozone."[118] On March 12, 2008, the EPA finalized the primary/secondary ozone standard of 75 ppb. Two months later, both environmentalists and industry groups petitioned the D.C. Circuit for a review, and in early 2009, the court granted the EPA's request for a stay so the Obama administration could review the standards.

Bush's EPA was also under pressure to revise the ambient air quality standard for small (2.5 microns or smaller) particulates downward in response to new scientific evidence. The agency's science advisory committee suggested an annual standard of between 13 and 14 micrograms per cubic meter of air and a twenty-four-hour threshold of between 30 and 35 micrograms per cubic meter. In December 2005, the EPA proposed lowering the primary standard for fine particulates, but not to the levels proposed by its scientific advisors: it would retain the annual standard of 15 micrograms per cubic meter and lower the twenty-four-hour threshold from 65 to 35 micrograms per cubic meter. The EPA's analysis suggested that its proposal would have a negligible effect on polluters, whereas the stricter standards recommended by the science panel would force substantial changes. On September 29, 2006, in an unusually harsh letter, the seven charter members of the scientific advisory committee accused the EPA of ignoring several aspects of the panel's advice when issuing its final rule on small particulates.[119] Undeterred, on December 18, the EPA finalized the primary/secondary standards for small particulates at the levels originally proposed. In early 2009, however, the D.C. Circuit threw out the Bush administration standards, saying the agency had made a decision that was "contrary to law and unsupported by adequately reasoned decision making."[120]

In a third rule change that reflected the administration's propensity to adopt an environmentally risk-tolerant position, in the summer of 2008, the EPA finalized new air quality rules that made it easier to build power plants, oil refineries, and other major industrial facilities near national parks and wilderness areas. Specifically, the new rule averaged pollution levels in the nation's cleanest areas over a year. By contrast, the status quo was to measure levels over both three-hour and twenty-four-hour periods, to capture the consequences of spikes in emissions that occur during peak energy demand. The agency adopted the rule change over the objections of its own staff; half of EPA's ten regional administrators formally dissented from the decision, and four of them criticized the rule in writing.[121] Defending the agency's decision, Jeffrey Holmstead explained, "The question from a policy perspective was: Do you need to have models based on the absolute worst-case conditions that [are] unlikely ever to occur in the real world?"[122]

### Enforcement Gives Way to Voluntary Compliance

The effects of the Bush administration's low-profile challenges to the air pollution regime were evident in the realm of enforcement as well. Like previous conservative administrations, the Bush administration preferred state to federal oversight and voluntary compliance to enforcement. This propensity was consistent with the stated opinion of Bush appointees that that industry executives were generally inclined to go beyond compliance without prodding from government. As one former Bush EPA appointee put it, "most companies have smart people at the top . . . who do understand that there are legitimate environmental concerns."[123] Some veteran EPA staff were also sympathetic to the concerns of business. For example, one staffer explained, "There are companies where their environmental performance is key to their success in the marketplace and their stock price. It's not this external, compliance-oriented thing they have to do." Having spent time with plant managers and corporate environmental health and safety executives, he added, "I might be more inclined to trust them" than would an environmental activist.[124]

As a first step toward instituting a more business-friendly enforcement policy, in July 2001, Whitman announced her intention to cut the agency's federal and regional environmental enforcement staff by 8 percent, or the equivalent of 270 positions, while shifting $25 million from federal enforcement to the states. (Athough not negligible, this was not as draconian a shift as it appeared. State agencies were already handling most enforcement. Moreover, of the 270 positions to be cut, only 70 were actually filled at the time.) In a June speech to the National Association of Manufacturers, Whitman explained that the states were better equipped to address environmental degradation in partnership with industry—although a December 1998 report by the EPA's inspector general had concluded that state environmental agencies substantially underreported local Clean Air Action violations. Congress restored funding for the enforcement office, but the administration made some of the proposed cuts anyway. According to former EPA official Eric Schaeffer, even after Congress replaced the money, the administration cut thirty enforcement positions, ostensibly to pay for counterterrorism activities—even though Congress had provided special funding for counterterrorism.[125] In early 2002, the EPA requested a $16 million increase for enforcement (from $387 million in fiscal year 2002 to $402 million in fiscal year 2003), but again proposed sending a large chunk of that money to the states. Congress did not accede to this funding request, however, and resisted the agency's efforts to devolve enforcement.

Despite efforts by Congress to hold the line, watchdog groups argued that enforcement slowed under Bush. For example, the nonprofit Public Employees for Environmental Responsibility (PEER) reported that in 2000, the agency made 105 referrals to the Justice Department for criminal prosecution; in 2001, by contrast, it made only 42 referrals, and that number dropped to 26 in 2002.[126] The Environmental Integrity Project, a D.C.-based nonprofit started by Eric Schaeffer, determined that in fiscal year 2002, the penalties levied against polluters fell dramatically: in the three years preceding the Bush administration takeover, the amount of money recovered from polluting companies in federal court averaged about $103 million per year; in 2002, that figure dropped to $51 million.

Even as it repudiated enforcement as a means of gaining compliance, the EPA fought back against assertions that it was retreating on enforcement. In early 2003, the EPA changed course and requested additional funding and staff time to enhance compliance monitoring and civil enforcement. Then, in December, shortly after Knight Ridder published a story critical of the agency's enforcement record, the agency released a new set of statistics that showed its enforcement efforts in a positive light. According to J. P. Suarez, the numbers highlighted the agency's "smart enforcement" campaign to focus on the most significant violators and obtain the most environmentally beneficial results. (The agency adjusted the way it tallied some enforcement statistics, making comparisons with earlier eras difficult.) The EPA continued to tout its enforcement record in 2004, pointing out that it had collected a record $4.8 billion in fines and penalties from individuals, companies, and municipal governments.[127]

Critics challenged this interpretation of the data and pointed to a drop in key EPA enforcement indicators, such as civil penalties, the number of cases referred to the Justice Department for prosecution, and closed-out cases. Criticism continued for the remainder of the Bush administration's tenure. In 2007, the *Washington Post* reported that the EPA's pursuit of criminal cases against polluters had dropped off sharply under Bush, with the number of prosecutions, new investigations, and total convictions all down by more than one-third, based on data from the EPA and Department of Justice.[128] The *Post* claimed that White House and top EPA officials had strongly discouraged enforcement activity and instead opted to pursue more settlements and plea bargains. As a result, although the agency pursued a small number of high-profile cases, overall, environmental prosecutions by U.S. attorneys declined by more than one-third, from 919 in 2001 to 584 in 2006.[129]

Beyond shifting its emphasis away from sanctions, the administration sought more subtle means of reducing the EPA's enforcement capacity. According to legal scholar Joel Mintz, from the opening months of the administration it was apparent to career staff that enforcement would be devalued at the agency. In addition to demonstrating a desire to devolve enforcement to the states, Whitman rarely identified enforcement as a high priority, and senior officials almost never consulted career staff in making decisions.[130] In a particularly low-profile maneuver, the administration's budget request for fiscal year 2007 proposed an 80 percent cut in the EPA's library budget—from $2.5 million to $500,000—to be achieved by eliminating its electronic catalogue and shutting down several of its regional libraries. The libraries were used primarily by EPA scientists, regulators, and attorneys for enforcing regulations under the Clean Air Act and other statutes. In October, after quietly closing several regional libraries and boxing up or destroying their contents, the EPA announced it was closing its headquarters library and began ordering its regional offices to cancel subscriptions to several technical journals and environmental publications used by its scientists. According to a GAO report released in February 2008, some libraries tossed out documents and sold office equipment at fire-sale prices in their rush to meet shutdown deadlines. Although the agency promised that it would post much of the lost material online, the GAO noted that, because of copyright restrictions, only 10 percent of EPA data could be digitized for Internet access.[131] In early 2007, in response to congressional concerns, the EPA enacted an indefinite moratorium on further changes.

In December, Congress approved an additional $1 million for the libraries and ordered the EPA to reopen them.[132]

In lieu of enforcement, and consistent with the administration's "new environmentalism," the EPA emphasized a positive, voluntary approach to gaining compliance, as exemplified by the Performance Track program. Initiated under Carol Browner in 2000, Performance Track allowed companies that enrolled voluntarily to face fewer inspections and more permissive regulatory requirements, as well as to garner beneficial publicity, in exchange for a promise to adopt cutting-edge environmental practices. Performance Track blossomed during the eight years of the Bush administration: after accepting 227 charter members a month before Bush became president, during Bush's tenure the program doubled its membership to 548; the office swelled from five to eighteen employees, while its annual budget grew from $910,000 to $4.7 million.[133]

According to the EPA, between 2000 and 2006, Performance Track's accomplishments were impressive. Members reduced water consumption by 3.7 billion gallons, energy use by 4.3 million Btus, and hazardous waste generation by 52,266 tons, while conserving some 16,809 acres of land.[134] But as policy scholars Cary Coglianese and Jennifer Nash point out in their analysis of Performance Track, it is difficult to determine how many of these improvements would have occurred in the absence of the program. More importantly, a 2006 analysis by EPA enforcement officials detected "considerable non-compliance among [Performance Track] facilities and [found] that many members who are widely touted as meeting or exceeding regulatory requirements actually are not."[135] Those findings were based on mediocre data, but an audit by the EPA's inspector general confirmed at least some of them. In a 2007 report, the inspector general pointed out that only two of the thirty Performance Track members her office investigated actually met all of their environmental commitments. While some Performance Track members' compliance and toxic-release records were better than the average for their sector, others were not.[136] In fact, according to the Environmental Integrity Project, some Performance Track members' emissions actually increased.[137]

An investigative report by the *Philadelphia Inquirer* charged that what started out as an innovative stewardship program had by December 2008 "become little more than smoke and mirrors."[138] Among the authors' findings:

[T]he EPA had recruited companies with mixed, even dismal, environmental records; despite offering regulatory breaks, the EPA had failed to verify independently that Performance-Track companies actually reached their goals; some Performance-Track companies had paid fines to settle EPA accusations that they broke environmental rules (since 2003, participants had racked up more than 100 violations and paid $15.25 million in fines); at least a dozen Performance-Track members had increased the amount of toxic chemicals they emitted; and, desperate for new members, the program had turned to gift shops and post offices to pad its numbers.[139]

## Making the Endangered Species Act More Permissive

A second major target of Bush administration hostility was any regulatory program that sought to conserve biodiversity, particularly the Endangered Species Act. Consistent with the antiregulatory storyline, Bush administration officials depicted the act as an effort by environmentalists to "lock up" excessive amounts of land and productive resources, to the detriment of the economy and national security.[140] They argued that highly valued species and landscapes should be protected through voluntary stewardship by landowners and local governments. Therefore, the administration's primary mechanism for implementing the Endangered Species Act was financial incentives for local, private, and collaboratively formulated conservation initiatives, approaches it could foster without changing the law. Stewardship initiatives supplemented a variety of low-profile challenges to the process of listing and designating critical habitat under the act. Complementing the administration's efforts to relax the regulatory aspects of the act were a series of withering, if ultimately unsuccessful, attacks on the law by conservatives in Congress.

## Conversion of the Endangered Species Act through Low-Profile Challenges

One way the Bush administration' made the Endangered Species Act more permissive was by allowing regulatory actions under the act to languish. The first step was to curb endangered species listings, which trigger a host of regulatory restrictions. The Clinton administration had set the stage for such a retreat: in response to a surge in lawsuits by environmentalists, the Fish and Wildlife Service announced in November 2000 that it would be unable to consider listing any new species, since it was expending all of its time and money responding to legal actions. But Secretary Norton's Fish and Wildlife Service took such resistance even further: it was the first ever not to voluntarily list a single species as endangered or threatened; all listings were undertaken in response to lawsuits.[141] It also kept listings to a minimum. In late August 2001, the

Bush administration reached an agreement with environmental groups, promising quick action on twenty-nine species in exchange for environmentalists' consent not to demand immediate compliance with court orders affecting other species.[142] Prior to this accord, the administration listed only one species, the milk vetch plant. After finalizing eleven listings in its first year, the wildlife agencies listed only eight species per year on average, compared to sixty-five per year under Clinton and fifty-nine per year under George H. W. Bush.[143]

According to journalist Juliet Eilperin, the administration accomplished this low rate of listing "through a variety of little-noticed procedural and policy moves."[144] Internal documents revealed that the administration had erected "pervasive bureaucratic obstacles" to limit the number of species listed. For example, under Norton, the Interior Department no longer rated the threat to particular species based primarily on the status of populations within the United States. In a second reversal, the department's solicitor declared that when officials were considering whether a significant portion of a species' range was in peril, they should consider only "the range in which a species currently exists, not the historical range of the species where it once existed."[145] The Fish and Wildlife Service took another step to raise the bar for listing as well: it decreed that its files on proposed listings should include only evidence from petitions, along with any information in agency records that could undercut, as opposed to support, a decision to list the species.

In a particularly subtle maneuver, in May 2005, Dale Hall, southwest regional director for the Fish and Wildlife Service, issued a new policy forbidding biologists from using wildlife genetics to protect or aid recovery of endangered and threatened species. Specifically, Hall said that all decisions about how to increase species populations must use only the genetic data available at the time the species was placed on the endangered species list, even if the scientific understanding of its genetic makeup had improved in subsequent years. The policy was timed to block the listing of the lesser prairie chicken and to water down recovery plans for the Mexican spotted owl and the southwestern willow flycatcher, as well as a number of desert fish species. It allowed the service to permit development that would extirpate whole populations or declare wildlife species secure based on the status of a single population, even if a majority of populations were on the brink of extinction. Ralph Morgenweck, Mountain-Prairie regional director for the Fish and Wildlife Service, sharply rebutted Hall's memo, which he said "could run counter to the purpose of the ESA" and "may contradict our direction to use the best available science in endangered species decisions in some cases."[146] But Morgenweck's memo was ignored, and shortly thereafter Hall was elevated to director of the service.[147]

The administration also sought to make it more difficult for environmentalists to force listings. At the behest of the Fish and Wildlife Service, the Interior appropriations bill for fiscal year 2002 contained a rider that discouraged citizens from suing the service to act on listing petitions by allowing the agency's funds to be spent only to comply with existing court orders or to list species deemed priorities by the interior secretary, and by prohibiting the department from spending money to carry out court orders or settlements after its enactment. In addition, the service took the position that if the agency identified a species as a candidate for the list, citizens could not file a petition for that species, thereby eliminating the legal deadlines that environmentalists had used to gain leverage in court. (In 2003, U.S. District Court judge Reggie Walton overturned this policy on the grounds that it allowed the agency to avoid its "mandatory, non-discretionary duties to issue findings" under the act.)

In addition to curbing listing, the Bush administration scaled back on recovery planning.[148] Under Reagan, the wildlife agencies approved some thirty recovery plans per year, under George H. W. Bush they approved just over forty, under Clinton around seventy. Under George W. Bush that number was twelve. The recovery plans developed during George W. Bush's administration were also minimally restrictive. For example, the Fish and Wildlife Service proposed to reduce by 1.5 million acres (from 6.9 million acres to 5.3 million acres) the amount of habitat set aside for the northern spotted owl and instead focus recovery efforts on culling the barred owl, which preys on the spotted owl. In mid-August 2007, an agency-ordered peer review charged that in drafting its spotted owl recovery plan the service had ignored the best-available science. The scientists found that the service selectively cited reports and data to justify its proposal to reduce protection for old-growth forests and to emphasize the threat posed by the barred owl.[149] In 2008, the Fish and Wildlife Service unveiled a revised recovery plan for the spotted owl. This one called for a network of 133 managed owl-conservation areas totaling nearly 6 million acres, while opening up to increased logging 23 percent of the 1.6 million acres designated as critical habitat in Oregon.[150]

Under Bush, the wildlife agencies also resisted designating large swaths of critical habitat, and gave greater weight than their predecessors had to economic factors when issuing such designations. In this regard, the administration got a boost from the Tenth Circuit, which ruled in 2001 that economic impacts must be considered at the time critical habitat is designated regardless of whether those impacts are attributable to another cause, such as the species listing (*New Mexico Cattlegrowers Association v. U.S. FWS*). In the process, the court invalidated nearly six hundred miles of protected stream- and riverbed habitat for the southwestern willow flycatcher. The service responded with alacrity to this ruling, asking judges across the West to remand dozens of critical habitat designations in response to challenges by development interests, in order to conduct more detailed and quantitative economic analyses.[151] It also interpreted the ruling to require identifying every economic downside to a listing decision while minimizing consideration of the benefits.

Between 2001 and 2003, the Bush administration designated some 38 million acres of critical habitat for 115 species—more species than any previous administration—largely as a result of successful litigation by environmentalists.[152] But an analysis of federal data by the National Wildlife Federation found that, during this period, the wildlife agencies designated as critical habitat only half the acreage recommended by federal biologists. It also found that in 2003, biologists' proposals were reduced by one-third, with 69 percent of those reductions based on economic factors, up from less than 1 percent in 2001.[153] According to the Center for Biological Diversity, by the end of the Bush administration two-thirds of critical habitat designations covering 178 species had been reduced between proposed and final by an average of 49 percent, shrinking the total designated acreage by nearly 63 million acres. Only seven designations were increased.[154]

In mid-2003, the Fish and Wildlife Service announced it was temporarily halting designations of critical habitat altogether because it was out of money. (In October 2003, the GAO confirmed that the service faced severe fiscal and management challenges as a result of mounting litigation by environmentalists over critical habitat.[155]) Critics pointed out that, despite its chronic budget woes, the service had not requested more money from Congress and had received all it had asked for in the budget for fiscal year 2003.[156] When they resumed designating critical habitat, the wildlife agencies routinely inserted a statement that critical habitat "provides little real conservation benefit, is driven by litigation rather than biology," is established "before complete scientific information is available," and "imposes huge social and economic costs"— caveats that invited industry to challenge the designation.[157] (Although the Bush administration derided critical habitat as useless, reports to Congress from the wildlife agencies showed that species with critical habitat were less likely to be declining than and twice as likely to be recovering as those without.)

In lieu of the traditional tools of regulation, enforcement, and fee-simple land acquisition, in implementing the Endangered Species Act the Interior Department drew on the principles of free-market environmentalism.[158] In this, they built on the administrative practices initiated by Secretary Babbitt: compensating landowners for protecting endangered species, creating conservation easements, and forging partnerships with private landowners and states. As Lynn Scarlett explained, "we looked at the ESA and asked how, within the context of the existing law, we could increase the incentives and strengthen what the previous administration had done on safe harbor, assurances, rules, and guidelines for conservation banking. All to enable landowners to actively engage in conservation without the fear that their livelihoods would be extinguished."[159] Interior Secretary Norton labeled this approach "the four Cs"—communication, consultation, and cooperation, in the service of conservation. "Successful conservation is a partnership between the government and the people," Norton argued. "The government's role is to empower the people to take conservation into their own hands."[160]

The department used organizational mechanisms—such as training staff in mediation, collaboration, facilitation, and negotiation—to encourage employees to engage in the partnerships that were central to the four Cs.[161] Department officials also tried to shift from input measures to performance-based measures to assess progress, while seeking to ensure that those performance measures rewarded collaboration. And they created a large number of additional "service-first" locations, in which agencies working in a common landscape on common problems could be in the same place and share resources. In August 2004, the president put his imprimatur on the four Cs by signing Executive Order 13352, Facilitation of Cooperative Conservation, which directed the Departments of the Interior, Agriculture, and Commerce, as well as the EPA, to implement laws related to the environment and natural resources in a manner that promoted cooperative conservation, with an emphasis on local inclusion.

To finance the four Cs, in 2002, President Bush launched the $100 million Cooperative Conservation Initiative, which comprised two main elements: the Landowner Incentive Program and the Private Stewardship Grant Program. According to the Interior Department, between 2001 and 2006, nearly $2.5 billion in grants went to states, private landowners, hunting and fishing groups, and others to preserve open space, restore habitat, and conserve species. As a result, sixteen million acres of habitat were restored, protected, or extended. Defending this approach, Secretary Norton remarked, "These grants are very much in line with my philosophy that states should be given more resources and greater flexibility to protect habitat and conserve threatened and endangered species."[162] Most of the money devoted to voluntary land conservation was reallocated from other Interior Department programs, however, and even supporters acknowledged that the administration's cooperative conservation programs received increasingly inadequate funding as Bush's tenure wore on, largely because of resistance from the OMB and conservatives in Congress.[163] Furthermore, Bush's campaign promise notwithstanding, the Land and Water Conservation Fund, which supports fee-simple land acquisition, never received close to full funding.[164]

In addition to shifting resources away from the regulatory pillars of the Endangered Species Act and into voluntary conservation, the administration devolved responsibility for endangered species conservation to states and regions. For example, in preparation for downgrading federal protection for the gray wolf in the Northern Rockies, the Fish and Wildlife Service sought to turn responsibility for managing wolves over to Montana, Wyoming, and Idaho. In early 2005, the service issued new rules giving state wildlife officials greater flexibility in controlling wolf populations, and in February 2008, the agency delisted the wolf in all three states. The administration was not entirely consistent in its emphasis on local solutions, however. For example, in mid-June 2001, Secretary Norton announced the department was abandoning a Clinton-era plan to reintroduce twenty-five grizzly bears into the Selway-Bitterroot and Frank Church-River of No Return wilderness areas in Idaho and Montana. That plan was the result of an intensive, seven-year collaborative planning process among local stakeholders and included the first-ever citizen management committee, to be appointed by the governors of Idaho and Montana. Norton acted at the behest of Idaho governor Dirk Kempthorne, who worried about introducing the "massive, flesh-eating carnivores" into his state."[165] Justifying her decision, she said that "[b]uilding support from state leaders is an important element to any potential partnership of this size and scope."[166]

Even as she fended off criticism by environmentalists, Lynn Scarlett staunchly defended the administration's approach to implementing the Endangered Species Act against criticism by conservatives who thought it was insufficiently market oriented. For example, after the Property and

Environment Research Center gave the administration a C- for its application of free-market principles to environmental issues, Scarlett argued that the department's actions actually met the center's criteria: respect for property rights, enhancement of local decision making, use of market forces, and application of fees for service. "The effect of [the administration's] efforts," she wrote, "is to help focus the nation's attention on private stewardship and away from a long-standing presumption that conservation requires federal (or state) dominion over lands." Instead, she explained, the administration was fostering partnerships with locals. "In essence," she explained, "the four Cs vision seeks to advance personal stewardship." Whereas "the 'old environmentalism' turned to Washington for answers, focusing on top-down prescriptions, paperwork, and process, and tended to view the 'stick'—fees, fines, and punishment—as the primary tools with which to achieve environmental results," she added, the Bush administration relied on cooperation, innovation, and entrepreneurship.[167]

### More Low-Profile Challenges: Substituting Risk-Tolerant for Precautionary Judgment

A more subtle low-profile tactic employed by Bush administration officials to avoid regulation of development interests under the Endangered Species Act was to substitute their own environmentally risk-tolerant views for the more precautionary judgments of agency scientists. The first manifestation of this practice concerned the Arctic National Wildlife Refuge. In an op-ed piece in the *New York Times*, Secretary Norton described the high-tech world of energy exploration that American ingenuity had produced, and promised oil and gas development would have no significant impact on the refuge. In the fall of 2001, at the behest of Alaska senator Frank Murkowski, Norton furnished the Senate Energy and Natural Resources Committee with Interior's assessment that drilling in ANWR would not harm the hundreds of thousands of caribou that roamed the refuge.

Fish and Wildlife Service biologists pointed out, however, that Norton had made seventeen alterations to the report they had given her, substantially changing its emphasis by substituting key words in order to minimize the potential impacts. In fact, the scientific report, which had been vetted by five offices before landing on Norton's desk, concluded that although caribou had mostly thrived in the years since oil drilling in the region began, they gravitated toward ANWR's so-called 1002 Area (the undeveloped portion that was proposed for drilling) and tended to avoid oil fields when calving. Norton inserted a statement that caribou had been concentrated "outside" the 1002 Area for eleven of the past eighteen years, when the correct word was "inside"; she also left out data showing that calf production and early survival were lower in the years when the caribou did not calve in the 1002 Area.[168] When asked about the changes, Norton claimed they were typographical errors.

Norton also ordered the rewriting of an exhaustive twelve-year study by federal biologists detailing the effects that Arctic drilling would have on populations of caribou, musk oxen, and snow geese. The original study warned that caribou "may be particularly sensitive" to oil exploration in the refuge. By contrast, a two-page supplemental report written by the same scientists but employing more modest development scenarios showed no negative impact on wildlife.[169] Similarly, Norton ordered the suppression of two studies by the Fish and Wildlife Service concluding that the drilling would threaten polar bear populations and violate the international treaty protecting the bears. She then instructed the agency to redo the report to "reflect the Interior Department's position."[170] (Despite Norton's efforts, opponents in Congress managed to prevent oil exploration in ANWR throughout the Bush administration.)

A second case in which Bush administration appointees substituted their risk-tolerant judgment for that of agency scientists involved the sage grouse, a large bird native to the western United States. Sage grouse numbers plummeted in the twentieth century as its habitat—the sage steppe ecosystem—disappeared, much of it destroyed by energy exploration and development. The Fish and Wildlife Service estimated the grouse population was at between 1 percent and 31 percent of its historical levels, largely as a result of habitat loss. In late December 2003, the Sierra Club and nineteen other environmental groups petitioned the service to list the sage grouse as endangered, pointing out that its population had declined 80 percent over the previous two decades and that accelerating oil and gas development threatened much of its remaining habitat. But the service was reluctant to list the bird because it did not want to discourage state and local collaborative entities that had sprung up across the West in hopes of preventing such a listing through voluntary conservation. As of the fall of 2004, all eleven states in the range of the sage grouse had completed or were working on cooperative conservation plans, and the service anticipated that by the winter of 2004–2005, more than seventy stakeholder groups would have similar plans.

In early December 2004, a team of Fish and Wildlife Service biologists and managers concluded that the sage grouse was *not* threatened with extinction because the rate of population decline had slowed, several core populations were healthy, and plenty of habitat still existed. Environmentalists attacked that decision, however, when it was revealed that Julie MacDonald—a top aide to Craig Manson, the Interior assistant secretary who oversaw the service—had edited the source material for the panel that recommended against listing the bird. In her critique, MacDonald, who had no background in wildlife biology, dismissed studies that indicated significant declines in the grouse population or its habitat, denigrating them as mere "opinion." She also highlighted industry comments she found more persuasive. At the same time, she eliminated more than half of the references to a pessimistic conservation assessment conducted by a group of scientists on behalf of the Western Association of Fish and Wildlife Agencies, saying "We should treat it as we would an industry publication."[171]

Despite efforts by environmentalists to create a flap over MacDonald's editing, in January 2005, the service announced that the sage grouse would not be placed on the endangered species list. In response, environmentalists sued. While the case was pending, MacDonald resigned, after the Interior Department's inspector general Earl Devaney issued a scathing report that found she had improperly edited scientific decisions on endangered species issues. (She had also violated ethics rules and passed internal agency information to outside parties that were suing the department, including the Pacific Legal Foundation and the California Farm Bureau Federation.) In early December 2007, Judge B. Lynn Winmill of the U.S. District Court in Idaho ordered the Fish and Wildlife Service to reconsider its refusal to list the sage grouse (*Western Watersheds Project v. United States Fish and Wildlife Service*). The court found that while the service had consulted with experts, it excluded them from the listing decision; it also created no detailed report of the experts' opinions, while ignoring the portion of those opinions that was preserved on the record. "What an odd process," Winmill wrote. "Right at the moment where the 'best science' was most needed, it was locked out of the room." Winmill chastised top Interior Department officials for meddling in the listing process, using pressure and intimidation, and criticized MacDonald's conduct as "inexcusable."[172] Just weeks before Winmill's decision, the Fish and Wildlife Service announced it would revise seven rulings that denied endangered species listings or limited critical habitat designations because they were "inappropriately influenced" by MacDonald, and in early 2008, the service began the listing process for the sage grouse anew.

A third case in which political appointees adopted an environmentally risk-tolerant interpretation of the available science over the recommendations of agency experts involved the Klamath River Basin. In early April 2001, in the midst of a record drought, the Bureau of Reclamation halted irrigation of 90 percent of the 200,000 acres served by the Klamath Project in order to protect sucker fish in Upper Klamath Lake and coho salmon that spawn in the Klamath River. At the time, although sympathetic to the plight of the 1,400 affected farmers, Secretary Norton felt she had no choice but to comply with the law and allow the restrictions to be put in place. Farmers reacted furiously: on three separate occasions in late June and early July, locals used saws and welding torches to reopen the headgate of an irrigation canal and restore the flow of water. Local authorities refused to intervene.

Vice President Cheney expressed concern for the farmers, telling a radio host, "We need to have more flexibility built into the statutes so we don't end up in these situations where we are literally affecting the livelihood of thousands of people—good, hardworking farmers—in order to protect the so-called sucker fish."[173] Environmentalists, of course, saw the situation differently. "The problem in the Klamath Basin," said Todd True of the Earthjustice Legal Defense Fund, "is not the Endangered Species Act, and seeking an exemption from the act is not going to solve the problem. The problem is decades of overuse of water and a federal project that is simply out of scale to what the basin can sustain and not suffer an ecological collapse."[174]

On the advice of Cheney, Norton sought to resolve the controversy by commissioning a report by the National Research Council (NRC) of the National Academy of Sciences that would examine the science underpinning the biological opinions (BiOps) for salmon and sucker fish. The NRC's preliminary report, delivered in early February 2002, concluded that the BiOps on which the Bureau of Reclamation had based its decision were not supported by firm science—or, more precisely, that there was not enough science to *prove* that agency scientists' precautionary judgments were correct.[175] The report prompted triumphant statements like that of Republican James Hansen of Utah, who crowed, "A handful of U.S. Fish and Wildlife Service bureaucrats withheld desperately needed water from farmers in the Klamath Basin last summer. Now we find out that that decision was based on sloppy science and apparent guesswork. . . .This latest travesty in the enforcement of the Endangered Species Act should be one more nail in the coffin of that broken law."[176]

Shortly after the report's release, Norton authorized diverting more water to farmers.[177] Six months later, tens of thousands of salmon washed up on the banks of the Klamath River. According to biologist and whistleblower Michael Kelly, the massive fish kill was not surprising because NMFS never performed the scientific analysis necessary to verify that water levels in the new BiOp would not jeopardize the coho's continued existence.[178] Both the Fish and Wildlife Service and the California Department of Fish and Game subsequently concluded that a combination of low river flows, high water temperatures, and crowding of fish precipitated the disease outbreak that caused the fish kill.[179] In mid-July 2003, District Court judge Saundra B. Armstrong ruled that portions of the administration's ten-year irrigation plan for the Klamath were "arbitrary and capricious" (*Pacific Coast Federation of Fishermen's Association v. Bureau of Reclamation*). Specifically, she said the plan did not adequately provide for sucker fish and coho salmon. Nevertheless, the Bureau of Reclamation continued to deny water to the salmon until, in early spring 2006, Judge Armstrong directed it to give salmon top priority when the irrigation season began that April.

### Taking a Development-Friendly Approach to Litigation

Another low-profile tactic the Interior Department employed in hopes of reducing the restrictiveness of federal conservation efforts was encouraging and then settling lawsuits on development-friendly terms. For example, in November 2000, the National Association of Homebuilders and sixteen other groups filed a lawsuit alleging that NMFS had failed to conduct an economic impact analysis when it designated critical habitat for nineteen salmon and steelhead populations (*National Association of Home Builders v. Evans*). Nick Cammarota, general council for the California Building Industry Association, one of the plaintiffs, explained the lawsuit was "part of a strategy of many lawsuits we're involved in," which were intended to force the agencies to reduce the amount of land designated as critical habitat.[180] In early March 2002, NMFS agreed to settle the case, announcing it would withdraw the existing designations and open them to public comment. In November 2004, NMFS proposed designating some 40,000 river miles of West Coast streams and estuaries as critical habitat for the fish—an area that comprised only one-fifth of what the agency had previously designated because it included only currently occupied areas.

In December 2004, in a case that held enormous importance for property rights advocates, the administration settled a suit with California farmers who claimed their property rights had been violated by the reservation of water to protect fish under the Endangered Species Act. In 2001, U.S. Court of Federal Claims judge John Paul Wiese had sided with farmers in Tulare and Kern counties, who argued their water contracts were equivalent to property rights (*Tulare Lake Basin Water Storage v. United States*). Defending his decision, Wiese said, "The federal government is certainly free to preserve the fish; it must simply pay for the water it takes to do so."[181] Prior to Wiese's ruling, the case law had been on the side of government, and most observers thought the claims court decision was likely to be overruled. Both California authorities and NMFS lawyers urged the Justice Department to appeal the verdict, fearing that a settlement would invite new legal challenges.[182] Instead, however, the Justice Department agreed to pay the farmers $16.7 million—the original award plus interest.

Yet another way the administration enabled a risk-tolerant orientation to prevail was by declining to appeal development-friendly judicial rulings. For example, federal officials decided not to appeal a September 2001 ruling by Judge Michael R. Hogan, of the U.S. District Court in Eugene, Oregon, that NMFS regulators "arbitrarily and capriciously" distinguished between wild and hatchery salmon when listing wild salmon as endangered (*Alsea Valley Alliance v. Evans*). Based on that ruling, which stripped the Oregon coastal coho of its threatened status, NMFS declared that it would review the listings of twenty-five out of twenty-six groups of Pacific salmon and steelhead. Then, in late May 2004, the agency announced it would routinely count hatchery-bred fish when assessing the health of wild stocks. (It made this decision under Mark Rutzick, a legal advisor to NMFS who had been the timber industry's top lawyer when it sought to overturn fish and wildlife regulations it viewed as overly restrictive.)

NMFS's hatchery listing policy met with the near-universal disapprobation of fishery scientists. Six of the world's leading experts on salmon ecology complained to the journal *Science* in March 2004 that fish produced in hatcheries could not be counted on to save wild salmon. When asked to comment on the federal government's salmon recovery program, the scientists pointed out that while hatchery fish often boost absolute numbers, they also erode genetic diversity, have smaller spatial distribution, do not have reproductive success, lack the ability to avoid predators, and have poor rates of survival at sea; in fact, the scientists said, studies indicate that hatchery salmon can actually hamper recovery efforts for naturally spawning fish. NMFS staff seemed to agree with the scientists' conclusions: in a policy draft written ten months after the court decision, they indicated that counting hatchery fish did not help assess the health of wild salmon. The law, they wrote, required them to list species "based on whether they are likely to be self-sustaining in their native ecosystem."[183]

Ultimately, NMFS downgraded only two species of salmon under its new hatchery listing policy. Nonetheless, several environmental groups sued the agency, and in mid-June 2007, Seattle District Court judge John C. Coughenour nullified the policy, pointing out that NMFS's counting method "departs from the [ESA's] central purpose, which is to promote and conserve naturally self-sustaining populations" (*Trout Unlimited v. Lohn*).[184] Judge Coughenour agreed with the plaintiffs that to commingle the numbers of hatchery and wild populations when deciding on protections "is, in fact, contrary to the best available scientific evidence" and inconsistent with the Endangered Species Act, which has "a central purpose of preserving and promoting self-sustaining natural populations." Noting that six years earlier a federal judge in Eugene, Oregon, had endorsed the opposite interpretation, Coughenour wrote in his order that he would welcome the "happy result" of a review by the Ninth Circuit. In this case, however, the Bush administration eventually prevailed: in March 2009, the Ninth Circuit upheld NMFS's decision to downgrade the steelhead, which it regarded as based on a permissible interpretation of the existing science.

### Environmentalists Fight Back

In response to environmentalists' lawsuits, the courts ultimately rejected many of the Bush administration's risk-tolerant Endangered Species Act interpretations. For example, in a landmark ruling in 2004, the Ninth Circuit rejected the Fish and Wildlife Service's implementation of the act's critical habitat provisions. In *Gifford Pinchot Task Force v. U.S. Fish and Wildlife Service*, environmental organizations petitioned the Ninth Circuit to review six BiOps issued by the service authorizing the incidental "take" of northern spotted owls in the Pacific Northwest. The Ninth Circuit held that the service's critical habitat analysis was fatally flawed because the service's definition of "destruction or adverse modification" of habitat equated species "recovery" with "survival." As a result, adverse modification would not occur until habitat modification threatened the survival of a species, rather than just its recovery. According to the court, this interpretation contradicted the statutory requirement that the service find an adverse modification if there is appreciable diminishment in the value of the habitat for survival *or* recovery.

In another case, decided in May 2005, Judge James Redden, of the U.S. District Court in Portland, Oregon, ruled that a NMFS BiOp for salmon in the Columbia River Basin had arbitrarily limited and skewed its analysis of the harm that fourteen federal dams cause to twelve endangered species of Columbia River and Snake River salmon and steelhead (*National Wildlife Federation et al. v. National Marine Fisheries Service et al.*). As a result, the judge said, the Bush administration had shirked its duty under the Endangered Species Act to ensure that federal actions did not jeopardize the survival of the species. This decision actually marked the third time the courts had rejected NMFS's analysis of how federal actions might affect salmon and what could be done to mitigate that harm. The first two analyses were conducted under the Clinton administration. In 2003, the court ruled that the previous BiOp, released in 2000, relied too heavily on actions taken by nonfederal actors. Although it acknowledged, "Breaching the four lower Snake River dams would provide more certainty of long-term [salmon] survival and recovery than would other measures," the success of the 2000 BiOp depended entirely on measures to improve upstream habitat and upgrade hatcheries.[185]

The Bush administration's Columbia River Basin BiOp, however, was even more risk-tolerant. It treated dams as immutable features of the landscape and therefore simply analyzed their operations. In late November 2004, shortly before NMFS released its final BiOp, 250 scientists sent a letter to President Bush blasting the document. "This new analysis is an alarming sea change in approach with no supporting scientific justification," they said.[186] As Judge Redden wrote, under the new interpretation, the agency "would be able to exempt itself from accountability by characterizing some, even lethal, elements of any proposed action as 'nondiscretionary.'"[187] In April 2007, the Ninth Circuit affirmed Judge Redden's ruling, noting that under the administration's theory, "a listed species could be gradually destroyed, so long as each step on the path to destruction is sufficiently modest. This type of slow slide into oblivion is one of the very ills the Endangered Species Act seeks to prevent."[188] The BiOp went back to the drawing board, while the dams continued to operate. In late 2007, NMFS released a fourth BiOp that again declined to consider removing the dams, inviting yet another legal challenge.

In two additional cases, decided in August 2005, federal judges ruled that the Fish and Wildlife Service had acted arbitrarily and violated the Endangered Species Act when it cut back protections for the gray wolf and the tiger salamander. As journalist Felicity Barringer explained, "In both instances, the administration had combined sparser, distinct populations of species with larger, robust populations, and then said legal protection could be reduced."[189] In the case of the tiger salamander, Judge William Alsup invalidated the 2004 rule reducing protections for separate populations, saying it was "bereft of any analysis" (*Center for Biological Diversity v. U.S. Fish and Wildlife Service*). He chastised the Fish and Wildlife Service because agency scientists "were overruled and directed to eliminate" their earlier finding that the two populations of salamanders were distinct subgroups.[190]

In a third such case, decided in mid-July 2008, Federal District Court judge Donald W. Molloy issued a preliminary injunction against delisting the gray wolf in Montana, Idaho, and Wyoming (*Defenders of Wildlife et al. v. Department of Interior et al.*). The Fish and Wildlife Service had ended federal protection for the wolves in February and turned management responsibility over to the states, which planned to institute wolf hunts that would dramatically reduce the wolf population. The judge was persuaded that there was a possibility of irreparable harm to the species under the states' plans. He expressed particular concern about the service's decision to approve Wyoming's plan for maintaining just eight breeding pairs, instead of the fifteen the federal government had required. He said the decision—which ran counter to the government's earlier rejection of the Wyoming wolf-management plan—"represents an agency change of course unsupported by adequate reasoning."[191] (In late September, the service rescinded the delisting decision, but just before leaving office it lifted protections for the gray wolf again.)

Environmentalists' efforts to block the Bush administration's Endangered Species Act policies got a boost when, in March 2007, Interior Department inspector general Earl Devaney issued his report saying that Julie MacDonald had run roughshod over agency scientists. In it, he asserted that 75 percent of the findings by the western office of the Fish and Wildlife Service on endangered species status reviews and critical habitat determinations had been sent to Washington, D.C. without any assurances from career lawyers and biologists that they were valid.[192] In late November, Devaney released a followup report documenting MacDonald's efforts to remove the Sacramento splittail from the endangered species list, despite owning a property and business that could be affected by the decision. In December 2008, Devaney issued an even more sweeping critique, which found that Interior Department officials routinely interfered with scientific work in order to limit protection of at-risk species. Although the report identified MacDonald as the main culprit, it also indicted several of her colleagues, whom Devaney said aided and abetted "her attempts to interfere with the science" and "the unwritten policy to exclude as many areas as practicable from Critical Habitat Determinations."[193]

The inspector general's reports buttressed allegations by the Union of Concerned Scientists (UCS), a Cambridge-based nonprofit that in early 2004 issued its own report charging the Bush administration with "unprecedented" levels of political interference in science. The UCS charged the White House with "repeatedly censoring and suppressing reports by its own scientists, stacking advisory committees with unqualified political appointees, disbanding government panels that provided unwanted advice, and refusing to seek any independent scientific expertise in some cases."[194] (White House science advisor John H. Marburger III contested the UCS's allegations, but they were consistent with anecdotal reports that had been emerging during the administration's first three years in office.)

In an effort to determine how routine was the interference of political appointees into scientists' work, in 2005, the UCS joined forces with the whistleblower group Public Employees for Environmental Responsibility (PEER) to survey more than 1,400 Fish and Wildlife Service biologists, ecologists, and botanists in field offices across the country.[195] Forty-four percent of those whose work was related to endangered species reported that they "[had] been directed, for non-scientific reasons, to refrain from making jeopardy or other findings that are protective of species." One in five said they had been "directed to inappropriately exclude or alter technical information from a Fish and Wildlife Service scientific document." And 56 percent cited cases where "commercial interests have inappropriately induced the reversal or withdrawal of scientific conclusions or decisions through political intervention." Furthermore, 42 percent said they could not publicly express "concerns about the biological needs of species and habitats without fear of retaliation," while nearly one-third felt they could not do so even within the agency.[196] A survey of 460 scientists from the National Oceanic and Atmospheric Administration, returned by 27 percent of them, revealed similar patterns: about two-thirds of those who responded said they did not believe the agency was doing its job, and more than one-half said they knew of cases in which "commercial interests" or senior administration officials had "inappropriately influenced" agency decisions.[197]

Although environmentalists succeeded in deflecting many of the Bush administration's low-profile challenges through litigation and negative publicity, in 2007, the restrictive interpretation of the Endangered Species Act suffered a major setback. In *National Association of Homebuilders v. Defenders of Wildlife*, the first substantive Endangered Species Act case before the Supreme Court in a decade, environmental groups argued that the EPA had improperly delegated authority to issue water pollution permits to the State of Arizona because it did not consult with the Fish and Wildlife Service to ensure the delegation would not jeopardize any of the state's sixty threatened and endangered species. But a 5–4 majority reversed the Ninth Circuit, ruling that the service had reasonably interpreted the act's Section 7 consultation procedure as applying only to discretionary action that federal agencies take under their authorizing statutes. Justice Alito, writing for the majority, argued that the Clean Water Act makes delegation of permitting authority non-discretionary, once specific criteria are met. Therefore, the EPA was not required to consult with the wildlife agencies. According to legal scholar J. B. Ruhl, this ruling marked a complete about-face from the position articulated by the Court in *Hill v. TVA* three decades earlier.[198] No longer would the Endangered Species Act trump all other federal action.

### Challenging the Endangered Species Act Directly

Despite Babbitt's administrative reforms in the mid-1990s, the Bush administration's even more aggressive deregulatory initiatives, and declining support for the act by the Supreme Court, the Endangered Species Act continued to be a thorn in the side of conservative activists, who demanded a full-blown legislative revision. In March 2002, the House Resources Committee considered two bills aimed at reforming the act that reflected many of the concerns raised by conservative critics: one sponsored by Oregon Republican Greg Walden and the other by Richard Pombo. To foster an image of the Endangered Species Act as ineffective and punitive, committee chair James Hansen held field hearings throughout the West at which witnesses told horror stories about the law's enforcement. "This is the only act in the country that…elevates species of flies, rats, slimy slugs and a host of other creatures nobody has heard of over the needs, desires and the pursuit of happiness of American citizens," Hansen declared.[199] "In an economy that is struggling to take off, we should be seeking ways to improve economic growth, not hinder it," complained Sam Graves of Missouri, who chaired the Rural Enterprises, Agriculture and Technology Subcommittee. "We must get the ESA off the backs of farmers and small businesses."[200]

There were ample signs that members of both parties were receptive to such complaints. In July 2004, the Resources Committee voted 28–14 to approve a bill sponsored by California Democrat Dennis Cardoza that gave the Fish and Wildlife Service more time and leeway in selecting critical habitat. The committee also approved (26–15) a bill sponsored by Representative Walden that required peer review by panels of outside scientists of government listings and critical habitat designations, codifying a practice the wildlife agencies had already embraced. There was considerable agreement on a couple of other modifications as well, such as changing the process of designating critical habitat so that land-use restrictions would take effect only *after* federal scientists had devised a formal recovery plan, and providing federal grants or tax incentives to landowners for maintaining key habitat for imperiled plants and animals.

But sharp differences remained. In particular, experts like Michael Bean pointed out that some proposed "reforms" reflected a misapprehension of science; for example, some of the bills would reduce the agencies' reliance on models and increase their dependence on "peer reviewed" data. But data are not peer reviewed, and models are essential to population viability analysis. Some bills also required extensive and concrete evidence of threats to a species' viability, although it is well understood that listing decisions are matters of judgment, not fact. Moreover, many environmentalists feared that in a Republican Congress *any* effort to rewrite the law would be an excuse to eviscerate it. So attempts at reform were stymied in both sessions of the 108th Congress.

After gaining seats in the November 2004 elections, however, congressional Republicans signaled their intention to proceed with an Endangered Species Act reform that incorporated "free-market principles."[201] Pombo moved quickly to capitalize on the opportunity afforded by the election while avoiding negative publicity. Pombo's bill contained numerous provisions that were noxious to environmentalists. It jettisoned critical habitat altogether, replacing it with "recovery teams"—comprising landowners, environmentalists, and government officials—that would prepare recovery plans based on the best available scientific data (alternatively, the interior secretary could prepare the plan); allowed the secretary of the interior to decide on the science the agency would use in listing a species; gave the Fish and Wildlife Service no more than 180 days to decide whether to block a development on sensitive habitat; created a program to compensate landowners if they could not develop their property because of Endangered Species Act restrictions; and repealed provisions that protected endangered species from pesticides. During the debate on the bill, the House accepted a manager's amendment from Pombo that narrowed the definition of what constitutes harm to a species, restricted the agency's use of science to sources that were peer reviewed by individuals recommended by the National Academy of Sciences, and required the Interior Department to prepare an analysis of a listing on the economy and national security—three measures that dramatically reduced the 'act's restrictiveness by raising hurdles to regulatory action. (In order to get the bill passed, Pombo dropped some even more radical proposals, including one that would have automatically taken the law off the books in 2015.)

In late September 2005, the House passed Pombo's Endangered Species Act revision while rejecting a bill sponsored by moderate Republican Sherwood Boehlert. Pombo managed to move his bill through committee (26–12) and to the House floor, where it passed by 229–193, in just nine days. Reflecting the importance of regional, in addition to partisan/ideological, divisions, thirty-six Democrats (mostly rural, and many from the Rocky Mountain West) approved the measure, while thirty-four Republicans voted against it. Property rights advocates were elated. "A critical mass is developing of people who are now aware of the problems that the existing Endangered Species Act imposes on landowners and communities and understands that it's counterproductive to recovering species," said property rights activist Chuck Cushman.[202] In fact, however, the bill's narrow passage—a result of frantic lobbying by environmentalists and scientists to undercut support for it—dampened its momentum, and a coalition of conservation biologists lost no time in working with Senate allies to stop it.[203]

Ultimately, Republican senator Lincoln Chafee, chair of the Environment and Public Works Committee, bottled up the bill so it could not get to the floor. (One tactic Chafee employed was to ask the Keystone Center, a nonprofit organization, to convene and facilitate a working group to build a consensus on reforms to the act—a process that effectively delayed action.) Contributing to a growing reluctance among Senate Republicans to gut the act was the unexpected mobilization of evangelicals. In 2004, twenty-nine representatives of evangelical groups convened in Maryland to produce a document that laid out the key principles of "creation care" and called on evangelicals to fight global warming and species extinction. In the fall of 2005, after the House passed its bill, the Academy of Evangelical Scientists and Ethicists ran an ad likening the act to Noah's Ark, saying, "Don't Let Congress Sink the Endangered Species Act."[204]

Despairing of legislative action, conservatives in the Bush administration tried to achieve many of the results advocated by Pombo and his allies through low-profile administrative means. As an Idaho senator,

Interior Secretary Kempthorne had authored legislation that would have allowed government agencies to exempt their actions from Endangered Species Act regulations and required the wildlife agencies to conduct cost-benefit analyses prior to listing a species. In 2007, with prospects for legislative reform dimming, the Interior Department generated a 117-page administrative-strategy document that incorporated language from Kempthorne's bill, as well as from Pombo's more recent one. Among the most significant changes was a proposal to give state governors the authority and funding to create recovery plans, veto the reintroduction of species within state boundaries, and even determine which plants and animals would get protection.

Many Fish and Wildlife Service employees, although they did not support the proposals in the draft document, were reluctant to speak up for fear of reprisals. But Bob Hallock—a recently retired thirty-four-year veteran of the service who worked with state agencies in Washington, Idaho, and Montana as an endangered species specialist—told journalist Rebecca Clarren, "If states are involved, the act [will] only get minimally enforced. States are, if anything, closer to special economic interests. They're more manipulated. The states have not demonstrated the will or interest in upholding the act. It's why we created a federal law in the first place."[205] Kempthorne's regulatory initiative was aborted after the draft proposal was leaked and Democrats in Congress threatened to cut Interior Department funding.

In another effort to accomplish administratively what conservatives in Congress had failed to achieve, in October 2008, as the administration was wrapping up its tenure, Kempthorne issued a draft rule to eliminate mandatory scientific reviews by the Fish and Wildlife Service of federal projects that could imperil listed plants and animals. Under the new regulations, which were finalized in December, consultations would not be required if an agency judged there would be little harm to a species. Kempthorne justified the rule as a means of "streamlining" the regulatory process in order to expedite domestic energy projects. In particular, Kempthorne said, the changes were needed to ensure that the Endangered Species Act was not used as a "back door" tool to regulate greenhouse gases—a veiled reference to advocates' effort to list the polar bear.[206] Earlier in 2008, after being sued twice, the service had listed the polar bear as threatened, but explicitly ruled out seeking to reduce greenhouse gases as part of the bear's recovery plan, which Secretary Kempthorne said would be "wholly inappropriate." In fact, in order to allow continued oil and gas exploration and development in the bears' habitat, the listing decision employed the act's 4(d) rule, which permits flexibility in species management as long as chances of conservation are enhanced, or at least not diminished.

## Preventing Action on Climate Change

Conservatives' greatest success came not in weakening or delaying implementation and enforcement of the Endangered Species Act but in preventing federal action to address climate change—in particular, blocking federally mandated greenhouse gas reductions. The administration's rhetorical strategy in defense of the permissive status quo involved questioning environmentalists' definition of the climate change problem by discrediting and suppressing worrisome scientific information, while tarnishing the image of environmentalists' preferred solution by highlighting the potential costs of federal controls. Complementing the skeptical rhetoric was a series of efforts to scrub risk-averse scientific language from federal reports. Meanwhile, in Congress, conservative legislators thwarted attempts to pass domestic greenhouse gas emissions controls, refusing to endorse even the voluntary programs put forth by the administration.

## Bush Takes an Antiregulatory Position on Climate Change

Initially, it appeared as though the Bush administration would act aggressively on climate change in response to an increasingly firm scientific consensus. Upon taking office, EPA administrator Whitman affirmed the president's commitment to reducing carbon dioxide emissions from coal-fired power plants as part of the multipollutant strategy introduced during the presidential campaign.[207] In February 2001, just a month into her tenure, Whitman told a Senate subcommittee, "There's no question but that global warming is a real phenomenon, that it is occurring. The science is strong there."[208] She also declared on CNN's "Crossfire" that the president was "very sensitive to the issue of global warming."[209]

Whitman's comments immediately sparked objections from some prominent GOP senators, however, as well as intense lobbying from the oil and gas industries. In hopes of prompting a reversal, the conservative Competitive Enterprise Institute and the Greening Earth Society, a coalition of coal-fired power plant operators, sent an e-mail message to top members of Congress and their aides referring to Whitman disparagingly as "Christine Todd Browner."[210] Larry Craig of Idaho, one of four

Republican senators who wrote to the president expressing opposition to carbon dioxide limits, said, "If you attempt to regulate carbon dioxide, you will regulate us into a permanent energy crisis in this country."[211] A small team of White House aides proceeded to draft a six-page memo to John Bridgeland, the president's deputy assistant for domestic policy, listing the potential impacts of regulating carbon dioxide emissions on the coal industry while devoting only six sentences to the science of climate change.[212]

In response to this barrage, Whitman urged the president to acknowledge climate change because it was an important "credibility issue" for the United States abroad, as well as "an issue that is resonating here at home."[213] Nevertheless, in mid-March 2001, Bush reversed his campaign pledge. He explained that the original promise had been a mistake and was inconsistent with the administration's broader goal of increasing domestic energy production. "At a time when California has already experienced energy shortages, and other Western states are worried about price and availability of energy this summer, we must be very careful not to take actions that could harm consumers," Bush wrote in a letter to the disgruntled Republican senators. "This is especially true given the incomplete state of scientific knowledge of the causes of, and solutions to, global climate change and the lack of commercially available technologies for removing and storing carbon dioxide."[214] Asked by reporters what had changed since the campaign, Bush replied, "We're in an energy crisis now."[215] A chastened Whitman elaborated that there was "still some science that is unclear. As we move forward and decide on actions we need to take, it would be helpful to have real science behind what those levels [of carbon dioxide] should be."[216]

Shortly after backing away from the idea of domestic greenhouse gas regulation, the president announced that the United States would withdraw from negotiations over the Kyoto Protocol, which he called "fatally flawed." European officials pleaded with the president to reconsider, but to no avail. Whitman and Secretary of State Colin Powell also encouraged the president to change course. But other members of the administration—notably Vice President Cheney—were adamantly opposed to mandatory greenhouse gas limits, which they argued would force utilities to switch from oil and coal to natural gas, causing increases in the price of natural gas and shortages of the kind that had occurred in California. As White House spokesman Ari Fleischer explained, the president unequivocally "does not support the Kyoto treaty. It exempts the developing nations around the world, and it is not in the United

States' economic best interest."[217] Officials from the coal and oil industry hailed the decision. "[R]equiring mandatory controls would drive a stake through the heart of a balanced energy program," said John Grasser of the National Mining Association.[218] A *Wall Street Journal* editorial also endorsed the president's move, commenting, "The whole idea behind Kyoto is puzzling at best, outrageous at worst. Why require the nations of this planet to spend the hundreds of billions of dollars necessary to reduce carbon dioxide and other emissions when we don't even know if the earth's climate is getting permanently hotter or if that temperature change is caused by human activity or if that change is even dangerous?"[219]

### Redefining the Problem and Creating a Negative Policy Image

With public concern about global warming escalating—a January 2001 Gallup poll found that 40 percent of Americans worried about global warming "a great deal," up five points since 1989 and much higher than the level of concern reported (27 percent) in 1997[220]—Bush's decision to withdraw from the Kyoto Protocol triggered a flurry of critical media coverage. The administration sought to defuse concern about the issue by framing its position in a way that would be credible and legitimate, recognizing—in the words of presidential counselor Karen Hughes—that green issues "are killing us."[221] To this end, White House communications officials embraced the strategy of raising doubts about the scientific consensus. Once again, they followed the dictates of Frank Luntz, who pointed out, "Should the public come to believe that the scientific issues are settled, their views about global warming will change accordingly. Therefore you need to continue to make the lack of scientific certainty a primary issue." Among the ways to "challenge the science," Luntz suggested, was to "be even more active in recruiting experts who are sympathetic to your view and much more active in making them part of your message" because "people are more willing to trust scientists than politicians."[222]

At first, however, the administration lacked a systematic plan for dealing the science of climate change. The third assessment by the Intergovernmental Panel on Climate Change, released in the winter of 2001, expressed greater certainty than its predecessors that human activities were responsible for climate change. The IPCC noted that atmospheric concentrations of carbon dioxide had increased by almost one-third since 1750, to a level higher than at any time during the preceding 420,00 years—and possibly the last 20 million years—and were continuing to rise, with potentially catastrophic consequences. Unconvinced, the White House asked the National Academy of Sciences' National Research Council to review the scientific consensus. The resulting twenty-four-page report, released in early June 2001, "reaffirmed the mainstream scientific view that the earth's atmosphere was getting warmer and that human activity was largely responsible."[223] To the dismay of many conservatives, the president proceeded to acknowledge that climate change was a problem, although he emphasized that its magnitude and seriousness were uncertain, and vowed to take "a leadership role" in addressing it."[224] Presidential spokesman Ari Fleischer told reporters that when Bush headed to Europe he would stress that he took the issue of global climate change seriously, that it was an issue all nations needed to deal with, and that "through technologies and through growth and through other measures, the world has a responsibility to face up to this."[225]

Then, in June 2002, the administration surprised some observers by forwarding to the United Nations a report written by the EPA and the State Department—the *U.S. Climate Action Report*—acknowledging that human activities were a cause of climate change and warning about the deleterious consequences. The report proposed no major new policies, however; instead it recommended adapting to the inevitable shifts accompanying climate change. Moreover, President Bush—facing intense criticism from conservative activists—dismissed the report as a product of "the bureaucracy" and reiterated his opposition to the Kyoto Protocol. "I accept the alternative we put out," he said, "that we can grow our economy and, at the same time, through technologies, improve our environment."[226]

Subsequently, however, the White House became more proactive in shaping the science that underpinned the administration's position. In September 2002, the EPA excised the entire section on global warming from its annual report on air pollution trends after the White House insisted on edits that, according to EPA staff, distorted the scientific information to such a degree that the report "no longer accurately represent[ed] the scientific consensus on climate change."[227] The White House took a similar tack with respect to an EPA report released in June 2003; the agency's first comprehensive analysis of the quality of the environment in the United States gave only scant treatment to climate change because the section had been heavily edited by the White House. The edits, made by Philip A. Cooney, a staff member for the Council on Environmental Quality, had reduced the climate change section from two pages to one paragraph, deleted concerns about the health and environmental effects of climate change, and eliminated references to many studies that concluded the phenomenon was caused at least partly by human activity. According to journalist Andrew Revkin, the changes were sometimes as subtle as inserting the phrase "significant and fundamental" before the word "uncertainties," but they created an air of doubt about what most climate scientists said were robust findings.[228] Upon learning of the edits, former EPA administrator Russell Train wrote in a *Washington Post* op-ed, "I can state categorically that there never was such White House intrusion into the business of the EPA during my tenure. . . . There appears to be a steady erosion in [the agency's] independent status."[229]

Another tactic employed by the administration was to prevent scientists doing climate research for the federal government from speaking forthrightly to the public about global warming.[230] The first major complaint about high-level censorship of scientists came when James Hansen told the *New York Times* and the *Washington Post* that the administration had tried to muzzle him after he gave a lecture in December 2003, in which he called for cuts in greenhouse gas emissions. Subsequently, scientists from the National Oceanic and Atmospheric Administration reported that the administration was routinely playing down the threat of climate change in their documents and news releases. Scientists told journalists that, as of the summer of 2004, they were required to clear all media requests with administration officials, who dictated the language they could use.

## Obstructing Action on Climate Change in Congress
While the Bush White House sought to downplay the seriousness of climate change, conservatives in Congress struggled to ensure that Democrats and moderate Republicans would not take meaningful action to reduce the nation's greenhouse gas emissions. In the spring of 2001, after the president pulled out of the Kyoto Protocol negotiations, the Senate held hearings to educate its members about climate change science and mitigation options. The Senate also considered several bills on climate change that, although largely symbolic, reflected the issue's rising salience among the public. One option was Senator Jeffords' four-pollutant bill (S. 556), an alternative to Clear Skies, that established a cap-and-trade system for carbon dioxide. In June 2002, after a rancorous and largely partisan debate, the Environment and Public Works Committee narrowly approved S. 556, but the bill stood little chance in the chamber as a whole because of the carbon dioxide provision. Another

proposal, introduced during the debate on the Bush administration's comprehensive energy bill, would have created a Department of Energy office and data-analysis center for climate change policy, modified greenhouse-gas-emissions reporting, and authorized billions of dollars for climate change research. A third bill would have created an office in the White House to oversee policy on climate change and authorized $4.8 billion over ten years for research.

Although the Senate failed to pass any of these measures, in early August 2001, the Senate Foreign Relations Committee unanimously approved a resolution calling on President Bush to return to the bargaining table with specific proposals for either revising the Kyoto Protocol or negotiating a new binding agreement for reducing greenhouse gas emissions. The 19–0 vote, which included members from coal-producing states, marked a significant shift in a body that until recently had appeared hostile to international climate negotiations. Meanwhile, supporters of emissions controls tried to circumvent opposition with low-profile maneuvers of their own, attaching riders seeking increased funding for climate-related programs to a variety of bills. For example, the Senate approved a bipartisan amendment to the budget resolution for fiscal year 2002 that restored $4.5 billion for climate change programs over the coming decade.[231] House appropriators also stripped language from several spending bills that banned the use of federal money to implement the Kyoto Protocol in fiscal year 2002.

In mid-February 2002, even as his administration downplayed climate change science, Bush announced his response to these legislative gambits: a plan to reduce the rate of greenhouse gas production relative to economic output by 18 percent by 2012. According to the White House, the president's scheme would cut greenhouse gas emissions from an estimated 183 million metric tons per million dollars of GDP in 2002 to 151 million metric tons by 2012. (Critics pointed out the United States was already on this trajectory, which fell well short of what the Kyoto Protocol would have required.) Under the president's proposal, which the White House characterized as "rational and balanced," the federal government would disburse $4.6 billion in tax credits over five years to companies that invested in alternative energy technologies, conservation, or other emissions-reducing practices, and agreed to participate in a voluntary emissions-tracking program. The reporting system was contentious in Congress, but eventually a compromise was reached: companies would report their emissions voluntarily for five years, after which, if more than 60 percent of emissions went undeclared, the reporting system would become mandatory. To appease moderate Republicans, Bush also created a cabinet-level office on climate change and proposed adding $700 million to climate change programs in the fiscal year 2003 budget.

Bush explained that his go-slow approach was based on "the common-sense idea that sustainable economic growth is key to environmental progress—because it is growth that provides the resources for investment in clean technologies."[232] The Edison Electric Institute, the American Power Association, the National Mining Association, the National Association of Manufacturers, and other business groups applauded his plan, calling it "balanced and realistic."[233] A *Wall Street Journal* editorial also praised the Bush approach as more than adequate, pointing out that Bush "made a large concession by suggesting that global warming might be a problem. . . . For the truth is that all science really knows about climate change is that the Earth has been getting a little warmer; whether the cause is manmade or just part of the world's periodic warming and cooling pattern is still hotly debated. And we certainly don't understand the impact of warming—are longer growing seasons so awful?—much less if there's anything we can or should do about it."[234]

On the one-year anniversary of its voluntary greenhouse-gas-reduction program, the administration staged a celebration to mark its achievements. "There is a perception by many that if environmental programs are not mandatory, they're not real," said Whitman. "I'm here to tell you that these programs are very real and they're getting real results."[235] In early 2004, however, *Washington Post* reporters Guy Gugliotta and Eric Pianin evaluated the efficacy of the Bush administration's voluntary climate programs and found few beneficial outcomes. At the heart of Bush's strategy was "Climate Leaders," a program that recruited the nation's industrial polluters to devise ways to curb their greenhouse gas emissions voluntarily by 10 percent or more over ten years. Two years into the program, only fifty companies had joined Climate Leaders, and of those only fourteen had set goals. Some of those that volunteered said they did so because it made good economic sense; others were nudged to join by state or federal regulators. Meanwhile, the utilities with the highest emissions remained aloof.[236] A GAO report issued in May 2006 confirmed that neither Climate Leaders nor Climate Vision, administered by the Department of Energy, had delivered promised results. As of November 2005, only thirty-eight of seventy-four companies in the EPA program had set greenhouse-gas-reduction goals. Eleven of fifteen trade groups participating in the Energy Department program had established targets, but only five had reported their emissions.[237]

The president's actions, although almost entirely symbolic, irritated conservatives in Congress because they suggested he was conceding that climate change was a genuine problem. On April 11, 2003, the House passed its version of the comprehensive energy legislation initiated by the White House, including provisions to implement elements of the Bush climate change program. But in the Senate, Republican Larry Craig of Idaho insisted on dropping the president's climate-related measures, saying they constituted a first step toward mandatory greenhouse gas curbs and that he did not want to endorse "bad science based on unproven claims about climate change or impose mandates that would impede economic growth."[238] On July 31, the Senate passed its version of the comprehensive energy bill with no climate change provision. In any case, the conference committee bill that reconciled the House and Senate versions died in the Senate after a failed cloture vote in November 2003.

In exchange for agreeing to drop the climate-change provisions during the Senate debate, Republican senator John McCain of Arizona extracted a promise from Senate majority leader Bill Frist to grant a stand-alone climate change bill six hours of floor time in the fall—in what would be the Senate's first substantive debate on the issue. With Democratic senator Joe Lieberman of Connecticut, McCain then seized the opportunity to introduce the Climate Stewardship Act, which would cap overall greenhouse gas emissions at 2000 levels by 2025, beginning in 2010, by rolling back emissions from the energy, manufacturing, and transportation sectors.[239] In the run-up to the debate on the Climate Stewardship Act, conservative politicians adhered to their script, insisting that the science of climate change was inconclusive and the costs of addressing it prohibitive. For example, in a floor speech on July 28, 2003, Senator Inhofe ridiculed the forecasts of "global warming alarmists. . . . After studying the issue over the last several years," he said, "I believe the balance of evidence offers strong proof that natural variability, not man-made, is the overwhelming factor influencing climate, and that man-made gases are virtually irrelevant."[240] In another memorable speech, delivered in early August, Inhofe asked, "With all of the hysteria, all of the fear, all of the phony science, could it be that man-made global warming is the greatest hoax ever perpetrated on the American people?"[241] Inhofe's staffer, Marc Morano, worked tirelessly to disseminate the conservative view on climate change, "sending out a blizzard of e-mails to journalists covering the issue."[242] On October 30, 2003, the Senate rejected the Climate Stewardship Act by a vote of forty-three to fifty-five, with opponents claiming the legislation would eliminate jobs and force people to pay higher utility bills. "The science underlying this bill has been repudiated," Inhofe declared. "[T]he economic costs are far too high and the environmental benefits are nonexistent."[243]

When Republicans gained seats in the November 2004 elections, prospects for the administration's comprehensive energy legislation brightened. Sure enough, in late July 2005, Congress finally passed an omnibus energy bill, the Energy Policy Act of 2005. The new law focused primarily on enhancing energy supplies: it expanded oil and gas production, initiated the first-ever inventory of offshore oil and gas resources, provided incentives and tax breaks for nuclear power and coal production, and extended tax incentives for renewable energy. During deliberations on the bill, the Senate once again considered including provisions to implement the president's voluntary plan to address climate change. As he did prior to the vote on the Climate Stewardship Act, Senator Inhofe held hearings and gave speeches aimed at defusing concern about climate change. For example, in floor remarks in early January 2005, he criticized the scientific consensus as "alarmist" and "emanating from environmental extremists and their elitist organizations"; he cited studies that he said proved that human activities were not causing the earth's climate to warm.[244] In April, he told his colleagues, "For the alarmists, global warming has nothing to do with science or scientific inquiry. Science is not about the inquiry to discover truth, but a mask to achieve an ideological agenda. For some, this issue has become a secular religion, pure and simple."[245] In the House, Texas representative Joe Barton, chair of the Energy and Commerce Committee, was also vocal in denouncing climate science. In the summer of 2005, in an effort to discredit proponents of the prevailing view, Barton sent a letter to climate scientists requesting information about their research and questioning the integrity of the IPCC review process.

On June 22, in the midst of the debate on the omnibus energy bill, the Senate took a second vote on a modified version of the McCain-Lieberman Climate Stewardship Act, this time defeating it 60–38. Some senators clearly felt uncomfortable moving on an issue surrounded by so much highly visible controversy; others who had previously supported the bill withdrew their backing in response to provisions creating $500 million in incentives to build nuclear power plants. On the other hand, only two hours later, the chamber approved (53–44) a "Sense of the Senate" resolution that explicitly rejected the conservative definition of the problem. First, it officially acknowledged that greenhouse gases were contributing to global warming, and second, it urged Congress to "enact a comprehensive and effective national program of mandatory, market-based limits on emissions of greenhouse gases that slow, stop and reverse the growth of such emissions." (In deference to ongoing opposition, the resolution also stated that any policy enacted by Congress should not significantly harm the U.S. economy and should encourage comparable action by other nations.)

In passing the resolution, senators may have been motivated by poll numbers suggesting that a growing proportion of Americans believed that global warming was a serious problem and wanted government to do something about it. More likely, though, they were influenced by more tangible expressions of dismay. In particular, core Republican constituencies were voicing alarm about climate change. In late March 2001, after Bush withdrew from the Kyoto Protocol, a coalition of religious groups had mobilized to challenge his decision. "If credible evidence exists to indicate our present course could threaten the quality of life for God's creation and children, this becomes an issue of paramount moral concern," the group's leaders wrote in a letter to the president.[246] In 2005, journalist Laurie Goodstein reported that a core group of evangelicals was putting its muscle behind the fight against global warming; nearly one hundred evangelical leaders had signed a platform entitled "For the Health of the Nation: An Evangelical Call to Civic Responsibility," which included a plank on "creation care."[247]

Executives of some of the nation's largest corporations were also lobbying for mandatory greenhouse-gas emissions curbs. A handful of prominent CEOs had become convinced that greenhouse gas regulations were inevitable, and they preferred a single federal framework to a patchwork of state regulations; others were getting pressure from shareholders to address climate risks. Whatever their motivation, some had already taken steps to cut their companies' emissions. In May 2001, for example, New Orleans–based Entergy Corporation—one of the nation's largest electric utilities—announced it would cap its carbon dioxide emissions at 2000 levels over five years. Entergy joined DuPont, BP Amoco, and Royal Dutch/Shell, along with the Environmental Defense Fund, to form the Partnership for Climate Action (the precursor to the U.S. Climate Action Partnership), whose members pledged to reduce their carbon dioxide emissions at least 80 metric tons annually by 2010. In January 2004, hoping to establish a framework that the federal government would eventually adopt, a group of major corporations launched the Chicago Climate Exchange, a mechanism to enable trades of greenhouse-gas-emissions credits earned by firms that exceeded their emissions-reduction goals. Founding members of the exchange—all of whom pledged to reduce their average greenhouse gas emissions by 4 percent in four years from a 1999–2001 baseline—included DuPont, Ford Motor Company, American Electric Power, and Motorola.

As the 2000s wore on, corporate leaders became more vocal about their desire for a federal program to address climate change. At a Senate Energy and Natural Resources Committee hearing in April 2006, representatives of several major corporations—including Exelon, Duke Energy, GNM Resources, Sempa Energy, Shell Oil Company, and Walmart—expressed interest in a cap-and-trade system for greenhouse gas emissions. According to one environmental activist, many executives simply did not buy the conservative arguments that the impact of carbon dioxide regulations on the overall economy was likely to be severe. Instead, they focused on figuring out how to design a palatable policy mechanism. "What they are worried about is their firms and the rate of change, and that you can handle with allowance allocation," he explained.[248]

A final source of pressure on members of Congress was the fact that, with the federal government gridlocked, states and localities across the country had begun to curb their greenhouse gas emissions. Between 2000 and 2003, state legislatures passed at least twenty-nine bills to combat climate change. Some capped greenhouse gas emissions; others created registries to track emissions or devised plans to diversify fuel sources or sequester carbon in cropland. Activity was not limited to traditionally "environmental" states: Texas and Nevada created renewable portfolio standards, while Nebraska, Oklahoma, and Wyoming passed laws to promote carbon sequestration in cropland and forests. Even cities were getting on the bandwagon: in 2005, Seattle mayor Greg Nickels launched an initiative in which U.S. mayors would sign a Climate Protection Agreement, pledging to reduce their greenhouse gas emissions to the levels required by the Kyoto Protocol. By 2007, five hundred mayors had signed the agreement, and dozens of cities had already begun to prepare climate action plans.

### Defending the Permissive Status Quo at the White House
Recognizing that voluntary action by corporations or state and local programs would be insufficient, environmentalists and several states pressed the EPA to address climate change using its authority under the Clean Air Act. But conservatives in the administration foiled that tactic as well. In late August 2003, in response to a petition filed four years

earlier by three environmental groups, the EPA announced it did not have the legal authority to regulate greenhouse gases from automobiles under the Clean Air Act. That decision contradicted assessments by two Clinton-era general counsels, who had said the gases could be regulated if they could reasonably be expected to harm human welfare.[249] The U.S. Chamber of Commerce, the National Association of Manufacturers, and other industry groups cheered the EPA's decision.

As well as resisting mandates on domestic greenhouse gas emissions, the administration continued to obstruct international negotiations on climate change. In the Buenos Aires climate talks in 2004, the Bush administration tried to convince other nations that fostering the development of technology, not mandating emissions limits, offered the best chance of preserving both economic growth and environmental health. "The U.S. position is maybe the only rational position, to identify and promulgate application of new technologies," said White House science adviser John Marburger. "To do anything meaningful [on limiting greenhouse gas emissions] requires a dramatic cessation or reduction of economic activity. It's simply not practical at the present time."[250] In 2005, U.S. diplomats pressured negotiators from the eight major industrialized nations to weaken key sections of a proposal for joint action on climate change, including details on the projected impacts of climate change and statements about the risks of adverse effects unless urgent action was taken. And when world leaders met in Montreal in late 2005 to discuss a successor to the Kyoto Protocol, the Bush administration agreed to participate only in a nonbinding dialogue.

In spring 2007, however, the Supreme Court dealt a sharp blow to the administration's position. In mid-July 2005, the D.C. Circuit had dismissed a 2003 lawsuit by eleven states and fourteen environmental groups that sought to compel the administration to issue mandatory greenhouse gas controls for cars and trucks after the EPA declined to do so. But in early April 2007, the justices overturned the lower court, ruling 5–4 that the Bush administration had failed to provide legitimate reasons for declining to decide whether to regulate greenhouse gas emissions under the Clean Air Act (*Massachusetts v. EPA*). The four dissenting justices were largely sympathetic to the administration's arguments that (1) carbon dioxide was not a pollutant; (2) even if it was, the EPA retained discretion over how to address it—in this case, through voluntary standards and further research; and (3) in any case, the suit should be thrown out because the plaintiffs lacked standing to sue.[251] But the majority upheld the plaintiffs' standing, observing that Massachusetts had a clear stake in the outcome, since the projected sea-level rise would be catastrophic. The majority also argued that "greenhouse gases fit well within the Clean Air Act's capacious definition of air pollutant." Moreover, they ruled that the EPA could "avoid taking further action" only "if it determine[d] that greenhouse gases do not contribute to climate change," or if it "provide[d] a reasonable explanation as to why it could not or would not determine whether they do."[252]

At first, the White House seemed to respond with alacrity to the Supreme Court ruling. In May 2007, the president issued an executive order calling on the EPA to begin writing regulations to reduce greenhouse gas emissions from cars and trucks in coordination with the departments of Transportation, Energy, and Agriculture. The following month, he proposed for the first time setting "a long-term global goal" for cutting greenhouse gas emissions and called on other industrialized nations to join the United States in negotiations aimed at reaching an agreement by the end of the year. In September, Bush convened the first conference of the world's seventeen major economies to work on a post-Kyoto accord. At that meeting he tried to persuade the major emitters to embrace "aspirational" (nonbinding) greenhouse gas emissions goals. Then, on December 19, 2007, Bush signed the Energy Independence and Security Act of 2007, which contained several provisions that would reduce fossil fuel consumption and therefore greenhouse gas emissions. The new law set an automotive fuel efficiency standard of 35 mpg by 2020—a 40 percent increase over the existing standard. It also required the Energy Department to establish more stringent standards for appliances and light bulbs. And it required the federal government to make all of its buildings carbon-neutral by 2030, through the adoption of energy-efficiency and clean-energy technologies.

Yet at the international talks in Bali held in December 2007, U.S. negotiators flatly rejected the idea of setting even provisional targets for greenhouse gas emission reductions. (Once again, they were roundly booed at the end of the meeting.) That same month, at the urging of the White House, the EPA rebuffed a request by California and sixteen other states for a waiver that would allow them to set their own carbon dioxide standards for automobiles.[253] To justify his decision, which went against the recommendations of his staff, EPA administrator Stephen Johnson had to make the awkward argument that, on the one hand, climate posed "no compelling and extraordinary" risk to California, but, on the other hand, climate change would be serious not just for California but for the entire country—and therefore a global, or at least a national, solution was warranted.[254] Johnson further pointed out the federal government was already raising automotive fuel economy standards through the energy bill Bush had just signed. Also that month the White House refused to open an e-mail that contained a document supporting the EPA's conclusion that greenhouse gases are pollutants that endanger public welfare and therefore must be controlled—an "endangerment finding" that would mark the first step toward regulating greenhouse gases under the Clean Air Act. The document, which the White House subsequently ordered the EPA to rescind, concluded that it would be cost-effective to require motor vehicles to be more fuel-efficient than currently required, and that the benefit of regulating carbon dioxide emissions from automobiles could amount to $2 trillion over thirty-two years.

In mid-April 2008, President Bush went on record for the first time in support of limiting greenhouse gas emissions. But he continued to oppose any legislation that "raises taxes, duplicates mandates already in place, abandons nuclear power or coal, imposes trade barriers or calls for drastic emission cuts that aren't realistic and will hurt American consumers through higher costs."[255] Frustrated, in April a coalition of cities, states, and environmental groups petitioned the D.C. Circuit to order the EPA to publish its endangerment finding. Finally, in July 2008, the agency released a watered-down version of its original proposal, after the White House successfully pressured it to eliminate large sections of the analysis that supported regulation. The revised document dramatically reduced the estimate of the economic benefits of regulating greenhouse gas emissions, to no more than $830 billion, while emphasizing the costs of controlling those emissions. It reached no conclusion about whether global warming posed a threat to human health or public welfare.

Administrator Johnson's comments in the preface to the report affirmed the administration's resistance. Johnson rejected any obligation to regulate greenhouse gases, saying that to do so would involve an "unprecedented expansion" of the agency's authority that would have "a profound effect on virtually every sector of the economy," touching "every household in the land."[256] James Connaughton, chair of the Council on Environmental Quality, also repudiated the EPA's findings, saying the agency's staff "myopically focuses on the Clean Air Act and ignores or understates major intended and unintended consequences that would flow from misapplying decades-old regulatory tools."[257] The EPA announced it would seek months of public comment on the document, essentially punting the issue to the next administration.

## Quietly Undermining Environmental Protection

In sum, although it enacted several restrictive measures to counter air pollution, the Bush administration's main focus was making environmental regulation more permissive and blocking new legislation. Their efforts to institutionalize antiregulatory ideas yielded mixed results. Attempts to reduce the burden of Clean Air Act regulations on coal-fired electric utilities through legislation ultimately failed. Many of the administration's low-profile tactics on air pollution were also unsuccessful. Between 2001 and 2008, the federal courts threw out all or part of seventeen of the twenty-seven air-pollution-control regulations issued by the EPA. Many of those decisions were made by relatively conservative panels of the D.C. Circuit, which repeatedly chastised the administration for failing to follow precedent and the plain language of the statute. The Bush administration's low-profile initiatives facilitated drift, however, by allowing utilities to continue operating for several additional years without installing pollution control equipment.

With respect to the Endangered Species Act, the Bush administration continued the process of conversion begun under Clinton. The Interior Department opted to promote collaborative, voluntary conservation measures while declining to exercise, or even subverting, its own regulatory authority. In addition, political appointees rendered a series of environmentally risk-tolerant decisions. Although many were ultimately reversed by the courts, these decisions had lasting impacts because once development is under way, it is difficult if not impossible to reverse; simply delaying listing makes recovery more costly and difficult and has, in some cases, resulted in extinction.

Conservatives in Congress and the White House were most effective in blocking efforts to address climate change at the federal level. Although industry lobbying and legislators' regional economic considerations also played a significant role, conservative politicians took the lead in obstructing initiatives aimed at curbing greenhouse gas emissions. In the process, they furnished a rationale that, thanks to the persistence of conservative advocates, became increasingly familiar.

In addition to their tangible policy impacts, conservatives in the Bush administration had more subtle, long-term effects on environmental institutions. They infused agency decision making with the cost-benefit paradigm, emphasizing quantification and costs over qualitative and benefit considerations.[258] According to several members of the administration, a primary focus at both the EPA and Interior was establishing performance measures and judging policy outputs accordingly.[259] But some officials charged that the administration's tactics were actually intended to provoke the exodus of veteran analysts and create reporting and accountability mechanisms that gummed up the works.[260] The administration also devalued precautionary scientific analysis by having all major decisions rewritten by political appointees.[261] This approach had a particularly severe effect on the wildlife agencies. In response to the 2005 survey of Fish and Wildlife Service scientists by the Union of Concerned Scientists and PEER, one biologist wrote, "We are not allowed to be forthright and honest. I have 20 years of federal service in this [agency] and this is the worst it has been."[262] Demoralized, many of the most experienced staff left the Interior Department. In addition, because it treated scientific advice so poorly, the department's relationship with the scientific community was strained, a result that further hamstrung its efforts to perform high-quality scientific analyses.[263]

The administration also used the budget to weaken environmental protection. During Bush's tenure, the EPA's funding dropped 27 percent, while personnel numbers fell 4.2 percent.[264] As a result, according to journalist Margaret Kriz, agency morale was almost as bad as it had been in the early Reagan years.[265] "Whoever comes in is going to take a long time to sort this out," worried one former EPA official.[266] Similarly, the landowner-incentive programs that formed the backbone of Endangered Species Act implementation were chronically underfunded, while the administration's unwillingness to request additional funding to implement the regulatory features of the act perpetuated the wildlife agencies' inability to meet their statutory requirements.[267]

The Bush administration was able to fulfill conservative objectives through administrative changes in part because there was a Republican or narrowly Democratic Congress during much of its tenure, so Congress provided few checks on its activities. The administration also reaped the benefits of a decades-long campaign to create skepticism about environmental regulations and convey the idea that regulatory "streamlining" is essential to the nation's economic well-being. And it benefited from political learning: rather than tackle the status quo directly, as Watt and Gorsuch did in the early 1980s, the Bush team relied heavily on making "subtle tweaks that [carried] large consequences."[268] And, even as they defended conservative priorities, such as enhancing the domestic energy supply, Bush administration officials adopted environmentally friendly language. They reconciled the two by simply asserting that they were compatible.

Initially, environmentalists were able to limit the administration's discretion by directing media attention to its low-profile actions. For example, in March 2001, after the administration suspended the arsenic standards for drinking water, CNN's headlines blared, "Bush Declares War on the Environment." Such headlines appear to have influenced public opinion: a *Washington Post*/ABC News poll taken in March 2001 found that Americans thought Bush cared more about the interests of large corporations than those of ordinary people by 61 percent to 31 percent.[269] As one environmental activist pointed out, "If you go back and look at the newspapers from January to August [2001], it was the environmental issues more than any other domestic or international issues that got all the play and drove [Bush's poll] numbers down."[270] Some members of the president's own party were shaken by his early actions on the environment; prior to September 11, 2001, Bush's approval ratings were falling fast among independents and moderate Republicans. When the Bush administration released its National Energy Policy in May 2001, Republican representative Christopher Shays of Connecticut asked, "What is happening to our Republican Party when it comes to the environment? I think it's a very bad mistake. Exploiting [the Arctic National Wildlife Refuge] and not having a sound conservation policy is backwards. It confirms our worst fear that this is an administration with a Texas oil perspective."[271]

The events of September 11 and the subsequent war in Iraq shifted media attention to national security, however, and the combination of distraction, low-profile maneuvers, and eco-friendly language made it difficult for journalists to deliver incisive coverage of environmental policy changes. The administration also had a propensity to release information about rule changes late on Friday afternoons or just before holidays, when it was less likely to draw press attention. As a result, environmentalists spent most of their time and resources during the Bush administration, as they had in the mid-1990s, playing defense—either taking the administration to court or lobbying members of Congress to thwart its administrative or legislative initiatives. As one environmental activist noted, this tactic worked when it was employed, but it was difficult to get the courts to act on day-to-day decisions that change the way a law is implemented.[272] It was also costly and time-consuming—and displaced efforts to move on new or festering problems.

Some observers were puzzled by the Bush administration's apparent indifference toward the environment. One-third of Americans declared themselves independents, and in a *New York Times*/CBS News poll taken in early March 2001, 64 percent of independents agreed the environment should take precedence over energy production.[273] The environment was a particularly salient issue among women and suburban voters, with whom Bush had fared poorly in 2000. Given his slim margin of victory, many analysts argued that he should adopt a green stance in order to appeal to the center. But Gerald Seib pointed out in the *Wall Street Journal* that Bush had fared well in blue-collar states where voters were inclined to worry about losing their jobs to environmental regulations. Seib suggested that Bush's strategy might therefore be to solidify his support among those voters, many of whom lived in the fastest-growing states.[274] Whatever the reason, Bush appointees who genuinely cared about environmental protection often found themselves at odds with the White House and rebuffed by conservative members of Congress, who were either indifferent or downright hostile.[275] In her book *It's My Party, Too*, Christine Todd Whitman writes that White House antipathy toward the EPA was so intense that even when the agency was allowed to pursue environmentally friendly policies, White House officials refused to let her publicize them for fear of alienating the conservative base.

In part, the low priority accorded to the environment within the White House reflected a belief among conservative officials that environmental protection would take care of itself, and that activism aimed at increasing government involvement was a thinly disguised attempt to increase regulation of all kinds. In part it was a belief that economic growth, enabled by cheap energy, was the key to human well-being. According to Lynn Scarlett, some Republicans came to conflate the regulatory mechanisms, which they disliked, with environmental values themselves.[276] More prosaically, as former EPA officials explained, many in the Republican leadership believed that environmentalists would never support a Republican, so there was no point in catering to them.[277] That view was confirmed by Glen Bolger, a Republican pollster, who told Katharine Seelye of the *New York Times*, "The environment resonates most strongly with the beats, the backpackers and the bangles crowd. And they are pretty well on the far left of the Democratic party."[278] Similarly, a *Wall Street Journal* editorial concluded, "Mr. Bush can chase the approval of the greens from here to the end of his Presidency, but he'll never get it."[279]

# 8

---

# The Consequences of a Conservative Era

A conservative insurgency pushed its way to power, transformed national discourse, and brought new priorities to the fore. No longer consigned to bit parts in political developments driven by their opponents, conservatives have written a new script and claimed a leading role for themselves in determining the shape of things to come.[1]

In the realm of environmental policy, conservatives' primary goal is to ensure that the nation's public land and natural resources are "open for business." To this end, their strategy is to roll back existing regulations and prevent new ones. Their stated rationale is that government intrusion in the market impinges on individual freedom, restrains business, and is inherently inefficient. In the rare instances when government intervention is unavoidable, conservatives favor the assignment of property rights and the creation of positive inducements over the imposition of rules and sanctions. In an effort to make the nation's environmental regulatory framework more consistent with these ideals, conservatives have sought to change the context in which policy decisions are made. They have created and disseminated a storyline that undermines the environmental narrative by discrediting environmentalists and furnishing a principled basis for disputing their claims. Conservative advocates have also worked assiduously to elect sympathizers to positions of power. In the White House, conservative presidents have used centralized regulatory oversight to raise the hurdles facing new rules and adjusted budget priorities to reduce the emphasis on regulatory enforcement. They have also used appointments to the federal bureaucracy and the courts to reorient agency decision making. In Congress, conservative legislators have sought leadership positions on key congressional committees, held hearings to showcase their views, and fought for procedural laws they expect will improve the prospects for their substantive policy preferences.

Beyond altering the policymaking context, conservative officials have sought to make environmentally restrictive policies more permissive. They have proposed legislative reforms based on problem definitions and policy images that are consistent with the antiregulatory storyline. They have learned from experience, however, that direct challenges to environmental laws rarely succeed. Such attacks may nevertheless be effective: those responsible for implementing the law, reluctant to bring on another attack, may become more conciliatory. But direct challenges often generate political costs for the attackers and can confer political benefits for defenders of the status quo.

Recognizing the drawbacks of direct challenges, conservatives have learned to modify restrictive policies in low-profile ways—by adding riders to budget and other must-pass legislation; changing the wording, interpretation, or enforcement of existing rules; devolving greater responsibility for interpreting and enforcing those rules to the states, regardless of their regulatory capacity or inclination; encouraging lawsuits by development interests, declining to appeal judicial rulings that benefit development, or settling lawsuits on terms favorable to industry; and downplaying, denying, or even modifying scientific analysis when it conflicts with development priorities. Recently, conservatives have employed another tactic as well: they have adopted the language of moderation, or even environmental improvement, confusing all but the most expert observers while making it extraordinarily difficult to raise public concern about both their direct and low-profile challenges.[2]

At the same time, conservatives have defended the permissive status quo against further restrictions. To do this, they have deployed antiregulatory problem definitions and policy images that downplay the magnitude of environmental damage while highlighting the economic risks posed by restrictive policies. They understand that, in the case of newly identified problems for which no statutory protections exist, the ability to sow confusion among the public is often sufficient to defuse the momentum behind environmentalists' proposals.

## Conservatives' Impact on Environmental Policy, 1970–2008

How effective has this combination of a consistent storyline and a multipronged assault on the levers of policymaking been? Although largely successful in attaining positions of political power, conservatives' ability to roll back environmental regulations between 1980 and 2008 varied. Their effectiveness depended on whether the challenge was direct or low profile, the extent to which environmentally risk-averse ideas were already institutionalized, and the ability of environmentalists to raise the salience of a competing problem definition. In general, direct challenges to institutionalized environmental protection fared poorly. Whether the issue was air pollution control or endangered species conservation, environmentalists were able to mobilize enough public opposition to thwart frontal attacks on existing laws.

When it came to low-profile challenges, however, the air-pollution-control framework proved more robust than the endangered-species-conservation framework. This is partly because air pollution falls within the purview of the EPA, which has a clear mission to protect the environment and well-positioned allies in Congress who defend its prerogatives during budget and authorizing negotiations. What is more, the courts historically have supported a restrictive interpretation of the Clean Air Act, even when the majority of judges has been conservative. By contrast, although the Fish and Wildlife Service has a protective mission, it is a relatively weak agency within the Interior Department, where probusiness ideas were institutionalized long before environmentally protective ones.[3] Moreover, the courts have become progressively less inclined toward a restrictive interpretation of the Endangered Species Act since *TVA v. Hill* in the mid-1970s.[4] In other words, despite the fact that both statutes contain stringent language and ambitious goals, administrators have considerably more latitude to implement the Endangered Species Act permissively than they do the Clean Air Act.

Contemporary ideas, which can bolster vetoes by allies in Congress or the White House, also influenced the relative vulnerability of policies on air pollution and endangered species. In terms of defining the problem, pollution has the potential to pose a direct and imminent threat to human health; it is more difficult to frame the extinction of a species, or even the depletion of biodiversity, as an immediate hazard.[5] Moreover, the possibilities for characterizing solutions are different for the Clean Air Act and the Endangered Species Act. Perhaps, as Joseph Sax has observed, whereas many regard pollution control as compatible with economic growth, conserving biodiversity is more readily portrayed as inescapably limiting or prohibiting some commercial activity.[6] Or perhaps it is simply easier to tell a story about ordinary individuals being harmed by Endangered Species Act restrictions. Whatever the reason, these differences in contemporary salience help to explain why, as Sheldon Kamieniecki observes, decisions to regulate pollution tend to be shaped by national political and economic considerations, while issues related to natural resources are more susceptible to regional political and economic forces.[7]

### Conservatives' Impacts on Environmental Policy

Because of administrators' relatively low discretion and the ability of environmentalists and their institutional allies to veto hostile challenges, between 1980 and 2008, conservatives did little more than slow the advance of restrictive policies to address air pollution by delaying the imposition of rules and layering new analytic requirements on top of them. In response to the implementation of a stringent new statutory framework in the 1970s, conservatives crafted and propagated an alternative problem definition: extremist environmentalists exaggerated the weak science underpinning regulatory decisions on air pollution. Conservatives also sought to damage the image of the Clean Air Act by claiming that unduly restrictive pollution control policies threatened industrial competitiveness, jobs, and consumer prices while offering minimal environmental and health benefits. Environmentalists retaliated with a vigorous defense of their own problem definition, highlighting the health consequences of air pollution for children, asthmatics, and other vulnerable populations; identifying large, old coal-fired utilities as the villains; and portraying clean air as a basic human right. They succeeded in using scientific research that identified and quantified human health threats to raise the salience of air pollution and defend the necessity for restrictive pollution control policies. To bolster their case in the administrative and judicial arenas, they mastered the arcane legal and technical details of policy, as well as the scientific and policy analyses that underpin regulation.

As a consequence, environmentalists' allies in Congress managed to repudiate the Reagan administration's legislative principles as well as President George W. Bush's Clear Skies bill, both of which would have relaxed protection relative to a strictly enforced status quo. The courts proved to be crucial backstops for the Clean Air Act as well, rebuffing efforts to take costs into consideration when setting air quality standards, rejecting changes to the New Source Review program, and generally requiring the EPA to adhere to a risk-averse interpretation of the law. That said, conservatives did have an impact on air pollution policy. Pressure from conservatives and their industrial allies prompted policy learning among pollution control advocates, who came to accept arguments about the importance of quantifying the costs and benefits of pollution control policies, as well as the desirability of market-based mechanisms and other flexible approaches to reducing industrial emissions. The EPA itself, although limited by statute, began employing such approaches in the late 1970s and by the 2000s was doing so regularly. In addition, conservative political appointees succeeded in tightening evidentiary standards, so that proponents of new or more stringent rules had to demonstrate to a far greater extent than before that a substance or activity caused harm. And, despite a brief resurgence during the Clinton administration, enforcement of existing rules declined, reaching a nadir under George W. Bush.

The net result was drift: although air pollution controls became more stringent over time, they did so more slowly than environmentalists and many scientists believed was warranted. This trend was most evident in the prolonged debates over acid rain in the 1980s, ozone and small particulates in the 1990s, and mercury in the 1990s and 2000s. Still, in the three decades after the Clean Air Act was passed, although the U.S. economy grew 164 percent, population grew 39 percent, and energy consumption increased 42 percent, air pollution from the six major pollutants identified by the act decreased by 48 percent.[8]

By contrast, conservatives managed to render the Endangered Species Act significantly more permissive between 1980 and 2008, even as the threats posed by development of both terrestrial and aquatic ecosystems increased. Challenges to the act first arose in the late 1970s with the case of the snail darter but became more virulent in the late 1980s, when implementation began to affect a wider swath of landowners, developers, and motorized recreationists. Wise use advocates reawakened the antigovernment sentiments that had motivated the Sagebrush Rebellion a decade earlier, mobilizing a potent coalition that opposed regulation on federal land. At the same time, drawing on a legal theory of "regulatory takings," property rights advocates launched a two-pronged attack that included a public relations campaign against the Endangered Species Act, as well as a series of lawsuits challenging local, state, and federal restrictions on private land use. Although they failed to bring about a legislative rewrite of the act, these attacks bore fruit: officials at the federal and regional levels tasked with administering the law became reluctant to enforce restrictive measures for fear of provoking a backlash.

Even more significant were low-profile challenges to the implementation of the Endangered Species Act. In Congress, conservative legislators instigated moratoria on species listings while resisting funding increases for the endangered species program, despite a series of reports indicating that its budget was woefully inadequate to the task required by the statute. Within the Interior Department, conservative political appointees raised hurdles to listing species based on local economic considerations, notwithstanding the act's clear mandate to consider only the best available science in making listing decisions. The service also demonstrated a growing willingness to delegate species conservation decisions to state and local decision makers, despite concerns that doing so would reduce the emphasis on precautionary science. Even officials in the Clinton administration, many of whom were deeply concerned about biodiversity, emphasized local- and regional-scale conservation mechanisms and incentives for landowners, rather than the prescriptive measures allowed by the act, partly in hopes of deflecting conservative attacks. Although policy innovations like safe harbor agreements and habitat conservation plans enabled proactive conservation, many of the mechanisms put in place under Clinton were vulnerable to exploitation by Bush administration appointees, who were more inclined than their predecessors to devolve responsibility for species protection without providing a regulatory backstop. Meanwhile, in response to litigation by industry trade associations and conservative law firms, the courts were increasingly inclined to require the wildlife agencies to consider the economic costs of conserving habitat.

As a result of these administrative changes, which amounted to conversion of the Endangered Species Act from prohibitive to permissive,[9] the level of endangered species conservation weakened over time relative to the risks posed by development. The act itself continued to afford substantial protection to listed species, and species given more protection under the act fared better than those given less.[10] In fact, thanks partly to the Endangered Species Act, a handful of species once in danger of extinction, including the iconic bald eagle and the American alligator, rebounded, and millions of acres of habitat were preserved. But the pressures on species, both listed and unlisted, grew dramatically between 1973, when the act was passed, and 2008. During that period, the U.S. population increased 40 percent, from 212 million to 293 million, and economic activity, as measured by GDP, grew nearly eightfold. As a consequence of rising income levels and builders' preference for suburban sites, the amount of land consumed for development grew at an even faster rate than the population. Habitat loss and fragmentation—the single most important threat to biodiversity—increased commensurately.[11]

Even more notable than their ability to ease restrictions aimed at saving endangered species was conservatives' success at rebuffing new environmental policy initiatives. In the 1970s and early 1980s, environmentalists were extraordinarily successful at drawing on science to tell stories that raised the salience of environmental problems. By the early 1980s, however, conservatives had devised a storytelling strategy of their own for preventing the enactment of policies they abhorred. They capitalized on the unavoidable uncertainty of conclusions drawn from scientific data and modeling to challenge environmentalists' depictions of problems, portraying environmentalists themselves as antihuman extremists who—abetted by a sympathetic media—aimed to impose their values on an ill-informed public. Through this new storyline, they shifted public attention to the impact of restrictive policies, depicting the victims as ordinary people, small businesses, and individual landowners; the villains as an overweening federal government and its army of out-of-touch bureaucrats; and the likelihood of economic damage more imminent and serious than any possibility of environmental harm. Although they mimicked the tactics developed by environmentalists, conservatives had a critical advantage: because their stories so often dovetailed with the interests of business, they had virtually unlimited resources with which to propagate them.[12]

The U.S. experience with the issue of climate change illustrates both the defensive strategy employed by conservatives and its impact. Throughout the 1990s, conservative activists joined forces with industry to discredit the problem definition and policy image proffered by environmentalists. In response to the view that global warming posed a serious threat and government ought to impose curbs on greenhouse gas emissions, conservatives argued that climate change science was highly uncertain and rested on unreliable models, notwithstanding steady improvements in the scientific understanding of climate dynamics. They also suggested—without much evidence—that increasing levels of carbon dioxide would be beneficial, while any efforts by the United States to curb greenhouse gas emissions would be exorbitantly costly and unfair. Conservative think tanks disseminated these assertions on talk radio and Web sites and in op-ed pieces, popular books, and magazine articles. Conservative members of Congress convened hearings to showcase the views of climate change contrarians and vigorously opposed legislation that would limit greenhouse gas emissions; they also used legislative riders to prevent federal agencies from spending money on practices aimed at reducing those emissions. Once in office, conservatives in the George W. Bush administration adopted many of the techniques of suppressing or distorting climate science that Reagan had used to delay action on acid rain. Although President Bush eventually acknowledged that human-caused global warming was real, he continued to downplay its potential severity and highlighted the costs associated with enacting restrictive policy. While the president declined to set the legislative agenda, his vice president and political appointees—particularly in the Energy Department and the OMB, but also in the EPA—strove to ensure that effective measures to combat climate change did not emerge from the bureaucracy.

The policy consequences of conservative opposition were plainly evident: federal action to address climate change was delayed by more than two decades, even as the risks of inaction continued to grow. The environmental effects were clear as well. Between 1990 and 2008, U.S. greenhouse gas emissions rose by 16 percent.[13] According to data collected at the federal observatory in Mauna Loa, Hawaii, the concentration of carbon dioxide in the atmosphere rose from 354 parts per million (ppm) to more than 385 ppm between 1990 and 2008. Ominously, the rate of growth in carbon dioxide emissions accelerated in the 2000s: having grown at an average rate of 1.5 ppm between 1970 and 2000, the annual rate increased to over 2 ppm after 2000.[14] Delay in acting to curb emissions exacerbated the risks posed by climate change. Because carbon dioxide has a prolonged half-life in the atmosphere, its steady accumulation greatly increases the likelihood of dangerous consequences; the later measures to reduce emissions are taken, the less likely they are to mitigate the worst effects of climate change.

In short, although some scholars have discerned a "greenward" trend in U.S. policy,[15] the real question is whether that trend—to the extent it exists—has kept pace with the severity of the environmental problems we face. Jacob Hacker and Paul Pierson observe that congressional inability to pass new social welfare laws or reform existing ones has left a growing number of American families vulnerable to economic risk.[16] Hacker points out that "critics of existing programs have not had to enact major reforms to move toward many of their favored ends. Merely by delegitimizing and blocking compensatory intervention designed to correct policy drift, opponents of the welfare state have gradually transformed the orientation of social policy."[17] In the same way, the federal government's inability to pass legislation that addresses climate change, its reluctance to impose restrictive measures under the Endangered

Species Act, and its dilatory implementation of Clean Air Act controls effectively increased the risks from biodiversity loss and a changing climate, while allowing risks from air pollution to persist long after they were identified by scientists.

To understand how unwillingness to take precautionary action in the face of a changing context can snowball, consider the impact of the proliferation of electronic gadgets, combined with a lack of regulatory constraints, on Americans' energy consumption. Evidence from experience with household appliance standards strongly suggests that mandatory efficiency rules yield substantial reductions in energy use. But federal efforts to tighten appliance efficiency lagged during the George W. Bush administration, as the Department of Energy missed a string of deadlines set by Congress. Moreover, because the federal government declined to put a price on carbon emissions, there was no incentive for consumers to rethink their overall consumption. Meanwhile, a new generation of energy-consuming appliances came into use, so that by 2009, there were about twenty-five consumer electronic products in every American household, compared with just three in 1980. As a consequence, according to the Energy Information Administration, despite advances in energy efficiency and conservation, U.S. per-capita energy consumption in 2008 was 327 million Btus per year, almost exactly the same as it was in 1970.[18]

## Not Just Conservatives: Industry, Environmentalists, Public Opinion, and the Economy

Some observers, including many environmentalists, argue that the central cause of environmental policy change, or lack thereof, is not conservatives' ability to either persuade or prevail over their opponents—that is, the interplay among conservative activism, existing institutions, and environmentalists' responses—but the clout of industry. From this perspective, every administration regardless of its ideology is deferential to development interests, so environmental policy is driven primarily by the desire of business to make a profit.[19] As one former EPA official put it: "[academics] do provide some theological rationales, but there's an energy underneath that's darker and more primitive."[20]

Clearly, as the villain in most definitions of environmental problems and the entity most often identified as responsible for the cost of repairs, industry plays a central role in environmental policymaking. In the late 1970s, political scientist Charles Lindblom warned about the privileged position of business in the governance of a market economy. Because it provides jobs and prosperity, he argued, business is able "to obstruct policies such as those on environmental pollution and decay, energy shortage, inflation and unemployment, and distribution of income and wealth. . . . [B]usiness need do no more than persuade government officials that reforms will damage business. Their vetoes are powerful and ubiquitous."[21] A decade later, Curtis Moore, Republican counsel to the Senate Environment and Public Works Committee, described industry's participation in environmental policymaking in the following way: "They fight at every stage of the process, from the moment legislation is being formulated, continuing to the stage legislation is actually being considered, through markups and into committee. If you succeed in enacting something, they will immediately be at the agency. When regulations are proposed, they are fighting them. When [rules] are final, they challenge them in court. Then they start the process all over again and find the loopholes."[22]

Scholars have had difficulty discerning evidence to support the notion that business systematically dictates policy, however, particularly on issues that are widely salient.[23] For example, political scientist David Vogel finds that, over time, the political fortunes of U.S. businesses have varied depending on the public's perception of the strength of the economy, the degree of cooperation among different firms and industries, and the disposition of politicians.[24] Scholars have also struggled to demonstrate that business consistently determines environmental policy in particular. In fact, political scientist Sheldon Kamieniecki contends, "business interests do not participate in environmental policy debates at a high rate, and when they do, they have mixed success in influencing policy outcomes."[25] In their review of the literature on this topic, Kamieniecki and his coauthor, political scientist Michael Kraft, conclude that given the adversarial nature of U.S. policymaking and the diversity of the interest-group universe, it is no surprise that "[a]lthough business interests represent a powerful, countervailing force in Washington, D.C., it is not true that they always get their way at the national level."[26]

These counterintuitive findings may reflect the reality that business exerts much of its influence in subtle ways that are difficult to detect using conventional social science methods. In addition to financing the campaigns of politicians who are sympathetic to their views, corporations fund public relations efforts that seek to shape public opinion or simply prevent an issue from becoming widely salient.[27] Business lobbyists also work to determine how members of Congress formulate problems or interpret the constraints they face,[28] participate actively in agency

rulemaking and enforcement,[29] and litigate relentlessly.[30] Further complicating matters, environmental controversies typically feature contests
between two (and occasionally more) coalitions, each of which may
include an industry component.[31] In fact, veteran environmental activist
Joe Browder maintains that most environmental debates pit one industry
against another.[32] For example, when the state of California sued the
Bush administration over the right to regulate greenhouse gas emissions
from cars in early 2007, the electric utilities cheered because they wanted
to shift the regulatory burden away from themselves.[33]

Conflicts among different industries or within industrial sectors arise
because businesspeople are not monolithic in their attitude toward regulation. Some industrialists perceive a benefit from regulation—because it
raises the barriers to entry for competitors, enhances the prospects of
businesses that aim to meet the needs of regulated entities (such as waste-
management firms, manufacturers of devices that enhance energy efficiency or water conservation, and environmental compliance consultants),
or enables an alternative industry (such as tourism or alternative energy
development and installation) to flourish. Furthermore, increasingly
powerful sectors of the U.S. economy, including the financial and high-
tech industries, do not rely directly on extraction or pollution; CEOs in
these industries are disposed to support environmental regulations that
improve quality of life for them and their employees.[34] More fundamentally, industrialists do not always know their own interests or the best
way to attain them, and their perceptions can change, as illustrated by
the behavior of "clean" utilities in the case of acid rain and, more recently,
by CEOs concerned about climate change.[35]

That said, the arguments made by conservatives have furnished industry lobbyists with abundant intellectual cover and enhanced their political efficacy. Wealthy business leaders were vocal critics of the New Deal,
but for many years they were ineffectual because their conservatism
appeared to be entirely self-serving.[36] If they hoped to be persuasive,
businessmen could not simply complain that their profits were threatened; they needed more widely compelling stories to advance their
interests—and more credible storytellers. Therefore, businessmen provided financial backing for the inchoate conservative movement, and the
industry-conservative nexus that ensued greatly enhanced the ability of
antiregulatory conservatives to translate their ideas into action. Collaboration between conservatives and business interests has sometimes alienated libertarian members of the conservative coalition. But for most
conservatives, contempt for government overwhelms any skepticism

about "big business," and the notion of businesspeople as virtuous entrepreneurs who create jobs resonates widely.

Other observers blame environmentalists for the federal government's
inability to advance restrictive environmental policy, particularly with
respect to climate change. They proffer several (often contradictory)
explanations for this indictment. In the late 1980s, Douglas Wheeler, vice
president of the Conservation Foundation, chastised the environmental
community for allowing the public to become apathetic for the better
part of a decade.[37] He exhorted environmentalists to eschew alarming
rhetoric, enlist support from progressive politicians regardless of their
party, narrow their agenda, and participate in developing partial
solutions—in other words, to be pragmatic. Nearly twenty years later,
Paul W. Hansen, executive director of the Izaak Walton League of
America, blamed environmentalists' uncivil rhetoric and tactics for the
stalemate in Congress. They needed, he said, to stop letting the perfect
be the enemy of the good.[38]

By contrast, Joe Browder attributes environmentalists' political failures partly to their efforts to be pragmatic. In particular, he contends
that environmentalists' dependence on foundations for funding has
forced them to narrow their agenda and thereby has undermined their
ability to cultivate (and demonstrate to their congressional representatives) a palpable connection with their local supporters.[39] Such criticisms
were common in the 1990s. For example, a 1995 op-ed by Karyn Strickler, former director of the National Endangered Species Coalition, decried
the "Big Ten" environmental groups as "comatose"—unwilling to craft
accessible narratives or mobilize the grassroots, and unable to forswear
inter-group competition for members and donations.[40] Similarly, Mark
Dowie's 1996 book *Losing Ground* derided mainstream environmentalists for being detached from the concerns of ordinary people. In 2004,
public relations experts Michael Shellenberger and Ted Nordhaus reprised
these charges in a paper purporting to demonstrate that environmentalists' inordinate emphasis on narrow environmental concerns and technical policy issues, and their consequent inability to mobilize the public,
was the central cause of policy paralysis on climate change.[41] These
authors ignore the central importance of implementation, however. In
fact, during the conservative era environmentalists were able to prevent
further reductions in environmental protection only *because* of their
ability to navigate agencies, courts, and the details of legislative procedure. More important, critics pay insufficient attention to the nationwide
conservative mobilization between 1980 and 2008, which severely con-

strained the ability of *all* liberal groups, not just environmentalists, to advance their causes.[42]

While critics overstate the case, environmentalists certainly bear some responsibility for the policy evolution of the last thirty years. They were caught flat-footed by conservative activism and largely reacted to, rather than creating, the new policymaking context. To minimize the damage of conservatives' attacks and maintain influence within an increasingly hostile political environment, mainstream environmentalists felt compelled to master the arcane mechanisms of implementation. Doing so came at a cost, however: they diverted limited resources from grassroots organizing to litigating, lobbying, and participating in agency rulemaking. As a result, they expended insufficient resources on storytelling and failed to promote the more fundamental societal transformation that many had envisioned when the contemporary environmental movement emerged in the late 1960s. Even those grassroots groups that worked outside the mainstream, using more militant tactics, were largely limited to enforcing the laws on the books in their efforts to hold back a tidal wave of development.[43]

Industry and environmentalists clearly exerted a powerful influence on environmental politics and policy between 1970 and 2008, interacting with conservative activism in critical ways. But two additional explanations for the decline in environmental protection—fluctuations in public support for environmental protection and variation in economic conditions—have played more subtle and ambiguous roles. Of course, public opinion and economic conditions are related: public support for aggressive environmental protection tends to wax and wane with economic conditions—although not as much as one might expect. But public opinion is primarily a consequence, rather than a cause, of advocacy, media coverage, and the positions taken by public officials. This is particularly true for problems about which people have no firsthand knowledge, such as climate change. When public officials attack environmental regulations, environmentalists mobilize in order to increase media coverage, and public support for those laws tends to rise; when public officials are supportive, activists and the media become quiescent and the public tends to become complacent. When scientists identify new problems, environmental advocates try to focus sympathetic media coverage in hopes of persuading politicians that the public is concerned, while conservatives try to defuse the impetus for action by feeding journalists competing scientific analyses and economic claims about the cost of enacting policy. Not surprisingly, except in cases where an issue becomes overwhelmingly salient, scholars have detected little direct correlation between public opinion, crudely measured by polls, and legislative outcomes. It is even more difficult to explain how public opinion on a particular issue would affect administrative or judicial decision making, about which most of the public is chronically unaware.

It would seem self-evident that poor economic conditions constrain politicians' willingness to enact policies that impinge on economic activity. In fact, however, Congress continued to pass restrictive environmental legislation throughout the 1970s despite the stuttering economy and the furious objections of affected industries. It became more difficult to enact such legislation in the 1980s, even though the economy was recovering from recession; Congress passed the Clean Air Act of 1990 in the midst of an economic downturn; and legislative gridlock finally became the norm in the go-go 1990s. Perhaps this is because whether or not an environmental policy is *perceived* as economically damaging depends on the success of advocates' efforts to portray it as such. That said, poor economic conditions can certainly lend credence to conservative claims about the economic threat posed by restrictive policies—particularly when, as in the case of climate change, the link between a proposed policy and costs to consumers is readily apparent.

### Conservatives' Political Impacts

Beyond their policy-level impacts, conservatives' efforts have yielded political results that are likely to be even more enduring than many of the policy changes they have wrought. Most importantly, conservatives have influenced the environmental debate in critical ways. They have drawn attention to the cost of regulations, an impact that many in the policy community have lauded. While former EPA officials have (sometimes grudgingly) acknowledged that serious consideration of regulatory costs is warranted, several have pointed out that there has been little appetite among conservative appointees for a "fair" cost-benefit analysis—one that would account for the diffuse or distant benefits that environmental regulation is likely to provide.[44] Similarly, many moderates have lauded attempts to improve the scientific basis for environmental risk assessments. But as often as not, conservative demands for "sound science" have reflected at best a misapprehension of what role science can play in the regulatory process and, at worst, a cynical desire to gum up the regulatory process by imposing excessive analytical requirements on or shifting the burden of proof to proponents of environmental protection.

The conservative mobilization has also prompted both bureaucrats and environmentalists to learn about policy mechanisms. As a result, incentives, devolution, collaboration, and voluntary stewardship are now viewed favorably, while rules and deadlines—elements of the "command-and-control" framework—are almost universally scorned.[45] A potent illustration of this phenomenon is the fact that the only legislative solution seriously considered to address climate change has been a carbon cap-and-trade mechanism. Yet, as journalist John Broder points out, "not long ago, many of today's supporters of cap-and-trade dismissed the idea of tradable emissions permits as an industry-inspired scheme to avoid the real costs of cutting air pollution."[46]

While many regard these developments as positive, other impacts are more problematic. In particular, following the advice of their public-relations consultants, conservatives have learned to couch antiregulatory measures in proenvironmental language. The George W. Bush administration fine-tuned this strategy with its Clear Skies and Healthy Forests initiatives. At the same time, as Thomas O. McGarity, Sidney Shapiro, and David Bollier point out, conservatives have "deliberately shift[ed] the political terms of debate away from the morally charged terrain of human tragedy and corporate blame, substituting in its stead an impersonal, 'objective' lexicon of economic and statistical analysis." They have disseminated a storyline that depicts environmentalists and antihuman extremists, and environmental regulation as "a relentless and irrational . . . attack on efficiency . . . a subversive, property-destroying crusade against the free market and . . . a paternalistic intrusion on our personal freedoms."[47] In large measure, these efforts have succeeded. Environmental pragmatists have conceded vast swaths of rhetorical territory; as a result of political learning, they have found themselves maneuvering within an extremely cramped rhetorical space, one in which both sides elevate "balance," "common sense," and "reason," over strong ecological values and the precautionary principle. The federal government is demonized and regulatory enforcement (coercion) is seen as a last resort rather than as a crucial foundation on which change can be constructed.

The rhetoric of self-interest and financial gain, although incommensurate with progressive environmental ideas, is now pervasive in environmental politics. For instance, in the pages of the progressive *Planning* magazine, a Fish and Wildlife Service officer describes a 1,000-acre "conservation bank" created by an Alabama-based land management company as "a good thing for landowners" because "[i]t turns endangered species into an asset."[48] Lou Leonard, director of international

climate policy for the World Wildlife Fund, relates his struggle to formulate an effective message explaining why the United States ought to fund
efforts directed toward climate change adaptation in poor countries,
saying, "There's an education lift in explaining to people why this is good
for American jobs and American people. There are good stories to tell
about why this should be included [in an energy and climate change bill]
even with a frame that this is about the American consumer and the
American economy."[49]

By the same token, thanks in part to the efforts of conservatives,
proenvironmental officials have become increasingly averse to citing the
environment as a rationale for environmental protection and take pains
to craft arguments that do not sound "extreme." They emphasize the
economic benefits of environmentally sustainable development and, to
avoid being cast as doomsayers, focus on opportunities rather than
hazards. For example, Democratic senator John Kerry of Massachusetts
said during his presidential campaign in 2003, "I want to change the
entire debate and discussion about the environment in this country. It's
about jobs, it's about health, it's about our legacy as a generation, and
it's about national security."[50] (The Obama administration adopted this
rhetorical strategy wholesale as it tried to drum up support for comprehensive energy and climate change legislation: they avoided the environmental rationale almost entirely, instead justifying policy change as a way
of stimulating a "clean-energy economy" that would furnish jobs for
working-class voters and more sustainable economic growth.[51]) Both
within and outside of the environmental community, many regard even
these developments as positive; they are sympathetic to the critiques of
conservatives and hear a ring of truth in even some of the more biting
critiques. But others find the rhetorical constrictions stifling.

An even more unambiguously negative political consequence of the
conservative era is that the environment has become a deeply partisan
issue.[52] Between 1970 and 2008, conservatives squeezed moderates out
of the Republican Party, and the two parties became dramatically more
homogeneous.[53] This trend was reinforced by the polarization of the
news media. As broadcast television lost viewers to cable and Internet
news sources, cable TV news outlets grew more partisan.[54] Liberal and
conservative political blogs linked almost exclusively to one another.[55]
The consequences of the growing partisan divide were readily apparent
on the issue of climate change, about which sociologists Riley Dunlap
and Aaron McCright described a large and growing gap, both at the elite
level and among the electorate.[56] According to Gallup, for example,

between 1997 and 2008, the percentage of Democrats who believed global warming was already happening rose from forty-six to seventy-six; during the same period, the percentage of Republicans who believed this remained essentially the same, falling from forty-eight to forty-seven. Similarly, the Pew Research Center found that between 2007 and 2008, the number of Americans who believed there was "solid evidence" of global warming declined from 77 percent to 71 percent, mainly as a result of increased skepticism among Republicans.[57]

One result of this polarization and partisanship: Republican leaders calculate that they cannot win environmental votes no matter what they do, so do not bother cultivating them, and Democrats take environmentalists' votes for granted. Another result is that even reforms with near-universal support are stymied. Environmentalists and their allies are loath to open up laws for reconsideration, fearing that conservatives will find ways to enact severe modifications. Polarization among activists and politicians has also curtailed the ability of federal agencies to adjust their practices to new realities, while an expanding population and a growing economy have undermined progress made since the 1970s. More than thirty years of withering attacks on the nation's environmental regulatory framework have left it strained, with few vocal defenders. Even as they faced additional regulatory responsibilities and procedural requirements, federal officials charged with implementing that framework experienced periodic budget cuts (or inadequate budget increases), reorganizations, and disparagement by politicians of every stripe.

A final consequence of the conservative mobilization is that by 2008, the Supreme Court was a more conservative venue. Journalist Adam Liptak points out that the side supported by the U.S. Chamber of Commerce, which files briefs in most major business cases, prevailed in thirteen of sixteen cases in the 2010 term. A study by legal scholars at Northwestern University and the University of Chicago that analyzed some 1,450 decisions between 1953 and 2010 found that the percentage of business cases on the Supreme Court docket grew under Chief Justice Roberts, as did the percentage of cases won by business interests. The Roberts Court ruled for business 61 percent of the time, compared with 46 percent in the last five years of the Court led by Rehnquist and 42 percent by all the Courts included in the analysis. In a separate study, the liberal Constitutional Accountability Center found a growing ideological divide in the Court: in the last eleven terms of the Rehnquist Court, the five conservative justices voted for the position taken by the U.S. Chamber of Commerce 61 percent of the time, while the four liberal justices voted for it 48 percent of the time. In the first five terms of the Roberts Court, by contrast, the five conservative justices voted for the chamber's position 74 percent of the time and the four liberal justices 43 percent of the time.[58]

Conservative appointments affected the appeals courts as well. With the Supreme Court deciding fewer than one hundred cases each year, the lower courts have the final say in more than 99 percent of cases. Eight months into Obama's presidency, Republicans had an eighty-eight to sixty advantage on the thirteen circuit courts. There were nineteen vacancies and more than two-dozen potential openings for senior judges, so Obama had an opportunity to reshape the federal judiciary.[59] But Republicans were determined to obstruct his efforts to do so.

### Environmental Politics and Policy under Obama

Although the prolonged period of conservative challenge had taken its toll, environmentalists had much to celebrate in 2008. Local environmental conditions in many parts of the United States had improved dramatically since the first Earth Day; environmental awareness among the public and corporations was high; and environmental advocacy groups were on a sound footing, organizationally and financially. Moreover, after the election of 2008, many analysts believed that environmental issues were straining the unity of the Republican Party. As voters turned away from Republicans in growing numbers,[60] some in the party reassessed their deference to the conservative position on the environment.[61] Journalist Jackie Calmes reported that both Republicans and Democrats saw more regulation as inevitable, and the only question was how far the pendulum would swing.[62] Political scientists Deborah Guber and Christopher Bosso speculated that, on the paramount issue of climate change, a political tipping point had been reached.[63]

### President Obama's First Term: Transformation or Tweaking?
Upon taking office, the Obama administration was prepared to capitalize on what appeared to be pent up demand for action on the environment. Obama appointed Lisa Jackson, former head of the New Jersey Department of Environmental Protection, as EPA administrator, and under her leadership the agency moved aggressively to address air pollution. Out of the gate, the EPA rescinded several Bush-era New Source Review regulations.[64] It also began work on stricter limits on mercury and other

hazardous air emissions from coal-fired power plants. And it eliminated a Bush-era rule allowing more than 3,500 factories to avoid giving a full public accounting of their toxic air emissions. Meanwhile, the Department of Justice launched three new NSR lawsuits.

In early 2010, the EPA set a restrictive new air quality standard for sulfur dioxide, establishing a one-hour maximum of 75 parts per billion (ppb) in order to protect human health from short-term spikes; at the same time, the agency revised sulfur dioxide monitoring requirements to ensure that monitors were located in areas where pollution affects large numbers of people. That summer, the EPA finalized rules limiting mercury, chemical-laden soot, and acid gases from cement kilns. (After failing to persuade Congress to overturn the rules through the rescissions process, cement manufacturers filed suit.) The EPA's actions delighted environmentalists but enraged conservatives, who charged the agency with trying to do "too much too fast," in the process threatening to cripple the already-weak U.S. economy.

Less praiseworthy, from environmentalists' point of view, were the administration's actions under the Endangered Species Act. There, Obama's Interior Department, led by the moderate Ken Salazar, departed only modestly from the path established under President Bush. Obama took an important first step: in April 2009, after a brief review, the administration threw out the last-minute rule issued by the Bush administration eliminating the requirement that federal officials consult with wildlife experts before taking actions that might harm endangered species. Then, in July 2009, the Interior Department withdrew the minimally protective Bush-era recovery plan for the spotted owl, saying it was "legally indefensible." (In June 2011, the Fish and Wildlife Service issued a new recovery plan that, although it deferred mapping critical habitat, proposed expanding owl protection beyond existing set-asides.)

In short order, however, Salazar made a series of decisions that exasperated environmentalists. He ignored the pleas of more than a thousand scientists and retained the relatively permissive Bush-era 4(d) rule for the polar bear, saying—as Secretary Kempthorne had—that the Endangered Species Act was not the appropriate tool for dealing with climate change. In October 2011, U.S. District Court judge Emmet G. Sullivan ruled that the service was within its authority in failing to consider greenhouse gas emissions in issuing a rule allowing "incidental take" of polar bears as a result of oil and gas activities in the Arctic. Nevertheless, the judge remanded the rule for review because the service had not completed an

environmental impact statement before issuing it in 2008. Like Kempthorne, Salazar also declined to list the sage grouse as endangered;
instead, the Fish and Wildlife Service concluded that a listing was "warranted but precluded" by a lack of resources. The decision was typical
of Salazar's compromising style; he said that development in the West
"has provided important benefits, but we must find common-sense ways
of protecting, restoring, and reconnecting the western lands that are most
important to the species' survival while responsibly developing much-
needed energy resources."[65]

The Obama administration followed in the Bush administration's
footsteps by once again removing gray wolves from the endangered
species list in Montana and Idaho, although not in Wyoming. After
Federal District Court judge Donald W. Molloy ruled that, as members
of a regional population, gray wolves in Montana and Idaho had to
receive the same protection under the Endangered Species Act as their
cousins in Wyoming, the Fish and Wildlife Service relisted the wolves.
But in April 2011, Congress—intervening for the first time in the endangered species list—approved a budget rider that delisted the wolves in
five states, including Montana and Idaho.[66] The Obama administration
also retained the essence of Bush's recovery plan for salmon on the
Columbia River. In May 2010, NMFS released a new salmon BiOp, but
three months later Oregon District Court judge James Redden rejected
it and urged the Obama administration—as he had Clinton and Bush—to
consider dam removal as an option.

More generally, the Obama administration disappointed environmentalists by maintaining the slow pace of endangered species listing established under Bush. During its first year, the administration listed only
two domestic species. Those numbers gradually increased as the Fish and
Wildlife Service adopted an ecosystem-based approach to listing, and in
just over two years the agency had listed fifty-nine species. (The rate of
listing was expected to increase after September 2011, when Judge Sullivan approved a pair of settlements that required the federal government
to list more than seven hundred species.) Still, biodiversity conservation
advocates were dismayed. "There is no longer a clear ideological opposition to endangered species," complained Noah Greenwald of the Center
for Biological Diversity in Tucson. "But they have not exactly made it
their priority either."[67]

Initially, environmentalists counseled patience with the Obama administration, taking comfort in the fact that they had not yet made any "bad"
policies. Most were reluctant to criticize their Democratic allies for fear

of losing any modicum of influence.[68] Even after the massive 2010 oil spill in the Gulf of Mexico, environmentalists "essentially [gave the president] a pass—all but refusing to unleash any vocal criticism against the president even as the public [grew] more frustrated by Obama's performance."[69] Carl Pope, chair of the Sierra Club, went further, suggesting that although the president had failed to address problems at the Minerals Management Service, overall, "his agencies [had] done a phenomenally good job."[70]

Environmentalists' were biting their tongues in part because they were focusing on climate change. They were ecstatic when President Obama took office promising to curb climate change and restore prosperity by converting the United States from a fossil-fuel-based to a clean-energy economy. The country appeared ripe for such a transformation: Obama was extraordinarily popular; public support for tackling energy and climate change was strong; industry was divided, with many prominent CEOs advocating a cap-and-trade system for greenhouse gas emissions; and the conservative opposition was beleaguered. What is more, the strength of the scientific consensus surrounding the causes and consequences of climate change was unprecedented. Dozens of prestigious scientific societies around the world had published official statements in support of controlling greenhouse gas emissions, while no reputable scientific body had taken a dissenting position.[71]

Obama's first steps were auspicious. In his State of the Union address, he argued that the nation's economic recovery would rest on a dramatic shift in its energy supply. "To truly transform our economy, protect our security, and save our planet from the ravages of climate change," he declared, "we need to ultimately make clean, renewable energy the profitable kind of energy. So I ask this Congress to send me legislation that places a market-based cap on carbon pollution." Obama's budget for fiscal year 2010 affirmed his support for curbing greenhouse gas emissions. It estimated revenue of $150 billion over ten years, beginning in 2012, from a carbon cap-and-trade bill that would cut U.S. emissions by more than 80 percent by 2050. It also included large increases in spending on energy efficiency and alternative energy by the Department of Energy as part of a $787 billion stimulus package. In addition, the EPA was slated for a 34 percent budget increase for fiscal year 2010, to about $10.5 billion from $7.2 billion in fiscal year 2008, including $19 million to establish a greenhouse gas inventory.[72]

Almost immediately after Obama's election, however, the prospects for climate change legislation began to deteriorate. Faced with a common enemy, conservatives abandoned their analysis of the Republican Party's failures in favor of a renewed focus on propagating core principles.[73] Within two months of Obama's inauguration, the Tea Party revitalized antiregulatory conservatism.[74] Bill Wilson, leader of the Tea Party group America for Limited Government, seemed to relish the prospect of a fight. "Obama has so heightened the debate over the proper role of government," Wilson said, "that it's inspired a lot of people to get involved." It is not any particular issue, he went on to say. "It's that government consumes more and more of what we call personal liberty."[75]

The Tea Party soon gained the backing of a variety of ultra-conservative donors, most prominently the libertarian billionaires Charles and David Koch, who—under the auspices of their group, Americans for Prosperity—encouraged activists to target cap-and-trade proposals.[76] As conservative activist Myron Ebell explained, the conservative strategy was simply to label cap-and-trade a tax. "It would be the biggest tax increase in the history of the world," he argued. "OK, it's indirect and sneaky; it's rationing rather than an actual tax," he added, so activists would have to reframe it. "I think we win the debate as long as we focus on who's going to pay for this," he said.[77] It was not long before "cap-and-tax" had become a Tea Party mantra.

Conservative activism that tarnished the image of cap-and-trade was accompanied by a resurgence in activity aimed at contesting environmentalists' definition of the problem by discrediting climate change science. In March 2009, the conservative Heartland Institute convened its annual three-day International Conference on Climate Change, where S. Fred Singer launched his Nongovernmental International Panel on Climate Change. MIT atmospheric physicist Richard Lindzen gave the keynote talk, beginning with "a biting attack" on what he called the "climate alarm movement" and proceeding to reiterate his position that "[t]he only place where this alleged climate catastrophe is happening is in the virtual world of computer models, not the real world."[78] In September 2009, a new Montana-based organization called "CO2 is Green" began running television ads that claimed, astonishingly, "There is no scientific evidence that CO2 is a pollutant. In fact, higher CO2 levels than we have today would help Earth's ecosystems."[79]

In mid-November 2009, climate change skeptics caused a furor with an episode they gleefully labeled "climate-gate": the theft and public release of hundreds of hacked e-mail messages from a computer server at the University of East Anglia in the United Kingdom. Critics charged that the exchanges between prominent American and British researchers revealed efforts to manipulate and distort data in order to make climate change appear more certain. "This is not a smoking gun, it is a mushroom cloud," declared climate contrarian Patrick Michaels.[80] A series of independent reviews concluded that the charges against the scientists were baseless, but intensive and derisive coverage by Fox News and other conservative outlets had already created an indelible sense of scandal. Then, in January and February 2010, the Intergovernmental Panel on Climate Change acknowledged that its 2007 assessment of climate change science contained a handful of mistakes. Researchers pointed out that minor errors in a three-thousand-page report were unavoidable. But again, coverage by the conservative media amplified the errors, which they portrayed as intentional distortions. Conservative politicians like Senator James Inhofe seized the opportunity to portray climate change science as "far from settled."

Meanwhile, the fossil fuel industries continued to lobby heavily both inside and outside of Congress on the issue of climate change. While some companies, including most electric utilities, as well as dozens of large manufacturers, focused on negotiating policies that would work in their favor, the major trade associations—particularly the National Association of Manufacturers and the U.S. Chamber of Commerce—were outspoken in their opposition to legislation that would curb greenhouse gas emissions.[81] Throughout the summer of 2009, for example, an outfit calling itself Energy Citizen organized anti-cap-and-trade rallies in southern and oil-producing states. The group, which was backed by the American Petroleum Institute, bussed employees of oil companies from their workplaces to the rally sites.[82] In October, the U.S. Chamber of Commerce launched a $100 million campaign aimed at "defend[ing] and advanc[ing] America's free-enterprise values in the face of the Obama administration's effort to expand the size and scope of the federal government."[83] The chamber's primary target was the cap-and-trade bill under consideration in Congress.

Conservative and fossil fuel industry opposition was accompanied by growing public apathy, largely a consequence of the deepening recession. A poll taken by the Pew Research Center in early 2009 suggested that Americans were less concerned about rising global temperatures than they had been a year earlier. In the poll, global warming came in dead last among twenty voter concerns; only 30 percent of the voters deemed it to be a "top priority," compared with 35 percent in 2008. "Protecting the environment," which had surged in the rankings from 2006 to 2008, dropped even more precipitously; only 41 percent called it a top priority, compared with 56 percent in 2008.[84]

Heightened interest group controversy and declining salience among the public dramatically lengthened the odds facing comprehensive energy and climate change legislation in the 111th Congress (2009–2010). In June 2009, following a frenzied push by Speaker Nancy Pelosi, as well as Obama and his top advisors, the House narrowly passed a comprehensive energy and climate change bill, the American Clean Energy and Security Act. But, despite concessions by the president on nuclear power and offshore drilling to attract holdouts, a companion bill foundered in the Senate. After a rancorous battle over health care and in the face of a prolonged recession, fence-sitting senators chose to postpone action rather than risk supporting a bill that would inevitably be portrayed as imposing tangible costs on their constituents. For his part, Obama declined to press the issue, bowing to the advice of economists in the White House that acting aggressively on carbon emissions would further weaken the faltering economy.

Ironically, then, the Obama administration found itself relying, just as the Bush administration had done, on low-profile administrative actions to advance its climate change goals. At the direction of the White House, federal officials began investigating whether the Securities and Exchange Commission should require publicly traded corporations to disclose financial risks related to global warming and how to integrate concerns about sea-level rise into national security planning. At the president's behest, the EPA, Department of Housing and Urban Development, and Department of Transportation launched an initiative to foster the creation of more sustainable communities. The Council on Environmental Quality issued guidance to federal agencies on how to incorporate climate change impacts into environmental impact statements. And both the Interior Department and the Forest Service began integrating climate change considerations into their management of public lands.

More problematic from the perspective of conservatives were steps taken by the EPA to address climate change under the Clean Air Act. Shortly after taking office, EPA administrator Jackson began reversing the Bush administration's actions to obstruct regulation of greenhouse gas emissions. During Obama's first year, the EPA granted California a waiver to regulate greenhouse gas emissions from motor vehicles, issued the "endangerment" finding necessary to begin regulating greenhouse gas emissions under the Clean Air Act, and proposed the first-ever greenhouse-gas-emissions standards for cars and light trucks (35 mpg by

2016). In January 2010, the EPA began tracking the carbon dioxide emissions of large industrial polluters, further paving the way for an emissions cap on factories, utilities, and other stationary sources. And in May, the EPA finalized a "tailoring" rule that would shield small businesses, households, and hospitals from greenhouse-gas-permit requirements. (After pushback from Congress, the EPA made its tailoring rule more permissive than the original proposal: it went from regulating industrial sources that emit more than 25,000 tons of carbon dioxide per year to a threshold of 75,000 tons per year.)

The EPA's moves to regulate greenhouse gas emissions inflamed the agency's critics, and it soon became a favorite target of conservative blogs and Tea Party rallies. One petition, circulated by Americans for Prosperity, described the EPA as "an out-of-control bureaucracy attempting an unprecedented power grab, seeking to regulate every aspect of our lives and take control of the U.S. economy."[85] Representative Michelle Bachmann of Minnesota wrote in a blog post on townhall.com, "In an attempt by the Environmental Protection Agency to establish a national energy tax by circumventing the legislative process, the EPA (with the backing of the Obama Administration) is pushing emission regulations which will destroy jobs and further impact our already struggling economy." Republican senator Lisa Murkowski of Alaska organized a drive to pass a "resolution of disapproval" under the Congressional Review Act that would veto the EPA's endangerment finding, and House Republicans responded by proposing a parallel resolution. At the same time, coal-state Democrats led by Jay Rockefeller of West Virginia sought a two-year delay in greenhouse gas limits for stationary sources.

### The 2010 Elections and Their Aftermath
The 2010 congressional election vaulted Republicans back into the majority in the House (which went from 255–179 to 193–242) and significantly narrowed the Democratic majority in the Senate (from 56–42–2 to 51–47–2). It seemed to constitute a stark repudiation of the Obama administration's agenda—although only around 38 percent of the electorate actually turned out to vote.[86] Ebullient congressional Republicans vowed to pursue expanded oil and gas drilling and fight the Obama administration's attempts to regulate energy production. In an effort at conciliation with industry groups and Republicans who charged that red tape was delaying the economic recovery, shortly after the new Congress was seated Obama issued an executive order requiring federal agencies to conduct a comprehensive review of regulations, with the goal

of eliminating unnecessary rules. The executive order also required agencies to consider ways to reduce the burden on business when developing new rules.

Obama's gesture elicited a tepid response, however, and conservative members of Congress continued to tout the antiregulatory storyline, taking particular aim at the EPA. For example, Republican Fred Upton of Michigan circulated a memo in January 2011 saying that his committee planned to review the EPA's activities closely because "we believe the agency has been regulating 'too much too fast' without fully analyzing the feasibility and economic and job impacts of the new rules."[87] In early February, the House Oversight and Government Reform Committee held a hearing entitled "Regulatory Impediments to Job Creation," and Republican sponsors introduced legislation to require that all rules costing more than $100 million be approved by Congress before taking effect. In the meantime, the House Energy and Commerce Committee announced a hearing to examine whether environmental agencies were doing enough to assess the impact of their rules on jobs. The House overwhelmingly (391–28) passed a resolution requiring ten committees to review new federal regulations to determine whether they were slowing down the economy. And in March, Republicans added another to a long list of bills targeting EPA regulations. The bill, sponsored by Senators Inhofe and Mike Johanns of Nebraska, would order the Commerce Department to review the "cumulative energy and economic impacts" of more than a half-dozen EPA rules. (Of course, these antiregulatory bills were symbolic; none had the votes to reach cloture in the Democratic-controlled Senate, and all faced a certain White House veto.) By August 2011, the EPA had become a favorite target of the Republican presidential candidates, all of whom depicted it as a heavy-handed bureaucracy whose regulatory agenda was strangling the economy.

Republicans also took a variety of lower-profile steps to curb the administration's regulatory powers through the budget process. A continuing resolution passed by the House in early 2011 slashed the EPA's fiscal year 2011 budget by $3 billion and cut the Energy Department's efficiency, renewables, and research accounts by more than $1 billion; it also stripped the EPA of its ability to regulate carbon dioxide emissions and cut funding for energy and climate research across the government.[88] After a standoff with the White House, many of those riders were deleted; likewise, Senate Democrats succeeded in removing more than a dozen antienvironmental riders from the GOP's rescissions bill for fiscal year 2011. Undeterred, the GOP once again attached antienvironmental riders to fiscal year 2012 spending bills for both the EPA and the Interior Department.

To the consternation of the party's moderates, after the 2010 elections it was apparent that skepticism about climate change had become a litmus test for Republicans, thanks largely to Tea Party and industry activism.[89] In the face of a revitalized conservative movement and increasingly strident and unified Republican attacks, Obama promised to continue pursuing his clean-energy agenda, albeit in a less comprehensive fashion.[90] In January 2011, for example, Obama released a plan to promote renewables by slashing $4 billion per year in subsidies to oil and gas companies. He also pledged to use the savings to finance a drive to obtain 80 percent of the nation's electricity from renewables by 2035. Despite Obama's efforts at conciliation—he included nuclear energy, "clean coal," and natural gas among qualifying renewables—Republicans described the bill as "job-slashing overreach."[91]

The EPA continued to issue air pollution rules after the 2010 elections, although its pace was slowed by resistance. For instance, on March 16, 2011, the agency unveiled a plan to require coal- and oil-fired power plants to reduce emissions of mercury and eighty-three other toxic air pollutants by 2016. Power plants, their trade associations, and members of Congress—including some Democrats—lobbied intensely against the so-called Utility MACT, arguing that the rule would cost the economy 144,000 jobs over the next decade.[92] In response, the EPA extended the comment period. In July, with little fanfare, the EPA issued new standards for power plants in the twenty-seven eastern states and D.C. to replace the Bush administration's Clean Air Interstate Rule (CAIR), which had been invalidated by the courts. When the new requirements take effect in 2014, power plants will have to cut sulfur dioxide emissions by 73 percent and nitrogen oxides by 54 percent from 2005 levels. The Cross-State Air Pollution Rule is more restrictive than CAIR because it does not allow interstate trading unless the whole state remains below its emissions limits. Holding its ground, the EPA declined to adopt the gradual phase-in of the new rule, as demanded by the utility industry and many Republicans in Congress. Industry sued, however, and in December 2011, the D.C. Circuit suspended the new rule until the litigation played out; in the interim, CAIR remains in effect.

Just two months after issuing the cross-state rule, to the dismay of environmentalists, President Obama decided not to issue a revised air quality standard for ozone that the agency had devised after two years of work. Jackson had pushed hard for the lower standard, but she lost

a battle with top White House political and economic advisors—
particularly William Daley, Obama's chief of staff, and OIRA administrator Cass Sunstein—who were concerned about compliance costs.[93]
Perhaps to demonstrate the administration would not always bow to
pressure from industry and its allies, on December 21, 2011, the EPA
finalized the new standards for mercury and other toxic pollutants from
coal- and oil-burning power plants. In terms of its economic impact, this
was the most significant rule enacted by the EPA in decades. Not surprisingly, Senator Inhofe bemoaned the rule. "Sadly, this rule isn't about
public health," he said. "It's a thinly veiled electricity tax that continues
the Obama administration's war on affordable energy and is the latest
in an unprecedented barrage of regulations that make up EPA's job-
killing regulatory agenda."[94]

### Engineering a Progressive Transformation

As the foregoing history makes clear, conservatives have had a substantial, though complicated, impact on U.S. environmental politics and
policy. For scholars, this analysis provides strong empirical support for
the notion that subterranean challenges to the status quo can effect
incremental institutional change. As James Mahoney and Kathleen
Thelen observe, "Although less dramatic than abrupt and wholesale
transitions, these slow and piecemeal changes can be equally consequen-
tial for patterning human behavior and for shaping substantive political
outcomes."[95] This narrative also illuminates the pathways of policy and
political learning. In response to tactical innovation by their opponents,
both conservatives and environmentalists have adjusted their own
tactics—sometimes reframing their positions or adjusting their priorities,
at other times repositioning, in hopes of capturing political support.
Advocates on both sides have also learned about the desirability of different policy mechanisms. This policy learning has occurred partly as a
result of experience with and assessments of particular mechanisms, and
partly in response to the gridlock that has accompanied partisan polarization. More generally, the story recounted in the preceding chapters
reinforces the growing preoccupation among many scholars with the
influence of ideas, whose impacts on politics and policy can be elusive
in the short run but more evident over time.

The question of how conservatives have affected U.S. environmental
politics and policy is more than academic, however. There is overwhelming evidence that human pressure on the world's natural systems has

increased dramatically during the late twentieth and early twenty-first centuries, an era of conservative dominance in U.S. politics. Between 1970 and 2008, the global population more than doubled, as did world-wide energy consumption.[96] On October 31, 2011, the world's seven billionth person was born, and population growth continues apace; by 2100, the United Nations projects, there will be ten billion people living on earth. As a result of this global population boom, the world's natural resource stocks have come under siege since 1970. Between 1970 and 1995, annual global consumption of raw materials—such as minerals, timber, metals, and sand—rose precipitously,[97] and with the accelerating industrialization of India and China since the early 2000s, world materials consumption has shown no signs of leveling off, let alone declining.[98] In 2001, the United Nations estimated, "By 2050, humanity could devour an estimated 140 billion tons of mineral ores, fossil fuels and biomass per year—three times its current appetite—unless the economic growth rate is 'decoupled' from the rate of natural resource consumption."[99] To put this in perspective, according to ecologist Fridolin Krausmann and his colleagues, global use of raw materials by humans is already "the same order of magnitude as . . . the amount of biomass produced annually by green plants through photosynthesis."[100]

The environmental consequences of this level of human consumption are widely evident. Despite massive conservation campaigns, tropical regions continue to lose millions of hectares of forests annually.[101] Marine fisheries and their corresponding ecosystems have experienced severe decline.[102] Most experts agree that the rate of biodiversity loss is increasing worldwide, a trend that will be exacerbated by climate change; in fact, biologists argue that we are in the midst of the sixth great extinction.[103] (The last mass extinction event, the Cretaceous-Palogene, occurred 65.5 million years ago.) In many regions of the world, including several parts of the United States, development has greatly exceeded the water supply, and countries now face dire trade-offs between conserving natural systems and supplying human demands—choices that promise to become more acute in the coming decades as the population grows and the global climate changes.

In late 2007, the United Nations issued a report warning that population growth, combined with unsustainable consumption patterns, was inflicting environmental damage that was nearing the point of irreversibility.[104] The worldwide recession that began in the summer of 2008 delayed the reckoning, but most experts assumed that—in the absence of a dramatic shift in consumption patterns—demand for food, energy, and materials would resume as the global economy rebounded. Sure enough, global energy consumption increased dramatically in 2010. Even more troubling, according to the Global Carbon Project, global emissions of carbon dioxide jumped by the largest amount ever recorded—5.9 percent—and in 2011 reached 393 parts per million, their highest level in history.[105]

It is worth adding that, even with rapid growth in China and other developing countries, the United States remains the world leader by far in terms of per capita energy use, greenhouse gas emissions, materials consumption, and ecological footprint—in other words, however you measure impact. We also set the standard that others strive to attain, even as we devour the resources necessary for them to do so. It is imperative, therefore, that the United States finds ways to reduce its ecological impact dramatically. Recognizing this, and frustrated with the gridlock and backsliding at the federal level, many U.S. environmentalists are opting to bypass government altogether and pursue environmental sustainability through alternative means.

For some, the venue of choice has been the private sector. Some of the world's largest corporations have, in fact, made sustainability a priority. In 2007, Google announced it would invest hundreds of millions of dollars in the development of alternative energy, partly in an effort to reduce the environmental impact of its power-hungry data centers, but also in the hope of promoting more widespread change. As Google founder Sergey Brin explained in a conference call with reporters, "We do like to take advantage of our noted . . . position to motivate the world and do things that are good."[106] "Our over-arching vision," Google's Web site states, "is to one day transform the global economy from one running on fossil fuels to one largely based on clean energy."

A few years before Google launched its alternative energy drive, Walmart kicked off its own sustainability initiative. According to writer Edward Humes, in 2004, the world's largest retailer began to explore the possibility that "making and selling green, sustainable products [could] become the most profitable business model there could be."[107] Since then, Walmart has taken significant steps to transform its core business. By 2010, it had become the world's largest buyer of organic cotton; prompted laundry detergent manufacturers to cut their packaging radically by using concentrated formulations, thereby saving vast quantities of cardboard, diesel fuel, water, and plastic resin; promoted the use of compact fluorescent light bulbs by millions of consumers; and donated millions of pounds of food that would otherwise have been wasted.

The actions taken by Google, Walmart, and other major corporations can stimulate innovation and create new markets for environmentally benign products. They are not likely to bring about the kind of transformation that appears necessary to attain a genuinely sustainable economy, however. Fundamentally, Walmart's business model rests on ever-increasing consumption, which in turn is rooted in the notion that citizens are primarily consumers—values antithetical to sustainability. In fact, although its 2010 sustainability report showed that Walmart had cut carbon emissions from its stores, trucks, and other operations by 16 percent, its overall emissions had risen because of increased sales.[108] Moreover, even the most motivated business is constrained by the need to get a competitive return on investment (ROI). As Humes explains, "as long as renewable energy could not compete on price with dirtier conventional options, Walmart would never make a significant switch to green power, no matter how great the environmental benefits."[109] In an era of "supercapitalism," in which global competition among corporate giants is unrelenting, companies have little leeway within which to pursue sustainability measures that are not profitable.[110]

Even when there is an ROI case to be made, obstacles to sustainability arise. According to Auden Schendler, executive director of sustainability at the Aspen Skiing Company, efforts to green his Aspen hotel were constrained by two things: first, a mental model that says hotels make money by selling rooms and other services, not by saving energy; and second, a simple lack of adequate up-front capital.[111] Furthermore, corporate sustainability efforts in many realms are derailed by government policies that subsidize (or at least do not discourage) environmentally damaging behavior. Walmart has acknowledged that its ability to operate more sustainably is limited by a lack of federal policies to structure various markets. For example, the company has struggled to provide sustainable wild-caught seafood, convince Americans to wash clothes in cold water, or source environmentally benign jewelry. Given such obstacles, Schendler reluctantly concludes, "only government action—on a global scale—can drive the level of change at the speed we require."[112]

Another option environmentalists who are alienated by the national political debate have pursued is fostering individual behavior change. Sociologist Thomas Dietz and his colleagues estimate that the United States could reduce its total carbon emissions by 7.4 percent over a decade through behavior-change programs that target residential energy use and nonbusiness travel.[113] To effect behavior change, particularly among consumers and homeowners, nonprofits have created dozens of certification and labeling schemes, like those that identify sustainably harvested wood, fish, and other commodities. Such information-based campaigns rest on the premise that if people understand the damaging effects of what they are doing or buying, they will change their behavior. Yet a wealth of research suggests this assumption is unfounded; in fact, studies show that even projects that emphasize the financial advantages of sustainable behavior have negligible impacts.[114] The most effective behavior-change initiatives appear to involve community-based social marketing, which focuses on eliminating barriers to change, and social networking, which is rooted in the recognition that human behavior is habitual and contagious. Critical to the success of either approach are policies that structure the incentives people face. Because, as Jonathan Rowson observes, "We have to shape the world around us to bring out the best in ourselves."[115]

Other environmentalists, alienated by the national political debate and hoping to reestablish their connection to ordinary people, have focused on local activism. For instance, the Sierra Club more than doubled the number of local community organizers nationwide, from forty to about one hundred between 2002 and 2004.[116] As journalist Leslie Kaufman reports, local, grassroots activism—to thwart coal-fired power plants, prevent construction of the Keystone XL Pipeline to transport oil from Canada's tar sands, or repel new hydraulic fracturing ventures—is particularly attractive to young environmentalists who are frustrated by national politics.[117] In addition, across the country, environmentalists are working with state and municipal governments on climate change mitigation and adaptation plans, filling the vacuum left by the federal government. Local sustainability initiatives are not exempt from right-wing attacks, however. Tea Party activists have begun disrupting community-based efforts to control sprawl and conserve energy, characterizing them as part of a "big government blueprint against individual rights."[118] In January 2012, the Republican Party adopted a resolution against local sustainability initiatives, decrying the "destructive and insidious nature" of the "plan of radical so-called 'sustainable development,'" which "views the American way of life of private property ownership, single family homes, private car ownership and individual travel choices, and privately owned farms; all as destructive to the environment."[119]

In addition to building grassroots organizations, many environmentalists are choosing to patronize local, small-scale enterprises, which generate jobs that are stable and relatively low-impact, albeit unproductive in the traditional sense.[120] Such establishments provide options for consumers who want to escape the big-box-store, consumption-oriented economy. Localism can demonstrate that a locally rooted economy is more satisfying than one in which an abundance of cheap goods comes at the expense of jobs and environmental quality. It may also foster the creation of new social networks needed to change mindsets and values.[121] There are limits to the transformative power of participating in locally based economic activity, however. Just as efforts to change individual behavior are undermined by collective action problems, local enterprises are routinely thwarted by perverse incentives embedded in national and international policies. In addition, large corporations can easily undermine smaller local entities by taking advantage of economies of scale. There is a more subtle barrier to localism as well: the marginalization of those who resist pressures to conform to mainstream values. Given the hostility of the global economic system and the values and structures that underpin it, only the hardiest examples of localism will survive, and even they will always be vulnerable. More important, they will remain boutique exceptions, available primarily to the well-to-do, not the norm. As political scientist David Hess explains, "opting out" of the global economic system, even if many people do it, is not enough to change the world; instead, localism must be rooted in a larger project to construct an alternative, locally based global economy—one that is driven by environmental and equity concerns, rather than the interests of global multinational corporations.[122]

And finally, during the 2000s, in an effort to reinvigorate the environmental movement and enhance its clout, many environmentalists formed pragmatic alliances with traditional adversaries. For example, in Nebraska, the Sierra Club collaborated with local farmers to pass state legislation that blocked implementation of EPA rules reducing public scrutiny of animal feedlot operations.[123] The Environmental Defense Fund, the Natural Resources Defense Council, and the Nature Conservancy forged alliances with business leaders in the U.S. Climate Action Partnership, with the goal of crafting legislation to address climate change. Environmentalists also joined forces with labor unions; for example, the Apollo Alliance and the Blue Green Alliance came together around combating global warming by creating jobs in energy efficiency and alternative fuels. In the West, environmentalists worked with the "hook-and-bullet" crowd (hunters and fishermen) to thwart oil and gas exploration.[124] Such pragmatic partnerships can bring about improvements in specific policies and practices but rarely prompt more fundamental change. Perhaps more important, they are often ephemeral because they are rooted in common interests around a particular issue, rather than in the discovery of deeply held shared values and beliefs.

In the early twenty-first century, it is apparent that meeting the challenges posed by the rapid environmental deterioration associated with worldwide industrialization will require more than corporate sustainability initiatives, voluntary behavior change, localism, and pragmatic coalition building. As Gus Speth, a long-time leader in the environmental movement, observes, "The main body of environmental action is carried out within the system as currently designed, but working within the system puts off-limits major efforts to correct many underlying drivers of deterioration. . . . Working only within the system will, in the end, not succeed when what is needed is transformative change in the system itself."[125] If such a systemic transformation is to be effected, environmentalists and their allies need to fight antiregulatory ideas with ideas of their own. They need to expose and challenge the fundamental values that underpin contemporary conservative activism. They also need to offer a coherent public philosophy that can serve as a basis for political and policy change—one that can readily be translated into compelling storylines that are starkly different from those proffered by the conservative coalition. Because, as political activists David Bollier and Jonathan Rowe point out, although a variety of individual factions have a beef with the current system, "there is no contemporary master narrative that unifies such movements; nor a challenge to market fundamentalism that does not carry the echoes of old, discredited [liberal] ideology."[126]

The intellectual framework to undergird such a public philosophy already exists. One element of this framework is a thoroughgoing critique of the reigning economic paradigm. The primary target of that critique is the idea that *economic growth is essential to human well-being*. Scholars have documented how the idea of economic growth became inextricable from our understanding of progress and even fetishized.[127] For much of the twentieth century, economic growth led to better quality of life for many in the industrialized world. By the 1970s, however, the ecological limits to growth were becoming apparent, and forty years later they are even more so. Just as important, contrary to the predictions of mainstream economic theory, in recent decades, technological advances have *not* resulted in reduced consumption of materials or energy.[128] In fact, as economist Juliet Schor points out, increased consumption enabled by affluence has swamped the benefits of fuel- and materials-saving technological advances.[129] Furthermore, economic growth has increasingly generated what Herman Daly and others call "illth"—that is, costs that are counted as benefits because money is spent to address them. The concept of illth is dramatically illustrated by the aftermath of Hurricane Katrina and by the months-long oil spill in the Gulf of Mexico in 2010.[130]

What is more, at least in developed countries, economic growth has not enhanced equity; in fact, by the turn of the twenty-first century the distribution of wealth in the United States had become dramatically more unequal than it was just decades earlier.[131] During the latter half of the twentieth century, the correlation between growth and well-being—as measured in a welter of "happiness" studies—disintegrated:[132] real per-capita income tripled in the United States between 1950 and 2005, but the percentage of people reporting themselves very happy barely budged, and actually declined after the mid-1970s.[133] The near collapse of the global financial system in 2008 provided a potent illustration of the flaws and risks inherent in a global economy driven by growth. But the evidence was there already in the rapidly rising inequality, social isolation, and environmental degradation that economic system promoted, even when it appeared to be healthy.

A second, and related, target of the critique of the status quo is its reliance on consumption, which—as writer Tim Jackson observes—is not so much a consequence of consumer greed as "a structural prerequisite for survival."[134] Yet abundant research has made clear that ever-increasing consumption leads not to satisfaction but to status anxiety.[135] A third target is the obsession with productivity, which rests on the hope of extracting the maximum output from the minimum expenditure of human labor. Such an aspiration seemed logical in a world of seemingly unlimited natural resources, but in the twenty-first century—with pressing limits on natural systems and a vast surplus of workers—it rarely makes sense to conserve labor by using more energy and raw materials (except, of course, in terms of corporate profits). A fourth target is the failure of free-market capitalism to value the services of ecological systems and the natural capital stocks that produce them, even though they are essential to human health and well-being. In the late 1990s, Robert Costanza and his colleagues estimated the global monetary worth of such services at between $16 trillion and $54 trillion, compared with a global GNP of $18 trillion per year.[136]

In addition to a critique of the status quo, progressive thinkers have furnished a rough roadmap for building a more socially equitable and ecologically sustainable economy. Beginning with Nicholas Georgescu-Roegen and continuing with Kenneth Boulding, Herman Daly, Douglas Booth, Juliet Schor, and others, a small set of dissenting economists have long advocated for a macroeconomic model that does not rely on growth but rather has human development as its ultimate aim. This alternative would promote not ever-increasing consumption but a broader and more equitable distribution of the benefits of development—that is, improvements in human well-being—primarily through full employment combined with more leisure time. Such an economy would also be more stable and resilient than the current one, and would operate within ecological limits. Using a simulation model of the Canadian economy called LowGrow, ecological economist Peter Victor has demonstrated that it is possible to structure an economy "in which full employment prevails, poverty is essentially eliminated, people enjoy more leisure, greenhouse-gas emissions are drastically reduced, and the level of government indebtedness declines, all in the context of low and ultimately no growth."[137] Even some mainstream economists have come to terms with the possibility of a steady-state economy. In 2008, Robert Solow, who three decades earlier won the Nobel Prize for innovation in growth theory, conceded, "There is no reason at all why capitalism could not survive with slow or even no growth. . . . There is nothing intrinsic in the system that says it cannot exist happily in a stationary state."[138]

Of course, an economy that is not based on unfettered markets, perpetual growth, and ever-increasing consumption not only poses a threat to the conservative doctrine but also challenges the assumptions of many moderate Democrats and Republicans. To build support for the broad reforms that will be needed, for more than a decade, scholars, practitioners, and writers—including Paul Hawken and Amory and Hunter Lovins, Edward Goldsmith and Jerry Mander, Gar Alperovitz, Clive Hamilton, Jonathon Porritt, Bill McKibben, Gus Speth, Annie Leonard, Tim Jackson, Paul Gilding, and many others—have been weaving together the elements described above to produce a progressive public philosophy that can provide the foundation for a broad coalition.[139] At its core, the first argument of that public philosophy is that the current system not only degrades the environment but also corrodes social bonds and undermines individual and collective security. The second argument of the progressive philosophy is equally important: we will not only survive, but thrive, if we dispense with our single-minded focus on economic growth and the barren politics that underpin it. Such a vision should appeal not only to liberals and independents, but also to many conservatives, particularly traditionalists who are disaffected with the philosophy expounded by the contemporary conservative movement.[140] Still, proponents of political transformation face long odds and a daunting struggle; they are up against powerful vested interests, as well as a formidable set of habits, mental models, and social norms. To overcome that resistance, they need not mimic the tactics of the conservative movement. But they would do well to recall—as the history recounted in this book makes clear—that much of what conservatives were saying seemed outlandish and inconceivable in the early 1970s, but in 2011 seems commonsensical.

# Notes

## Preface

1. Alfred S. Regnery, *Upstream: The Ascendance of American Conservatism* (New York: Threshold Editions, 2008), 25.

2. Samuel P. Hays, "Introduction: An Environmental Historian Amid the Thickets of Environmental Politics," in *Explorations in Environmental History* (Pittsburgh, PA: University of Pittsburgh Press, 1998), xxxv.

3. Ibid., xxvii.

4. Ibid., xxviii.

## Chapter 1

1. A cap-and-trade system involves setting a cap on total greenhouse gas emission, allocating emission allowances among polluters, and enabling polluters to bank or trade those allowances.

2. It was also inconsistent with McCain's own environmental record. In his twenty-five years in the Senate, McCain voted with environmentalists only 24 percent of the time. By contrast, Obama, though in the Senate only a few years, voted with environmentalists 86 percent of the time. See Ray Ring, "A Fractured Party," *High Country News*, July 21, 2004. Furthermore, there were differences in the candidates' climate change prescriptions: Obama called for an 80 percent cut in carbon dioxide emissions by 2050 and wanted to auction off all permits; McCain called for a 66 percent cut and did not support a full-blown permit auction.

3. These beliefs are consistent with neoliberalism, an economic and political theory rooted in three assumptions. First, private institutions can always be expected to do a better job of providing public services than public institutions, so government should restrict itself to providing a legal environment conducive to private sector activity and maintaining the necessary infrastructure. Second, reducing trade barriers is always beneficial to all parties; therefore, rather than trying to develop autonomously, each nation should pursue its competitive advantage in the global marketplace. And third, spending policies meant to

benefit the poor are counterproductive and should be eliminated or pared back, since they distort the workings of the market; instead, governments should limit spending and maintain a balanced budget, in order to create an environment hospitable to foreign investment. See David Graeber, "Neoliberalism, or The Bureaucratization of the World," in *The Insecure American: How We Got Here and What We Should Do About It*, ed. Hugh Gusterson and Catherine Besteman (Berkeley: University of California Press, 2010), 79–96. The American conservative movement is less coherent ideologically than the term *neoliberalism* implies, however, and is more accurately defined as the product of pragmatic alliances. See Brian J. Glenn and Steven M. Teles, "Studying the Role of Conservatives in American Political Development," in *Conservatism and American Political Development*, ed. Brian J. Glenn and Steven M. Teles (New York: Oxford University Press, 2009), 3–17.

4. A third group of conservatives, traditionalists, have been distinctly subordinate within the U.S. coalition. Following Edmund Burke, traditionalists not only share patriotism, a belief in individual liberty, and suspicion of central government; they also value hierarchy and established institutions and are skeptical of the idea of progress. Journalists John Micklethwait and Adrian Wooldridge argue the latter two qualities are not present in contemporary U.S. conservatism because the phenomenon is rooted in the American West, where populism and optimism about the future are entrenched cultural attitudes. See John Micklethwait and Adrian Wooldridge, *The Right Nation: Conservative Power in America* (New York: Penguin Press, 2004).

5. American conservatism is distinctively probusiness. Its emphasis, in practice, is more on facilitating wealth creation than on ensuring well-functioning markets. Dissenters have called this "pseudo-conservatism" and charged its adherents with hypocrisy. For example, Independent presidential candidate John B. Anderson, formerly a Republican, argued passionately that "real" conservatives would oppose subsidies for big business and public works that damage the environment; they would support imposing prices on pollution and restricting development in fragile ecosystems. See John B. Anderson, "Real Conservatives, Pseudo-Conservatives" *New York Times*, December 2, 1980, A19.

6. Alfred S. Regnery, *Upstream: The Ascendance of American Conservatism* (New York: Threshold Editions, 2008).

7. David Mastio, "The GOP's Enviro-rut," *Policy Review* 101 (June–July 2000).

8. For instance, since 1984, the Gallup organization has asked: "With which one of these statements about the environment and the economy do you most agree—protection of the environment should be given priority even at the risk of curbing economic growth (or) economic growth should be given priority, even if the environment suffers to some extent?" Between 1984 and 2000, more than 60 percent of respondents consistently agreed with the first option. See http://www.gallup.com/poll/1615/environment.aspx.

9. After Vermont Republican Jim Jeffords became an Independent in May 2001, the Senate was split 50–49–1. The 2002 elections once again gave Republicans a Senate majority.

10. Julian E. Zelizer, "Seizing Power: Conservatives and Congress since the 1970s," in *The Transformation of American Politics: Activist Government and the Rise of Conservatism*, ed. Paul Pierson and Theda Skocpol (Princeton, NJ: Princeton University Press, 2007), 105–134.

11. Christopher McGrory Klyza and David Sousa, *American Environmental Politics, 1990–2006: Beyond Gridlock* (Cambridge, MA: MIT Press, 2008). Those assessments echo the results of numerous studies of the welfare state, which—as Jacob Hacker characterizes them—conclude that "welfare states are under strain, cuts have occurred, but their social policy framework remains secure, anchored by their enduring popularity, their powerful constituencies, and their centrality within the postwar order." See Jacob S. Hacker, "Privatizing Risk without Privatizing the Welfare State: The Hidden Politics of Social Policy Retrenchment in the United States," *American Political Science Review* 98, no. 2 (2004): 243.

12. Hacker, "Privatizing Risk."

13. Cary Coglianese and Jennifer Nash, "Government Clubs: Theory and Evidence from Voluntary Environmental Programs," University of Pennsylvania Law School, Public Law and Legal Theory Research Paper Series, Research Paper No. 08–49 (2008); Nicole Darnall and Stephen Sides, "Assessing the Performance of Voluntary Environmental Programs: Does Certification Matter?" *Policy Studies Journal* 36, no. 1 (2008): 95–117; Richard D. Morgenstern and William A. Pizer, *Reality Check: The Nature and Performance of Voluntary Environmental Programs in the United States, Europe, and Japan* (Washington, D.C.: Resources for the Future, 2007); Jorge Rivera and Peter deLeon, "Is Greener Whiter? Voluntary Environmental Performance of Western Ski Areas," *Policy Studies Journal* 32, no. 3 (2004): 417–437; David Vogel, *The Market for Virtue: The Potential and Limits of Corporate Social Responsibility* (Washington, D.C.: Brookings Institution Press, 2005).

14. Ben Furnas, "Idea of the Day: Seize the Energy Opportunity or Slip Further Behind," Center for American Progress, April 24, 2009. See http://www.americanprogress.org/issues/ideas/2009/04/042409.html; Evan Osnos, "Green Giant: Beijing's Crash Program for Clean Energy," *New Yorker*, December 31, 2009; Elizabeth Rosenthal, "U.S. Is Falling Behind in the Business of 'Green,'" *New York Times*, June 8, 2011.

15. Stephen Skowronek, "An Attenuated Reconstruction: The Conservative Turn in American Political Development," in *Conservatism and American Political Development*, ed. Brian J. Glenn and Steven M. Teles (New York: Oxford University Press), 352.

16. Paul Pierson, *Politics in Time: History, Institutions, and Social Analysis* (Princeton, NJ: Princeton University Press, 2004).

17. Daniel Beland and Robert Henry Cox, "Ideas and Politics," in *Ideas and Politics in Social Science Research*, ed. Daniel Beland and Robert Henry Cox (New York: Oxford University Press, 2011), 3–21; Mark Blyth, *Great Transformations: Economic Ideas and Institutional Change in the Twentieth Century* (New York: Cambridge University Press, 2002); G. John Ikenberry, "A

World Economy Restored: Expert Consensus and the Anglo-American Postwar Settlement," *International Organization* 46 (Winter 1992): 289–321; John W. Kingdon, *Agendas, Alternatives, and Public Policies*, 2nd ed. (New York: HarperCollins College Publishers, 1995).

18. Hacker, "Privatizing Risk"; James Mahoney and Kathleen Thelen, "A Theory of Gradual Institutional Change," in *Explaining Institutional Change: Ambiguity, Agency, and Power*, ed. James Mahoney and Kathleen Thelen (New York: Cambridge University Press, 2010), 1–37; Wolfgang Streeck and Kathleen Ann Thelen, eds., *Beyond Continuity: Institutional Change in Advanced Political Economies* (New York: Oxford University Press, 2005).

19. I focus on federal policymaking partly for reasons of space, but also because—as J. Clarence Davies and Jan Mazurek note—"Federal pollution control laws are the bedrock, the driving force, of the country's pollution control system." See J. Clarence Davies and Jan Mazurek, *Pollution Control in the United States: Evaluating the System* (Washington, DC: Resources for the Future, 1998), 11. Similarly, since the 1970s biodiversity conservation has been driven primarily by federal law.

## Chapter 2

1. William Genieys and Marc Smyrl, *Elites, Ideas, and the Evolution of Public Policy* (New York: Palgrave Macmillan, 2008); Paul Pierson and Theda Skocpol, "American Politics in the Long Run," in *The Transformation of American Politics: Activist Government and the Rise of Conservatism*, ed. Paul Pierson and Theda Skocpol (Princeton, NJ: Princeton University Press, 2007), 3–16. The notion of a policy system simplifies what is in reality a complex and messy world. In practice, what constitutes a policy system is a matter of continual debate, as is whether a particular policy belongs within one system or another. Moreover, most policy systems contain distinct policy areas. For example, within the education policy system, different sets of advocates and experts focus on K–12 education and higher education.

2. Jacob S. Hacker, "Privatizing Risk without Privatizing the Welfare State: The Hidden Politics of Social Policy Retrenchment in the United States," *American Political Science Review* 98, no. 2 (2004): 243.

3. Peter Bachrach and Morton S. Baratz, "Two Faces of Power," *American Political Science Review* 56 (1962): 947–952; Hacker, "Privatizing Risk"; Steven Lukes, *Power: A Radical View* (London: Macmillan, 1974).

4. In practice, the distinctions between popular and technical discourses are blurred, often intentionally. In addition, other distinctions are possible. For example, Vivien Schmidt makes the point that even in the "public" realm one can discern different kinds of rhetoric, so that communication among political colleagues (coordinative discourse) is different from communication between a political official and the public (communicative discourse). See Vivien A. Schmidt, *Democracy in Europe: The Impact of European Integration* (New York: Oxford University Press, 2006).

5. Many scholars distinguish between the normative and cognitive content of political ideas. See, for example, Erik Bleich, *Race Politics in Britain and France: Ideas and Policymaking since the 1960s* (New York: Cambridge University Press, 2003); John L. Campbell, "Institutional Analysis and the Role of Ideas in Political Economy," *Theory and Society* 27, no. 3 (1998): 377–409; and Robert C. Lieberman, "Ideas, Institutions, and Political Order: Explaining Political Change," *American Political Science Review* 96, no. 4 (2002): 697–712. My view is that causal beliefs and values are virtually inseparable in practice and that distinguishing between them, even for analytic purposes, can be misleading.

6. Judith Goldstein and Robert O. Keohane, "Ideas and Foreign Policy: An Analytical Framework," in *Ideas and Foreign Policy: Beliefs, Institutions, and Political Change*, ed. Judith Goldstein and Robert O. Keohane (Ithaca, NY: Cornell University Press, 1993), 8.

7. Quoted in Hugh Heclo, "Ronald Reagan and the American Public Philosophy," in *The Reagan Presidency: Pragmatic Conservatism & Its Legacies*, ed. W. Elliot Brownlee and Hugh Davis Graham (Lawrence: University of Kansas Press, 2003), 17.

8. As table 2.1 indicates, scholars have coined a host of terms for these different kinds of ideas, although they rarely distinguish between technical and public audiences. There is rough correspondence between what I label a worldview and what William Rees calls a "pre-analytic vision" and what William Hudson calls an ideology, which he defines as "provid[ing] the underlying rationale, in terms of political values and principles, for choosing one policy option over another." See William Rees, "Achieving Sustainability: Reform or Transformation?" in *The Earthscan Reader in Sustainable Cities*, ed. David Satterthwaite (London: Earthscan, 1999), 22–52; and William E. Hudson, *The Libertarian Illusion: Ideology, Public Policy, and the Assault on the Common Good* (Washington, DC: CQ Press, 2008), 4. Similarly, what I label principled beliefs, following Goldstein and Keohane, is analogous to Sabatier and Jenkins-Smith's "core beliefs." See Goldstein and Keohane, "Ideas and Foreign Policy"; and Paul A. Sabatier and Hank C. Jenkins-Smith, "The Advocacy Coalition Framework: Assessment, Revisions, and Implications for Scholars and Practitioners," in *Policy Change and Learning*, ed. Paul Sabatier and Hank C. Jenkins-Smith (Boulder, CO: Westview Press, 1993), 211–235. What Peter Hall and John Campbell refer to as policy paradigms, I have divided into analytic frameworks (equivalent to Genieys and Smyrl's systemic frameworks) and storylines. See Peter Hall, "Policy Paradigms, Social Learning, and the State: The Case of Economic Policymaking in Britain," *Comparative Politics* 25, no. 3 (1993): 275–296; John L. Campbell, "Institutional Analysis"; and Genieys and Smyrl, *Elites, Ideas, and the Evolution of Public Policy*. My term storyline is reasonably equivalent to linguist George Lakoff's "commonsense reasoning." See George Lakoff, *Moral Politics: What Conservatives Know That Liberals Don't* (Chicago: University of Chicago Press, 1996). What I refer to as policy images, following Baumgartner and Jones, is related but not identical to what others have defined as a secondary belief or a programmatic or sectoral idea. See Frank R. Baumgartner and Bryan D. Jones, *Agendas and Instability in American Politics* (Chicago: University of Chicago Press, 1993);

Sabatier and Jenkins-Smith, "The Advocacy Coalition Framework"; Genieys and Smyrl, *Elites, Ideas, and the Evolution of Public Policy*; and Margaret Weir, "Ideas and the Politics of Bounded Innovation," in *Structuring Politics: Historical Institutionalism in Comparative Analysis*, ed. Kathleen Thelen and Sven Steinmo (New York: Cambridge University Press, 1992), 188–216.

9.  Kenneth A. Shepsle, "Comment" in *Regulatory Policy and the Social Sciences*, ed. Roger Noll (Berkeley: University of California Press, 1985), 231–237. Similarly, Stephen Krasner contends that "Ideas have been one among several instruments that actors have invoked to promote their own, usually mundane interests." See Stephen D. Krasner, "Westphalia and All That," in Goldstein and Keohane, *Ideas and Foreign Policy*, 238. Some scholars have sought to find a role for ideas in rational-choice theory. Barry Weingast argues that ideas such as sovereignty provide shared expectations, which help reduce ambiguity and thereby allow members of an international community to cooperate. See Barry Weingast, "A Rational Choice Perspective on the Role of Ideas: Shared Belief Systems and State Sovereignty in International Cooperation," *Politics & Society* 23, no. 4 (1995): 449–464. Bates, De Figueiredo, and Weingast try to reconcile interpretive and game-theoretic approaches by suggesting that to construct a coherent and valid rational-choice account of history, game theorists need "detailed knowledge of the values of individuals, of the expectations that individuals have of each other's reactions, and of the ways in which these expectations have been shaped by history." See Robert H. Bates, Rui J. P. De Figueiredo Jr., and Barry R. Weingast, "The Politics of Interpretation: Rationality, Culture, and Transition," *Politics & Society* 26, no. 2: 244.

10.  John W. Kingdon, *Agendas, Alternatives, and Public Policies*, 2nd ed. (New York: HarperCollins College Publishers, 1995).

11.  Deborah Stone, *Policy Paradox: The Art of Political Decision Making*, rev. ed. (New York: W.W. Norton, 2002), 10.

12.  James Mahoney and Kathleen Thelen, "A Theory of Gradual Institutional Change," in *Explaining Institutional Change: Ambiguity, Agency, and Power*, ed. James Mahoney and Kathleen Thelen (New York: Cambridge University Press, 2010), 4.

13.  Karen Orren and Stephen Skowronek, *The Search for American Political Development* (New York: Cambridge University Press, 2004).

14.  Kathleen Thelen and Sven Steinmo. 1992. "Historical Institutionalism in Comparative Politics," in *Structuring Politics: Historical Institutionalism in Comparative Analysis*, ed. Sven Steinmo, Kathleen Thelen, and Frank Longstreth (New York: Cambridge University Press, 1992), 2. All three major schools of institutionalism—historical, sociological, and rational-choice—regard institutions as relatively enduring features of political and social life, but they differ in their precise definitions. Rational-choice institutionalists define institutions as mechanisms that coordinate behavior by structuring actors' behavior. Sociological institutionalists define institutions as the scripts, cues, and routines by which policies are executed or the "structures of meaning that explain and justify behavior—roles, identities and belongings, common purposes, and causal and

normative beliefs." For more on scripts, cues, and routines, see Paul J. DiMaggio and Walter W. Powell, "Introduction," in *The New Institutionalism in Organizational Analysis*, ed. Walter W. Powell and Paul J. DiMaggio (Chicago: University of Chicago Press, 1991), 1–38; on structures of meaning, see James G. March and Johan P. Olsen, "The Logic of Appropriateness," in *The Oxford Handbook of Public Policy*, ed. Michael Moran, Martin Rein, and Robert E. Goodin (New York: Oxford University Press, 2006), 691. Historical institutionalists define institutions "first and foremost as the political legacies of concrete historical struggles." See Mahoney and Thelen, "A Theory of Gradual Institutional Change," 7. Based on this definition, Paul Pierson wonders whether policies ought to be considered institutions. See Paul Pierson, "Public Policies as Institutions," in *Rethinking Political Institutions: The Art of the State*, ed. Ian Shapiro, Stephen Skowroneck, and Daniel Galvin (New York: New York University Press), 114–131. Wolfgang Streeck and Kathleen Thelen include policies in their definition of institutions "to the extent that they constitute rules for actors other than for the policymakers themselves—rules that can and need to be implemented and that are legitimate in the sense that they will if necessary be enforced by agents acting on behalf of the society as a whole." See Wolfgang Streeck and Kathleen Thelen, "Introduction: Institutional Change and Advanced Political Economies," in *Beyond Continuity: Institutional Change in Advanced Political Economies*, ed. Wolfgang Streeck and Kathleen Thelen (New York: Oxford University Press, 2005), 12.

15. Judith Goldstein, "Ideas, Institutions, and American Trade Policy," *International Organization* 42 (Winter, 1988): 179–217.

16. Andrea Campbell, *How Policies Make Citizens: Senior Political Activism and the American Welfare State* (Princeton, NJ: Princeton University Press, 2005); Robert C. Lieberman, "Ideas, Institutions, and Political Order: Explaining Political Change," *American Political Science Review* 96, no. 4 (2002): 697–712; Theda Skocpol, *Protecting Soldiers and Mothers: The Political Origins of Social Policy in the United States* (Cambridge, MA: Harvard University Press, 1992).

17. Paul Pierson, *Politics in Time: History, Institutions, and Social Analysis* (Princeton, NJ: Princeton University Press, 2004). The term "path dependence" refers to the phenomenon in which initial steps in a particular direction induce further movement in the same direction, as the cost of switching to a previously plausible alternative rises over time.

18. Ellen M. Immergut, "Institutional Constraints on Policy," in *The Oxford Handbook of Public Policy*, ed. Michael Moran, Martin Rein, and Robert E. Goodin (New York: Oxford University Press, 2006), 557–571.

19. G. John Ikenberry, "A World Economy Restored: Expert Consensus and the Anglo-American Postwar Settlement." *International Organization* 46 (Winter, 1992): 318–319.

20. Mark Blyth, *Great Transformations: Economic Ideas and Institutional Change in the Twentieth Century* (New York: Cambridge University Press, 2002), 10.

21. Blyth, *Great Transformations*.

22. Mahoney and Thelen, "A Theory of Gradual Institutional Change."

23. Peter Hall, "Policy Paradigms, Social Learning, and the State: The Case of Economic Policymaking in Britain," *Comparative Politics* 25, no. 3 (1993): 278.

24. Hugh Heclo formulated the original policy-learning construct, when he said, "Politics finds its sources not only in power but in uncertainty—men collectively wondering what to do. . . . Much political interaction has constituted a process of social learning expressed through policy." See Hugh Heclo, *Modern Social Politics in Britain and Sweden* (New Haven: Yale University Press, 1974), 305–306. Peter Hall suggests that policymakers and advocates can adjust their views about goals, policy instruments, and the settings of those instruments. See Hall, "Policy Paradigms." But Paul Sabatier, who defines policy learning as "relatively enduring alterations of thought or behavioral intentions which result from experience and/or new information which are concerned with the attainment or revision of policy objectives," argues that policy learning almost always results in changes to means (policy instruments and their settings), not ends. See Paul A. Sabatier, "An Advocacy Coalition Framework of Policy Change and the Role of Policy-Oriented Learning Therein," *Policy Sciences* 21 (1988): 133.

25. Phillip J. Cooper, *The War against Regulation: From Jimmy Carter to George W. Bush* (Lawrence: University Press of Kansas, 2009).

26. William E. Kovacic, "The Reagan Judiciary and Environmental Policy: The Impact of Appointments to the Federal Courts of Appeals," *Environmental Affairs* 18, no. 4 (1991): 669–713.

27. Peter A. Hall, "Foreword," in *Elites, Ideas, and the Evolution of Public Policy*, ed. William Genieys and Marc Smyrl (New York: Palgrave Macmillan, 2008), ix–xv.

28. Martin A. Hajer, *The Politics of Environmental Discourse: Ecological Modernization and the Policy Process* (New York: Oxford University Press, 1995); John S. Dryzek, *The Politics of the Earth: Environmental Discourses* (New York: Oxford University Press, 1997).

29. Mark H. Moore, "What Sort of Ideas Become Public Ideas," in *The Power of Public Ideas*, ed. Robert Reich (Cambridge, MA: Ballinger, 1988); Robert D. Benford and David A. Snow, "Framing Processes and Social Movements: An Overview and Assessment," *Annual Review of Sociology* 26 (2000): 611–639.

30. Frank R. Baumgartner and Bryan D. Jones, *Agendas and Instability in American Politics* (Chicago: University of Chicago Press, 1993).

31. Robert E. Goodin, Martin Rein, and Michael Moran, "The Public and Its Policies," in *The Oxford Handbook of Public Policy*, ed. Michael Moran, Martin Rein, and Robert E. Goodin (New York: Oxford University Press, 2006), 3–35.

32. Deborah Stone, *Policy Paradox: The Art of Political Decision Making*, rev. ed. (New York: W.W. Norton, 2002); Anne Schneider and Helen Ingram, "Social Construction of Target Populations: Implications for Politics and Policy," *American Political Science Review* 87 (1993): 334–347.

33. Joseph R. Gusfield, *The Culture of Public Problems: Drinking-Driving and the Symbolic Order* (Chicago: University of Chicago Press, 1981); Giandomenico Majone, *Evidence, Argument, and Persuasion in the Policy Process* (New Haven, CT: Yale University Press, 1989); Stone, *Policy Paradox*; David A. Rochefort and Roger W. Cobb, eds., *The Politics of Problem Definition: Shaping the Policy Agenda* (Lawrence: University Press of Kansas, 1994).

34. Sarah B. Pralle, *Branching Out, Digging In: Environmental Advocacy and Agenda Setting* (Washington, DC: Georgetown University Press, 2006); David A. Snow and Robert D. Benford, "Ideology, Frame Resonance, and Participant Mobilization," *International Social Movement Research* vol. 1 (Greenwich, CT: JAI Press): 197–217; Rochefort and Cobb, *Politics of Problem Definition*; Stone, *Policy Paradox*; James Q. Wilson, *The Politics of Regulation* (New York: Basic Books, 1980).

35. Baumgartner and Jones, *Agendas and Instability*; Goldstein, "Ideas, institutions, and American Trade Policy"; Kingdon, *Agendas, Alternatives, and Public Policies*; Gary Mucciaroni, *Reversals of Fortune: Public Policy and Private Interests* (Washington, DC: The Brookings Institution, 1995).

36. Kingdon, *Agendas, Alternatives, and Public Policies*; Moore, "What Sort of Ideas"; E. E. Schattschneider, *The Semisovereign People: A Realist's View of Democracy in America* (New York: Holt, Reinhart and Winston, 1960); Stone, *Policy Paradox*.

37. Timothy J. Conlan, Margaret T. Wrightson, and David R. Beam, *Taxing Choices: The Politics of Tax Reform* (Washington, DC: CQ Press, 1990); Mucciaroni, *Reversals of Fortune*.

38. John B. Gilmour, *Strategic Disagreement: Stalemate in American Politics* (Pittsburgh, PA: University of Pittsburgh Press, 1995).

39. Lawrence R. Jacobs and Robert Y. Shapiro, *Politicians Don't Pander: Political Manipulation and the Loss of Democratic Responsiveness* (Chicago: University of Chicago Press, 2000).

40. During the period analyzed in this book, the nature of the media changed dramatically, as did our ability to talk credibly about "the media" as an entity. In particular, the Internet facilitated the proliferation of political Web sites, while the disappearance of the fairness doctrine in the mid-1980s enabled the reemergence of a partisan news and talk radio programming. I discuss these developments in chapter five.

41. Doris A. Graber, *Media Power in Politics*, 5th ed. (Washington, DC: CQ Press, 2006); Shanto Iyengar, "Framing Responsibility for Political Issues," in *Do the Media Govern?*, ed. Shanto Iyengar and Richard Reeves (Thousand Oaks, CA: Sage Publications, 1997).

42. Henry Waxman, *The Waxman Report: How Congress Really Works* (New York: Twelve, 2009).

43. Schneider and Ingram, "Social Construction of Target Populations," 336.

44. Kingdon, *Agendas, Alternatives, and Public Policies*.

45. Moore, "What Sort of Ideas," 79.

46. Conlan, Wrightson and Beam, *Taxing Choices*.

47. Ibid. 250, 251.

48. Martha Derthick and Paul J. Quirk, *The Politics of Deregulation* (Washington, DC: The Brookings Institution, 1985).

49. Genieys and Smyrl, *Elites, Ideas, and the Evolution of Public Policy*; B. Guy Peters, Jon Pierre, and Desmond S. King, "The Politics of Path Dependency: Political Conflict in Historical Institutionalism," *Journal of Politics* 67, no. 4 (2005): 1275–1300; Sabatier and Jenkins-Smith, "The Advocacy Coalition Framework."

50. Benford and Snow, "Framing Processes"; Roger W. Cobb and Marc Howard Ross, "Agenda Setting and the Denial of Agenda Access: Key Concepts," in *Cultural Strategies of Agenda Denial: Avoidance, Attack, and Redefinition*, ed. Roger W. Cobb and Marc Howard Ross (Lawrence: University of Kansas, 1997), 3–24; Malcolm Spector and John I. Kitsuse, *Constructing Social Problems* (New York: Aldine de Gruyter, 1977).

51. Hacker, "Privatizing Risk," 344.

52. Christopher McGrory Klyza and David Sousa, *American Environmental Politics, 1990–2006: Beyond Gridlock* (Cambridge, MA: MIT Press, 2008), 63. The Line Item Veto Act of 1996 gave the president the authority to veto individual items within a bill passed by Congress, potentially eliminating the effectiveness of riders, but the U.S. Supreme Court struck down that law as unconstitutional in 1998.

53. Schattschneider, *Semisovereign People*.

54. Phillip J. Cooper, *By Order of the President: The Use and Abuse of Executive Direct Action* (Lawrence: University Press of Kansas, 2002), 58.

55. Alexis Simendinger, "The Paper Wars," *National Journal*, July 25, 1998.

56. Joanne Omang, "The Clean Air Act: Straightening Out a Regulatory Maze," *Washington Post*, February 22, 1981.

57. Richard Waterman, *Presidential Influence and the Administrative State* (Knoxville: University of Tennessee Press, 1989), 37.

58. Pralle, *Branching Out, Digging In*.

59. Daniel P. Carpenter, *The Forging of Bureaucratic Autonomy: Reputations, Networks, and Policy Innovation in Executive Agencies, 1862–1928* (Princeton, NJ: Princeton University Press, 2001).

60. Craig W. Thomas, *Bureaucratic Landscapes* (Cambridge, MA: MIT Press, 2003).

61. Jon Cannon, "Bargaining, Politics, and Law in Environmental Regulation," in *Environmental Contracts*, ed. Eric W. Orts and Kurt Deketelaere (Boston: Kluwer Law International, 2001), 39–70.

62. Martin A. Linsky, "The Media and Public Deliberation," in *The Power of Public Ideas*, ed. Robert Reich (Cambridge, MA: Ballinger, 1988).

63. The Congressional Review Act, passed in the spring of 1996, enables Congress to reject a rule if a "resolution of disapproval" gets a simple majority vote

in both houses of Congress and is signed by the president. The resolution must be introduced within sixty legislative days of the submission of a rule. As of June 2010, Congress had used its authority under the Congressional Review Act only once: in early 2001, it repealed an ergonomics rule, which established new workplace rules to combat repetitive stress injuries, issued by the Occupational Safety and Health Administration.

64. Eileen Braman, *Law, Politics, & Perception: How Policy Preferences Influence Legal Reasoning* (Charlottesville: University of Virginia Press, 2009); Frank B. Cross, *Decision Making in the U.S. Court of Appeals* (Stanford, CA: Stanford University Press, 2007); Cass R. Sunstein, David Schkade, Lisa M. Ellman, and Andres Sawicki, *Are Judges Political? An Empirical Analysis of the Federal Judiciary* (Washington, DC: Brookings Institution Press, 2006).

65. John D. Echeverria, personal communication, 2011.

66. Frank B. Cross and Emerson H. Tiller, "Judicial Partisanship and Obedience to Legal Doctrine: Whistleblowing on the Federal Court of Appeals," *Yale Law Journal* 107 (1998): 2155; Richard J. Pierce Sr., "Is Standing Law or Politics?" *North Carolina Law Review* 77 (June 1999): 1741; Richard Revesz, "Environmental Regulation, Ideology, and the D.C. Circuit," *Virginia Law Review* 83 (1997): 1717–1772; Christopher H. Schroeder and Robert Glicksman, "Chevron, State Farm, and EPA in the Courts of Appeals During the 1990s," *Environment Law Reporter* 31 (2001): 10371; Sidney A. Shapiro and Richard E. Levy, "Judicial Incentives and Indeterminacy in Substantive Review of Administrative Decisions," *Duke Law Journal* 44 (1995): 1051; Sunstein et al., *Are Judges Political?*.

67. Kingdon, *Agendas, Alternatives, and Public Policies*; Michael Mintrom and Sandra Vergari, "Advocacy Coalitions, Policy Entrepreneurs, and Policy Change," *Policy Studies Journal* 24 (1996): 420–434.

68. A. Campbell, *How Policies Make Citizens*; Hacker, "Privatizing Risk."

69. Streeck and Thelen, "Introduction," 8.

70. Mahoney and Thelen, "A Theory of Gradual Institutional Change."

71. Thelen, "How Institutions Evolve," 226.

72. Hacker, "Privatizing Risk," 246.

73. Ibid.

74. Mahoney and Thelen, "A Theory of Gradual Institutional Change."

75. Hacker "Privatizing Risk," citing Steven M. Teles.

76. Mark A. Smith, *The Right Talk: How Conservatives Transformed the Great Society Into the Economic Society* (Princeton, NJ: Princeton University Press, 2007).

77. Smith, *The Right Talk*, 41.

78. I have categorized these interviews by type in the chapter endnotes: EPA refers to an EPA official, DOI refers to an Interior Department official, ENV refers to an environmental activist, and CON refers to a conservative activist. For example, the citation EPA1 2009 denotes an interview held in 2009 with an

EPA official; EPA2 2009 denotes an interview held in 2009 with a different EPA official. The categories are imprecise; some former EPA officials, for example, now work as environmental activists or industry lobbyists. With a few exceptions, in the narrative that follows I quote informants by category, rather than by name.

79. Martin F. J. Taylor, Kieran Suckling, and Jeffrey T. Rachlinski, "The Effectiveness of the Endangered Species Act: A Quantitative Analysis," *Bioscience 55*, no. 4 (2005): 360–367. Note that I focus exclusively on domestic implementation of the Endangered Species Act, although the law also requires the wildlife agencies to participate in the Convention on International Trade in Endangered Species (CITES).

80. See Joel A. Mintz, *Enforcement at the EPA: High Stakes and Hard Choices* (Austin: University of Texas Press, 1995).

81. Alexander L. George and Andrew Bennett, *Case Studies and Theory Development in the Social Sciences* (Cambridge, MA: MIT Press, 2005); Alexander L. George and Timothy McKeown, "Case Studies and Theories of Organizational Decision Making," *Advances in Information Processing in Organizations* 2 (1985): 21–58.

82. John D. Leshy, "Natural Resource Policy," in *Natural Resources and the Environment*, ed. Paul R. Portney (Washington, DC: Urban Institute Press, 1984), 16.

## Chapter 3

1. John C. Whitaker, *Striking a Balance: Environment and Natural Resources Policy in the Nixon-Ford Years* (Washington, DC: AEI-Hoover Policy Studies, 1976).

2. Samuel P. Hays, *Beauty, Health, and Permanence: Environmental Politics in the United States, 1955–1985* (New York: Cambridge University Press, 1987), 27.

3. For an excellent history of U.S. environmental politics and policy prior to the 1960s, as well as its subsequent evolution, see Richard N. L. Andrews' *Managing the Environment, Managing Ourselves* (New Haven, CT: Yale University Press, 2006). On the rise of environmentalism in the United States, see Samuel P. Hays, *Beauty, Health and Permanence*.

4. Unless otherwise noted, all presidential quotations are drawn from the online database of presidential documents assembled by John Woolley and Gerhard Peters as part of the American Presidency Project at the University of California Santa Barbara. See http://www.presidency.ucsb.edu/ws/?pid_3731.

5. Quoted in David Bird, "Udall Says Nation Must Curb Growth to Spare Environment," *New York Times*, January 15, 1970.

6. Lynn E. Blais, "Beyond Cost Benefit: The Maturation of Economic Analysis of the Law and Its Consequences for Environmental Policymaking," *University of Illinois Law Review* 2000, no. 1 (2000): 237.

7. E. W. Kenworthy, "Citizen Lawsuits on Ecology Urged," *New York Times*, July 4, 1970.

8. Richard J. Lazarus, "The Tragedy of Distrust in the Implementation of Environmental Law," *Law & Contemporary Problems* 54, no. 4 (1991): 323.

9. Douglas Costle, paraphrased in Richard A. Harris and Sidney M. Milkis, *The Politics of Regulatory Change: A Tale of Two Agencies*, 2nd ed. (New York: Oxford University Press, 1996), 241.

10. Helen Ingram, "The Political Rationality of Innovation: The Clean Air Act Amendments of 1970," in *Approaches to Controlling Air Pollution*, ed. Anne F. Friedlander (Cambridge, MA: MIT Press, 1978), 14.

11. The first major biodiversity conservation law of this era was the 1972 Marine Mammal Protection Act (MMPA), which prohibited the "take" of marine mammals in U.S. waters by U.S. citizens on the high seas, and the importation of marine mammals and marine mammal products into the United States. Ultimately, the Endangered Species Act has had a broader impact than the MMPA, however, and so has been a more significant political target.

12. Jeanne Nienaber Clark and Daniel C. McCool, *Staking Out the Terrain: Power and Performance Among Natural Resource Agencies*, 2nd ed. (Albany: State University of New York Press, 1996).

13. Richard N. L. Andrews, *Managing the Environment, Managing Ourselves*; J. Brooks Flippen, *Nixon and the Environment* (Albuquerque: University of New Mexico Press, 2000); Hays, *Beauty, Health, and Permanence*; Whitaker, *Striking a Balance*.

14. Russell Train, *Politics, Pollution, and Pandas* (Washington, DC: Island Press, 2003), 79.

15. During the fall of 1970, a *New York Times* survey reported the environment was a key issue in twenty-five states. See Flippen, *Nixon and the Environment*.

16. Quoted in ibid., 149.

17. Elsie Carper, "Environment Made Football by Two Major Parties," *Washington Post*, September 21, 1972. The administration submitted a land-use bill to Congress, but conservatives gutted it with Nixon's acquiescence, and its original supporters backed away from it. See J. Brooks Flippen, *Conservative Conservationist* (Baton Rouge: Louisiana State University Press, 2006). The sulfur dioxide tax provoked heavy opposition, not just from the fossil fuel industry but also from environmentalists, who feared it would be used as a "license to pollute." See E. W. Kenworthy, "Nixon Plan to Tax Sulphur Content of Coal Meets Unexpected Opposition," *New York Times*, April 4, 1971.

18. Quoted in Flippen, *Nixon and the Environment*, 182.

19. Gladwin Hill, "The 'Offensive' Against the Environmental Agency," *New York Times*, August 6, 1971.

20. Joe Browder, "Decision-Making in the White House," in *Nixon and the Environment: The Politics of Devastation*, ed. James Rathlesberger (New York: Taurus Communications, Inc., 1973), 257–269; Flippen, *Nixon and the*

*Environment*; James Miller, "Air Pollution," in *Nixon and the Environment: The Politics of Devastation*, ed. James Rathlesberger (New York: Taurus Communications, Inc., 1973), 9–29; John Quarles, *Cleaning Up America: An Insider's View of the Environmental Protection Agency* (New York: Houghton Mifflin Company, 1976).

21. Quarles, *Cleaning Up America*, 142.

22. Nixon established the OMB in 1970. It replaced the Bureau of the Budget and greatly broadened the executive capacity for coordinating and controlling government policy.

23. Marc Allen Eisner, *Regulatory Politics in Transition*, 2nd ed. (Baltimore: Johns Hopkins University Press, 2000). In the summer of 1973, after Ruckelshaus left to head the FBI, Russell Train, the newly appointed EPA administrator, received written confirmation that he had ultimate authority over the content of EPA regulations. See Quarles, *Cleaning Up America*.

24. E. W. Kenworthy, "Nixon Gets the 'Message,' But Path Is Not Easy," *New York Times*, February 14, 1971.

25. Whitaker, *Striking a Balance*.

26. E. W. Kenworthy, "5 Programs under New Agency Listed for Double the Funds," *New York Times*, January 30, 1971.

27. E. W. Kenworthy, "Request for Antipollution Funds Is Lower than Was Authorized," *New York Times*, January 25 1972.

28. E. W. Kenworthy, "Ecological Retrenching," *New York Times*, January 17, 1973.

29. Lou Cannon, "Ecology Drive Draws Near Collision with Fiscal Barrier," *Washington Post*, February 14, 1973.

30. George C. Wilson, "Environmental Gains Threatened by Crisis," *Washington Post*, December 11, 1973.

31. Quarles, *Cleaning Up America*.

32. Train, *Politics, Pollution, and Pandas*.

33. As part of the Energy Supply and Coordination Act of 1974, however, Congress did extend the automobile emission-control deadlines for another year and granted the EPA administrator the discretion to delay them yet another year if warranted.

34. Flippen, *Conservative Conservationist*.

35. Quoted in Train, *Politics, Pollution, and Pandas*, 203–204.

36. Quoted in Flippen, *Conservative Conservationist*, 172.

37. Lewis Regenstein, "The Candidates and the Environment: An Analysis," *Washington Post*, October 19, 1975.

38. In January 1975, EPA administrator Train granted the automakers another one-year extension, concerned that the use of catalytic converters might create a new emission hazard: sulfates. Shortly thereafter, the "sulfate problem" all but disappeared, and General Motors acknowledged that its cars ran better and more

economically with a catalytic converter. See "The Fight Over Curbing Automobile Emissions," *National Journal*, January 1, 1977.

39. Train, *Politics, Pollution, and Pandas*, 232.

40. Joel A. Mintz, *Enforcement at the EPA: High Stakes and Hard Choices* (Austin: University of Texas Press, 1995).

41. R. Shep Melnick, *Regulation and the Courts: The Case of the Clean Air Act* (Washington, DC: Brookings Institution, 1983).

42. Quoted in "EPA Curb on Lead in Gas Upheld," Facts on File World News Digest, March 27, 1976. Contrary to popular perception, the great majority of lawsuits were brought by industry, not environmentalists. Environmentalists were strategic in their litigation, however, choosing cases to affect general problems of rulemaking and administrative policy. See Hays, *Beauty, Health, and Permanence*. They also brought as many cases as possible to the D.C. Circuit, which came to be identified as proenvironment. Regardless of which side sued, the government won the majority of cases in which it was the defendant (63 percent against industry and 62 percent against environmentalists) between 1970 and 1982. See Lettie M. Wenner, "Judicial Oversight of Environmental Deregulation," in *Environmental Policy in the 1980s: Reagan's New Agenda*, ed. Norman J. Vig and Michael E. Kraft (Washington, DC: CQ Press, 1984), 181–199.

43. The district court concluded that Congress had intended a policy of nondegradation, so that industries would not simply move to clean-air regions to avoid investing in pollution control equipment. The D.C. Circuit upheld the decision without writing an opinion. The Supreme Court reviewed the case but split 4–4, leaving the lower court decision intact. Ruckelshaus had modified Clean Air Act regulations to disallow significant deterioration, but the revised rules, due to be issued in late June 1971, were never released. Environmentalists alleged that the OMB had stopped the nondegradation clause. See E. W. Kenworthy, "Air Standards: Should They Make Things Worse?" *New York Times*, June 4, 1972.

44. Quoted in Steven M. Teles, *The Rise of the Conservative Legal Movement: The Battle for Control of the Law* (Princeton, NJ: Princeton University Press, 2008), 55.

45. Jack McWethy, "After Setbacks—New Tactics in Environmental Crusade," *U.S. News & World Report*, June 6, 1975.

46. "The Environmental Complex," Heritage Foundation Report, November 1977.

47. McWethy, "After Setbacks"; "The Environmental Complex."

48. "A Turn in the Tide—Pollution Battle Being Won," *U.S. News & World Report*, August 4, 1975.

49. For the sake of comprehensibility, the narrative that follows is linear and relatively orderly, but—as historian Gregory Schneider reminds us—"Rancorous disputes over how to translate ideas into action dominate any social or political movement," and the conservative movement was no exception. See Gregory L. Schneider, ed., *Conservatism in America since 1930* (New York: New York University Press, 2003), 2. Journalist Lee Edwards provides a lively account of the

various setbacks and struggles the inchoate movement endured. That said, he expresses little doubt that by the late 1970s conservatives of various stripes considered themselves part of a movement. See Lee Edwards, *The Conservative Revolution: The Movement That Remade America* (New York: Free Press, 1999). In his foreword to James Roberts' book, *The Conservative Decade*, Ronald Reagan contends, "As a rule you won't find references to the conservative movement in the *New York Times* or the *Washington Post*. But with few exceptions, the people involved—whether they're members of Congress or congressional staffs, whether they write for conservative periodicals or the general mass media, whether they work in 'think tanks' or universities or the many issue-oriented conservative organizations—view themselves as being part of a movement." See Ronald Reagan, "Forward," [sic] in James C. Roberts, *The Conservative Decade: Emerging Leaders of the 1980s* (Westport, CT: Arlington House Publishers, 1980), viii.

50. For a discussion of how conservative businessmen who opposed the New Deal gravitated toward the ideas of Austrian economists Friedrich von Hayek and Ludwig von Mises, see Kim Phillips-Fein, *Invisible Hands: The Businessmen's Crusade Against the New Deal* (New York: W. W. Norton, 2009).

51. George H. Nash, *The Conservative Intellectual Movement in America since 1945* (New York: Basic Books. 1976), xiii.

52. Ibid.

53. Richard Hofstadter, "The Paranoid Style in American Politics," *Harper's*, November 1964, 81.

54. Sidney Blumenthal, *The Rise of the Counter-Establishment: From Conservative Ideology to Political Power* (New York: Times Books, 1986).

55. Edwards, *Conservative Revolution*, 80.

56. Nash, *Conservative Intellectual Movement*.

57. Chip Berlet, "The New Political Right in the United States: Reaction, Rollback, and Resentment," in *Confronting the New Conservatism: The Rise of the Right in America*, ed. Michael J. Thompson (New York: New York University Press, 2007), 71–106.

58. Ted V. McAllister, "Reagan and the Transformation of American Conservatism," in *The Reagan Presidency: Pragmatic Conservatism and Its Legacies*, ed. W. Elliot Brownlee and Hugh Davis Graham (Lawrence: University of Kansas Press, 2003), 40–60. As McAllister points out, however, that resolution was uneasy. "The American right," he says, "is caught in a dialectic struggle between the primacy of the group and the primacy of the individual, between the call to Return and the lure of Progress" (43).

59. Nash, *Conservative Intellectual Movement*, 319. As Nash explains, "There was a fascinating heterogeneity in conservative thought, yet most right-wing intellectuals readily agreed on certain fundamental 'prejudices' . . .; a presumption in favor of private property and a free enterprise economy; opposition to Communism, socialism, and utopian schemes of all kinds; support of strong national defense; belief in Christianity or Judaism (or at least the utility of

such belief); acceptance of traditional morality and the need for an inelastic moral code; hostility to positivism and relativism; a 'gut affirmation' of the goodness of America and the West. These were but a few constituent elements of the working conservative consensus." See Nash, *Conservative Intellectual Movement*, 342.

60. Blaine Harden, "The Editor Who Claims to Think Like a President," *Washington Post Magazine*, July 11, 1982; Dan Morgan, "Getting Our Ideology in the Wall Street Journal," *Washington Post*, February 15, 1981.

61. Ibid.

62. Edwards, *Conservative Revolution*.

63. Alice O'Connor, "Financing the Counterrevolution," in *Rightward Bound: Making American Conservative in the 1970s*, ed. Bruce J. Schulman and Julian E. Zelizer (Cambridge, MA: Harvard University Press, 2008), 148–168.

64. David Callahan, "Liberal Policy's Weak Foundations," *The Nation*, November 13, 1995; Alfred S. Regnery, *Upstream: The Ascendance of American Conservatism* (New York: Threshold Editions, 2008); Beth Schulman, "Foundations for a Movement: How the Right Wing Subsidizes Its Press," *Extra! Newsletter of Fairness and Accuracy in Reporting*, March/April 1995.

65. Callahan,"Liberal Policy's Weak Foundations"; Jean Hardisty, *Mobilizing Resentment: Conservative Resurgence from the John Birch Society to the Promise Keepers* (Boston: Beacon Press, 1999).

66. George E. Jones, K. M. Chrysler, and Carey W. English, "The Conservative Network: How It Plans to Keep on Winning," *U.S. News & World Report*, July 20, 1981.

67. Phillips-Fein, *Invisible Hands*.

68. John Stefancik and Richard Delgado, *No Mercy: How Conservative Think Tanks and Foundations Changed America's Social Agenda* (Philadelphia: Temple University Press, 1996).

69. Mission statements were drawn from organizations' Web pages. See http://www.aei.org/about/; http://www.heritage.org/about; http://www.cato.org/about.php; and http://reason.org/about/.

70. Donald T. Critchlow, *The Conservative Ascendancy: How the GOP Right Made Political History* (Cambridge, MA: Harvard University Press, 2007).

71. Initially, *The Public Interest*—founded by Daniel Bell and Irving Kristol—was a forum for a variety of views. In the early 1970s, however, Bell left the magazine and it became a more reliably conservative outlet.

72. Andrew Rich and R. Kent Weaver, "Advocates and Analysts: Think Tanks and the Politicization of Expertise," in *Interest Group Politics*, 5th ed., ed. Allan J. Cigler and Burdett A. Loomis (Washington, DC: CQ Press, 1998), 235–253.

73. Donald T. Critchlow, *The Conservative Ascendancy: How the GOP Right Made Political History* (Cambridge, MA: Harvard University Press, 2007), 122.

74. Phillips-Fein, *Invisible Hands*.

75. Matthew N. Lyons, "Business Conflict and Right-Wing Movements," in *Unraveling the Right: The New Conservatism in American Thought and Politics*, ed. Amy E. Ansell (Boulder, CO: Westview Press, 1998).

76. Gladwin Hill, "Man and His Environment: Some Basic Facts about a Growing National Problem," *New York Times*, April 20, 1970.

77. Quoted in Joseph G. Peschek, *Policy-Planning Organizations: Elite Agendas and America's Rightward Turn* (Philadelphia: Temple University Press, 1987), 190.

78. Ibid., 190–191.

79. The chamber became more aggressively political around 1977 and subsequently expanded rapidly, going from only 100,000 members in 1980 to 250,000 by 1982. See Ann Crittenden, "A Stubborn Chamber of Commerce Roils the Waters," *New York Times*, June 27, 1982.

80. Phillips-Fein, *Invisible Hands*.

81. David Vogel, "The Power of Business in America: A Reappraisal," *British Journal of Political Science* 13 (January 1983): 19–43, cited in Peschek, *Policy-Planning Organizations*, 64.

82. Philip Shabecoff, "Big Business on the Offensive," *New York Times Magazine*, December 9, 1979. Data collected by political scientist Kay Lehman Schlozman confirms that while that there was an explosion in the number of public interest, civil rights, and social welfare organizations between 1960 and 1980, there was an even greater increase in the representation of business. As a result, "For all organizations having representation in Washington, the proportion representing the interests of business rose from 57 percent to 72 percent [between 1960 and 1980]. The proportion of public interest groups decreased from 9 percent to 5 percent of all organizations, and the proportion representing labor plummeted from 11 percent to 2 percent." See Kay Lehman Schlozman, "What Accent the Heavenly Chorus? Political Equality and the American Pressure System," *Journal of Politics* 46, no. 4 (November 1984): 1021.

83. Richard J. Lazarus, *The Making of Environmental Law* (Chicago: University of Chicago Press, 2004).

84. John B. Judis, *The Paradox of American Democracy: Elites, Special Interests, and the Betrayal of Public Trust* (New York: Pantheon Books, 2000).

85. Karen Dewitt, "More Concerns Sponsor Political-Education Plans," *New York Times*, March 3, 1980.

86. John S. Saloma III, *Ominous Politics: The New Conservative Labyrinth* (New York: Hill and Wang, 1984), 72.

87. Bethany E. Moreton, "Make Payroll, Not War," in *Rightward Bound: Making America Conservative in the 1970s*, ed. Bruce J. Schulman and Julian E. Zelizer (Cambridge MA: Harvard University Press, 2008), 52–70; Roberts, *The Conservative Decade*.

88. Jerry M. Flint, "Auto Industry, Changing Strategies, Opens Counterattack on Environmental and Co.," *New York Times*, November 18, 1970; Jerry M. Flint, "Auto Men Assail Air Quality Rules," *New York Times*, March 17, 1971;

Jerry M. Flint, "G.M. Cites Gains in Clean-Air Cars," *New York Times*, January 11, 1973.

89. Quoted in Flint, "Auto Industry, Changing Strategies."

90. Quarles, *Cleaning Up America*.

91. Ibid.

92. E. W. Kenworthy, "Concerns and Doubts over the Nixon Program," *New York Times*, February 15, 1970; Wilson, "Environmental Gains Threatened"; Margot Hornblower, "Decade-Long Regulation vs. Inflation Fight Continues," *Washington Post*, January 2, 1979.

93. Phillips-Fein, *Invisible Hands*, 166.

94. To read the complete memo, see http://reclaimdemocracy.org/corporate _accountability/powell_memo_lewis.html.

95. George Lakoff, *Moral Politics: What Conservatives Know That Liberals Don't* (Chicago: University of Chicago Press, 1996).

96. Phillips-Fein, *Invisible Hands*, 178.

97. The "new class" was first described in a 1965 book by M. Stanton Evans, *The Liberal Establishment*. According to Evans, the "liberal establishment" was the consequence of a liberal education in the American academy, where students were taught the characteristic liberal ideas of centralized power, "accommodation" of foreign adversaries, moral relativism, and the conviction that anyone who disagreed with those views was ignorant. Ultimately, Evans concluded, the liberal establishment was an enemy of freedom.

98. William E. Simon, *A Time for Truth* (New York: Reader's Digest Press, 1978), 5.

99. Norman Podhoretz, "The New Defenders of Capitalism," *Harvard Business Review*, March–April (1981), 96.

100. Quoted in Peschek, *Policy-Planning Organizations*, 229.

101. Mark A. Smith, *The Right Talk: How Conservatives Transformed the Great Society into the Economic Society* (Princeton, NJ: Princeton University Press, 2007), 77.

102. Peschek, *Policy-Planning Organizations*. In 1977, the American Enterprise Institute began publishing the journal *Regulation*, which was replete with articles critical of the EPA, the Occupational Health and Safety Administration, and other regulatory agencies.

103. Peschek, *Policy-Planning Organizations*, 203, 205.

104. Hardisty, *Mobilizing Resistance*; Peschek, *Policy-Planning Organizations*; Smith, *Right Talk*. For example, journalist Thomas Frank attributes Republicans' electoral success to campaigns built around social and cultural issues. See Thomas Frank, *What's the Matter with Kansas?: How Conservatives Won the Heart of America* (New York: Metropolitan Books, 2004). But political scientist Mark Smith finds that in six of eight presidential elections between 1976 and 2004, Republicans benefited most from the public perception that they would be better on the economy. See Smith, *Right Talk*. They probably both have a point:

politicians—particularly those running for national office—were reluctant to deliver speeches on social issues. Fund-raisers and party activists were less cautious, however.

105. Alan Ehrenhalt, "The Right in Congress: Seeking a Strategy," *Congressional Quarterly Weekly Report*, August 5, 1978, 2022–2028.

106. Lisa McGirr, *Suburban Warriors: The Origins of the New American Right* (Princeton, NJ: Princeton University Press, 2001).

107. Regnery, *Upstream*; Roberts, *Conservative Decade.*

108. Nash, *Conservative Intellectual Movement*, 294.

109. The Democrats retained the majority, however: 248–187.

110. George Packer, "The Fall of Conservatism," *New Yorker*, May 26, 2008, 47–55.

111. Edwards, *Conservative Revolution*; Regnery, *Upstream.*

112. Quoted in Critchlow, *Conservative Ascendancy*, 103.

113. Alan Crawford, *Thunder on the Right: The "New Right" and the Politics of Resentment* (New York: Pantheon Books, 1980).

114. Lawrence Martin, "U.S. Veers Toward the Right on Anti-Government Wave," *Globe and Mail*, December 28, 1978.

115. Richard A. Viguerie, *The New Right: We're Ready to Lead* (Falls Church, VA: The Viguerie Company, 1981).

116. Paul L. Martin, "The Conservatives' Drive for a Stronger Voice," *U.S. News & World Report*, July 11, 1977.

117. "The New Right's Strong Ambition Is Fueled by Huge Mail Campaign," *New York Times*, December 4, 1977.

118. Crawford, *Thunder on the Right*; Packer, "Fall of Conservatism." Conservative activist and author James Roberts dismisses strong distinctions between the Old Right and the New Right. The terms have meaning only in a chronological sense, he asserts; on matters of principle, there is little to distinguish the two. See Roberts, *Conservative Decade.*

119. Viguerie may be referring to the use of direct mail in a national campaign. California congressman Henry Waxman used direct-mail solicitation in his campaign for state assemblymen in the 1970s.

120. Quoted in Crawford, *Thunder on the Right*, 166.

121. Exploiting a loophole in the campaign finance laws that put no limit on the amount a group could spend *against* a candidate, in 1978–1979, the NCPAC spent $8.5 million on attack ads—more than any other nonparty organization. Some funders worried about the "incitement strategy" of the New Right. "Without the New Right, the Republicans could not be elected," said Leslie Levkowsky of the Smith Richardson Foundation. "With it, they may not be able to govern." Quoted in Jones, Chrysler, and English, "The Conservative Network."

122. Viguerie, *New Right.*

123. Adam Clymer, *Drawing the Line at the Big Ditch: The Panama Canal Treaties and the Rise of the Right* (Lawrence: University of Kansas, 2008).

124. Saloma, *Ominous Politics*, 81.

125. Ehrenhalt, "The Right in Congress," 2022.

126. Francis J. Flaherty, "Right-Wing Firms Pick Up Steam," *National Law Journal* (1983), 1.

127. Jeffrey Rosen, "The Unregulated Offensive," *New York Times Magazine*, April 17, 2005.

128. Quoted in A. O. Sulzberger, "The Naderites on the Other Side," *New York Times*, September 30, 1979.

129. Quoted in James W. Singer, "Liberal Public Interest Law Firms Face Budgetary, Ideological Challenges," *National Journal*, December 8, 1979, 2052.

130. Teles, *Rise of the Conservative Legal Movement*.

131. "The Horowitz Report," *Wall Street Journal*, March 19, 1981; Saloma, *Ominous Politics*.

132. Nevertheless, the liberal public interest law firms dwarfed the conservative ones. In 1983, there were some 120 liberal public interest law firms with 700 attorneys and an annual budget of $50 million. By contrast, there were about 20 conservative public interest law firms with 100 lawyers and an annual budget of $15 million. See Flaherty, "Right-Wing Firms."

133. Saloma, *Ominous Politics*; Teles, *Rise of the Conservative Legal Movement*.

134. Henry Manne, "Foreword," in *The Attack on Corporate America: The Corporate Issues Sourcebook*, ed. Bruce M. Johnson (New York: McGraw-Hill Book Company, 1978), xiii.

135. Ibid.

136. Larry Ruff, "The Economic Common Sense of Pollution," *The Public Interest* (Spring 1970), 69–85; A. Myrick Freeman III and Robert H. Haveman, "Clean Rhetoric and Dirty Water," *Public Interest* 28 (Summer 1972), 51–65; Lawrence White, "The Auto Pollution Muddle," *Public Interest* 32 (Summer 1973), 97–112.

137. Allen V. Kneese and Charles L. Schultze, *Pollution, Prices, and Public Policy* (Washington, DC: Brookings Institution, 1975), 1.

138. Frederick R. Anderson, Allen V. Kneese, Phillip D. Reed, Russell B. Stevenson, and Serge Taylor, *Environmental Improvement through Economic Incentives* (Baltimore: Johns Hopkins University Press/Resources for the Future, 1977).

139. Thomas O. McGarity, Sidney Shapiro, and David Bollier, *Sophisticated Sabotage: The Intellectual Games Used to Subvert Responsible Regulation* (Washington, DC: Environmental Law Institute, 2004).

140. Quoted in Edwin L. Dale Jr., "White House Aide Criticizes Heavy 'Social Cost' of Environmentalists' Goals," *New York Times*, April 20, 1971.

141. Lewis J. Perl, "Ecology's Missing Price Tag," *Wall Street Journal*, August 10, 1976.

142. Lewis J. Perl, "How to Talk Business to the E.P.A.," *New York Times*, January 29, 1978.

143. Murray L. Weidenbaum and Robert DeFina, "The Costs of Federal Regulation of Economic Activity," Reprint No. 88 (Washington, DC: American Enterprise Institute, 1978); Murray L. Weidenbaum, "On Estimating Regulatory Costs," *Regulation* (May/June 1978).

144. Murray L. Weidenbaum, *The Future of Business Regulation: Private Action and Public Demand* (New York: Amacom, 1979), 5, v.

145. "Questions on Environment," *Wall Street Journal*, February 16, 1970.

146. Irving Kristol, "The Environmentalist Crusade," *Wall Street Journal*, December 16, 1974.

147. Irving Kristol, "The Hidden Costs of Regulation," *Wall Street Journal*, January 12, 1977.

148. "A 'Tough' Bill," *Wall Street Journal*, July 5, 1972.

149. "A Most Important Review," *Wall Street Journal*, July 23, 1973.

150. "EPA's Clean Air Proposal," *Wall Street Journal*, August 20, 1974.

151. Karen Elliott House, "Lost in a Smog Bank," *Wall Street Journal*, January 16, 1976.

152. John Maddox, *The Doomsday Syndrome* (New York: Macmillan, 1972), 5.

153. Melvin J. Grayson and Thomas R. Shepard Jr., *The Disaster Lobby: Prophets of Ecological Doom and Other Absurdities* (Chicago: Follett Publishing Company, 1973), 3–4, 7, 9–10, 12–13.

154. Kristol, "The Environmentalist Crusade."

155. William Tucker, "Environmentalism and the Leisure Class," *Harper's*, December 1977, 49–56, 73–80.

156. William E. Leuchtenburg, "Jimmy Carter and the Post–New Deal Presidency," in *The Carter Presidency: Policy Choices in the Post–New Deal Era*, ed. Gary M. Fink and Hugh Davis Graham (Lawrence: University of Kansas Press, 1998), 7–28.

157. Howard Gold, *Hollow Mandates: American Public Opinion and the Conservative Shift* (Boulder, CO: Westview Press, 1992), 27.

158. Gladwin Hill, "Conservationists Expecting Carter to Open New Era for Environment," *New York Times*, November 5, 1976.

159. Quoted in Philip Shabecoff, "Carter Record Mixed on the Environment," *New York Times*, January 3, 1978.

160. Quoted in Margot Hornblower, "New Chief of EPA Promises Tough Anti-Pollution Stance," *Washington Post*, April 12, 1977.

161. U.S. Environmental Protection Agency, "Douglas M. Costle: Oral History Interview," EPA 202-K-01–002 (2001). See http://www.epa.gov/history/publications/print/costle.html.

162. Quoted in Ron Arnold, *At the Eye of the Storm: James Watt and the Environmentalists* (Chicago: Regnery Gateway, 1982), 94.

163. Quoted in Margot Hornblower, "A New Breed Shakes Old Order at Interior Dept.," *Washington Post*, April 3, 1977.

164. Jeffrey K. Stine, "Environmental Policy Choices During the Carter Presidency," in *The Carter Presidency: Policy Choices in the Post–New Deal Era*, ed. Gary M. Fink and Hugh Davis Graham (Lawrence: University of Kansas Press, 1998), 184.

165. Carter's avowed environmental concern notwithstanding, the topic received almost no mention in his 600-page memoir, *Keeping Faith*.

166. David Gelman, James Doyne, Michael J. Sniffen, Phyllis Malamud, and Gerald C. Lubenow, "Is America Turning Right?" *Newsweek*, November 7, 1977.

167. Mary Russell, "'Liberal' Democratic House is Surprisingly Conservative," *Washington Post*, July 5, 1977; Michael J. Malbin, "New Democrats Don't See Eye to Eye With Their Senior Comrades," *National Journal*, July 9, 1977, 1080.

168. Frank K. Armour, Joseph Ives, George F. Polzer, Floyd Stiles, and S. L. Terry, Testimony before the Subcommittee on Environmental Pollution of the Committee on Environment and Public Works, United States Senate, 95th Congress, First Session on S. 251, S. 252, and S. 253, bill to amend the Clean Air Act, as amended, February 10–11, 1977, Serial No. 95-H7.

169. Quoted in Margot Hornblower, "Decade-Long Regulation vs. Inflation Fight Continues," *Washington Post*, January 2, 1979.

170. Ibid.

171. Quoted in Bill Richards and Helen Dewar, "EPA Is Pressed to Relax Clean Air Rules in Fight on Inflation," *Washington Post*, June 17, 1978.

172. Timothy B. Clark, "Carter's Assault on the Costs of Regulation," *National Journal*, August 12, 1978.

173. In setting the new standard, Costle changed the basis for the standard from photochemical oxidant to ozone, the principal measurable ingredient in smog. Ozone is not emitted directly; it is a product of a series of complex reactions that occur when hydrocarbons and nitrogen oxides are exposed to sunlight. Costle also insisted that cost was not a factor in setting the standard.

174. Quoted in Margot Hornblower, "EPA Set to Ease Smog Standards for Urban Areas," *Washington Post*, January 21, 1979.

175. Robert W. Crandall and Lester Lave, "The Cost of Controlling Smog," *Washington Post*, January 6, 1979.

176. Larry Kramer, "Tougher Clean-Air Rule," *Washington Post*, September 12, 1978.

177. Margot Hornblower, "EPA Issues Rules on Power Plant Coal Emissions," *Washington Post*, May 26, 1979; Dick Kirschten, "Politics at the Heart of the Clean Air Debate," *National Journal*, May 19, 1979. Btus are British thermal units, a measure of the energy content of fuel.

178. Quoted in Bayard Webster, "U.S. Said to Delay Action on Endangered Species," *New York Times*, December 30, 1975.

179. "The Furbish Lousewort," *Wall Street Journal*, November 12, 1976.

180. Les Gapay, "Will the Protection of Animals, Plants Peril Homo Sapiens?" *Wall Street Journal*, January 9, 1976.

181. P. J. Wingate, "Of Snail Darters and Diamondback Rattlers," *Wall Street Journal*, July 6, 1978.

182. "Scopes Prosecution Vindicated," *Wall Street Journal*, June 16, 1978.

183. "Unnatural Selection," *Wall Street Journal*, October 2, 1978.

184. Margot Hornblower, "Wildlife Species Act Endangers Projects," *Washington Post*, July 21, 1977.

185. Quoted in Charles Mohr, "Hearings Open on Amending the Endangered Species Act," *New York Times*, April 14, 1978.

186. Quoted in Ward Sinclair, "'Pork Panic' Sweeping Congress in Wake of Darter's Rescue," *Washington Post*, June 28, 1978.

187. D. Noah Greenwald, Kieran F. Suckling, and Martin Taylor, "The Listing Record," in *The Endangered Species Act at Thirty: Renewing the Conservation Promise*, ed. Dale D. Goble, J. Michael Scott, and Frank W. Davis (Washington, DC: Island Press, 2006), 51–67; J. Michael Scott, Dale D. Goble, Leona K. Svancara, and Anna Pidgorna, "By the Numbers," in Goble, Scott, and Davis, *The Endangered Species Act at Thirty*, 16–35.

188. Quoted in Philip Shabecoff, "Interior Dept. Assailed on Missing a Deadline for Species Protection," *New York Times*, November 7, 1979.

189. After failing several times to win congressional approval for overruling the God Squad decision, in late 1979, proponents of the Tellico Dam succeeded in attaching a rider to the energy and water development appropriations bill mandating its completion and exempting it from the Endangered Species Act and all other environmental laws. Carter infuriated environmentalists by signing the bill.

190. Quoted in John C. Barrow, "An Age of Limits: Jimmy Carter and the Quest for a National Energy Policy," in *The Carter Presidency: Policy Choices in the Post–New Deal Era*," ed. Gary M. Fink and Hugh Davis Graham (Lawrence: University of Kansas Press, 1998), 163.

191. Bruce J. Schulman, *The Seventies* (New York: Free Press, 2001), 127.

192. Ibid.

193. Peter Goldman, James Doyle, Thomas M. DeFrank, Eleanor Clift, and Gerald C. Lubnow, "The New Tilt," *Newsweek*, November 20, 1978.

194. Quoted in ibid.

195. Mintz, *Enforcement at the EPA*.

196. Hays, *Beauty, Health, and Permanence*, 59.

197. Quoted in Timothy B. Clark, "The Year of Regulation," *National Journal*, January 20, 1979.

198. Quoted in Leuchtenburg, "Jimmy Carter," 16.

199. Quoted in "Washington Regulators Do Some Tightening of Their Own Belts," *Chemical Week*, November 8, 1978.

200. Phillip J. Cooper, *The War against Regulation: From Jimmy Carter to George W. Bush* (Lawrence: University Press of Kansas, 2009), 27.

201. Quoted in Margot Hornblower, "White House to Propose 'Regulatory Experiment Bill," *Washington Post*, February 7, 1979.

202. Quoted in Harris and Milkis, *Politics of Regulatory Change*, 250.

203. Quoted in Peter Nulty, "A Brave Experiment in Pollution Control," *Business Week*, February 12, 1979, 120–123.

204. Quoted in Timothy B. Clark, "New Approaches to Regulatory Reform—Letting the Market Do the Job," *National Journal*, August 11, 1979, 1316.

205. The Natural Resources Defense Council successfully challenged the netting program in the lower courts, but in 1984, the Supreme Court reversed those rulings in *Chevron v. Natural Resources Defense Council*. The netting program eventually became the most widely used element of the EPA's trading portfolio.

206. Martin Crutsinger, "EPA Girds for Reagan, Congressional Assault on Clean Air Act," Associated Press, October 18, 1980.

207. Richard L. Lesher, "Getting the Overkill Out of Environmental Regulation," *National Journal*, September 29, 1979, 1625.

208. Quarles, *Cleaning Up America*, 58.

209. "Earth Choice," *Wall Street Journal*, April 22, 1980.

210. Norman J. Vig and Michael E. Kraft, "Environmental Policy from the Seventies to the Eighties," in *Environmental Policy in the 1980s: Reagan's New Agenda*, ed. Norman J. Vig and Michael E. Kraft (Washington, DC: CQ Press, 1984), 3–26.

211. Michael E. Kraft, "U.S. Environmental Policy and Politics: From the 1960s to the 1990s," *Journal of Policy History* 12, no. 1 (2000): 17–39.

212. Hornblower, "Decade-Long Inflation Fight Continues."

213. Keith Schneider, "The Environment: The Public Wants More Protection, Not Less," *National Journal*, March 26, 1983.

214. Robert A. Jones, "U.S. Environmental Efforts Face Erosion," *Los Angeles Times*, November 25, 1979.

215. Gladwin Hill, "Environmentalists Unafraid of Conservative Trend," *New York Times*, February 5, 1979.

216. Alfred Marcus, "EPA's Successes and Failures," in *Controversies in Environmental Policy*, ed. Sheldon Kamieniecki, Robert O'Brien, and Michael Clarke (Abany: State University of New York Press, 1986), 153–173.

217. McAllister, "Reagan and the Transformation," 47.

## Chapter 4

1. Theodore White, "Summing Up," *New York Times Magazine*, April 25, 1982. The figures supplied by White are inaccurate. He says the *Federal Register* went from 54,482 pages in 1970 to 87,012 pages in 1980. According to the Office of the Federal Register, the actual number of pages was 20,036 in 1970 and 87,012 in 1980.

2. George C. Eads and Michael Fix, *Relief or Reform? Reagan's Regulatory Dilemma* (Washington, DC: Urban Institute Press, 1984), 87.

3. Lester B. Lave and Gilbert S. Omenn, *Clearing the Air: Reforming the Clean Air Act* (Washington, DC: Brookings Institution, 1981).

4. Robert W. Crandall, *Controlling Industrial Pollution: The Economics and Politics of Clean Air* (Washington, DC: Brookings Institution, 1983).

5. "Breathing Easier," *Wall Street Journal*, August 25, 1981.

6. Quoted in Edwin McDowell, "OSHA, E.P.A.: The Heydey is Over," *New York Times*, January 4, 1981.

7. Eugene Bardach and Robert A. Kagan, *Going by the Book: The Problem of Regulatory Unreasonableness* (Philadelphia: Temple University Press, 1982).

8. R. Shep Melnick, *Regulation and the Courts: The Case of the Clean Air Act* (Washington, DC: Brookings Institution, 1983), 343.

9. Ibid., 344.

10. John Quarles, "Its Goals Safe, EPA Must Tend to Valid Beefs," *Wall Street Journal*, May 5, 1983.

11. John Quarles, "Congress Must Decide Soon on Clean Air Act," *Wall Street Journal*, September 16, 1981.

12. Ronald Taylor, "In Clean Air Drive, A Pause to Help Industry," *U.S. News & World Report*, December 15, 1980.

13. Merrill Brown, "Regulatory 'Balance' May Shift to Dismantlers," *Washington Post*, January 11, 1981.

14. Alfred Marcus, "EPA's Successes and Failures," in *Controversies in Environmental Policy*, ed. Sheldon Kamieniecki, Robert O'Brien, and Michael Clarke (Abany: State University of New York Press, 1986), 153–173.

15. Ibid.

16. Lawrence Mosher, "Environmentalists Question Whether to Retreat or Stay on the Offensive," *National Journal*, December 30, 1980, 2116.

17. Henry C. Kenski and Helen M. Ingram, "The Reagan Administration and Environmental Regulation: The Constraint of the Political Market," in *Controversies in Environmental Policy*, ed. Sheldon Kamieniecki, Robert O'Brien, and Michael Clark (Albany: State University of New York Press, 1986), 275–299.

18. Richard N. L. Andrews, "Deregulation: The Failure at EPA," in *Environmental Policy in the 1980s: Reagan's New Agenda*, ed. Norman J. Vig and Michael E. Kraft (Washington, DC: CQ Press, 1984), 161–180; Stephen Breyer, *Regula-*

*tion and Its Reform* (Cambridge, MA: Harvard University Press, 1982); Lou Cannon, *President Reagan: The Role of a Lifetime* (New York: Simon & Schuster, 1991); Robert W. Crandall and Paul R. Portney, "Environmental Policy," in *Natural Resources and the Environment: The Reagan Approach*, ed. Paul R. Portney (Washington, DC: Urban Institute Press, 1984), 47–81; Eads and Fix, *Relief or Reform*; Robert E. Litan and William D. Nordhaus, *Reforming Federal Regulation* (New Haven, CT: Yale University Press, 1983); Philip Shabecoff, "Environmental Action Enters New Era," *New York Times*, January 20, 1981.

19. Crandall and Portney, "Environmental Policy."

20. Charles Wolf Jr., "A Theory of Nonmarket Failure: Framework for Implementation Analysis," *Journal of Law and Economics* 22, no. 1 (1979): 107–139. The typical rationale for regulation is "market failure." Wolf argued that government action to address market failure could distort behavior with results even more pernicious than those caused by the original market failure.

21. Peter H. Aranson, "Pollution Control: The Case for Competition," in *Instead of Regulation*, ed. Robert W. Poole Jr. (Lexington, MA: Lexington Books, 1982), 339–393.

22. Aaron Wildavsky, "Richer is Safer," *Public Interest* (Summer 1980), 23–39.

23. Julian L. Simon, *The Ultimate Resource* (Princeton, NJ: Princeton University Press, 1981), 3.

24. Ibid., 345.

25. Edwin J. Feulner, "Foreword," in *Mandate for Leadership*, ed. Charles Heatherly (Washington, DC: Heritage Foundation, 1981), viii.

26. James E. Hinish Jr., "Regulatory Reform: An Overview," in Heatherly, *Mandate for Leadership*, 697, 698, 700.

27. Louis J. Cordia, "Environmental Protection Agency," in Heatherly, *Mandate for Leadership*, 1023.

28. "Clean Air Act Is Given Backing of Federal Panel," *Wall Street Journal*, March 3, 1981.

29. "Clean Air Realism," *Wall Street Journal*, December 31, 1981.

30. "Clean Air Inertia," *Wall Street Journal*, April 5, 1982, 1982.

31. "Clean Air Farce," *Wall Street Journal*, December 15, 1982.

32. According to political scientist Jacqueline Vaughn Switzer, a Nevada journalist coined the term "Sagebrush Rebellion," which is typically applied to activity undertaken from 1978 to 1981. See Jacqueline Vaughn Switzer, *Green Backlash: The History and Politics of Environmental Opposition in the U.S.* (Boulder, CO: Lynne Rienner Publishers, 1997).

33. Charles E. Wilkinson, *Crossing the Next Meridian: Land, Water, and the Future of the West* (Washington, DC: Island Press, 1993).

34. Robert H. Nelson, *Public Lands and Private Rights* (Lanham, MD: Rowman & Littlefield, 1995).

35. R. McGreggor Cawley, *Federal Land, Western Anger: The Sagebrush Rebellion and Environmental Politics* (Lawrence: University Press of Kansas, 1993).

36. Switzer, *Green Backlash.*

37. There was no national leadership or formal administrative structure for the rebellion. The only national meeting occurred in 1980, at a conference sponsored by the League for the Advancement of States' Rights. See Cawley, *Federal Land, Western Anger.*

38. Lou Cannon, "Governors Sense New U.S. Mood on Environment," *Washington Post*, March 1, 1977.

39. John Herbers, "West Taking South's Place as Most Alienated Area," *New York Times*, March 18, 1979.

40. Cawley, *Federal Land, Western Anger*, 14.

41. Lou Cannon, *Reagan* (New York: G.P. Putnam's Sons, 1982), 358.

42. Quoted in ibid., 358.

43. Lee Edwards, *Conservative Revolution: The Movement That Remade America* (New York: Free Press, 1999), 22.

44. Robert L. Terrell, "The Department of the Interior," in Heatherly, *Mandate for Leadership*, 380.

45. White, "Summing Up," 75.

46. Burton Yale Pines, "The Ten Legacies of Reagan," *Policy Review*, April 1, 1989. Murray Weidenbaum described Reagan's philosophy in more technical terms, as an artful fusing of individual liberty and economic efficiency: "[T]he basic objective of Reaganomics is to shift the balance of power between the Government and the rest of society. In its fundamentals, that shift is to be accomplished by slowing down the growth rate of Federal spending, cutting tax rates, curtailing the burden of regulation and reducing the growth of the money supply. The moral and conceptual foundations of this approach should not be ignored: the strengthening of individual freedom in the belief that economic liberty is a key requisite for personal liberty. But the benefits of these actions are intended to be more than philosophical. The Reagan four-point program was developed to strengthen the economy—specifically to reduce inflation, increase economic growth and stabilize what had been a stop-and-go history of economic policy and economic performance." See Murray Weidenbaum, "Assessing Reagan's Economic Program," *New York Times*, August 22, 1982.

47. Cannon, *Reagan*, 1991.

48. Quoted in Douglas E. Kneeland, "Teamsters Back Republican," *New York Times*, October 10, 1980.

49. Joanne Omang, "Reagan Criticizes Clean Air Laws and EPA as Obstacles to Growth," *Washington Post*, October 9, 1980.

50. Quoted in Merrill Brown, "Regulatory 'Balance' May Shift to Dismantlers," *Washington Post*, January 11, 1981.

51. Quoted in Martin Crutsinger, "Battle Over Clean-Air Rules Begins With Industry Attack," Associated Press, November 22, 1980.

52. "Carter vs. Reagan," *Washington Post*, October 28, 1980; Crutsinger, "Battle Over Clean-Air Rules."

53. Walter Shapiro, "The New, Republican Senate: Still Moderate In Spite of Itself," *Washington Post*, January 20, 1981.

54. Melissa Martino Golden, *What Motivates Bureaucrats? Politics and Administration during the Reagan Years* (New York: Columbia University Press, 2000).

55. Lawrence Mosher, "Clean Air Act an Inviting Target for Industry Critics Next Year," *National Journal*, November 15, 1980, 1927.

56. Crutsinger, "Battle Over Clean-Air Rules."

57. The EPA had already granted more than a dozen waivers of carbon monoxide standards, backed away from requiring 1982-model vehicles to meet exhaust standards at all possible idle-speed settings, and delayed until 1984 new rules for controlling pollution from light-duty trucks and heavy-duty vehicles. See Taylor, "In Clean Air Drive."

58. Philip Shabecoff, "Unions Divided on Revision of Clean Air Act," *New York Times*, March 8, 1982.

59. Lewis Regenstein, "Clean Air: Defending a Law in Peril," *Washington Post*, August 4, 1981. Regenstein noted that according to economist A. Myrick Freeman, the Clean Air Act had yielded national benefits of between $5 billion and $51 billion per year, clearly exceeding the cost of about $21.4 billion since 1970. An earlier analysis by economists Lester Lave and Eugene Seskin had similarly found that the Clean Air Act's benefits greatly outweighed its costs.

60. Joanne Omang, "Commissions Back Easing Rules for Controlling Pollution," *Washington Post*, March 3, 1981.

61. "Breathing Easier," *Wall Street Journal*, August 25, 1981.

62. Quoted in Philip Shabecoff, "Democrats Disclose Reagan Draft Document Easing Clean Air Standards," *New York Times*, June 20, 1981.

63. Ibid.

64. Quoted in Joanne Omang, "EPA Revision of Clean Air Act Leaves a 'Shell,' Waxman Says," *Washington Post*, June 20, 1981.

65. Philip Shabecoff, "Clean Air Act: A Barometer of Changes," *New York Times*, July 1, 1981.

66. Quoted in "It's a Depression at EPA," *Washington Post*, November 3, 1981.

67. Quoted in Philip Shabecoff, "Politics Clouds Clean Air Act Debate," *New York Times*, November 3, 1981.

68. Kathy Koch, "Reagan Switches Strategy on Clean Air," *Congressional Quarterly Weekly Report*, August 8, 1981, 1454.

69. Quoted in Robert D. Hershey, "Changes Proposed for Clean Air Act," *New York Times*, August 6, 1981.

70. "Breathing Easier," *Wall Street Journal*, August 25, 1981.

71. Quoted in "Administration in Switch, Takes Tough Line on Clean Air Rules," *New York Times*, May 1, 1982.

72. In June 1974, under pressure from industry, Congress passed legislation that permitted temporary reliance on tall stacks on a case-by-case basis; efforts to allow tall stacks as a permanent control strategy were soundly defeated, however. In 1976, the EPA issued new guidelines that grandfathered all stacks raised before 1972 and set a height limit of 2.5 times that of the boiler house for new stacks. In the 1977 Clean Air Act amendments, Congress tried to close a loophole in the 1976 guideline, by saying that utilities could rely on stack height to meet sulfur dioxide standards only if "necessary" to avoid "excessive concentrations" of pollution caused by air turbulence. Power companies interpreted that clause as giving them a blanket right to raise stacks to 2.5 times the height of the pollution source, and they proceeded to do so. In 1980, the EPA, citing acid rain concerns, turned down a request by a Cleveland utility to raise its stacks. But one of Gorsuch's first decisions was to rescind the Cleveland decision. Then, in 1982, she issued a new regulation affirming the industry's view of the 1977 amendments. The Natural Resources Defense Council sued, and in 1983, the D.C. Circuit ruled that utilities were *not* entitled to raise their stacks. See Michael Weisskopf, "Administration in Switch, Takes Tough Line on Clean Air Rules," *New York Times*, May 1, 1982.

73. Quoted in William Kronholm, "Destructive Potential of Acid Rain Detailed," Associated Press, April 8, 1980.

74. Cass Peterson, "Acid Rain vs. Cleanup Costs Seen as Choice of Poisons," *Washington Post*, September 28, 1982.

75. National Research Council, *Atmosphere-Biosphere Interactions: Toward a Better Understanding of the Ecological Consequences of Fossil Fuel Combustion* (Washington, DC: National Academy of Sciences, 1981), 7, 3.

76. Judith A. Layzer, *The Environmental Case: Translating Values into Policy*, 3rd ed. (Washington, DC: CQ Press, 2012). In early June 1982, the administration cut off funds to the National Academy for acid rain research.

77. Quoted in Philip Shabecoff, "Acid Rain Debate Tells As Much about Washington As Science," *New York Times*, February 9, 1982.

78. Quoted in Russell W. Peterson, "Laissez-Faire Landscape," *New York Times Magazine*, October 31, 1982.

79. Richard J. Tobin, "Revising the Clean Air Act: Legislative Failure and Administrative Success," in *Environmental Policy in the 1980s: Reagan's New Agenda*, ed. Norman J. Vig and Michael E. Kraft (Washington, DC: CQ Press, 1984), 243–244.

80. Chester A. Newland, "The Reagan Presidency: Limited Government and Political Administration," *Public Administration Review* 43, no. 1 (1983): 1–21.

81. Quoted in Clyde H. Farnsworth, "Reagan Signs Order to Curb Regulations," *New York Times*, February 18, 1981.

82. Reagan's approach differed from Carter's in other respects as well: it was extraordinarily shielded from public view, it gave OIRA two opportunities to

impede the progress of a rule, and it created "sunset" procedures for existing rules. See Eads and Fix, *Relief or Reform?*

83. Quoted in Peter Behr, "Regulation Target List Being Prepared," *Washington Post*, February 21, 1981. The environmental regulations on the lists included: lead phasedown rules that limited lead in gasoline to 0.5 micrograms per cubic liter, the Endangered Species Act consultation rule, the emissions standard for carbon monoxide on 1982-model cars, rules for certifying and testing to ensure that emissions controls were working properly, emissions controls on small industrial power plants, and proposed rules requiring industries to treat wastes before discharging them into municipal sewage systems.

84. Andrews, "Deregulation."

85. Eads and Fix, *Relief or Reform?* The task force was disbanded in 1983, after its actions became too controversial for White House pragmatists, particularly James Baker.

86. Peter Behr, "OMB Now a Regulator in Historic Power Shift," *Washington Post*, May 4, 1981.

87. Quoted in Felicity Barringer, "30 More Regulations Targeted for Review," *Washington Post*, August 13, 1981.

88. Quoted in Eads and Fix, *Relief or Reform?*, 137–138.

89. Quoted in Mary Thornton, "Rules Leaked to Industry," *Washington Post*, September 28, 1983.

90. Quoted in Michael E. Kraft, "A New Environmental Policy Agenda: The 1980 Presidential Campaign and Its Aftermath," in *Environmental Policy in the 1980s: Reagan's New Agenda*, ed. Norman J. Vig and Michael E. Kraft (Washington, DC: CQ Press, 1984), 38.

91. James E. Hinish Jr., "Regulatory Reform," 701.

92. Newland, "Reagan Presidency," 3.

93. John H. Kessel, "The Structures of the Reagan White House," *American Journal of Political Science* 28, no. 2 (May 1984): 231–258.

94. Howell Raines, "Reagan Reversing Many U.S. Policies," *New York Times*, July 3, 1981.

95. Philip J. Hilts, "Will Bush Pay Attention to Science?" *Washington Post*, November 28, 1988.

96. Quoted in Cannon, *Reagan*, 359.

97. Quoted in Cawley, *Federal Land, Western Anger*, 130.

98. Quoted in Pamela Fessler, "A Quarter-Century of Activism Erected a Bulwark of Laws," *CQ Weekly*, January 20, 1990, 156.

99. Quoted in Angus Phillips, "Environmentalists United Against Watt," *Washington Post*, August 30, 1981.

100. Quoted in "Confirmation Seems Likely to Administrator of EPA," *New York Times*, May 2, 1981.

101. "Trying to Make 'The New Federalism' Work at EPA," *Journal (Water Pollution Control Federation)* 54, no. 2 (February 1982): 119–124.

102. Quoted in Philip Shabecoff, "New Environmental Chief Vows to Lift Regulatory 'Overburden,'" *New York Times*, June 21, 1981.

103. Quoted in Howell Raines, "Reagan Reversing Many U.S. Policies," *New York Times*, July 3, 1981.

104. When he named Miller to chair the Federal Trade Commission, Reagan replaced him with Christopher DeMuth, who shared Miller's and Stockman's belief that "there are scores, hundreds of regulations on the books that are imposing costs without much positive result in terms of environmental or health improvement." Quoted in Jonathan Lash, Katherine Gillman, and David Sheridan, *A Season of Spoils: The Reagan Administration's Attack on the Environment* (New York: Pantheon Books, 1984), 25.

105. Supply-side economics is a school of thought that argues the most effective way to stimulate economic growth is to (1) lower income and capital gains taxes, and (2) relax regulations. According to supply-siders, such measures boost growth by increasing investment in the production of goods and services.

106. David Stockman and Jack Kemp, "Memo to Reagan: 'Avoiding a GOP Economic Dunkirk,'" *New York Times*, December 14, 1980.

107. Al Kamen, "Federalist Society Quickly Comes of Age," *Washington Post*, February 1, 1987.

108. David M. O'Brien, "Federal Judgeships in Retrospect," in *The Reagan Presidency: Pragmatic Conservatism and Its Legacies*, ed. W. Elliot Brownlee and Hugh Davis Graham (Lawrence: University Press of Kansas, 2003), 330.

109. Robert Pear, "Convention in Dallas," *New York Times*, August 20, 1984; Philip Shabecoff, "The President and the Environment," *New York Times*, July 14, 1984.

110. Michael E. Kraft and Norman J. Vig, "Environmental Policy from the 1970s to 1990," in *Environmental Policy in the 1990s: Reform or Reaction?*, 3rd ed., ed. Norman J. Vig and Michael E. Kraft (Washington, DC: CQ Press, 1994), 19.

111. Norman J. Vig and Michael E. Kraft, "Environmental Policy from the Seventies to the Eighties," in Vig and Kraft, *Environmental Policy in the 1980s*, 3–26.

112. Richard N. L. Andrews, *Managing the Environment, Managing Ourselves* (New Haven, CT: Yale University Press, 2006).

113. Lash, Gillman, and Sheridan, *A Season of Spoils*.

114. Robert V. Bartlett, "The Budgetary Process and Environmental Policy," in Vig and Kraft, *Environmental Policy in the 1980s*, 121–141.

115. Lawrence Mosher, "More Cuts in EPA Research Threaten Its Regulatory Goals, Critics Warn," *National Journal*, April 10, 1982.

116. Lawrence Mosher, "Endangered Species Act May Be Off Endangered List, At Least For Now," *National Journal*, April 24, 1982.

117. Figures supplied to the House Appropriations Committee by the EPA showed that 4,129 employees left during fiscal year 1981, and 236 were subject

to a Reduction in Force—amounting to a loss of almost one-third of the agency's staff. Because some employees were replaced, the total reduction between January and September of 1981 was 1,859. See Lash, Gillman, and Sheridan, *A Season of Spoils.*

118. Marc K. Landy, Marc J. Roberts, and Stephen R. Thomas, *The Environmental Protection Agency: Asking the Wrong Questions,* expanded ed. (New York: Oxford University Press, 1984), 249.

119. Russell Train, "The Destruction of the EPA," *Washington Post,* February 2, 1982.

120. Quoted in Philip Shabecoff, "Nearing Complete Renovation of Interior Department Rules," *New York Times,* January 23, 1983.

121. Ron Arnold, *At the Eye of the Storm: James Watt and the Environmentalists* (Chicago: Regnery Gateway, 1982), 131.

122. Cass Peterson, "It's Open Season on Endangered Species Act," *Washington Post,* March 8, 1982.

123. Quoted in Shabecoff, "Nearing Complete Renovation."

124. Melinda Beck, "Battle over the Wilderness," *Newsweek,* July 25, 1983. In 1982 alone, Watt sold leases for 1.7 billion tons of coal—the amount the Carter administration had proposed to lease over four years. He established a five-year program to make available 200 million acres of offshore waters each year for oil and gas leasing; the Carter administration had proposed 55 million acres over the same period. The Bureau of Land Management leased more acres of federal land for oil and gas development in 1982 than the Carter administration leased in four years. And, for the first time in twenty-five years, the secretary directed that the Interior Department consider oil and gas lease applications in more than 1 million acres of national wildlife refuges. Watt's aides also directed refuge managers to find new "economic uses" for the refuges, such as haying, grazing, mineral exploration, and recreation. See Dale Russakoff, "Watt Submits Resignation as Interior Secretary," *Washington Post,* October 10, 1983.

125. Stanford Environmental Law Society, *The Endangered Species Act* (Stanford, CA: Stanford University Press, 2001), 24.

126. Michael J. Scott, Dale D. Goble, Leona K. Svancara, and Anna Pidgorna, "By the Numbers," in *The Endangered Species Act at Thirty: Renewing the Conservation Promise,* ed. Dale D. Goble, J. Michael Scott, and Frank W. Davis (Washington, DC: Island Press, 2006), 16–35.

127. Peterson, "It's Open Season."

128. Philip Shabecoff, "Placing Species on Danger List De-emphasized," *New York Times,* January 31, 1981.

129. Philip Shabecoff, "Environmental Unit Plans to Sue Watt to Speed Species Protection," *New York Times,* July 23, 1981.

130. Walter Pincus, "Clearing Up the Fine Points on 'Harm' to an Endangered Species," *Washington Post,* June 8, 1981.

131. Felicity Barringer, "After 8 Years, Rule Is a Victory for Environmentalists," *New York Times*, November 9, 1981.

132. Philip Shabecoff, "Environmental Action Enters New Era," *New York Times*, January 20, 1981.

133. Quoted in Linda Greenhouse, "Court Upholds Reagan on Air Standard," *New York Times*, June 26, 1984.

134. Tobin, "Revising the Clean Air Act"

135. Richard N. L. Andrews, *Managing the Environment, Managing Ourselves* (New Haven, CT: Yale University Press, 2006).

136. J. Clarence Davies, "Environmental Institutions and the Reagan Administration," in Vig and Kraft, *Environmental Policy in the 1980s* 143–160.

137. Quoted in Lash, Gillman, and Sheridan, *A Season of Spoils*, 47.

138. Ibid.

139. Eads and Fix, *Relief or Reform?*

140. Mintz, *Enforcement at the EPA*.

141. Philip Shabecoff, "Higher Risks Seen in New E.P.A. Rules," *New York Times*, September 18, 1983.

142. Quoted in Davies, "Environmental Institutions," 151.

143. Ibid.

144. Andrews, "Deregulation," 173.

145. Andy Pasztor, "Transfer of Power," *Wall Street Journal*, August 24, 1982.

146. Quoted in Steve H. Hanke, "The Privatization Debate: An Insider's View," *Cato Journal* 2, no. 3 (Winter 1982).

147. Robert H. Nelson, *Public Lands and Private Rights* (Lanham, MD: Rowman & Littlefield, 1995).

148. Quoted in Christopher McGrory Klyza, *Who Controls Public Lands? Mining, Forestry, and Grazing Policy, 1870–1990* (Chapel Hill: University of North Carolina Press, 1994), 102.

149. Landy, Roberts, and Thomas, *The Environmental Protection Agency*.

150. Quoted in Samuel P. Hays, *Beauty, Health, and Permanence: Environmental Politics in the United States, 1955–1985* (New York: Cambridge University Press, 1987), 504.

151. Quoted in Philip Shabecoff, "Memo: Meese and Environmentalists," *New York Times*, February 5, 1982.

152. Eads and Fix, *Relief or Reform?*

153. Dale Russakoff, "The Unforcer: Strip Mining Agency Falls Victim to Reagan's Reforms," *Washington Post*, June 6, 1982.

154. Quoted in Cass Peterson, "Cleaner Diesel Engine Rule Postponed 2 Years by EPA," *Washington Post*, January 18, 1984.

155. Quoted in Philip Shabecoff, "Bad Faith on Ecology Laid to Reagan," *New York Times*, April 1, 1982.

156. Quoted in "State of the Environment 1982," *Washington Post*, June 24, 1982.

157. Caroline Mayer, "Economists Call Regulatory Reform Too Slow, Narrow," *Washington Post*, December 9, 1981.

158. Quoted in John B. Oakes, "Reagan Making Bad Start on Nature," *New York Times*, August 31, 1981.

159. Quoted in Coleman McCarthy, "Where Does Burford's Failure End and Reagan's Begin?" *Washington Post*, March 30, 1983.

160. John D. Leshy, "Natural Resource Policy," in *Natural Resources and the Environment*, ed. Paul R. Portney (Washington, DC: Urban Institute Press, 1984), 13–46.

161. Andy Pasztor, "Reagan Goal of Easing Environmental Laws Is Largely Unattained," *Wall Street Journal*, February 18, 1983.

162. Philip Shabecoff, "Crisis: Environment Emerges As a Mainstream Issue," *New York Times*, April 29, 1983.

163. Dale Russakoff, "Poll Finds Broad Support for Environmental Laws," *Washington Post*, November 11, 1982.

164. Quoted in "A Call for Tougher—Not Weaker—Antipollution Laws," *Business Week*, January 24, 1983.

165. Quoted in Pazstor, "Reagan Goal of Easing Environmental Laws."

166. Haynes Johnson, Cass Peterson, Eric Pianin, and Ward Sinclair, "Environment Is Potent Political Issue Despite State's Economic Hardships," *Washington Post*, July 17, 1983.

167. Avoiding election-year politics, the administration declined to present a specific position on reauthorization of the Endangered Species Act.

168. President Reagan reluctantly signed the only other major piece of environmental legislation passed by Congress in his first term—the reauthorization of the Resource Conservation and Recovery Act, which extended hazardous waste reporting requirements to "small quantity generators" and mandated the replacement of thousands of corroded and leaking underground storage tanks.

169. Cannon, *Reagan*.

170. Cannon, *Reagan*, 364.

171. Quoted in Steven V. Roberts, "Congress's Intent Held as Violated," *New York Times*, March 14, 1983.

172. Shabecoff, "Crisis: Environment Emerges as a Mainstream Issue."

173. Quoted in Philip Shabecoff, "Ruckelshaus Said to Have Wanted Air Rules Eased," *New York Times*, April 28, 1983.

174. Philip Shabecoff, "Ruckelshaus Planning Few Major Policy Changes," *New York Times*, May 6, 1983.

175. Philip Shabecoff, "Ruckelshaus Ends First Year Back at E.P.A.," *New York Times*, May 20, 1984.

176. Philip Shabecoff, "Higher Risks Seen in New E.P.A. Rules," *New York Times*, September 18, 1983.

177. Philip Shabecoff, "E.P.A. Is Assailed on Acid Rain Plan," *New York Times*, November 15, 1983.

178. Quoted in Philip Shabecoff, "The President and the Environment," *New York Times*, July 14, 1984.

179. Quoted in "U.S. Judge Rules E.P.A. In Contempt," *New York Times*, December 12, 1984.

180. Philip Shabecoff, "Watt Says He'll Shift toward Conservation," *New York Times*, June 26, 1983.

181. Philip Shabecoff, "Clark Praised and Assailed on Environmental Issues," *New York Times*, October 15, 1983.

182. Ibid.; Dale Russakoff, "Critics Vow to Focus on Environment," *Washington Post*, October 15, 1983.

183. Jeffrey K. Stine, "Environmental Policy Choices during the Carter Presidency," in *The Carter Presidency: Policy Choices in the Post–New Deal Era*, ed. Gary M. Fink and Hugh Davis Graham (Lawrence: University of Kansas Press, 1998), 179–201.

184. Philip Shabecoff, "Earth, Wind, and Loss of Momentum," *New York Times*, April 28, 1984.

185. Andrews, *Managing the Environment*; Richard J. Lazarus, "The Tragedy of Distrust in the Implementation of Environmental Law," *Law & Contemporary Problems* 54, no. 4 (1991): 311–374.

186. Philip Shabecoff, "Watt's Goals at Interior, But in a Different Style," *New York Times*, March 3, 1986; Rochelle Stanfield, "Protecting Public Lands," *National Journal*, December 20, 1986, 3065–3067.

187. Ronald B. Taylor, "Two Battles Over Different Visions of the Future,"*Los Angeles Times*, May 24, 1987.

188. James G. Watt, Oral History, Center for the American West (February 11, 2004). See http://centerwest.org/wp-content/uploads/2011/01/watt1.pdf.

189. Quoted in Philip Shabecoff, "With 2 Years Left, Many Reagan Goals on Environmental Policy Are Unmet," *New York Times*, December 30, 1986.

190. Philip Shabecoff, "New Wilderness Rules May Reopen Dispute," *New York Times*, February 26, 1985.

191. Quoted Shabecoff, "Watt's Goals at Interior."

192. Philip Shabecoff, "Bush Tells Environmentalists He'll Listen to Them," *New York Times*, December 1, 1988; Philip Shabecoff, "Reagan and Environment: To Many, a Stalemate," *New York Times*, January 2, 1989.

193. Philip Shabecoff, "At the Wildlife Service, an Extinction with Irony," *New York Times*, November 25, 1987.

194. Thomas was the first administrator drawn from within the agency's ranks; he was unanimously confirmed by the Senate and was seen as having integrity, if not political clout.

195. Philip Shabecoff, "Of Trees and Laws and Bad Reps," *New York Times*, July 17, 1987.

196. David Burnham, "EPA Seeks Shift in Fight on Toxic Air Pollution," *New York Times*, June 5, 1985.

197. Philip Shabecoff, "E.P.A. Reassesses the Cancer Risks of Many Chemicals," *New York Times*, January 4, 1988; Michael Weisskopf, "EPA Panel Shifts Course on Pollutant," *Washington Post*, October 5, 1987.

198. Philip Shabecoff, "E.P.A. Declines to Toughen Rules on Sulfur Dioxide," *New York Times*, April 15, 1988.

199. Michael Weisskopf, "Legal Pollution That Makes Students Sick," *Washington Post*, Jun 6, 1989.

200. John N. Maclean, "Acid-rain Measure Dealt Critical Blow," *Chicago Tribune*, April 30, 1986.

201. According to a study by the NRDC, between the passage of the Clean Air Act in 1970 and the mid-1980s, 212 tall stacks were erected at 95 power plants in 25 states. See "E.P.A. and Utilities Assailed on Tall Smokestacks," *New York Times*, March 16, 1985. Journalist Michael Weisskopf reports a considerably smaller number—108 between 1970 and 1989. See Michael Weisskopf, "Administration in Switch, Takes Tough Line on Clean Air Rules," *New York Times*, May 1, 1989.

202. Quoted in Philip Shabecoff, "The Environment as Local Jurisdiction," *New York Times*, January 22, 1989.

203. Ibid.

204. Haynes Johnson, "Talk about . . . a Very Fearful Thing," *Washington Post*, July 24, 1977.

205. Philip Shabecoff, "U.S. Study Warns of Extensive Problems from Carbon Dioxide Pollution," *New York Times*, January 14, 1981.

206. Spencer Weart, "Government: The View from Washington, D.C." in *The Discovery of Global Warming* (College Park, MD: American Institute of Physics, 2009). See http://www.aip.org/history/climate/Govt.htm.

207. Quoted in Philip Shabecoff, "E.P.A. Report Says Earth Will Heat Up Beginning in 1990's," *New York Times*, October 18, 1983.

208. Quoted in Philip Shabecoff, "Haste of Global Warming Trend Opposed," *New York Times*, October 21, 1983.

209. Philip Shabecoff, "Ozone Agreement Is Hailed as a First Step in Cooperation," *New York Times*, May 5, 1987.

210. Cooper, *War against Regulation*, 40.

211. Philip Shabecoff, "E.P.A. Faces Test on Truck Pollution," *New York Times*, March 8, 1985; Philip Shabecoff, "Judge Bars U.S. Plea for Secrecy in Suit over Budget Office Delay," *New York Times*, December 20, 1985; Cass Peterson, "EPA Reverses Position on Asbestos Regulation," *Washington Post*, March 12, 1985; Cass Peterson, "Asbestos Rule 'Sabotage' Alleged," *Washington Post*, April 16, 1985; Cass Peterson, "Senate Calls OMB's Bluff on Regulatory Review,"

*Washington Post*, September 23, 1985; Cass Peterson, "OMB Illegally Blocked EPA Plan for Asbestos Ban, Report Says," *Washington Post*, October 4, 1985; Michael Weisskopf, "Few Hazardous Wastes Controlled by EPA," *Washington Post*, January 17, 1987.

212. Judith Havemann, "OMB Cracks Whip on Rule-Making," *Washington Post*, June 17, 1987. The OMB said the percentages changed because the office was no longer even looking at rules that it routinely cleared early on. Wendy Gramm said she believed a trend line of the previous two years would be essentially flat, with more than two-thirds of rules passing muster without change.

213. Lazarus, "Tragedy of Distrust."

214. "Justice Agency Plans Greater Opposition to Environmental Suits," *Wall Street Journal*, May 13, 1981.

215. Richard A. Harris and Sidney M. Milkis, *The Politics of Regulatory Change: A Tale of Two Agencies*, rev. ed. (New York: Oxford University Press, 1996).

216. Charles Fried, *Order and Law: Arguing the Reagan Revolution—a First-hand Account* (New York: Simon & Schuster, 1991).

217. Andrews, *Managing the Environment*, 262.

218. Philip Shabecoff, "100th Congress Is Expected to Put Environment at Top of Priorities," *New York Times*, November 16, 1986.

219. Quoted in Michael Weisskopf, "Clean-Water Compromise to Be Sought," *Washington Post*, January 1, 1987.

220. Alan C. Miller, "Hodel Takes Aim at the Endangered Species Act," *Los Angeles Times*, February 4, 1988.

221. Weart, "Government: The View from Washington."

222. Michael Weisskopf, "Reagan Aide Blocks 'Greenhouse' Rule," *Washington Post*, January 11, 1989.

223. Conservatives were also disappointed with Reagan's failure to shrink the government more generally; in fact, during his tenure the federal workforce increased by about 1.6 percent. See Clyde H. Farnsworth, "Promise of Deregulation Proved Tough to Keep," *New York Times*, August 18, 1988.

224. Quoted in Philip Shabecoff, "Reagan and Environment: To Many, a Stalemate," *New York Times*, January 2, 1989.

225. Frank Swoboda, "The Legacy of Deregulation," *Washington Post*, October 2, 1988.

226. Judith Havemann, "OMB Cracks Whip on Rule-Making," *Washington Post*, June 17, 1987.

227. EPA1, personal communication, 2009; EPA3, personal communication, 2009; EPA4, personal communication, 2008; EPA5, personal communication, 2008.

228. EPA1, personal communication, 2009.

229. Norman J. Vig and Michael E. Kraft, "Presidential Leadership and the Environment: From Reagan and Bush to Clinton," in *Environmental Policy in the 1990s: Toward a New Agenda*, 2nd ed., ed. Norman J. Vig and Michael E. Kraft (Washington, DC: CQ Press, 1994), 71–95.

230. Cooper, *War against Regulation.*

231. Andrews, *Managing the Environment*, 259.

232. Peterson, "Laissez-Faire Landscape."

233. Bruce Ingersoll, "Tough Environment," *Wall Street Journal*, January 20, 1989.

234. Quoted in ibid.

235. Quoted in Philip Shabecoff, "Watt Says He'll Shift Toward Conservation," *New York Times*, June 26, 1983. In late 1988, the U.S. General Accounting Office (GAO) issued a series of unusually critical reports about the legacy of the Reagan administration. Among other things, the GAO urged President-elect Bush to abandon Reagan's practice of denouncing federal agencies and bureaucrats—a practice that made it difficult for the government to "attract, motivate and retain committed people." See Robert Pear, "Reagan Leaving Many Costly Domestic Problems, G.A.O. Tells Bush," *New York Times*, November 22, 1988.

236. Watt, Oral history.

237. Quoted in Bernard Weinraub, "The Reagan Legacy," *New York Times Magazine*, June 22, 1986.

238. David M. O'Brien, "Federal Judgeships in Retrospect," in *The Reagan Presidency: Pragmatic Conservatism & Its Legacies*, ed. W. Elliot Brownlee and Hugh Davis Graham (Lawrence: University Press of Kansas, 2003), 327.

239. Andrews, *Managing the Environment*, 259.

240. Philip Shabecoff, "Ruckelshaus Planning Few Major Policy Changes," *New York Times*, May 6, 1983.

241. Constance Holden, "Public Fear of Watt is Environmentalists' Gain," *Science*, April 24, 1981, 422.

242. Christopher J. Bosso, *Environment, Inc.: From Grassroots to Beltway* (Lawrence: University Press of Kansas, 2005).

## Chapter 5

1. In the 101st Congress (1989–1990), Democrats controlled the Senate by 55–45 and the House by 251–183. Democrats increased their majorities in the 102nd Congress: by the end of 1992, Democrats held 58 seats in the Senate and 270 seats in the House.

2. Henry C. Kenski and Helen M. Ingram, "The Reagan Administration and Environmental Regulation: The Constraint of the Political Market," in

*Controversies in Environmental Policy*, ed. Sheldon Kamieniecki, Robert O'Brien, and Michael Clark (Albany: State University of New York Press, 1986), 275–299; Andy Pasztor, "Reagan Goal of Easing Environmental Laws Is Largely Unattained," *Wall Street Journal*, February 18, 1983; Edward P. Weber, *Pluralism by the Rules: Conflict and Cooperation in Environmental Regulation* (Washington, DC: Georgetown University Press, 1998).

3. Daniel J. Fiorino, *The New Environmental Regulation* (Cambridge, MA: MIT Press, 2006), citing Johan Schot and Kurt Fischer, "Introduction: The Greening of the Industrial Firm," in *Environmental Strategies for Industry: International Perspectives on Research Needs and Policy Implications*, ed. Kurt Fischer and Johan Schot (Washington, DC: Island Press, 1993), 3–33.

4. William Greider, "The Rise of Corporate Environmentalism," *Washington Post*, January 4, 1981.

5. Richard N. L. Andrews, *Managing the Environment, Managing Ourselves* (New Haven, CT: Yale University Press, 2006).

6. Ibid, 266.

7. Fiorino, *New Environmental Regulation*. Skeptical commentators, including science and technology scholar Sharon Beder, were sharply critical of the notion that business had genuinely evolved, instead positing that the majority of business activity consisted of public relations and greenwashing. See Sharon Beder, *Global Spin: The Corporate Assault on Environmentalism*, rev. ed. (White River Junction, VT: Chelsea Green Publishing Company, 2002).

8. Michael H. Levin, "Anti-Smog Bill Won't Clear the Air," *Wall Street Journal*, June 20, 1987.

9. Michael H. Levin, Barry Elman, and Tapio Kuusinen, "Make Pollution Control Easy and Cheap," *Washington Post*, March 1, 1988.

10. Richard J. Lazarus, *The Making of Environmental Law* (Chicago: University of Chicago Press, 2004).

11. Michael Levin, "Statutes and Stopping Points: Building a Better Bubble at EPA," *Regulation*, March/April 1985, 33–42.

12. Matthew L. Wald, "U.S. Agencies Use Negotiations to Pre-empt Lawsuits Over Rules," *New York Times*, September 23, 1991.

13. Some businesspeople also resisted a shift to incentive-based policies. For them, permits and fees threatened uncertainty and double payments—first for the pollution control system and then for the permit or fee; furthermore, many large firms appreciated the barrier to entry provided by regulation. See Steven Kelman, "Economists and the Environmental Muddle," *Public Interest* 64 (Summer 1981): 106–123; Michael H. Levin, "Getting There: Implementing the 'Bubble' Policy," in *Social Regulation: Strategies for Reform*, ed. Eugene Bardach and Robert A. Kagan (New Brunswick, NJ: Transaction Books, 1982), 59–92. Moreover, as economist George Eads points out, because pollution charges are less susceptible to manipulation than complex prescriptive regulation, "those businesses that have spent a lot of money understanding regulation are reluctant

to abandon it." Quoted in Timothy B. Clark, "New Approaches to Regulatory Reform—Letting the Market Do The Job," *National Journal*, August 11, 1979, 1316.

14. Quoted in Philip Shabecoff, "Bush Tells Environmentalists He'll Listen to Them," *New York Times*, December 1, 1988.

15. Philip Shabecoff, "New Leaders and a New Era for Environmentalists," *New York Times*, November 29, 1985; Rochelle Stanfield, "Environmental Lobby's Changing of the Guard Is Part of Movement's Evolution," *National Journal*, June 8, 1985.

16. Kirkpatrick Sale, *The Green Revolution: The American Environmental Movement 1962–1992* (New York: Hill and Wang, 1993), 54.

17. Keith Schneider, "Selling Out? Pushed and Pulled, Environment Inc. is on the Defensive," *New York Times*, March 29, 1992; Philip Shabecoff, "Aide Sees Need to Head Off Global Warming," *New York Times*, June 12, 1986; Michael Weisskop, "How on Earth to Turn Off the Heat," *Washington Post*, March 21, 1989.

18. The environmental movement had always been heterogeneous, with some groups focusing more on analysis than on advocacy, and advocacy groups ranging from those who sought marginal changes to the status quo to those who demanded more fundamental transformation. Increasingly, groups also specialized in particular problems, from wilderness preservation to remediation of abandoned hazardous waste sites. See Christopher J. Bosso, *Environment, Inc.: From Grassroots to Beltway* (Lawrence: University Press of Kansas, 2005).

19. Doug Bandow, "Economic Means for Environmental Ends," *Wall Street Journal*, March 5, 1990.

20. Andrews, *Managing the Environment.*

21. Mary Douglas and Aaron Wildavsky, *Risk and Culture: An Essay on the Selection of Technological and Environmental Dangers* (Berkeley: University of California Press, 1982).

22. Aaron Wildavsky, *Searching for Safety* (New Brunswick, NJ: Transaction Books, 1988), 2.

23. Morrall's article was widely cited and received little scrutiny until 1998, when legal scholar Lisa Heinzerling published an extensive critique of his analysis. See Lisa Heinzerling, "Regulatory Costs of Mythic Proportions," *Yale Law Journal* 107 (1998): 1981. In 2003, Morrall answered Heinzerling's challenges with a detailed rebuttal. See John F. Morrall III, "Saving Lives: A Review of the Record," Working Paper 03–6, July (AEI-Brookings Joint Center for Regulatory Studies, 2003), http://biotech.law.lsu.edu/cases/adlaw/cba/Morrall-Saving-Lives-2003.pdf. Richard Parker, also a legal scholar, subsequently issued a rejoinder in which he sought to discredit the whole notion of regulatory scorecards. See Richard W. Parker, "Is Government Irrational?: A Reply to Morrall and Hahn," University of Connecticut School of Law, Articles and Working Papers (2004), http://lsr.nellco.org/uconn_wps/31/.

24. Ralph L. Keeney, "Mortality Risks Induced by Economic Expenditures," *Risk Analysis* 10 (1990): 147–159.

25. Edith Efron, *The Apocalyptics: Cancer and the Big Lie* (New York: Simon & Schuster, 1984), 60–61.

26. D. Keith Mano, "On Environmentalism," *National Review*, February 10, 1989, 64.

27. Dixy Lee Ray and Lou Guzzo, *Trashing the Planet* (Washington, DC: Regnery Gateway, 1990), 163.

28. David Horowitz, "Making the Green One Red," *National Review*, March 19, 1990, 40.

29. Ralph De Toledano, "Chicken Little is Wrong," *National Review*, June 11, 1990, 48.

30. Bruce Frohnen, "Humans Last!" *National Review*, September 17, 1990, 50.

31. "Clean Air and Hot Air," *Wall Street Journal*, November 19, 1987.

32. Jane S. Shaw, "Greens Learn to Stay Clear of the Ballot Box," *Wall Street Journal*, November 13, 1990.

33. Public choice practitioners use the tools of economics to analyze political phenomena.

34. John Baden, "Crimes Against Nature: Public Funding of Environmental Destruction," *Policy Review* (Winter 1987), 36.

35. Richard L. Stroup and Jane S. Shaw, "The Free Market and the Environment," *Public Interest* 97 (Fall 1989), 30–43; William Tucker, "Conservation in Deed," *Reason*, May 1983, 34–39.

36. Joseph G. Peschek, *Policy-Planning Organizations: Elite Agendas and America's Rightward Turn* (Philadelphia: Temple University Press, 1987).

37. John Stefancik and Richard Delgado, *No Mercy: How Conservative Think Tanks and Foundations Changed America's Social Agenda* (Philadelphia: Temple University Press, 1996).

38. Andrew Rich and R. Kent Weaver, "Advocates and Analysts: Think Tanks and the Politicization of Expertise," in *Interest Group Politics*, 5th ed., ed. Allan J. Cigler and Burdett A. Loomis (Washington, DC: CQ Press, 1998), 235–253.

39. Stefancik and Delgado, *No Mercy*.

40. Quoted in David Helvarg, *The War Against the Greens* (San Francisco: Sierra Club Books, 1994), 20.

41. http://www.perc.org/whatis.php.

42. http://www.free-eco.org/about/

43. Terry L. Anderson, "New Resource Economics: Old Ideas and New Applications," *American Journal of Agricultural Economics* 64, no. 5 (December 1982): 928–934.

44. John S. Saloma III, *Ominous Politics: The New Conservative Labyrinth* (New York: Hill and Wang, 1984), 21–22.

45. Beth Schulman, "Foundations for a Movement: How the Right Wing Subsidizes Its Press," *Extra! Newletter of Fairness and Accuracy in Reporting*, March/April, 1995.

46. David Callahan, "Liberal Policy's Weak Foundations," *The Nation*, November 13, 1995. Peter Jaques, Riley Dunlap, and Mark Freeman argue that conservative think tanks have been the key organizational component of the conservative countermovement, which in turn "has been central to the reversal of U.S. support for environmental protection, both domestically and internationally." They find that advocates of environmental skepticism are overwhelmingly conservative and, in a vast majority of cases, are directly linked to one or more conservative think tanks. See Peter J. Jacques, Riley E. Dunlap and Mark Freeman, "The Organization of Denial: Conservative Think Tanks and Environmental Skepticism," *Environmental Politics* 17, no. 3 (2008): 351.

47. Clifford D. May, "Pollution Ills Stir Support for Environmental Groups," *New York Times*, August 21, 1988.

48. Bill Peterson, "Bush Vows to Fight Pollution, Install 'Conservation Ethic,'" *Washington Post*, September 1, 1988.

49. David Hoffman, "Bush Calls Civil Servants Unsung Heroes," *Washington Post*, January 27, 1989.

50. Quoted in Michael Weisskopf, "Visit with President-Elect Cheers Environmentalists," *Washington Post*, December 1, 1988.

51. Norman J. Vig, "Presidential Leadership: From the Reagan to the Bush Administration," in *Environmental Policy in the 1990s: Toward a New Agenda*, ed. Norman J. Vig and Michael E. Kraft (Washington, DC: CQ Press, 1990), 33–58.

52. Quoted in Michael Weisskopf, "Bush's EPA Choice Declares 'New Era,'" *Washington Post*, February 1, 1989.

53. Quoted in Philip Shabecoff, "Bush Is Urged to Fight Threat of Global Warming," *New York Times*, January 6, 1989.

54. Ibid.

55. ENV2, personal communication, 2008.

56. Martin Tolchin, "New Faces for 4 Cabinet Posts and Top Environmental Job," *New York Times*, December 23, 1988. LCV scores represent the percentage of times an official votes with environmentalists on a sample of environmental bills deemed significant by the League of Conservation Voters.

57. Cass Peterson, "Bush Cabinet's Weak Link: Affable, Gaffe-Prone Lujan," *Washington Post*, May 15, 1989.

58. Quoted in McGreggor Cawley, *Federal Land, Western Anger: The Sagebrush Rebellion and Environmental Politics* (Lawrence: University Press of Kansas, 1993), 165.

59. John B. Oakes, "Bush's Shell Game," *New York Times*, January 12, 1989; John B. Oakes, "Bush's 'Environmentalists'—Who's Watt, and Why," *New York Times*, April 29, 1989; Peterson, "Bush Cabinet's Weak Link"; Tolchin "New

Faces." Most controversial was Bush's selection of James E. Cason, a former real estate developer, to head the Forest Service, which resides in the Department of Agriculture. As acting assistant secretary for land and minerals management at Interior, Cason had been involved in below-market sales of oil shale lands and attempts to open national parks and wilderness areas to strip mining and oil drilling. Cason ultimately withdrew from consideration as Forest Service chief because he faced insurmountable opposition in the Senate. Dale Bosworth, who had taken the post in 1987, remained as Forest Service chief for the rest of the Bush administration.

60. David E. Rosenbaum, "Bush's First Budget: Like Reagan's Last," *New York Times*, February 10, 1989.

61. John Lancaster, "'92 Budget Plan Reasonably Earth-Friendly," *Washington Post*, February 14, 1991.

62. Alvin Alm, "On Outside Looking In, Former Officials Rate Bush Budget," *Washington Post*, February 5, 1991.

63. Lancaster, "92 Budget Plan."

64. John Lancaster, "New Look, Old Mission at Lujan's Department," *Washington Post*, January 19, 1990.

65. Quoted in Cass Peterson, "Questioning Lujan's Interior Motives," *Washington Post*, March 22, 1989.

66. Quoted in Rogers Worthington, "Lujan Zips In, Out," *Chicago Tribune*, April 21, 1989.

67. Quoted in John Lancaster, "Lujan: Endangered Species Act 'Too Tough,'" Needs Changes," *Washington Post*, May 12, 1990.

68. The main statutes at issue were the National Forest Management Act (NFMA) and Federal Land Policy and Management Act (FLPMA), which require the Forest Service and the BLM to develop comprehensive forest- and district-level management plans and which formally designate wildlife as a major use of both Forest Service and BLM lands. NFMA regulations also require the Forest Service to identify indicator species, whose health reflects the condition of the entire forest ecosystem, and to ensure the viability of those species' populations.

69. "Endangered Species: Spotted Owl Petition Evaluation Beset by Problems," GAO/RCED-89-79, February 1989.

70. Quoted in Christopher Hanson, "Spotted Owl Joins Threatened List," *Seattle Post-Intelligencer*, June 23, 1990.

71. Timothy Egan, "Administration Offers Plan to Limit Northwest Logging," *New York Times*, September 22, 1990.

72. Quoted in Christopher Hanson, "Spotted Owl Joins Threatened List," *Seattle Post-Intelligencer*, June 23, 1990.

73. Keith Schneider, "Bush and Congress Facing a Showdown on Forests," *New York Times*, May 12, 1992.

74. Warren E. Leary, "Interior Secretary Questions Law on Endangered Species," *New York Times*, May 12, 1990.

75. Quoted in Phillip A. Davis, "BLM Calls on 'God Squad' to Let Its Timber Go," *CQ Weekly*, September 1991.

76. Quoted in Andrew Rosenthal, "Bush, on West Coast, Skirts Two Conservation Issues," *New York Times*, May 22, 1990.

77. Quoted in Jane Gross, "A Dying Fish May Force California to Break Its Water Habits," *New York Times*, October 27, 1991.

78. Quoted in Schneider, "Bush and Congress."

79. EPA1, personal communication, 2009; EPA2, personal communication, 2009; EPA3, personal communication, 2009.

80. The EPA has the responsibility under the Clean Air Act to protect visibility within national parks, but did nothing to implement that provision until a lawsuit by the EDF forced it to formulate a program in 1984. The restriction on the Navajo Generating Station, owned by the Bureau of Reclamation, was the first enforcement action.

81. Brad Knickerbocker, "Candidates Compete for Top 'Green' Spot," *Christian Science Monitor*, October 1, 1992.

82. Joel A. Mintz, *Enforcement at the EPA: High Stakes and Hard Choices* (Austin: University of Texas Press, 1995).

83. Andrews, *Managing the Environment*.

84. Trip Gabriel, "Greening the White House," *New York Times*, August 13, 1989.

85. Michael Weisskopf, "Administration Split on Clean Air Plan," *Washington Post*, June 10, 1989.

86. John Lancaster, "Clean Air Proposal Weakened," *Washington Post*, July 12, 1989.

87. Michael Weisskopf, "Bush Weakens Clean Air Proposal," *Washington Post*, July 21, 1989.

88. Michael Weisskopf, "With Pen, Bush to Seal Administration Split on Clean Air Act," *Washington Post*, November 15, 1989.

89. President Bush also oversaw a major expansion in cleanup efforts by the departments of Energy and Defense of nuclear and other hazardous waste on weapons production sites.

90. Quoted in Michael Weisskopf, "Bush Pledges Research on Global Warming," *Washington Post*, February 6, 1990.

91. Quoted in Michael Weisskopf, "White House Aides Overshadow EPA Chief," *Washington Post*, February 13, 1990.

92. John Noble Wilford, "His Bold Statement Transforms the Debate on Greenhouse Effect," *New York Times*, August 23, 1988.

93. George Bush, "From Afar, Both Candidates Are Environmentalists . . .," *New York Times*, September 24, 1988.

94. Philip Shabecoff, "The Environment as Local Jurisdiction," *New York Times*, January 22, 1989.

95. Quoted in Rochelle Stanfield, "Greenhouse Diplomacy," *National Journal*, March 4, 1989, 510.

96. Quoted in Michael Weisskopf, "How on Earth to Turn Off the Heat," *Washington Post*, March 21, 1989.

97. Cass Peterson, "Experts, OMB Spar on Global Warming," *Washington Post*, May 9, 1989.

98. Philip Shabecoff, "Scientist Says Budget Office Altered His Testimony," *New York Times*, May 8, 1989.

99. William Booth, "U.S. Details Global Warming Study," *Washington Post*, September 1, 1989.

100. Ibid. According to Daniel Lashof, formerly an EPA official, the administration simply renamed a lot of existing programs "global climate" but did not actually provide much new money.

101. William Booth, "Action Urged Against Global Warming," *Washington Post*, February 2, 1990.

102. Philip Shabecoff, "Team of Scientists Sees Substantial Warming of Earth," *New York Times*, April 16, 1990.

103. Quoted in Weisskopf, "White House Aides Overshadow EPA Chief."

104. Ibid.

105. Leonard Silk, "A Global Program for the Environment," *New York Times*, April 27, 1990.

106. Craig Whitney, "Scientists Urge Rapid Action on Global Warming," *New York Times*, May 26, 1990.

107. Bob Woodward and David S. Broder, "Quayle's Quest: Curb Rules, Leave 'No Fingerprints,'" *Washington Post*, January 9, 1992.

108. Quoted in Keith Schneider, "Administration's Regulation Slayer Has Achieved a Perilous Prominence," *New York Times*, June 30, 1992.

109. Gerry Sikorski, "Posturing about Lead Poisoning," *Washington Post*, October 21, 1991.

110. Michael Weisskopf, "Wetlands Protection and the Struggle over Environmental Policy," *Washington Post*, August 8, 1991. The council backed off its wetland regulation reforms after encountering resistance from EPA administrator Reilly. As the Bush administration drew to a close, the EPA announced wetlands regulations that, although less restrictive than those initially proposed by the administration, were far more restrictive than the ones suggested by Quayle.

111. Philip J. Hilts, "At the Heart of Debate on Quayle Council: Who Controls Federal Regulations?" *New York Times*, December 16, 1991.

112. Michael Weisskopf, "Rule-Making Process Could Soften Clean Air Act," *Washington Post*, September 21, 1991.

113. Michael Weisskopf, "Bush Curbs Clean Air Provision," *Washington Post*, May 17, 1992. The EPA's legal counsel, E. Donald Elliot, had concluded the rule change—which affected roughly 35,000 factories, chemical and phar-

maceutical plants, power plants, and other stationary sources—was *not* legally defensible.

114. Quoted in Michael Weisskopf, "Rule-Making Process Could Soften Clean Air Act," *Washington Post*, September 21, 1991.

115. Ibid.

116. Michael Weisskopf, "Quayle Council Official Had Role in Acid Rain Rule," *Washington Post*, December 6, 1991.

117. Woodward and Broder, "Quayle's Quest."

118. Jessica Mathews, "Bush's Double Game," *Washington Post*, November 22, 1991.

119. Quoted in Dana Priest, "Competitiveness Council Suspected of Unduly Influencing Regulators," *Washington Post*, November 18, 1991.

120. Ibid.

121. Dan Quayle, "Protecting America's Greatness," *Washington Post*, December 8, 1991.

122. "Justice Dept. Says It's Tough on Crimes Against the Earth," *Washington Post*, December 28, 1989.

123. Frank Swoboda, "EPA and OSHA Joining Forces," *Washington Post*, November 29, 1990.

124. Keith Shabecoff, "In Thicket of Environmental Policy, Bush Uses Balance as His Compass," *New York Times*, July 1, 1990.

125. Quoted in Keith Schneider, "The Environmental Impact of President Bush," *New York Times*, August 25, 1991.

126. Quoted in Andrew Rosenthal, "Bush, on West Coast, Skirts Two Conservation Issues," *New York Times*, May 22, 1990.

127. Quoted in John E. Yang, "Regulation of Business May Ease," *Washington Post*, January 21, 1992.

128. David E. Rosenbaum, "Bush's First Budget: Like Reagan's Last," *New York Times*, February 10, 1989.

129. This decision, announced at a campaign stop in Michigan, resolved what was in part a long-running dispute between the car industry and the oil industry. Seventeen years earlier the government had begun considering controlling fumes from refueling, and the question was whether to modify cars or fuel pumps. Bush's decision meant that the EPA would require gas station owners in about forty-five cities to install rubber collars on nozzles and vapor recovery systems on pumps. Environmentalists wanted *both* cars and gas stations to install devices, however. In January 1993, the D.C. Circuit ordered the EPA to draft rules requiring automakers to install canisters, saying the EPA administrator did not have the discretion to suspend publication of the standard.

130. Michael Weisskopf, "EPA Won't Tighten Urban Ozone Standard," *Washington Post*, August 4, 1992.

131. Michael Weisskopf, "Administration Considers Weaker Protections for Unpolluted Air," *Washington Post*, October 29, 1992.

132. Quoted in Michael Weisskopf, "Bush Curbs Clean Air Provision," *Washington Post*, May 17, 1992.

133. Quoted in Keith Schneider, "Courthouse Is a Citadel No Longer," *New York Times*, March 23, 1992.

134. Ibid.

135. Philip J. Hilts, "Senate Backs Faster Protection of Ozone Layer as Bush Relents," *New York Times*, February 7, 1992.

136. Specifically, a NASA satellite had detected exceptionally high levels of CFCs over a wide area of the Northern Hemisphere. In an early February 1992 press conference, scientists warned that the probability of significant ozone loss was higher than previously believed, and such losses could occur over populated regions, not just Antarctica. The press conference triggered alarming coverage by the *New York Times*, *Washington Post*, and *Time* magazine. The Senate quickly voted to accelerate the phaseout, and the White House acquiesced.

137. Thomas W. Lippman, "Energy Plan Emphasizes Production," *Washington Post*, February 9, 1991.

138. Tom Kenworthy and Ann Devroy, "Memo Shows Emission Cuts by U.S. Are Within Reach," *Washington Post*, April 25, 1992.

139. Steven Greenhouse, "Ecology, the Economy and Bush," *New York Times*, June 14, 1992.

140. The framework convention did impose some national obligations. It required all parties to formulate and regularly update a national program to mitigate climate change by addressing human-generated emissions of greenhouse gases. It further required industrialized countries to limit their greenhouse gas emissions and demonstrate they were taking steps to do so. Within six months of the treaty taking effect and periodically thereafter, all parties were required to report on progress "with the aim of returning individually or jointly to their 1990 levels" of emissions. In addition, industrial countries agreed to help finance and provide technology to developing countries through the Global Environmental Facility, a new international aid program. See William K. Stevens, "With Climate Treaty Signed, All Say They'll Do Even More," *New York Times*, June 13, 1992.

141. Schneider, "Administration's Regulation Slayer."

142. Quoted in Michael Wines, "Bush Says He Seeks Balance on the Environment," *New York Times*, May 31, 1992.

143. Quoted in Michael Wines, "Bush, Trying to Counter Criticism, Offers Plan to Save Earth's Forests," *New York Times*, June 2, 1992.

144. Richard L. Berke, "Oratory of Environmentalism Becomes the Sound of Politics," *New York Times*, April 17, 1990.

145. Matthew L. Wald, "Earth Day at 20: How Green the Globe?" *New York Times*, April 22, 1990.

146. D'Vera Cohn, "From Fringe to Political Mainstream," *Washington Post*, April 19, 1990.

147. Berke, "Oratory of Environmentalism."

148. Michael Weisskopf, "Environment Fades as Political Issue," *Washington Post*, February 1, 1992.

149. Matthew L. Wald, "Oil Industry Lashes Out at Restrictions," *New York Times*, November 19, 1991.

150. Keith Schneider, "Selling Out? Pushed and Pulled, Environment Inc. is on the Defensive," *New York Times*, March 29, 1992.

151. Quoted in Joel Connelly, "Bush Blames Owl for Lost Jobs; State Campaign Speech Goes After the Blue-Collar Vote," *Seattle Post-Intelligencer*, September 15, 1992.

152. Quoted in Michael Wines, "Bush, in Far West, Sides with Loggers," *New York Times*, September 15, 1992.

153. Quoted in Keith Schneider, "Bush and Congress Facing a Showdown on Forests," *New York Times*, May 12, 1992.

154. Tom Kenworthy, "Some Environmental Rules Loosened, Some Tightened," *Washington Post*, September 24, 1992.

155. Keith Schneider, "Environment Laws Are Eased by Bush As Election Nears," *New York Times*, May 20, 1992.

156. Quoted in ibid.

157. Quoted in John Lancaster, "Western Industries Fuel Grass-Roots Drive for 'Wise Use' of Resources," *Washington Post*, May 16, 1991.

158. Quoted in Jacqueline Vaughn Switzer, *Green Backlash: The History and Politics of Environmental Opposition in the U.S.* (Boulder, CO: Lynne Rienner Publishers, 1997), 200. Arnold appropriated the phrase "wise use" from conservationist Gifford Pinchot because it was both headline-friendly and rich in symbolism. See Thomas Lewis, "Cloaked in a Wise Disguise," in *Let the People Judge: Wise Use and the Private Property Rights Movement*, ed. John Echeverria and Raymond Booth Eby (Lanham, MD: Rowman & Littlefield, 1995).

159. The Blue Ribbon Coalition represented some 500,000 users of off-road vehicles. Founded in 1976 by Alan Gottlieb and Ron Arnold, the tiny but effective Center for the Defense of Free Enterprise sought to promote and defend a capitalist economy unfettered by regulations. Formed by mining companies in 1989, the Western States Public Lands Coalition and its subsidiary, People for the West!, sought to improve the public image of extractive industries. See MacWilliams Cosgrove Snider, *The Wise Use Movement: Strategic Analysis and the Fifty State Review* (Washington, DC: Environmental Working Group, 1993).

160. Wayne Hage, *Storm over Rangelands: Private Rights in Federal Lands* (Bellevue, WA: Free Enterprise Press, 1989), 20.

161. Quoted in Marla Williams, "Save the People!" *Boston Globe*, January 13, 1992.

162. Ibid.

163. Ibid.

164. Quoted in Frederick Buell, *Apocalypse as Way of Life* (New York: Routledge, 2003), 23.

165. Tom Kenworthy, "Showdown in Big Sky Country," *Washington Post Magazine*, September 27, 1992.

166. Quoted in Kate O'Callaghan, "Whose Agenda for America," *Audubon*, September–October 1992, 84.

167. Quoted in Tom Kenworthy, "Saving Plant and Animal Life," *Washington Post*, June 1, 1992.

168. Quoted in Robert B. Keiter, *Keeping Faith with Nature: Ecosystems, Democracy, and America's Public Lands* (New Haven, CT: Yale University Press, 2003), 235.

169. Nancie G. Marzulla, "The Property Rights Movement: How It Began and Where It Is Headed," in Bruce Yandle, ed., *Land Rights: The 1990s Property Rights Rebellion* (Lanham, MD: Rowman & Littlefield, 1995); Jeff Ruch, personal communication, 2009; Joseph L. Sax, "Environmental Law at the Turn of the Century: A Reportorial Fragment of Contemporary History," *California Law Review* 88, no. 6 (2000): 2375–2402.

170. Quoted in H. Jane Lehman, "Landowners Drawing the Battle Lines," *Los Angeles Times*, October 11, 1992.

171. Quoted in Keith Schneider, "As Earth Day Turns 25, Life Gets Complicated," *New York Times*, April 16, 1995.

172. Quoted in Keith Schneider, "When the Bad Guy Is Seen as the One in the Green Hat," *New York Times*, February 16, 1992.

173. Quoted in Kenneth Jost, "Property Rights," *CQ Researcher*, June 16, 1995, 516.

174. Quoted in O'Callaghan, "Whose Agenda for America," 84.

175. Marzulla, "Property Rights Movement," 22.

176. Quoted in Tom Kenworthy and Bill McAllister, "Environmentalists See Roadblock in 'Taking' Appraisals," *Washington Post*, November 6, 1991.

177. Lehman, "Landowners Drawing the Battle Lines."

178. The delta smelt population declined 90 percent between 1979 and 1991. Because it lives only one year and reproduces between February and May, which is prime pumping season, the smelt is a particularly good indicator of the health of the San-Joaquin-Sacramento-River Delta. NMFS listed the Snake River Sockeye after just four of them returned to their ancestral spawning grounds in Idaho's Sawtooth Mountains. Sea turtles have swum the world's oceans since the age of the dinosaurs, but their numbers dwindled rapidly during the mid-twentieth century. In the 1970s, NMFS listed five of the world's remaining sea turtle species as endangered or threatened under the Endangered Species Act. The service required shrimpers to install turtle excluder devices in response to data suggesting that shrimp trawlers were drowning 150,000 sea turtles each year. Environmentalists argue that the well-being of the human species is tied to the health of

ecosystems, and the precipitous declines in these species are ominous signals of ecosystem collapse.

179. A 1992 study by the World Wildlife Federation found that only 19 federal activities and projects out of a pool of almost 75,000 had been blocked or terminated in the preceding five years because of irreconcilable conflicts over species protection. See Tom Kenworthy, "Wildlife Protection Stops Few Projects, Study Asserts," *Washington Post*, February 11, 1992. Similarly, the federal government calculated that between 1987 and 1991, 34,203 projects had been proposed in areas where there was potential harm to endangered species. In only 367 cases did the government say the project would harm a species, and only 18 of those projects were actually canceled because of incompatibility with the Endangered Species Act. See Timothy Egan, "Strongest U.S. Environmental Law May Become Endangered Species," *New York Times*, May 26, 1992.

180. Ann Reilly Dowd, "Environmentalists Are on the Run," *Fortune*, September 19, 1994, 91–92, 96–100. The fine was issued not by the EPA but by the Fish and Wildlife Service, which enforces the Endangered Species Act; others put the fine at $7,000. See, for example, William Perry Pendley, "Doing Everything by the Book," American Policy Center (2008), http://americanpolicy.org/1999/03/29/doing-everything-by-the-book.

181. Jost, " Property Rights."

182. Quoted in Schneider, "Bush and Congress."

183. Quoted in Phillip A. Davis, "Economy, Politics Threaten Species Act Renewal," *CQ Weekly*, January 4, 1992.

184. Charles Oliver, "Tyrannosaurus Lex: Is Every Species Worth Saving?" *Reason*, April 1992, 23, 27.

185. Robert J. Smith, "Resolving the Tragedy of the Commons by Creating Private Property Rights in Wildlife. *Cato Journal* 1, no. 2 (Fall 1981), 444, 456.

186. Ike C. Sugg, "To Save an Endangered Species, Own One," *Wall Street Journal*, August 31, 1992.

187. Schneider, "Courthouse Is a Citadel No Longer."

188. William E. Kovacic, "The Reagan Judiciary and Environmental Policy: The Impact of Appointments to the Federal Courts of Appeals," *Environmental Affairs* 18, no. 4 (1991): 669–713; ibid.

189. Kovacic, "The Reagan Judiciary."

190. Michael S. Greve, *The Demise of Environmentalism in American Law* (Washington, DC: AEI Press, 1996).

191. William Glaberson, "Novel Antipollution Tool is Being Upset by Courts," *New York Times*, June 5, 1999.

192. The Bureau of Reclamation was overseeing construction of the Aswan Dam, which affected the habitat of the Nile crocodile and peregrine falcons. In Sri Lanka, the U.S. Agency for International Development was assisting with the construction of the Mahaweli Dam, which threatened the Indian elephant, the

leopard, and the red-faced Malkoha. The plaintiffs, who were studying the species in question, had asserted that the projects would threaten their enjoyment of wildlife.

193. Keith Schneider, "Environment Laws Face a Stiff Test from Landowners," *New York Times*, January 20, 1992.

194. In 1982, the original Court of Claims—created to hear financial claims against the federal government—was upgraded into the U.S. Court of Appeals for the Federal Circuit, and a new U.S. Court of Federal Claims was created at the next-highest level of the judicial system.

195. W. John Moore, "Just Compensation," *National Journal*, June 19, 1992.

196. Quoted in ibid.

197. Political scientist Mark Kann describes this perspective as a "corporate ideology," in which fears of environmental disaster are exaggerated, environmental problems are equated to a set of consumer demands (robbing them of their moral urgency), and corporations rather than government are best able to secure Americans' well being. See Mark E. Kann, "Environmental Democracy in the United States," in *Controversies in Environmental Policy*, ed. Sheldon Kamieniecki, Robert O'Brien, and Michael Clarke (Abany: State University of New York Press, 1986), 252–274.

198. John H. Cushman Jr., "Federal Regulations Growing Despite Quayle Panel's Role," *New York Times*, December 24, 1991. According to a report issued by the Heritage Foundation, the total annual length of the Federal Register grew from 53,376 pages in 1988 to 67,716 pages in 1991—the third highest ever. The number of federal employees devoted to issuing and enforcing regulations rose from 104,360 in 1988 to a new all-time high of 124,994. And the amount of money the federal government spent on regulatory programs each year increased 18 percent, from $9.558 billion in 1988 to $11.276 billion in 1992, in constant 1987 dollars. See William G. Laffer III, "George Bush's Hidden Tax: The Explosion in Regulation," Paper No. 905, July 1992.

199. Michael E. Kraft and Norman J. Vig, "Environmental Policy from the 1970s to 1990," in *Environmental Policy in the 1990s: Reform or Reaction?*, 3rd ed., ed. Norman J. Vig and Michael E. Kraft (Washington, D.C.: CQ Press, 1994), 3–29.

200. EPA4, personal communication, 2008.

201. Warren T. Brookes, 1990. "Chaining the Economy: America Dragged Down," *National Review*, October 15, 1990, 40.

202. Switzer, *Green Backlash*.

## Chapter 6

1. Christopher J. Bosso, "Seizing Back the Day: The Challenge to Environmental Activism in the 1990s," in *Environmental Policy in the 1990s: Reform or Reaction?*, 3rd ed., ed. Norman J. Vig and Michael E. Kraft (Washington, DC: CQ Press, 1997), 63.

2. The Environmental Defense Fund's annual revenue jumped nearly six-fold, from $3.4 million in 1985 to $20.2 million in 1992. Jim Maddy, executive director of the League of Conservation Voters, estimated the twenty largest groups combined could raise $1 billion per year. See Brad Knickerbocker, "Environmentalism Extends Its Reach," *Christian Science Monitor*, January 12, 1993.

3. Keith Schneider, "How a Rebellion over Environmental Rules Grew from a Patch of Weeds," *New York Times*, March 24, 1993.

4. "Bill Clinton, Environmentalist?" *New York Times*, January 5, 1993.

5. Norman J. Vig, "Presidential Leadership and the Environment: From Reagan to Clinton," in Vig and Kraft, *Environmental Policy in the 1990s*, 95–118.

6. Quoted in William Booth, "Everglades Accord Indicative of EPA Designee's Approach," *Washington Post*, January 11, 1993.

7. Despite purported improvements in transparency, a review by the U.S. Government Accountability Office (GAO) in 1998 found that complete documentation of substantive changes made in rules was available for only half of the 122 rules reviewed. The GAO recommended that the director of the OMB provide the agencies with guidance on how to implement the transparency requirements, but he declined to do so. See U.S. Government Accountability Office, *Regulatory Reform: Changes Made to Agencies' Rules Are Not Always Clearly Documented*, GAO/GGD-98-31, January 8, 1998.

8. EPA1, personal communication, 2009.

9. Joseph E. Stiglitz, *Globalization and Its Discontents* (New York: W. W. Norton & Company, 2003); Bob Woodward, *The Agenda: Inside the Clinton White House* (New York: Simon & Schuster, 1994). According to journalist Bob Woodward, Clinton's economic team converged on deficit reduction as a way of boosting financial markets and fending off inflation, while his pollster, Stanley Greenberg, told him the public was more concerned about job creation, health care reform, and welfare reform.

10. John Hart, "President Clinton and the Politics of Symbolism: Cutting the White House Staff," *Political Science Quarterly* 110, no. 3 (Fall 1995): 385–408.

11. Gary Lee, "Browner Strengthens Enforcement Office," *Washington Post*, October 14, 1993.

12. Phillip Cooper, *The War against Regulation: From Jimmy Carter to George W. Bush* (Lawrence: University Press of Kansas, 2009).

13. Quoted in Ibid., 61.

14. Robert Stavins and Thomas Grumbly, "The Greening of the Market: Making the Polluter Pay," in *Mandate for Change*, ed. Will Marshall and Martin Schram (New York: Berkeley Books, 1993), 197.

15. Quoted in Robert Pear, "In a Final Draft, Democrats Reject Part of Their Past," *New York Times*, June 26, 1992.

16. Tom Kenworthy, "Environmental Policy Overhaul Proposed," *Washington Post*, December 10, 1992.

17. David Callahan, "$1 Billion for Conservative Ideas," *The Nation*, April 26, 1999.

18. Ibid.

19. Peter J. Jacques, Riley E. Dunlap, and Mark Freeman, "The Organization of Denial: Conservative Think Tanks and Environmental Skepticism," *Environmental Politics* 17, no. 3 (2008): 349–385.

20. Michael Fumento, *Science Under Siege: How the Environmental Misinformation Campaign Is Affecting Our Law, Taxes, and Our Daily Life* (New York: Quill), 1993.

21. Ben Bolch and Harold Lyons, *Apocalypse Not* (Washington, DC: Cato Institute, 1993), 12.

22. Fred L. Smith, "Conclusion: Environmental Policy at the Crossroads," in *Environmental Politics: Public Costs, Private Rewards*, ed. Michael S. Greve and Fred L. Smith (New York: Praeger, 1992), 179–180.

23. Michael S. Greve, "Introduction: Environmental Politics Without Romance," in Greve and Smith, *Environmental Politics: Public Costs, Private Rewards*, 2.

24. Rush Limbaugh, *The Way Things Ought to Be* (New York: Simon & Schuster, 1992), 152, 155, 166–168.

25. Ibid, 156, 157, 164, 168.

26. Chlorine from natural sources is soluble, so it gets rained out of the lower atmosphere. CFCs, by contrast, are insoluble and inert, and thus make it to the stratosphere where they release their chlorine. Moreover, volcanic eruptions—the main natural source of chlorine—do not reach high enough to push chlorine into the stratosphere.

27. Gregg Easterbrook, *A Moment on the Earth: The Coming Age of Environmental Optimism* (New York: Viking Penguin, 1995); Ronald Bailey, ed., *The True State of the Planet* (New York: The Free Press, 1995).

28. Ronald Bailey, "Prologue: Environmentalism for the Twenty-First Century," in Bailey *The True State of the Planet*, 1, 3, 6.

29. James R. Dunn and John E. Kinney, *Conservative Environmentalism: Reassessing the Means, Redefining the Ends* (Westport, CT: Quorum Books, 1996), xv, 9, 138, 247–248.

30. Robert W. Crandall, Christopher DeMuth, Robert W. Hahn, Robert E. Litan, Pietro S. Nivola, and Paul R. Portney, *An Agenda for Federal Regulatory Reform* (Washington, DC: AEI/Brookings, 1997), 1.

31. Robert W. Hahn and Robert E. Litan, *Improving Regulatory Accountability* (Washington, DC: AEI/Brookings), 2.

32. Fred L. Smith, "Conclusion: Environmental Policy at the Crossroads," 190, 192.

33. Fred L. Smith, "Epilogue: Reappraising Humanity's Challenges, Humanity's Opportunities," in Bailey, *True State of the Planet*.

34. Kathleen Hall Jamieson and Joseph N. Capella, *Echo Chamber: Rush Limbaugh and the Conservative Media Establishment* (New York: Oxford University Press, 2008).

35. Ibid.; Katharine Q. Seelye, "Republicans Get a Pep Talk from Rush Limbaugh," *New York Times*, December 12, 1994.

36. Jamieson and Cappella, *Echo Chamber*.

37. Ibid., 4.

38. Markus Prior, *Post-Broadcast Democracy: How Media Choice Increases Inequality in Political Involvement and Polarizes Elections* (New York: Cambridge University Press, 2007), 228.

39. Richard Lazarus, *The Making of Environmental Law* (Chicago: University of Chicago Press, 2004). Political scientists Nolan McCarty, Keith Poole, and Howard Rosenthal find that the average positions of Republican and Democratic legislators began to diverge markedly in the 1970s, following a fifty-year period in which partisan divisions were blurred. See Nolan McCarty, Keith T. Poole, and Howard Rosenthal, *Polarized America: the Dance of Ideology and Unequal Riches* (Cambridge, MA: MIT Press, 2006).

40. Jessica Mathews, "Scorched Earth," *Washington Post*, October 18, 1994.

41. Quoted in Keith Schneider, "Second Chance on the Environment," *New York Times*, March 26, 1993.

42. Ibid.

43. Quoted in John H. Cushman Jr., "E.P.A. Critics Get Boost in Congress," *New York Times*, February 7, 1994.

44. Quoted in John H. Cushman Jr., "Environmental Lobby Beats Tactical Retreat," *New York Times*, March 30, 1994.

45. Ibid.

46. Frank Clifford, "GOP Divided on Environmental Regulation," *Los Angeles Times*, September 25, 1995.

47. Timothy Egan, "Campaigns Focus on 2 Views of West," *New York Times*, November 4, 1994.

48. Ibid. Egan explains that westerners seemed to be of two minds about the land; even in the urbanized West, cowboy symbolism retained a hold on the imagination, according to Democratic pollster Celinda Lake. But Republicans also benefited from the fact that only the most motivated vote in the midterm elections—and often against the party in power. See Timothy Egan, "Look Who's Hugging Trees Now," *New York Times*, July 7, 1996.

49. Egan, "Look Who's Hugging Trees."

50. Gary Younge, "Conservationists Unite to Send GOP a Message," *Washington Post*, August 17, 1996.

51. Quoted in Bob Benenson, "GOP Sets the 104th Congress on a New Regulatory Course," *CQ Weekly*, June 17, 1995.

52. Quoted in John H. Cushman Jr., "Alaska Delegation Pushes Agenda of Development," *New York Times*, September 13, 1998.

53. Ibid.

54. Quoted in Serge F. Kovaleski, "Gingrich's Guru: Corporate Psychotherapist Enlisted to Shape Message," *Washington Post*, December 8, 1994. Gingrich had

long recognized the importance of language; in 1990, when he was head of GOPAC, the Republican political action committee, the organization urged candidates to draw from a list of 133 labels it had devised. Some were invectives, to be deployed against the opposition, such as sick, pathetic, liberal, shallow, incompetent, permissive, destructive, insecure, and insensitive; others were plaudits to be used in describing oneself, such as moral, candid, humane, pristine, confident, and passionate.

55. Quoted in John H. Cushman Jr., "Congressional Republicans Take Aim at Extensive List of Environmental Statutes," *New York Times*, February 22, 1995.

56. Quoted in Cindy Skrzycki, "Hill Republicans Promise a Regulatory Revolution," *Washington Post*, January 4, 1995.

57. Ibid.

58. Ibid.

59. The moratorium spanned the period from November 20, 1994 to December 31, 1995.

60. Quoted in Michael Weisskopf and David Maraniss, "Forging an Alliance for Deregulation," *Washington Post*, March 12, 1995.

61. John H. Cushman Jr., "Republicans Plan Sweeping Barriers to New U.S. Rules," *New York Times*, December 25, 1994; Frank Swoboda, "Plan Combines a Revival of Reaganomics, Reins on Regulation," *Washington Post*, December 14, 1994; Jessica Mathews, "Green Sweep," *Washington Post*, December 18, 1994.

62. Quoted in Swoboda, "Plan Combines a Revival of Reaganomics."

63. Quoted in Gary Lee, "Gingrich Lashes Out at EPA," *Washington Post*, February 17, 1995.

64. Quoted in John H. Cushman Jr., "Backed by Business, G.O.P. Takes Steps to Overhaul Environmental Regulations," *New York Times*, February 10, 1995.

65. John H. Cushman Jr., "House Endorses Deep Cutbacks in Regulations," *New York Times*, March 4, 1995.

66. Senator John Chafee of Rhode Island had an LCV score of 57 in 1995; James Jeffords of Vermont had a score of 64; Olympia Snowe of Maine had a score of 64; and William Roth of Delaware had a score of 50. In addition, Arlen Specter of Pennsylvania had a score of 50.

67. David Cloud, "Industry, Politics Intertwined in Dole's Regulatory Bill," *CQ Weekly*, May 6, 1995.

68. Orrin Hatch and John Kyl, "Stop the Regulation Machine," *New York Times*, July 18, 1995.

69. Quoted in Christopher Georges, "House GOP Hopes to Cut Funding Used to Enforce Dozens of U.S. Regulations," *Wall Street Journal*, June 1, 1995.

70. Ibid.

71. Jessica Mathews, "Green Sweep."

72. Ibid.

73. John Skow, "Earth Day Blues," *Time*, April 24, 1995.

74. John H. Cushman Jr., "Environment Gets a Push from Clinton," *New York Times*, July 5, 1995.

75. Michael E. Kraft, "Environmental Policy in Congress: Revolution, Reform, or Gridlock?" in Vig and Kraft, *Environmental Policy in the 1990s*, 129.

76. Gary Lee, "Environmental Groups Launch Counterattack After Losses on Hill," *Washington Post*, August 19, 1995.

77. Bosso, "Seizing Back the Day."

78. Gary Lee, "GOP Is Warned of Backlash on Environment," *Washington Post*, January 24, 1996.

79. John H. Cushman Jr., "E.P.A. Bill, Modified, Still Faces Veto Threat," *New York Times*, November 19, 1995.

80. Quoted in Todd S. Purdum, "Clinton Says G.O.P. Rule Cutting Would Cost Lives," *New York Times*, February 22, 1995.

81. John H. Cushman Jr., "Proposed Changes Simplify Rules on Pollution Control," *New York Times*, March 17, 1995.

82. Quoted in Gary Lee, "Clinton Counters GOP Regulation Proposal," *Washington Post*, March 17, 1995.

83. Quoted in Timothy Noah and Michael Selz, "Clinton Acts to Ease Regulatory Burdens in Latest Attempt to Derail GOP Bills," *Wall Street Journal*, March 17, 1995.

84. Ibid.

85. John H. Cushman Jr., "Battles on Conservation Are Reaping Dividends," *New York Times*, July 31, 1996.

86. Quoted in Anne Devroy, "Clinton Issues Broadside on Environment," *Washington Post*, April 22, 1995.

87. Kraft, "Environmental Policy in Congress."

88. The $16 billion rescissions bill signed in the summer of 1995 directed the Forest Service and Bureau of Land Management to proceed within forty-five days with long-delayed timber sales involving 270 million board feet of timber. In addition to the timber salvage rider, the rescissions bill included restrictions on listing new hazardous waste sites, reduced protections for wildlife, and relieved the states of having to comply with some Clean Air Act provisions.

89. Quoted in Tom Kenworthy and Gary Lee, "Divided GOP Falters on Environmental Agenda," *Washington Post*, November 24, 1995.

90. John H. Cushman Jr., "Business Scaling Back Plans to Defang Regulations," *New York Times*, February 3, 1996.

91. Quoted in John H. Cushman Jr., "G.O.P. Backing Off from Tough Stand Over Environment," *New York Times*, January 26, 1996.

92. Quoted in Timothy Noah, "GOP's Rep. DeLay Is Working in Every Corner to Exterminate Regulations That Bug Business," *Wall Street Journal*, March 6, 1995.

93. Quoted in Bosso, "Seizing Back the Day," 58.

94. Quoted in Gary Lee, "GOP is Warned of Backlash on Environment," *Washington Post*, January 24, 1996.

95. EPA4, personal communication, 2008.

96. Quoted in John H. Cushman Jr., "Battles on Conservation Are Reaping Dividends," *New York Times*, July 31, 1996.

97. Albert Gore Jr., "Earth Days Have Become Earth Years," *New York Times*, April 23, 1995.

98. Some Democrats continued to work on regulatory reform as well. Senator Carl Levin of Michigan, the second-ranking Democrat on the Senate Governmental Affairs Committee, sponsored a comprehensive regulatory reform bill, the Regulatory Improvement Act of 1997. This bill required federal regulators to consider the costs of major new rules but was more modest than Dole's. It made little headway in the polarized 104th Congress.

99. Quoted in John H. Cushman Jr., "House G.O.P. Chiefs Back Off on Stiff Antiregulatory Plan," *New York Times*, March 6, 1996.

100. Kenneth J. Arrow, Maureen L. Cropper, George C. Eads, and Robert W. Hahn et al., "Is There a Role for Benefit-Cost Analysis in Environmental, Health, and Safety Regulations?" *Science* (April 12, 1996): 221–222.

101. John H. Cushman Jr., "Gingrich, Like the President, Calls for a 'New Environmentalism,'" *New York Times*, April 25, 1996.

102. Quoted in John H. Cushman Jr., "House G.O.P., Softening Stance, Issues Manifesto on the Environment," *New York Times*, May 16, 1996.

103. Quoted in Timothy Egan, "Look Who's Hugging Trees Now."

104. Timothy Egan, "The Congress and the Issues," *New York Times*, September 15, 1996.

105. John Shanahan, "Regulating the Regulators: Regulatory Process Reform in the 104th Congress," *Regulation* 20, no. 1 (Winter 1997).

106. Tom Kenworthy, "A Pesticide Balancing Act," *Washington Post*, August 2, 1999.

107. Margaret Kriz, "A Peace Treaty Over the Delaney Clause," *National Journal*, August 3, 1996.

108. Richard L. Berke, "In a Reversal, G.O.P. Courts the 'Greens,'" *New York Times*, July 2, 1997.

109. Quoted in Juliet Eilperin, "GOP Group Forms to Promote Free-Market Environmentalism," *Washington Post*, June 15, 1998.

110. Quoted in John M. Broder, "Deregulation: Crusade Shifts to Compromise," *New York Times*, January 31, 1997.

111. Joby Warrick, "Clinton Claims Environmental Gains in Interior Bill," *Washington Post*, November 15, 1997.

112. Tom Kenworthy, "Differences on Environment Are Often a Matter of Degree," *Washington Post*, October 8, 1996.

113. Sally Katzen, "We've Been Shredding the Red Tape," *Wall Street Journal*, July 19, 1995.

114. Broder, "Deregulation."

115. Quoted in Gary Lee, "Analyzing Risk Assessment at EPA," *Washington Post*, March 8, 1994.

116. Quoted in John H. Cushman Jr., "House Approves Sweeping Changes on Regulations," *New York Times*, March 1, 1995.

117. Mintz, *Enforcement at the EPA*; Brad Knickerbocker, "Pragmatism Beats Out Ideology in Clinton Environmental Policy," *Christian Science Monitor*, December 27, 1993.

118. Quoted in John H. Cushman Jr., "States Neglecting Pollution Rules, White House Says," *New York Times*, December 15, 1996.

119. The EPA was taking a heavy hand because of states' recent tendencies to adopt pro-industry environmental policies. For instance, legislatures in twenty-three states had adopted environmental audit laws granting amnesty to companies that admitted to having violated state environmental requirements. Such laws allowed companies to keep their pollution records secret and immunized firms from future legal challenges. That said, overall, Browner's EPA accelerated the trend initiated by her Republican predecessors of delegating responsibility for regulatory programs to the states; as a result, by 1998, the EPA had devolved responsibility for 757 environmental programs, an increase of nearly 75 percent over five years earlier. See John H. Cushman Jr., "Clinton Backs Environmental Power-Sharing," *New York Times*, January 31, 1999.

120. Specifically, Congress required preconstruction review and a permit for major modifications of existing pollution sources. (If a modification was found to be major, the source would be subject to NSPS and PSD rules.) Congress defined "modification" as "any physical change in, or change in the method of operation of, a stationary source which increases the amount of any air pollutant emitted by such source or which results in the emission of any air pollutant not previously emitted." Between 1975 and 1980, the EPA advanced regulations to elaborate the meaning of "modification," establishing a two-step test to determine whether the change was physical or operational and whether emissions would increase as a result. The EPA also established a policy to exempt routine maintenance activities based on "common sense," case-by-case reviews of industry requests.

121. The reasoning behind the sector-based approach was that in many industries competition was so intense that if one figured out how to evade compliance, the others followed suit, so it was critical to look at performance across an entire industry sector. According to Eric Schaeffer, former head of enforcement at the

EPA, many in industry resented the sector-based approach, which suggested to him that entire industries were systematically ignoring the law. Eric Schaeffer, "Clearing the Air: Why I Quit Bush's EPA," *Washington Monthly*, July/August 2002, www.washingtonmonthly.com/features/2001/0207.schaeffer.html.

122. Ground-level ozone is formed by a reaction of nitrogen oxides, volatile organic compounds, carbon monoxide, and methane. These pollutants have numerous sources, from power plants and factories to motor vehicles and gasoline vapors. Because sunlight is a catalyst for ozone, it is worst in summer.

123. Jon Cannon, "Bargaining, Politics, and Law in Environmental Regulation," in *Environmental Contracts*, ed. Eric W. Orts and Kurt Deketelaere (Boston: Kluwer Law International, 2001), 39–70.

124. C. Boyden Gray, "Superfund of the Sky," *Wall Street Journal*, June 24, 1997; Thomas D. Hopkins, "Proof? Who Needs Proof? We're the EPA!," *Wall Street Journal*, April 21, 1997; Steven J. Milloy and Michael Gough, "The EPA's Clean Air-ogance," *Wall Street Journal*, January 7, 1997.

125. Wendy L. Gramm and Susan E. Dudley, "The Human Cost of EPA Standards," *Wall Street Journal*, June 9, 1997; Kenneth Chilton and Christopher Boerner, "Health and Smog: No Cause for Alarm," *Regulation*, Summer 1995; Michael Fumento, "Polluted Science," *Reason*, August/September 1997, 28–42.

126. Broder, "Deregulation."

127. Quoted in John Fialka, "Clinton Backs Rules Covering Air Pollution—Standards Split Difference Between Positions Held by U.S. Agencies," *Wall Street Journal*, June 26, 1997.

128. Quoted in John H. Cushman Jr., "Administration Issues Its Proposal for Tightening of Air Standards," *New York Times*, November 28, 1996.

129. Quoted in Margaret Kriz, "Heavy Breathing," *National Journal*, January 4, 1997.

130. Claudia Deutsch, "Still Defiant, But Subtler, Industry Awaits E.P.A. Rules," *New York Times*, May 27, 1997.

131. Quoted in John H. Cushman Jr., "Clinton Sharply Tightens Air Pollution Regulations Despite Concerns over Cost," *New York Times*, June 26, 1997.

132. Quoted in Joseph B. White, "EPA Extends Olive Branches to Auto Makers," *Wall Street Journal*, March 23, 1993.

133. Quoted in Hobart Rowen, "Browner's Fresh Breeze of Candor at EPA," *Washington Post*, October 3, 1993.

134. Cannon, "Bargaining, Politics, and Law," 39.

135. EPA1, personal communication, 2009; EPA2, personal communication, 2009; EPA4, personal communication, 2008; EPA5, personal communication, 2008; EPA6, personal communication, 2009.

136. Gary Lee, "EPA Chief Plans Major 'New Direction,'" *Washington Post*, July 20, 1994.

137. Gary Lee, "Compromising on Clean Air Act," *Washington Post*, February 21, 1996.

138. Cindy Skrzycki, "Critics See a Playground for Polluters in EPA's XL Plan," *Washington Post*, January 24, 1997.

139. EPA1, personal communication, 2009; EPA2, personal communication, 2009; EPA4, personal commuication, 2008; EPA5, personal communication, 2008. Ultimately, however, according to one EPA official, the Common Sense Initiative "led to zero change."

140. Gary Lee, "Regulatory Reform Effort Helps Industry Hit Targets," *Washington Post*, April 4, 1996.

141. Quoted in Lee, "Compromising in Clean Air Act."

142. Gary Lee, "EPA Tells Chemical Plants to Cut Toxic Emissions 88%," *Washington Post*, March 2, 1994.

143. Matthew L. Wald, "E.P.A. Steps into Auto Pollution Dispute," *New York Times*, December 17, 1997.

144. The Clean Air Act Amendments of 1990 gave state officials until November 1994 to submit revised state implementation plans. When state officials protested, the EPA extended the deadline until late 1996. Nevertheless, a coalition of GOP governors, legislators, and corporate lobbyists mounted a vigorous campaign against the new requirements, particularly the centralized emissions testing programs. In a tense session with Browner in 1995, the governors threatened to mobilize for a legislative repeal of the act unless she relaxed some of the law's requirements.

145. John Fialka, "EPA Plans to Offer Incentives to Curb 'Sprawl' Pollution," *Wall Street Journal*, October 18, 2000. This voluntary program built on a tax law change passed in 1998 that let employers either provide workers with as much as $65 per month in tax-free commuter vouchers or allow them buy up to $65 per month in transit passes with pretax payroll deductions.

146. John Fialka, "EPA Is Considering Increased Flexibility in Issuing Industry Air-Pollution Permits," *Wall Street Journal*, June 5, 2000.

147. Quoted in Cindy Skryzycki, "Slowing the Flow of Federal Rules," *Washington Post*, February 18, 1996.

148. Ibid.

149. John Leshy, "The Babbitt Legacy at the Department of the Interior: a Preliminary View," *Environmental Law* (Spring 2001).

150. Ellen Gamerman, "Poll Shows Widespread Support for Endangered Species Act," States News Service, January 27, 1992; "Species Act: New Poll Finds Widespread Support," *Greenwire*, March 26, 1993.

151. Ike Sugg, "The Timber Summit: Ecosystem Babbitt-babble," *Wall Street Journal*, April 2, 1993.

152. David Gelertner, "In Rats We Trust," *Washington Post*, November 17, 1996.

153. Julian Simon and Aaron Wildavsky, "Facts, Not Species, Are Periled," *New York Times*, May 13, 1993.

154. David Wilcove and Michael Bean, "Before Skies Become Entirely Barren of Birds," *New York Times*, May 25, 1993.

155. Gregg Easterbrook, "The Birds," *New Republic*, March 28, 1994.

156. Charles C. Mann and Mark L. Plummer, "The Butterfly Problem," *Atlantic Magazine*, January 1992.

157. Quoted in William K. Stevens, "Battle Looms over U.S. Policy on Species," *New York Times*, November 16, 1993.

158. Quoted in Mark Dowie, *Losing Ground: American Environmentalism at the Close of the Twentieth Century* (Cambridge, MA: MIT Press, 1995), 64.

159. Erik Larson, "Unrest in the West," *Time*, October 23, 1995.

160. Peter D. Coppelman, "The Federal Government's Response to the County Supremacy Movement," *NR&E*, Summer 1997, 30–33, 79–80.

161. Brad Knickerbocker, "The Radical Element: Violent Conflict Over Resources," *Christian Science Monitor*, May 2, 1995.

162. Maura Dolan, "Nature At Risk in Quiet War," *Los Angeles Times*, December 20, 1992.

163. Kenneth R. Harney, "Senate Bill Would Give Property Owners New Weapons in Battle with Regulators," *Washington Post*, May 13, 1995.

164. John H. Cushman Jr., "Senate Halts Property Bill Backed by G.O.P.," *New York Times*, July 14, 1998.

165. Quoted in John H. Cushman Jr., "Senate Halts Property Bill Backed by G.O.P.," *New York Times*, July 14, 1998.

166. ENV1, personal communication, 2009.

167. Dolan, "Nature At Risk in Quiet War."

168. William K. Stevens, "Future of Endangered Species Act in Doubt as Law is Debated," *New York Times*, May 16, 1995.

169. Quoted in Timothy Egan, "Industries Affected by Endangered Species Act Help a Senator Rewrite Its Provisions," *New York Times*, April 13, 1995.

170. DOI1, personal communication, 2009.

171. National Research Council, *Science and the Endangered Species Act* (Washington, DC: The National Academies Press, 1995); Tom Kenworthy, "Panel Supports Stronger Species Act," *Washington Post*, May 25, 1995.

172. Tom Kenworthy, "Interior Report Says Species Law Works," *Washington Post*, October 31, 1995.

173. Quoted in Richard Lacayo, "This Land Is Whose Land?" *Time*, October 23, 1995.

174. Quoted in Peter Steinfels, "Evangelical Group Defends Laws Protecting Endangered Species as a Modern 'Noah's Ark,'" *New York Times*, January 31, 1996.

175. Legal scholar J. B. Ruhl describes the ruling in this case as a "pyrrhic victory" for environmentalists because the decision also said that a proof-of-harm violation requires proximate causation and foreseeability and must establish "injury to particular animals"—a tort-law approach that rules out accidental harm. See J. B. Ruhl, "The Endangered Species Act's Fall From Grace in the

Supreme Court," Vanderbilt University Law School, Public Law & Legal Theory, Working Paper No. 11-29, 2011.

176. Ibid.

177. For example, in mid-December 1992, shortly before leaving office, the George H. W. Bush administration settled a lawsuit with environmentalists that required the government to list four hundred species of plants and animals over the next four years—increasing by 53 percent the number of species receiving federal protection. The agency also agreed to expedite consideration of nine hundred species that it believed were worthy of protection but for which definitive scientific evidence had not been collected.

178. Joseph L. Sax, "Environmental Law at the Turn of the Century: A Reportorial Fragment of Contemporary History," *California Law Review* 88, no. 6 (2000): 2375–2402. Once a species is listed, a property owner must apply for a permit to the Fish and Wildlife Service to conduct any activity on her land that might harm that species. The property owner can protect herself from civil suits or criminal penalties by obtaining an "incidental take" permit. To get such a permit, she must file a plan that satisfies the service that she is doing her best not to destroy the species or its habitat. Litigation also irked Fish and Wildlife Service officials because it allowed environmentalists to set their priorities, and because they feared litigation-driven activities would consume their entire budget.

179. Public Employees for Environmental Responsibility, "War of Attrition: Sabotage of the Endangered Species Act by the U.S. Department of Interior," White Paper, December 1997, http://www.peer.org/pubs/whitepapers/1997_war _of_attrition.pdf.

180. Marcilynn Burke, "Klamath Farmers and Cappuccino Cowboys: The Rhetoric of the Endangered Species Act and Why It (Still) Matters," *Duke Environmental Law & Policy Forum* 14 (Spring 2004): 441.

181. Noah D. Greenwald, Kieran F. Suckling, and Martin Taylor, "The Listing Record," in *The Endangered Species Act at Thirty: Renewing the Conservation Promise*, ed. Dale D. Goble, J. Michael Scott, and Frank W. Davis (Washington, DC: Island Press, 2006), 51–67.

182. Quoted in Rob Taylor and Mike Merritt, "Clinton Promises Action," *Seattle Post-Intelligencer*, April 3, 1993.

183. Quoted in William K. Stevens, "Interior Secretary Is Pushing a New Way to Save Species," *New York Times*, February 17, 1993.

184. Specifically, the ten principles were: (1) treat landowners fairly and with consideration; (2) minimize social and economic impacts; (3) create incentives for landowners to conserve species; (4) provide quick, responsive answers and certainty to landowners; (5) base Endangered Species Act decisions on sound and objective scientific information; (6) prevent species from becoming endangered or threatened; (7) promptly recover and delist threatened or endangered species; (8) provide state, tribal, and local governments with opportunities to play a greater role in carrying out the Endangered Species Act; (9) make effective use of limited public and private resources by focusing on groups of species

dependent on the same habitat; and (10) promote efficiency and consistency in the Departments of Interior and Commerce.

185. Quoted in Tom Kenworthy, "Administration Moves to Ease Opposition to Biodiversity Act," *Washington Post*, June 15, 1994.

186. Quoted in Kostyak, "Tipping the Balance," 345.

187. DOI1, personal communication, 2009. Although environmentalists initially prevailed in court when they challenged the No Surprises and Permit Revocation rules, both were eventually reissued by the George W. Bush administration and upheld by the Federal District Court for the District of Columbia.

188. Laura Hood Watchman, Martha Groom, and John D. Perrine, "Science and Uncertainty in Habitat Conservation Planning," *American Scientist* 89, no. 4 (July/August 2001).

189. Quoted in Skrzycki, "Slowing the Flow of Federal Rules."

190. Karen Donovan, "HCPs—Important Tools for Conserving Habitat and Species," in *The Endangered Species Act: Law, Policy, and Perspectives*, ed. Donald C. Baur and William Robert Irvin (Chicago: American Bar Association, 2002), 326–327.

191. Bruce Babbitt, personal communication, 2008.

192. John Kostyack, "Tipping the Balance," in Baur and Irvin, *The Endangered Species Act: Law, Policy, and Perspectives*, 339.

193. Michael O'Connell, "Response to: 'Six Biological Reasons Why the Endangered Species Act Doesn't Work and What to Do About It,'" *Conservation Biology* 6, no. 1: 142.

194. Rodger Schlickeissen, personal communication, 2009.

195. Michael J. Bean, personal communication, 2008.

196. Michael J. Bean, "Endangered Species Act and Private Land: Four Lessons Learned From the Past Quarter Century," *Environmental Law Reporter* 28 (1998): 10701–10710; Michael J. Bean, "Lessons From Leopold in Assessing the ESA," *Endangered Species Bulletin*, November/December 1999, 18–19; Michael J. Bean, "Overcoming Unintended Consequences of Endangered Species Regulation," *Idaho Law Review* 38 (2002), 409–420.

197. Bean, "Endangered Species Act and Private Land," 10702.

198. Quoted in Peter Chilson, "Lawmakers Struggle to Rewrite the Endangered Species Act," *High Country News*, March 16, 1998. One pragmatist, David Wilcove of the Environmental Defense Fund, wrote one of the signatories of the scientific letter asking him to reconsider his position, arguing that unless concessions were made, landowners would simply not report endangered species or, even worse, would destroy species on their land to avoid discovery.

199. Robert C. Balling, "Global Warming: Messy Models, Decent Data, and Pointless Policy," in *True State of the Planet*, ed. Ronald Bailey (New York: The Free Press, 1995), 84.

200. Warren T. Brookes, "Chaining the Economy: America Dragged Down," *National Review*, October 15, 43.

201. Ben Bolch and Harold Lyons, *Apocalypse Not* (Washington, DC: Cato Institute), 80, 81.

202. S. Fred Singer, "Benefits of Global Warming," *Society* 29 (March–April 1993), 33.

203. Jane S. Shaw and Richard L. Stroup, "Getting Warmer?" *National Review*, July 14, 1989, 27, 28.

204. Wilfred Beckerman and Jesse Malkin, "How Much Does Global Warming Matter?" *Public Interest*, Winter 1994, 3–16.

205. Thomas Gale Moore, "Why Global Warming Would Be Good for You," *Public Interest* (Winter 1995), 83–99.

206. Quoted in Margaret Kriz, "The Selling of 'the Green President,'" *National Journal*, September 19, 1992.

207. Quoted in Gregg Easterbrook, Kent Jenkins Jr., and Kenneth T. Walsh, "Hot Air Treaty," *U.S. News & World Report*, December 22, 1997, 46.

208. Quoted in Ross Gelbspan, *The Heat Is On: The Climate Crisis, The Cover Up, the Prescription*, updated ed. (New York: Perseus Books 1998), 34.

209. The Western Fuels Association was undaunted, however. In 1998, it formed the Greening Earth Society, to advance the notion that carbon dioxide emissions would benefit mankind. That same year, the American Petroleum Institute reprised the idea of a media campaign to discredit climate change science; it devised the "Global Science Communications Plan" with the aim of making doubt about climate change the conventional wisdom.

210. In early 1996, the organization's advisory committee gave it a seventeen-page primer that found unpersuasive the contrarian arguments and theories challenging the conventional model of greenhouse gas–induced climate change.

211. A Danish journalist who investigated the story found that twelve of the thirty-three European signatories denied signing the petition. See Eric Pooley, *The Climate War: True Believers, Power Brokers, and the Fight to Save the Earth* (New York: Hyperion, 2010).

212. See the petition at http://www.petitionproject.org/instructions_for_signing _petition.php.

213. Quoted in Seth Schliesel, "Kyoto? Rio? Al Gore? Cyberviews of the Eco-Fatigued," *New York Times*, December 8, 1997.

214. Maxwell T. Boykoff and Jules M. Boykoff, "Balance as Bias: Global Warming and the U.S. Prestige Press," *Global Environmental Change* 14 (2004): 125–136.

215. Mike Mills, "Tough Talk Is Heating Up; Specific Action Unlikely," *CQ Weekly*, January 20, 1990.

216. George Gallup Jr., and F. Newport, "Americans Strongly in Tune with the Purpose of Earth Day 1990," *The Gallup Poll Monthly* 295, April, 5–9, 1990.

217. Craig Trumbo, "Constructing Climate Change: Claims and Frames in US News Coverage of an Environmental Issue," *Public Understanding of Science* 5 (1996): 269–283.

218. Boykoff and Boykoff, "Balance As Bias," 133.

219. Keith Schneider, "Gore Meets Resistance in Efforts for Steps on Global Warming," *New York Times*, April 19, 1993.

220. Elizabeth Drew, *On the Edge: The Clinton Presidency* (New York: Simon & Schuster, 1994); Margaret Kriz, "A Green Tax," *National Journal*, April 17, 1993.

221. Jon Healey, "Deficit, Environmental Worries Push Fuel Taxes to Forefront," *CQ Weekly*, January 9, 1993; Bob Woodward, *The Agenda: Inside the Clinton White House* (New York: Simon & Schuster, 1994).

222. Woodward, *The Agenda*.

223. Pooley, *Climate War*.

224. Gary Lee, "Clinton Offers Package to 'Halt Global Warming,'" *Washington Post*, October 20, 1993.

225. Catalina Camia, "Clinton Offers Plan on Global Warming," *CQ Weekly*, October 23, 1993.

226. Quoted in George E. Brown Jr., "Environmental Science under Siege in the U.S. Congress," *Environment* 39, no. 2 (1997): 14.

227. Ibid.

228. Quoted in Dan Morgan, "Strengthened U.S. Commitment Lights a Fire under Global Warming Debate," *Washington Post*, September 13, 1996.

229. Ibid.

230. Allan Freedman, "'Greenhouse' Issue Heats Up as Kyoto Talks Approach," *CQ Weekly*, November 29, 1997.

231. Gale E. Christianson, *Greenhouse: The 200-Year Story of Global Warming* (New York: Penguin Books 1999), 258.

232. Pooley, *Climate War*. Pooley notes that treaty supporters engaged in a scripted discussion in order to provide a legislative history that would clarify the intent of the resolution, but to no avail.

233. Phillip A. Davis, "Congress Calls on President to Fight Global Warming," *CQ Weekly*, April 11, 1992.

234. Quoted in Joby Warrick and Peter Baker, "Clinton Details Global Warming Plan," *Washington Post*, October 23, 1997.

235. John H. Cushman Jr. and David E. Sanger, "No Simple Fight: The Forces That Shaped the Clinton Plan," *New York Times*, December 1, 1997.

236. After struggling for two years to come up with a single, credible analysis of the economic effects of moving away from fossil fuels, in the summer of 1997, the administration declared the effort a failure. See ibid.

237. Quoted in Allan Freedman, "Coalition Behind Bill Faces Pressure All Around," *CQ Weekly*, September 27, 1997.

238. Quoted in Allan Freedman, "Presidential Issues: Seeking Middle Ground on Divisive Issues," *CQ Weekly*, October 5, 1996.

239. Quoted in Warrick and Baker, "Clinton Details Global Warming Plan."

240. Ronald D. Elving, "Saving the Earth, Losing Peoria," *CQ Weekly*, December 13, 1997. The industry campaign did not appear to have affected the public: a *New York Times* poll taken in November 1997 found that only 6 percent nationwide recalled seeing industry ads opposing a treaty; of those who recalled the ads, two-thirds said they were not influenced, and the remainder said they were as likely to have been swayed in favor of as against the treaty. See John H. Cushman Jr., "Intense Lobbying against Global Warming Treaty," *New York Times*, December 7, 1997.

241. Quoted in Allan Freedman, "'Greenhouse' Issue Heats Up."

242. Quoted in Eric Schmitt, "Congress, the Kibbitzers at the Climate Table, Waits for Its Turn," *New York Times*, December 1, 1997.

243. Quoted in Alison Mitchell, "G.O.P. Hopes Climate Fight Echoes Health Care Outcome," *New York Times*, December 13, 1997.

244. Quoted in Charles Pope, "Fresh Focus on Global Warming Does Not Dispel Doubts about Kyoto Treaty's Future," *CQ Weekly*, June 6, 1998.

245. Ibid.

246. There were sharp debates over climate change language in fiscal year 1999 appropriations bills for the Departments of Energy and Interior as well.

247. Quoted in Lori Nitschke, "Battles over Kyoto Treaty May Delay House Action on VA-HUD Spending Bill," *CQ Weekly*, June 27, 1998.

248. Quoted in Charles Pope, "Opposition to Global Warming Treaty Is Cropping Up in Spending Bills," *CQ Weekly*, August 1, 1998.

249. Joby Warrick, "Administration Signs Global Warming Pact," *Washington Post*, November 13, 1998.

250. Quoted in Charles Pope, "A Year after Kyoto Pact's Completion, the Political Heat Is Unabated," *CQ Weekly*, November 21, 1998.

251. The U.S. federal government is the world's largest energy user; it consumes more than $8 billion worth each year, about half of that to heat, cool, and light buildings.

252. John D. Echeverria, personal communication, 2011.

253. Rosemary O'Leary, "Environmental Policy in the Courts," in *Environmental Policy: New Directions for the Twenty-First Century*, 7th ed., ed. Norman J. Vig and Michael E. Kraft (Washington, DC: CQ Press, 2010), 140.

254. Although it concerned physical, rather than regulatory, takings, the Court's 2005 ruling in *Kelo et al. v. City of New London et al.* devastated conservative activists and provoked heated debate among urban planners and legal scholars over the use of eminent domain. In the Kelo case, the city of New London, Connecticut, after approving an urban redevelopment plan, purchased a large swath of property, mostly from willing sellers. When fifteen residents refused to sell, however, the city initiated condemnation proceedings, with the goal of transferring the land to a private developer. The plaintiffs sued, on the grounds that taking their property violated the "public use" restriction on the Fifth Amendment's Takings Clause ("nor shall private property be taken for public use, without just compensation"). In his opinion for the 5–4 majority, Justice John

Paul Stevens argued that the city's proposed plan did, in fact, qualify as a "public use" within the meaning of the Takings Clause because the property was to be used for the "public purpose" of economic development.

255. William Glaberson, "Novel Antipollution Tool Is Being Upset by Courts," *New York Times*, June 5, 1999.

256. John D. Echeverria and Jon T. Zeidler, "Barely Standing," *Environmental Forum* 16, no. 4 (1999): 27.

257. Ruth Marcus, "Issues Groups Fund Seminars for Judges," *Washington Post*, April 9, 1998.

258. Cited in Abner Mikva, "The Wooing of Our Judges," *New York Times*, August 28, 2000.

259. Mikva, "Wooing of Our Judges."

260. Michael E. Greve, *The Demise of Environmentalism in American Law* (Washington, DC: AEI Press, 1996), 19.

261. Frank B. Cross and Emerson H. Tiller, "Judicial Partisanship and Obedience to Legal Doctrine: Whistleblowing on the Federal Court of Appeals," *Yale Law Journal* 107 (1986): 2155+; Richard J. Pierce Sr., "Is Standing Law or Politics?" 77 *North Carolina Law Review* (June 1999): 1741; Richard Revesz, "Environmental Regulation, Ideology, and the D.C. Circuit," 83 *Virginia Law Review* (1997), 1717–1772; Cass R. Sunstein, David Schkade, Lisa M. Ellman, and Andres Sawicki, *Are Judges Political? An Empirical Analysis of the Federal Judiciary* (Washington, DC: Brookings Institution Press, 2006).

262. John Leshy, "The Babbitt Legacy at the Department of the Interior: a Preliminary View," *Environmental Law* (Spring 2001).

263. Cindy Skzrycki, "White House Initiatives Hit Roadblocks," *Washington Post*, June 20, 2000.

264. Quoted in Dan Morgan, "Clinton's Last Regulatory Rush," *Washington Post*, December 6, 2000.

265. Keith Schneider, "For the Environment, Compassion Fatigue," *New York Times*, November 6, 1994.

266. Bruce A. Ackerman and Richard B. Stewart, "Reforming Environmental Law: The Democratic Case for Market Incentives," *Columbia Journal of Environmental Law* 13, no. 2 (1998): 171–200; Stephen Breyer, *Breaking the Vicious Circle* (Cambridge, MA : Harvard University Press, 1993); Marion R. Chertow and Daniel C. Esty, eds., *Thinking Ecologically: The Next Generation of Environmental Policy* (New Haven, CT: Yale University Press, 1997); J. Clarence Davies and Jan Mazurek, *Pollution Control in the United States: Evaluating the System* (Washington, DC: Resources for the Future, 1998); Jeremy B. Hockenstein, Robert N. Stavins, and Bradley W. Whitehead, "Crafting the Next Generation of Market-Based Environmental Tools," *Environment* 39, no. 4 (May 1997): 13–20, 30–3; C.S. Holling and Gary K. Meffe, "Command and Control and the Pathology of Natural Resource Management," *Conservation Biology* 10, no. 2 (April 1996): 328–337; Dewitt John, *Civic Environmentalism: Alternatives to*

*Regulation in States and Communities* (Washington, DC: CQ Press, 1994); Debra Knopman, "Second Generation: A New Strategy for Environmental Protection," Policy Report, Progressive Policy Institute, April 19, 1996, http://www.dlc.org/documents/2ndGen.pdf; Jessica Mathews, "Scorched Earth," *Washington Post*, October 18, 1994; Paul R. Portney, "Chain-Saw Surgery," *Washington Post*, January 15, 1995; David A. Salvesen and Douglas R. Porter. 1995. "Introduction" in *Collaborative Planning for Wetlands and Wildlife*, ed. Douglas R. Porter and David A. Salvesen (Washington, DC: Island Press, 1995), 1–6; James G. Speth, Russell E. Train, and Douglas M. Costle, "A National Strategy for Helping America Clean Up by Cleaning Up," *Washington Post*, October 4, 1992; Richard B. Stewart, "United States Environmental Regulation: A Failing Paradigm," *Journal of Law and Commerce* 15 (1996): 585+; Cass R. Sunstein, "Paradoxes of the Regulatory State," *University of Chicago Law Review* 57, no. 2 (1990): 407–441. For descriptions of the process by which the consensus on the need for reform evolved in the environmental policy community, see Daniel A. Mazmanian and Michael E. Kraft, eds., *Toward Sustainable Communities: Transition and Transformations in Environmental Policy* (Cambridge, MA: MIT Press, 1999); and Daniel J. Fiorino, *The New Environmental Regulation* (Cambridge, MA: MIT Press, 2006).

267. Iwin M. Stelzer and Paul R. Portney, *Making Environmental Policy: Two Views* (Washington, DC: AEI Press, 1998), 24–25.

268. Keith Schneider, "As Earth Day Turns 25, Life Gets Complicated," *New York Times*, April 16, 1995.

269. Cary Coglianese, "Limits of Consensus," *Environment* 41, no.3 (April 1999), 28-33.

270. Quoted in Cindy Skrzycki, "New President's Choices at Regulatory Agencies Will Set the Course," *Washington Post*, November 5, 2000.

## Chapter 7

1. Andrew C. Revkin, "Bush vs. the Laureates: How Science Became a Partisan Issue," *New York Times*, October 19, 2004. Although every administration interprets scientific information in ways that are consistent with its political philosophy, the Bush administration provoked an unusually widespread and strident backlash among scientists inside and outside of government for its efforts to control information. See Union of Concerned Scientists, *Scientific Integrity in Policymaking: An Investigation into the Bush Administration's Misuse of Science* (March 2004), http://www.ucsusa.org/assets/documents/scientific_integrity/rsi_final_fullreport_1.pdf; United States House of Representatives, Committee on Oversight and Government Reform, *Political Interference With Climate Change Science* (December 2007), http://oversight-archive.waxman.house.gov/documents/20071210101633.pdf.

2. Mike Allen and Eric Pianin, "Democrats See Environment as a Bush Liability," *Washington Post*, March 24, 2001.

3. Quoted in Jim Yardley, "Governor Bush and the Environment," *New York Times*, November 9, 1999.

4. Norman J. Vig, "Presidential Leadership and the Environment," in *Environmental Policy: New Directions for the Twenty-First Century*, 5th ed., ed. Norman J. Vig and Michael E. Kraft (Washington, DC: CQ Press, 2003), 103–125.

5. Quoted in Frank Bruni, "Flexibility on Nature Is Needed, Bush Says," *New York Times*, June 2, 2000.

6. Frank Bruni, "Bush, in Energy Plan, Endorses New U.S. Drilling to Curb Prices," *New York Times*, September 30, 2000.

7. Eric Pianin and Amy Goldstein, "Bush Drops a Call for Emissions Cuts," *Washington Post*, March 14, 2001.

8. Quoted in Joseph Kahn and David E. Sanger, "President Offers Plan to Promote Oil Exploration," *New York Times*, January 30, 2001. Between 2000 and 2001, California faced a series of large-scale blackouts that affected hundreds of thousands of electricity customers.

9. Ibid.

10. Quoted in Katharine Q. Seelye, "Industry Seeking Rewards from G.O.P.-Led Congress," *New York Times*, December 3, 2002.

11. Quoted in Douglas Jehl, "On Environmental Rules, Bush Sees a Balance, Critics a Threat," *New York Times*, February 23, 2003.

12. Although he focused on language professionally, Luntz appeared to be a genuine believer in the conservative position and warned that the public had erroneously come to regard Republicans as against the environment because they were against existing laws or regulations. In a December 2003 *Frontline* interview, when asked whether the phrase "healthy forests" was an example of using language to obfuscate, Luntz said, "thanks to environmentalists who are extreme and radical in their approach, who say that we must not touch anything at any time in any way, we lose thousands, thousands, hundreds of thousands of acres of forests and all the wildlife that was inside it. And they don't come back again. It takes generations for it to regenerate. So don't tell me about language, because 'healthy forests' actually is what it means."

13. The entire memo—part of a larger briefing book—is available at the Web site of the Environmental Working Group, http://www.ewg.org/files/LuntzResearch_environment.pdf.

14. In fact, the Clinton administration did write a record number of new regulations, publishing 26,542 pages in the *Federal Register* in its final three months in office. See Darren Samuelsohn, "As Bush Administration Winds Down, Washington Awaits 'Midnight' Rules," *Greenwire*, September 23, 2008. The flurry of new rules put in place by the Clinton administration was nothing new, however. Beginning with Reagan, finalizing rules that had been in the pipeline during an administration's final months was standard practice. A study by the Mercatus Center entitled "Midnight Rules" found that beginning in 1948, no matter which party held the White House, when power shifted to the other party the page count in the *Federal Register* was, on average, 17 percent higher than in nonelec-

tion years. See Cindy Skrzycki, "Bush Wants Sun to Set on Midnight Regulations," *Washington Post*, June 3, 2008.

15. Bruce Barcott, "Changing All the Rules," *New York Times Magazine*, April 4, 2004.

16. ENV7, personal communication, 2008.

17. Grunwald and Pianin, "A Mixed Environmental Bag," *Washington Post*, December 23, 2000; David M. Halbfinger and Andrew C. Revkin, "Whitman Seen as Strong Choice for E.P.A.," *New York Times*, December 21, 2000; Douglas Jehl, "Whitman Promises Latitude to States on Pollution Rules," *New York Times*, January 18, 2001; John Sullivan, "As Mrs. Whitman Begins Her New Job, There Is Debate over Her Commitment to the Environment in the Past," *New York Times*, February 4, 2001.

18. Grunwald and Pianin, "A Mixed Environmental Bag."

19. Quoted in Melinda Henneberger, "Despite Appearances, Whitman Says She and Bush Agree on Environment," *New York Times*, April 17, 2001.

20. Quoted in Douglas Jehl, "Whitman Promises Latitude to States on Pollution Rules," *New York Times*, January 18, 2001.

21. "EPA in the Balance," *Wall Street Journal*, May 22, 2003.

22. Robert F. Kennedy Jr., "Crimes Against Nature," *Rolling Stone*, December 11, 2003.

23. Quoted in Felicity Barringer, "Bush's Record: New Priorities in Environment," *New York Times*, September 14, 2004.

24. Quoted in Katharine Q. Seelye, "Bush Choice to Head E.P.A. Asks Clinton Administrator for Reference," *New York Times*, August 13, 2003.

25. EPA2, personal communication, 2009.

26. Quoted in Stephen Labaton, "Bush Is Putting Team in Place for a Full-Bore Assault on Regulation," *New York Times*, May 23, 2001.

27. Quoted in Douglas Jehl, "Interior Choice Sends a Signal on Land Policy," *New York Times*, December 30, 2000.

28. Rebecca Adams, "Environmentalists Question Norton's Conciliatory Stands, but Confirmation Expected," *CQ Weekly*, January 20, 2001; Douglas Jehl, "Environmental Groups Join in Opposing Choice for Interior Secretary," *New York Times*, January 12, 2001; Douglas Jehl, "Norton Record Often at Odds with Laws She Would Enforce," *New York Times*, January 13, 2001.

29. Quoted in "Norton Sticks to 'Collaborative' Theme Throughout Questioning," *Environment and Energy Daily*, January 19, 2001.

30. Lynn Scarlett, "New Environmentalism," National Center for Policy Analysis, January 1, 1997, http://www.ncpa.org/pub/st201?pg=12.

31. Quoted in Katharine Q. Seelye, "Bush Is Choosing Industry Insiders to Fill Several Environmental Positions," *New York Times*, May 12, 2001.

32. Eric Pianin, "In Pollution Debates, Bush's Man Seeks Harmony Amid the Storm," *Washington Post*, August 5, 2003.

33. Quoted in Douglas Jehl, "Regulations Czar Prefers New Path," *New York Times*, March 25, 2001.

34. Quoted in Katharine Q. Seelye, "White House Identifies Regulations That May Change," *New York Times*, December 20, 2002.

35. The proposed cuts came in the wake of extraordinary increases in some environmental agencies' budgets between fiscal year 2000 and fiscal year 2001. See John D. McKinnon, "Bush Mulls Cutting Budget Outlays for Environment," *Wall Street Journal*, February 22, 2001.

36. Stephen Power and Jacob M. Schlesinger, "Redrawing the Lines: Bush's Rules Czar Brings Long Knife to New Regulations," *Wall Street Journal*, June 12, 2002.

37. Quoted in Amy Goldstein, "'Last-Minute' Spin on Regulatory Rite," *Washington Post*, June 9, 2001.

38. EPA2, personal communication, 2009.

39. Marty Coyne, "White House Calls for External Review of Science Behind Agency Rules," *Greenwire*, September 4, 2003.

40. Michael Grunwald, "Business Lobbyists Asked to Discuss Onerous Rules," *Washington Post*, December 4, 2001.

41. Cindy Skrzycki, "Report Sheds Light on Changing Role of Regulation," January 25, *Washington Post*, 2005.

42. U.S. GAO, *OMB's Role in Reviews of Agencies' Draft Rules and the Transparency of Those Reviews*, GAO-03-929, September 2003.

43. Quoted in Rebecca Adams, "GOP Adds New Tactics to War on Regulations," *CQ Weekly*, January 31, 2005.

44. Tasha Eichenseher, "White House Seeks to Ease Rules on Manufacturers," *Greenwire*, March 15, 2005.

45. Colin Macilwain, "Safe and Sound," *Nature* 442 (July 20, 2006): 242–243.

46. Quoted in John J. Fialka, "White House, in Rare Move, Yields to Scientific Panel on Policy Plan," *Wall Street Journal*, January 12, 2007.

47. Susan E. Dudley and Sharon L. Hays, "Updated Principles for Risk Analysis," Memorandum for the Heads of Executive Departments and Agencies, September 19, 2007.

48. Enacted on December 21, 2000, the law occupied twenty-seven lines (227 words) in a 712-page Treasury and General Government Appropriations Act, the year's omnibus spending bill. It took effect on October 1, 2002.

49. Tozzi pioneered the practice of attacking the science underpinning proposed regulations. According to journalist Rick Weiss, Tozzi crafted key sentences in the Data Quality Act and then gave the bill to Republican representative Jo Ann Emerson of Missouri, who in turn inserted it into the Treasury and General Government Appropriations Act. See Rick Weiss, "'Data Quality' Law is Nemesis of Regulation," *Washington Post*, August 16, 2004.

50. Quoted in Rebecca Adams, "Federal Regulations Face Assault on Their Foundation," *CQ Weekly*, August 10, 2002.

51. Quoted in Andrew C. Revkin, "Law Revises Standards for Scientific Study," *New York Times*, March 21, 2002.

52. Weiss, "'Data Quality' Law."

53. Ibid. Between 2002 and 2005, the U.S. Chamber of Commerce submitted twenty-eight requests for corrections of EPA data. See Cindy Skrzycki, "EPA Data Not Reliable, Business Lobby Says," *Washington Post*, June 7, 2005.

54. Margaret Kriz, "Bush's Quiet Plan," *National Journal*, November 30, 2002.

55. Robert W. Hahn and Robert E. Litan, "Improving Regulatory Accountability" (Washington, DC: AEI & Brookings, 2007), www.brookings.edu/papers/2007/01_execorder_litan.aspx?p=1.

56. Quoted in Robert Pear, "Bush Directive Increases Sway on Regulation," *New York Times*, January 30, 2007.

57. After several senators died or resigned, by the end of the 107th Congress, the party balance was 49–50–1, with Republicans holding a slim majority.

58. Jacqueline Vaughn and Hanna J. Cortner, *George W. Bush's Healthy Forests Act: Reframing the Environmental Debate* (Boulder: University Press of Colorado, 2006).

59. Quoted in Felicity Barringer and Michael Janofsky, "Republicans Plan to Give Environment Rules a Free-Market Tilt," *New York Times*, November 8, 2004.

60. Ibid.

61. Felicity Barringer, "Environmentalists, Though Winners in the Election, Warn against Expected Vast Changes," *New York Times*, November 14, 2006.

62. Margaret Kriz, "Vanishing Act," *National Journal*, April 12, 2008.

63. Felicity Barringer, "Greater Role for Nonscientists in E.P.A. Pollution Decisions," *New York Times*, December 8, 2006.

64. Eric Pianin and Juliet Eilperin, "Lawmakers Join Effort to Fight Diesel Rule," *Washington Post*, July 24, 2002.

65. Gregg Easterbrook, "Hostile Environment," *New York Times Magazine*, August 19, 2001.

66. Quoted in John J. Fialka, "Off-Road Vehicles Fueled by Diesel Targeted by EPA," *Wall Street Journal*, April 16, 2003.

67. Ibid.

68. David Stout, "In Revising Clean Air Rules, E.P.A. Draws Praise and Criticism in the Same Week," *New York Times*, March 15, 2008. In 2002, the EPA proposed to curb emissions from U.S. ships and began building a case to regulate foreign ships, which account for 95 percent of calls on U.S. ports. But after its consultation with the OMB, the agency issued a much less restrictive proposal that postponed action on foreign-flagged vessels while imposing regulations for U.S. ships that mirrored what those ships were already doing.

69. Gina Solomon, a senior scientist at the NRDC, pointed out, however, that because the EPA had dismantled half of the nation's air-monitoring stations, it would be difficult to ascertain how much lead was actually in the air in many communities. See Juliet Eilperin, "EPA Places Stricter Regulations on Lead," *Washington Post*, October 17, 2008.

70. John J. Fialka and David S. Cloud, "White House Review Freezes EPA Inquiry," *Wall Street Journal*, June 28, 2001.

71. John J. Fialka, "Coal Industries Seek Fewer EPA Reviews—Utilities, Mining Firms Say Clean Air Rule Damps Overhaul of Power Plants," *Wall Street Journal*, May 1, 2001.

72. Joseph Kahn, "A New Role for Greens: Public Enemy," *New York Times*, March 25, 2001.

73. Quoted in Richard Benedetto, "Cheney's Energy Plan Focuses on Production," *USA Today*, May 1, 2001. Consistent with this view, the president's budget framework envisioned cutting funding for energy efficiency and renewable energy programs by 30 percent. See Kahn, "A New Role for Greens." In late June, however, the administration added a proposal for nearly $300 million to finance Clinton-era energy conservation programs—money the administration had struck from the budget earlier in the year. The White House maintained the move was not political—polls had shown Americans believed the administration's energy plan was primarily to help oil companies—but rather the result of a review by Energy Secretary Abraham. See David E. Sanger and Lizette Alvarez, "Conservation-Mindful Bush Turns to Energy Research," *New York Times*, June 29, 2001.

74. Douglas Jehl, "A New Focus on Supply," *New York Times*, May 18, 2001.

75. Joseph Kahn and Jeff Gerth, "Energy Industry Raises Production at a Record Pace," *New York Times*, May 13, 2001.

76. Quoted in Thomas Frank, *The Wrecking Crew: How Conservatives Rule* (New York: Metropolitan Books, 2008), 160.

77. Quoted in David A. Sanger, "Bush Shows His Green Side to Sell Agenda," *New York Times*, May 19, 2001.

78. Quoted in Bruce Barcott, "Changing All the Rules," *New York Times Magazine*, April 4, 2004.

79. Katharine Q. Seelye, "The Art of Turning a Sow's Ear Into a Silk Purse," *New York Times*, January 13, 2002; Katharine Q. Seelye, "E.P.A. and Energy Department War Over Clean Air Rules," *New York Times*, February 19, 2002.

80. Quoted in Seelye, "E.P.A. and Energy Department War."

81. Quoted in Katharine Q. Seelye, "Top E.P.A. Official Quits, Criticizing Bush's Policies," *New York Times*, March 1, 2002.

82. Quoted in Seelye, "E.P.A. and Energy Department War." In October 2003, the *Washington Post* reported that Jeffrey Holmstead had misled Congress about the impact of changing NSR rules on pending lawsuits. Apparently, Holmstead told two Senate committees in 2002 that the EPA did not expect the proposed

rule changes to have a negative effect on enforcement cases. But EPA enforcement officials Eric Schaeffer and Sylvia Lowrance claimed they had told Holmstead repeatedly that the rule changes *would* undermine ongoing enforcement cases. Former EPA enforcement official Bruce Buckheit also told Congress that he had briefed Holmstead about the likely impact of the rule changes. See Eric Pianin, "Ex-EPA Officials Question Clean Air Suits," *Washington Post*, October 10, 2003; Darren Samuelsohn, "Bush NSR Reforms Face Inspector General Scrutiny," *Greenwire*, August 12, 2004.

83. Ryan Dezember, "EPA's Air-Pollution Action Keeps Industry in a Fog," *Wall Street Journal*, November 25, 2002.

84. Quoted in Katharine Q. Seelye, "White House Seeks a Change in Rules on Air Pollution," *New York Times*, June 14, 2002.

85. Quoted in John J. Fialka, "EPA's New Rules Ease Power-Plant Upgrades," *Wall Street Journal*, August 28, 2003.

86. Environmental Integrity Project and Council of State Governments/Eastern Regional Conference, "Reform or Rollback? How EPA's Changes to New Source Review Could Affect Air Pollution in 12 States," October 2003, http://www.environmentalintegrity.org/pdf/publications/ReformOrRollbackSummary_final.pdf. At the behest of the Rockefeller Family Fund, the nonpartisan National Academy of Public Administration reviewed the study and characterized its methodology as "appropriate, reasonable, and fair."

87. U.S. Government Accountability Office, *New Source Review Revisions Could Affect Utility Enforcement Cases and Public Access to Emissions Data*, GAO-04-58, October 2003.

88. Quoted in Darren Samuelsohn, "Bush Presses Air Pollution Reforms, Legislation," *Greenwire*, September 16, 2003; Rachel L. Swarns, "Bush Defends New Environmental Rules," *New York Times*, September 16, 2003; Barcott, "Changing All the Rules."

89. For example, in mid-April 2003, the Dominion Virginia Power Company agreed to spend $1.2 billion installing pollution control technology in eight coal-burning power plants in Virginia and West Virginia, pay $5.3 million in federal fines, and spend $14 million for various states' environmental projects. See Jennifer 8. Lee, "Utility to Spend $1.2 Billion to Cut Emissions," *New York Times*, April 19, 2003. The settlement was the same as the one reached in 2000, under the Clinton administration, but delayed for several years due to confusion about the Bush administration's position. Two weeks after the Dominion settlement, the Wisconsin Electric Power Company agreed to spend $600 million over ten years to reduce pollution at five plants in Wisconsin and Michigan. It also agreed to pay $3.2 million in fines and spend at least $20 million to test technology to remove mercury from coal. See "Wisconsin Utility Reaches Pollution Accord," *New York Times*, April 3, 2003.

90. Quoted in Darren Samuelsohn, "Former EPA Enforcement Chief Questioned NSR Reform Package," *Greenwire*, October 2004.

91. Eric Pianin, "Bush Moves to Defuse Environmental Criticism," *Washington Post*, February 2, 2004.

92. Darren Samuelsohn, "No New Electric Utility Lawsuits in the Offing, DOJ Official Says," *Greenwire*, March 21, 2005.

93. Darren Samuelsohn, "Bush NSR Reforms Face Inspector General Scrutiny," *Greenwire*, August 12, 2004.

94. U.S. Environmental Protection Agency, Office of Inspector General, New Source Review Rule Change Harms EPA's Ability to Enforce Against Coal-fired Electric Utilities, 2004-P-00034, September 30, 2004.

95. Ohio Edison agreed to spend $1.1 billion on pollution controls that would reduce emissions by 212,000 tons annually. It also agreed to pay an $8.5 million civil penalty and spend $25 million in environmental mitigation.

96. As the case returned to the Fourth Circuit, the utilities were planning to adopt a new legal strategy. They intended to argue—as they had in the late 1990s—that the EPA's enforcement activities "retroactively targeted 20 years of accepted practice" by utilities; they also planned to rejuvenate the argument that the changes they made were "routine maintenance," not major modifications—an issue the Supreme Court had not addressed. See Daniel Cusick, "Industry Establishes Blueprint for Future NSR Legal Arguments," *Greenwire*, April 4, 2007.

97. Matthew L. Wald and Stephanie Saul, "Big Utility Says It Will Settle 8-Year-Old Pollution Suit," *New York Times*, October 9, 2007.

98. In February 2002, however, the EPA changed its stance and claimed that under existing regulations nitrogen oxides would only be cut to 4 million tons, sulfur dioxide to 9.1 million tons, and mercury to 43 tons.

99. Quoted in Katharine Q. Seelye, "White House Rejected a Stricter E.P.A. Alternative to the President's Clear Skies Plan," *New York Times*, April 28, 2002.

100. Jeffords's bill (S. 556) set a 2008 deadline for a 75 percent reduction in sulfur dioxide and nitrogen oxides from current regulation and 1997 baselines respectively, as well as a 90 percent cut in mercury from 1990 levels. Carbon dioxide emissions would fall to 1990 levels. Carper's more modest bill (S. 3135) required a cut in nitrogen oxides of 54 percent by 2008 and 58 percent by 2012; reductions in sulfur dioxide emissions of 50 percent by 2008, 61 percent by 2012, and 75 percent by 2015; and a cut in mercury of 68 percent by 2008, along with source-by-source controls to achieve required reductions of 50 percent by 2008 and 70 percent by 2012. Carper's bill would also stabilize carbon dioxide emissions at 2005 levels by 2008, and by 2012, would cap carbon dioxide at 2001 levels.

101. Guy Gugliotta and Eric Pianin, "Senate Plan Found More Effective, Slightly More Costly Than Bush Proposal," *Washington Post*, July 1, 2003.

102. Quoted in Guy Gugliotta and Eric Pianin, "EPA Issues Rosier 'Clear Skies' Analysis, Based on New Model," *Washington Post*, July 2, 2003.

103. Documents from a meeting between Energy Secretary Abraham, Interior Secretary Norton, and other cabinet officials revealed discussions about "how to achieve the goals of the president's Clear Skies Initiative through the administrative approach, using existing Clean Air Act authority." Quoted in Jennifer 8. Lee,

"E.P.A. Plans to Expand Pollution Markets," *New York Times*, December 15, 2003.

104. Quoted in John J. Fialka, "EPA Sets Strict Limits on Power-Plant Emissions," *Wall Street Journal*, March 11, 2005.

105. Quoted in Christopher Drew and Richard A. Oppel Jr., "How Power Lobby Won Battle of Pollution Control at E.P.A.," *New York Times*, March 6, 2004.

106. Juliet Eilperin, "Bush Pollution Curbs are Rated Equal to Clinton's," *Washington Post*, July 22, 2006.

107. "Decisions Shut Door on Bush Clean-Air Steps," *New York Times*, July 12, 2008.

108. According to the National Academy of Sciences, 60,000 children born each year may suffer from learning disabilities if their mothers ate mercury-laden food while pregnant. See National Research Council, *Toxicological Effects of Methylmercury* (Washington, DC: National Academies Press, 2000).

109. Greg Hitt, "Mercury Issue Takes Wing," *Wall Street Journal*, June 9, 2004. The Clinton EPA had considered cap-and-trade for mercury as well, in response to pressure from the OMB, but EPA lawyers had concluded the approach would be legally vulnerable.

110. Jennifer 8. Lee, "U.S. Proposes Easing Rules on Emissions of Mercury," *New York Times*, December 3, 2003.

111. Quoted in Eric Pianin, "EPA Led Mercury Policy Shift," *Washington Post*, December 30, 2003.

112. Juliet Eilperin, "Further Study Ordered on Mercury Regulation," *Washington Post*, March 17, 2004.

113. Eric Pianin, "Mercury Rules Work, Study Finds," *Washington Post*, November 6, 2003.

114. Jennifer 8. Lee, "White House Minimized Risks of Mercury in Proposed Rules, Scientists Say," *New York Times*, April 7, 2004.

115. U.S. Environmental Protection Agency, Office of the Inspector General, *Additional Analyses of Mercury Emissions Needed Before EPA Finalizes Rules for Coal-Fired Electric Utilities*, 2005-P-00003, February 3, 2005.

116. U.S. Government Accountability Office, Observations on EPA's Cost-Benefit Analysis of Its Mercury Control Options, GAO-05-252, February 2005.

117. Quoted in Juliet Eilperin, "Ozone Rules Weakened at Bush's Behest," *Washington Post*, March 14, 2008.

118. Ibid.

119. Daniel Cusick, "EPA Science Advisers Fire Missive to Administrator Over Soot Rule," *Greenwire*, October 3, 2006.

120. Quoted in Gabriel Nelson, "EPA Staffers Recommend a Crackdown on Soot," *Greenwire*, April 20, 2011.

121. Juliet Eilperin, "EPA Moves to Ease Air Rules for Parks," *Washington Post*, November 19, 2008.

122. Quoted in Juliet Eilperin, "Clean-Air Rules Protecting Parks Set to be Eased," *Washington Post*, May 16, 2008.

123. EPA9, personal communication, 2009.

124. EPA6, personal communication, 2009.

125. Schaeffer, "Clearing the Air."

126. Juliet Eilperin, "EPA Faulted on Clean-Water Violations," *Washington Post*, March 31, 2004.

127. Marty Coyne, "Agency Touts Record Year for Enforcement-Related Penalties," *Greenwire*, November 16, 2004.

128. John Solomon and Juliet Eilperin, "Bush's EPA is Pursuing Fewer Polluters," *Washington Post*, September 30, 2007.

129. The same data showed that the number of people convicted of environmental crimes dropped from 738 in 2001 to 470 in 2006, and the number of cases opened by EPA investigators fell 37 percent from 482 in 2001 to 305 in 2006.

130. Joel Mintz, "'Treading Water': A Preliminary Assessment of EPA Enforcement During the Bush II Administration," *Environmental Law Reporter* 34 (October 2004): 10933.

131. U.S. Government Accountability Office, *The EPA Needs to Ensure That Best Practices and Procedures Are Followed When Making Further Changes to Its Library Network*, GAO-08-304, February 2008; Margaret Kriz, "Vanishing Act," *National Journal*, April 12, 2008.

132. Christopher Lee, "EPA Closure of Libraries Faulted for Curbing Access to Data," *Washington Post*, March 14, 2008. The Obama administration began to restore the library system in 2009, and in 2011, they initiated a strategic planning process to rejuvenate the system.

133. John Sullivan and John Shiffman, "Green Club and EPA Charade," *Philadelphia Inquirer*, December 9, 2008.

134. Cary Coglianese and Jennifer Nash, "Government Clubs: Theory and Evidence from Voluntary Environmental Programs," University of Pennsylvania Law School, Public Law and Legal Theory Research Paper Series, Research Paper No. #08–49 (2008).

135. Quoted in Sullivan and Shiffman, "Green Club and EPA Charade."

136. U.S. Environmental Protection Agency, Office of Inspector General, *Performance Track Could Improve Program Design and Management to Ensure Value*, Report No. 2007-P-00013, March 29, 2007.

137. Sullivan and Shiffman, "Green Club and EPA Charade."

138. Ibid.

139. Ibid.

140. The administration argued that increasing domestic production of oil, gas, and other natural resources was the best way to maintain rural jobs, stimulate the economy, and free the United States from dependence on foreign sources.

They applied this prescription to the national forests, where they sought rule changes that would loosen restrictions on timber harvesting, and to western land controlled by the Interior Department, where they created incentives to promote energy development while "streamlining" environmental review. With respect to forest policy, for example, the administration replaced the Clinton-era roadless-area rule with a policy that allowed governors to petition the federal government if they wished to keep certain areas roadless; gave forest managers more discretion to approve logging, drilling, off-road vehicle use, and other commercial activities with less evaluation of environmental damage; and weakened requirements aimed at preventing fish and wildlife in national forests from becoming endangered or threatened—changes that were justified in the name of efficiency. With respect to energy development, the Interior Department revised land-use plans to allow more development in oil- and gas-rich areas, and Bureau of Land Management officials offered incentives to employees who were able to speed approval of new drilling permits. Although the courts blocked some high-profile permits, the net result was that the number of approved permits for new wells soared, from slightly more than 1,900 wells in 2000 to nearly 6,000 by 2004. See Joby Warrick and Juliet Eilperin, "Oil and Gas Hold the Reins in the Wild West," *Washington Post*, September 25, 2004.

141. Between 1995 and 2001, the Fish and Wildlife Service listed 315 species under court order. By contrast, between 2001 and 2007, the service listed only 55 species, all under court order. See Noah Greenwald, "Implementation of the Endangered Species Act by the Bush Administration: A Case Study in Abuse of Executive Authority," 2008, http://www.cspinet.org/integrity/pdf/Greenwald.ESA%20talk%202008%20three.pdf.

142. Katharine Q. Seelye, "Ending Logjam, U.S. Reaches Accord on Endangered Species," *New York Times*, August 30, 2001.

143. Allison Winter, "New Listings Wait as Obama Administration Charts New Course," *Greenwire*, November 24, 2009. Although the Bush administration cited budget woes and litigation as reasons for its slow pace of listing, the facts belied this explanation. Between 2000 and 2006, the Fish and Wildlife Service's listing budget increased from $6.2 million to $17.6 million. To take another measure, the number of species protected per dollar declined dramatically under Bush. The service listed nearly thirty species per million dollars in 1997 and over seven species per million dollars in 1998. Between 2002 and 2006, the agency listed an average of just 2.4 species per million dollars. Similarly, the Clinton administration completed many more court-ordered determinations (290) between 1995 and 2001 than the Bush administration completed (178) between 2001 and 2007. And finally, the Bush administration had a greater propensity to reject listings than did the Clinton administration. Between 1995 and 2001, of the 692 listing determinations completed, only 13 percent denied protection to candidate species. Of the 206 listing determinations completed between 2001 and 2007, 52 percent denied protection. See Noah Greenwald, "Politicizing Extinction: The Bush Administration's Dangerous Approach to Endangered Wildlife," Center for Biological Diversity, n.d., http://www.biologicaldiversity.org/publications/papers/PoliticizingExtinction.pdf.

144. Juliet Eilperin, "Since '01, Guarding Species Is Harder," *Washington Post*, March 23, 2008.

145. Quoted in ibid.

146. Quoted in Felicity Barringer, "New Rule on Endangered Species in Southwest," *New York Times*, May 24, 2005.

147. Jeff Ruch, "Endangered Species Act Implementation: Science or Politics?" Testimony Before the House Natural Resources Committee, May 9, 2007.

148. According to the GAO, recovery plans play an important role in species recovery efforts by identifying many of the actions that biologists deem most important to species' recovery. See U.S. Government Accountability Office, *Many Factors Affect the Length of Time to Recover Select Species*, GAO-06-730, September 2006.

149. Dan Berman, "FWS's Spotted Owl Plan Based on Shaky Science—Review Panel," *Greenwire*, August 14, 2007.

150. April Reese, "New Threats Could Undermine Obama Admin's Plan for Northern Spotted Owl," *Land Letter*, April 9, 2009.

151. Greg Winter, "U.S. Acts to Shrink Endangered Species Habitats," *New York Times*, March 20, 2002; Amy Sinden, "The Economics of Endangered Species: Why Less is More in the Economic Analysis of Critical Habitat Designations," *Harvard Environmental Law Review* 28 (2004): 129–214.

152. Douglas Jehl, "Rare Arizona Owl (All 7 Inches of It) Is in Habitat Furor," *New York Times*, March 17, 2003.

153. Felicity Barringer, "Endangered Species Act Faces Broad New Challenges," *New York Times*, June 26, 2005; Juliet Eilperin, "Endangered Species Act's Protections Are Trimmed," *Washington Post*, July 4, 2004.

154. Noah Greenwald, "Politicizing Extinction."

155. U.S. Government Accountability Office, *Fish and Wildlife Service Uses Best Available Science to Make Listing Decisions, but Additional Guidance Needed for Critical Habitat Designations*, GAO-03-803, August 2003.

156. Center for Biological Diversity et al., "Bush Administration Attacks Endangered Species Act," n.d., http://www.biologicaldiversity.org/publications/papers/esa_attack.pdf.

157. Quoted in Felicity Barringer, "Endangered Species Act Faces Broad New Challenges," *New York Times*, June 26, 2005. Legal scholar Amy Sinden notes that the Fish and Wildlife Service resisted designating critical habitat under the Clinton administration as well. She points out, however, that the Bush administration went much further, giving the ruling in the *New Mexico Cattlegrowers* case the broadest possible reach. See Sinden, "The Economics of Endangered Species."

158. Eric Pianin, "Free-Market Environmentalists Gaining Stature," *Washington Post*, June 4, 2001.

159. Lynn Scarlett, personal communication, 2009.

160. Quoted in Natalie M. Henry, "Norton Touts Private Conservation in 'New Environmentalism,'" *Greenwire*, February 21, 2002.

161. Scarlett, 2009.

162. Quoted in Tim Breen, "FWS Releases First of New Conservation Funds," *Greenwire*, September 27, 2001.

163. DOI3, personal communication, 2009; ENV2, personal communication, 2008.

164. The administration claimed it was fully funding the LWCF, but the numbers it cited included programs beyond those for land acquisition and state matching grants—the only two activities authorized under the program. In fiscal year 2003, the Bush administration requested $532 million for the LWCF but received only $414 million. In fiscal year 2004, the administration requested $348 million but Congress cut that to $225 million. In fiscal year 2005, the federal acquisition program received $166 million, while state grants amounted to $92.5 million; in fiscal year 2006, the federal pot contained $114.5 million, and the state pot was $30 million; in fiscal year 2007 the numbers were nearly identical ($113 million for federal land acquisition and $30 million for state grants).

165. Quoted in Michael Grunwald, "Plan for Grizzlies May Be Shelved," *Washington Post*, April 25, 2001.

166. Quoted in Douglas Jehl, "Interior Dept. Halting Plan for Grizzlies in 2 States," *New York Times*, June 21, 2001.

167. Lynn Scarlett, "A Closer Look at Interior," *PERC Reports*, 2003, 21,4, 12–14.

168. Michael Grunwald, "Departmental Differences Show over ANWR Drilling," *Washington Post*, October 19, 2001.

169. Michael Grunwald, "Warnings on Drilling Reversed," *Washington Post*, April 17, 2002.

170. Kennedy, "Crimes Against Nature."

171. Quoted in Felicity Barringer, "Interior Aide and Biologists Clashed over Protecting Bird," *New York Times*, December 5, 2004.

172. Quoted in Allison Winter, "Judge Orders FWS to Reconsider Rejection of Sage Grouse," *Land Letter*, December 6, 2007.

173. Quoted in "BuRec Blocks Irrigation Flow Needed for Fish," *Greenwire*, July 3, 2001.

174. Ibid.

175. More specifically, the NRC criticized the recommendations concerning minimum water levels for Upper Klamath Lake on the grounds that a substantial data-collection effort and analysis by the Fish and Wildlife Service had not shown a clear connection between lake levels and conditions that were adverse to suckers; in fact, high populations of the fish had occurred in low-water years. Similarly, with respect to NMFS's BiOp for salmon, the panel did not find "clear scientific or technical support for increased minimum flows in the Klamath River main stem"; instead, it found the water released into the river from Upper Klamath Lake was too warm. See Natalie M. Henry and Damon Franz, "Panel to Say Klamath Study Shows ESA Needs Reform," *Environment*

*& Energy Daily*, March 11, 2002. A subsequent study conducted by two Oregon State University researchers and published in the journal *Fisheries* charged that the NRC panel's finding was riddled with errors. Specifically, Douglas Markle and Jacob Kann argued that the panel's analyses failed to take into account the region's complex ecological conditions. The real problem, as writer Robert Service points out, is that the panel was asked to determine whether there was scientific proof that the policies embraced by the wildlife agencies would save the fish. But the agencies' mandates require them to use the best-available science to protect the fish, and to err on the side of conservation when in doubt. See Robert F. Service, "Combat Biology on the Klamath," *Science*, April 4, 2003.

176. Quoted in Service, "Combat Biology."

177. Journalist Tom Hamburger claimed that the water-delivery policy also changed in response to pressure from Karl Rove, Bush's political advisor, who raised the issue with federal officials on several occasions. See Tom Hamburger, "Water Saga Illuminates Rove's Methods," *Wall Street Journal*, July 30, 2003. The Interior Department's inspector general cleared the department of allegations that it succumbed to pressure from Rove. But a subsequent investigation by the *Washington Post*, confirmed that Vice President Cheney played a key role in the decision. Apparently, he intervened after receiving an appeal from Robert F. Smith, a former Republican congressman from Oregon. Cheney urged Norton to consult the National Academy of Sciences rather than convene the God Squad in order to avoid putting the administration on record as advocating the extinction of an endangered species. See Jo Becker and Barton Gellman, "Leaving No Tracks," *Washington Post*, June 27, 2007.

178. Natalie Henry, "Whistleblower Says NMFS Violated ESA When Deciding How to Protect Salmon," *Greenwire*, March 20, 2003.

179. Patrick Parenteau, "Anything Industry Wants: Environmental Policy under Bush II," *Duke Environmental Law & Policy Forum* 14 (Spring 2004): 363.

180. Quoted in Julie Elliott, "Habitat Protection Takes a Critical Hit," *High Country News*, April 15, 2002.

181. Quoted in Juliet Eilperin, "Water Rights Case Threatens Species Protection," *Washington Post*, December 7, 2004.

182. Juliet Eilperin, "U.S. Pact May Alter Protection of Endangered Species," *Washington Post*, December 22, 2004; Dean E. Murphy, "In Fish vs. Farmer Cases, the Fish Loses Its Edge," *New York Times*, February 22, 2005.

183. Quoted in Timothy Egan, "Shift on Salmon Reignites Fight on Species Law," *New York Times*, May 9, 2004.

184. Quoted in Felicity Barringer, "Only Wild Fish Matter in 'Endangered' Count, Judge Rules," *New York Times*, June 14, 2007.

185. Quoted in Blaine Harden, "Judge Rules Plan Is Insufficient to Save Salmon," *Washington Post*, May 8, 2003.

186. Quoted in Natalie M. Henry, "Scientists Blast Admin's New Strategy for Fish, Dams," *Greenwire*, November 24, 2004.

187. Quoted in Felicity Barringer, "Government Shirked Its Duty to Wild Fish, a Judge Rules," *New York Times*, May 27, 2005.

188. Quoted in Felicity Barringer, "On the Snake River, Dam's Natural Allies Seem to Have a Change of Heart," *New York Times*, May 13, 2007.

189. Felicity Barringer, "Judges Rebuff Government on Endangered Species," *New York Times*, August 20, 2005.

190. Quoted in ibid.

191. Quoted in Felicity Barringer, "Judge Returns Gray Wolves to Endangered List," *New York Times*, July 19, 2008.

192. Felicity Barringer, "Report Says Interior Official Overrode Work of Scientists," *New York Times*, March 29, 2007.

193. Earl E. Devaney, *Investigative Report: The Endangered Species Act and the Conflict between Science and Policy*, December 10, 2008.

194. Union of Concerned Scientists, *Scientific Integrity in Policymaking: An Investigation Into the Bush Administration's Misuse of Science*, March 2004.

195. Given its response rate of only 30 percent, the survey's findings should be considered suggestive rather than definitive.

196. Ruch, "Endangered Species Act Implementation."

197. Blaine Harden, "Future of Salmon Leads to Dispute over Federal Dams," *Washington Post*, July 2, 2005.

198. J. B. Ruhl, "The Endangered Species Act's Fall From Grace in the Supreme Court," Vanderbilt Public Law Research Paper No. 11-29, November 3, 2011, http://papers.ssrn.com/sol3/papers.cfm?abstract_id=1953339. Ruhl argues that the Court changed its position not because of a change in its composition but because the Endangered Species Act had been transformed from a "values" statute to a legalistic regulatory regime in the years since *TVA v. Hill*.

199. Natalie M. Henry, "Two Bills to Amend ESA Science Receive Mixed Reaction," *Environment & Energy Daily*, March 21, 2002.

200. Quoted in Dan Berman, "Farmers, Ranchers Call for ESA Reform," *Environment & Energy Daily*, July 18, 2003.

201. Felicity Barringer and Michael Janofsky, "Republicans Plan to Give Environment Rules a Free-Market Tilt," *New York Times*, November 8, 2004.

202. Quoted in Erica Werner, "House Approves Major Overhaul of Endangered Species Act," *Seattle Times*, September 30, 2005.

203. ENV1, personal communication, 2008.

204. John Cochran, "New Heaven, New Earth," *CQ Weekly*, October 17, 2005.

205. Quoted in Rebecca Clarren, "Inside the Secretive Plan to Gut the Endangered Species Act," Salon.com, March 27, 2007, http://www.salon.com/2007/03/27/endangered_species_2/.

206. Quoted in Felicity Barringer, "Rule Eases a Mandate under a Law on Wildlife," *New York Times*, December 12, 2008.

207. Christine Todd Whitman, *It's My Party Too: The Battle for the Heart of the GOP and the Future of America* (New York: Penguin Books, 2006).

208. Quoted in Lou Cannon and Carl M. Cannon, *Reagan's Disciple: George W. Bush's Troubled Quest for a Presidential Legacy* (New York: Public Affairs, 2008), 85–86.

209. Quoted in Amy Goldstein and Eric Pianin, "Hill Pressure Fueled Bush's Emissions Shift," *Washington Post*, March 15, 2001.

210. CON1, personal communication, 2009; Rebecca Adams, "Bush's Decision Not to Curb Carbon Dioxide Casts Shadow on Emission Control Legislation," *CQ Weekly*, March 17, 2001.

211. Quoted in Eric Pianin and Amy Goldstein, "Bush Drops a Call for Emissions Cuts," *Washington Post*, March 14, 2001.

212. Jeremy Symons, "How Bush and Co. Obscure the Science," *Washington Post*, July 13, 2003.

213. Quoted in Eric Pianin, "EPA Chief Lobbied on Warming Before Bush's Emissions Switch," *Washington Post*, March 27, 2001.

214. Quoted in Douglas Jehl and Andrew C. Revkin, "Bush, In Reversal, Won't Seek Cut in Emissions of Carbon Dioxide," *New York Times*, March 14, 2001.

215. Quoted in Goldstein and Pianin, "Hill Pressure Fueled Bush's Emissions Shift."

216. Quoted in Rebecca Adams, "Senate Democrats Will Turn Up Heat on Bush to Deliver Proposals for Reducing Global Warming," *CQ Weekly*, June 2001.

217. Quoted in William Drozdiak and Eric Pianin, "U.S. Angers Allies Over Climate Pact," *Washington Post*, March 29, 2001.

218. Quoted in Pianin and Goldstein, "Bush Drops a Call for Emissions Cuts."

219. "Emissions Impossible?" *Wall Street Journal*, July 23, 2001.

220. Darren K. Carlson, "Scientists Deliver Serious Warning about Effects of Gobal Warming," Gallup Poll Releases, January 23, 2001.

221. Quoted in Symons, "How Bush and Co. Obscure the Science."

222. Frank Luntz, "The Environment: A Cleaner, Safer, Healthier America," http://www.ewg.org/files/LuntzResearch_environment.pdf.

223. Katharine Q. Seelye and Andrew C. Revkin, "Panel Tells Bush Global Warming Is Getting Worse," *New York Times*, June 7, 2001.

224. Quoted in Mike Allen and Eric Pianin, "Bush to Set Climate Pact Alternative," *Washington Post*, June 10, 2001.

225. Quoted in Katharine Q. Seelye, "In a Shift, White House Cites Global Warming as a Problem," *New York Times*, June 8, 2001.

226. "Bush Withholds Backing of EPA Report on Warming," *Washington Post*, June 5, 2002.

227. Symons, "How Bush and Co. Obscure the Science."

228. Andrew C. Revkin, "Bush Aide Edited Climate Reports," *New York Times*, June 8, 2005.

229. Quoted in Symons, "How Bush and Co. Obscure the Science."

230. Juliet Eilperin, "Climate Researchers Feeling Heat from White House," *Washington Post*, April 6, 2006.

231. Eric Pianin, "Senate Budget Vote Rebuffs Bush on Global Warming," *Washington Post*, April 7, 2001.

232. Quoted in Rebecca Adams, "Lack of Carbon Dioxide Regulation Spurs Criticism of Bush's Clean-Air Plan," *CQ Weekly*, February 16, 2002.

233. Ibid.

234. "Never Green Enough."

235. Quoted in Edward Walsh, "Emissions Reduction Plan Touted," *Washington Post*, February 13, 2003.

236. Guy Gugliotta and Eric Pianin, "Bush Plans on Global Warming Alter Little," *Washington Post*, January 1, 2004.

237. U.S. Government Accountability Office, *Climate Change: EPA and DOE Should Do More to Encourage Progress Under Two Voluntary Programs*, GAO-06–97, April 2006.

238. Quoted in Samuel Goldreich, "Flash Points in Energy Bill Versions Threaten Another Fatal Conference," *CQ Weekly*, April 12, 2003.

239. Emissions from these three sectors, which together make up 85 percent of the economy, would be capped while emissions of other sectors would grow; the net result would be overall emissions at 2000 levels by 2025.

240. Quoted in Mary Clare Jalonick, "Ominous Forecast Predicted for Greenhouse Emissions Bill in Upcoming Senate Debate," *CQ Weekly*, October 25, 2003.

241. Quoted in Andrew C. Revkin, "Politics Reasserts Itself in the Debate over Climate Change and Its Hazards," *New York Times*, August 5, 2003.

242. Leslie Kaufman, "Dissenter on Warming Expands His Campaign," *New York Times*, April 9, 2009. In April 2009, Morano left Inhofe's office to start his own Web site, ClimateDepot.com, which was financed by the Committee for a Constructive Tomorrow, a Washington, D.C.–based nonprofit that advocates "free-market" solutions to environmental issues.

243. Quoted in Eric Pianin, "Senate Rejects Mandatory Cap on Greenhouse Gas Emissions," *Washington Post*, October 31, 2003.

244. Andrew Freedman, "Sen. Inhofe Denounces Climate 'Alarmism' as Clear Skies Debate Looms," *Environment & Energy Daily*, January 6, 2005.

245. Quoted in Jeff Tollefson, "Warming Skeptics Few But Powerful," *CQ Weekly*, December 5, 2005.

246. Eric Pianin, "Coalition Raps Bush on Global Warming," *Washington Post*, March 30, 2001.

247. Laurie Goodstein, "Evangelical Leaders Swing Influence Behind Effort to Combat Global Warming," *Washington Post*, March 10, 2005.

248. ENV4, personal communication, 2009.

249. At issue was section 202 of the Clean Air Act, which says the EPA administrator "shall" regulate any pollutant from any new vehicles that "may reasonably be anticipated to endanger public health or welfare."

250. Quoted in Juliet Eilperin, "Climate Talks Bring Bush's Policy to Fore," *Washington Post*, December 5, 2004.

251. Specifically, they argued that because greenhouse gas emissions inflict widespread harm, the plaintiffs could not possibly demonstrate a particularized injury, actual or imminent, traceable to the defendant, as precedent requires. They also argued that the EPA's decision not to regulate greenhouse gas emissions from motor vehicles contributed so insignificantly to any alleged injuries that the agency could not be made to answer for them.

252. Quoted in Linda Greenhouse, "Justices Say E.P.A. Has Power to Act on Harmful Gases," *New York Times*, April 3, 2007.

253. The Clean Air Act gives California special authority to enact stricter air pollution standards for motor vehicles than the federal government's. The EPA must approve a waiver, however, before California's rules may go into effect. The 2007 decision marked the first time California had been denied a Clean Air Act waiver.

254. Quoted in Matthew L. Wald, "E.P.A. Chief Defends His Decision on California," *New York Times*, January 25, 2008.

255. Quoted in Darren Samuelsohn, "U.S. Emissions Must Stop Growing by 2025," *Greenwire*, April 16, 2008.

256. Quoted in Felicity Barringer, "2 Decisions Shut Door on Bush Clean-Air Steps," *New York Times*, July 12, 2008.

257. Ibid.

258. EPA4, personal communication, 2008.

259. EPA6, personal communication, 2009; DOI3, personal communication, 2009.

260. EPA1, personal communication, 2009; EPA2, personal communication, 2009; EPA3, personal communication, 2009.

261. ENV7, personal communication, 2008; DOI1, personal communication, 2009; DOI6, personal communication, 2009.

262. Quoted in Clarren, "Inside the Secretive Plan."

263. DOI1, personal communication, 2009; DOI2, personal communication, 2009.

264. John B. Judis, "The Quiet Revolution," *New Republic*, February 18, 2010.

265. Kriz, "Vanishing Act."

266. EPA1, personal communication, 2009.

267. ENV1, personal communication, 2009.

268. Joby Warrick, "Appalachia Is Paying Price for White House Rule Change," *Washington Post*, August 17, 2004.

269. Dana Milbank and Eric Pianin, "Bush to Counter Environmental Criticism," *Washington Post*, March 31, 2001.

270. ENV1, personal communication, 2009.

271. Quoted in Lizette Alvarez and Joseph Kahn, "House Republicans Gather Support for Alaska Drilling," *New York Times*, August 1, 2001.

272. ENV1, personal communication, 2009.

273. Robin Toner, "Environmental Reversals Leave Moderate Republicans Hoping for Greener Times," *New York Times*, April 4, 2001.

274. Gerald Seib, "On Green Affairs, Politics Aren't All Black and White," *Wall Street Journal*, April 1, 2001.

275. DOI1, personal communication, 2009; EPA6, personal communication, 2009; EPA7, personal communication, 2009.

276. Scarlett, personal communication, 2009..

277. EPA6, personal communication, 2009; EPA7, personal communication, 2009.

278. Quoted in Katharine Q. Seelye, "President to Use Earth Day to Sell Environmental Plan," *New York Times*, April 22, 2002.

279. "Never Green Enough."

# Chapter 8

1. Stephen Skowronek, "An Attenuated Reconstruction: The Conservative Turn in American Political Development," in *Conservatism and American Political Development*, ed. Brian J. Glenn and Steven M. Teles (New York: Oxford University Press, 2009), 348.

2. Industry groups quickly cottoned on to the importance of language, particularly the value of nature-friendly names. For example, a coalition of big utilities and other companies in the Pacific Northwest coined the name Northwesterners for More Fish; the National Wetlands Coalition was a group of oil and gas interests aiming to explore the Arctic National Wildlife Refuge; Californians for Balanced Wildlife Management supported hunting mountain lions; the National Wilderness Institute opposed the Endangered Species Act; the Wilderness Impact Research Foundation represented logging, ranching, and related interests; and an association of fossil fuel interested dedicated to preventing action on global warming called itself the Global Climate Coalition. See Jane Fritsch, "Nature Groups Say Foes Bear Friendly Names," *New York Times*, March 25, 1996.

3. Likewise, the National Marine Fisheries Service (NMFS), which administers the Endangered Species Act for anadromous fish, is housed within the development-friendly Department of Commerce.

4. J. B. Ruhl, "The Endangered Species Act's Fall From Grace in the Supreme Court," Vanderbilt University Law School, Public Law & Legal Theory, Working Paper No. 11-29, November 3, 2011.

5. There is, of course, variation within the realm of pollution control, and it is easier to raise the salience of some pollution problems than others. This complexity is revealed in efforts to regulate concentrated animal feeding operations (CAFOs). Pollution from CAFOs poses obvious threats to natural systems but less obvious (though real) hazards to human health. Moreover, jurisdiction over CAFOs is split between the EPA, which has a protective mission, and the Department of Agriculture, which is more development oriented. Even within the EPA, CAFOs have benefited from the positive image of "farmers" that advantages all the beneficiaries of agricultural policy.

6. Joseph L. Sax, "Environmental Law at the Turn of the Century: A Reportorial Fragment of Contemporary History," *California Law Review* 88, no. 6 (2000): 2375–2402.

7. Sheldon Kamieniecki, *Corporate America and Environmental Policy: How Often Does Business Get Its Way?* (Palo Alto, CA: Stanford Law and Politics, 2006).

8. "Key Bush Environmental Accomplishments" (2004), http://georgewbush-whitehouse.archives.gov/news/releases/2004/07/20040714-2.html. The six criteria pollutants under the 1970 Clean Air Act are carbon monoxide, ground-level ozone, lead, nitrogen dioxide, sulfur dioxide, and particulates.

9. Michael J. Scott, Dale D. Goble, and Frank W. Davis, "Introduction," in *The Endangered Species Act at Thirty: Renewing the Conservation Promise*, ed. Dale D. Goble, J. Michael Scott, and Frank W. Davis (Washington, DC: Island Press, 2006), 3–15.

10. Martin F. J. Taylor, Kieran Suckling, and Jeffrey T. Rachlinski, "The Effectiveness of the Endangered Species Act: A Quantitative Analysis," *Bioscience 55*, no. 4 (2005): 360–367.

11. For example, a study by the Brookings Institution found that the amount of urbanized land in the United States almost doubled between 1982 and 1997, while the country's population grew by only 17 percent. See April Reese, "Development No. 1 Cause of Habitat Loss, Scientists Say," *Greenwire*, July 19, 2001.

12. Darrell M. West and Burdett A. Loomis, *The Sound of Money: How Political Interests Get What They Want* (New York: W.W. Norton & Company, 1999).

13. U.S. Environmental Protection Agency, "Executive Summary, Inventory of U.S. Greenhouse Gas Emissions and Sinks: 1990–2008," http://www.epa.gov/climatechange/emissions/downloads10/US-GHG-Inventory-2010_ExecutiveSummary.pdf.

14. David Adam, "World Carbon Dioxide Levels Highest for 650,000 Years, Says U.S. Report," *The Guardian* [UK], May 13, 2008.

15. Christopher McGrory Klyza and David Sousa, *American Environmental Politics, 1990–2006: Beyond Gridlock* (Cambridge, MA: MIT Press, 2008).

16. Jacob S. Hacker and Paul Pierson, *Off Center: The Republican Revolution and the Erosion of American Democracy* (New Haven, CT: Yale University Press, 2005).

17. Jacob S. Hacker, "Privatizing Risk without Privatizing the Welfare State: The Hidden Politics of Social Policy Retrenchment in the United States," *American Political Science Review* 98, no. 2 (2004): 257.

18. Jad Mouawad and Kate Galbraith, "Plugged-in Age Feeds a Hunger for Electricity," *New York Times*, September 20, 2009. In 1970, per-capita energy consumption was 331 million Btus. Between 1970 and 2008, it fluctuated, depending on economic conditions, reaching 359 million Btus in 1978 and 1979 before falling gradually back to 327 Btus in 2008. See U.S. Energy Information Administration, *Annual Energy Review*, October 19, 2011, http://www.eia.doe.gov/emeu/aer/pdf/pages/sec1_13.pdf.

19. Sharon Beder, *Global Spin: The Corporate Assault on Environmentalism*, rev. ed. (White River Junction, VT: Chelsea Green Publishing Company, 2002); ENV3, personal communication, 2009; ENV4, personal communication, 2009; ENV7, personal communication, 2009; EPA1, personal communication, 2008; EPA8, personal communication, 2008.

20. EPA8, personal communication, 2008.

21. Charles E. Lindblom, *Politics and Markets: The World's Political-Economic Systems* (New York: Basic Books, 1977), 347.

22. Quoted in Michael Weisskopf, "Administration Split on Clean Air Plan," *Washington Post*, June 10, 1989.

23. Mark A. Smith, *American Business and Political Power: Public Opinion, Elections, and Democracy* (Chicago: University of Chicago Press, 2000).

24. David Vogel, *Fluctuating Fortunes: The Political Power of Business in America* (New York: Basic Books, 1989); David Vogel, *Kindred Strangers: The Uneasy Relationship between Politics and Business in America* (Princeton, NJ: Princeton University Press, 1996).

25. Kamieniecki, *Corporate America and Environmental Policy*, viii.

26. Michael E. Kraft and Sheldon Kamieniecki, "Conclusions: The Influence of Business on Environmental Policy and Politics," in *Business and Environmental Policy: Corporate Interests in the American Political System*, ed. Michael E. Kraft and Sheldon Kamieniecki (Cambridge, MA: MIT Press, 2007), 337.

27. Beder, *Global Spin*; Smith, *American Business and Political Power*.

28. Judith A. Layzer, "Deep Freeze: How Business Has Shaped the Global Warming Debate in Congress," in Kraft and Kamieniecki, *Business and Environmental Policy*, 93–125.

29. Scott R. Furlong, "Businesses and the Environment: Influencing Agency Policymaking," in Kraft and Kamieniecki, *Business and Environmental Policy*, 155–184.

30. Lettie McSpadden, "Industry's Use of the Courts," in Kraft and Kamieniecki, *Business and Environmental Policy*, 233–262.

31. Elizabeth R. DeSombre, *Domestic Sources of International Environmental Policy: Industry, Environmentalists, and U.S. Power* (Cambridge, MA: MIT Press, 2001).

32. Joe Browder, personal communication, 2009.

33. Jeffrey Ball, "Utilities Back California in Auto-Emissions Suit," *Wall Street Journal*, November 9, 2007. By contrast, Kamieniecki contends that "[a]lthough companies may express different attitudes toward environmental protection (or none at all), they rarely oppose one another in the legislative process." See Kamieniecki, *Corporate America and Environmental Policy*, 257.

34. Amy Cortese, "Can Entrepreneurs and Environmentalists Mix?" *New York Times*, May 6, 2001; David Callahan, "Traitors to Their Class," *New Republic*, July 8, 2010.

35. Judith A. Layzer, *The Environmental Case: Translating Values into Policy*, 3rd ed. (Washington, DC: CQ Press); Layzer, "Deep Freeze."

36. Kim Phillips-Fein, *Invisible Hands: The Businessmen's Crusade against the New Deal* (New York: W.W. Norton, 2009).

37. Douglas P. Wheeler, "Why America Fell Asleep over the Environment," *Washington Post*, September 11, 1988.

38. Paul W. Hansen, 2005. "Green in Gridlock," *Washington Post*, March 15, 2005.

39. Browder, personal communication.

40. Karyn Strickler, "Environmental Towers Built Too High to Keep Grass Roots," *Christian Science Monitor*, April 21, 1995.

41. Michael Shellenberger and Ted Nordhaus, "The Death of Environmentalism: Global Warming Politics in a Post-Environmental World," http://www.thebreakthrough.org/PDF/Death_of_Environmentalism.pdf.

42. ENV1, personal communication, 2009; ENV8, personal communication, 2008; John Micklethwait and Adrian Wooldridge, *The Right Nation: Conservative Power in America* (New York: Penguin Press, 2004).

43. Douglas Bevington, *The Rebirth of Environmentalism: Grassroots Activism from the Spotted Owl to the Polar Bear* (Washington, DC: Island Press, 2009).

44. EPA1, personal communication, 2009; EPA2, personal communication, 2009; EPA4, personal communication, 2008; EPA5, personal communication, 2008.

45. Economist Denny Ellerman says, "If ever economics has managed a semantic triumph, it is with command and control, for it is hard to imagine a less appealing term." See Denny Ellerman, "Are Cap-and-Trade Programs More Environmentally Effective Than Conventional Regulation?" in *Moving to Markets*, ed. Jody Freeman and Charles D. Kolstad (New York: Oxford University Press, 2007), 48.

46. John M. Broder, "From a Theory to a Consensus on Emissions," *New York Times*, May 17, 2009.

47. Thomas O. McGarity, Sidney Shapiro, and David Bollier, "Sophisticated Sabotage," Center for American Progress blog (2004), http://www.americanprogress.org/issues/kfiles/b187072.html.

48. Quoted in Justin Fritscher, "Conservation Bank Protects Tortoises in the South," *Planning*, January, 7, 2010.

49. Quoted in Anne C. Mulkern, "WWF Emerges as Leading Lobbyist on Senate Emissions Bill," *Environment & Energy Daily*, May 18, 2010.

50. Quoted in Katharine Q. Seelye, "Democratic Field Tries to Add Punch to Environment Issue," *New York Times*, July 2, 2003.

51. In an op-ed piece in the *New York Times*, political scientists Theodore Marmor and Jerry Mashaw describe a similar phenomenon in the realm of social policy. See Theodore R. Marmor and Jerry L. Mashaw, "How Do You Say 'Economic Security?'" *New York Times*, September 23, 2011.

52. This polarization is not limited to environmental issues, of course. As McCarty, Poole, and Rosenthal explain, since the 1970s, moderates within parties have been vanishing, while the parties have been pulling apart. See Nolan McCarty, Keith T. Poole, and Howard Rosenthal, *Polarized America: the Dance of Ideology and Unequal Riches* (Cambridge, MA: MIT Press, 2006).

53. The elimination of moderates was not accidental but a purposeful result of the activities of groups like the Club for Growth, which funds candidates that promise to cut taxes and reduce government spending. See Matt Bai, "Fight Club," *New York Times Magazine*, August 10, 2003.

54. Ken Auletta, "Non-Stop News," *New Yorker*, January 25, 2010, 38–47.

55. Linda A. Adamic and Natalie Glance, "The Political Blogosphere and the 2004 U.S. Election: Divided They Blog," International Conference on Knowledge Discovery and Data Mining, *Proceedings of the 3rd International Workshop on Link Discovery* (2005): 36–43.

56. Riley E. Dunlap and Aaron McCright, "A Widening Gap: Republican and Democratic Views on Climate Change," *Environment*, September/October 2008, 26–36.

57. Deborah Lynn Guber and Christopher J. Bosso, "Past the Tipping Point? Public Discourse and the Role of the Environmental Movement in a Post-Bush Era," in *Environmental Policy: New Directions for the Twenty-First Century*, ed. Norman J. Vig and Michael E. Kraft (Washington, DC: CQ Press, 2010), 51–74.

58. Adam Liptak, "Justices Offer Receptive Ear to Business Interests," *New York Times*, December 18, 2010.

59. Jennifer Koons, "Obama Nominees Could Reshape Industry-Friendly Judiciary," *Greenwire*, August 20, 2009.

60. Dan Balz, "Will GOP Sleep through Wake-Up Call?" *Washington Post*, April 29, 2009; Jennifer Steinhauer, "G.O.P. Drops in Voting Rolls in Many States," *New York Times*, August 5, 2008.

61. Mark Fisher, "Gilchrest Unloads on Know-Nothing Pols and the Rest of Us," *Washington Post*, October 2, 2008; David Frum, *Comeback: Conservatism That Can Win Again* (New York: Doubleday, 2008).

62. Jackie Calmes, "Both Sides of the Aisle See More Regulation, and Not Just of Banks," *New York Times*, October 14, 2008.

63. Guber and Bosso, "Past the Tipping Point?"

64. Specifically, one rule had instituted an industry-friendly test that would allow utilities to treat several modifications at a single facility as separate, rather than having to consider the overall emissions increases. The second rule exempted "fugitive" emissions (leaks) from consideration in determining whether NSR was triggered. The third allowed "batch process facilities" like oil refineries and chemical plants to ignore certain emissions when determining whether NSR was triggered.

65. Quoted in John M. Broder, "No Endangered Status for Plains Bird," *New York Times*, March 6, 2010.

66. In the fall of 2011, the wolf hunts began, to dramatic effect. As of early December, the Idaho Department of Fish and Game reported that 154 of its approximately 750 wolves had been "harvested" and that legal hunting—using both snares to strangle and leg traps to capture—would continue through the spring. The aim was to reduce the wolf population to less than 150. In Montana, hunters were allowed to kill up to 220 of the state's estimated 550 wolves. And in Wyoming, hunters were permitted to kill wolves year round, with about 60 percent of the state's 350 wolves to be targeted for elimination. See J. William Gibson, "The War on Wolves," *Los Angeles Times*, December 8, 2011.

67. Quoted in Allison Winter, "New Listings Wait as Obama Administration Charts New Course," *Greenwire*, November 24, 2009.

68. ENV3, personal communication, 2009; ENV1, personal communication, 2009.

69. Josh Gerstein, "Environmentalists Give Barack Obama a Pass on Oil Spill," *Politico*, June 12, 2010.

70. Quoted in ibid.

71. The only ominous sign was that the most recent—admittedly symbolic—attempt to pass climate change legislation had failed in the Senate. In late 2007, Connecticut Independent Joseph Lieberman and Republican John Warner of Virginia had introduced a bill to cut greenhouse gas emissions to about 63 percent of 2005 levels by 2050. Despite frantic lobbying by the coal industry and its allies, in 2008, forty-eight senators had voted to break the Republican filibuster of America's Climate Security Act, while thirty-six voted against cloture. But nine out of a group of ten moderate Democrats promptly published a letter explaining that, although they had voted for the bill, they did not actually support it. See Eric Pooley, *The Climate War: True Believers, Power Brokers, and the Fight to Save the Earth* (New York: Hyperion, 2010).

72. John M. Broder, "Setting 'Green' Goals," *New York Times*, February 27, 2009; Gabriel Nelson, "Officials Hit the Hill in Bid to Salvage Budget," *Greenwire*, January 12, 2011.

73. Patricia Cohen, "Conservative Magazines: Their Vision Isn't G.O.P.'s," *New York Times*, June 13, 2009.

74. According to a poll conducted by the Yale Project on Climate Change Communication, the Tea Party was outside the mainstream on environmental issues. In September 2011, majorities of Democrats (78 percent), Independents (71 percent), and Republicans (53 percent) said they believe global warming is happening; by contrast, only 34 percent of Tea Party members said they believe this. See Andrew C. Revkin, "Survey: Tea Part Isolated on Climate, But Wide Accord on Most Energy Policies," *New York Times* blogs (Dot Earth), September 7, 2011. Majorities of Democrats, Independents, and Republicans also support requiring electric utilities to produce at least 20 percent of their electricity from renewable energy sources, whereas a majority of Tea Party members oppose this policy. And majorities of Democrats, Independents, and Republicans support an international treaty to cut carbon dioxide emissions, while a large majority of Tea Party members oppose such a treaty.

75. Quoted in Scott Shane, "A Critic Finds Obama Policies a Perfect Target," *New York Times*, September 26, 2009.

76. Kate Zernike, "Secretive Republican Donors Are Planning Ahead," *New York Times*, October 19, 2010; Jane Mayer, "Covert Operations," *New Yorker*, August 30, 2010.

77. Myron Ebell, personal communication, 2009.

78. Quoted in Andrew C. Revkin, "Skeptics Dispute Climate Worries and Each Other," *New York Times*, March 8, 2009.

79. Quoted in Steven Mufson, "New Groups Revive the Debate over Causes of Climate Change," *Washington Post*, September 25, 2009. The cofounders of CO2 is Green, as well as of the education-oriented Plants Need CO2, are H. Leighton Steward and Corbin J. Robertson Jr., fossil-fuel industry executives who invested $1 million to launch their new groups.

80. Quoted in Andrew C. Revkin, "Hacked E-Mail Is New Fodder for Climate Dispute," *New York Times*, November 20, 2009.

81. As Democratic congressman Henry Waxman observes, "Trade groups always push to weaken a bill to the point where none of their members object to it, which is why they are so often such a negative force in the process." See Henry Waxman, *The Waxman Report: How Congress Really Works* (New York: Twelve, 2009), 61.

82. Earlier in the summer, a public relations company hired by a pro-coal industry group, the American Coalition for Clean Coal Electricity, sent fifty-eight fake letters opposing new climate laws to members of Congress. The letters, which were forged by the public relations company Bonner & Associates, purported to be from groups like the National Association for the Advancement of Colored People and Hispanic organizations. See Clifford Krauss and Jad Mouawad, "Oil Industry Backs Protests of Emissions Bill," *New York Times*, August 19, 2009.

83. Michael Burnham, "U.S. Chamber Launches $100M 'Campaign for Free Enterprise,'" *E&E News PM*, June 10, 2009.

84. Andrew C. Revkin, "Environmental Issues Slide in Poll of Public's Concern," *New York Times*, January 23, 2009. A series of polls taken by Yale University

and George Mason University confirmed that conservative activism was having an impact, but suggested it might be temporary. Between November 2008 and January 2010, the percentage of people who believe global warming is happening fell from 71 percent to 27 percent, but rose again to 61 percent in June 2010. Similarly, the question of whether global warming is caused by human activity went from 57 percent in November 2008 to 47 percent in January 2010, and then back up to 50 percent in June 2010. What did persist was uncertainty about the extent of scientific agreement on climate change science and lower levels of concern. See A. Leiserowitz, E. Maibach, C. Roser-Renouf, and N. Smith, "Climate Change in the American Mind: Americans' Global Warming Beliefs and Attitudes in June 2010," Yale Project on Climate Change Communication, http://environment.yale.edu/climate/files/ClimateBeliefsJune2010.pdf.

85. Alex Kaplun, "Looming Regulations Put EPA in Conservatives' Cross Hairs," *Greenwire*, March 5, 2010.

86. Conservatives gained influence at the state level as well, and after the 2010 elections, Republican governors were pushing to roll back conservation, cut the budgets and personnel of regulatory agencies, and prevent the issuance of new regulations. Governor Rick Scott of Florida, a Tea Party ally, proposed eliminating millions of dollars for land conservation and cutting drastically the budget allocated for Everglades restoration; he also asked to downsize the Department of Community Affairs, which regulates land use in the state, from 358 staff members to 40. In North Carolina, where Republicans won control of both houses of the legislature, leaders proposed to cut the operating funds for the state's Department of Environment and Natural Resources by 22 percent. And in Maine, Tea Party favorite Paul LePage announced a sixty-three-point plan to cut environmental regulations, including opening 3 million acres of the North Woods for development. Governor LePage summed up his rationale, saying: "Maine's working families and small businesses are endangered. It is time we start defending the interests of those who want to work and invest in Maine with the same vigor that we defend the tree frogs and Canadian lynx." Quoted in Leslie Kaufman, "G.O.P. Pushes to Deregulate Environment at State Level," *New York Times*, April 15, 2011.

Governors were also adopting a favorite tactic of presidents: choosing environmental appointees with probusiness credentials. In Ohio, Governor John Kasich named David Mustine, former senior vice president at American Electric Power and director of the Dubai-based oil and gas company Terrasis, as head of the Natural Resources Department. To direct the state's Environmental Protection Agency, Kasich chose Scott Nally, a former regional manager for Perdue Farms Inc. Governor Rick Scott appointed shipbuilding executive Herschel Vinyard Jr. to lead Florida's Department of Environmental Protection and Billy Buzzett, a land-use lawyer who worked for the state's second-largest developer, to head the Department of Community Affairs. Governor Susana Martinez of New Mexico appointed global-warming skeptic Harrison "Jack" Schmitt to lead the state's Energy, Minerals, and Natural Resources Department. See Amanda Peterka, "New Governors Use Environmental Appointees to Advance Agendas," *Greenwire*, January 10, 2011.

87. Quoted in Jean Chemnick, "Is the Climate Debate Providing Cover for Other Clean Air Act Changes," *Environment & Energy Daily*, January 20, 2011.

88. Lauren Morello et al., "Republicans Gut EPA Climate Rules, Slash Deeply into Climate Research, Aid and Technology Programs," *New York Times*, February 14, 2011. Congress passes short-term continuing resolutions to fund the federal government when it has failed to pass a final spending bill for the year.

89. Coral Davenport, "Heads in the Sand," *National Journal*, December 11, 2011; Jim Tankersley, "GOP is Warming to Skepticism," *Los Angeles Times*, March 10, 2012.

90. Jann Wenner, "Obama in Command: The Rolling Stone Interview," *Rolling Stone*, September 28, 2010.

91. Quoted in Evan Lehman, "Obama Announcing Clean Energy Standard, Looks for Compromise," *ClimateWire*, January 26, 2011.

92. Gabriel Nelson, "Utility Groups Trade Blows on New EPA Emissions Rules," *Greenwire*, June 8, 2011.

93. John M. Broder, "Obama Abandons a Stricter Limit on Air Pollution," *New York Times*, September 3, 2011.

94. Quoted in John M. Broder, "E.P.A. Issues Limits on Mercury Emissions," *New York Times*, December 21, 2011.

95. James Mahoney and Kathleen Thelen, "A Theory of Gradual Institutional Change," in *Explaining Institutional Change: Ambiguity, Agency, and Power*, ed. James Mahoney and Kathleen Thelen (New York: Cambridge University Press), 1.

96. According to the U.S. Energy Information Agency, global energy consumption went from 206.72 quadrillion Btus to 493.014 quadrillion Btus between 1970 and 2008. The vast majority of that total was attributable to the combustion of fossil fuels—petroleum, coal, and natural gas. See energy consumption statistics at www.eia.doe.gov/iea/wecbtu.html. Although efficiency increased during this period, rising consumption overall negated the energy savings.

97. Grecia Matos and Lorie Wagner, "Consumption of Materials in the United States, 1900–1995," *Annual Review of Energy and the Environment* 23 (1998): 107–122.

98. Fridolin Krausmann et al., "The Global Sociometabolic Transition," *Journal of Industrial Ecology* 12, no. 5/6 (2008): 637–656; Fridolin Krausmann et al, "Growth in Global Materials Use, GDP, and Population during the 20th Century," *Ecological Economics* 68 (2009): 2696–2705. Matos and Wagner include fibers, plastics, feedstocks, metals, paper, cement, and sand and gravel in their definition of raw materials. See Matos and Wagner, "Consumption of Materials." Krausmann and her colleagues use a more expansive definition in their analyses.

99. United National Environment Program, "Decoupling Natural Resources and Environmental Impacts From Environmental Growth" (2011), http://www.unep.org/resourcepanel/decoupling/files/pdf/Decoupling_Report_English.pdf. The quote is from the UNEP Decoupling Report Web page, http://www.unep.org/resourcepanel/Publications/Decoupling/tabid/56048/Default.aspx

100. Krausmann et al., "Growth in Global Materials Use," 2701.

101. P. Mayaux et al., "Tropical Forest Cover Change in the 1990's and Options for Future Monitoring," *Philosophical Transactions of the Royal Society B: Biological Sciences* 360, no. 1454 (2005): 373–384; Michael Williams, *Deforesting the Earth: From Prehistory to Global Crisis* (Chicago: University of Chicago Press, 2003). Estimates of annual tropical deforestation remain highly uncertain, ranging from nearly 6 million hectares to about 15 million hectares. The United Nations Food and Agriculture Organization estimates that in the 2000s, approximately 13 million hectares per year were converted or lost to natural causes, compared to 16 million hectares per year in the 1990s. See United National Food and Agriculture Organization, "Key Findings from the Global Forest Resource Assessment" (2010), http://foris.fao.org/static/dta/fra2010/KeyFindings_en.pdf.

102. Boris Worm et al., "Impacts of Biodiversity Loss on Ocean Ecosystem Services," *Science* 314, no. 5800 (November 3, 2006): 787–790; United Nations Food and Agriculture Organization, "State of World Fisheries and Agriculture" (2010), http://www.fao.org/docrep/013/i1820e/i1820e00.htm. According to the United Nations Food and Agriculture Organization, the proportion of fully exploited fish stocks has remained stable at about 50 percent since the 1970s. Between 1974 and 2008, however, the proportion of marine fish stocks estimated to be underexploited or moderately exploited declined from 40 percent to 15 percent, whereas the proportion of overexploited, depleted, or recovering stocks increased from 10 percent to 32 percent. As Worm and his colleagues explain, the elimination of locally adapted populations and species not only impairs the ability of marine ecosystems to feed a growing human population but also impairs the stability and recovery potential of those ecosystems.

103. Ann Gibbons, "Study Foresees a Rapid and Widespread Extinction of Species," *Washington Post*, March 8, 2011; Millennium Ecosystem Assessment, *Ecosystems and Human Well-Being: Synthesis* (Washington, DC: Island Press, 2005); United National Environment Program, "Executive Summary," *Global Biodiversity Outlook*, 3rd ed (2010), http://www.cbd.int./gbo/gbo3/GBO3 -Summary-final-en.pdf.; Ariel Zirulnick, "The Extinction Risk for Birds, Mammals and Amphibians," *Christian Science Monitor*, October 27, 2010.

104. James Kanter, "U.N. Warns of Rapid Decay of Environment," *New York Times*, October 26, 2007.

105. http://www.enerdta/net/enerdatauk/publications/pages/g-20-2010-strongly -energy-demand-increase.php.

106. Quoted in "Google Expands into Alternative Energy," Associated Press, January 27, 2007.

107. Edward Humes, *Force of Nature: The Unlikely Story of Wal-Mart's Green Revolution* (New York: HarperBusiness, 2011), 7.

108. Ibid.

109. Ibid, 76.

110. Robert B. Reich, *Supercapitalism: The Transformation of Business, Democracy, and Everyday Life* (New York: Alfred A. Knopf, 2007).

111. Auden Schendler, *Getting Green Done: Hard Truths from the Front Lines of the Sustainability Revolution* (New York: PublicAffairs, 2009).

112. Ibid, 21.

113. Thomas Dietz, Gerald T. Gardner, Jonathan Gilligan, Paul Stern, and Michael P. Vanderbergh, "Household Actions Can Provide a Behavioral Wedge to Rapidly Reduce U.S. Carbon Emissions," *Proceedings of the National Academy of Science* 106, no.4 (November 3, 2009), 18452–18456.

114. E. Scott Geller, "It Takes More Than Information to Save Energy," *American Psychologist* (June 1992): 814–815; Matthias Finger, "From Knowledge to Action? Exploring the Relationships Between Environmental Experiences, Learning, and Behavior," *Journal of Social Issues* 50, issue 3 (1994): 141–160; Alexa Spence and Nick Pidgeon, "Psychology, Climate Change & Sustainable Behavior," *Environment*, November–December 2009; Mark Costanzo, Dane Archer, Elliot Aronson, and Thomas Pettigrew, "Energy Conservation Behavior: The Difficult Path from Information to Action," *American Psychologist* 41 (1986): 521–528.

115. Jonathan Rowson, "Social Networks and Behavior Change," Talk delivered at the Garrison Institute, Garrison, New York, March 11, 2011.

116. Ibid.

117. Leslie Kaufman, "Environmentalists Get Down to Earth," *New York Times*, December 17, 2011.

118. Leslie Kaufman and Kate Zernike, "Activists Fight Green Projects, Seeing U.N. Plot," *New York Times*, February 3, 2012.

119. Quoted in ibid.

120. In response to an analysis of local-sector productivity, Tim Jackson wryly observes, "We're getting perilously close here to the lunacy at the heart of the growth-obsessed, resource-intensive, consumer economy. Here is a sector which could provide meaningful work, offer people capabilities for flourishing, contribute positively to community and have a decent chance of being materially light. And yet it's denigrated as worthless because it's actually employing people." See Tim Jackson, *Prosperity without Growth: Economics for a Finite Planet* (Sterling, VA: Earthscan, 2009), 132.

121. Reflecting the current level of civil disengagement, a poll conducted by faculty at George Mason, Yale, and American Universities found that Americans who were most alarmed about climate change were more than eight times more likely to express their concern through shopping for green products than by contacting an elected official multiple times about it. See David A. Fahrenthold and Juliet Eilperin, "Born in 1970, Event Has Cause for Celebration," *Washington Post*, April 22, 2010.

122. David J. Hess, *Localist Movements in a Global Economy* (Cambridge, MA: MIT Press, 2009).

123. Jim Carlton, "It's Easier Being Green at the Local Level," *Wall Street Journal*, May 17, 2006.

124. ENV6, personal communication, 2009. A nationwide poll by the National Wildlife Federation in 2004 found that hunters and anglers—68 percent of whom voted for President Bush in 2000—believed the administration was too attentive to developers and the energy industry. Sixty-eight percent of those polled agreed with the statement that natural wetlands should not be destroyed, even if they could be replaced through mitigation banking. See Alex Kaplun, "Traditionally Conservative Sportsmen No Longer Certain for GOP—Poll," *Greenwire*, July 15, 2004.

125. James Gustave Speth, *The Bridge at the End of the World: Capitalism, the Environment, and Crossing from Crisis to Sustainability* (New Haven, CT: Yale University Press, 2008), 86.

126. David Bollier and Jonathan Rowe, "The Illth of Nations: Enlarging Our Sense of the Economy," *Boston Review*, March 30, 2011.

127. H. W. Arndt, *The Rise and Fall of Economic Growth* (Chicago: University of Chicago Press, 1984); Robert M. Collins, *More: The Politics of Economic Growth in Postwar America* (New York: Oxford University Press, 2000); Clive Hamilton, *Growth Fetish* (Sterling, VA: Pluto Press, 2004); Steven Stoll, "Fear of Fallowing," *Harper's*, March 2008, 88–94. As historian J. R. McNeill writes, "After the Depression, economic rationality trumped all other concerns except security. Those who promised to deliver the holy grail became high priests. These were economists, mostly Anglo-American economists." Environmental ideas have proven enduring as well, but the idea of economic growth is far more powerful, as evidenced by our willingness to accept claims about the compatibility of growth and the environment despite overwhelming evidence to the contrary. See J. R. McNeill, *Something New under the Sun: An Environmental History of the Twentieth-Century World* (New York: W. W. Norton & Company, Inc.), 335.

128. Jackson, *Prosperity without Growth*; Krausmann et al., "Growth in Global Materials Use." Although advanced economies have become more efficient in their use of energy, overall energy consumption—and hence carbon dioxide emissions—have continued to increase. (Even in economies where emissions appear to be stabilizing, calculations fail to account for rising imports of goods that embed carbon.) When it comes to materials use, there is little evidence of either relative or absolute decoupling of materials or energy from economic growth (except during periods of recession, when consumption declines). The point is that technological advances cannot be relied on to mitigate the impacts of economic growth, as suggested by mainstream economic theory; in practice, population growth and affluence have undermined gains from dematerialization and efficiency.

129. Juliet Schor, "The Impact of Consumption & Working Hours on Climate," Talk presented at the Garrison Institute, Garrison, New York, February 2012.

130. Unfortunately, the most widely used measure of economic well-being, GDP, treats illth as a benefit because money is spent on it. Some economists complain that GDP not only fails to capture the well-being of society but also skews global political objectives toward the single-minded pursuit of economic growth. See

John Gertner, "The Rise and Fall of GDP," *New York Times Magazine*, May 16, 2010.

131. The top 1 percent garners more income than the bottom 100 million Americans combined; ownership of wealth is even more concentrated: the richest 1 percent of American households own half of all outstanding stock, financial securities, trust equity, and business equity; a mere 5 percent owns more than two-thirds of America's financial assets. See Gar Alperovitz, *America beyond Capitalism: Reclaiming Our Wealth, Our Liberty, and Our Democracy* (New York: John Wiley & Sons, Inc., 2005). Inequality has been rising over time: the top 20 percent of Americans went from earning 30 times what the bottom 20 percent earned in 1960 to earning 75 times as much by 2006; the top 100 executives received 30 times the pay of the average worker in 1960, but by 2006 it was 1,000 times as much. See Catherine Besteman and Hugh Gusterson, "Introduction," in *The Insecure American: How We Got Here and What We Should Do about It*, ed. Hugh Gusterson and Catherine Besteman (Berkeley: University of California Press, 2009), 1–23.

132. Ed Diener and Robert Biswas-Diener, *Happiness: Unlocking the Mysteries of Psychological Wealth* (Malden, MA: Blackwell Publishing, 2008); Richard Layard, *Happiness: Lessons from a New Science* (New York: Penguin Press, 2005).

133. Jackson, *Prosperity without Growth*. The relationship between life satisfaction and income vanishes after about $15,000. This is because people adapt to new circumstances and adjust their expectations upward; they also measure their wealth relative to those around them.

134. Jackson, *Prosperity without Growth*, 97.

135. Robert H. Frank, *Luxury Fever: Why Money Fails to Satisfy in an Era of Excess* (New York: Free Press, 1999); Greider, *Soul of Capitalism*; Juliet B. Schor, *The Overspent American: Upscaling, Downshifting, and the New Consumer* (New York: Basic Books, 1998).

136. Robert Costanza et al., "The Value of the World's Ecosystem Services and Natural Capital," *Nature* 387 (May 15, 1997): 253–260.

137. Peter A. Victor, *Managing without Growth: Slower by Design, Not Disaster* (Northampton, MA: Edward Elgar, 2008), 192–193.

138. Quoted in Stoll, "Fear of Fallowing," 92, 94.

139. Paul Gilding, *The Great Disruption: Why the Climate Crisis Will Bring On the End of Shopping and the Birth of a New World Order* (New York: Bloomsbury Press, 2011); Edward Goldsmith and Jerry Mander, *The Case against the Global Economy & for a Turn toward Localization* (San Francisco: Sierra Club Books, 2001); Clive Hamilton, *Growth Fetish* (Sterling, VA: Pluto Press, 2004); Paul Hawken, Amory Lovins, and L. Hunter Lovins, *Natural Capitalism: Creating the Next Industrial Revolution* (Boston: Little, Brown and Company, 1997); Tim Jackson, *Prosperity without Growth*; Bill McKibben, *Deep Economy* (New York: Times Books, 2007); Jonathan Porritt, *Capitalism As If the World Matters*, rev. ed. (Sterling, VA: Earthscan, 2007); James Gustave Speth, *The Bridge at the*

*End of the World: Capitalism, the Environment, and Crossing from Crisis to Sustainability* (New Haven, CT: Yale University Press, 2008); Annie Leonard, *The Story of Stuff: How Our Obsession with Stuff Is Trashing the Planet, Our Communities, and Our Health—and a Vision for Change* (New York: Simon & Schuster 2010).

140. John B. Anderson, "Real Conservatives, Pseudo-Conservatives" *New York Times*, December 2, 1980; Rod Dreher, *Crunchy Cons: The New Conservative Counterculture and Its Return to Roots* (New York: Three Rivers Press, 2006). Thanks to my colleague Nathan Dinneen for pointing this out.

# Selected References

Ackerman, Bruce A., and Richard B. Stewart. 1988. "Reforming Environmental Law: The Democratic Case for Market Incentives." *Columbia Journal of Environmental Law* 13 (2): 171–200.

Alperovitz, Gar. 2005. *America beyond Capitalism: Reclaiming Our Wealth, Our Liberty, and Our Democracy*. New York: John Wiley & Sons, Inc.

Anderson, Frederick R., Allen V. Kneese, Phillip D. Reed, Russell B. Stevenson, and Serge Taylor. 1977. *Environmental Improvement through Economic Incentives*. Baltimore: Johns Hopkins University Press/Resources for the Future.

Anderson, Terry L. 1982. "New Resource Economics: Old Ideas and New Applications." *American Journal of Agricultural Economics* 64 (5): 928–934.

Andrews, Richard N. L. 2006. *Managing the Environment, Managing Ourselves*. New Haven, CT: Yale University Press.

Ansell, Amy E., ed. 1998. *Unraveling the Right: The New Conservatism in American Thought and Politics*. Boulder, CO: Westview Press.

Arndt, H. W. 1984. *The Rise and Fall of Economic Growth*. Chicago: University of Chicago Press.

Arnold, Ron. 1982. *At the Eye of the Storm: James Watt and the Environmentalists*. Chicago: Regnery Gateway.

Bachrach, Peter, and Morton S. Baratz. 1962. "Two Faces of Power." *American Political Science Review* 56: 947–952.

Baden, John, and Richard Stroup. 1981. *Bureaucracy vs. Environment: The Environmental Costs of Bureaucratic Governance*. Ann Arbor: University of Michigan Press.

Bailey, Ronald, ed. 1995. *The True State of the Planet*. New York: The Free Press.

Bardach, Eugene and Robert A. Kagan. 1982. *Going by the Book: The Problem of Regulatory Unreasonableness*. Philadelphia: Temple University Press.

Bardach, Eugene, and Robert A. Kagan, eds. 1982. *Social Regulation: Strategies for Reform*. New Brunswick, NJ: Transaction Books.

Bates, Robert H., Rui J. P. De Figueiredo Jr., and Barry R. Weingast. 1998. "The Politics of Interpretation: Rationality, Culture, and Transition." *Politics & Society* 26 (2): 221–256.

Baumgartner, Frank R., and Bryan D. Jones. 1993. *Agendas and Instability in American Politics*. Chicago: University of Chicago Press.

Baur, Donald C., and William Robert Irvin, eds. 2002. *The Endangered Species Act: Law, Policy, and Perspectives*. Chicago: American Bar Association.

Bean, Michael J. 1998. "Endangered Species Act and Private Land: Four Lessons Learned from the Past Quarter Century." *Environmental Law Reporter* 28: 10701–10710.

Bean, Michael J. 2002. "Overcoming Unintended Consequences of Endangered Species Regulation." *Idaho Law Review* 38: 409–420.

Beder, Sharon. 2002. *Global Spin: The Corporate Assault on Environmentalism*. rev. ed. White River Junction, VT: Chelsea Green Publishing Company.

Beland, Daniel, and Robert Henry Cox, eds. 2010. *Ideas and Politics in Social Science Research*. New York: Oxford University Press.

Benford, Robert D., and David A. Snow. 2000. "Framing Processes and Social Movements: An Overview and Assessment." *Annual Review of Sociology* 26: 611–639.

Bevington, Douglas. 2009. *The Rebirth of Environmentalism: Grassroots Activism from the Spotted Owl to the Polar Bear*. Washington, DC: Island Press.

Blais, Lynn E. 2000. "Beyond Cost Benefit: The Maturation of Economic Analysis of the Law and Its Consequences for Environmental Policymaking." *University of Illinois Law Review* v.2000, no.1: 237–253.

Bleich, Erik. 2003. *Race Politics in Britain and France: Ideas and Policymaking since the 1960s*. New York: Cambridge University Press.

Blumenthal, Sidney. 1986. *The Rise of the Counter-Establishment: From Conservative Ideology to Political Power*. New York: Times Books.

Blyth, Mark. 2002. *Great Transformations: Economic Ideas and Institutional Change in the Twentieth Century*. New York: Cambridge University Press

Bolch, Ben, and Harold Lyons. 1993. *Apocalypse Not*. Washington, DC: Cato Institute.

Bollier, David, and Jonathan Rowe. 2011. "The Illth of Nations: Enlarging Our Sense of the Economy." *Boston Review*, March 30.

Bosso, Christopher J. 2005. *Environment, Inc.: From Grassroots to Beltway*. Lawrence: University Press of Kansas.

Boykoff, Maxwell T., and Jules M. Boykoff. 2004. "Balance as Bias: Global Warming and the U.S. Prestige Press." *Global Environmental Change* 14: 125–136.

Braman, Eileen. 2009. *Law, Politics, & Perception: How Policy Preferences Influence Legal Reasoning*. Charlottesville, VA: University of Virginia Press.

Breyer, Stephen. 1982. *Regulation and Its Reform*. Cambridge, MA: Harvard University Press.

Breyer, Stephen. 1993. *Breaking the Vicious Circle*. Cambridge, MA: Harvard University Press.

Brookes, Warren T. 1990. "Chaining the Economy: America Dragged Down." *National Review*, October 15, 34–43.

Brown, George E., Jr. 1997. "Environmental Science under Siege in the U.S. Congress." *Environment* 39 (2): 12–20, 29–31.

Brownlee, W. Elliot, and Hugh Davis Graham, eds. 2003. *The Reagan Presidency: Pragmatic Conservatism & Its Legacies*. Lawrence: University of Kansas Press.

Buell, Frederick. 2003. *Apocalypse as Way of Life*. New York: Routledge.

Burke, Marcilynn. 2004. "Klamath Farmers and Cappuccino Cowboys: The Rhetoric of the Endangered Species Act and Why It (Still) Matters." *Duke Environmental Law & Policy Forum* 14: 441.

Callahan, David. 1995. "Liberal Policy's Weak Foundations." *Nation*, November 13.

Callahan, David. 1999. "$1 Billion for Conservative Ideas." *Nation*, April 26.

Callahan, David. 2010. "Traitors to Their Class." *New Republic*, July 8.

Campbell, Andrea. 2005. *How Policies Make Citizens: Senior Political Activism and the American Welfare State*. Princeton, NJ: Princeton University Press.

Campbell, John L. 1998. "Institutional Analysis and the Role of Ideas in Political Economy." *Theory and Society* 27 (3): 377–409.

Cannon, Lou. 1982. *Reagan*. New York: G.P. Putnam's Sons.

Cannon, Lou. 1991. *President Reagan: The Role of a Lifetime*. New York: Simon & Schuster.

Cannon, Lou, and Carl M. Cannon. 2008. *Reagan's Disciple: George W. Bush's Troubled Quest for a Presidential Legacy*. New York: Public Affairs.

Carpenter, Daniel P. 2001. *The Forging of Bureaucratic Autonomy: Reputations, Networks, and Policy Innovation in Executive Agencies, 1862–1928*. Princeton, NJ: Princeton University Press.

Cawley, R. McGreggor. 1993. *Federal Land, Western Anger: The Sagebrush Rebellion and Environmental Politics*. Lawrence: University Press of Kansas.

Chertow, Marion R., and Daniel C. Esty, eds. 1997. *Thinking Ecologically: The Next Generation of Environmental Policy*. New Haven, CT: Yale University Press.

Christianson, Gale E. 1999. *Greenhouse: The 200-Year Story of Global Warming*. New York: Penguin Books.

Cigler, Allan J., and Burdett A. Loomis, eds. 1998. *Interest Group Politics*. 5th ed. Washington, DC: CQ Press.

Clark, Jeanne Nienaber, and Daniel C. McCool. 1996. *Staking Out the Terrain: Power and Performance Among Natural Resource Agencies*. 2nd ed. Albany: SUNY Press.

Clymer, Adam. 2008. *Drawing the Line at the Big Ditch: The Panama Canal Treaties and the Rise of the Right*. Lawrence: University of Kansas.

Cobb, Roger W., and Marc Howard Ross, eds. 1997. *Cultural Strategies of Agenda Denial: Avoidance, Attack, and Redefinition*. Lawrence: University of Kansas.

Coglianese, Cary. 1999. "Limits of Consensus." *Environment* (April), 29–33

Collins, Robert M. 2000. *More: The Politics of Economic Growth in Postwar America*. New York: Oxford University Press.

Conlan, Timothy J., Margaret T. Wrightson, and David R. Beam. 1990. *Taxing Choices: The Politics of Tax Reform*. Washington, DC: CQ Press.

Cooper, Phillip J. . 2002. *By Order of the President: The Use and Abuse of Executive Direct Action*. Lawrence: University Press of Kansas.

Cooper, Phillip J. 2009. *The War against Regulation: From Jimmy Carter to George W. Bush*. Lawrence: University Press of Kansas.

Costanza, Robert, Ralph d'Arge, Rudolf de Groots, Stephen Farber, Monica Grasso, Bruce Hannon, Karin Limburg, Shahid Naeem, Robert V. O'Neill, Jose Paruelo, Robert G. Raskin, Paul Sutton, and Marjan van den Belt. 1997. "The Value of the World's Ecosystem Services and Natural Capital." *Nature* 387 (May 15): 253–260.

Crandall, Robert W. 1983. *Controlling Industrial Pollution: The Economics and Politics of Clean Air*. Washington, DC. Brookings Institution.

Crawford, Alan. 1980. *Thunder on the Right: The "New Right" and the Politics of Resentment*. New York: Pantheon Books.

Critchlow, Donald T. 2007. *The Conservative Ascendancy: How the GOP Right Made Political History*. Cambridge, MA: Harvard University Press.

Cross, Frank B. 2007. *Decision Making in the U.S. Court of Appeals*. Stanford, CA: Stanford University Press.

Cross, Frank B., and Emerson H. Tiller. 1998. "Judicial Partisanship and Obedience to Legal Doctrine: Whistleblowing on the Federal Court of Appeals." *Yale Law Journal* 107: 2155.

Darnall, Nicole, and Stephen Sides. 2008. "Assessing the Performance of Voluntary Environmental Programs: Does Certification Matter?" *Policy Studies Journal* 36 (1): 95–117.

Davies, J. Clarence and Jan Mazurek. 1998. *Pollution Control in the United States: Evaluating the System.* Washington, DC: Resources for the Future.

Derthick, Martha, and Paul J. Quirk. 1985. *The Politics of Deregulation*. Washington, DC: The Brookings Institution.

DeSombre, Elizabeth R. 2001. *Domestic Sources of International Environmental Policy: Industry, Environmentalists, and U.S. Power*. Cambridge, MA: MIT Press.

Devine, Robert S. 2004. *Bush vs. the Environment*. New York: Anchor Books.

Diener, Ed, and Robert Biswas-Diener. 2008. *Happiness: Unlocking the Mysteries of Psychological Wealth*. Malden, MA: Blackwell Publishing.

Dorrien, Gary. 1993. *The Neoconservative Mind: Politics, Culture, and the War of Ideology*. Philadelphia: Temple University Press.

Douglas, Mary, and Aaron Wildavsky. 1982. *Risk and Culture: An Essay on the Selection of Technological and Environmental Dangers*. Berkeley: University of California Press.

Dowie, Mark. 1996. *Losing Ground: American Environmentalism at the Close of the Twentieth Century.* Cambridge, MA: MIT Press.

Dreher, Rod. 2006. *Crunchy Cons: The New Conservative Counterculture and Its Return to Roots.* New York: Three Rivers Press.

Drew, Elizabeth. 1994. *On the Edge: The Clinton Presidency.* New York: Simon & Schuster.

Dunlap, Riley E., and Aaron McCright. 2008. "A Widening Gap: Republican and Democratic Views on Climate Change." *Environment* (September/October): 26–36.

Dunn, James R., and John E.Kinney. 1996. *Conservative Environmentalism: Reassessing the Means, Redefining the Ends.* Westport, CT: Quorum Books.

Durant, Robert F., Daniel J. Fiorino, and Rosemary O'Leary, eds. 2004. *Environmental Governance Reconsidered: Challenges, Choices, and Opportunities.* Cambridge, MA: MIT Press.

Eads, George C., and Michael Fix. 1984. *Relief or Reform? Reagan's Regulatory Dilemma.* Washington, DC: Urban Institute Press.

Easterbrook, Gregg. 1995. *A Moment on the Earth: The Coming Age of Environmental Optimism.* New York: Viking Penguin.

Echeverria, John, and Raymond Booth Eby, eds. 1995. *Let the People Judge: Wise Use and the Private Property Rights Movement.* Lanham, MD: Rowman & Littlefield.

Echeverria, John D., and Jon T. Zeidler. 1999. "Barely Standing." *Environmental Forum* 16 (4): 21–30.

Edwards, Lee. 1999. *Conservative Revolution: The Movement That Remade America.* New York: Free Press.

Efron, Edith. 1984. *The Apocalyptics: Cancer and the Big Lie.* New York: Simon & Schuster.

Eisner, Marc Allen. 2000. *Regulatory Politics in Transition.* 2nd ed. Baltimore: Johns Hopkins University Press.

Evans, M. Stanton. 1965. *The Liberal Establishment.* New York: The Devin-Adair Company.

Evans, Peter B., Dietrich Rueschmeyer, and Theda Skocpol, eds. 1985. *Bringing the State Back In.* New York: Cambridge University Press.

Fink, Gary M., and Hugh Davis Graham, eds. 1998. *The Carter Presidency: Policy Choices in the Post–New Deal Era.* Lawrence: University of Kansas Press.

Fiorino, Daniel J. 2006. *The New Environmental Regulation.* Cambridge, MA: MIT Press.

Fischer, Kurt, and Johan Schot, eds. 1993. *Environmental Strategies for Industry: International Perspectives on Research Needs and Policy Implications.* Washington, DC: Island Press.

Flaherty, Francis J. 1983. "Right-Wing Firms Pick Up Steam." *National Law Journal* (May 25): 1–35.

Flippen, J. Brooks. 2000. *Nixon and the Environment.* Albuquerque: University of New Mexico Press.

Flippen, J. 2006. *Conservative Conservationist.* Baton Rouge: Louisiana State University Press.

Frank, Robert H. 1999. *Luxury Fever: Why Money Fails to Satisfy in an Era of Excess.* New York: Free Press.

Frank, Thomas. 2004. *What's the Matter with Kansas? How Conservatives Won the Heart of America.* New York: Metropolitan Books.

Frank, Thomas. 2008. *The Wrecking Crew: How Conservatives Rule.* New York: Metropolitan Books.

Fried, Charles. 1991. *Order and Law: Arguing the Reagan Revolution—a First-hand Account.* New York: Simon & Schuster.

Friedlander, Anne F., ed. 1978. *Approaches to Controlling Air Pollution.* Cambridge, MA: MIT Press.

Frum, David. 2008. *Comeback: Conservatism That Can Win Again.* New York: Doubleday.

Fumento, Michael. 1993. *Science under Siege: How the Environmental Misinformation Campaign Is Affecting Our Law, Taxes, and Our Daily Life.* New York: Quill.

Galbraith, James K. 2008. *The Predator State: How Conservatives Abandoned the Free Market and Why Liberals Should Too.* New York: Free Press.

Gelbspan, Ross. 1998. *The Heat Is On: The Climate Crisis, the Cover Up, the Prescription.* Updated ed. New York: Perseus Books.

Genieys, William, and Marc Smyrl. 2008. *Elites, Ideas, and the Evolution of Public Policy.* New York: Palgrave Macmillan.

George, Alexander L., and Andrew Bennett. 2005. *Case Studies and Theory Development in the Social Sciences.* Cambridge, MA: MIT Press.

George, Alexander L., and Timothy McKeown. 1985. "Case Studies and Theories of Organizational Decision Making." *Advances in Information Processing in Organizations* 2: 21–58.

Gilding, Paul. 2011. *The Great Disruption: Why the Climate Crisis Will Bring On the End of Shopping and the Birth of a New World Order.* New York: Bloomsbury Press.

Gilmour, John B. 1995. *Strategic Disagreement: Stalemate in American Politics.* Pittsburgh: University of Pittsburgh Press.

Glenn, Brian J., and Steven M. Teles, eds. 2008. *Conservatism and American Political Development.* New York: Oxford University Press.

Goble, Dale D., J. Michael Scott, and Frank W. Davis, eds. 2006. *The Endangered Species Act at Thirty: Renewing the Conservation Promise.* Washington, DC: Island Press.

Gold, Howard. 1992. *Hollow Mandates: American Public Opinion and the Conservative Shift.* Boulder, CO: Westview Press.

Golden, Melissa Martino. 2000. *What Motivates Bureaucrats? Politics and Administration during the Reagan Years*. New York: Columbia University Press.

Goldsmith, Edward, and Jerry Mander. 2001. *The Case against the Global Economy & for a Turn toward Localization*. San Francisco: Sierra Club Books.

Goldstein, Judith. 1988. "Ideas, Institutions, and American Trade Policy." *International Organization* 42 (Winter): 179–217.

Goldstein, Judith, and Robert O. Keohane, eds. 1993. *Ideas and Foreign Policy: Elites, Institutions, and Political Change*. Ithaca, NY: Cornell University Press.

Graber, Doris A. 2006. *Media Power in Politics*. 5th ed. Washington, DC: CQ Press.

Grayson, Melvin J., and Thomas R. Shepard Jr. 1973. *The Disaster Lobby: Prophets of Ecological Doom and Other Absurdities*. Chicago: Follett Publishing Company.

Greider, William. 2003. *The Soul of Capitalism: Opening Paths to a Moral Economy*. New York: Simon & Schuster.

Greve, Michael S. 1996. *The Demise of Environmentalism in American Law*. Washington, DC: AEI Press.

Greve, Michael S., and Fred L. Smith, eds. 1992. *Environmental Politics: Public Costs, Private Rewards*. New York: Praeger.

Gusfield, Joseph R. 1981. *The Culture of Public Problems: Drinking-Driving and the Symbolic Order*. Chicago: University of Chicago Press.

Gusterson, Hugh, and Catherine Besteman, eds. 2009. *The Insecure American: How We Got Here and What We Should Do about It*. Berkeley: University of California Press.

Haas, Peter M. 1992. "Introduction: Epistemic Communities and International Policy Coordination." *International Organization* 46 (1): 1–35.

Hacker, Jacob S. 2004. "Privatizing Risk without Privatizing the Welfare State: The Hidden Politics of Social Policy Retrenchment in the United States." *American Political Science Review* 98 (2): 243–260.

Hacker, Jacob S., and Paul Pierson. 2005. *Off Center: The Republican Revolution and the Erosion of American Democracy*. New Haven, CT: Yale University Press.

Hage, Wayne. 1989. *Storm over Rangelands: Private Rights in Federal Lands*. Bellevue, WA: Free Enterprise Press.

Hall, Peter A., ed. 1989. *The Political Power of Economic Ideas: Keynesianism across Nations*. Princeton, NJ: Princeton University Press.

Hall, Peter A., ed. 1993. "Policy Paradigms, Social Learning, and the State: The Case of Economic Policymaking in Britain." *Comparative Politics* 25 (3): 275–296.

Hamilton, Clive. 2004. *Growth Fetish*. Sterling, VA: Pluto Press.

Hardisty, Jean. 1999. *Mobilizing Resentment: Conservative Resurgence from the John Birch Society to the Promise Keepers*. Boston: Beacon Press.

Harris, Richard A., and Sidney M. Milkis. 1996. *The Politics of Regulatory Change: A Tale of Two Agencies*. Revised ed. New York: Oxford University Press.

Hart, John. 1995. "President Clinton and the Politics of Symbolism: Cutting the White House Staff." *Political Science Quarterly* 110 (3): 385–408.

Hawken, Paul. 2007. *Blessed Unrest: How the Largest Movement in the World Came into Being and Why No One Saw It Coming*. New York: Viking.

Hawken, Paul, Amory Lovins, and L. Hunter Lovins. 1997. *Natural Capitalism: Creating the Next Industrial Revolution*. Boston: Little, Brown and Company.

Hays, Samuel P. 1987. *Beauty, Health, and Permanence: Environmental Politics in the United States, 1955–1985*. New York: Cambridge University Press.

Hays, Samuel P. 1998. *Explorations in Environmental History*. Pittsburgh: University of Pittsburgh Press.

Heatherly, Charles, ed. 1981. *Mandate for Leadership*. Washington, DC: Heritage Foundation.

Heclo, Hugh. 1974. *Modern Social Politics in Britain and Sweden*. New Haven, CT: Yale University Press.

Heinzerling, Lisa. 1998. "Regulatory Costs of Mythic Proportions." *Yale Law Journal* 107 (May): 1981-2070.

Helvarg, David. 1997. *The War against the Greens*. San Francisco: Sierra Club Books.

Hess, David J. 2009. *Localist Movements in a Global Economy*. Cambridge, MA: MIT Press.

Hockenstein, Jeremy B., Robert N. Stavins, and Bradley W. Whitehead. 1997. "Crafting the Next Generation of Market-Based Environmental Tools." *Environment* 39 (May): 13–20, 30–33.

Hofstadter, Richard. 1964. "The Paranoid Style in American Politics." *Harper's*, November, 77–86.

Holden, Constance. 1981. "Public Fear of Watt Is Environmentalists' Gain." *Science* (April 24): 422.

Holling, C.S. and Gary K. Meffe. 1996. "Command and Control and the Pathology of Natural Resource Management." *Conservation Biology* 10 (2): 328–337.

Hudson, William E. 2008. *The Libertarian Illusion: Ideology, Public Policy, and the Assault on the Common Good*. Washington, DC: CQ Press.

Humes, Edward. 2011. *Force of Nature: The Unlikely Story of Wal-Mart's Green Revolution*. New York: HarperBusiness.

Ikenberry, G. John. 1992. "A World Economy Restored: Expert Consensus and the Anglo-American Postwar Settlement." *International Organization* 46: 289–321.

Iyengar, Shanto, and Richard Reeves, eds. 1997. *Do the Media Govern?* Thousand Oaks, CA: Sage Publications.

Jackson, Tim. 2009. *Prosperity without Growth: Economics for a Finite Planet.* Sterling, VA: Earthscan.

Jacobs, Lawrence R., and Robert Y. Shapiro. 2000. *Politicians Don't Pander: Political Manipulation and the Loss of Democratic Responsiveness.* Chicago: University of Chicago Press.

Jacques, Peter J., Riley E.Dunlap, and Mark Freeman. 2008. "The Organization of Denial: Conservative Think Tanks and Environmental Skepticism." *Environmental Politics* 17 (3): 349–385.

Jamieson, Kathleen Hall, and Joseph N. Capella. 2008. *Echo Chamber: Rush Limbaugh and the Conservative Media Establishment.* New York: Oxford University Press.

John, Dewitt. 1994. *Civic Environmentalism: Alternatives to Regulation in States and Communities.* Washington, DC: CQ Press.

Johnson, M. Bruce. 1978. *The Attack on Corporate America: The Corporate Issues Sourcebook.* New York: McGraw-Hill Book Company.

Judis, John B. 2000. *The Paradox of American Democracy: Elites, Special Interests, and the Betrayal of Public Trust.* New York: Pantheon Books.

Kamieniecki, Sheldon. 2006. *Corporate America and Environmental Policy: How Often Does Business Get Its Way?* Palo Alto, CA: Stanford University Press.

Kamieniecki, Sheldon, Robert O'Brien, and Michael Clarke, eds. 1986. *Controversies in Environmental Policy.* Albany: State University of New York Press.

Keeney, Ralph L. 1990. "Mortality Risks Induced by Economic Expenditures." *Risk Analysis* 10: 147–159.

Keiter, Robert B. 2003. *Keeping Faith with Nature: Ecosystems, Democracy, and America's Public Lands.* New Haven: Yale University Press.

Kessel, John H. 1984. "The Structures of the Reagan White House." *American Journal of Political Science* 28 (2): 231–258.

Kingdon, John W. 1995. *Agendas, Alternatives, and Public Policies.* 2nd ed. New York: HarperCollins College Publishers.

Klyza, Christopher McGrory. 1994. *Who Controls Public Lands? Mining, Forestry, and Grazing Policy, 1870–1990.* Chapel Hill: University of North Carolina Press.

Klyza, Christopher McGrory and David Sousa. 2008. *American Environmental Politics, 1990–2006: Beyond Gridlock.* Cambridge, MA: MIT Press.

Kneese, Allen V., and Charles L. Schultze. 1975. *Pollution, Prices, and Public Policy.* Washington, DC: Brookings Institution.

Kovacic, William E. 1991. "The Reagan Judiciary and Environmental Policy: The Impact of Appointments to the Federal Courts of Appeals." *Environmental Affairs* 18 (4): 669–713.

Kraft, Michael E. 2000. "U.S. Environmental Policy and Politics: From the 1960s to the 1990s." *Journal of Policy History* 12 (1): 17–39.

Kraft, Michael E., and Sheldon Kamieniecki, eds. 2007. *Business in Environmental Policy: Corporate Interests in the American Political System*. Cambridge, MA: MIT Press.

Krausmann, Fridolin, Marina Fischer-Kowalski, Heinz Schandl, and Nina Eisenmenger. 2008. "The Global Sociometabolic Transition." *Journal of Industrial Ecology* 12 (5/6): 637–656.

Krausmann, Fridolin, Simone Gingrich, Nina Eisenmenger, Karl-Heinz Erb, Helmut Haberl, and Marina Fischer-Kowalski. 2009. "Growth in Global Materials Use, GDP, and Population during the 20th Century." *Ecological Economics* 68: 2696–2705.

Kristol, Irving. 1978. *Two Cheers for Capitalism*. New York: Basic Books.

Lakoff, George. 1996. *Moral Politics: What Conservatives Know That Liberals Don't*. Chicago: University of Chicago Press.

Landy, Marc K., Marc J. Roberts, and Stephen R. Thomas. 1994. *The Environmental Protection Agency: Asking the Wrong Questions*. Expanded ed. New York: Oxford University Press.

Lash, Jonathan, Katherine Gillman, and David Sheridan. 1984. *A Season of Spoils: The Reagan Administration's Attack on the Environment*. New York: Pantheon Books.

Lave, Lester B., and Gilbert S. Omenn. 1981. *Clearing the Air: Reforming the Clean Air Act*. Washington, DC: Brookings Institution.

Layard, Richard. 2005. *Happiness: Lessons from a New Science*. New York: Penguin Press.

Layzer, Judith A. 2006. "Fish Stories: Science, Advocacy, and Policy Change in New England Fishery Management." *Policy Studies Journal* 34 (1): 59–80.

Layzer, Judith A. 2012. *The Environmental Case: Translating Values into Policy*. 3rd ed. Washington, DC: CQ Press.

Lazarus, Richard J. 1991. "The Tragedy of Distrust in the Implementation of Environmental Law." *Law and Contemporary Problems* 54 (4): 311–374.

Lazarus, Richard J. 2004. *The Making of Environmental Law*. Chicago: University of Chicago Press.

Leshy, John D. 2001. "The Babbitt Legacy at the Department of the Interior: Preliminary View." *Environmental Law* 31 (Spring): 199–227..

Leshy, John D. 2004. "Natural Resources Policy in the Bush (II) Administration: An Outsider's Somewhat Jaundiced View." *Duke Environmental Law & Policy Forum* 14 (Spring): 347–361.

Lieberman, Robert C. 2002. "Ideas, Institutions, and Political Order: Explaining Political Change." *American Political Science Review* 96 (4): 697–712.

Limbaugh, Rush. 1992. *The Way Things Ought to Be*. New York: Simon & Schuster.

Lindblom, Charles E. 1959. "The Science of Muddling Through." *Public Administration Review* 14:79–88.

Lindblom, Charles E. 1977. *Politics and Markets: The World's Political-Economic Systems*. New York: Basic Books.

Litan, Robert E., and William D. Nordhaus. 1983. *Reforming Federal Regulation*. New Haven, CT: Yale University Press.

Lukes, Steven. 1974. *Power: A Radical View*. London: Macmillan Press.

Macilwain, Colin. 2006. "Safe and Sound." *Nature* 442 (July 20): 242–243.

MacWilliams, Cosgrove Snider. 1993. *The Wise Use Movement: Strategic Analysis and the Fifty State Review*. Washington, DC: Environmental Working Group.

Maddox, John. 1972. *The Doomsday Syndrome*. New York: Macmillan.

Mahoney, James, and Dietrich Reuschmeyer, eds. 2003. *Comparative Historical Analysis in the Social Sciences*. New York: Cambridge University Press.

Mahoney, James, and Kathleen Thelen, eds. 2010. *Explaining Institutional Change: Ambiguity, Agency, and Power*. New York: Cambridge University Press.

Majone, Giandomenico. 1989. *Evidence, Argument, and Persuasion in the Policy Process*. New Haven, CT: Yale University Press.

March, James G., and Johan P. Olsen. 1989. *Rediscovering Institutions: The Organizational Basis of Politics*. New York: Free Press.

Marshall, Will, and Martin Schram, eds. 1993. *Mandate for Change*. New York: Berkeley Books.

Matos, Grecia, and Lorie Wagner. 1998. "Consumption of Materials in the United States, 1900–1995." *Annual Review of Energy and the Environment* 23: 107–122.

Mayaux, P., P. Holmgren, F. Acard, H. Eve, H. Stibig, and A. Branthomme. 2005. "Tropical Forest Cover Change in the 1990's and Options for Future Monitoring." *Philosophical Transactions of the Royal Society. SeriesB. Biological Sciences* 360 (1454): 373–384.

Mazmanian, Daniel A., and Michael E. Kraft, eds. 1999. *Toward Sustainable Communities: Transition and Transformations in Environmental Policy*. Cambridge, MA: MIT Press.

McCarty, Nolan, Keith T. Poole, and Howard Rosenthal. 2006. *Polarized America: The Dance of Ideology and Unequal Riches*. Cambridge, MA: MIT Press.

McCright, Aaron M., and Riley E. Dunlap. 2000. "Challenging Global Warming as a Social Problem: An Analysis of the Conservative Movement's Counter-Claims." *Social Problems* 47 (4): 499–522.

McCright, Aaron M., and Riley E. Dunlap. 2010. "Anti-Reflexivity: The American Conservative Movement's Success in Undermining Climate Change Science and Policy." *Theory, Culture & Society*. 27 (May 24): 100–133.

McGarity, Thomas O., Sidney Shapiro, and David Bollier. 2004. *Sophisticated Sabotage: The Intellectual Games Used to Subvert Responsible Regulation*. Washington, DC: Environmental Law Institute.

McGirr, Lisa. 2001. *Suburban Warriors: The Origins of the New American Right*. Princeton, NJ: Princeton University Press.

McKibben, Bill. 2007. *Deep Economy*. New York: Times Books.

McNeill, J. R. 2000. *Something New under the Sun: An Environmental History of the Twentieth-Century World*. New York: W.W. Norton & Company, Inc.

Melnick, R. Shep. 1983. *Regulation and the Courts: The Case of the Clean Air Act*. Washington, DC: Brookings Institution.

Micklethwait, John, and Adrian Woolridge. 2004. *The Right Nation: Conservative Power in America*. New York: Penguin Press.

Millennium Ecosystem Assessment. 2005. *Ecosystems and Human Well-Being: Synthesis*. Washington, DC: Island Press.

Mintrom, Michael, and Sandra Vergari. 1996. "Advocacy Coalitions, Policy Entrepreneurs, and Policy Change." *Policy Studies Journal* 24: 420–434.

Mintz, Joel A. 1995. *Enforcement at the EPA: High Stakes and Hard Choices*. Austin: University of Texas Press.

Moran, Michael, Martin Rein, and Robert E. Goodin, eds. 2006. *The Oxford Handbook of Public Policy*. New York: Oxford University Press.

Morgenstein, Richard D., and William A. Pizer. 2007. *Reality Check: The Nature and Performance of Voluntary Environmental Programs in the United States, Europe, and Japan*. Washington, DC: Resources for the Future.

Mucciaroni, Gary. 1995. *Reversals of Fortune: Public Policy and Private Interests*. Washington, DC: The Brookings Institution.

Nash, George H. 1976. *The Conservative Intellectual Movement in America since 1945*. New York: Basic Books.

Nelkin, Dorothy. 1995. *Selling Science: How the Press Covers Science and Technology*. New York: W.H. Freeman.

Nelson, Robert H. 1995. *Public Lands and Private Rights*. Lanham, MD: Rowman & Littlefield.

Newland, Chester A. 1983. "The Reagan Presidency: Limited Government and Political Administration." *Public Administration Review* 43 (1): 1–21.

Noll, Roger, ed. 1985. *Regulatory Policy and the Social Sciences*. Berkeley: University of California Press.

Novak, Michael. 1978. *An American Vision: An Essay on the Future of Democratic Capitalism*. Washington, DC: American Enterprise Institute for Public Policy Research.

O'Connell, Michael. 1992. "Response to: 'Six Biological Reasons Why the Endangered Species Act Doesn't Work and What to Do About It.'" *Conservation Biology* 6 (1): 140–143.

Orren, Karen, and Stephen Skowronek. 2004. *The Search for American Political Development*. New York: Cambridge University Press.

Orts, Eric W., and Kurt Deketelaere, eds. 2001. *Environmental Contracts*. Boston: Kluwer Law International.

Parenteau, Patrick. 2004. "Anything Industry Wants: Environmental Policy under Bush II." *Duke Environmental Law & Policy Forum* 14 (Spring): 363-405.

Peschek, Joseph G. 1987. *Policy-Planning Organizations: Elite Agendas and America's Rightward Turn*. Philadelphia: Temple University Press.

Peters, B. Guy, Jon Pierre, and Desmond S. King. 2005. "The Politics of Path Dependency: Political Conflict in Historical Institutionalism." *Journal of Politics* 67 (4): 1275–1300.

Petracca, Mark P., ed. 1992. *The Politics of Interests: Interest Groups Transformed*. Boulder, CO: Westview Press.

Phillips-Fein, Kim. 2009. *Invisible Hands: The Businessmen's Crusade against the New Deal*. New York: W.W. Norton.

Pierce, Richard J., Sr. 1999. "Is Standing Law or Politics?" *North Carolina Law Review* 77 (June): 1741–1789.

Pierson, Paul. 2004. *Politics in Time: History, Institutions, and Social Analysis*. Princeton, NJ: Princeton University Press.

Pierson, Paul, and Theda Skocpol, eds. 2007. *The Transformation of American Politics: Activist Government and the Rise of Conservatism*. Princeton, NJ: Princeton University Press.

Podhoretz, Norman. 1981. "The New Defenders of Capitalism." *Harvard Business Review* (March–April): 96–106.

Poole, Robert W., Jr., ed. 1982. *Instead of Regulation*. Lexington, MA: Lexington Books.

Pooley, Eric. 2010. *The Climate War: True Believers, Power Brokers, and the Fight to Save the Earth*. New York: Hyperion.

Pope, Carl, and Paul Rauber. 2004. *Strategic Ignorance: Why the Bush Administration Is Recklessly Destroying a Century of Environmental Progress*. San Francisco: Sierra Club Books.

Porritt, Jonathon. 2007. *Capitalism As If the World Matters*. Revised ed. Sterling, VA: Earthscan.

Portney, Paul R., ed. 1984. *Natural Resources and the Environment: The Reagan Approach*. Washington, DC: Urban Institute Press.

Powell, Walter W., and Paul J. DiMaggio, eds. 1991. *The New Institutionalism in Organizational Analysis*. Chicago: University of Chicago Press.

Porter, Douglas R., and David A. Salvesen, eds. 1995. *Collaborative Planning for Wetlands and Wildlife*. Washington, DC: Island Press.

Pralle, Sarah B. 2006. *Branching Out, Digging In: Environmental Advocacy and Agenda Setting*. Washington, DC: Georgetown University Press.

Prior, Markus. 2007. *Post-Broadcast Democracy: How Media Choice Increases Inequality in Political Involvement and Polarizes Elections*. New York: Cambridge University Press.

Quarles, John. 1976. *Cleaning Up America: An Insider's View of the Environmental Protection Agency*. New York: Houghton Mifflin Company.

Rathlesberger, James, ed. 1973. *Nixon and the Environment: The Politics of Devastation.* New York: Taurus Communications, Inc.

Ray, Dixy Lee, and Lou Guzzo. 1990. *Trashing the Planet.* Washington, DC: Regnery Gateway.

Regnery, Alfred S. 2008. *Upstream: The Ascendance of American Conservatism.* New York: Threshold Editions.

Reich, Robert B., ed. 1988. *The Power of Public Ideas.* Cambridge, MA: Ballinger.

Reich, Robert B. 2007. *Supercapitalism: The Transformation of Business, Democracy, and Everyday Life.* New York: Alfred A. Knopf.

Revesz, Richard. 1997. "Environmental Regulation, Ideology, and the D.C. Circuit." *Virginia Law Review* 83: 1717–1772.

Rivera, Jorge, and Peter deLeon. 2004. "Is Greener Whiter? Voluntary Environmental Performance of Western Ski Areas." *Policy Studies Journal* 32 (3): 417–437.

Roberts, James C. 1980. *The Conservative Decade: Emerging Leaders of the 1980s.* Westport, CT: Arlington House Publishers.

Rochefort, David A., and Roger W. Cobb, eds. 1994. *The Politics of Problem Definition: Shaping the Policy Agenda.* Lawrence: University Press of Kansas.

Sabatier, Paul A. 1988. "An Advocacy Coalition Framework of Policy Change and the Role of Policy-Oriented Learning Therein." *Policy Sciences* 21: 129–168.

Sabatier, Paul A., and Hank C. Jenkins-Smith, eds. 1993. *Policy Change and Learning.* Boulder, CO: Westview Press.

Sale, Kirkpatrick. 1993. *The Green Revolution: The American Environmental Movement 1962–1992.* New York: Hill and Wang.

Saloma, John S., III. 1984. *Ominous Politics: The New Conservative Labyrinth.* New York: Hill and Wang.

Satterthwaite, David, ed. 1999. *The Earthscan Reader in Sustainable Cities.* London: Earthscan.

Sax, Joseph L. 2000. "Environmental Law at the Turn of the Century: A Reportorial Fragment of Contemporary History." *California Law Review* 88 (6): 2375–2402.

Schattschneider, E. E. 1960. *The Semisovereign People: A Realist's View of Democracy in America.* New York: Holt, Reinhart and Winston.

Schendler, Auden. 2009. *Getting Green Done: Hard Truths from the Front Lines of the Sustainability Revolution.* New York: PublicAffairs.

Schlozman, Kay Lehman. 1984. "What Accent the Heavenly Chorus? Political Equality and the American Pressure System." *Journal of Politics* 46 (4): 1006–1032.

Schmidt, Vivien A. 2006. *Democracy in Europe: The Impact of European Integration.* New York: Oxford University Press.

Schneider, Anne, and Helen Ingram. 1993. "Social Construction of Target Populations: Implications for Politics and Policy." *American Political Science Review* 87: 334–347.

Schneider, Gregory L., ed. 2003. *Conservatism in America since 1930*. New York: New York University Press.

Schor, Juliet B. 1998. *The Overspent American: Upscaling, Downshifting, and the New Consumer*. New York: Basic Books.

Schroeder, Christopher H., and Robert Glicksman. 2001. "Chevron, State Farm, and EPA in the Courts of Appeals during the 1990s." *Environmental Law Reporter* 31: 10371.

Schulman, Bruce J., and Julian E. Zelizer, eds. 2008. *Rightward Bound: Making American Conservative in the 1970s*. Cambridge, MA: Harvard University Press.

Schultze, Charles. 1977. *The Public Use of Private Interest*. Washington, DC: Brookings Institution Press.

Schwartz, Herman. 2004. *Right Wing Justice: The Conservative Campaign to Take Over the Courts*. New York: Nation Books.

Seidman, Harold, and Robert Gilmour. 1986. *Politics, Position, and Power: From the Positive to the Regulatory State*. 4th ed. New York: Oxford University Press.

Shanley, Robert A. 1992. *Presidential Influence and Environmental Policy*. Westport, CT: Greenwood Press.

Shapiro, Ian, Stephen Skowronek, and Daniel Galvin, eds. 2006. *Rethinking Political Institutions: The Art of the State*. New York: New York University Press.

Shapiro, Sidney A., and Richard E. Levy. 1995. "Judicial Incentives and Indeterminacy in Substantive Review of Administrative Decisions." *Duke Law Journal* 44 (April): 1051–1080.

Simon, Julian L. 1981. *The Ultimate Resource*. Princeton, NJ: Princeton University Press.

Simon, William E. 1978. *A Time for Truth*. New York: Reader's Digest Press.

Sinden, Amy. 2004. "The Economics of Endangered Species: Why Less Is More in the Economic Analysis of Critical Habitat Designations." *Harvard Environmental Law Review* 28: 129–214.

Skocpol, Theda. 1992. *Protecting Soldiers and Mothers: The Political Origins of Social Policy in the United States*. Cambridge, MA: Harvard University Press.

Smith, Mark A. 2000. *American Business and Political Power: Public Opinion, Elections, and Democracy*. Chicago: University of Chicago Press.

Smith, Mark A. 2007. *The Right Talk: How Conservatives Transformed the Great Society into the Economic Society*. Princeton, NJ: Princeton University Press.

Snow, David A., and Robert D. Benford. 1988. "Ideology, Frame Resonance, and Participant Mobilization." *International Social Movement Research*. vol. 1., 197–217. Greenwich, CT: JAI Press.

Spector, Malcolm, and John I. Kitsuse. 1977. *Constructing Social Problems*. New York: Aldine de Gruyter.

Speth, James Gustave. 2004. *Red Sky at Morning: America and the Crisis of the Global Environment*. New Haven, CT: Yale University Press.

Speth, James Gustave. 2008. *The Bridge at the End of the World: Capitalism, the Environment, and Crossing from Crisis to Sustainability*. New Haven, CT: Yale University Press.

Stanford Environmental Law Society. 2001. *The Endangered Species Act*. Stanford, CA: Stanford University Press.

Stefancik, John, and Richard Delgado. 1996. *No Mercy: How Conservative Think Tanks and Foundations Changed America's Social Agenda*. Philadelphia: Temple University Press.

Steinmo, Sven, Kathleen Thelen, and Frank Longstreth, eds. 1992. *Structuring Politics: Historical Institutionalism in Comparative Analysis*. New York: Cambridge University Press.

Stelzer, Irwin M., and Paul R. Portney. 1998. *Making Environmental Policy: Two Views*. Washington, DC: American Enterprise Institute.

Stewart, Richard B. 1996. "United States Environmental Regulation: A Failing Paradigm." *Journal of Law and Commerce* 15: 585-596.

Stiglitz, Joseph E. 2003. *Globalization and Its Discontents*. New York: W. W. Norton & Company.

Stone, Deborah. [1988] 2002. *Policy Paradox: The Art of Political Decision Making*. New York: W.W. Norton.

Streeck, Wolfgang, and Kathleen Thelen, eds. 2005. *Beyond Continuity: Institutional Change in Advanced Political Economies*. New York: Oxford University Press.

Sunstein, Cass R. 1990. "Paradoxes of the Regulatory State." *University of Chicago Law Review* 57 (2): 407–441.

Sunstein, Cass R., David Schkade, Lisa M. Ellman, and Andres Sawicki. 2006. *Are Judges Political? An Empirical Analysis of the Federal Judiciary*. Washington, DC: Brookings Institution Press.

Switzer, Jacqueline Vaughn. 1997. *Green Backlash: The History and Politics of Environmental Opposition in the U.S.* Boulder, CO: Lynne Rienner Publishers.

Tamanaha, Brian Z. 2010. *Beyond the Formalist-Realist Divide: The Role of Politics in Judging*. Princeton, NJ: Princeton University Press.

Taylor, Martin F.J., Kieran Suckling, and Jeffrey T. Rachlinski. 2005. "The Effectiveness of the Endangered Species Act: A Quantitative Analysis." *Bioscience* 55 (4): 360–367.

Teles, Steven M. 2008. *The Rise of the Conservative Legal Movement: The Battle for Control of the Law*. Princeton, NJ: Princeton University Press.

Thomas, Craig W. 2003. *Bureaucratic Landscapes*. Cambridge, MA: MIT Press.

Thompson, Michael J., ed. 2007. *Confronting the New Conservatism: The Rise of the Right in America.* New York: New York University Press.

Train, Russell. 2003. *Politics, Pollution, and Pandas.* Washington, DC: Island Press.

Trumbo, Craig. 1996. "Constructing Climate Change: Claims and Frames in US News Coverage of an Environmental Issue." *Public Understanding of Science* 5: 269–283.

Tucker, William. 1982. *Progress and Privilege: America in the Age of Environmentalism.* New York: Doubleday.

Vaughn, Jacqueline, and Hanna J. Cortner. 2006. *George W. Bush's Healthy Forests Act: Reframing the Environmental Debate.* Boulder, CO: University Press of Colorado.

Victor, Peter A. 2008. *Managing without Growth: Slower by Design, Not Disaster.* Northampton, MA: Edward Elgar.

Vig, Norman J., and Michael E. Kraft, eds. 1984. *Environmental Policy in the 1980s: Reagan's New Agenda.* Washington, DC: CQ Press.

Vig, Norman J., and Michael E. Kraft, eds. 1994. *Environmental Policy in the 1990s: Toward a New Agenda.* 2nd ed. Washington, DC: CQ Press.

Vig, Norman J., and Michael E. Kraft, eds. 1997. *Environmental Policy in the 1990s: Reform or Reaction?* 3rd ed. Washington, DC: CQ Press.

Vig, Norman J., and Michael E. Kraft, eds. 2003. *Environmental Policy: New Directions for the Twenty-First Century.* 5th ed. Washington, DC: CQ Press.

Vig, Norman J., and Michael E. Kraft, eds. 2006. *Environmental Policy: New Directions for the Twenty-First Century.* 6th ed. Washington, DC: CQ Press.

Vig, Norman J., and Michael E. Kraft, eds. 2010. *Environmental Policy: New Directions for the Twenty-First Century.* 7th ed. Washington, DC: CQ Press.

Vig, Norman J., and Michael G. Faure, eds. 2004. *Green Giants: Environmental Policies of the United States and the European Union.* Cambridge, MA: MIT Press.

Viguerie, Richard A. 1981. *The New Right: We're Ready to Lead.* Falls Church, VA: The Viguerie Company.

Vogel, David. 1989. *Fluctuating Fortunes: The Political Power of Business in America.* New York: Basic Books.

Vogel, David. 1996. *Kindred Strangers: The Uneasy Relationship between Politics and Business in America.* Princeton, NJ: Princeton University Press.

Vogel, David. 2005. *The Market for Virtue: The Potential and Limits of Corporate Social Responsibility.* Washington, DC: Brookings Institution Press.

Wagner, Frederic H. 1999. "Whatever Happened to the National Biological Survey?" *Bioscience* 49 (3): 219–222.

Watchman, Laura Hood, Martha Groom, and John D. Perrine. 2001. "Science and Uncertainty in Habitat Conservation Planning." *American Scientist* 89 (4): 351–359.

Waterman, Richard. 1989. *Presidential Influence and the Administrative State.* Knoxville: University of Tennessee Press.

Watt, James. 2004. Oral history, Center for the American West (February 11). Available at http://centerwest.org/wp-content/uploads/2011/01/watt1.pdf.

Waxman, Henry. 2009. *The Waxman Report: How Congress Really Works.* New York: Twelve.

Weart, Spencer. 2009. "Government: The View from Washington, D.C." in The Discovery of Global Warming. Available at http://www.aip.org/history/climate/Govt.htm.

Weber, Edward P. 1998. *Pluralism by the Rules: Conflict and Cooperation in Environmental Regulation.* Washington, DC: Georgetown University Press.

Weidenbaum, Murray L. 1979. *The Future of Business Regulation: Private Action and Public Demand.* New York: Amacom.

Weingast, Barry. 1995. "A Rational Choice Perspective on the Role of Ideas: Shared Belief Systems and State Sovereignty in International Cooperation." *Politics & Society* 23 (4): 449–464.

West, Darrell M., and Burdett A. Loomis. 1999. *The Sound of Money: How Political Interests Get What They Want.* New York: W.W. Norton & Company.

Whitaker, John C. 1976. *Striking a Balance: Environment and Natural Resources Policy in the Nixon-Ford Years.* Washington, DC: AEI-Hoover Policy Studies.

Whitman, Christine Todd. 2005. *It's My Party Too: The Battle for the Heart of the GOP and the Future of America.* New York: Penguin Books.

Wildavsky, Aaron. 1988. *Searching for Safety.* New Brunswick, NJ: Transaction Books.

Wilkinson, Richard, and Kate Pickett. 2009. *The* Spirit *Level: Why Greater Equality Makes Societies Stronger.* New York: Bloomsbury Press.

Williams, Michael. 2003. *Deforesting the Earth: From Prehistory to Global Crisis.* Chicago: University of Chicago Press.

Wilson, James Q. 1980. *The Politics of Regulation.* New York: Basic Books.

Wilson, James Q. 1989. *Bureaucracy.* New York: Basic Books.

Woodward, Bob. 1994. *The Agenda: Inside the Clinton White House.* New York: Simon & Schuster.

Wolf, Charles Jr. 1979. "A Theory of Nonmarket Failure: Framework for Implementation Analysis." *Journal of Law & Economics* 22 (1): 107–139.

Worm, Boris, Edward J. Barbier, Nicola Beaumont, J. Emmett Duffy, Carl Folke, Benjamin S. Halpern, Jeremy B. C. Jackson, Heike K. Lotze, Fiorenza Micheli, Sephen R. Palumbi, Enric Sala, Kimberley A. Selkoe, John J. Stachowicz, and Reg Watson. 2006. "Impacts of Biodiversity Loss on Ocean Ecosystem Services." *Science* 314 (November 3): 787–790.

Yandle, Bruce, ed. 1995. *Land Rights: The 1990s Property Rights Rebellion.* Lanham, MD: Rowman and Littlefield.

# Index

# American and Comparative Environmental Policy

Sheldon Kamieniecki and Michael E. Kraft, series editors